Developing Web-Enabled Decision Support Systems

Using Access, VB .NET, and ASP .NET

Abhijit A. Pol

Computer and Information Science and Engineering
University of Florida, Gainesville

Ravindra K. Ahuja

Industrial and Systems Engineering
University of Florida, Gainesville
and
Innovative Scheduling, Inc., Gainesville

Dynamic Ideas
Belmont, Massachusetts

Dynamic Ideas
43 Lantern Road
Belmont, Mass. 02478
U.S.A.
WWW information and orders: http://www.dynamic-ideas.com

Cover Design: *Saumya Ahuja*

Publisher's Cataloging-in-Publication Data

Pol, Abhijit, Ahuja, Ravindra K.
Developing Web-Enabled Decision Support Systems
Includes bibliographical references and index
1. Database Design.   2. Visual basic.NET.   3. Decision Support Systems.

HD30.213.A38   2007

ISBN: 0-9759146-4-2

Abhijit dedicates this book to his model-base: his father, Ashok; to his knowledge-base: his mother, Anagha; and to his data-base: his brother Amit.

Ravi dedicates this book to his favorite decision support network: Smita, Saumya, and Shaman.

Together, we dedicate this book to Professor Don Hearn, who inspired us to write books on decision support systems and remained a constant source of encouragement throughout their evolution.

Contents

Preface

OVERVIEW

- Motivation
- Book Contents
- Required Background
- Suggestions for Instructors
- Web site Contents
- Acknowledgments

Motivation

Developing Web-Based Decision Support Systems is intended to be a textbook that describes database design and development, illustrates the programming topics (basic as well as advanced) in Visual Basic .NET and database connectivity, demonstrates Web-enabling using ASP .NET, and applies these techniques to building decision support systems arising in several disciplines. This book can also be used as a supplementary reference book for courses or as a self-study manual by practitioners.

Information systems based on decision models are called *Decision Support Systems* (DSS). A DSS uses the data residing in databases, models it, processes or analyzes it using problem-specific methodologies, and assists the user in the decision-making process through a graphical user interface. Industrial Engineering and Operations Research (IE/OR) and business school graduates are frequently being employed in positions that require developing DSS. We believe that decision support systems will gain widespread popularity in the future, and knowing how to develop such systems will make our students highly desirable in the workplace.

IE/OR departments and business schools teach its students decision models-based courses that impart spreadsheet modeling, optimization, and simulation skills. Most of these departments require its students to take a computer-programming course, often in C++, Java, or Visual Basic (VB). Several departments require its students to take a database course as well. Thus, students acquire background in modeling, optimization, simulation, database, and programming, but there are no courses that teach students how to integrate the technologies learned in these different courses to build complete decision support systems. Students are given many components, but they cannot assemble them into a complete package suitable for use by a customer. Decision support systems combine these technologies, and teaching how to build such systems is ideally suited to be an integral part of the IE/OR and business school curriculum.

Developing courses that teach our students how to build decision support systems has been a demanding task so far, since it requires the availability of platforms that allow the integration of various technologies (data, models, and programming). However, in the past decade, several platforms that allow such integration have become available. One such platform is Microsoft's .NET technology.

The *Visual Basic .NET* (VB .NET) package of the .NET platform can be used in conjunction with *Microsoft Access* databases to build Windows-based, single-user database applications. The Microsoft Access database allows data storage, and VB .NET—an easy-to-learn yet powerful object-oriented programming (OOP) language—provides a mechanism for data analysis, implementing optimization and simulation models, and building graphical user interfaces. Further, Web programming has also become easier with the introduction of *Active Server Pages .NET* (ASP .NET). This .NET package makes use of standard *HyperText Markup Language* or HTML (the front-end) and VB .NET (the back-end) to deploy elegant and easy-to-build database-connected, Web-enabled applications. Another powerful .NET package is *Crystal Report .NET*. The Crystal Report package provides an ideal environment for creating reports and charts that can effectively summarize data. Thus, we have developed a complete set of course material in the Access and .NET framework for a course on Web-Enabled Decision Support Systems. This textbook is a byproduct of this effort. One can alternatively build spreadsheet-based decision support systems using the Microsoft Excel spreadsheet package, which is the subject of our parallel effort and which led to the companion book, "*Developing Spreadsheet-Based Decision Support Systems*," by Michelle M.H. Seref, Ravindra K. Ahuja, and Wayne L. Winston.

The DSS development skills are important to all IE/OR and business school graduates for several reasons. First, having these skills will allow them to develop simple tools that might increase their productivity. Second, many graduates will be involved in information systems development during their career, and having a better understanding of the underlying technology will allow them to play a more useful role in the development process. Third, our graduates can develop a prototype system using the techniques learned here to establish the system proof-of-concept before it is turned over to the professional programmers. Fourth, several graduates are often employed in departments that are service organizations catering to the modeling and optimization needs of other departments such as manufacturing, sales, marketing, accounting, and purchasing. These departments often request decision tools to be built to meet their business needs. The users in this department are not modeling experts, and the mathematical complexity of these models becomes an impediment to their use. If our graduates are well versed in the DSS building process, they can build optimization and simulation models and package these models within friendly interfaces so that the modeling complexity is hidden from the user. This will make modeling and optimization approaches more popular in the workplace. Finally, with data mining becoming increasingly important, industries are realizing a critical need for persons who understand data, models, algorithms, and IT, and our graduates can fulfill this need. Our students possess modeling and algorithmic skills to analyze the data but lack information systems development skills, and providing them these skills will make them ideally suited for this task.

Book Contents

Building a Web-enabled, data-driven decision support system requires four skills: knowledge of database design, database development, database programming language, and Web programming. We also need to illustrate through some practical applications how to build such decision support systems. Currently, there are no books available in the market that covers all of the five areas. Our book is intended to meet this need. There are five parts of this textbook: learning database design; getting familiar with database development with Microsoft Access; learning how to program with VB .NET and build Windows-based database applications; making them Web-enabled with ASP .NET; and learning how to develop DSS applications through several case studies.

Part I—Principles of Good Database Design

We start this part of the book with an introduction to decision support systems and an introduction to databases (Chapters 1 and 2). We then cover principles of good database design. The database design process primarily involves two kinds of data modeling: Object-Based Modeling and Record-Based Modeling. The *entity-relationship (E-R) model*—an object-based data model—describes the data in the form of an E-R diagram, entities, attributes, and relationships and is the subject of Chapter 3. The *relational data model*—a record-based data model—is based on the mathematical concept of *relations* and uses tables (or relations) to represent data and relationships and is the subject of Chapter 4.

Part II—Database Development with MS Access

This part of the book introduces the database development process using the Microsoft Access package. In Chapter 5, we provide a tour of Access's development environment. We introduce the development window, various menus and toolbars, and the architecture of Access and its main components. In Chapter 6, we give a detailed explanation of Access tables, the central element of relational databases. Access tables store data and provide an effective grid structure for data organization. We also discuss how to design and modify Access tables in this chapter. Chapter 7 is dedicated to relationships among Access tables. Once we have populated them with data, we can query tables to retrieve useful information. We do this through Access queries, which are the subject of Chapter 8. Chapter 9 introduces SQL, the standard language used to write database queries. We have also written two comprehensive chapters on Access Forms and Access Reports, which are available on the book Web site: www.dssbooks.com.

Part III—Developing Windows Applications with VB .NET

With potential uses of a database application in mind, we present VB .NET as a database programming language in this part of the book. We first introduce, in Chapter 10, the Visual Studio environment—Integrated Development Environment (IDE)—that provides all the tools we need to develop a database application. In Chapter 11, we introduce VB .NET along with its programming language constructs: variables, data types, control structures, operators, and arrays. Chapter 12 presents a discussion of the object-oriented support features of VB .NET, namely, Classes, Modules, Procedures, Methods, and Properties. In Chapter 13, we formally introduce Windows forms and controls. Forms and controls constitute the building blocks of a GUI. In Chapter 14, we discuss database connectivity using ADO .NET. In Chapter 15, we illustrate more advanced database connectivity topics. Finally, in Chapter 16, we introduce Crystal Reports, a powerful tool that can summarize data in the form of reports and graphs, and discuss its integration with Windows forms.

Part IV—Web Application Development with ASP .NET

The Internet era has taken information-sharing to new heights, allowing billions of users to share information on the World Wide Web (WWW). This development has created the need for Web-enabled applications that are accessible to a large number of users over a network. Today's information systems involving databases are pervasive, and a growing number of them are Web-enabled. In this part of the book, we illustrate the process of developing Web applications. We discuss Hyper Text Markup Language (HTML), a Web interface standard, in Chapter 17. We introduce a Web programming language, ASP .NET, in Chapter 18. We then introduce database connectivity in Web applications using VB .NET and ADO .NET in Chapter 19 to build a complete Web-enabled DSS.

Part V—Case Studies

This part presents five fully developed DSS applications arising in IE/OR, business, and general engineering. These case studies walk through the complete process of developing a Web-enabled decision support system. Through these case studies, students will learn how IE/OR and business techniques apply to real-life decision problems and how we can effectively use those techniques to build DSS applications. Our case studies include Online Book Store, Portfolio Management and Optimization, Television Advertisement Allocation, Voyage Prophesy, and ADO .NET and MS Excel. Each case study also lists extensions that students can do as additional projects or practice assignments. We have developed a few more case studies that are available on the book Web site: www.dssbooks.com. The space limitation did not permit us to include these case studies in this printed form of the book.

This book explains all topics through classical examples selected from IE/OR, business school, data management, and engineering curriculums. Each new concept or idea is illustrated through examples or hands-on tutorials and reinforced through exercises at the end of the chapter. Each chapter contains an in-class assignment, several review questions, and many hands-on exercises. We also have created an extensive list and description of student course projects (over 50 such projects), which will further enhance students' learning experience. These projects are available at the book Web site.

Required Background

The book does not require any prior experience with databases and can be used as an introductory text for novices in database design, development, and implementation. For readers familiar with the design process and the Access environment, this book provides a comprehensive review of these topics.

Prior experience in programming is not mandatory to use this book. We instruct readers on how to create variables, define functions, use basic programming structures, and work with arrays using Visual Basic language. Readers will also learn how to create good graphical user interfaces in the Visual Studio environment. This material also includes several applications that may be considered "mini" DSS applications. Therefore, even for an experienced programmer, it is useful to review these chapters to strengthen the reader's skills in using VB .NET and ASP .NET in the context of developing a DSS.

We hope that after learning the database background and application development material in *Parts I–IV* of the book, readers will be able to develop any of the case studies found in *Part V*. The case studies construct prototypes of data-driven, Web-enabled decision support systems that are simple enough to be understood by undergraduates and complex enough to be reasonably accurate representatives of real-world problems. The case studies require that you have picked up good database design, development, and programming skills from *Parts I–IV* of the book.

Suggestions for Instructors

This book is primarily intended as a textbook for undergraduate and graduate students in the IE/OR and business school curriculums. This book can also be used as a reference book to supplement other textbooks in courses and as a self-study manual. DSS are great tools for consulting, and consultants can use the skills learned profitably in developing their consulting practice.

As a textbook, this book can be used in a variety of ways to teach different courses. It can be used to offer courses for undergraduate and graduate students. In an undergraduate-level course, instructors can cover topics at a slower pace. In a graduate-level course, instructors can spend less time on some topics such as programming basics or HTML, and focus more on case studies. Instructors can offer semester-long courses (covering all the material), or half-semester/quarter courses on either database design and development or Windows and Web application development.

The Web-enabled DSS course may be taught in different formats including or excluding several different chapters from our text. We propose that the general structure of the course begin by teaching database design and development to students to ensure that they are familiar with the databases; then teach VB .NET programming, database connectivity, and ASP .NET to show students how to work with Windows and Web-enabled database applications; the course should then end with a full discussion of decision support systems and instructing students how to combine their acquired database and programming skills to develop a DSS application. The text has been designed to follow this general course structure.

From our experience, it seems most productive to hold this course in a computer laboratory or require students to bring laptops to the class. We recommend that the instructor illustrate concepts, hands-on examples, or tutorials on the computer screen while students are watching them and trying to do them themselves on their computers. We suggest that the instructor end each class by conducting one of the hands-on examples or tutorials as an illustration of all the concepts taught in that class. We also recommend that there be a teaching assistant available to help students as they are doing the hands-on examples on their personal computers, while the instructor may illustrate the example simultaneously at the front of the class. We have found that students learn much more in this manner as they experiment with Access, VB .NET, and ASP .NET themselves along with the instructor, with the teaching assistant readily available to answer questions or address their difficulties.

In this suggested setting of a computer laboratory or class with laptops, we also suggest that the course be taught in two-hour sessions instead of one-hour sessions. This allows students enough time to set up their computers and instructors enough time to illustrate a full example during the class. The course material can be adjusted to teach semester long courses or half-semester/quarter courses. The material can be covered in different rigors and at different paces, and some of the material can be assigned for self-study.

We have discovered by teaching these courses over the years that students learn the most by doing course projects. Lectures teach them the technology and how to use it, but unless they apply it themselves to build complete systems, they do not assimilate the material. In addition, the process of developing a full system from conception to completion and seeing the fruits of their labor gives them tremendous satisfaction and confidence. Course projects may be done by teams of students, in which case they promote teamwork—an essential skill in any workplace. We have developed over 50 course projects from different application areas in IE/OR, business, and engineering curriculums. These projects are available at the book Web site. Course projects can be assigned on an individual basis or in groups depending on the course size and course format. Students can select a project from our list, or they can create their own project as long as it is sufficiently interesting and challenging. We require our students to present these projects before the entire class when completed. Many students have told us that doing these projects and building complete decision support systems was the most educative experience for them in the course. We can't recommend them more highly!

Web site Contents

We have developed a Web site for this textbook that contains valuable resources for both students and instructors. The URL of this Web site is: www.dssbooks.com

This Web site contains the following material:

- Database files, VB .NET and ASP .NET source code, and application files for all the Hands-On tutorials covered in all chapters
- PowerPoint presentations for all book chapters
- Source code and the complete application package including database files for all five case studies discussed in Part V of the book
- Additional case study chapters that could not be included in the book
- Database files for Hands-On exercises for required chapters
- Additional chapters on Access Forms and Reports that could not be included in the book
- A booklet containing about 50 student projects
- Sample course schedules

A Solutions Manual of the book is also available and will be provided to instructors offering courses using this book as the principle textbook. The Web site provides the email addresses for requesting the Solution Manual and giving your feedback to the book authors.

Acknowledgments

There are many people whom we would like to thank for making significant contributions to this book-writing project. First and foremost, we would like to thank Dr. Donald Hearn, Chair of the Industrial and Systems Engineering Department at the University of Florida, who has been the driving force in this book-writing initiative. He motivated us to teach courses that incorporate greater levels of information technology in the IE/OR curriculum at the University of Florida. He also inspired us to write this book and provided constant encouragement throughout its evolution from a concept to a reality. We are truly thankful to him for his encouragement and support.

Next, we would like to offer many thanks to Sandra Duni Eksioglu. Sandra received her doctorate in Industrial and Systems Engineering from the University of Florida and has been working with us since the inception of the project. She has developed several exercises, their solutions, and team projects for the book. Sandra has taken a lead role in organizing all the team projects into a booklet and in preparing the solutions manual for the book. Her hard work and dedication is much appreciated.

Several students of the Industrial and Systems Engineering, Computer Science, and English Departments at the University of Florida helped us in the development of the book at different stages. In particular, we would like to thank Margaret Reece and Padmavati Sridhar for the contributions they made in developing several exercises and their solutions for the book; and Krishna Jha, and Burak Eksioglu for developing several team projects. Our special thanks to the programming junta of Rakesh Desai, Siddharth Gaitonde, Kunal Gandhi, Tapasvi Moturu, and Mohammad Jaradat for the contributions they made in developing case studies and examples for the book. Ruben Galbraith assisted us in preparing the PowerPoint presentations for the book chapters, and we appreciate his help. We extend our sincere thanks to Dean Swinford, Tamara Johnston, Carolyn Houston, and Krystal Harriot for their copy editing of the text. We would also like to thank students of the DSS courses offered at the University of Florida who served as guinea pigs to test early versions of book chapters and who gave valuable feedback. We are indeed indebted for their feedback. Several students who assisted us in the book-writing project were supported by the National Science Foundation Course Curriculum Development Grant 0341203.

Finally, we thank our families for their constant support and encouragement.

Abhijit A. Pol
Ravindra K. Ahuja

PART ONE

Principles of Good Database Design

CHAPTER

one Introduction

chapter OVERVIEW

3

1.1   *Introduction*

As a new graduate, equipped with the modeling and algorithmic skills taught in a standard operations management curriculum, Susan is ready to solve real-world problems. With a knowledge and understanding of theory and applications of mathematical programming, simulation techniques, supply-chain management and other IE/OR and business topics, she is ready to help her company solve distribution problems by linear programming, inventory problems by applying the EOQ model, and manpower planning problems by integer programming. However, as she works on projects with her experienced colleagues and presents results to management, she realizes that she needs more than her models and equations. The management needs Susan to help solve decision problems, but they only want to know the final analysis; they have no time or interest in understanding the mathematical model for these problems. They want this decision analysis tool to be available as a software system in which they can modify parameters and see different results for various scenarios. However, Susan is clueless about how to develop such a system. She knows the right model but she does not know how to package her model and how to present it with friendly graphical user interface. She feels that her education did not impart to her the skills she needs to meet her job requirements.

Susan is not the only one facing problems in her job as an operations research (OR) or business decision analyst. This is a widely prevalent problem that is not addressed in the current IE/OR or business curriculums. As OR practitioners and business analysts, students are support staff members and are required to build systems for non-OR users. They must know how to package OR/business models so that they can be comfortably used by top managers and other co-workers. Real-life decision making often requires building interactive systems, which students must know how to design and implement. To summarize, students must learn sufficient information technology skills so that they can build intelligent information systems, alternatively, called *decision support systems*, which can run sophisticated models at the back end, but are friendly enough at the front end to be used comfortably by any user.

A decision support system (DSS) gives its users access to a variety of data sources, modeling techniques, and stored domain knowledge via an easy to use *graphical user interface* (GUI). For example, a DSS can use the data residing in *databases*, prepare a mathematical model using this data, solve or analyze this model using problem-specific methodologies, and can assist the user in the decision-making process through a GUI. Students are frequently being employed in positions that require developing DSS, which are gaining widespread popularity. As more and more companies install enterprise resource planning (ERP) packages and invest in building data warehouses, those who are able to create decision technology-driven applications that interface with these systems and analyze the data they provide will become increasingly valuable. Indeed, imparting DSS development skills, which combine OR/business skills with *information technology* (IT) skills, will make students highly sought after in the modern workplace.

Developing courses that teach our students how to build decision support systems has been a challenging task so far since it requires the availability of platforms that allow the integration of various technologies (data, models, codes, etc.). However, in the past few years, several platforms have become available that allow such integration. One such platform is Microsoft's .NET framework. The *Visual Basic .NET* (VB .NET) package of the .NET platform can be used in conjunction with *Microsoft Access* databases to build Windows-based, single-user database applications. The Microsoft Access database allows data storage and VB .NET, an easy to learn and yet powerful object-oriented programming (OOP) language, allows us to design and build object models and develop professional quality GUI for applications. Further, Web programming has also become easier with the introduction of *Active Server Pages .NET* (ASP .NET). This .NET package makes use of standard *HyperText Markup Language* or HTML (the front end) and VB .NET (the back-end) to deploy elegant and easy-to-build database connected Web-enabled applications. Another powerful .NET package is *Crystal Report .NET*. Crystal Report package provides an ideal environment for creating reports and charts that can effectively summarize data. Thus, Microsoft .NET and Microsoft Access provides a platform in which fairly sophisticated DSS applications can be built. This book imparts the skills needed to build such systems.

1.1.1 Topics

This chapter discusses the following topics:

- Definition and components of decision support system and Web-enabled decision support system.
- Decision support system applications.
- An overview of the textbook.

1.2 *Defining a Decision Support System*

A *decision support system* (DSS) is a model-based or knowledge-based system intended to support managerial decision making in semi-structured or unstructured situations. A DSS is not meant to replace a decision maker, but to extend his/her decision making capabilities. It uses data, provides a clear user interface, and can incorporate the decision maker's own insights. Some of the major DSS capabilities are the following:

1. A DSS brings together human judgment and computerized information for semi-structured decision situations. Such problems cannot be conveniently solved by standard quantitative techniques or computerized systems.
2. A DSS is designed to be easy to use. User friendliness, graphical capabilities, and an interactive human-machine interface greatly increase the effectiveness of a DSS.
3. A DSS usually uses models for analyzing decision-making situations and may also include a knowledge component.
4. A DSS attempts to improve the effectiveness of decision making rather than its efficiency.
5. A DSS provides support for various managerial levels from line mangers to top executives. It provides support to individuals as well as groups. It can be PC-based or Web-based.

A DSS application contains five components: database, model base, knowledge base, GUI, and user (see Figure 1.1). The database stores the data, model and knowledge bases store the collections of models and knowledge, respectively, and the GUI allows the user to interact with the database, model base, and knowledge base. The database and knowledge base can be found in a basic information system. The knowledge base may contain simple search results for analyzing the data in the database. For example, the knowledge base may contain how many employees in a company database have worked at the company for over ten years. A decision support system is an *intelligent information system* because of the addition of the model base. The model base has the models used to perform optimization, simulation, or other algorithms for advanced calculations and analysis. These models allow the decision support system to not only supply information to the user but aid the user in making a decision. We now present a more detailed look at each of these components.

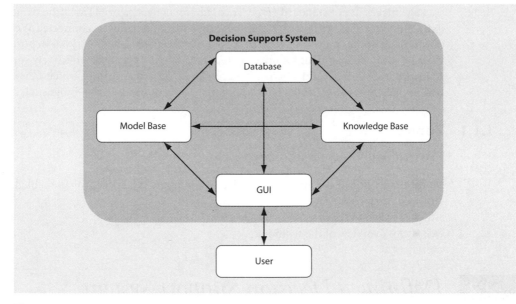

Figure 1.1 A schematic view of a decision support system.

Database: The database provides the data with which decisions are made. The data may reside in databases or even in a data warehouse, a repository for decision-making data relevant to a corporation. The database allows a user to access, manipulate, and query data. Some examples of databases include an MS Access file containing personal banking account information and a data warehouse containing shipment records of various products.

Model Base: A model base contains statistical, financial, optimization, or simulation models that provide the analysis capabilities in a DSS. Some popular optimization models include linear programming, integer programming, and nonlinear programming. The DSS allows the ability to invoke, run, and change any model or combine multiple models. An example of a model base would be an integer programming model used to solve a capital budgeting problem.

Knowledge Base: Many managerial decision-making problems are so complex that they require special expertise for their solution. The knowledge base part of a DSS allows this expertise to be stored and accessed to enhance the operation of other DSS components. For example, credit card companies use a DSS to identify credit card thefts. They store in their knowledge base the spending patterns that usually follow credit card thefts; any abnormal activity in an account would trigger checking for the presence of those patterns and a possible suspension of the account.

GUI: The graphical user interface (GUI) covers all aspects of communication between a user and a DSS application. The user interface interacts with the database, model base, and knowledge base. It allows the user to enter data or update data, run the chosen model, view the results of the model, and possibly rerun the application with different data and/or model combinations. The user interface is perhaps one of the most important components of a DSS because much of the flexibility and ease of use of a DSS are derived from this component.

User: The person who uses the DSS to support the decision-making process is called the user, or decision maker. A DSS has two broad classes of users: managers and staff specialists, or engineers. When designing a DSS, it is important to know for which class of users the DSS is being designed. In general, managers expect a DSS to be more user-friendly than do staff specialists.

A DSS should be distinguished from more common *management information systems* (MIS). An MIS can be viewed as an information system that can generate standard and exception reports and summaries for managers, provide answers to queries, and help in monitoring the performance of a system using simple data processing. A DSS can be viewed as a more sophisticated MIS in which we allow the use of models and knowledge bases to process the data and perform analysis.

1.3 *Web-Enabled Decision Support Systems*

Traditionally, MIS have been used for relatively simple data processing and data presentation. However, as these systems have become more popular and organizations have become larger and more complex, an enormous amount of data is generated routinely. That is when a need for well-developed DSS is felt that can assimilate this data and derive meaningful decisions of managerial and economic significance. Today, the era of the *Internet* has taken information sharing to new heights, allowing billions of users to share information on the *World Wide Web* (WWW) simultaneously. DSS, which are now critical to the efficient functioning of any organization, need to be upgraded and must be Web-enabled. In this book, we will discuss the development of such *Web-enabled decision support systems*.

A **Web-enabled decision support system** is a DSS that can be accessed on the World Wide Web via Internet. A typical Web-enabled decision support system requires data, a *database management system* (DBMS), a programming language, and a mechanism for Web-enabling. A DBMS is used to store, manage, and process the data, while a programming language is used to build graphical user interfaces (GUI), to do complex data processing and presentation, and to incorporate external optimization engines. Several different software packages can be used to build such a DSS. We believe that the combination of Microsoft Access (a DBMS), VB .NET (a programming language), and ASP .NET (a scripting language for Web-enabling) provides the best way to teach these concepts to students in a single course.

1.4 *Decision Support System Applications*

Given the above definition of a Web-enabled decision support system, we have developed several complete, Web-enabled DSS applications using MS Access, VB .NET, and ASP .NET. As IE/OR or business graduates, students will discover opportunities in their careers to develop and use DSS applications. Many students who have taken DSS courses have reported that their skills of combining modeling with an information technology (IT) packaging have truly helped them be outstanding at their jobs. Let us consider three examples of DSS applications that may be found in industry.

Online Shopping: Consider an example of online shopping Web sites like Amazon.com and Buy.com. Typically, for these kinds of industries, its "Web site" is the main or only way to interact with its customers. Customers visit the Web sites, browse ten hundreds of products or even search the product of interest in specific product category. They can read a detailed description of the product, view product images and reviews left by previous buyers before placing an order. Let us consider an interesting DSS application for online shopping. As customers buy products, the Web site can make some recommendations to the buyers. For example, if a customer buys a laptop of a particular brand, the Web site can suggest that people who bought this laptop also shopped for these compatible printers and accessories. Giving such online recommendations requires sophisticated DSS support. The DSS keeps tracks of all past transactions in a database. A business model then dictates which products within a transaction are really related to each other (e.g., laptop and printer), how popular they are, discount for combined package, what is the inventory level of recommended products, and so forth. The output or decision is then displayed to the user in online manner. The system evolves as more and more transactions are made and stored in the database.

Car Production: Consider a factory that produces cars. The manager of the factory, probably a business or IE/OR graduate, may need to make some important decisions about ordering parts, hiring/firing employees, finding new suppliers, or making changes to the production process. Let us focus on a production process DSS application. The manager may be deciding where to place a new piece of equipment or how to add a new product part to the production sequence. With the use of some basic simulation and analysis tools, one could develop a DSS that allows the manager to enter the parameters to describe a possible scenario and see how it would affect production. The manager may not want to know the details of the models used, but rather what would be the effect on cost and production time and quantity if a specific change was made. One can imagine having this system accessible via internal Internet or Intranet through a Web browser within a factory to different decision makers. This is just one example of how a DSS could be used to aid in the car production industry.

Railroad Car Management: Consider a railroad company that owns several trains on which they place several thousand railroad cars that ship to several cities in the country. A distribution manager, again with an IE/OR or business background, may need to decide which cars should go on which trains to which cities. He would benefit from using an optimization model that allows him to modify certain constraints or focus on various objectives and compare the resulting distribution plans. He may want to display the car and train plans visually and may project them on a country map, to have a better understanding of the effects of one solution compared to another. A DSS would aid him in accomplishing this analysis and making a decision that considers all scenarios and possible outcomes.

The applications we develop are basic illustrations of decisions that are made in IE/OR and business industries. Two examples, selected from the DSS applications developed in Part V of this book, are described below.

Portfolio Management and Optimization: In this application, we allow users to create and/or edit their portfolios as well as to optimize their investments. To create a portfolio, users can choose from a list of stocks in an MS Access database and add or remove them to/from their portfolios. The stocks are listed by name and category. These stocks can also be compared using their historical annual returns and changes in market price. Once users have created their portfolios, they may also edit them at any time. Users may then optimize their investments by specifying a desired return on their portfolios and the amount available for investing. The application then solves an optimization problem that minimizes users' risk on their selected portfolios. The suggested investment strategy is then displayed to the users. This application allows users to interact with the database of stock information and the knowledge base of comparative statistics. The model base for this DSS uses a heuristic algorithm coded in VB .NET to perform an optimization that minimizes the user's risk on the portfolio investments.

Advertisement Allocation Problem: Television is the most popular media of entertainment. Considering its impact on us, it is natural to make optimal use of this media for advertisement and entertainment programs. Generally, a cable service provider can track information for each household; which channel and the period the viewer is tuned in on any particular channel. This information along with the data about customer, television programs, episodes, and the show times, can be used to develop a decision support system. As one of the functionalities of the DSS, we allocate advertisement and episode based on some predetermined criteria. For example, given a set of advertisements, their target age group, race, and income group, an advertisement budget, and cost of advertising per program, we optimally allocate these advertisements to different TV programs to maximize the viewership per dollar spent. The model base for the advertisement allocation problem makes use of a greedy algorithm of knapsack problems programmed in VB .NET.

1.5 *Textbook Overview*

Developing Web-Enabled Decision Support Systems describes how to design a database, how to implement databases using Microsoft Access database management system, and how to add additional application functionalities using the VB .NET programming language. We also demonstrate how to Web-enable these decision support systems using ASP .NET scripting language. We illustrate this development process through five case studies based on practical situations taken from the domains of science, engineering, and management. The book contains the following five modules:

- Part I: Principles of Good Database Design
- Part II: Database Development with Microsoft Access
- Part III: Windows Application Development with VB .NET
- Part IV: Web Application Development with ASP .NET
- Part V: Case Studies

We now present an overview of these modules.

1.5.1 Overview of Principles of Good Database Design

The desire to collect and organize information for easy access predates computer technology. Before the advent of computers, or even writing, civilizations preserved important information in stories, myths, and proverbs. These civilizations honored storytellers, who maintained a verbal record of events ranging from battles to harvests. The advent of print technology gave rise to systematic data collection that promoted scribes over storytellers. From this perspective, we can view books and libraries as the initial models for the databases of today. In an era in which information technology and communication are of paramount importance, databases are pervasive. We access databases for a variety of everyday activities such as shopping online, getting driving directions, or registering for classes. This discussion emphasizes the need to master the concepts, design, and development of databases.

Part I of this book covers principles of good database design. The database design process primarily involves two kinds of data modeling: object-based modeling and record-based modeling. The object-based data modeling use entities, attributes, and relationships to present the information. The *entity-relationship* (E-R) *model* is an example of an object-based data model and has emerged as one of the most popular and widely used techniques. It describes the data in the form of an E-R diagram, which is the subject of Chapter 3. Record-based data modeling use records to present the data. The *relational data model* is an example of a record-based model. Relational data modeling is based on the mathematical concept of *relations* and uses relations to represent data and relationships. This is dealt with in detail in Chapter 4.

1.5.2   Overview of Database Development with MS Access

Having introduced the fundamentals of database design, we next delineate the process of database development based on the relational data model. There are several relational database management system (DBMS) software packages available. Some of the most popular DBMS packages are Microsoft Access, Oracle and SQL Server.

We have selected the Access DBMS to work with for several reasons. Access DBMS is immensely popular in small to medium size industries. It is easy to learn and can be used in conjunction with many other applications for Microsoft Windows. It is simple and compatible, yet powerful enough to compete with relational database management systems, such as Oracle and SQL Server, which are used by major corporations. Part II of this book is devoted to Access DBMS.

In Chapter 5, we provide a tour of Access's development environment. We introduce the development window, various menus and toolbars, and the architecture of Access and its main components. In Chapter 6, we give a detailed explanation of Access tables, the central element of relational databases. Access tables store data and provide an effective grid structure for data organization. We also discuss how to design and modify Access tables in this chapter. Chapter 7 is dedicated to relationships among Access tables. Once we have populated them with data, we can query tables to retrieve useful information. We do this through Access queries, which are the subject of Chapter 8. Chapter 9 introduces SQL, the standard language used to write database queries.

1.5.3   Overview of Windows Application Development with VB .NET

Knowledge of database design and development alone won't suffice to meet today's business needs. There is a need for an additional tool that can present processed data effectively and efficiently to the user. Presenting the data in a legitimate format is as important as processing it. A presentation tool not only broadens audience perception of our information, but also enhances the efficiency of data editing, processing, and printing operations. A *database application* allows us to achieve these goals.

With potential uses of a database application in mind, we present VB .NET as a database programming language in Part III of the book. We have organized this part as follows. In Chapter 10, we introduce the Visual Studio environment. Visual Studio is an *integrated development environment* (IDE) that provides all the tools we need to develop a database application. In Chapter 11, we introduce VB .NET along with its programming language constructs: variables, data types, control structures, operators, and arrays. Chapter 12 presents a discussion of the object-oriented support features of VB .NET, namely, classes, modules, procedures, methods, and properties. In Chapter 13, we formally introduce Windows forms and controls. Forms and controls constitute the building blocks of a GUI. In Chapter 14, we discuss database connectivity using ADO .NET. In Chapter 15, we illustrate advance database connectivity topics. Finally, in Chapter 16, we introduce Crystal Reports .NET, a powerful tool that can summarize data in the form of reports and graphs, and discuss its integration with Windows forms.

1.5.4   Overview of Web Application Development with ASP .NET

Though Windows applications are highly effective for single-user personal computers, they do not completely meet today's networking needs. The Internet era has taken information sharing to new heights, allowing billions of users to share information on the World Wide Web (WWW). This development has created the need for Web-enabled applications that are accessible to a large number of users over the Internet. Today's information systems involving databases are pervasive, and a growing number of them are Web-enabled.

In Part IV of this book, we illustrate the process of developing Web applications. With the introduction of Microsoft's new technology—ASP .NET—the Web application development process became very similar to Windows application development. The database connectivity and data processing needs of an application are handled using VB .NET as in Windows applications. Thus, VB .NET forms the back-end of Web applications. As we drag and drop Windows controls on Windows forms to create Windows application GUI, ASP .NET allows us to drag and drop Web controls on Web forms to create Web GUI. As we build Web GUI, ASP .NET automatically writes HTML code of our actions. HTML is a Web standard for displaying data on Web pages. Thus, HTML forms the front-end of Web applications. We briefly discuss HTML in Chapter 17 and introduce ASP .NET in Chapter 18. In Chapter 19, we illustrate development of complete, database connected Web applications.

1.5.5   Overview of Case Studies

Part V of the book illustrates the relevance and importance of decision support systems and Web-DSS in the fields of industrial and systems engineering, business, and general engineering. We demonstrate the significance of DSS in various disciplines and showcase the development of DSS applications that integrate databases, models, methodologies, and user interfaces.

We have developed and presented five case studies, which are described in detail in this part of the book. These case studies walk through the complete process of developing a Web-enabled decision support system and are based on important applications of IE/OR and business. Through these case studies, students will learn how IE/OR and business techniques apply to real-life decision problems and how we can effectively use those techniques to build DSS applications. Our case studies include: Online Book Shopping, Television Channel—A Data Mining Application, Portfolio Management and Optimization, Voyage Prophecy—A Map Point Based Application, Accessing MS Excel Features in .NET Application—Forecasting and Optimization. Each case study also lists extensions that reader can use as additional projects or practice assignments.

1.6   *Summary*

- *Decision support systems* (DSS) are model-based or knowledge-based systems that support managerial decision making; they are not meant to replace decision makers, but to extend their decision-making capabilities.

- There are five components to a DSS: database, model base, knowledge base, GUI, and user.

- A *Web-enabled decision support system* is a DSS that can be accessed on WWW via Internet.

- Part I of the book covers the principles of good database design. We discuss the entity-relationship model (an example of object-based data modeling) and the relational data model (an example of record-based data modeling) in this part.

- Part II of the book is dedicated to Microsoft Access, a relational database management system (DBMS). We discuss Access tables, relationships, queries, and SQL in this part.

- A tool that can present processed data effectively and efficiently is crucial. Presentation tools not only improve audience perception of our information, but also enhance the efficiency of data editing, processing, and printing operations. Database applications allow us to achieve these goals. With potential uses of a database application in mind, we present VB .NET as a database programming language in Part III of the book.

- Web applications can be shared globally by billions of users over the Internet. In Part IV of this book, we illustrate the Web application development process with ASP .NET. We discuss HTML and VB .NET database connectivity in Web applications in this part.

- The case studies are intended to illustrate to the reader how to develop DSS applications that integrate databases, models, methodologies, and user interfaces. Part V of the book features five case studies.

1.7 *Exercises*

1.7.1 Review Questions

1. What are the components of a decision support system?
2. What is the difference between an information system and a decision support system?
3. What are some industrial engineering or business problems that may use databases and database applications? Which applications are suitable for extension to the Web?
4. What user interface would be necessary to communicate with a user who does not have a background in databases?
5. What are some industrial engineering applications that could require a decision support system?

two Introduction to Databases

chapter OVERVIEW

2.1   *Introduction*

The desire to collect, organize, and easily access information predates computer technology. Before computers, or even writing, civilizations preserved important information in stories, myths, and proverbs. These civilizations honored storytellers, who maintained an oral record of events ranging from battles to harvests. The advent of print technology displaced data collection from the domain of storytellers to that of scribes. To this extent, we can view written language, books, and even libraries as the initial models for the electronic databases of today.

Computers, like books, have altered the way we collect, store, and retrieve information. *Database* is a computer solution for fast, efficient, accurate, and secure data access. Programmers have modified databases from their initial applications in large mainframe computers to their current usage in today's personal computers (PCs). Databases are used for a variety of purposes, ranging from business applications in packages such as Oracle and SQL Server to PC-based applications in packages such as Microsoft Access and FoxPro. A database can be so complex that it can handle the demanding data of a NASA satellite or simple enough to manage personal accounts. Databases have played a crucial role in the growing dominance of Internet-based technology.

In today's information age, databases are pervasive. We use databases, or collections of related data, for a variety of routine transactions. For example, while shopping online, getting driving directions, or registering for classes, chances are that we are accessing a database to do so. We elaborate upon these situations below.

Online Purchasing   When customers visit an online retail Website, an underlying database provides access to product information. The database contains data related to products while a Web interface serves as a database application that interacts with the product database. Additionally, information required when placing an order, such as mailing and billing addresses and credit card numbers, is entered into the database and can be accessed by the various departments that collaboratively process and ship an order.

Driving Directions   People also use database applications to find driving directions to and from any destination in the country. After users provide information about specific locations, database applications interact with a large database that contains information about every highway and street in the nation. These databases also store distance, traffic, and speed limit information to determine the best possible route.

Class Enrollment and Online Grades   Most universities maintain databases of students, faculty, and classes. One of the database applications controls class enrollment, handling constraints such as prerequisite courses and classroom capacity. The other applications allow faculty members to input student grades at the end of the semester. Students can then access their grades online through another Web-based database application.

Discussion on these example applications emphasizes the need to master the concepts, design, and development of databases. In this chapter, we take the first step and introduce database concepts to provide a general overview and to promote a better understanding of the subject.

2.1.1   Topics

This chapter discusses the following topics:

- ■ Terms like data, information, and metadata.
- ■ Data handling using file-based approach and database approach.

- Components of a database environment: the physical storage, the database management system, the database application, and the database personnel.
- Data modeling: entity-relationship (E-R) and relational modeling.

2.2   *Data, Information, and Metadata*

The term ***data*** refers to known facts that can be recorded and preserved. Facts can take different forms, which often include text, graphics, images, and/or video. Figure 2.1(a) presents an example of data in a text format.

Information is the processed data presented in a form suitable for human interpretation. The same data can be processed in a variety of ways to generate different kinds of information. For example, we can filter university data to retain information for students from Florida and New York. We can also summarize data and present it in a graphical format; Figure 2.1(b) displays a pie chart that indicates the total number of students from different states.

Processed data (information) gives meaning to raw data, for which to be processed, information-building demands an additional description of the data. This description of data, or data about a data, is known as ***metadata***. Figure 2.1(c) illustrates the concept of metadata.

ID	Name	Address	City	State
1	Andrew	SW 16th Ave	Orlando	FL
2	Robert	23rd Terrace	Boston	MA
3	Bob	52nd Avenue	Bronx	NY
4	Lee Hung	52nd Avenue	Albany	NY
5	Richard	999 Palm Bay	Detroit	MI
6	Tony	15th Avenue	Austin	TX

(a)

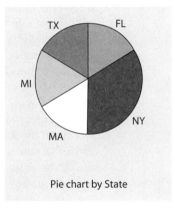

Pie chart by State

(b)

Name	Data Type	Size	Description
ID	Number	4	Unique Student ID
Name	Text	50	Student name
Address	Text	200	Mailing Address
City	Text	50	Residential City
State	Text	2	Residential State
ZIP	Number	5	ZIP Code

(c)

Figure 2.1 (a) Data in context; (b) Information; (c) Metadata.

Definitions

Data refers to known facts that can be recorded and preserved.

Information is the processed data presented in a form suitable for human interpretation.

Metadata is data about a data.

Generally, we wish to accomplish more than just storing and presenting raw data. As it is defined, we need to systematically process data and present it in a suitable format. To convert data into information, we can either employ the traditional file-based approach or a modern database approach. We will discuss these separately in the following sections.

2.3   *File-Based Approach*

During the late 60's, large mainframe computers were being used for business computations. These computers transformed the way business was conducted with their ability to store, manipulate, and retrieve data from large *text files*. In the file-based approach, a system is designed to store data in flat text files, and different computer programs are written to process these files and present information to the user.

Although file-based systems are now largely obsolete and used only for archive operations, we want to discuss this approach for two reasons. First, understanding file-based systems and their limitations helps us to appreciate the value of today's new systems. Second, if we wish to convert a file-based system to a better system (for example, a database system) it might be useful, if not essential, to understand it.

Consider the example of a university's file-based system (see Figure 2.2). This system stores data about the following: students and employees in the personnel file; available courses in the course file; student grades in the grade file; and student activities in the activity file. Each of these files can be viewed as a series of letter strings stored in a text file in some pre-defined format. For example, in the personnel file, each line represents information about exactly one student. Further, the student information within a line is represented by comma-separated values such as student name, home address, email address, and phone number. Similarly, a grade file might contain student name, email address, course number, semester, and grade information on each line.

Now consider an application program, Program-C or *View Grades*. The objective of this application is to display student information and grades to the student user. In other words, the application is designed to answer questions of the form, "What are the grades and postal address for John Adams?" In order to answer this question, the Program-C will perform following tasks:

- Read all the lines in the grade file; locate and output each of John's courses and grade information.
- Read personnel file; locate and output John's postal address.

Consider another application program, Program-B or *Update Grades*. This application allows faculty members to update student grades at the end of each semester. Like the *View Grades* application, *Update Grades* reads and manipulates the grades file. However, for security reasons the application might be accessing a copy of the grades file, as opposed to the original. After all the updates are completed, these files are copied to the location where *View Grades* is expecting them. Constraints such as this introduce data duplication in the file-based system. Managing duplicate data and ensuring consistency is a daunting and laborious task.

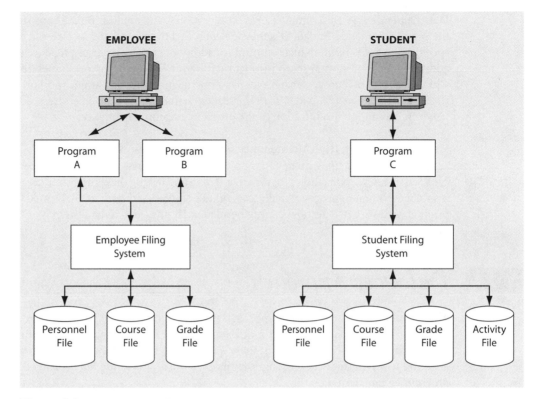

Figure 2.2 The university's file-based system.

Before we mention some of the obvious limitations of file-based systems, let's imagine the efforts required and difficulties faced to answer the following questions:

- What is the average grade for Dr. John Doe's students?
- List the activities for all students enrolled in EZZ 4162.
- Which personnel are students as well as staff?

Application programs for these tasks not only scan multiple files, but also might have to bring data from these files to temporary files for intermediate processing. This requires tremendous processing power, large developing and processing time, and significant computer resources, as well as skilled programmers.

2.3.1 Limitations of File-Based Approach

The file-based approach suffers primarily from the following three disadvantages:

Duplication of Data: Duplicating data is the rule, rather than the exception, of the file-based approach. Applications are often developed in isolation, leading to the decentralized development and uncontrolled creation of duplicate files. For example, *View Grades* and *Update Grades* applications duplicate the grade files for their own purposes. The production of duplicate files expends time and storage space and, therefore, money. Additionally, the file-based system jeopardizes data integrity. Because updates in one program are not automatically carried over to duplicate files, this system results in inconsistent records. For example, the *Update Grades* application may not update all the information accessed by the *View Grades* application.

Data Dependency: The computer programs written for an application are compatible only with the physical structure of data files they are supposed to manipulate. As a result, any changes to specific data fields result in huge amounts of additional work. For example, if we want to add an additional field of marital status just before the address field in the personnel file, we are faced with a monumental process that forces us to rewrite many existing application programs. All existing programs are designed to scan the student name followed by an address; adding a field in between demands a modification to the program's scanning sequence.

Slow Development, High Maintenance, and Fixed Queries: Above all, the file-based approach simply cannot keep up with the rapid pace of today's business. Almost every new task demands creation of a new application program. Designing and testing these programs greatly hinders the overall development process. Finally, capabilities of file-based systems are limited to the creator's original version; new questions cannot be adequately answered if the system is not appropriately prepared.

2.4 *Database Approach*

The limitations of the file-based approach provide some valuable lessons regarding data management: first, the parameters defining data should be stored separately and should not be embedded in the application; second, there should be a way to control and manipulate data in isolation from the application program. In other words, *we should not depend on an application program to manage data.*

2.4.1 The Database System

In response to the disadvantages of file-based systems evolved the radical new design of the database approach. Figure 2.3 depicts a database system for a university. In contrast to Figure 2.2, both filing systems are replaced by a single *Database Management System* (DBMS) and all physical files are collected and stored inside one repository, labeled as *Database*. All the application programs now interact with the DBMS, which centrally manages the database. A *database system* can be defined as the combination of a database, a DBMS, and application programs.

Unlike a filing system with scattered duplicate files, a database stores all its data in one location, thereby limiting data duplication. In our example, we can imagine a database with just one copy of each file for personnel, courses, grades, and activities. Furthermore, the database system stores the metadata in separate system files. This helps to decouple data definition from application programs, and thus reduces program-data dependency.

A *database management system* (DBMS) is a piece of software that allows a user to define, create, and manage access to a database. The DBMS actually decouples application programs from data, providing a logical view of the underlying data to the user or user program. For example, relational databases often allow a user or user program to view data in the form of tables. DBMS software enables this logical illusion by storing data on a computer disk. The DBMS allows for data abstraction as it hides unnecessary physical level details from the user. Also, as Figure 2.3 reveals, a special user, a *database administrator* (DBA), or a group of system developers must maintain the DBMS and ensure the accuracy of all user and application programs.

Because of the advantages offered by a DBMS, businesses and organizations prefer the database approach to the file-based approach of program-data dependency. With the database approach, application programs no longer depend on data; instead, the DBMS organizes it in a logical manner.

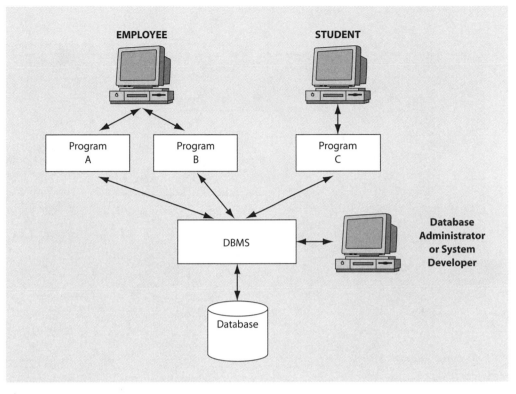

Figure 2.3 A university's database system.

2.4.2 Components of a Database System

The various components of the database environment and its relationships are depicted in Figure 2.4. This figure can be interpreted as a conceptual version of the information provided in Figure 2.3.

Database   A **database** is a collection of logically related data. Databases are designed to meet the data analysis needs of organizational users. The process of designing a database involves logical as well as physical composition. The following two chapters are devoted to logical database design. However, the physical design is omitted from this book.

Database Management System (DBMS)   We have defined a **DBMS** as software that allows users to define, create, and manage database access. We introduce one popular DBMS, MS Access, later in this text. Other examples of popular database management systems are Oracle, IBM's DB2, and SQL Server. We will discuss the functions of a DBMS later in this chapter.

Database Applications   **Database applications** are computer programs that allow users to manipulate the data in a DBMS through a user-friendly interface.

Database applications can be divided into four broad categories: personal, departmental, enterprise, and Internet. Personal applications are restricted to a single user. For example, many individuals maintain databases and applications to keep track of their expenses. Departmental applications are typically referenced by hundreds of users over a shared system or network. A

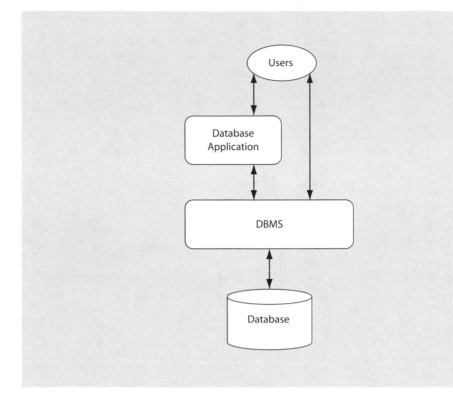

Figure 2.4 The components of a database system.

database application maintained by product development team is an excellent example of departmental application. The application can be accessed by design, orders, as well as payment teams to track the progress. Enterprise applications are extensions of departmental applications in which thousands of users share the information. ERP systems are examples of enterprise applications. Finally, Internet applications are the largest form of information sharing wherein billions of users are involved. Web sites like Amazon.com and Buy.com are excellent examples of Internet database applications.

Database Administrator, System Developer, and End User   A *database administrator* (DBA) is a person or group of people responsible for all the data resources of an organization. A DBA uses tools that come with a DBMS to improve the productivity and performance of database planning and design. Often, this job involves collecting statistics about the usage of a database and optimizing database indexing and queries to enhance the response time.

System developers are a group of people responsible for the creation of new application programs that cater to the user requirements. System developers use their own tools to write programs that communicate with the DBMS. For example, a developer can design a Visual Basic application to communicate with an Access DBMS that supports employee salary-related functions.

End-users in an organization can add, update, and delete data in a database through application programs or directly through a DBMS. End-users may or may not understand the intricacy of the application program, DBMS, or database concepts, but can use the application program to accomplish their day-to-day tasks.

> ## *Definitions*
>
> A **database** is a collection of logically related data.
>
> A **database management system** (DBMS) is a piece of software that allows a user to define, create, and manage access to a database.
>
> **Database applications** are computer programs that allow users to manipulate the data in a DBMS through a user-friendly interface.

2.4.3 Functions of a DBMS

A DBMS is primarily responsible for providing a logical view of underlying data. This task can be divided into fundamental functions like storage, retrieval, and updates. Each DBMS should allow its user to store, retrieve, and update data in the database and provide a clear, simple, and logical view of the process that manipulates the data. Some other DBMS functions are described below.

Data Independence   A DBMS should maintain segregation between the program and the data. It does so by creating a fixed interface for an application program but follows its own standards to store and update the data in the database. For example, in the MS Access DBMS, a user or a program can add an attribute to a table simply by inserting a column in a grid structure. Access then follows its own physical schema and makes the appropriate changes to actual database files through a series of actions that are hidden from the user.

Concurrency Control and Recovery Services   Concurrency control and recovery services are important functions supported by a DBMS; they are increasingly becoming a necessity with the advent of the Internet. To illustrate these concepts, let's consider the example of a banking database. Assume that a user makes a deposit to her account at the same time that her partner, a joint account holder, withdraws money from an ATM. A DBMS is capable of updating the account to reflect these concurrent changes. In addition, in the event of a power loss, a DBMS can recover the database and return it to its previous state.

Utility Services   All modern database management systems are equipped with utility services that allow a database administrator or a system developer to perform initialization and maintenance operations on a database. These include operations such as loading a large amount of data into a database from flat files, removing unused records, moving data from one physical device to another, monitoring the usage of a database, and statistical analysis.

2.4.4 Evolution of Database Systems

Database systems have enjoyed considerable popularity in the business world since the 1970s and have evolved to keep pace with the varying needs of companies and individuals worldwide. Figure 2.5 depicts this evolution on a time axis. The traditional file-based systems were introduced in the 1960s.

As we have discussed before, these systems were unable to handle the complexities of ever-growing business needs. Although early systems led to huge advances in data technology, the relational systems developed by IBM's E. F. Codd in the early 1980s were the first to gain

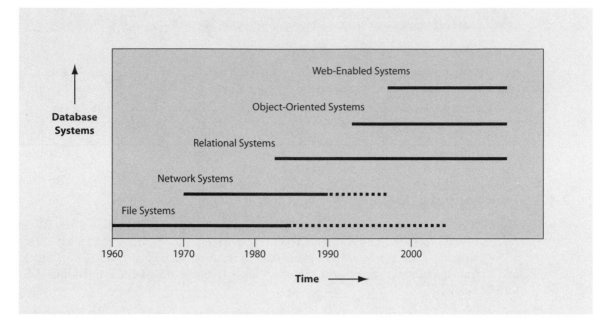

Figure 2.5 The evolution of database systems.

prominence in the business world. In fact, such relational systems are still widely used even today. We will discuss these systems in depth in Chapter 4. Around the mid-1990s, the structured use of data in a variety of formats (including audio, video, and graphical) became increasingly common. Object-oriented systems were developed to cope with this new prominence of large and complex data (a detailed discussion of object-oriented systems, however, exceeds the scope of this book). At around the same time, the Internet and Internet-based applications started to gain importance. Web-enabled systems evolved to meet these needs.

2.4.5   Advantages and Disadvantages of Database Approach

The segregation of the application program and the data remains the biggest advantage of the database approach. Database systems achieve this independence through a DBMS and metadata. The database approach results in minimal data duplication because all data files are integrated into a single logical structure. This avoids the duplication of data files for different programs; the DBMS knows where things are stored, how to retrieve them, and how to update them. As a result, modern relational databases provide inexperienced end-users with another important advantage: the ability to retrieve data easily. Because the database approach minimizes data dependency, users no longer have to rewrite application programs for small changes in the database. This reduces development time and maintenance needs considerably.

The main disadvantages of the database approach result from its complexity, size, and cost. The database approach is complicated and demands high skill levels to design and maintain the system. Because of the need for specialized software, such as database management systems, and for highly skilled personnel, this approach is expensive and, therefore, often not feasible for individuals and smaller businesses. However, in today's technology-driven marketplace, the long-term benefits of this approach more than compensate for its higher initial cost.

2.5 *Database Development Process*

We have presented the database approach and discussed various components of a database system. In this section, we give an overview of the database development process. The main goal of a database system is to provide users with an abstract view of data, while hiding unnecessary details of how data is stored and manipulated. The development process can be described through the following four steps (see Figure 2.6).

Step 1: Enterprise Modeling   This step describes, in general terms, the data needed for database system. This includes reviewing and analyzing any existing system and estimating the requirements for the database.

Step 2: Conceptual Database Modeling   This step takes the output of step 1 (the requirements) and outlines high-level categories of data (entities) and major relationships that are relevant to the organization. This is often done with the help of an entity-relationship (E-R) modeling. E-R modeling develops a conceptual data model in the form of an E-R diagram (see Chapter 3 for more details on this subject).

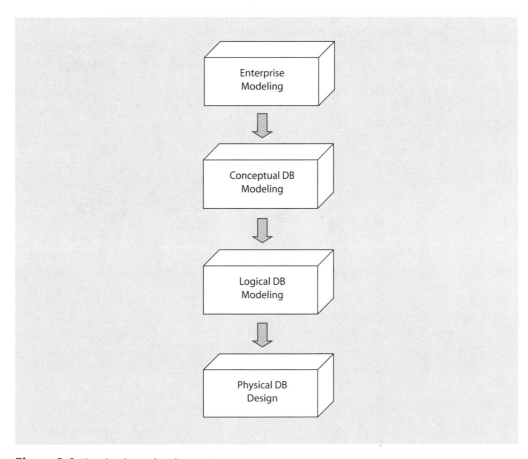

Figure 2.6 The database development process.

Step 3: Logical Database Design   In this step, the relational data modeling is used to transform the E-R diagram developed in Step 2 into a relational schema or a list of database tables (see Chapter 4 for more details on this subject).

Step 4: Physical Database Design and Creation   This step pertains to the selection of software (DBMS) and hardware. We define the physical structure of the database as an output of this step. We select the MS Access DBMS to create database tables and build queries (see Chapters 5-11).

The process of database development can also be explained using *schema*, an overall description of the database. A database can have three types of schemas defined by their levels of abstraction (see Figure 2.7).

At the highest level, multiple external schemas correspond to the data view. The *external schema* describes the database in terms of data viewed by different users. This abstraction separates the data view from the underlying technology used to store the data. For example, the external schema of user 1 indicates that the date field is in MM-DD-YYYY format; for user 2, on the other hand, this same date might be displayed in DD-MM-YY format, while the date might be stored in DD-MM-YYYY format in the database.

The *conceptual schema* describes the database in terms of entities, attributes, and relationships, along with its integrity constraints (see Chapter 4). This level is concerned with the actual data that a database stores. We do not deal with the format of the date field in this schema; instead, we decide that the database must include a date field. Entities, attributes, and relationships are tools that allow us to express what data we need for a database. This step requires us to conceptualize our design as we develop a database.

At the lowest level of abstraction, the *internal schema* describes the database in terms of stored records, data fields, and indexes. Continuing with the example of the date field, the in-

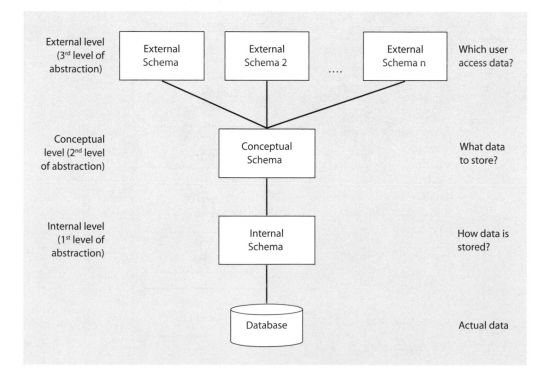

Figure 2.7 Three-tier (schema) architecture.

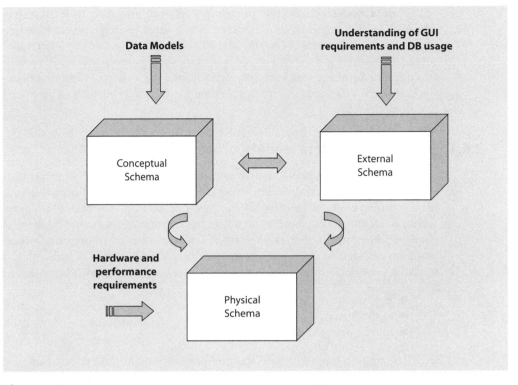

Figure 2.8 The database development process (schema model).

ternal schema is concerned with defining the date field as a date/time data type and with the disk space required for each data field. The display format of the date field or whether we need a data field is abstracted by higher-level schemas. The internal schema covers the physical aspects of database design and creation. Each database has exactly one conceptual schema, one internal schema, and multiple external schemas.

Now that we have defined the three database schemas, we are ready to describe the database development process in terms of these schemas. Figure 2.8 depicts this process. Although the three schemas appear in a hierarchically arranged tier in Figure 2.7, conceptual and external schemas are developed interactively in the development process. For example, we employ data models to develop the first form of a conceptual schema. Then, we consider the various GUI and database requirements that may require the addition or removal of attributes from the conceptual design. This process can mediate between different schematic categories until we have finalized our design. We then move to the physical schema with additional inputs of hardware and performance requirements.

2.6 *Data Models*

Schemas are complex and appear so to most end-users working with problem requirements. Data models, however, provide a clearer and more accurate description and representation of data, and they play an important role in the conceptual design of databases. Data models provide a standard platform that enables database designers and end-users to communicate.

A **data model** is a collection of concepts for describing data, its relationships, and its constraints. As with schemas, data models come in three varieties: object-based models, record-based models, and physical data models. These three types of data models parallel the three tiers of database schemas described above. The object-based and record-based models describe data at conceptual and external levels, respectively, and the physical model describes data at the internal level. For the remainder of this chapter, we will briefly introduce object-based and record-based modeling.

2.6.1   Object-Based Data Models

Object-based data models use entities, attributes, and relationships to present information. An *entity* is defined as a living or non-living object in the real world. For example, a person, place, or event is an entity. An *attribute* is a property of an entity. For example, a person's name and address can serve as attributes in an object-based model. A *relationship* is defined as an association between entities. For example, if a database contains information about the fact that students register for courses, *register* constitutes a relationship between the STUDENT and COURSE entities. Some common types of object-based data models include the following:

- Entity-relationship data model
- Functional data model
- Object-oriented data model

The *entity-relationship model* has emerged as one of the most popular and widely used techniques in today's databases. The entity-relationship model describes data in the form of an E-R diagram. Figure 2.9 depicts a part of an E-R diagram for a university organization. The participating entities, STUDENT and DEPARTMENT, are designated by rectangles. The relationship, *Belongs to*, is located within a diamond. The ovals are the properties of an entity and designate its attributes. This diagram also presents the cardinalities ("\>" and "|") associated with the relationship. Cardinalities operate like constraints. In this example, each student belongs to exactly one department, but a department can have one or more students. We concentrate only on the entity-relationship (E-R) model and discuss it in depth in Chapter 3. Entity-relationship models are best suited for conceptual database design.

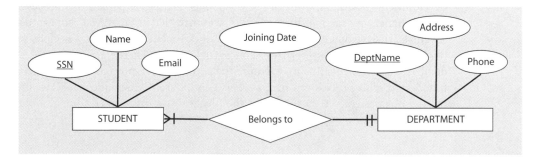

Figure 2.9 An entity-relationship diagram.

2.6.2   Record-Based Data Models

Record-based data models use records to present data. A *record* is a structure that contains a fixed number of fields to hold a piece of information (see Figure 2.10). There are three main types of record-based data models:

STUDENT

SSN	Name	Email	DeptName	JoiningDate
234-23-2535	John Doe	John.Doe@mail.com	ISE	7/4/99
545-28-2324	Samuel Ed	Samuel.Ed@mail.com	CISE	7/9/00
368-98-4234	Jay Leno	Jay.Leno@mail.com	ISE	7/2/01
975-34-3558	Ricky Grey	Ricky.Grey@mail.com	PHY	7/9/01

DEPARTMENT

DeptName	Address	Phone
ISE	Weil Hall, GNV, FL	352-222-1111
CISE	Marston Science, GNV, FL	352-333-9999
PHY	Physics Bldg, GNV, FL	352-444-8888
CHEM	Chemistry Bldg, GNV, FL	352-555-3333

Figure 2.10 A relational data model.

- Relational data models
- Network data models
- Hierarchical data models

Relational data models are based on mathematical concepts of relations. These models use tables (or relations) to represent data and relationships. Figure 2.10 depicts a relational data model as it might be implemented by a university.

The university relational data model in Figure 2.10 has two tables: a student table and a department table. Each table consists of a fixed number of named columns (attributes) and an arbitrary number of unnamed rows (records). The student table in the figure provides information about students, and the department table provides information about departments. For example, row 1 in the student table includes the social security number, name, email address, and department affiliation of student John Doe. The department table, on the other hand, provides information about the ISE department, including its address and phone. It is important to note that the relationship between the student and department tables is not as explicit as in the E-R model. We only know about the relationship by a common field, *DeptName*, in these tables. The *DeptName* attribute in the student table indicates that a student belongs to a particular department.

In this book, we concentrate only on the relational data model and discuss it depth in Chapter 4. The relational data model is best suited for logical database design.

It is not hard to realize that the E-R model and the relational model are actually closely related to each other. Entities in the E-R model become tables in the relational model; attributes of entities in the E-R model are the table columns in the relational model; and the relationships in the E-R model are represented by a common attribute in the relational model. In fact, the process of logical database design requires transforming the conceptual design (an E-R diagram) into the logical design (list of relations). This well-documented transformation follows systematic rules, which we explore in Chapter 4. Figure 2.11 depicts such a transformation for the student-department E-R diagram.

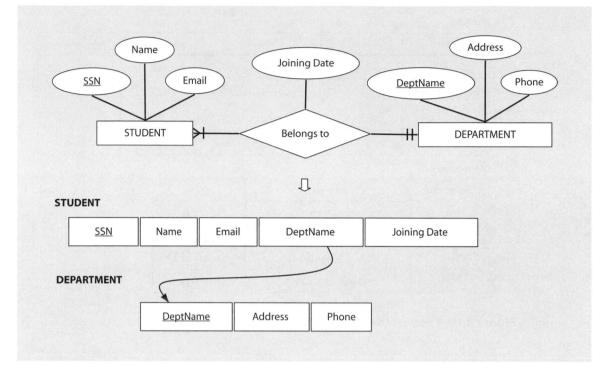

Figure 2.11 Transforming the E-R data model to the relational data model.

2.7 *Summary*

- *Data* are known facts that can be recorded and preserved. *Information* is the processed data presented in a form suitable for human interpretation. *Metadata* is data about data.

- There are two approaches to convert data to information: a traditional *file-based approach* and a modern *database approach*. A system of files and the collection of computer programs manipulating them is a file-based system. A database system consists of a combination of a database, a DBMS, and application programs.

- A *database* is an organized collection of logically related data.

- A *database management system* is software that allows users to define, create, and manage database access.

- *Database applications* are computer programs that allow users to manipulate data in a DBMS through a user-friendly interface.

- A *database administrator* (DBA) is a person or group of people responsible for all the data resources of an organization.

- The database development process consists of four steps. Step 1: Enterprise modeling; Step 2: Concep-

tual database modeling; Step 3: Logical database design; and Step 4: Physical database design and creation.

- The process of database development can also be explained through the *schema*, an overall description of the database. The external schema describes the database in terms of data viewed by different users. The conceptual schema describes the database in terms of entities, attributes, and relationships along with integrity constraints. At the lowest level of abstraction, the internal schema describes the database in terms of stored records, data fields, and indexes.

- A data model is a collection of concepts for describing data, its relationships, and its constraints. *Object-based* data models use entities, attributes, and relationships to present information. The *entity-relationship data model* is an example of an object-based model and describes data in the form of an E-R diagram. *Record-based* data models use records to present data. *Relational data model* is based on mathematical concepts of relations and is an example of record-based model.

2.8 *Exercises*

2.8.1 Review Questions

1. Define each of the following terms:
   a. Database
   b. Database System
   c. Database Application
   d. Database Management System

2. To what does the term "data" refer? Name the different formats that can present data.

3. Define "information." Explain the associations and the differences that exist between data and information.

4. Define "metadata." Explain how it relates to data and information.

5. Answer the following questions:
   a. What is a file-based system?
   b. What are the limitations of a file-based approach?

6. Name the database systems that have been developed so far. When was each system introduced?

7. What are the advantages of using the database approach versus the file-based approach for managing a database?

8. Answer the following questions:
   a. What are the functions of a database management system? Explain them.
   b. What are the advantages of using a database management system?
   c. What are the disadvantages of using a database management system?
   d. Name the popular database management software packages.
   e. Name four categories of database applications.

9. Answer the following questions:
   a. Name the three levels of abstraction of the three-tier architecture.
   b. What is a database schema?

10. Answer the following questions:
    a. What is a data model and why do we use it?
    b. What does an external data model represent?
    c. What does an internal data model represent?
    d. What does a conceptual data model represent?

11. Answer the following questions:
    a. What are the characteristics of object-based data models?
    b. Define the following terms: "entity," "attribute," and "relation." Provide an example for each term.
    c. Name some of the common types of object-based data models.

2.8.2 Hands-On Exercises

1. Answer the following questions related to the entity-relationship diagram below:

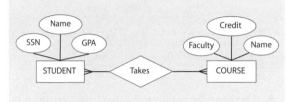

   a. What are the entities in the above E-R diagram? What are their attributes?
   b. What is the relationship between the entities?

2. Answer the following questions about the record-based data models:
   a. What is a record?
   b. What is the relationship between record-based data models and entity-relationship models?
   c. Name the three main types of record-based data modeling.

3. The Center of Higher Education summarized the information about the number of students in a particular state in the following table:

STUDENTS

University	No of Students
The State	40,567
JohnCorel	20,100
Western	17,267
Eastern University	30,000

Draw a pie chart (see Figure 2.1) to demonstrate the distribution of the students by university in this state.

4. The following table presents part of the data kept by a university. Answer the following questions:
   a. What does a row of table *Book* represents?
   b. What does a row of table *Publisher* represents?
   c. Is there a relationship between the two tables (*Book* and *Publisher*)?

BOOK

ISBN	TITLE	Author	Publisher
0-471-283665	Integer Programming	L.A. Wolsey	John Wiley & Sons
0-19-5108094	Investment Science	D.G.	Oxford University
3-540-653678	Approximation	V.V. Vazirani	Springer

PUBLISHER

Name	Address	Telephone
John Wiley & Sons	Atlanta	455-321-8899
Oxford University	New York	345-190-1283
Springer	New York	345-190-2234

5. The figure below presents the entity-relationship diagram for the College of Engineering in a university. Refer to the diagram to answer the following questions:
   a. Identify the entities of the above E-R diagram. What are their attributes?
   b. Which relationship shown in the diagram identifies the courses taken by a student?
   c. Which relationship identifies the courses taught by a professor?

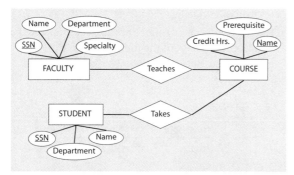

6. See Figure 2.10 to answer the following questions:
   a. What is the email address of the student with SSN 234-23-2535?
   b. In which department is Samuel Ed enrolled?

   c. What is the phone number of the PHY department?
   d. Name one of the students of the ISE department.
   e. Develop a metadata chart (see Figure 2.1) for the data attributes in Figure 2.10.

7. The figure below presents the product database of a large apparel manufacturer. Refer to the figure to answer the following questions:
   a. What order(s) is/are outstanding for January 2003?
   b. What product is included in order O1120? (Give the product name, size, color, and the quantity ordered.)
   c. Name some of the products produced in the production line "Jeans."

PRODUCT

P-ID	P-Name	Color	Size	PL-Name	Inventory
P101	Straight-leg	Black	30-32	Jeans	1,263
P102	Boot-leg cut	Blue	30-34	Jeans	2,713
P103	Boot-leg cut	White	34-38	Jeans	3,121

PRODUCTION LINE

PL-Name	Classification	Manager
Jeans	Menswear	K.L. Jim
T-shirts	Kids	M. Fang
Swimwear	Kids	D. Stan

ORDER

ID	Customer	P-ID	Due Date	Quantity
O1120	J.C. Penny	P101	Jan. 10, 2003	500
O1121	SEARS	P110	Feb. 15, 2003	1,200
O1122	Dillard	P230	March 5,	1,500

   d. Assume that straight-leg jeans will not be produced during the month of January 2003. What will the inventory level be for black straight-leg jeans of size 30–32 on January 31, 2003?
   e. Identify any relationships in this database.
   f. Develop a metadata chart (see Figure 2.1) for the data attributes in the tables *Product*, *Production Line*, and *Order*.

8. The following table summarizes total sales by product for year 2002. The apparel manufacturer wants to identify which product and which production line has been the most successful during

the last year (2002). Answer the following related questions:

a. Which product had the highest sales in 2002?

b. Which production line had the highest sales in 2002?

c. Develop a pie chart (see Figure 2.1) for the sales of 2002.

d. Develop a metadata chart (see Figure 2.1) for the data attributes in the table *Sales*.

SALES

ID	Sales
P101	12,130
P402	9,130
P103	7,267
P110	5,999
P213	1,109
P390	1,030
P320	550

three Entity-Relationship Modeling

chapter OVERVIEW

3.1   *Introduction*

In Chapter 2, we introduced data models. *A data model* is an integrated collection of concepts that represents real world objects, events, and their relationships. We also briefly discussed two types of data models: object-based data models and relation-based data models. It is a common practice in database design to develop an object-based model first and then to systematically convert the model into a relation-based model, which is more suitable for database implementation. In this chapter, we will focus on conceptual database design using object-based models. In Chapter 4, we will discuss the relational data models.

The three most popular object-based models discussed in database literature are the entity-relationship model, the functional model, and the object-oriented model. The entity-relationship model has emerged as one of the most popular techniques in the design of databases due to its inherent advantages. The entity-relationship (E-R) model is easy to learn, yet powerful enough to model complex, real-world scenarios. We have therefore chosen the E-R model for database design discussion.

3.1.1   Topics

This chapter discusses the following topics:

- Entities, attributes, and relationships in entity-relationship diagram.
- Degree of relationships: unary, binary, and ternary relationships.
- Cardinality of relationships: one-to-one relationships, one-to-many relationships, many-to-many relationships.
- Associative and weak entity types.
- Enhanced entity-relationship diagram: generalization and specialization process, and participation and disjoint constraints.

3.2   *The Entity-Relationship Model*

An *entity-relationship model* describes data in terms of the following:

1. Entities
2. Relationship between entities
3. Attributes of entities

We graphically display an E-R model using an **entity-relationship diagram** (or E-R diagram) like the sample in Figure 3.1. While this figure may seem to be confusing at first glance, its meaning should become very clear by the end of this chapter.

We will now discuss the components of an E-R diagram in detail.

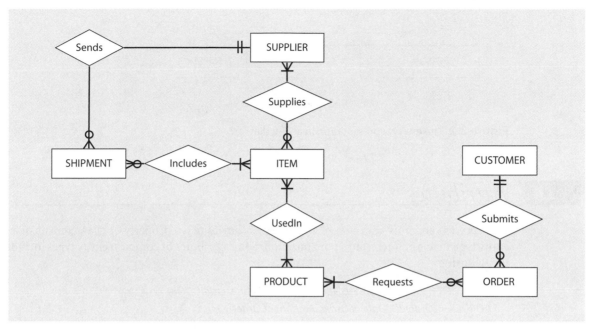

Figure 3.1 Example of an E-R diagram.

3.3 *Entity*

An ***entity*** is an object that exists and which is distinguishable from other objects. An entity can be a person, a place, an object, an event, or a concept about which an organization wishes to maintain data. The following are some examples of entities:

Person: STUDENT, EMPLOYEE, CLIENT
Object: COUCH, AIRPLANE, MACHINE
Place: CITY, NATIONAL PARK, ROOM, WAREHOUSE
Event: WAR, MARRIAGE, LEASE
Concept: PROJECT, ACCOUNT, COURSE

It is important to understand the distinction between an *entity type*, an *entity instance*, and an *entity set*. An ***entity type*** defines a collection of entities that have same attributes. An ***entity instance*** is a single item in this collection. An ***entity set*** is a set of entity instances. The following example will clarify this distinction: STUDENT is an entity type; a student with ID number 555-55-5555 is an entity instance; and a collection of all students is an entity set.

In the E-R diagram, we assign a name to each entity type. When assigning names to entity types, we follow certain naming conventions. An entity name should be a concise singular noun that captures the unique characteristics of the entity type. An E-R diagram depicts an entity type using a rectangle with the name of the entity inside (see Figure 3.2).

Figure 3.2 The entity representation in an E-R diagram.

3.4 *Attributes*

We represent an entity with a set of attributes. An ***attribute*** is a property or characteristic of an entity type that is of interest to an organization. Some attributes of common entity types include the following:

STUDENT = {Student ID, SSN, Name, Address, Phone, Email, DOB}
ORDER = {Order ID, Date of Order, Amount of Order}
ACCOUNT = {Account Number, Account Type, Date Opened, Balance}
CITY = {City Name, State, Population}

We use the following conventions while naming attributes:

1. Each word in a name starts with an uppercase letter followed by lower case letters.
2. If an attribute name contains two or more words, the first letter of each subsequent word is also in uppercase, unless it is an article or preposition, such as "a," "the," "of," or "about" (see Figure 3.3).

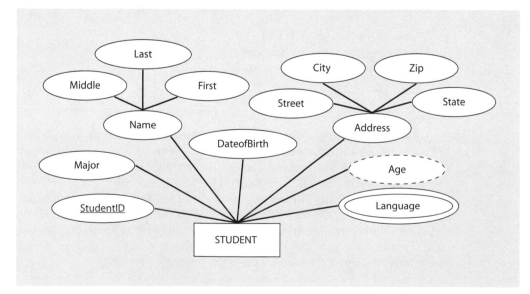

Figure 3.3 Attributes of the STUDENT entity type.

E-R diagrams depict an attribute inside an ellipse and connect the ellipse with a line to the associated entity type. Figure 3.3 illustrates some of the possible attributes in an E-R diagram for the entity STUDENT.

Notice that not all of the attributes in Figure 3.3 are marked in the same way. There are actually several types of attributes featured in this figure. These include: simple, composite, single-valued, multi-valued, stored, and derived attributes. In the following subsections, we discuss the distinctions between these types of attributes.

3.4.1 Simple and Composite Attributes

A **simple** or an **atomic attribute**, such as *City* or *State*, cannot be further divided into smaller components. A **composite attribute**, however, can be divided into smaller subparts in which each subpart represents an independent attribute. *Name* and *Address* are the only composite attributes in Figure 3.3. All other attributes, even those that are subcategories of *Name* and *Address*, are simple attributes. The figure also presents the notation that depicts a composite attribute.

3.4.2 Single-Valued and Multi-Valued Attributes

Most attributes have a single value for an entity instance; such attributes are called **single-valued attributes**. A **multi-valued attribute**, on the other hand, may have more than one value for an entity instance. Figure 3.3 features one multi-valued attribute, *Languages*, which stores the names of the languages that a student speaks. Since a student may speak several languages, it is a multi-valued attribute. All other attributes of the STUDENT entity type are single-valued attributes. For example, a student has only one date of birth and one student identification number. In the E-R diagram, we denote a multi-valued attribute with a double-lined ellipse. Note that in a multi-valued attribute, we always use a double-lined ellipse, regardless of the number of values.

3.4.3 Stored and Derived Attributes

The value of a **derived attribute** can be determined by analyzing other attributes. For example, in Figure 3.3 *Age* is a derived attribute because its value can be derived from the current date and the attribute *DateofBirth*. An attribute whose value cannot be derived from the values of other attributes is called a **stored attribute**. As we will learn, a derived attribute *Age* is not stored in the database. Derived attributes are depicted in the E-R diagram with a dashed ellipse.

3.4.4 Key Attribute

A **key attribute** (or identifier) is a single attribute or a combination of attributes that uniquely identify an individual instance of an entity type. No two instances within an entity set can have the same key attribute value. For the STUDENT entity shown in Figure 3.3, *StudentID* is the key attribute since each student identification number is unique. *Name*, by contrast, cannot be an identifier because two students can have the same name. We underline key attributes in an E-R diagram (also see Figure 3.4).

Sometimes no single attribute can uniquely identify an instance of an entity type. However, in these circumstances, we identify a set of attributes that, when combined, is unique for each entity instance. In this case the key attribute, also known as **composite key**, is not a simple attribute, but a composite attribute that uniquely identifies each entity instance.

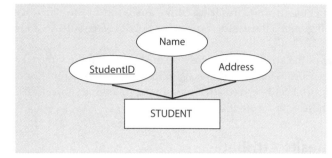

Figure 3.4 The key attribute.

A composite key must be minimal in the sense that no subset of a composite key can form the key of the entity instance. For example, if a composite key has four attributes, A1 to A4, then any subset, say A2, A4 or A2, A3 (or any of 16 combinations), should not form a key for an entity. In other words, we need all attributes, A1–A4, to identify each instance of an entity uniquely. In the E-R diagram, we underline each attribute in the composite key.

For example, consider the CITY entity type (see Figure 3.5). This category includes, potentially, all the cities in the United States. Notice that none of the attributes (i.e. *Name*, *State* or *Population*) can serve as a key attribute since there are many cities in each state and two cities could possibly have the same name or population. However, the composite attribute {*Name*, *State*} is a valid key attribute for the CITY entity as no two cities within a state can have the same name.

An entity can have more than one attribute that qualifies to be an identifier. For the entity shown in Figure 3.6, each of the attributes *Name*, *StateAbbr*, and *UnionOrder* (the order in which the state entered the union of the United States) can be an identifier. In this case, it is a matter of preference as to which attribute is made an identifier or key attribute.

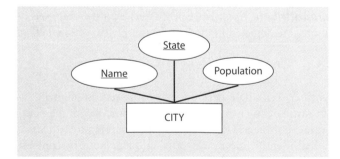

Figure 3.5 The composite key attribute.

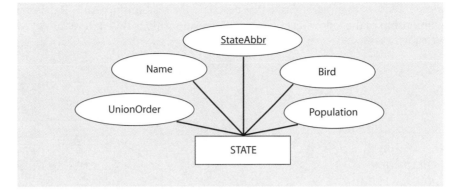

Figure 3.6 An example of more than one key attribute.

3.5 *Relationships*

Entities in an organization do not exist in isolation but are related to each other. Students take courses and each STUDENT entity is related to the COURSE entity. Faculty members teach courses and each FACULTY entity is also related to the COURSE entity. Consequently, the STUDENT entity is related to the FACULTY entity through the COURSE entity. E-R diagrams can also illustrate relationships between entities.

We define a ***relationship*** as an association among several entities. Consider, for example, an association between customers of a bank. If customer Williams has a bank account number 523, then the quality of ownership constitutes a ***relationship instance*** that associates the CUSTOMER instance Williams with the ACCOUNT instance *523*. We can think of the relationship instance as a verb that links a subject and an object: customer Williams *has* an account; student John *registers* for a course; professor Smith *teaches* a course. A ***relationship set*** is a grouping of all matching relationship instances, and the term ***relationship type*** refers to the relationship between entity types. For example, Figure 3.7 illustrates a relationship set between the CUSTOMER and the ACCOUNT instances.

In an E-R diagram, we represent relationship types with diamond-shaped boxes connected by straight lines to the rectangles that represent participating entity types. A relationship type is a given name that is displayed in this diamond-shaped box and typically takes the form of a

Definition

An **entity** is an object that exists and that is distinguishable from other objects.

An **attribute** is a property or characteristic of an entity type that is of interest to an organization.

A **relationship** is an association among several entities.

present tense verb or verb phrase that describes the relationship. An E-R diagram may depict a relationship as the following example of the relationship between the entities CUSTOMER and ACCOUNT does:

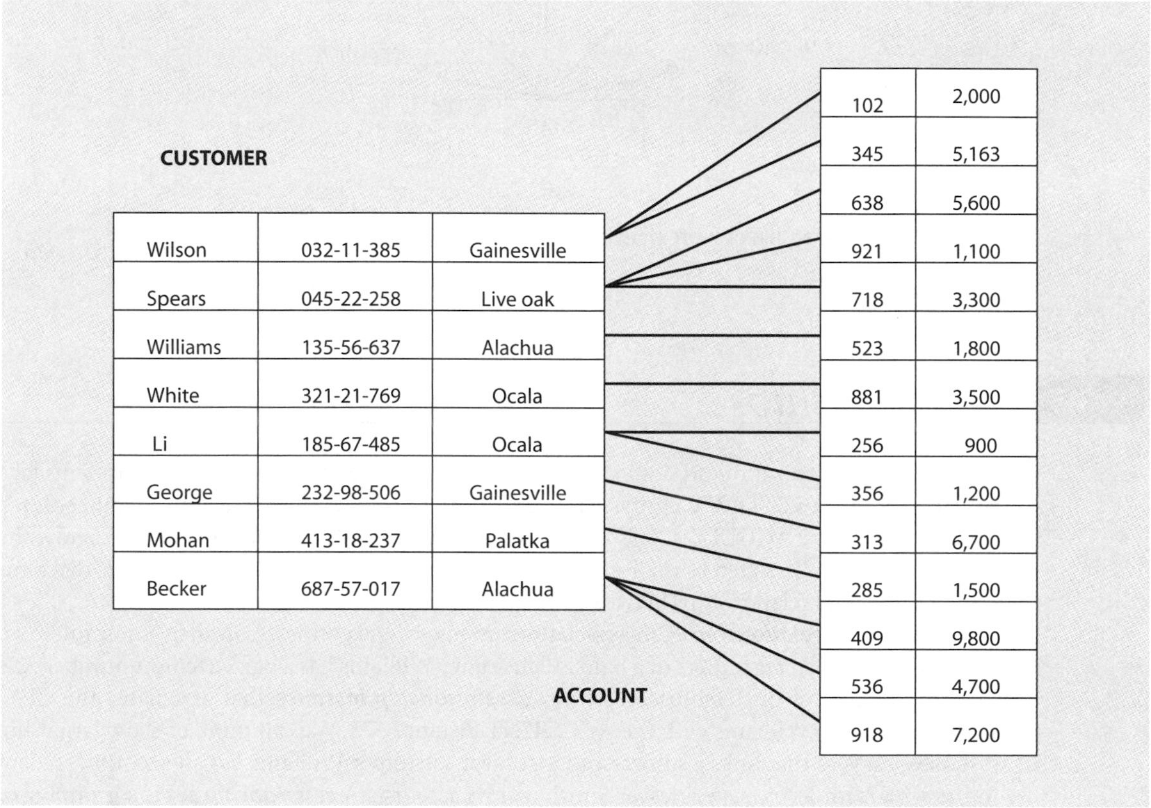

CUSTOMER				
			102	2,000
			345	5,163
			638	5,600
Wilson	032-11-385	Gainesville	921	1,100
Spears	045-22-258	Live oak	718	3,300
Williams	135-56-637	Alachua	523	1,800
White	321-21-769	Ocala	881	3,500
Li	185-67-485	Ocala	256	900
George	232-98-506	Gainesville	356	1,200
Mohan	413-18-237	Palatka	313	6,700
Becker	687-57-017	Alachua	285	1,500
			409	9,800
		ACCOUNT	536	4,700
			918	7,200

Figure 3.7 The relationship set between the CUSTOMER and ACCOUNT entities.

3.6   *Degree of a Relationship*

The number of entity sets that participate in a relationship is called the ***degree of relationship***. For example, the degree of the relationship featured in Figure 3.8 is two because CUSTOMER and ACCOUNT are two separate entity types that participate in the relationship. The three most common degrees of a relationship in a database are unary (degree 1), binary (degree 2), and ternary (degree 3). We will briefly define these degrees and then explore each kind of relationship in detail in subsequent sections.

Let E_1, E_2, . . . , E_n denote n entity sets and let R be the relationship. The degree of the relationship can also be expressed as follows:

Unary Relationship   A unary relationship R is an association between two instances of the same entity type (i.e., R $\in E_1 \times E_1$). For example, two students are roommates and stay together in an apartment. Because they share the same address, a unary relationship exists between them for the attribute *Address* in Figure 3.3.

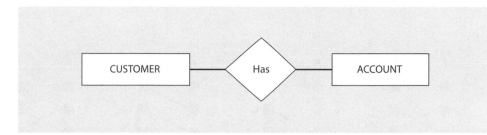

Figure 3.8 The relationship between CUSTOMER and ACCOUNT entities in an E-R diagram.

Binary Relationship   A binary relationship R is an association between two instances of two different entity types (i.e., $R \in E_1 \times E_2$). For example, in a university, a binary relationship exists between a student (STUDENT entity) and an instructor (FACULTY entity) of a single class; an instructor *teaches* a student.

Ternary Relationship   A ternary relationship R is an association between three instances of three different entity types (i.e., $R \in E_1 \times E_2 \times E_3$). For example, consider a student using certain equipment for a project. In this case, the STUDENT, PROJECT, and EQUIPMENT entity types relate to each other with ternary relationships: a student *checks out* equipment for a project.

3.7   *Cardinality of a Relationship*

The term *cardinal number* refers to the number used in counting. An *ordinal number*, by contrast, emphasizes the order of a number (1st, 7th, etc.). When we say cardinality of a relationship, we mean the ability to count the number of entities involved in that relationship. For example, if the entity types A and B are connected by a relationship, then the **maximum cardinality** represents the maximum number of instances of entity B that can be associated with any instance of entity A.

However, we don't need to assign a number value for every level of connection in a relationship. In fact, the term *maximum cardinality* refers to only two possible values: one or many. While this may seem to be too simple, the division between one and many allows us to categorize all of the permutations possible in any relationship. The maximum cardinality value of a relationship, then, allows us to define the four types of relationships possible between entity types A and B. Figure 3.9 illustrates these types of relationships.

One-to-One Relationship   In a one-to-one relationship, at most one instance of entity B can be associated with a given instance of entity A and vice versa.

One-to-Many Relationship   In a one-to-many relationship, many instances of entity B can be associated with a given instance of entity A. However, only one instance of entity A can be associated with a given instance of entity B. For example, while a customer of a company can make many orders, an order can only be related to a single customer.

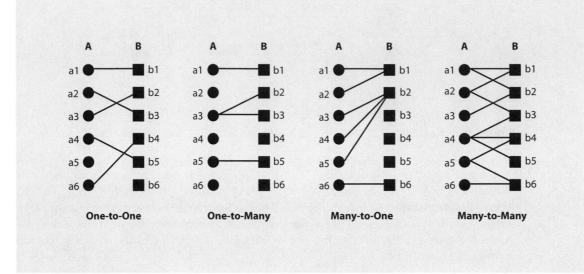

Figure 3.9 The four types of relationships between entity types A and B.

Many-to-Many Relationship   In a many-to-many relationship, many instances of entity A can be associated with a given instance of entity B, and, likewise, many instances of entity B can be associated with a given instance of entity A. For example, a machine may have different parts, while each individual part may be used in different machines.

Representing Relationship Types   Figure 3.10 displays how we represent different relationship types in an E-R diagram. An entity on the *one* side of the relationship is represented by a vertical line, "I," which intersects the line connecting the entity and the relationship. Entities on the *many* side of a relationship are designated by a crowfoot as depicted in Figure 3.10.

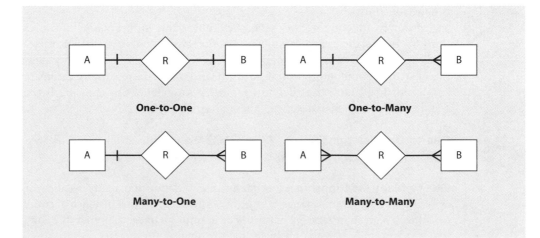

Figure 3.10 The relationship types based on maximum cardinality.

We will now discuss the minimum cardinality of a relationship. The ***minimum cardinality*** between two entity types A and B is defined as the minimum number of instances of entity B that must be associated with each instance of entity A. In an E-R diagram, we allow the minimum cardinality to take two values: zero or one. If the minimum cardinality is zero, we say that entity type B is an *optional* participant in the relationship; otherwise, it is a *mandatory* participant. An optional relationship is represented by an "O" and mandatory relationship is represented by "|" in an E-R diagram.

Figure 3.11 shows the four possibilities of the minimum cardinality of a relationship between two entity types A and B. Figure 3.11(a) depicts a situation in which no minimum cardinality constraints exist between the instances of entities A and B, meaning both entities A and B are optional participants in the relationship. Figure 3.11(b) illustrates a situation in which each instance of entity B must be associated with at least one instance of entity A, but no association is required for an instance of entity A. Figure 3.11(c) illustrates a situation in which each instance of entity A must be associated with at least one instance of entity B, but no association is required for an instance of entity B. Finally, Figure 3.11(d) illustrates a situation in which each instance of entity A and B must be associated with at least one instance of entity B and A, respectively.

An E-R diagram displays both the maximum and the minimum cardinalities of the relationships between two entities. Since there are four basic possibilities of maximum cardinalities and four possibilities of minimum cardinalities between two entities, there are 16 types of relationships possible between two entities in terms of cardinality. We will see several examples of these relationships while studying unary, binary, and ternary relationships.

Definition

The number (unary, binary, or ternary) of entity sets that participate in a relationship is called the **degree of relationship**.

The **cardinality of relationship** represents the minimum/maximum number of instances of entity B that must/can be associated with any instance of entity A.

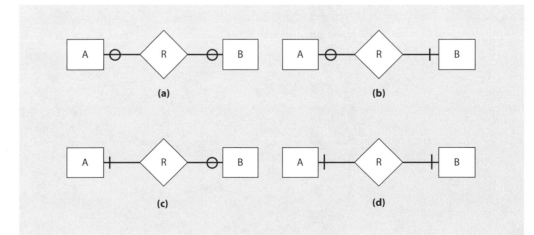

Figure 3.11 The relationship types based on minimum cardinality.

3.8 *Unary Relationship*

As we mentioned in Section 3.5, a unary relationship ($R \in E_1 \times E_1$) is an association between two entities of the same entity type. Figure 3.12(a) displays the E-R diagram of a unary relationship *IsMarriedTo*. Whenever two people in the entity type PERSON get married, the relationship instance *IsMarriedTo* is created. The *Date* of marriage is an attribute of this relationship. Since a person can only be married to one other person, marriage is a one-to-one relationship. Furthermore, since a person can be unmarried, the minimum cardinality of the *IsMarriedTo* relationship is zero.

Figure 3.12(b) depicts several relationship instances of this relationship type. Each relationship instance (r1, r2, r3, and r4) connects two instances in PERSON. The lines allow us to

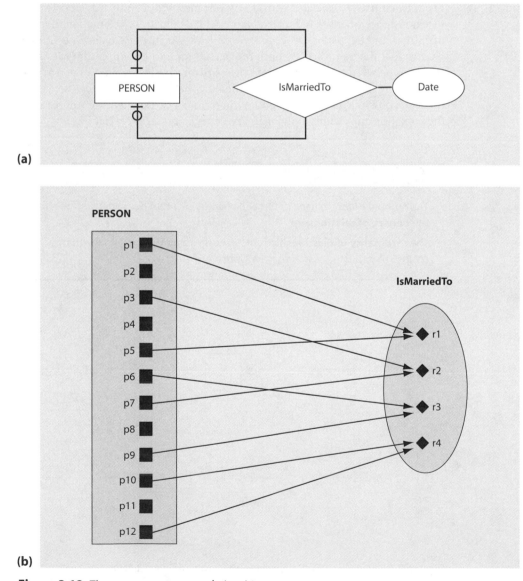

(a)

(b)

Figure 3.12 The unary one-to-one relationship.

read relationships between entity instances. For example, r1 suggests that person p1 is married to person p5, and so forth.

Figure 3.13(a) illustrates another example of a unary relationship, expressed by the relationship instance *Supervises*. This relationship instance exists whenever an employee supervises another employee. The relationship *Supervises* is a one-to-many relationship since an employer can supervise many employees but a supervisee can have only one supervisor. The minimum cardinality for supervising is zero (an employee may not supervise anyone) but the minimum cardinality of being supervised is one (every employee must be supervised).

Figure 3.13(b) shows several relationship instances of this relationship type. Each relationship instance (r1, r2, r3, and r4) connects two entity instances in EMPLOYEE; these are the supervisor instance and the supervisee instance. For example, r2 suggests that employee e3 supervises employee e7, and so forth.

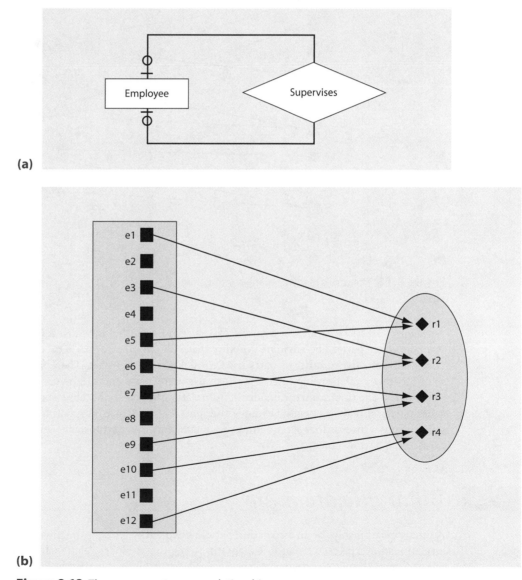

(a)

(b)

Figure 3.13 The unary one-to-many relationship.

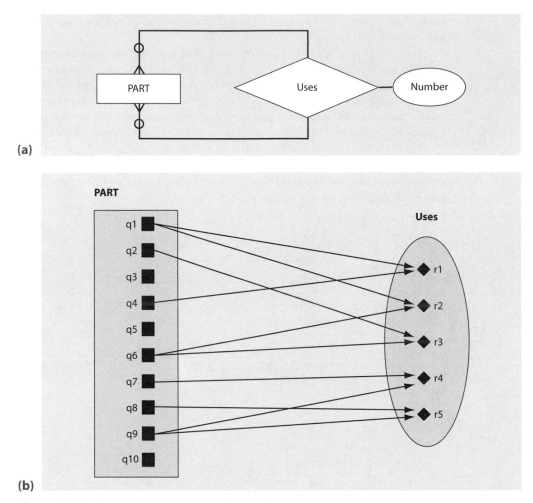

Figure 3.14 The unary many-to-many relationship.

Figure 3.14(a) provides an example of a unary relationship in which certain parts are used to make other parts. The attribute *Number* stores the number of parts used. The relationship *Uses* quantifies the number of parts used to make any other part. The *Uses* relationship is a many-to-many relationship since a part can use many parts and can be used in the making of many parts. The minimum cardinality of this relationship is zero because a part may not use any other part and may not be used by any other part. Figure 3.14(b) displays five instances of this relationship. Observe that several lines can emanate from a part instance and several lines terminate at a part instance.

3.9 *Binary Relationship*

A binary relationship, or an association between two entity types, is the most common form of a relationship expressed by an E-R diagram. Recall that a binary relationship is $R \in E_1 \times E_2$ in which E_1 and E_2 are two different entity types. The examples of binary relationships with the relationship instances are presented in Figure 3.15. Notice that each relationship instance obeys a basic characteristic of the binary relationships; in other words, each relationship instance is connected to exactly two entity instances of different entity types.

By applying what we have learned earlier in this chapter, we should be able to determine the cardinalities of these relationships quite easily. The relationship in Figure 3.15(a) is a one-to-one relationship since we assume that an employee can manage at most one department and each department is managed by at most one employee. The minimum cardinality can be determined

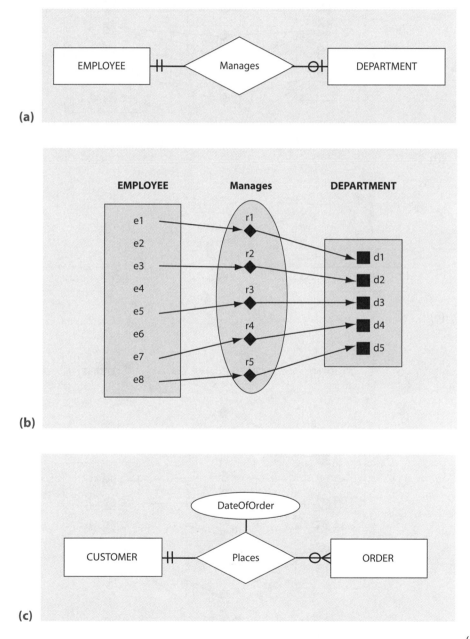

(a)

(b)

(c)

(continues)

Figure 3.15 (a) and (b): Binary one-to-one relationships; (c) and (d): Binary one-to-many relationships; (e) and (f): Binary many-many relationships.

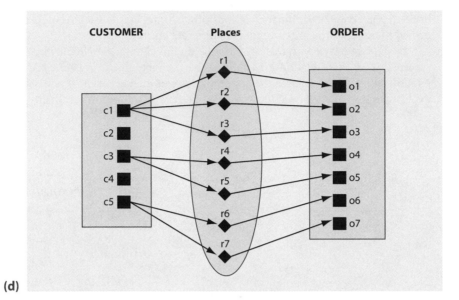

(d)

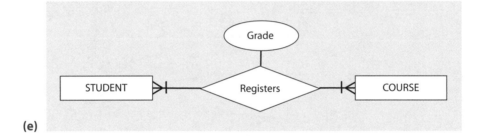

(e)

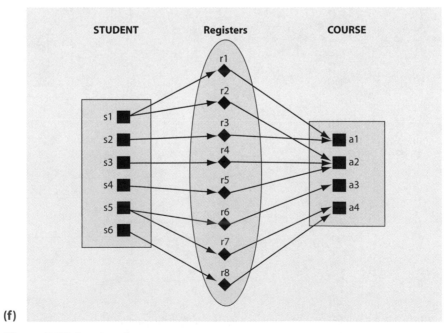

(f)

Figure 3.15 (*continued*)

since each department must be managed by an employee, but not all employees manage departments. For example, while some of the employees in Figure 3.15(b), such as e2, e4, and e6, do not manage a department, every department is managed by an employee.

The binary one-to-many relationship represented in Figure 3.15(c) features a slightly different arrangement. While a customer can place several orders or may choose not to order at all, each order must be placed by exactly one customer. Figure 3.15(d) shows us that, while each order is made by a single customer, not all customers place orders. However, Figure 3.15(d) differs from Figure 3.15(b) in that a single customer may place any number of orders; while the first customer places three orders, and the fifth customer places only two, both transactions represent a maximum cardinality of many.

Finally, Figure 3.15(e) and (f) illustrates a many-to-many relationship, featuring a minimum cardinality of zero and a maximum cardinality of many. In other words, each student can participate in many activities, a single activity, or no activity at all. Conversely, any number of students, from many to none, can participate in a given activity.

3.10 *Ternary Relationships*

Recall that a ternary relationship R is a relationship among instances of three different entity types, E_1, E_2, and E_3 ($R \in E_1 \times E_2 \times E_3$). Each instance of the ternary relationship R requires the participation of an instance from each of the entity types E_1, E_2, and E_3. See Figure 3.16 for examples of ternary relationships.

The examples in Figure 3.16(a) and (b) reveal the possible relationships associated with a competition for classical musicians. Let's suppose that at this competition, musicians perform individually and in small groups for judges who rate the performances. Each performance requires an artist, a composition, and a venue. Observe that each relationship instance, *Performs*, connects an entity instance of MUSICIAN, COMPOSITION, and VENUE. Each relationship instance also has an attribute, *Rating*, that stores the average rating of the performance by a panel of judges. Similarly, in Figure 3.16(c), students use equipment to work on projects; each instance of *Uses* involves an instance of STUDENT, PROJECT, and EQUIPMENT. If a student uses two pieces of equipment to work on a project, there are two instances of the relationship *Uses*. A campus lab may use the attribute in this ternary relationship, the *Date* of use, to log the equipment usage.

Ternary relationships differ significantly from the other kinds of relationships that we have examined so far. It is important to remember that a ternary relationship is not equivalent to two binary relationships. Suppose that we recognize this ternary relationship as a series of binary relationships, such as ARTIST-CONCERT, ARTIST-COMPOSITION, and CONCERT-COMPOSITION. These three binary relationships can store data about the artists who performed at different concerts, the compositions performed by artists, and the compositions performed at different concerts; however, the relationships cannot store the compositions performed by an artist at a particular concert. Therefore, three binary relationships cannot encapsulate the range of data stored by a single ternary relationship. A ternary relationship, though, can capture the data of three binary relationships.

Observe that the cardinalities of the relationships in Figure 3.16 are not expressed in the E-R diagrams. The cardinalities of a relationship are defined for a pair of entities; in a ternary relationship, there are three pairs of ternary relationships. We cannot express the cardinalities of these types of relationships in E-R diagrams. Instead, we can turn the ternary relationship into an associative entity, a process that we will discuss in Section 3.12. This technique allows us to demonstrate the cardinalities of the entities within the associative entity.

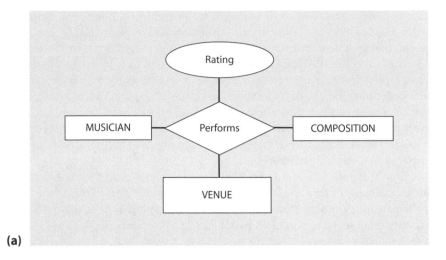

(a)

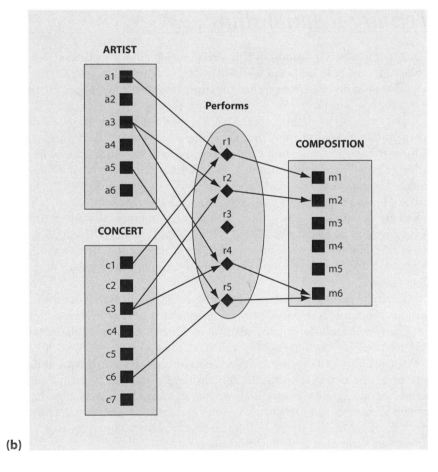

(b)

(continues)

Figure 3.16 Examples of ternary relationships.

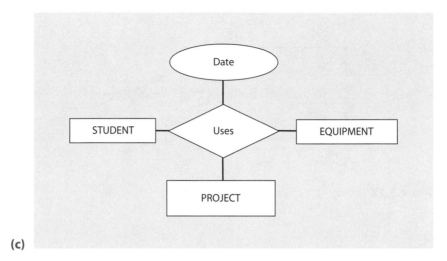

(c)

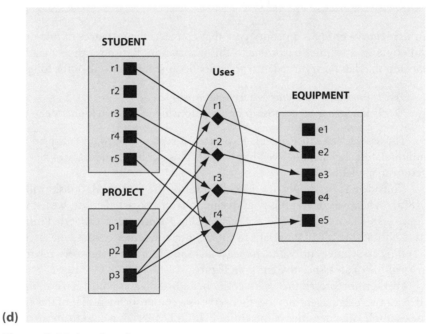

(d)

Figure 3.16 *(continued)*

3.11 *Attributes of Relationships*

We have already discussed examples of E-R diagrams that reveal attributes stemming off relationships. Recall Figure 3.15(c), for example. In that E-R diagram, the attribute *DateofOrder* collects data for the relationship CUSTOMER *places* ORDER. Attributes on relationships are like attributes on entity types we have seen so far. An attribute on a relationship stores information related to the relationship. In Figure 3.17, the attribute *Quantity* stores the number of components that make up an entity type ITEM. Note that the attribute *Quantity* stems from the relationship and not from the entity.

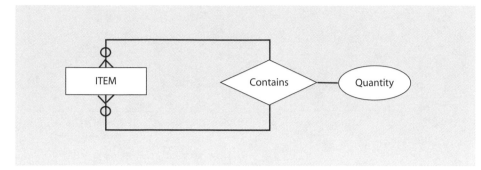

Figure 3.17 An example of attributes of relationships.

<h2> 3.12 *Associative Entities*</h2>

An ***associative entity*** is an entity type that connects the instances of one or more entity types and contains attributes particular to this association. Basically, an associative entity is a relationship that has been turned into an entity because it meets one of the following conditions:

1. It is a many-to-many binary relationship
2. It is a ternary relationship or a relationship of an even higher degree

The associative entity in an E-R diagram is represented by an entity box enclosing the diamond relationship symbol (see Figure 3.18). This symbol demonstrates that the entity is generated from a relationship.

Consider, for example, the E-R diagram of the binary relationship illustrated in Figure 3.18(a). When we convert this relationship into an associated entity, we get the E-R diagram in Figure 3.18(b). In the example, the relationship *Participates* is converted into an associated entity, ENROLLMENT. If the relationship has attributes, they become the attributes of the corresponding associative entity. *DateJoined* is an example of an attribute of a relationship turned into an attribute of an associative entity in Figure 3.18(b).

Furthermore, recall that every entity in an E-R diagram must have an identifier. The identifiers of two original entities together serve as a composite identifier of the associative entity. In our example, the identifier of the entity ENROLLMENT is a composite attribute comprised of the identifiers of the STUDENT and ACTIVITY entities. Since a student can enroll in every activity but can only enroll once in any given activity, the composite attribute {*StudentID, ActivityID*} is a valid identifier for the associated entity ENROLLMENT.

Now that ENROLLMENT is a new entity in Figure 3.18(b), note that there is no relationship diamond on the line between the entity STUDENT and the associative entity ENROLLMENT because the associative entity represents a relationship. Furthermore, the E-R diagram in Figure 3.18 (b) depicts the cardinalities. Each instance of the STUDENT entity is related to several instances of the ENROLLMENT entity; in fact, each instance of the STUDENT entity is related to as many instances of the ENROLLMENT entity as the number of activities in which the student participates. Therefore, there is a one-to-many relationship between the STUDENT entity type and the ENROLLMENT entity type. Similarly, there is a one-to-many relationship between the entity types ACTIVITY and ENROLLMENT because several students may enroll in one activity.

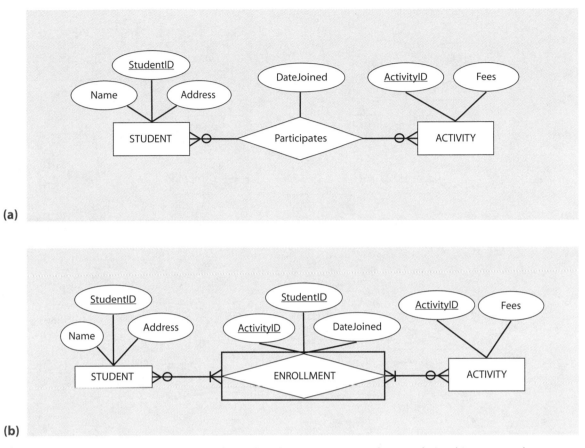

Figure 3.18 (a) A many-to-many binary relationship; (b) A many-to-many binary relationship converted to an associated entity.

Notice that when we convert a relationship into an associative entity, we change its name from a verb to a noun. Therefore, the relationship expressed by the verb participates in Figure 3.18(a) becomes the associative entity represented by the noun enrollment in Figure 3.18(b). This grammatical distinction parallels the main reason for turning a relationship into an associative entity. A verb expresses an action, a process. However, once we want to count, record, or analyze an instance of that process, we end up with a person, place, or thing. In short, by transforming a relationship into an associative entity, we can analyze and record a process in the same way that we analyze and record a noun.

In Chapter 4, we make it clear why we can only turn a many-to-many relationship into an associative entity. We convert a ternary relationship into an associative entity as it allows us to express the cardinalies of a relationship correctly. We will now consider another example of associative entity converted from a ternary relationship.

The E-R diagram shown in Figure 3.19 is similar to the one we first observed in Figure 3.16. Here, we convert the ternary relationship instance *Performs* into the associative entity PERFORMANCE. We change the verb performs, an action not necessarily related to a specific event, to performance, a noun that expresses an event that can be recorded, counted, and analyzed. Observe that the identifier of the associated entity PERFORMANCE is comprised of the union of the identifiers of the entities involved in the ternary relationship. One of the most important

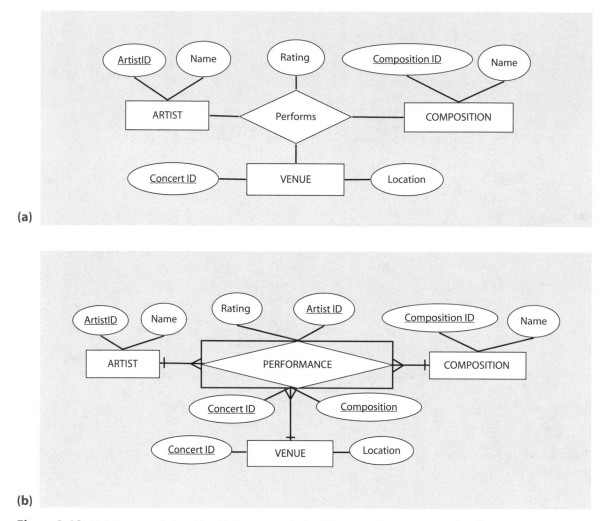

Figure 3.19 (a) A ternary relationship; (b) A ternary relationship converting to an associated entity.

characteristics of this arrangement is that each entity, ARTIST, VENUE, and COMPOSITION, has a one-to-many relationship (minimum cardinalities are omitted for clarity) with the associated entity PERFORMANCE.

3.13   *Weak Entity Types*

Entity types can be classified into two categories: *strong entity types* and *weak entity types*. A **strong entity type** exists independent of other entity types, while a **weak entity type** depends on another entity type. Consider a student database that includes an entity STUDENT. Suppose that we also record data about each student's dependents, such as a spouse or children, in this database. To do so, we must create the entity type DEPENDENT. The entity type DEPENDENT does not exist on its own and owes its existence to the STUDENT entity type. When students graduate and their records are removed from the STUDENT entity set, the records of their dependents are also removed from the DEPENDENT entity set. In the E-R diagram, a weak entity is indicated by a double-lined rectangle. The corresponding relationship diamond is also double-lined.

The entity type on which a weak entity type depends is called the *identifying owner* (or simply *owner*), and the relationship between a weak entity type and its owner is called an *identifying relationship*. In Figure 3.20, STUDENT is the owner and *Has* is the identifying relationship. For a weak entity, we define a *partial key attribute* that, when combined with the key attribute of its owner, provides the full identifier for the weak entity. In Figure 3.20, for example, *DependentName* is the partial identifying attribute. When we combine it with the *StudentID*, it uniquely identifies the dependent. Of course, in this example, we make an implicit assumption that people do not give the same name to more than one of their children.

Definition

An **associative entity** is an entity type that connects the instances of one or more entity types and contains attributes particular to this association.

A **strong entity type** exists independent of other entity types, while a **weak entity type** depends on another entity type.

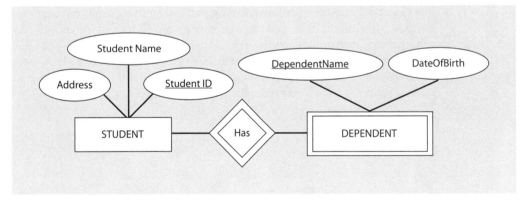

Figure 3.20 The weak entity in an E-R diagram.

3.14 | *Enhanced Entity-Relationship Modeling*

We have illustrated the basic concepts of the entity-relationship model. These concepts are generally adequate to design solutions for common business problems. However, since the early 1980s, business database applications and database requirements have changed dramatically. Business relationships and business data have become much more complex as applications such as multimedia systems, geographical information systems, and computer-aided engineering have gained prominence. These applications demand more complex database requirements than traditional applications, rendering the basic concepts of E-R modeling inadequate. As a result, researchers in the '80s enhanced the original E-R model to form the *enhanced entity-relationship (EE-R) model.*

In the remaining sections of this chapter, we will discuss the EE-R model by detailing superclass and subclass entities, the processes of specialization and generalization, and various constraints on these processes.

3.15 *Superclass, Subclass, and Relationships*

Recall that we have defined an *entity type* as a collection of entities that share the same attributes. In this section, we will introduce two special types of entities: superclass and subclass. We will also discuss the notations that allow us to include these special entities in a regular E-R diagram to create an enhanced entity-relationship (EE-R) diagram. We will also study superclass and subclass relationships as well as the process of attribute inheritance associated with superclass and subclass entity types.

3.15.1 Superclass and Subclass

All the instances of an entity type share the same set of attributes, but each single attribute may not be a required attribute of for each instance. For example, consider the PERSON entity type. The entity PERSON includes all personnel in a university. Specifically, it includes students, staff, and faculty members. The attributes of this entity, *SSN, Address, Email, Salary, Class, GPA*, and *Office Phone* are depicted in Figure 3.21. Although all these attributes are common to the PERSON entity, attributes such as *Class* and *GPA* are not required for faculty instances of PERSON. At the same time, the attribute *Salary* is required for staff and faculty but may not be relevant for students.

This distinction is important when we have a large number of instances for an entity type. In such a scenario, one or more attributes for each instance won't have any valid value. In our example, each faculty instance will have no valid value for *GPA* and *Class*, and many student instances won't have value for *Salary, Rank*, and *Designation*. As we will see in Chapter 4, having many redundant fields results in a data redundancy problem and degrades the database performance.

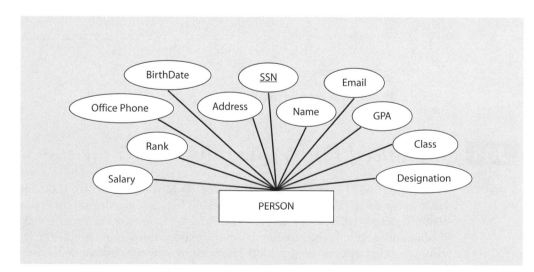

Figure 3.21 The E-R diagram for entity type PERSON.

One possible solution to this problem is to extend the E-R model to accurately represent the complex groupings that we encounter in everyday life. Let us begin our discussion by formally defining superclass and subclass entity types.

A **superclass** is an entity type that has one or more distinct subgroups with unique attributes. For example, the entity type PERSON in Figure 3.22 is a superclass that includes faculty, staff, and students as its subgroups. The superclass features only those attributes that are common for all its subgroups. For example, attributes of PERSON such as *SSN*, *Name*, *Address*, and *Email* are shared by all its subgroups regardless of an individual's position as student, faculty, or staff within the university. The subgroups with unique attributes are defined as **subclasses**. The PERSON superclass thus has three subclasses: STUDENT, STAFF, and FACULTY. A subclass entity type STUDENT has attributes of its superclass along with its own attributes such as *Major*, *GPA*, and *Class* that uniquely identify the subclass. Figure 3.22 depicts a superclass and subclasses.

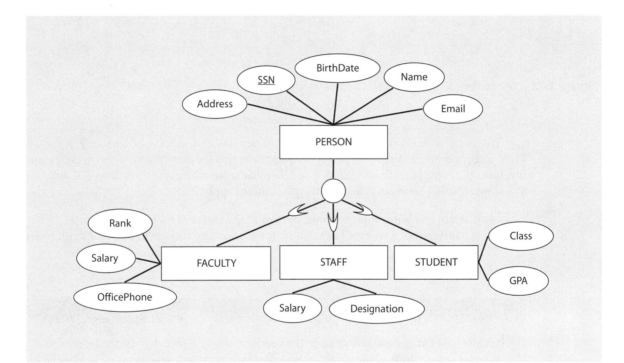

Figure 3.22 The enhanced E-R diagram for entity type PERSON.

Let us examine the formal notations used to represent a superclass and subclass. We represent both superclass and subclass entity types with the usual rectangle notation of an entity type. A superclass is connected to a circle by a short line. This circle, in turn, is connected to each of the subclass entity types with another line. An optional U-shaped symbol on each line that connects subclass entity types to the circle indicates that a subclass is a subset of a superclass entity type. This U-shaped symbol also indicates the direction of the superclass/subclass relationship. In that sense, it operates like an arrow pointing from the superclass to a subclass. Other notations of basic E-R diagrams prevail (see Figure 3.23 for general layout).

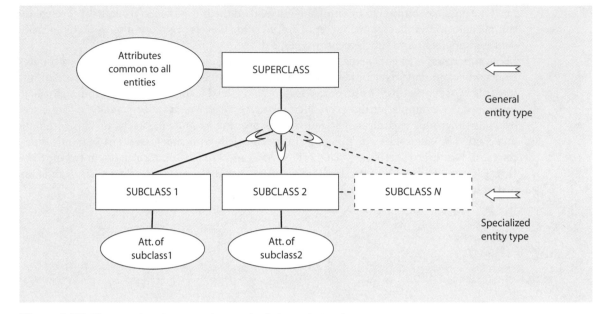

Figure 3.23 The notations for superclass and subclass relationships.

There are several reasons for introducing superclass and subclasses into an E-R model. First, incorporating a superclass and subclasses maintains the cleanliness of the structure and improves the conceptual flow. Second, it adds familiar semantic information to an E-R diagram. We consider using subtypes if the following conditions apply:

1. Certain attributes apply to some, but not all, instances of an entity type.
2. An instance of a subtype participates in a relationship unique to that relationship (see Figure 3.24).

Definition

The **Enhanced Entity-Relationships (EE-R) model** is a revised E-R model that extends the original E-R model and supports additional semantic concepts by providing new modeling constructs.

A **superclass** is an entity type that has one or more distinct sub groups with unique attributes.

A **subclass** is an entity type that shares common attributes or relationships distinct from other subclasses.

3.15.2 Attribute Inheritance and Subclass Relationships

Attribute Inheritance is the property by which subclass entities inherit attributes of the superclass. The subclass entity type is an entity type in itself with a set of attributes and relationships. In addition to its own attributes, a subclass entity inherits all the attributes of its superclass. For example, the STUDENT subclass has attributes such as *MajorDept*, *Class*, and *GPA*. It also inherits all the attributes of the PERSON entity type. In other words, if Chris Alto is an instance of the STUDENT subclass, then he is necessarily an instance of the PERSON superclass as well. Chris Alto is a value for the *Name* attribute for the entity PERSON, and the STUDENT subclass inherits it from the PERSON. Note that Chris's 4.0 *GPA* is an attribute of the STUDENT subclass only. Thus, the identifier of a superclass is also inherited by all its subclasses and serves as an identifier for subclasses. Subclasses don't need their own identifier. Thus, the relationship between a superclass and subclass is always a one-to-one relationship (notations are usually ignored in an E-R diagram).

Although, each subclass also possesses attributes of its superclass, each subclass entity expresses a distinct role in an E-R diagram. It can have its own attributes and relationships that distinguish one subclass from another. Figure 3.24 depicts relationships for the STUDENT and FACULTY subclasses.

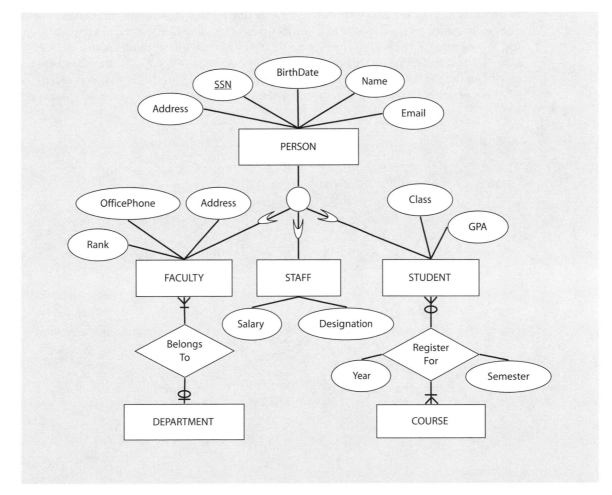

Figure 3.24 An example of the superclass/subclass relationships.

3.16   *Generalization and Specialization Process*

In the previous section we described the superclass/subclass model. However, in the process of modeling a complex real-word scenario, it is important to recognize when superclass and subclass entity types can be generated. The processes of *specialization* and *generalization* are used to find such opportunities. These processes serve as conceptual models for the development of superclass/subclass relationships.

3.16.1   Generalization

Generalization is the process of defining general entity types from a set of specialized entity types by identifying their common characteristics. In other words, this process minimizes the differences between entities by *identifying a general entity type* that features the common attributes of specialized entities. Generalization is a bottom-up approach as it starts with the specialized entity types (subclasses) and forms a generalized entity type (superclass).

For example, suppose that someone has given us the specialized entity types FACULTY, STAFF, and STUDENT, and we want to represent these entity types separately in the E-R model as depicted in Figure 3.25(a). However, if we examine them closely, we can observe that a number of attributes are common to all entity types, while others are specific to a particular entity. For example, FACULTY, STAFF, and STUDENT all share the attributes *Name*, *SSN*, *Birth Date*, *Address*, and *Email*. On the other hand, attributes such as *GPA*, *Class*, and *MajorDept* are specific to the STUDENTS; *OfficePhone* is specific to FACULTY, and *Designation* is specific to STAFF. Common attributes suggest that each of these three entity types is a form of a more gen-

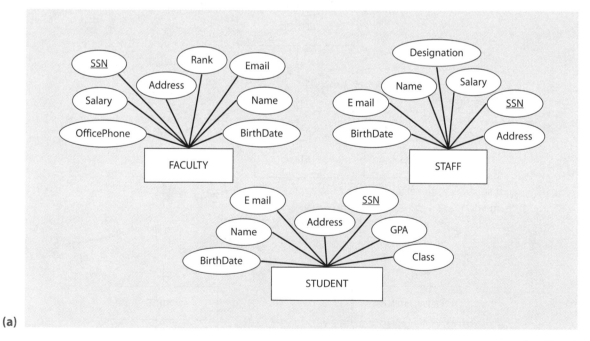

(a)

(continues)

Figure 3.25 (a) STAFF, FACULTY, and STUDENT entities before generalization; (b) PERSON superclass and FACULTY, STAFF, and STUDENT subclasses after generalization.

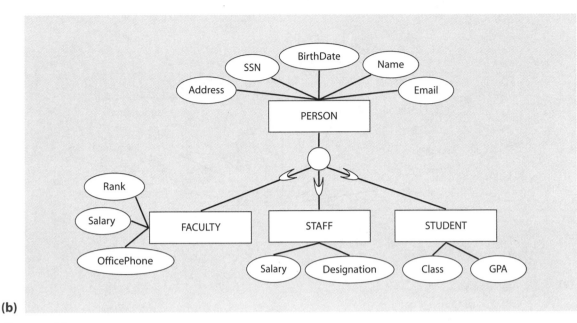

(b)

Figure 3.25 (*continued*)

eral entity type. This general entity type is simply a PERSON superclass entity with common attributes of three subclasses (see Figure 3.25(b)).

Thus, in the generalization process, we group specialized entity types to form one general entity type and identify common attributes of specialized entities as attributes of a general entity type. The general entity type is a superclass of specialized entity types or subclasses.

3.16.2 Specialization

Specialization is the process of defining one or more subclasses of a superclass by identifying its distinguishing characteristics. Unlike generalization, specialization is thus a top-down approach. It starts with the general entity (superclass) and forms specialized entity types (subclasses) based on specialized attributes or relationships specific to a subclass.

For example, consider Figure 3.26(a). LIBRARY ITEM is an entity type with several attributes such as *IdentificationNo*, *RecordingDate*, *Frequency*, and *Edition*. After careful review of these items, it should become clear that some items such as books do not have values for attributes such as *Frequency*, *RecordingDate*, and *CourseNo*, while Video CDs do not have an *Author* or an *Edition*.

In addition, all items have common attributes such as *IdentificationNo*, *Location*, and *Subject*. Someone creating a library database, then, could use the specialization process to identify superclass and subclass relationships. In this case, the original entity LIBRARY ITEM forms a superclass entity type made up of attributes shared by all items, while specialized items with distinguishing attributes, such as BOOK, JOURNALS, and VIDEOCD, form subclasses.

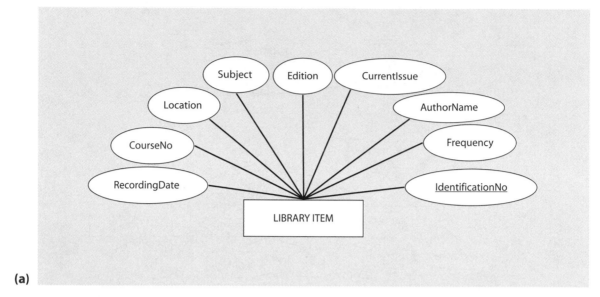

(a)

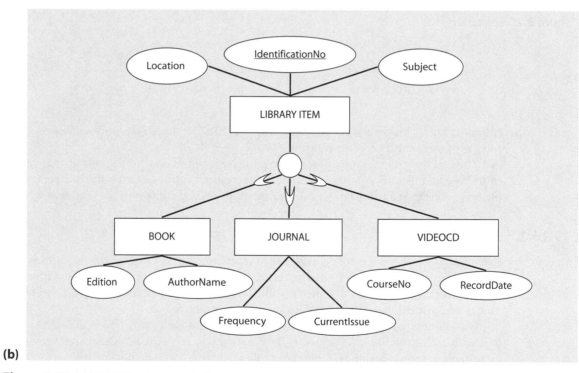

(b)

Figure 3.26 (a) LIBRARY ITEM entity before specialization; (b) LIBRARY ITEM superclass and BOOK, JOURNAL, and VIDEOCD subclasses after specialization.

> ### Definition
>
> **Attribute inheritance** is the property by which subclass entities inherit values for all attributes of the superclass.
>
> **Generalization** is the process of defining a general entity type from a set of specialized entity types by identifying their common characteristics.
>
> **Specialization** is a process of defining one or more subclasses of a superclass by identifying their distinguishing characteristics.

3.17 *Participation and Disjoint Constraints*

So far we have discussed superclass/subclass entity types, their relationships, and two processes to identify them. In this section, we will discuss constraints on superclass/subclass relationships. Specifically, we will introduce a *participation* constraint and a *disjoint* constraint. These constraints are intuitive and help us manifest business rules and incorporate them into the design of an EE-R.

3.17.1 Participation Constraints

Participation constraints dictate whether each instance (member) of a superclass must participate as an instance (member) of a subclass. A participation of superclass instance may be mandatory or optional in one or more subclasses. The mandatory constraint is also known as a total participation (constraint) or total specialization rule, while an optional constraint is known as a partial participation (constraint) or partial specialization rule.

Total Participation Rule   In total participation, membership is mandatory. Each instance of a superclass must be an instance of at least one subclass. For example, consider Figure 3.27.

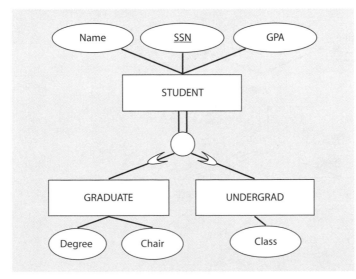

Figure 3.27 An example of the total participation rule.

Every instance of the superclass STUDENT must be an instance of either the GRADUATE student or UNDERGRAD student subclass. That is, if John Doe is an instance of a STUDENT, then John must be a graduate or undergraduate student. However, whether John Doe belongs to the graduate, undergraduate, or both entity types is answered by the disjoint rule, which we will define in a moment. We use a double line between the superclass entity type and the circle to represent the total participation.

Partial Participation Rule   Membership is optional in a partial participation. An instance of a superclass does not have to be an instance of any of the subclasses. For example, consider Figure 3.26. An instance of the LIBRARY ITEM superclass can be a member of BOOK, VIDEO CD, or JOURNALS; however it is not mandatory for an instance to belong to any of these subclasses. If the library item *Newspaper* is an instance of a superclass, it does not have to be included in one of the subclasses; it can stay at the superclass level without having values for any subclass attributes. We use a single line between the superclass entity type and the circle (the default notation) to represent partial participation.

3.17.2   Disjoint Constraints

Disjoint constraints define whether it is possible for an instance of a superclass to simultaneously be a member of one or more subclasses. Disjoint constraints indicate whether a superclass instance can be disjointed or overlap more than one subclass.

Disjoint Rule   The disjoint rule states that if an instance of a superclass is a member of any subclass, then it cannot be a member of more than one subtype (note that the participation rule will dictate whether the instance is a member of a subclass or not). For example, consider Figure 3.28. We put a constraint of disjoint rule to indicate that a student must be either a graduate or an undergraduate student but cannot belong to both subclasses simultaneously. We indicate the disjoint rule by putting a letter "D" in the joining circle of the superclass/subclass relationship (see Figure 3.28).

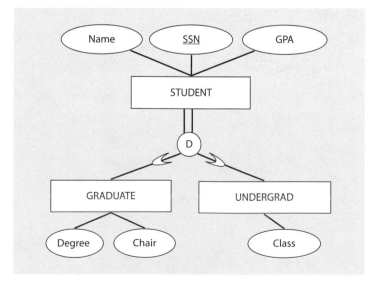

Figure 3.28 An example of the disjoint rule.

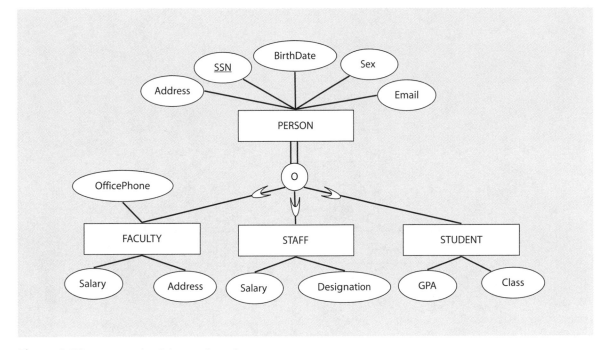

Figure 3.29 An example of the overlap rule.

Overlap Rule   The overlap rule states that if an instance of a superclass is a member of any subclass, then it can be a member (overlap) of more than one subtype. For example, consider Figure 3.29. It reveals that an instance of a PERSON must be FACULTY, STAFF, a STUDENT, or any combination of these three. A work-study person would overlap, for example, the STAFF and STUDENT entities. We indicate the overlap rule by putting a letter "O" in the joining circle of the superclass/subclass relationship.

3.17.3   Subclass Discriminators

The participation and disjoint constraints allow an instance of a superclass to be a member of one or more subclasses. We keep track of membership using a special attribute of a superclass, a ***subclass discriminator***. In other words, we put a discriminating attribute on a superclass that can record membership of superclass instances into one or more subclasses. Figure 3.30 provides an example of total participation with the disjoint rule. An instance of STUDENT item must be a member of exactly one subclass. For every instance of a superclass when it is assigned to either subclass, we record the membership in the *StudentType* attribute. For example, if John Doe is a graduate student, we assign a value, say "G," to *StudentType*. If Monica Adams is an undergraduate student, we assign *StudentType* "U," and so on.

There are two special cases with partial participation and overlap rules using a discriminating attribute. If the participation is partial and an instance of a superclass does not participate in any subclasses, we assign NULL value to the discriminating attribute. If an overlap rule is in effect and if an instance of a superclass participates in more than one subclass, we assign multiple values to the discriminating attribute. Thus, the discriminating attribute becomes a multi-valued attribute under the overlap rule.

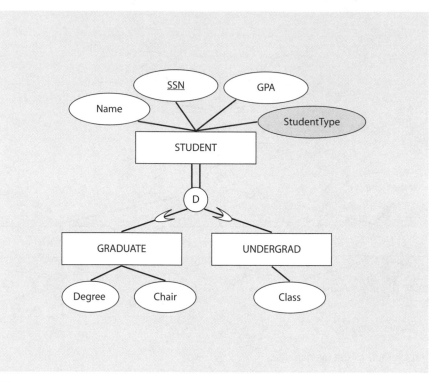

Figure 3.30 *StudentType* subclass discriminator.

Definition

Participation constraints dictate whether each instance (member) of a superclass must partici-pate as an instance (member) of a subclass.

Disjoint constraints define whether it is possible for an instance of a superclass to simultane-ously be a member of one or more subclasses.

A superclass/subclass hierarchy is a hierarchical structure of a superclass and its various sub-classes in which each subclass has exactly one superclass.

3.18   *Superclass/Subclass Hierarchy*

A subclass type can have one or more subclasses. In other words, a subclass can act as superclass for other entity types, resulting in a hierarchy of superclass and subclasses. A ***superclass/ subclass hierarchy*** is a hierarchical structure of a superclass and its various subclasses in which each subclass has exactly one superclass. For example, we have discussed PERSON and STU-DENT superclass entity types. We put these two examples together in Figure 3.31 to create a hi-erarchical structure.

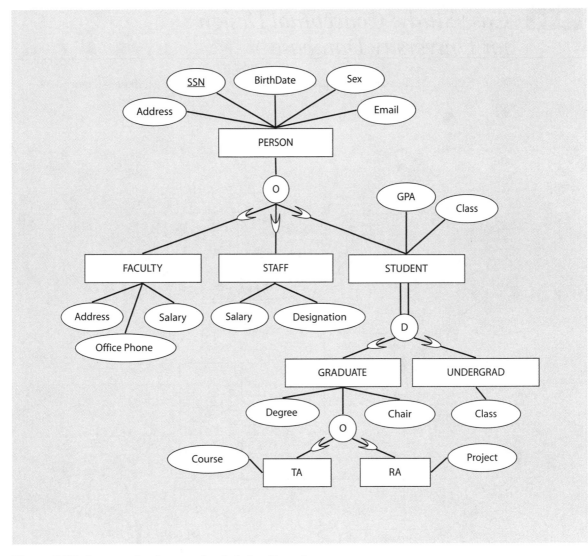

Figure 3.31 An example of a superclass/subclass hierarchy.

PERSON is the superclass with FACULTY, STAFF, and STUDENT as its subclasses. The relationship is partial participation with overlap rules. The STUDENT subclass has its own subclasses: GRADUATE student and UNDERGRAD student. Further, the GRADUATE subclass acts as a superclass for TA and RA subclasses; a graduate student can be a teaching assistant or a research assistant or both. Thus each level of a hierarchy can have its own set of entity types and relationships to depict the organizational requirements.

Case Study: Conceptual Design for University Database

In this section, we illustrate the conceptual design for a university database in Figure 3.32

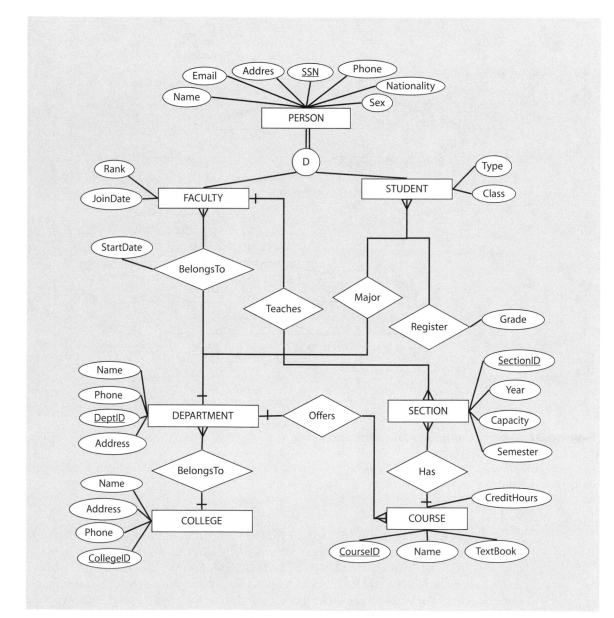

Figure 3.32 An EE-R diagram for the university database.

3.20 *In-Class Assignment*

Consider the following problem statement to draw an E-R diagram:

The annual Bolder Boulder is one of America's top 10 km races. The race is held each Memorial Day in Boulder, Colorado. This race attracts world-class runners as well as casual joggers. It is a point-to-point race beginning at the Bank of Boulder at the northeast corner of the city, winding throughout the city streets, and ending near the town center in the University of Colorado's football stadium.

The organizers record the following information for each race: the date of the race; the total number of runners registered for the race (on-line pre-registration is possible); the actual number of participants; the number of male runners; the number of female runners; the name of the male winner; the name of the female winner; the name of the male master (runner over the age of 40) winner; and the name of the female master winner. In addition, the following information about each participant is recorded: social security number, name, birth date, gender, address, age, and certified personal record (PR) running times for a 10 km race.

3.21 *Summary*

■ An *entity type* defines a collection of entities that have the same attributes. An *entity instance* is a single item in this collection, and an *entity set* is a set of entity instances.

■ An *attribute* is a property or characteristic of an entity type that is of interest to an organization.

■ Most attributes are *single-valued*, meaning they have a single value for an entity instance. A *multi-valued* attribute is an attribute that can take more than one value for an entity instance.

■ A *derived attribute* is one whose value can be derived from other attributes.

■ A *key attribute* is an attribute or a combination of several attributes that uniquely identify an individual instance of an entity type.

■ The *degree of the relationship* is the number of entity sets that participate in a relationship.

■ A *unary relationship* R is an association between two instances of the same entity types.

■ A *binary relationship* R is an association between two instances of two different entity types.

■ A *ternary relationship* R is an association between three instances of three different entity types.

■ The *maximum cardinality* represents the maximum number of instances of any entity B that can be associated with any instance of any entity A.

■ The *minimum cardinality* of a relationship between the entity types A and B is the minimum number of instances of entity B that must be associated with each instance of entity A.

■ An *associative entity* is an entity type that associates the instances of one or more entity types and contains attributes particular to this association.

■ A *strong entity type* exists independent of other entity types. A *weak entity type's* existence depends on another entity type.

■ The *Enhanced Entity-Relationships (EE-R) model* is a revised E-R model that extends the original E-R model and supports additional semantic concepts by providing new modeling constructs.

■ A *superclass* is an entity type that has one or more distinct sub groups with unique attributes. The subgroups should be of importance to the organization and are therefore necessarily represented in a data model.

■ A *subclass* is an entity type that shares common attributes or relationships distinct from other subclasses.

■ *Attribute inheritance* is the property by which subclass entities inherit values for all attributes of the superclass.

■ *Generalization* is the process of defining a general entity type from a set of specialized entity types by identifying their common characteristics.

■ *Specialization* is a process of defining one or more subclasses of a superclass by identifying their distinguishing characteristics.

■ *Participation constraints* dictate whether every instance of a superclass must participate as an instance of a subclass. If it is mandatory for a superclass instance to be a member of at least one subclass, it is known as the total participation rule. When some instances of a superclass are free to not participate in any of the subclasses, it is referred to as the partial participation rule.

■ *Disjoint constraints* dictate whether it is possible for an instance of a superclass to be a member of one or more subclasses simultaneously. The *disjoint rule* states that if the instance of superclass is a member of a subclass, then it must belong to ex-actly one subclass. The *overlap rule* states that members of a subclass can belong to more than one subclass.

■ A *subclass discriminator* is an attribute of a super-class that classifies its instance into the appropriate subclass. The value of a discriminator determines the target subclass for an instance of a superclass.

■ A superclass/subclass hierarchy is a hierarchical structure of a superclass and subclasses wherein each subclass has exactly one superclass.

3.22 *Exercises*

3.22.1 Review Questions

1. Explain the following terms using an example: entity-relationship model, entity type, weak entity, attribute, key attribute, derived attribute, multi-valued attribute.

2. Explain, using an example (other than the ones discussed in the book), the contrast between the following terms:
   a. entity type; entity instance
   b. strong entity type; weak entity type
   c. simple attribute; composite attribute
   d. stored attribute; derived attribute

3. Provide an example of multiple relationships between entities. Draw the E-R diagram.

4. Under what conditions is a relationship converted to an associative entity type? Give an example.

5. Explain why we study the E-R model of a database.

6. A department in a university stores the informa-tion about its students and courses in a database. The administrative assistant manages the database. At the end of the semester, he prepares a report about each course. Is the E-R diagram correct? If not, explain why and draw the correct diagram.

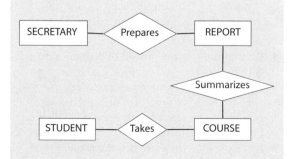

7. A veterinary doctor stores the information about his clients and their pets in a database. Complete the following E-R diagram.

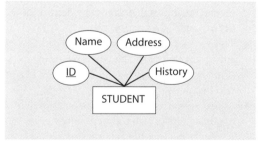

8. Explain the term "degree of a relationship." Provide a simple example for each of the three types of relationships described in this chapter and draw the corresponding E-R diagrams.

9. A university maintains a detailed database of its student information. The following is the E-R diagram of entity STUDENT. Draw an alternative E-R diagram for this database.

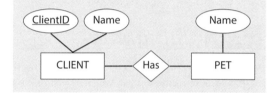

10. Discuss the reasons for choosing one of the at-tributes as an identifier of an entity type.

11. "Enhanced E-R diagrams provide more flexibility in designing a database than E-R diagrams." Support this statement with an example.

12. Using an example, define the following terms: subtype, subtype discriminator, disjoint rule, overlapping rule. Demonstrate how they relate to one another.

13. Using an example, explain the reasons why a database designer considers using subtype/supertype relationships.

14. The Admissions office in a university stores the information about the university entrance applications in a database. In order to facilitate processing the applications, the office classifies the applicants as freshman, transfer, graduate, and international students.

    a. Draw the EE-R diagram of this database. Identify a unique attribute for each entity subtype.

    b. Add a subtype discriminator for each of the subtypes of the entity APPLICANT.

15. Using an example, explain the difference between the generalization rule and the specialization rule.

16. The Accounting department in a company keeps the information about its employees in a database. The employees are classified as part-time employees, full-time employees, and interns. Interns are usually students who work with the company during the summers. Complete the EE-R diagram below by:

    a. Adding a unique attribute (relationship) for each entity subtype

    b. Adding an attribute shared by all entities

    c. Identifying whether the disjoint or overlap rule applies

    d. Identifying whether the total specialization or partial specialization rule applies

3.22.2 Hands-On Exercises

1. Savannah's family has owned and operated a 640-acre farm for several generations. Since the business is growing, Savannah is considering building a database that would make it easier to manage the farm's activities. She is considering the following requirements for the database:

    a. For each livestock classification group (for example: cow, horse, etc.), Savannah keeps track of each animal's identification number and classification.

    b. For each crop, she records the crop identification number and the classification.

    c. Savannah has recorded the yield of each crop classification group during the last ten years. The records consist of the year, yield, sales, crop price, and amount of money earned.

    d. Savannah has also recorded the yield of each livestock classification group during the last ten years. The records consist of the following historical data: the year, the (historical) selling price per head, the number of livestock in the end of the year, the number of livestock sold during a one-year period, and the total amount of money earned.

Draw an E-R diagram for this application. Specify the key attribute of each entity type.

2. The Coca Cola Company in Atlanta, Georgia produces a wide range of products that are delivered to its worldwide clientele once a week. The company stores information about its employees, products, and customers in a database that includes the following set of tables:

    a. The company records the following information about its customers: customer identification number, name, address, X (longitude) and Y (latitude) coordinates of their location, and the amount of time (in fractions of an hour) required making a stop at that location.

    b. Each employee has an employee identification number, name, address (which consists of a city, state, and zip code), gender, birth date, position in the company, wage earned per hour of regular time work, wage earned per hour of overtime work, number of dependents, and number of years worked for the Coca Cola Company.

    c. Each product has a product identification number, price, and number of units produced per day.

Products may be ordered by one or more customers, and a customer may order one or more products. Furthermore, employees produce one or more products, and a product may be produced by exactly one employee. Draw an E-R diagram for the above description and add the minimum and maximum relationship cardinalities. Identify the key attributes for each entity and the composite attributes.

3. Consider the database in Hands-On Exercise 2. Update the E-R diagram for the cases described below. For each entity, identify the key attribute(s).

a. For tax purposes, the Coca Cola Company extends the data kept for each employee to include additional information about their dependents. This information consists of each dependent's name, birth date, and age.

b. The company has decided to record information about its suppliers and the raw material(s) supplied by them. The following information is recorded for each supplier: the supplier identification number, the address, and the name of the contact person. The raw material information consists of the raw material identification number and the material's name.

c. The company keeps a fleet of vehicles to facilitate the distribution of the products to the customers. Each vehicle has an identification number, model, and capacity.

It should also be noted that employees use raw materials to produce one or more final products, which are delivered to the customer. A supplier supplies many raw materials, but a particular raw material is purchased from only one supplier. It is not necessary to include all the attributes and cardinalities from the previous question. Just be sure to include the entities to demonstrate the relationships and attributes for the new entities.

4. Again consider the database in Hands-On Exercise 2. The Coca Cola Company has a few plants that are distributed throughout Georgia. For each plant, the following information is stored in the database: a plant identification number, the address, and the X and Y coordinates of the plant location. Note that the inventory level, inventory capacity, and quantity produced of a particular product differ by plant.

   The systems of relationships that exist are as follows. A plant may have one or more employees, and an employee works in exactly one plant. Additionally, a plant produces one or more products, and a product may be produced in one or more plants. Also, an employee may contribute to one or more products, and a product is produced by exactly one employee. It is not necessary to include all the attributes and cardinalities from the previous question. Just be sure to include the entities to demonstrate the relationships and attributes for the new entities.

5. Major airline companies that provide passenger services in Taiwan are UniAir, TransAsia Airways, Far Eastern Transport, and Great China Airlines. Taiwan's Federal Aviation Administration (TFAA) maintains a database with information about all the airlines. This information is made accessible to all airlines in Taiwan with the intention of helping the companies assess their competitive position in the domestic market. The information consists of the following:

a. Each airline has an identification number, a name and address, a contact person's name, and a telephone number.

b. Each aircraft has an aircraft identification number, a capacity, and a model.

c. Each employee has an employee identification number, a name, an address, a birth date, a gender, a position within the company, and a qualification.

d. Each route has a route identification number, an origin, a destination, a classification (domestic or international route), a distance of the route, and a price charged per passenger.

e. Each airline records information about its buy/sell transactions. (For example, selling an airplane ticket is a sell transaction; paying for maintenance is a buy transaction.) Each transaction has a transaction identification number, a date, a description, and an amount of money paid/received.

The above information is related as follows. Each employee works for exactly one airline. Airlines assign different aircraft on different routes based on the availability. Furthermore, each airline makes one or more transactions; however, each transaction is associated with exactly one airline. Make the necessary assumptions about the other relationships and draw an E-R diagram.

6. Consider the database described in Hands-On Exercise 5. Each airline owns different aircraft models, each with a different capacity. Depending on the length of the route and flight classification (domestic or international) the aircraft are assigned to different routes. The relationship between the airlines, aircraft, and routes is a ternary relationship. Each flight carries a number of passengers, has a particular time length (which depends on the distance of the route and the model of the aircraft), and has a departure and arrival time. Draw the E-R diagram for this database.

7. "Electronic commerce" is one of the most common terms in the business world. It is the buying and selling of goods and services on the Internet. One of the most popular products in e-commerce, as it is more commonly known, is the compact disc. This exercise describes the database of a CD warehouse.

   The company's customers and employees access the database. Assume that customers have access to a company's Web site and that they are able to open an account by providing their social security number, name, address, and music preferences. For each employee, the following information is recorded: an employee identification number, a name, an address, a birth date, and the title of the position within the company.

   The products for the CD warehouse are the albums. The database records the following information about each album: an album identification number, the name, the group name, the musical category, the name of the vocalist, the names of the other band members, and the number of CDs in stock. The database also keeps the following information about suppliers: a supplier identification number, the address, the name of the company, and the name of the contact person.

   An album may be bought by one or more customers, and one customer may buy one or more albums. Additionally, an employee may monitor one or more albums; however, an album is monitored by exactly one employee. Suppliers may provide one or more albums; however, an album is supplied by exactly one supplier. Using the above information, draw an E-R diagram for the CD warehouse database. Identify the relationship cardinalities and the key attribute of each entity.

8. One of the three-star hotels in the Miami area is in the process of updating its database. The hotel has various room types on each of its floors. The rooms may be regular, deluxe, or a suite and each can be either a single, double, or triple. The suites have ocean views and are bigger than the regular rooms. The deluxe rooms are as big as suites, but they do not have an ocean view. All the rooms have air conditioning. Most of the rooms are non-smoking, but the hotel offers some smoking rooms as well. Each floor has a different number of a particular room type. The price of each room differs by the size of the room, the view, and the room's location (first floor, second floor, etc.).

   The customers are charged on a per-day basis. The number of days is computed based on the check-in time and the check-out time. The following details are stored for each customer: name, address, check-in date, check-out date, payment method, and final bill amount. In addition to the room charges, there may be extra fees, such as telephone usage, fax services, extra beds, and room service. For this application, we assume that a room can be booked by more than one customer as long as there is no overlap and that a customer can be assigned to any available room. Draw an E-R diagram for the hotel database and state any assumptions made in order to develop a complete diagram.

9. The Newark divisional office of the Life Insurance Corporation of America stores all the necessary information about its policyholders in a database. A policyholder pays a premium until the maturity of the policy or until his or her death, at which time the sum assured and the bonus are paid to the beneficiary. The premium to be paid is determined based on the age of the person proposed and the term of the policy. The Newark division records the following information about each policyholder: social security number, name, address, date of birth, maturity amount, and annual premium.

   The corporation has divided its Newark division into 15 zones for its convenience. For each zone, they store the Zone ID and the location. Each zone also has a manager. Every zone has a number of agents allotted, typically ranging from 10 to 20 and every agent must procure a minimum of 10 customers. Each policyholder in a particular zone is assigned to only one agent affiliated with that zone; this agent puts forth the terms of the policy. Additionally, an agent in a particular zone can serve multiple policyholders. Make assumptions for the remaining relationships and draw an E-R diagram for the corporation's database.

10. Ford distribution centers provide automotive parts to authorized dealers. The dealers then distribute the parts to customers throughout North America. Ford is under pressure to provide excellent customer service at a minimum cost. Maintaining a well-organized database of

information will contribute to achieving this goal.

Ford stores the following information about each of its distribution centers: the identification number, the location (X longitude coordinate and Y latitude coordinate), the address (city, state, zip code) and the name of the contact person. The following information is kept about each dealer: the identification number, the dealer's location (X longitude coordinate and Y latitude coordinate), the address (city, state, zip code) and the name of the contact person.

The following information is kept about each product: a product identification number, its name, its price, its weight and its value. Ford also records the following information about the flow and cost data for all the distribution centers to dealer channels: distribution center identification number; dealer identification number; product identification number; the number of miles between each distribution center and its dealers (determined using the road network); the quantity of products being shipped; and the dollar value of the shipment.

A distribution center can ship many products to different dealers. A dealer, meanwhile, can receive several products from different distribution centers. Every week, the distribution center sends to the dealer a shipment for which the following information is recorded: distance (using the road network); the quantity of products being shipped; the monetary value of the shipment; and the date of the shipment. Using this information, draw an E-R diagram for the Ford database. State any assumptions made in order to develop a complete diagram.

11. The University Housing Office receives many applications from graduate and married students requesting apartments on campus. The housing villages are located at five different locations, and each village has about 500 apartments. Each apartment falls into one of the apartment categories, which are determined based on the following criteria: village location; if the apartment has a dishwasher; whether it is a one- or two-bedroom; whether it has central air conditioning or a window unit; and if it is furnished.

The Housing Office records the following information about the head of each household: social security number, name, telephone number, marital status, and college and department in which he or she is enrolled. The Housing Office also keeps the following information about the students who have applied for on-campus housing but have not yet been assigned to an apartment: social security number, name, telephone number, marital status, college and department in which he or she is enrolled, and his or her apartment preference.

An applicant applies to one or more villages, and a resident resides in exactly one apartment. Make suitable assumptions for the other relationships, and draw an E-R diagram for the University Housing Office database.

12. A database is being developed to manage the course timetable of an academic institution. For each course, the following information is recorded: an identification number, the name of the course, the number of students attending the course, and the number of credits.

For each teacher, the following information is recorded: social security number, name, department, skills, and yearly salary. For each class period, the following information is recorded: period number, starting time, ending time. For each room, the following information is recorded: room number, room type (classroom, office, auditorium, or computer lab), and capacity.

Staff members refer to the above information in order to make appropriate assignments of a particular course to a specific time period, classroom, and professor. A professor teaches one or more courses; however, a course is taught by exactly one professor. Using this information, draw an E-R diagram for this database. Clearly state any assumptions made about other relationships in the diagram.

13. A database is being constructed to monitor the teams, players, and games of the national intercollegiate football championship. For each player, the following information is recorded: social security number, name, address, birth date, team position, and the number of years the player has been with the team.

For each team that participates in the football championship, the following information is recorded: the name of the team; the name of the university it represents; the rank of the team in the current season; the number of games that the team has won in the current season; and the number of games that the team has lost in the current season. The database also keeps information about the team coach. This information includes the following: social security number, name, age, number of years coaching the current team, total number of years coaching, and number of times that the team he or she has coached won the championship.

The following information is recorded about each game: the game identification number, the date and place of the event, the start time, the end time, and the winner. A coach can lead exactly one team, and a team can have exactly one coach. Each team may play one or more games in a season, and a game is played by one or more teams. Additionally, a team may have one or more players, and a player can play for exactly one team. A team may win more than one game in a season, and a game is won by exactly one team. Draw an E-R diagram for this database. Clearly state any assumptions made.

14. Consider the database described in Hands-On Exercise 13. Suppose that we want to design an attribute for the COACH entity type to keep track of previous employment. Such an attribute should have one entity for each college he or she worked for. Each entry should be composed of a college name, a start and end date of employment, and the title of the position (coach, assistant coach, etc.). Update the E-R diagram from Hands-On Exercise 13 to account for this modification.

15. Again consider the database described in Hands-On Exercise 13. Each player of a football team not only plays for a college, but, at the same time, is enrolled at that college. Each college has one or more players enrolled, and a player is enrolled in exactly one college. Additionally, each team belongs to exactly one college. Update the E-R diagram to account for this information. Include only the name of the university.

16. JobSearch.com is an Internet-based company. It provides information about open positions to students looking for a job as well as information about candidates to the companies. Both the companies and the students can access the database. Students access the database to post their resumes and to look for open positions in their area of interest. Companies access the database to post its job openings and to look for the candidates who best fit its needs.

For every student, the following information is recorded in the database: student identification number, name, birth date, address, gender, country of citizenship, immigration status, university, major department, degree program, and skills. For every company, the following information is recorded: identification number, name, address (city, state, and zip code), telephone number, Web site address, and industry. When a job opening is submitted, the companies specify the following: posted date, job description, type of job (full-time, part-time, co-op, etc.). A contact person, who works for the company then looks into the database, selects candidates, schedules the interviews, and conducts the interviews.

A particular job posting can belong to exactly one company; however, a company may post multiple jobs. Also, a student may be pursuing one or more jobs, and a job may be pursued by one or more students. Using the above information, draw an E-R diagram for the JobSearch.com database. Clearly state any assumptions made.

17. The Florida Bus Traveling Agency needs to computerize its reservation database systems. The corporation has 18 buses spread over 20 routes to various destinations in Florida. There are two types of buses: regular and super deluxe. It has 10 regular buses with a seating capacity of 48 and eight super deluxe buses with a seating capacity of 36.

For each bus the following information is stored in the database: bus number, capacity, and type. The buses travel certain routes. For each route, the following information is recorded: route identification number, city of origin, and city of destination. Customers usually book trips that do not necessarily have to correspond to bus routes. A trip begins in one of the cities that is visited by a route (not necessarily the city of the origin of the route) and ends at another city visited by that route (not necessarily the city of the destination of the route). For every trip a customer books his or her ticket for, the following information is recorded: trip identification number, city of origin, city of destination, departure time, and arrival time.

A bus is assigned to a particular route, which passes through the origin and destination cities of one or more trips. Many buses can pass through a particular route. Draw an E-R diagram for the

Florida Bus Traveling Agency database. Clearly state any assumptions made.

18. SunRise hotel is located in Palm Beach. The hotel keeps a detailed database of the rooms and special services offered, as well as a database of employees and customers. Keeping a detailed database of the rooms facilitates the management of the hotel's everyday activities.

    The hotel keeps the following information about each customer: social security number, name, and address. For every room, the following information is recorded: room identification number, location (first floor, second floor, etc.), status (available or not available), rate, and room type (regular or luxurious). The hotel offers special services to customers, if requested. For the special services, the following information is recorded: identification number, rate, and service type.

    A customer may occupy exactly one room, and a room may be occupied by more than one customer as long as there is no overlap. Additionally, a customer may use more than one special service. Make suitable assumptions for the remaining relationships, and draw an E-R diagram for the SunRise hotel database.

19. GERU is a regional multi-service utility providing electric (E), natural gas (NG), water (W), and telecommunications (T) services to its customers. GERU is interested in developing a database of customers, services provided, and rates. This database will help GERU to maintain its operations and also to enable customers to track their energy consumption, check their payment history, report power failures, and tap into an array of services and useful information.

    The customers are classified into four major groups: domestic (D), commercial (C), agricultural (A), and industrial (I). Currently, GERU has 4,500 domestic connections, 1,200 commercial connections, 100 agricultural connections, and 500 industrial connections. For each customer, the following information is recorded: identification number, name, address, classification, and sign-in date.

    Each connection offered by GERU has associated characteristics and rates that depend on the type of service and the customer classification. (For example, domestic rates differ from the industrial rates.) For each service, the following information is recorded: service identification,

type, and rate. GERU also sends a bill to its customers every month for using its services. This bill includes the consumption total, the money due, and the due date.

    Customers may use more than one service, and service may be requested by more than one customer. Using this information, draw an E-R diagram for the GERU database. Clearly state any assumptions made.

20. VedMed is a veterinary hospital. The hospital keeps a database of its clients, pets, employees, and inventory. This information is used to provide better customer service and to manage everyday operations.

    The database includes the following information about each of the customers: customer identification number, name, address, and e-mail address. The database records the following information about each pet that visits the hospital: name, species, and birth date. In addition, for each pet, a history of the visits to the doctor is maintained. For each visit, the date, type of service offered, additional comments, and payment amount are recorded.

    Detailed records about the doctors working for the hospital are also stored in the database. Part of this information is made available to the customers in order to help them choose the doctor who best fits their needs. The doctors' database includes the following: identification number, name, address, gender, area of specialization, and degree earned. The hospital has a pharmacy where the customers can purchase medications. For every item in the inventory, the following information is recorded: identification number, name, description, price, quantity on hand, and safety stock level.

    A pet may visit multiple doctors, and a doctor receives visits from one or more pets. Additionally, a customer may purchase one or more medications. Make suitable assumptions for the remaining relationships and draw an E-R diagram.

21. Memorabilia is an on-line company that buys sports products from various producers around the country and sells them to on-line customers. Customers visit Memorabilia's Web site, select an item, and make an order. As soon as the customer's order is received, the product is delivered to the customer, and the inventory level is updated. The company orders a particular product from a supplier when the inventory level drops

below a certain level. The company has decided to maintain a detailed database of the customers, suppliers, and products to manage the operations. The following information is stored in the database:

a. Customer: name, address, gender, and preferred sport.

b. Supplier: supplier identification number, name of the company, and address.

c. Product: product identification number, price per unit, amount in the inventory, amount requested of the suppliers but not yet received, amount ordered by the customers but not yet shipped.

A customer may order one or more products, and a product may be ordered by one or more customers. Additionally, products may be provided by one or more suppliers, and a supplier may provide more than one product. Using this information, draw an E-R diagram for Memorabilia's database. Clearly state any assumptions made.

22. A small bookstore has been keeping track of its business mainly on paper. The owner is planning to expand the business and would like to have a state-of-the-art database system to improve bookkeeping and customer service.

As a caring bookstore owner, she would like to send information about new books, new editions of a book, and deals to the customers based on their profiles. If the customer is a faculty member at a university, then she wants to offer free copies of a new textbook or a new edition of an existing textbook. If the customer is a student who likes reading science fiction, she wants to send monthly notices about new releases.

The system will help the store maintain details about books, publishers, and customers. A book may be a textbook, a novel, a comic, a children's book, or a cookbook. Publishers are the suppliers of the books. The bookstore buys books from many publishers. Typical customers of the store are libraries, institutions, and individuals such as students, faculty, and others. If they wish, customers can open an account with the store and be given a customer number. With their customer number and a password that they set, the customers are able to login to the database from their own PC. They are able to search books, place orders, check their account

status, and also submit reviews about books they have read. The database also maintains a record of the transactions. For example, when a customer places an order, a payment is made. In the case that the inventory level for a particular book drops below a certain limit, the bookstore places an order to the publishers for new copies.

A customer may buy one or more books, and a book may be bought by one or more customers. Additionally, each book is provided by exactly one publisher; however, a publisher may provide one or more books. For each entity type, identify corresponding attributes and draw an E-R diagram.

23. Medicare is a medical service program that provides acute care for hospitalization, visits to a doctor's office, medical tests, and a limited amount of skilled nursing care for patients recuperating from an acute illness. Medicare covers 12 federally mandated services and several optional services. Medicare is developing a database management system that will perform the following functions: confirm patient eligibility, assign doctors, and pay doctors, pharmacists and hospitals promptly. The system should be designed to structure, store, retrieve, and analyze such critical Medicare management information as information about patients, doctors, pharmacies, and prescription drugs. The system stores the following information:

a. Patients: identification number, name, address, birth date, gender, identification number, sign-up date, and annual income.

b. Patient history: date of the visit, duration of the visit, diagnosis, and medication prescribed.

c. Doctors: identification number, name, address, gender, birth date, specialization.

d. Pharmacy: identification number, address, telephone number, name of contact person.

e. Pharmacy inventory (for every drug kept in the inventory): identification number, name, price, date of the last purchase, amount in the inventory, and amount ordered (not yet received).

f. Sales at a pharmacy: identification number, date of the transaction, and quantity purchased.

A patient may visit multiple doctors, and a doctor is visited by one or more patients. Additionally, a patient may buy his or her medication from the pharmacy. Using this information, draw an E-R diagram for the Medicare database management system.

24. Wood paneling manufacturers face a number of complex decisions in their daily proceedings. For example, allocating production resources and combining various raw materials to meet production goals require real-time decision making. Due to changing supplies and costs, the management of a wood paneling manufacturer has decided to build a database system to fine-tune their production processes.

   Consider a wood paneling manufacturer that produces a furniture-grade particleboard. Each of the panels consists of a middle layer and two surface layers that are symmetrical. To enhance its mechanical properties, each panel has several strata of different materials, compositions, and specific gravity. A panel's quality can be controlled by specifying different density profiles and raw material requirements. There are eight different types of raw materials, and the database records information about the manufacturer's suppliers, the quantities available, and the maximum capacity of the bottleneck equipment. The raw material needs can be supplied by six different sources, including sawdust, shavings, sawmill, residual, chips, and short or long logs (softwoods or hardwoods). The database should also keep a detailed matrix of specifications that reveals the quantity of each individual raw material allowable in various layers of the different products.

   Another variable that affects the production schedule is the production capacity. The database keeps track of each piece of equipment's production capacity, the equipment type (name), the maintenance date, and a description of its activities.

   Given that each piece of equipment is assigned to produce a product from raw materials and that each raw material has exactly one supplier, draw an E-R diagram of the manufacturer database. Make suitable assumptions for the remaining relationships.

25. The housing office in a university is facing difficulties in assigning undergraduate students to dormitories. One problem it is facing is that the current system does not consider student preferences; therefore, once the assignment is completed and announced, students ask to be reassigned to a different room or even a different building. Also, the number of undergraduate students entering the university is increasing every year, yet the amount of dormitories remains the same.

   The housing office has decided to build a database management system to assign students to dormitories. In particular, the new system will review students' preferences, including air conditioning, dorm location, and room location. It will also review each student's record from previous years, including payment history and history of rule violations or damages, to determine placement. The database will record these factors as student information and residential history.

   There are ten dormitories on campus. Each dormitory is classified into the four following categories: married couples, males only, females only, and co-ed. Each dormitory has up to four floors and each floor has up to ten apartments. An apartment is classified as a single, double, or triple room. Some apartments have air conditioning. Each apartment has a pre-set yearly cost, and students make one payment for their one-year stay. A student can apply to exactly one dorm; however, a dorm houses more than one student. Draw an E-R diagram and state any assumptions made.

26. People have tried to earn large profits from betting on horse races by finding ways of outwitting other betters. A large variety of books has been published on horse races, and each author claims that following his or her methods will lead to profits. So far, Bert has not been able to make big profits using any of the existing methods. Therefore, he has decided to build his own system to place sophisticated bets.

   Horse racing is one of the most thoroughly documented sports. There are thousands of pieces of data published on each upcoming race. This data is available to Bert, and he needs to build a database to organize and store all this information.

   a. For each horse, the following information is recorded: name, owner, height, breed, and parents.

   b. For each jockey, the following information is recorded: social security number, name, weight, height, number of years the jockey has been racing, and age.

c. For each racetrack: name, location (address), type (dirt, turf, etc.), and distance.

d. For each race: name, attendance, prize amount, winner, distance, and location.

A jockey rides exactly one horse, and a horse is ridden by exactly one jockey. Additionally, a horse may participate in one or more races on a racetrack. Draw an E-R diagram of this database.

27. The United States Tennis Association (USTA) is concerned about developing a ranking system of the tennis players that is objective, consistent, and broad-based. These qualities are important in a ranking system since rankings directly affect the acceptance of a tennis player's entry into a tournament and his or her placement in the draw.

USTA use a particular formula to determine the ranking points for each player. The formula uses the following information: number of tournaments played by the player; tournament points earned; number of matches played; and number of wins of the player (say player "*i*") over player *j*. The new system's performance relies on the efficiency of the database, which records the following information:

a. For each player: social security number, name, tournament points earned, current ranking, weight, height, and birth date.

b. For each court: name, type (grass, clay, and hard surface), location.

c. For each tournament: name, location, and tournament strength.

The strength of a tournament is a function of the quality of the players and the size of the tournament. A player may play one or more matches in a tournament on one or more courts. Also, a tournament involves many matches with different players who may play on the same court. Using this information, build an E-R diagram for the database described above.

28. The traditional MBA program has been receiving criticism because it is focused on analytical training. However, potential employers are looking for executives with a broader education. The American Assembly of Collegiate Schools of Business (AACSB) requires the following components in an MBA curriculum: a common body of knowledge in management; a field of specialization; and general competence for overall management.

Due to the business world's growing interest in a broader curriculum, most of the schools are trying to improve their MBA programs, which is not an easy task. As a first step, AACSB has decided to build a database that contains information about students and alumni/alumnae, schools, and courses offered. This information will be useful in preparing the new curriculum for the MBA program. The database consists of the following entities:

a. For each school: name; budget allocated for the MBA program; location (suburban, urban, rural); and whether it is AACSB accredited or not. (AACSB accredits those schools that meet certain requirements. Being AACSB-accredited is important for schools as it indicates their quality.)

b. For each alumnus or alumna: name, social security number, gender, current position, current salary, and GPA at graduation.

c. For each course: name, code, type of course (foundational, functional, general, sectoral, or institutional), and topics covered.

d. For each current student: name, social security number, gender, current GPA, courses completed, and the date she or he began the program.

Each school has one or more students and alumni/alumnae, whereas each student or alumnus/alumna can belong to exactly one business school. Additionally, each school offers one or more courses, which are taken by one or more students. Make suitable assumptions for the remaining relationships and draw an E-R diagram for this database.

29. Blue Bell is a large apparel manufacturer. It produces jeans and several other lines of sports and casual apparel for men, women, and children in the USA and has a substantial international business. Each of the above production lines breaks down into styles, lots, sizes, and stock keeping units (SKU). With time, the management began to realize that the number of product lines, styles, and SKUs had grown tremendously. The production process had incorporated several new automated manufacturing operations in response to a change in customer tastes. The management was concerned about the high investment in working capital. A large part of the working capital goes toward inventories. In this process of extending the business, Blue Bell is eager to effectively coordinate its activities. A well-organized database management system will help Blue Bell to do so. The database includes the following entities:

a. Production line: name (for example, jeans, t-shirts, swimwear, etc.), identification number, and classification (for example, men's-wear, women's-wear, boy's-wear, and girl's-wear).

b. Lot: identification number and name (for example blue, green, etc.).

c. Product: identification number, name, size, and inventory level.

d. Customer: identification number, name, address, and telephone number.

The relationships are explained as follows. A customer may buy one or more products, and a product may be bought by one or more customers. For each transaction, the date and value are recorded. Additionally, each product comes from exactly one lot, and a lot contains one or more products. Each lot comes from exactly one production line, and a production line produces one or more lots. Given this information, draw an E-R diagram for the Blue Bell database. Clearly state any assumptions made.

30. The main library of a university is interested in developing a database management system. The library carries the following items: books, journals, conference proceedings, reference textbooks, and copies of some recorded lectures on CD. These items are loaned to members in various categories.

The library has a total of 250,000 items. The library uses a coding scheme for classifying the items. Using this code, the librarian is able to identify the type of the item (book, journal, CD), the subject, the title, the author(s), and whether the item is on loan, overdue, or on the shelf.

Members of the library are undergraduate and graduate students, faculty members, staff, part-time students, and visiting scholars. The university issues to all members an ID card that can also be used at the library. Students and visiting scholars renew their ID card every semester. Faculty and staff ID are valid as long as they are still employed. The database records the social security number, name, and address of each member.

A member who borrows a CD cannot take it outside the library and has to use the computers

in the library to watch it. Journals and conference proceedings can be borrowed for 2 days, and reference textbooks can be taken on loan overnight only. Faculty and graduate students can borrow books for a period of 3 weeks, other students and visiting scholars can borrow them for 2 weeks, and staff can borrow books for 1 week only. Note that journals, unlike books, do not have a single author. Journals are usually published a few times a year. An item may be borrowed by one or more members, and a member may borrow more than one item. Using this information, draw an EE-R diagram for the university library database. Clearly state any assumptions made.

31. A financial institution offers to its customers various investment schemes such as shares and debentures. The company also accepts fixed deposits from the general public, institutions, and its employees. The company maintains a database with valuable information about its customers (such as ID number, name, and address) and its financial investments.

Fixed deposits have varying terms of 1, 2, and 3 years. For fixed deposits, there are currently two payment schemes. Under the first scheme, the investors get the principal in addition to the interest on maturity. Under the second scheme, they get the principal on maturity, but interest is paid periodically. The interest rates for fixed deposits under the first scheme may be paid quarterly, semi-annually, or annually. Investors have the option to renew their deposits on maturity. The company also raises debentures periodically. The debentures may be either convertible or non-convertible. Convertible debentures can be converted to equity shares on completion of the period. Debentures are issued for periods of one, two, or three years. The company also calls for shares periodically. The company issues two kinds of shares: equity shares and preferred shares. The dividend is declared at the end of the year. The system keeps track of the dividend rates and the dividends issued to the shareholders.

The company records the name of the department for the employees and the name of the contact person for institutions. Draw the EE-R diagram of this database. Identify the subtypes (if any) of the entities FINANCIAL INVESTMENT and MEMBER. Identify one (or more) unique attribute (relationship) for each subtype as well as one (or more) attribute that is shared by all entity subtypes.

32. Great Marbles is a small company in Venezuela that produces two main types of products: gems and marbles. They produce two sizes of gems and six sizes of marbles. Both products are offered in 25 colors. The different kinds of decoration marbles are distinguished by color, size, and shape. Each gem is classified as a matte gem or a luster gem.

    The database system keeps track of the inventory levels, the backorder level (orders not satisfied yet), and the number of outstanding orders (orders that are not yet received). The management refers to this information to decide when, which, and how many products to produce. Other than the information about the products, the database records information about the raw materials, suppliers, and customers. For each type of raw material, the database keeps the following information: identification number, name, and price per unit. For each supplier, the database records the supplier identification number, name, and address.

    The company sells its products in Venezuela as well as in the US and other Latin American countries. For the international customers, the company provides special packaging and charges increased rates. For each customer, the following information is recorded: identification number, name, and address. A customer may order one or more products, and a product may be ordered by one or more customers. Additionally, each product is produced from one or more raw materials, and a particular raw material may be used in multiple products. Each raw material is supplied by exactly one supplier, and a supplier may supply one or more raw materials. Draw an EE-R diagram for the database described above. Clearly state any assumptions made.

33. The medical school at the University of Florida serves UF students as well as the general public as a moderately sized hospital. The hospital stores information about patients, including name, address, date of visit, and doctor's name, in a database. The hospital does not charge the students for its services and charges reduced rates if the patient is a UF faculty or staff member.

    Data about wards, equipment, and operating rooms are also recorded. The hospital has three types of operating rooms used for major, minor, and small operations, respectively. There are two types of wards: general and special. The hospital has 55 general wards and 35 special wards. The general wards have a capacity of eight beds each. The special wards have one or two beds. The hospital also has an intensive care unit with a capacity of four beds. The patients are charged on a per day basis, and the rates depend on the type of the wards.

    The hospital uses the following equipment to examine patients: an X-ray machine, a CT-Scan machine, and an ultrasonic imager. If any of this equipment is needed to examine the patient, the patient is charged extra. The charges are based on the number of hours that the machine is in use. The X-ray machine costs $350 an hour, the CT-Scan machine costs $750 an hour, and the ultrasonic imager costs $150 an hour. Patients may require one or more wards, pieces of equipment, and/or operating rooms. Make suitable assumptions for the remaining relationships and draw an EE-R diagram for this database.

34. National Car Rental maintains a detailed database of its inventory (cars to rent) and customers. Customers rent a car mainly for two purposes: business and leisure. For each customer, National records the social security number, name, and address. If the customer rents the car for business purposes, in addition to the above information, National records the name of the company and the work phone number of the customer. In order to provide better service to customers, National prioritizes bookings based on length-of-rent (LOR).

    National offers the following types of cars: luxury, midsize, and economy. For each type, the company calculates protection level. A protection level is the number of cars that should be reserved for the demand in the current class. The company monitors the number of cars of a particular type available, as well. National charges customers a daily rate depending on LOR and the type of car they rent. A customer may be assigned exactly one car, and a car may be assigned to one or more customers as long as there is no overlap. Draw an EE-R diagram for the above circumstances.

35. All academic departments in a university maintain a database of its students. Students are classified into undergraduate, graduate, and

international students. There are a few reasons for grouping the students into these three categories. For example, the department's administrative assistant informs the undergraduate students about undergraduate courses offered, the graduate students about graduate courses and professional conferences, and international students about new immigration laws. Identify the subtypes (if any) of the entity STUDENTS. Also identify a unique attribute (relationship) for each subtype. Draw an EE-R diagram for a department's database.

36. A blood bank serves a critical purpose in providing a required type of blood to patients at critical times. A blood bank's database monitors the inventory of the blood together with relevant information such as blood type, date received, location, date of expiry, and donor.

The database stores information such as name, address, and telephone number for a blood bank. Supplementary information about the donors is recorded as well. Donors are classified into occasional and regular donors. For the regular donors, the database keeps information such as identification number, blood type, and history of donations. The database also keeps a list of healthcare providers in the area along with their addresses and telephone numbers. The healthcare providers are the customers of the blood bank. They keep track of the blood transactions performed. These transactions are classified into normal transactions and unexpected transactions (for example, due to car accidents during the holiday season). The reason for keeping track of the unexpected transactions is to use this information to estimate the extra amount of blood needed in the inventory for each age group during the next holiday season. A blood bank receives a particular bag of blood from exactly one donor. The blood bank then distributes the blood to health care providers. Draw an EE-R diagram for this database.

37. YXZ is a construction company. The company keeps a list of employees as well as a list of jobs that are scheduled in a particular day. Every day, the management gets a list of required jobs and a list of employees available. A job is then assigned to the employee who has the skills needed to do the job. (In other words, an employee should have enough skills to perform the job assigned.) We want to build a database that will facilitate the process of assigning employees to jobs.

Employees are classified into three main groups: managers, engineers, and workers. Managers take care of managerial issues, engineers direct production processes, and workers perform labor-intensive jobs that require a certain level of technical skill. Jobs are classified into those that require a high level of technical skill, a moderate level of technical skill, and managerial skills. The classification of employees and jobs into groups facilitates the process of assigning an employee to a job.

An employee may perform one or more jobs, and a job is performed by exactly one employee. Draw an EE-R diagram for this database. Identify the subtypes (if any) of the entity EMPLOYEE. Identify one (or more) unique attribute (relationship) for each subtype as well as one (or more) attribute that is shared by all entity subtypes.

Relational Data Modeling and Normalization

chapter **OVERVIEW**

4.1   *Introduction*

In Chapter 3, we described conceptual database design using object-based *entity-relationships (E-R) data modeling*. In this chapter, we describe logical database design using record-based *relational data modeling*. The objective of a logical database design is to transform the conceptual data model into a set of relations that can be used in physical database design. The reason we picked relational data modeling is twofold: first, it is widely used in contemporary database applications, and second, it is a very general modeling approach, and many principles of the relational data modeling can be easily extended to other record-based modeling.

4.1.1   Topics

This chapter discusses the following topics:

- The relational data model, relational keys, and relational data integrity constraints.
- How to transform E-R diagrams into relational schemas.
- Database normalization and anomalies.
- Functional dependencies and forms of normalization.

4.2   *The Relational Data Model*

The relational data model was first introduced by IBM's E. F. Codd, the founder of relational theory, in the paper "*A relational model of data for large shared data banks,*" published in 1970. During the late 70s, "System R" and "Ingress" research projects were launched to prove the feasibility of the relational data model proposed by Codd. After successful prototype testing of the *relational database management system* (RDBMS), the relational model began to penetrate the commercial market in 1980. In today's world, RDBMS technology is pervasive, and there are literally hundreds of products developed to cater to various application needs.

The relational data model is based on the mathematical concept of a *relation* and has a solid theoretical foundation. The concept is physically represented as a relation or a table that stores data. The relational data model consists of three components:

- **Relational Data Structure**: where data is organized
- **Data Manipulation**: the operations used to manipulate data stored in the data structure
- **Relational Data Integrity**: the rules that maintain the integrity of data when manipulated

In this chapter, we discuss relational data structure and data integrity. We address data manipulation in Chapters 8 and 9.

4.2.1   Relational Data Structure

A **relation** is the main data structure that stores and organizes data in the relational data model. A relation is a two-dimensional grid that holds data about the object that is represented in the database. Each relation has a unique name and consists of a set of named columns and an arbitrary number of unnamed rows. A column of a relation is referred to as an **attribute**, while a row is referred to as a **record** or a **tuple**. If we compare the relational data model with the entity-relationship model, we see the correspondence. The entities of an E-R diagram are like relations in the relational data model. The attributes of an entity are columns of a relation, and instances of an entity type are rows of a relation.

Figure 4.1 presents a relation for the STUDENT entity. The tabular data structure holds the student records. The columns of the relation are the attributes that categorize the students, and each row features a specific instance of a student. The number of attributes in a relation is defined as the **_degree of the relation_**, and the number of records in a relation is defined as the **_cardinality of the relation_**. We use the following shorthand notation to represent this relation:

STUDENT (<u>SSN</u>, Name, Email, DeptName)

The notation begins with the relation name followed by a list of comma-separated attributes. The key attributes are underlined just as they are in an E-R diagram. The notation is also referred to as **_relational schema_**. We use relational schema to discuss a relation without referring to specific records. The table below presents some of the important properties of a relation.

Properties of a Relation

1. Each relation is uniquely identified by its name.
2. Each cell of a relation contains exactly one (atomic) value.
3. Each record (all the attributes together) of a relation is unique.
4. Each attribute in a relation has a distinct name.
5. The values of an attribute are from the same domain.
6. The order of attributes is irrelevant. Columns can be interchanged without changing the meaning of a relation.
7. The order of records is also irrelevant. Rows can be interchanged without changing the meaning of a relation.

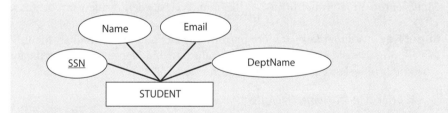

STUDENT

<u>SSN</u>	Name	Email	_DeptName_
234-23-2535	John Doe	John.Doe@mail.com	ISE
545-28-2324	Samuel Ed	Samuel.Ed@mail.com	CISE
368-98-4234	Jay Leno	Jay.Leno@mail.com	ISE
975-34-3558	Ricky Grey	Ricky.Grey@mail.com	PHY

Figure 4.1 E-R diagram and relational schema for the _Student_ relation.

4.2.2 Data Manipulation

Once we build a relation, we need a way to access and manipulate the data it contains. A data manipulation language, such as Structured Query Language (SQL), supports and facilitates data access and manipulation. The following is an example of an SQL statement that updates the faculty relation, *tblFaculty*. The salaries of all faculty members who joined the university before 1995 and have salary less than 70,000 are raised by 5%. We will cover specific details of SQL in Chapters 8 and 9.

```
UPDATE    tblFaculty
SET       Salary = Salary * 1.05
WHERE     JoinDate < #1/1/1995# AND Salary < 70000
```

4.2.3 Relational Data Integrity Constraints

Relational data integrity constraints maintain data integrity when a manipulation language is used to manipulate the data. These constraints emulate relationships and cardinalities in an E-R diagram. As entities in an E-R diagram are related to each other via a relationship, relations in the relational model are related to each other via an integrity constraint. Integrity constraints, therefore, allow us to incorporate business rules and constraints in the relational data model. Before examining integrity constraints in detail, we must define various relational keys, which have their own importance in the function and design of the relational databases.

4.3 *Relational Keys*

One of the properties of a relation is that no two records in a relation can be identical. In order to enforce this requirement, we identify one or more attributes that uniquely identify each record in the relation. These attributes are referred to as **relational keys**. Relational keys are equivalent to an identifier in an E-R diagram. We now define a few important relational keys.

Super Key   A **super key** is a set of one or more attributes that uniquely identifies each record in a relation. Consider the *Student* relation illustrated in Figure 4.1. Any of the following sets of attributes can serve as a super key for this relation.

> *Superkey1: {SSN, Name, Email, DeptName}*
> *Superkey2: {SSN, Name, DeptName}*
> *Superkey3: {Name, Email, DeptName}*
> *Superkey4: {SSN}*
> *SuperKey5: {Email}*

If we take all four attributes together, as defined in Superkey1, each record in the relation has a unique value for these fields as a set. Likewise, as Figure 4.1 indicates, Superkey4 and Superkey5 have unique values for each record as well. Conversely, the attributes *Name* and *DeptName* cannot serve as a super key by themselves because neither of the attributes guarantees uniqueness.

Candidate Key   It is clear from above example that a super key might contain additional attributes that are not required to uniquely identify each record. Efficient design requires a minimal number of attributes in the key set. A ***candidate key*** is a minimal super key (one that has a minimum number of attributes). In other words, a candidate key is a super key in which no subset of it can serve as a super key of a relation. In the previous example, both Superkey4 and Superkey5 are minimal super keys and thus are the candidate keys.

Candidatekey1: {SSN}
Candidatekey2: {Email}

Primary Key   While all candidate keys are minimal, we need only one key that satisfies the uniqueness property of the records. A ***primary key*** is a candidate key that has been selected to uniquely identify records in a relation. In the student example, we choose Candidatekey1 as the primary key.

Primarykey: {SSN}

Foreign Key   Recall that in an E-R diagram association between entities is expressed using relationships. The relational data model uses common attributes and constraints between common attributes to express relationships. For example, the STUDENT entity is related to the DEPARTMENT entity by the relationship *BelongsTo*. In the relational data model, we add a common attribute to the *Student* and *Department* relations. The Figure 4.2 depicts *DeptName* as a common attribute in these relations. Note that *DeptName* is the primary key in the *Department* relation. We refer to *DeptName* in the *Student* relation as the *foreign key*. A ***foreign key*** is an attribute or a set of attributes in a relation that serves as a primary key of the same or some other relation.

STUDENT

<u>SSN</u>	Name	Email	*DeptName*
234-23-2535	John Doe	John.Doe@mail.com	ISE
545-28-2324	Samuel Ed	Samuel.Ed@mail.com	CISE
368-98-4234	Jay Leno	Jay.Leno@mail.com	ISE
975-34-3558	Ricky Grey	Ricky.Grey@mail.com	PHY

DEPARTMENT

<u>DeptName</u>	Address	Phone	*College ID*
ISE	Weil Hall, GNV, FL	352-222-1111	COE
CISE	Marston Science, GNV, FL	352-333-9999	COE
PHY	Physics Bldg, GNV, FL	352-444-8888	CLAS
CHEM	Chemistry Bldg, GNV, FL	352-555-3333	CLAS

Figure 4.2 The *Student* and *Department* relations illustrating foreign keys.

We represent the primary key in the relational data model by underlining the attribute(s) and a foreign key by italicizing the attribute(s). In our example, the *SSN* attribute serves as the primary key and *DeptName* is the foreign key in the *Student* relation. *DeptName* serves as the primary key and *CollegeID* is the foreign key of the *Department* relation.

```
STUDENT (SSN, Name, Email, DeptName)
DEPARTMENT (DeptName, Address, Phone, CollegeID)
```

4.3.1   Selection of a Primary Key

We choose the primary key among candidate keys based on two simple guidelines. The first guideline for the selection of a primary key is that we choose a candidate key as a primary key that never changes its value. For example, while email addresses may be unique, students may change their email addresses during the course of the school years. A student's social security number, on the other hand, will never change. Second, we don't choose a candidate key that might get NULL values. The term *NULL value* does not mean a numeric zero or white space. Instead, a NULL value designates a non-existing or unknown value. For example, even if a fax number (not shown in the Figure 4.1) is unique for each student, it is not a valid primary key unless all students are guaranteed to have their own fax number, a scenario that is highly unlikely.

4.3.2   NULL Values

There are several situations in which a particular attribute of a relation cannot be assigned a data value. The first situation, which we encountered in our discussion of student fax numbers, occurs when there is no applicable data value for a particular attribute. Since all students do not have fax numbers, this attribute does not have an applicable data value for each record in the *Student* relation. In the second situation, the value for a particular attribute is unknown at the time of the assignment. For example, consider the attribute *PhoneNumber* for the *Student* relation. An administrative assistant entering a student's record into the database may not know a student's phone number and might add it at a later time.

The relational data model allows us to assign a NULL value to an attribute under these circumstances. NULL simply means that the value is either unknown or is not applicable, and it allows us to handle incomplete or exceptional data. Many readers confuse NULL with the numeric value zero or with blank text; however, NULL only represents the absence of a value.

Definitions

A **super key** is a set of one or more attributes that uniquely identifies each record in a relation.

A **candidate key** is a minimal super key.

A **primary key** is a selected candidate key.

A **foreign key** is an attribute or a set of attributes in a relation that serves as a primary key of the same or some other relation.

4.4 *Relational Data Integrity Constraints*

The relational data model includes several constraints and business rules that help maintain the accuracy and integrity of data that has been manipulated. In this section, we discuss three types of constraints: domain constraints, entity constraints, and referential constraints.

4.4.1 Domain Constraints

A *domain* is the set of values that can be assigned to an attribute. The definition of a domain consists of the domain name, the description, the data type, the size, and other information related to formatting and ranges. For example, the attribute SSN has the following domain:

Table 4.1 The domain definition.

Attribute	Domain Name	Description	Domain	Size	Format
SSN	SSNs	Set of all possible SSN values.	Number	9	xxx-xx-xxxx

The ***domain constraint*** states that all the values of an attribute must be from the same domain.

4.4.2 Entity Constraints

While discussing guidelines for the selection of a primary key, we mentioned that a candidate key that does not have NULL values is a good candidate for a primary key. Entity constraints enforce this guideline as a constraint in the relational data model. ***Entity constraints*** ensure that every relation of a relational data model has a primary key and that the value of the primary key cannot be NULL. In the *Student* relation, for example, we cannot possibly enter a student record with no value for the *SSN* attribute. Since *SSN* is a primary key, it cannot be NULL.

4.4.3 Referential Constraints

The third integrity constraint pertains to the foreign keys. *Referential integrity constraints* maintain consistency between two relations related to each other through the primary key-foreign key relationship. A ***referential integrity constraint*** ensures that the foreign key values of a relation must come from the primary key values of the related relation; otherwise, the value of a foreign key must be NULL.

For example, consider the relationship between the *Department* and *Student* relations depicted in Figure 4.2. The attribute *DeptName* is the foreign key in the *Student* relation and is the primary key in the *Department* relation. The definition of a referential integrity constraint suggests that the values for the *DeptName* attribute in the *Student* relation must come from the values of the *DeptName* attribute in the *Department* relation, or it must be NULL.

Let us discuss how the referential integrity constraint maintains data consistency. We use the *Department* relation to store the information about all the university's departments. When we add a new record to the *Student* relation, we should assign students to an existing department (from the *Department* relation). Assigning a department that is not in the *Department* relation clearly results in data inconsistency. If we are not sure about a student's department, then constraints allow us to provisionally assign a NULL value to the foreign key attributes. Figure 4.3 depicts an example of a violation of a referential integrity constraint.

STUDENT

<u>SSN</u>	Name	Email	*DeptName*
234-23-2535	John Doe	John.Doe@mail.com	ISE
545-28-2324	Samuel Ed	Samuel.Ed@mail.com	CISE
368-98-4234	Jay Leno	Jay.Leno@mail.com	ISE
975-34-3558	Ricky Grey	Ricky.Grey@mail.com	PHY
973-244-1111	Don Jose	Don.Jose@mail.com	BME

DEPARTMENT

<u>DeptName</u>	Address	Phone	*College ID*
ISE	Weil Hall, GNV, FL	352-222-1111	COE
CISE	Marston Science, GNV, FL	352-333-9999	COE
PHY	Physics Bldg, GNV, FL	352-444-8888	CLAS
CHEM	Chemistry Bldg, GNV, FL	352-555-3333	CLAS

Figure 4.3 A violation of a referential integrity constraint.

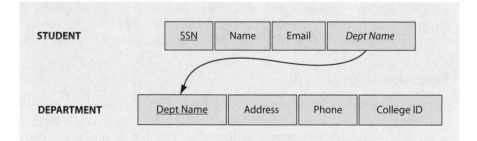

Figure 4.4 A graphical representation of a relational schema.

Definitions

The **domain constraint** states that all the values of an attribute must be from the same domain.

The **entity constraint** ensures that every relation of a relational data model has a primary key, and the values of a primary key cannot be NULL.

The **referential integrity constraint** ensures that the foreign key values of a relation must come from the primary key values in the related relation; otherwise, the value of a foreign key must be NULL.

4.5 *Transforming E-R Diagrams into Relational Schemas*

Recall the database development process discussed in Chapter 2. We mentioned that the process of logical database design requires transforming a conceptual data model into a set of relational schemas. We introduced conceptual database design in Chapter 3 and modeled database requirements in the form of E-R and EE-R diagrams. In this section, we systematically transform E-R and EE-R diagrams into a set of relational schemas. The transformation process follows a defined set of rules and is a fairly automatic process. In fact, there are software tools available that can convert E-R or EE-R diagrams into a set of relational schemas.

We examine the transformation process as a series of small tasks, each of which illustrates an aspect of an E-R diagram. These tasks can be put together or used in a series of transformations to convert larger diagrams into corresponding schemas.

4.5.1   Task 1: Transforming Regular Entities

Regular entities are independent entities that represent real-world objects such as people, activities, or products. We represent these entities with a rectangular block in an E-R diagram. To transform any regular entity from an E-R diagram into a relational schema, we follow these steps:

1. Transform a regular entity type in an E-R diagram into a relation.
2. Assign the entity name in an E-R diagram as a relation name.
3. Make each simple attribute of a regular entity an attribute of a relation.
4. Make the identifier of the regular entity type the primary key of a relation.

Figure 4.5 illustrates the transformation of the STUDENT entity type into a relational schema.

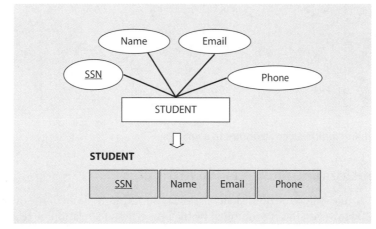

Figure 4.5 Transformation of a regular entity.

4.5.2   Task 2: Transforming Composite Attributes

When an entity type has composite attributes, we include simple attributes of a composite attribute in the relation. Figure 4.6 illustrates the transformation of a composite attribute. We add a composite attribute *Address* to the *Student* relation by adding its simple attributes: *Street*, *City*,

State, and *Zip*. Note that the composite attribute *Address* itself does not appear in the relational schema.

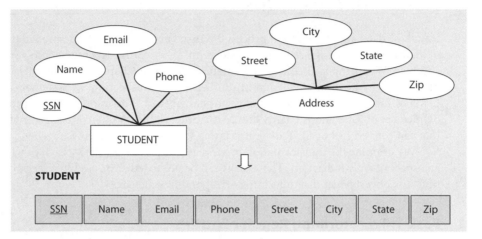

Figure 4.6 Transformation of a composite attribute.

STUDENT

SSN	Name	Email	Phone	Skills
234-23-2535	John Doe	John.Doe@mail.com	352-376-1234	Drawing, Football
545-28-2324	Samuel Ed	Samuel.Ed@mail.com	352-376-5678	Singing, Bowling
368-98-4234	Jay Leno	Jay.Leno@mail.com	352-376-0000	Acting, Sky diving
975-34-3558	Ricky Grey	Ricky.Grey@mail.com	352-376-9999	Swimming, Soccer

Figure 4.7 Adding multi-valued attributes to a relation.

4.5.3   Task 3: Transforming Multi-Valued Attributes

We could add a multi-valued attribute to a relation as we add a simple attribute of an entity type (see Figure 4.7). However, this is prohibited by the properties of a relation. A relation can have exactly one value for each of its cells (intersection of a row and a column). This property demands a slightly different set of rules for multi-valued attributes:

    1. Transform a regular entity as described in 4.5.1 and 4.5.2; however, do not add any multi-valued attributes to the relation.

2. Create a new relation (one for each multi-valued attribute). The new relation should have two attributes: the identifier of a regular entity and the multi-valued attribute. The name of the new relation should be a logical name that reflects the meaning of a multi-valued attribute.

3. The primary key of a new relation is a composite key. The two attributes of a new relation together serve as its primary key.

Consider the example in Figure 4.8. The *Skills* attribute is a multi-valued attribute of the STUDENT entity type. The *Skills* attribute stores data about various skills possessed by the students. We transform the STUDENT entity as described in Section 4.5.1 but without adding the *Skills* attribute. We now create a new relation named *StudentSkills*. We assign the attributes *SSN* and *Skills* to the new relation and also serve as the composite primary key of the new relation. The decomposition of relations allows us to store student skills in a new relation while maintaining the properties of the relation. The decomposition technique is frequently used in database design to reduce data redundancy and eliminates anomalies (discussed in detail later in this chapter—see sections on normalization).

As with entities, we must also transform relationships. The transformation rule varies based on degree and cardinality of a relationship. We will consider transformations from unary, binary, and ternary relationships. For each relationship type, we consider transformation for one-to-one, one-to-many, and many-to-many maximum cardinalities. Note that we are considering only maximum cardinalities for transformation cases as the minimum cardinalities have little or no effect on the transformation process.

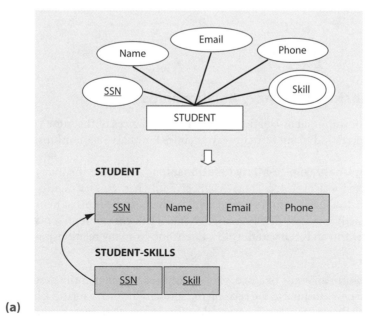

(a)

(continues)

Figure 4.8 (a) Transformation of multi-valued attribute; (b) Multi-valued attribute in the new relation *Student-Skills* after transformation.

STUDENT

SSN	Name	Email	Phone
234-23-2535	John Doe	John.Doe@mail.com	352-376-1234
545-28-2324	Samuel Ed	Samuel.Ed@mail.com	352-376-5678
368-98-4234	Jay Leno	Jay.Leno@mail.com	352-376-0000
975-34-3558	Ricky Grey	Ricky.Grey@mail.com	352-376-9999

STUDENT-SKILLS

SSN	Skills
234-23-2535	Drawing
234-23-2535	Football
545-28-2324	Singing
545-28-2324	Bowling
368-98-4234	Sky Diving
975-34-3558	Soccer

(b)

Figure 4.8 *(continued)*

4.5.4 Task 4: Transforming Unary Relationships

A unary relationship is an association between two instances of the same entity type. We consider one-to-many and many-to-many cardinalities for unary relationships.

Transforming Unary One-to-Many Relationships   Consider the unary one-to-many relationship depicted in Figure 4.9. The STUDENT entity has a unary one-to-many relationship, *Represents*, which associate a student with another student who is his or her representative. Each student has exactly one student representative, and a student can represents none or many students. To transform an E-R diagram with a unary one-to-many relationship, we use the following rules:

1. Transform an entity of a unary relationship as a regular entity described in Tasks 1–3.
2. Add a new attribute to the relation to represent the unary relationship. Specifically, duplicate the primary key. That is, add a foreign key that refers to the primary key of the same relation.
3. Draw an arrow that originates from the foreign key and points toward the primary key.

In our example, we add the attribute *StudentRepresentative* to the *Student* relation. We then point this attribute to the primary key *SSN*, indicating that the value of the foreign key comes from the SSN attribute. The foreign key value will be set to NULL for students who themselves are representatives. Figure 4.9 illustrates the transformation.

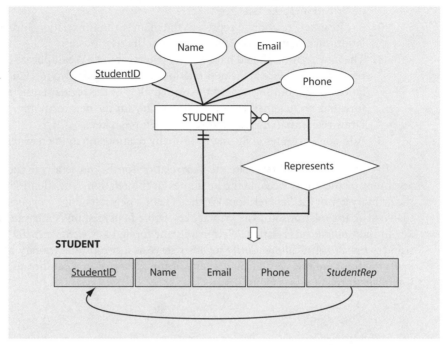

(a)

STUDENT

StudentID	Name	Email	Phone	Student Rep
100	John Doe	John.Doe@mail.com	352-376-1234	
200	Samuel Ed	Samuel.Ed@mail.com	352-376-5678	100
300	Jay Leno	Jay.Leno@mail.com	352-376-0000	100
400	Ricky Grey	Ricky.Grey@mail.com	352-376-9999	100
500	David Ray	David@mail.com	352-376-1111	
600	Rosy Ted	Rosy.Ted@mail.com	352-376-2222	500

(b)

Figure 4.9 (a) Transformation of a unary one-to-many relationship; (b) *Student* relation after transformation.

Transforming Unary Many-to-Many Relationship   Figure 4.10 provides an example of a unary many-to-many relationship. The ITEM entity is a regular entity with a unary many-to-many relationship, *Contains*, which represents the bill-of-material. The relationship is unary because items are assembled using other items. The relationship is many-to-many because an item can be assembled from one or more items, and conversely, an item can be used to assemble one or more items. To transform an E-R diagram with a unary many-to-many relationship, we follow these rules:

1. Transform the entity of a unary relationship as a regular entity according to the process described in Tasks 1–3.
2. Create a new relation to represent the many-to-many relationship. Name the new relation such that it reflects the meaning of the relationship.
3. The new relation should have at least two attributes. We duplicate the identifier of the regular entity twice in the new relation. That is, we add two foreign keys to the new relation, both pointing toward the primary key of the regular entity relation. These two foreign keys together serve as a primary key for the new relation.
4. Draw referential integrity arrows for the foreign keys.
5. Add any attributes of the many-to-many relationship in the new relation.

In our example, we first create the *Item* relation for the only entity in the E-R diagram. The attributes of the entity become the attributes of the relation. The identifier *ItemNo* serves as the primary key of the *Item* relation. We then create a new relation, *Components*, to represent the many-to-many relationship. The primary key of the *Item* relation is migrated twice as a foreign key in the *Components* relation. We rename one foreign key *ComponentID* for clarity. The attributes *ItemNo* and *ComponentID* together serve as a composite primary key for the *Components* relation. Finally, we add an attribute of the relationship, *Quantity*, as an attribute to the *Components* relation (see Figure 4.10).

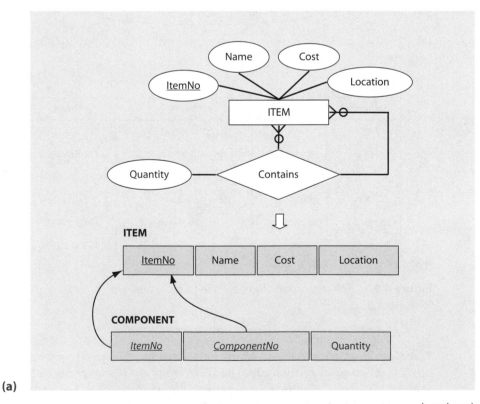

(a)

(continues)

Figure 4.10 (a) Transformation of a unary many-to-many relationship; (b) Relation *Item* and the new relation *Component* after transformation.

ITEM

ItemNo	Name	Cost	Location
1	Spindle	$1,200	Alachua
2	Rotor	$400	Ridge Rd
3	Fan Blade	$500	Stanton Hill
4	Capacitor	$700	Daytona

COMPONENT

ItemNo	ComponentNo	Quantity
1	3	1
1	4	2
2	1	3
2	3	1
2	4	5
3	2	10

(b)

Figure 4.10 (*continued*)

4.5.5 Task 5: Transforming Binary Relationships

A binary relationship is a relationship between two entity types. In this section, we consider transforming binary one-to-one, binary one-to-many, and binary many-to-many relationships.

Transforming Binary One-to-One Relationships   The entity types EMPLOYEE and WORK-STATION are related to each other with a binary one-to-one relationship (see Figure 4.11). Each employee is assigned to exactly one workstation, and each workstation is assigned to at most one employee. We transform such a binary one-to-one relationship using the following rules:

1. Create two relations, one for each entity in a binary relationship. Transform each regular entity into a relation using Tasks 1–3.
2. Include the primary key of one relation as a foreign key to the other relation. For one-to-one binary relationships, we can use minimum cardinalities to determine which relation should have a foreign key attribute. In such a pairing, the mandatory side migrates toward the optional side of the relationship.
3. Draw an arrow indicating the referential integrity constraint.
4. Any attributes of the relationship should also migrate toward the optional side of the relationship.

Our employee-workstation example has an optional cardinality on the employee side and a mandatory cardinality on the workstation side. During transformation, the primary key of the *Workstation* relation, *CompID*, migrates as a foreign key to the *Employee* relation. The *Date* attribute of a relationship also migrates to the *Employee* relation (see Figure 4.11).

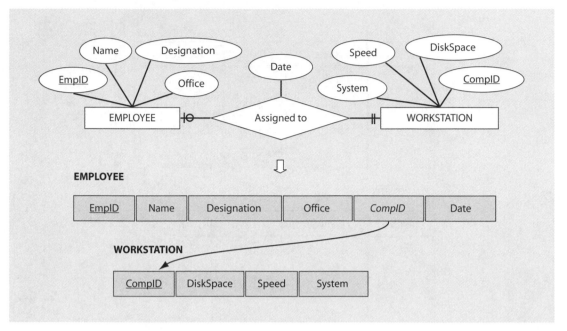

(a)

(b)

Figure 4.11 (a) Transformation of a binary one-to-one relationship; (b) *Employee* and *Workstation* relations after transformation.

Transforming Binary One-to-Many Relationships   Figure 4.12 depicts entity types STU-DENT and DEPARTMENT related to each other through a binary one-to-many relationship. Each student is associated with a maximum of one department, while every department has one or more students. We use the following rules to transform a binary one-to-many relationship:

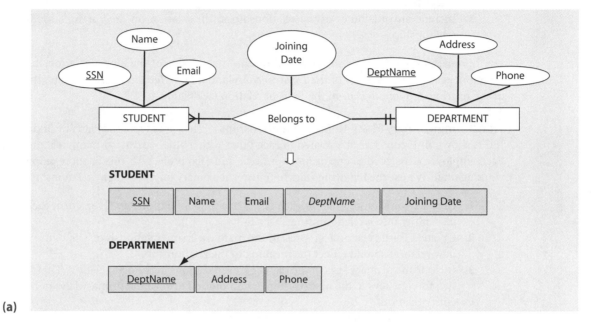

(a)

STUDENT

SSN	Name	Email	*DeptName*	Joining Date
234-23-2535	John Doe	John.Doe@mail.com	ISE	7/4/99
545-28-2324	Samuel Ed	Samuel.Ed@mail.com	CISE	7/9/00
368-98-4234	Jay Leno	Jay.Leno@mail.com	ISE	7/2/01
975-34-3558	Ricky Grey	Ricky.Grey@mail.com	PHY	7/9/01

DEPARTMENT

DeptName	Address	Phone
ISE	Weil Hall, GNV, FL	352-222-1111
CISE	Marston Science, GNV, FL	352-333-9999
PHY	Physics Bldg, GNV, FL	352-444-8888
CHEM	Chemistry Bldg, GNV, FL	352-555-3333

(b)

Figure 4.12 (a) Transformation of a binary one-to-many relationship; (b) *Student* and *Department* relations after transformation.

1. Create two relations, one for each entity in a binary relationship. Transform each regular entity into a relation using Tasks 1–3.
2. Include the primary key of a relation on the "one" side of the relationship in the relation on the "many" side of the relationship. Draw an arrow indicating the referential integrity constraint.
3. Include any attributes of the relationship in the relation on the "many" side of the relationship.

In our example, the *Student* relation is on the "many" side of the binary relationship and therefore gets the primary key of the *Department* relation, *DeptName*. We also add an attribute of the relationship *JoiningDate* in the *Student* relation (see Figure 4.12).

Transforming Binary Many-to-Many Relationships   The entity types EMPLOYEE and PROJECT, shown in Figure 4.13, are related to each other with a binary many-to-many relationship. Each employee is assigned to one or more projects, and each project has one or more employees working on it. We use the following rules to transform a binary many-to-many relationship:

1. Create two relations, one for each entity in a binary relationship. Transform each regular entity into a relation using Tasks 1–3.
2. Create a third relation to represent the many-to-many relationship. The name of the new relation should reflect the meaning of the relationship.
3. Include the primary keys of the regular entity relations in the new relation. That is, add two foreign keys to the new relation, each pointing toward the primary keys of regular entity relations.
4. Draw arrows for the referential integrity constraints.
5. The two foreign keys of the new relation together serve as a composite primary key.
6. Include any attributes of the relationship in the third intermediate relation that represent the relationship.

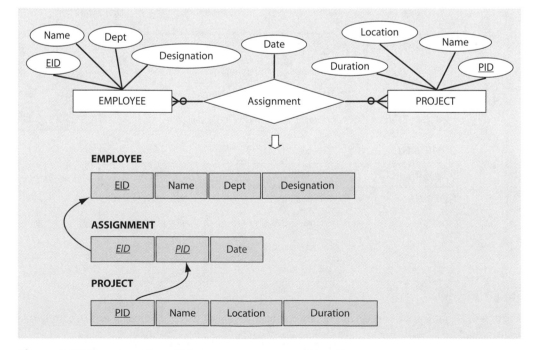

Figure 4.13 Transformation of binary many-to-many relationship.

In our example, we create a new relation, *Assignment*, to represent the many-to-many relationship. The new relation receives two attributes: *PID*, the primary key of the *Project* relation, and *EID*, the primary key of the *Employee* relation. *PID* and *EID* together serve as a primary key for the *Assignment* relation. Finally, we also add the attribute of the relationship *Date* to the *Assignment* relation (see Figure 4.14).

EMPLOYEE

EID	Name	Dept	Designation
2569	Larry	Design	Manager
3654	Ross	Manufacturing	Supervisor
9683	Paul	Quality Assurance	Officer

ASSIGNMENT

PID	EID	Date
1	2569	08/05/02
2	3654	09/23/99
3	9683	09/23/99

PROJECT

EID	Name	Location	Duration
1	MAHO	Florida	8
2	ULTRA	New York	9
3	DELTA	Vancouver	24

Figure 4.14 Transformed binary many-to-many relationship.

4.5.6 Task 6: Transforming Ternary Relationships

Figure 4.15 illustrates three entity types, TOURNAMENT, COURT, and PARTICIPANT, which are related to each other through the ternary relationship *Match*. Each participant plays a match on one or more courts in one or more different tournaments. Each court can host one or more different tournaments. We use the following rules to transform a ternary relationship:

1. Create three relations, one for each regular entity in a ternary relationship. Transform each regular entity using Tasks 1–3.
2. Create the fourth relation to represent the ternary relationship. The name of this new relation should reflect the meaning of the relationship.
3. Include the primary key from the three relations in the new relation. That is, add three foreign keys to the new relation, each pointing toward the primary keys of regular entity relations.
4. Draw arrows indicating the referential integrity constraint.

5. The three foreign keys of the new relation together serve as a composite primary key.
6. Include any attributes of the relationship in the fourth intermediate relation that represent the relationship.

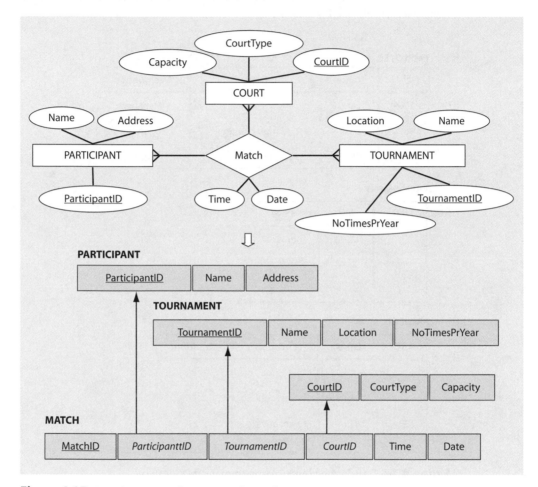

Figure 4.15 Transformation of a ternary relationship.

In our example, the fourth relation, *Match*, receives *CourtID*, the primary key of the *Court* relation; *ParticipantID*, the primary key of the *Participant* relation; and *TournamentID*, the primary key of the *Tournament* relation. These three fields also serve as a composite primary key of the *Match* relation. Finally, we add the *Date* and *Time* attributes of the relationship to the *Match* relation (see Figure 4.16).

PARTICIPANT

ParticipantID	Name	Address
1	Paul	12th Hill Rd, GNV
2	Sam	SW 16th Avenue, GNV
3	Steven	3rd Street, GNV

TOURNAMENT

TournamentID	Name	Location	NoTimesPrYear
T1	Tennis	Browards	2
V1	Volleyball	SCOC	1
B1	Basketball	SCOC	1

COURT

CourtID	CourtType	Capacity
100	Outdoor	1000
101	Indoor	1500
102	Indoor	5000

MATCH

MatchID	ParticipantID	TournamentID	CourtID	Time	Date
MT1	1	T1	100	11:00	2/8/03
MB1	2	B1	101	17:00	3/5/03
MB1	3	B1	101	17:00	3/5/03
MV1	3	V1	102	15:00	1/6/03

Figure 4.16 Transformed ternary relationship.

4.5.7 Task 7: Transforming Superclass/Subclass Relationships (EE-R)

In Chapter 3, we introduced Enhanced Entity-Relationship (EE-R) diagrams. EE-R employs Superclass/Subclass relationship to model complex real-world situations. Since EE-R is one-to-one relationship by default, they do not differ significantly from transformation rules seen before. We transform an EE-R using following rules:

1. Create a separate relation for the superclass and each subclass entity. Transform each regular entity into a relation using Tasks 1–3.

2. Assign all attributes of the superclass entity type along with the subclass discriminator attribute to the relation created for the superclass entity. The identifier of the superclass should serve as a primary key for the superclass relation.

3. For each subclass relation, assign the attributes unique to each subclass entity. Include the primary key of a superclass relation as a foreign key to each subclass relation. The foreign key also serves as a primary key for subclass relations. Draw the referential integrity arrows.

4. If we have the overlap rule employed in the EE-R diagram, the subclass discriminator is a multi-valued attribute and should be transformed using Task 3. The participation and disjoin rules do not affect the transformation.

Figure 4.17 provides an example of a superclass/subclass relationship. In this relationship, PERSON is a superclass entity, while STUDENT, STAFF, and FACULTY constitute its subclass entities. To transform this EE-R diagram, we first create relations for each entity type: *Person, Student, Staff,* and *Faculty.* The *SSN* serves as the primary key for the *Person* relation. We also include the discriminating attribute *Type* in the *Person* relation. The subclass relations, *Student, Staff,* and *Faculty,* each receive the primary key of the *Person* relation as a foreign key. We renamed these keys for clarity. The migrated *SSN* attribute serves as a primary key for the subclass entity relations.

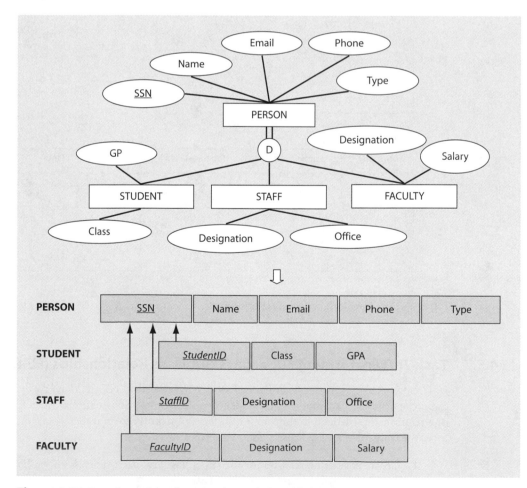

Figure 4.17 Transformation of a superclass/subclass relationship.

PERSON

SSN	Name	Email	Phone	Type
222-12-1234	Jim Ray	Jim@mail.com	352-377-1999	S100
321-12-1234	Robert Ed	Robert@mail.com	352-381-1111	O100
574-22-4555	Nick Brown	Nick@mail.com	352-321-1843	F102
549-24-5689	Cody Grey	Cody@mail.com	352-356-2124	S102
555-33-1344	Jack M.	Jack@mail.com	352-345-1236	F100

STUDENT

StudentID	Class	GPA
S100	ESI1111	3.5
S102	CSI1234	3.6

STAFF

StaffID	Designation	Office
O100	Accountant	Criser Hall

FACULTY

FacultyID	Designation	Salary
F100	Asst. Professor	$80,000
F102	Professor	$120,000

Figure 4.18 Transformed superclass/subclass relationship.

4.5.8   Task 8: Transforming Weak Entities

Weak entities are the entities that are dependent on other entity types. The entity on which a weak entity depends is referred to as the identifying owner or, simply, the owner. This relationship between a weak entity and its owner is called an identifying relationship. Weak entities have a partial key attribute which, when combined with the primary key of its owner, forms the primary key of the weak entity. We use the following rules to transform a weak entity:

1. Create a relation for the owner entity type using Tasks 1–3.
2. Create a new relation for the weak entity type.
3. Include the primary key of the owner relation as a foreign key in the weak entity relation. Draw an arrow indicating the referential integrity constraint.
4. The partial identifier of a weak entity and the identifier of the owner relation together serve as the composite primary key of a weak entity relation.

Consider the example in Figure 4.19. The PET is the weak entity that depends on the strong entity type, PATIENT. *PatientID* is the identifier for the PATIENT entity, and *PetName* is the partial identifier of the PET entity. We create a *Patient* relation with *PatientID* as the primary key. We also create a *Pet* relation with its own attributes including the partial key *PetName*. We add the *PatientID* attribute to the *Pet* relation as a foreign key. Finally, the *PatientID* and *Pet-Name* together serve as the primary key of the *Pet* relation.

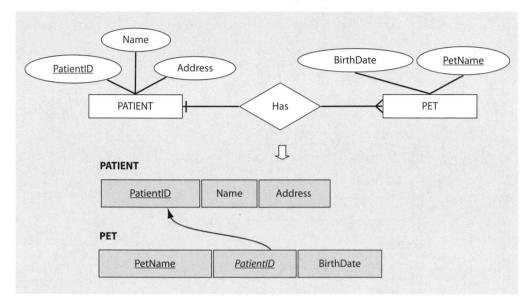

Figure 4.19 Transformation of a weak entity.

4.5.9 Task 9: Transforming Associative Entities

An associative entity is an entity type that associates the instances of one or more entity types and contains attributes particular to the association. An associate entity is a relationship turned into an entity when one of the following conditions exists:

a) It is a many-to-many binary relationship.
b) It is a ternary or higher degree relationship.

Consider the example of an associate entity type in Figure 4.20. The E-R diagram is for the office of academic support. The office keeps information about students who apply for summer internships as well as companies that are looking for interns. STUDENT and COMPANY are two distinct regular entities, while APPOINTMENT is an associate entity with its own attribute, *Date*. We use the following rules to transform an associate entity:

1. Create two relations, one for each of the two participating entity types. Transform participating regular entities using Tasks 1–.
2. Create another relation for the associate entity type and transform it into a regular entity.
3. Include the identifiers of participating entities as a foreign key in the relation for the associate entity. Draw the referential integrity arrows. For an associate entity with its own identifier, the identifier becomes its primary key (see Figure 4.21).

In our example, we create three relations: *Student*, *Company*, and *Appointment*. We include *StudentID* and *CompanyID*, the primary keys of two participating relations, as a foreign key in the *Appointment* relation. Two foreign keys together serve as the primary key of the relation.

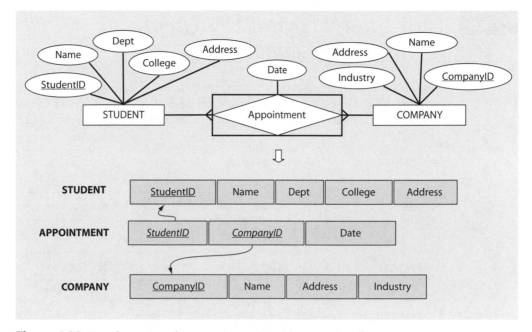

Figure 4.20 Transformation of an associate entity without an identifier.

Consider another example, depicted in Figure 4.21. The associate entity in this example has its own identifier, *ConnectionID*. We create a new relation for the associate entity with *ConnectionID* as a primary key. We add the attributes *ServiceID* and *CustomerID* as foreign keys to the relation for the associate entity to complete the transformation.

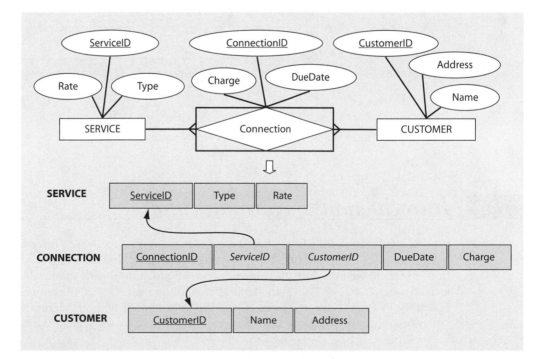

Figure 4.21 Transformation of an associate entity with an identifier.

4.6 *Case Study: Logical Design for a University Database*

In this section, we will transform the conceptual design (E-R diagram) from the case study presented at the end of Chapter 3 into a relational schema. We perform tasks one through nine to systematically transform the EE-R diagram into the relational schema shown in Figure 4.22.

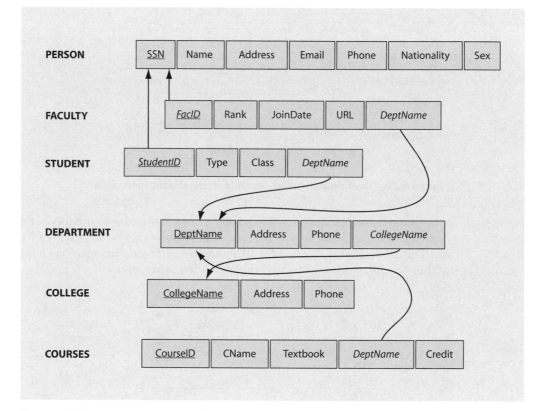

Figure 4.22 The relational schema for the university database.

4.7 *Introduction to Normalization*

We discussed the process of logical database design in previous sections of this chapter. We also mentioned several intuitive rules for converting a conceptual data model into a set of relations. In this section, we introduce the process of *normalization* to *validate* the transformation performed using Tasks 1–7. E.F. Codd first proposed this process in 1972. The term **normalization**, as defined by Codd, refers to a series of tests performed on relations to determine whether they satisfy or violate the requirements of a *normal form*. There are six popular normal forms: first normal form (1NF), second normal form (2NF), third normal form (3NF), Boyce-Codd normal form (BCNF), fourth normal form (4NF), and fifth normal form (5NF). We will discuss 1NF, 2NF, 3NF, and BCNF in depth in this chapter. Each normal form puts its own requirement on relations. A relation is said to be in a particular normal form if it satisfies the requirements of the normal form. For example, a relation is said to be in 2NF if it satisfies the requirements of second normal form. Further, these normal forms are inclusive in the sense that if a relation satisfies 3NF, then it must also satisfy 2NF and 1NF. The Fifth normal form is the highest form of normalization and is the strictest version (see Figure 4.23).

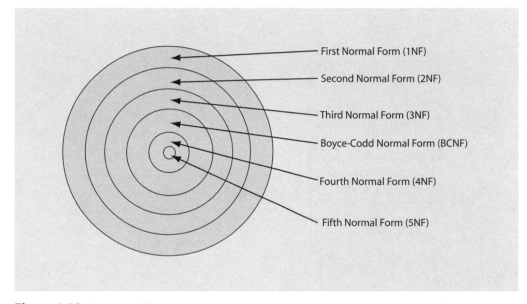

Figure 4.23 The normal forms.

The process of normalization is to convert a given relation to the predetermined normal form. For example, if we would like a relation that is currently in 1NF to be in BCNF, the process of normalization converts it from 2NF to 3NF to BCNF. In general, given a relation and target normal form, the normalization process use following steps (see Figure 4.24):

1. Test the given relation for a normal form starting with 1NF.
   - If satisfied, go to step 2.
   - If the test fails, convert the relation(s) to satisfy the normal form under consideration. Go to step 2.
2. If we have reached the target normal form, the set of relations is the desired set. Otherwise, go to step 1 with a higher normal form.

With each step of normalization, we actually improve and validate the logical database design. Each normalization step produces a set of well-structured relations with minimal data redundancy and data anomalies. Before we discuss normal forms and the process of normalization, we will set up a background with discussion on data redundancy, data anomalies, and functional dependency.

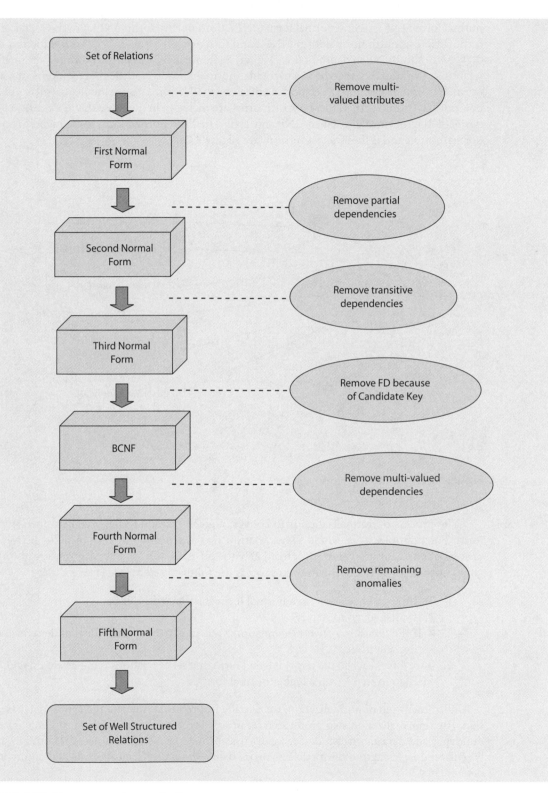

Figure 4.24 The process of normalization.

4.8   *Data Redundancy*

Data redundancy is having duplicate data in the database. The effective relational database design seeks to minimize data redundancy. Data redundancy creates two major problems: (1) it leads to increased use of disk storage space, and (2) it reduces the efficiency of data processing.

To understand the problems with data redundancy, consider the student-department E-R diagram in Figure 4.12. Consider an additional attribute, *DeptLogo*, for the department entity. Imagine that we do not use Task 5 rules to transform the binary relationships, but instead employ a different approach to group the attributes. We simply put all attributes of STUDENT and DEPARTMENT entities together in a single relation (see Figure 4.25). As the figure illustrates, we have redundant department information for each student in the department. With a large number of students in the department, duplicating fields such as *DeptLogo* (say a large image file) would certainly demand a large database size. Further, data redundancy slows down data processing. For example, updating a department phone number would require reading and updating all those student records in which students belong to the department under consideration.

On the other hand, if we follow the rules of Task 5 and create two separate relations for two entities, we avoid data redundancy and problems related to it. The department logo will be saved exactly once, and updating a department phone number would require updating exactly one record in the *Department* relation. The process of normalization simply validates rules of different tasks discussed before and ensures that we avoid any data redundancies.

STUDENT

SSN	Name	Email	DeptName	DeptAdd	DeptLogo
234-23-2535	John Doe	John@mail.com	ISE	Weil Hall	ISE.PSD
545-28-2324	Samuel Ed	Sam@mail.com	CISE	Marten Hall	CISE.JPG
368-98-4234	Jay Leno	Jay@mail.com	ISE	Weil Hall	ISE.PSD
975-34-3558	Ricky Grey	Ricky@mail.com	PHY	Rinker Hall	PHY.PSD
111-22-4444	Don Grey	Don@mail.com	ISE	Weil Hall	ISE.PSD
367-24-8384	Jim Ray	Jim@mail.com	CISE	Marten Hall	CISE.JPG
975-34-1558	Rick Flair	Rick@mail.com	PHY	Rinker Hall	PHY.PSD

Figure 4.25 Data redundancies.

4.9   *Database Anomalies*

Relations with redundant data may cause additional inconsistency problems known as ***anomalies***. We focus on three types of anomalies commonly encountered in a relational database design: insertion anomalies, deletion anomalies, and update anomalies. In this section, we refer to the examples from the *Vet* database to define database anomalies. A veterinarian's office uses the *Vet* database to keep track of *clients* who board their *pets* while on vacation. This office employs several *veterinarians* (or simply vet). Each client can have multiple pets and an assigned vet takes care of all of them. Thus, each client has exactly one vet assigned and each vet can be assigned to more than one client. Let us consider the VetOffice relation to explain anomalies:

VETOFFICE (<u>ClientID</u>, ClientName, <u>PetID</u>, PetName, PetWt, VetID, VetName)

Insertion Anomalies   *Insertion anomalies* refer to the abnormalities encountered while inserting new records in the relation. The anomaly is the side effect of data redundancy. Consider adding a new veterinarian, Jasper—*VetID 30*, to the *VetOffice* relation. When we insert this record in the relation, we may not have any associated client or pet data. Jasper may not have any assignments when he joins the office. This will leave the *ClientID* and *PetID* fields with NULLs, which is not allowed as per definition of a primary key. Consequently, we may not be able to insert new vets in the relation until we assign them to clients and their pets. This abnormality is referred as an *insertion anomaly*. If we were not duplicating all vet information for each client and storing it in a separate relation, we could add new vets to the separate relation without having them assigned to any client.

VETOFFICE

<u>ClientID</u>	Client Name	<u>PetID</u>	PetName	PetWt	VetID	VetName
2173	Barbara Hennesey	1	Sam	15	27	James
2173	Barbara Hennesey	2	Hoober	17	27	James
2173	Barbara Hennesey	3	Tom	18	27	James
4519	Vernon Noordsy	1	Charlie	11	31	John
8005	Sandra Amidon	1	Beefer	12	27	James
8005	Sandra Amidon	2	Kirby	15	27	James
8112	Helen Wandzell	1	Kirby	10	24	Chris

Figure 4.26 The *VetOffice* relation.

Deletion Anomalies   *Deletion anomalies* occur when data has been unintentionally removed from the relation. For example, the client Vernon decided not to leave his pets with this office, and so the office deletes his record (*ClientID 4519*, see Figure 4.26) from the relation. If all the records with *ClientID 4519* are removed, we also lose any information about the vet John (*VetID 31*, see Figure 4.26). Since vet *31* still works for the office, we unintentionally removed the valid data from the relation. Again, if there were no data redundancies, and if we had vet data in a separate relation, we could have removed the client record from the client relation without affecting the vet relation.

Update Anomalies   *Update anomalies* occur when there are multiple changes required to reflect a single attribute change. For example, if a client changes her name after marriage, we must update the client name attribute in multiple records, one for each of her pets. Any updating error (not updating one or more records or spelling mistakes) would leave the relation in an inconsistent format. If we don't repeat the same information in the multiple records, we require a single update to reflect a single attribute change, avoiding any update anomalies.

Definitions

Insertion anomalies occur when we want to add a new record into the relation and not all the information is available.

Deletion anomalies occur when critical data has been removed from the database.

Update anomalies occur when we must make multiple changes to reflect a single attribute change.

4.10 *Functional Dependencies*

A ***functional dependency*** is a relationship among *attributes*. Attribute B is functionally dependent on attribute A if given a value of attribute A, the value of attribute B is uniquely defined. We denote this functional dependency as A → B; the attribute A uniquely defines the attribute B, or the attribute B is functionally dependent on A.

Determining a functional dependency demands some knowledge about attributes and how they are related to one another. Consider the *VetOffice* relation introduced in the previous section (see Figure 4.26). Given a *ClientID*, we can uniquely determine the client's name and the information about the client's vet. The functional dependency is denoted thus:

```
FD1: ClientID → ClientName, VetID, VetName
```

A relation can have many functional dependencies. For example, in the *VetOffice* relation, given a *VetID* we can uniquely determine a vet's name. Also, the primary key {*ClientID*, *PetID*} uniquely determine all attributes of the relation.

```
FD2: VetID → VetName
FD3: ClientID, PetID → ClientName, PetName, PetWt, VetID, VetName
```

Consider following two dependencies in the *VetOffice* relation:

```
D1: ClientID — ClientName, PetName, PetWt
D2: VetID — ClientID, ClientName
```

D1 and D2 dependencies do not constitute functional dependencies. In D1, we cannot uniquely provide *ClientName*, *PetName*, and *PetWt* for a given *ClientID*. For example, *ClientID 2173* has more than one pet with a different *PetName*. In D2, we have the same vet working for more than one client.

Functional dependencies allow us to examine the relationships among the attributes of a relation. The process of normalization relies on inter-attribute relationships to decompose relations with anomalies into smaller, well-structured relations without anomalies. Interestingly, information about an attribute relationship can also be used to determine a primary key of a relation.

4.10.1 Primary Key and Functional Dependencies

Determinants are the attribute(s) on the left-hand side of the arrow in a functional dependency representation. For example, *ClientID* in FD1, *VetID* in FD2, and *ClientID* and *PetID* in FD3 are determinants. Thus, from the definition of a functional dependency, a determinant uniquely identifies all attributes on the right-hand side of the functional dependency arrow. For a given functional dependency, if the union of all its attributes is the set of attributes in the relation, then by definition of relational keys, the determinant of a functional dependency is actually a *super key*. For example, since the attributes involved in FD3 of the *VetOffice* relation is the complete set of attributes in the relation, {*ClientID, PetID*} is a super key. In other words, {*ClientID, PetID*} can uniquely identify any record of the *VetOffice* relation. Now recall that a minimal super key is a candidate key, and a chosen candidate key is a primary key of a relation. Thus, we can use functional dependencies to determine the primary key of a relation using following steps:

1. Write all the functional dependencies for a relation.
2. Choose those functional dependencies that feature all the attributes of a relation.
3. From selected functional dependencies, choose determinants with a minimal number of attributes as candidate keys.
4. Chose a primary key from a set of candidate keys as discussed in Section 4.3.1.

In the *VetOffice* relation, FD3 is the only dependency that features all the attributes of a relation. Therefore, {*ClientID, PetID*} is the only choice and, hence, is the primary key.

4.10.2 Dependency Diagram

A *dependency diagram* is a pictorial representation of a functional dependency. We use the following conventions to draw a dependency diagram:

- An attribute is represented by a rectangle.
- An arrow is drawn from the rectangle of attribute A to the rectangle of attribute B if and only if A → B.

The FD1 and FD3 for the *VetOffice* relation are depicted in Figure 4.27.

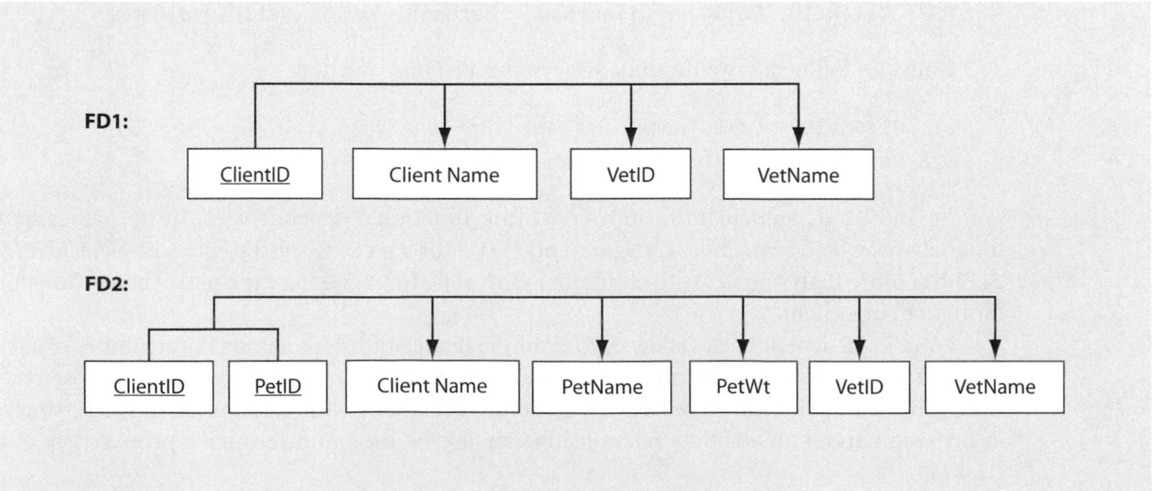

Figure 4.27 The dependency diagram for the *VetOffice* relation.

4.10.3 Types of Functional Dependencies

We consider two types of functional dependencies in this chapter: partial dependencies and transitive dependencies.

Partial Dependencies   A *partial dependency* is a functional dependency in which a non-primary key's attributes functionally depend on a part of (but not all) the primary key attributes. For example, consider FD1 in the *VetOffice* relation:

    FD1: ClientID → ClientName, VetID, VetName

In FD1, the non-primary key attributes *ClientName*, *VetID*, and *VetName* are functionally dependent on *ClientID*. However, the *ClientID* is only a part of the primary key. The primary key is a combination of the *ClientID* and *PetID* attributes. Consider FD3 from the same relation. FD3 is *not* a partial dependency as the non-primary key attributes on the right side of the arrow are depending on the entire primary key. The partial dependency can only exist in the relation with a composite primary key.

Transitive Dependencies   A *transitive dependency* is a functional dependency in which none of the attributes involves attributes of a primary key. For example, consider FD2 in the *VetOffice* relation:

    FD2: VetID → VetName

Since neither *VetID* nor *VetName* is a part of a primary key, FD2 is a transitive dependency. FD1 does not have transitive dependencies. See Figure 4.28 for the partial and transitive dependencies in the *VetOffice* relation.

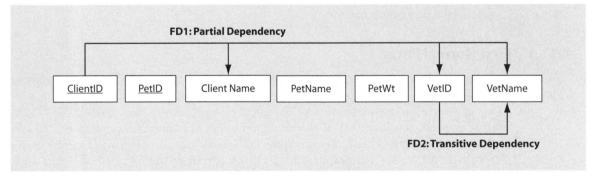

Figure 4.28 The partial and transitive dependencies.

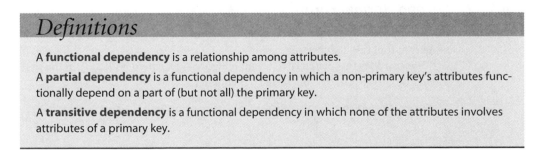

Definitions

A **functional dependency** is a relationship among attributes.

A **partial dependency** is a functional dependency in which a non-primary key's attributes functionally depend on a part of (but not all) the primary key.

A **transitive dependency** is a functional dependency in which none of the attributes involves attributes of a primary key.

4.10.4 Causes of Anomalies and Functional Dependencies

We know that anomalies are abnormalities that can occur while inserting, deleting, or updating data and that data redundancy is one of the main causes for anomalies. Functional dependencies are closely related to anomalies. Anomalies and their remedies can be explained with the help of partial and transitive dependencies.

Consider FD1 in the *VetOffice* relation (see Figure 4.28). FD1 is a partial dependency and is the reason for anomalies. For instance, when we delete a client from the relation, we may also lose his or her dependent data: *ClientName*, *VetID*, and *VetName*. This could result in a deletion anomaly. Similarly, consider the transitive dependency FD2 in Figure 4.28. A transitive dependency also causes anomalies. For example, inserting *VetID* and *VetName* in the relation results in an insertion anomaly as neither of the primary key attributes is involved in the insertion.

The aim of the normalization process is to produce well-structured relations without anomalies. We will see how the process of normalization makes use of functional dependencies to decompose the relations.

4.11 *Forms of Normalization*

We have defined normalization as a series of tests performed on relations to determine whether they satisfy or violate the requirements of a given *normal form*. In this section, we discuss the four most popular normal forms: first NF, second NF, third NF, and BCNF. The steps of normalization (see Figure 4.24) require relations to pass tests of normal forms in a sequential order. If a relation fails any particular test, we systematically decompose it into a new set of relations that satisfy the requirements of the normal form under consideration. We continue the process until the relations pass the test for the desired normal form. Third normal form and BCNF are considered good target normal forms.

4.11.1 First Normal Form

A relation is said to be in the **first normal form** if each cell in the relation contains exactly one value. Since this is one of the properties of a relation in the relational data model, relations are always considered in the first normal form.

For example, consider the *VetOffice* relation introduced in previous sections. For the sake of illustration, we present the *VetOffice* relation in the non-first normal form in Figure 4.29. We then convert it into the first normal form by decomposing its multi-valued cells into single value cells.

4.11.2 Second Normal Form

A relation is said to be in the **second normal form** if it is already in the first normal form and has no partial functional dependencies.

We consider the *VetOffice* relation in Figure 4.29, which is already in the first normal form. The relation has a partial functional dependency:

```
FD1: ClientID → ClientName, VetID, VetName
```

VETOFFICE

ClientID	Client Name	PetID	PetName	PetWt	VetID	VetName
2173	Barbara Hennesey	1 2 3	Sam Hobber Tom	15 17 18	27	James
4519	Vernon Noordsy	1	Charlie	11	31	John
8005	Sandra Amidon	1 2	Beefer Kirby	12 15	27	James
8112	Helen Wandzell	1	Kirby	10	24	Chris

(a)

VETOFFICE

ClientID	Client Name	PetID	PetName	PetWt	VetID	VetName
2173	Barbara Hennesey	1	Sam	15	27	James
2173	Barbara Hennesey	2	Hobber	17	27	James
2173	Barbara Hennesey	3	Tom	18	27	James
4519	Vernon Noordsy	1	Charlie	11	31	John
8005	Sandra Amidon	1	Beefer	12	27	James
8005	Sandra Amidon	2	Kirby	15	27	James
8112	Helen Wandzell	1	Kirby	10	24	Chris

(b)

Figure 4.29 (a) The *VetOffice* relation in non-1NF form; (b) The *VetOffice* relation in 1NF form.

Therefore, the *VetOffice* relation is not in the second normal form. To convert a relation into the second normal form, we decompose the relation into smaller relations based on the partial functional dependencies. Specifically, we perform the following steps:

1. We create a new relation for each partial dependency in the relation.
2. The determinant of the partial dependency forms the primary key of the new relation.
3. The attributes on the right side of arrow in the partial dependency form other attributes of the new relation.
4. We also remove non-primary key attributes of the new relation from the original relation.

The Figure 4.30 depicts the conversion to the second normal form for the *VetOffice* relation. We create the new relation *Client*. *ClientID* serves as the primary key for the new relation. The *ClientName*, *VetID*, and *VetName* are other attributes of the *Client* relation. These attributes are also removed from the *VetOffice* relation. Since the original relation now mainly stores the data about a client's pet, we rename the relation *Pet*. So, instead of a single *VetOffice* relation, we now have two relations: *Client* and *Pet*, with no partial dependencies.

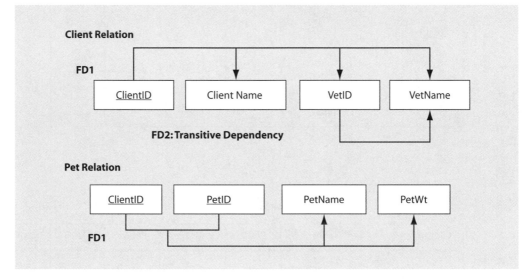

Figure 4.30 The second normal form: *Client* and *Pet* relations.

4.11.3 Third Normal Form

The *third normal form* is perhaps the most often used form of normalization and removes most of the dependencies from a relation. A relation is said to be in the **third normal form** if it is already in the second normal form and has no transitive dependencies. Since a relation in the third normal has no partial and transitive dependencies, it helps eliminate most anomalies.

Let us consider the *Client* and *Pet* relations in the second normal form as shown in Figure 4.30. The *Pet* relation is already in the third normal form as there are no transitive dependencies. However, the *Client* relation has the following transitive functional dependency:

```
FD2: VetID → VetName
```

Therefore, the *Client* relation is not in the third normal form. To convert a relation into the third normal form, we decompose the relation into smaller relations based on the transitive functional dependencies. Specifically, we perform the following steps:

1. We create a new relation for each transitive dependency in the relation.
2. The determinant of the transitive dependency forms the primary key of the new relation.
3. The attributes on the right side of the arrow in the transitive dependency form other attributes of the new relation.
4. We remove attributes of the new relation from the original relation. We add the primary key of the new relation as a foreign key in the original relation.

Figure 4.31 depicts the conversion to the third normal form for the *Client* relation. We create the new relation *Vet*. *VetID* serves as the primary key for the new relation. The *VetName* is the other attribute of the *Vet* relation. *VetID* and *VetName* are removed from the *Client* relation, and the primary key *VetID* is added as the foreign key in the *Client* relation. So, instead of two relations, we now have three relations: *Client*, *Vet*, and *Pet*, with no partial and transitive dependencies.

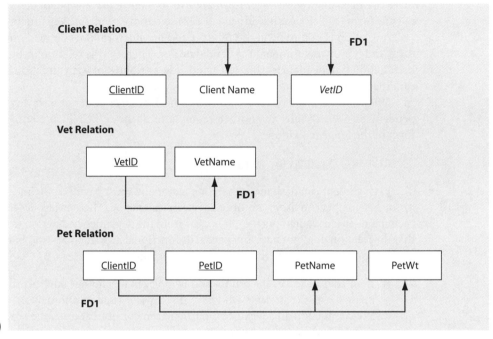

(a)

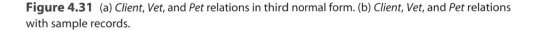

(b)

Figure 4.31 (a) *Client*, *Vet*, and *Pet* relations in third normal form. (b) *Client*, *Vet*, and *Pet* relations with sample records.

4.11.4   **Boyce-Codd Normal Form (BCNF)**

We have illustrated how the second and third normal forms remove partial and transitive dependencies. Note that the partial and transitive dependencies are defined in reference to the primary key. However, if a relation has more than one candidate key (from which we chose the primary key), we might have more functional dependencies defined in reference to candidate keys. As with primary key functional dependencies, these might also cause data redundancy. We therefore need an even stronger normal form to remove these dependencies. The Boyce-Codd normal form (BCNF) was introduced in 1974 to remove candidate key functional dependencies.

A relation is said to be in the ***Boyce-Codd normal form*** if it is already in the third normal form and if every determinant is a candidate key. Thus, for the relation in BCNF, if we write all its functional dependencies, the left-hand side attributes of each functional dependency is a candidate key of the relation.

Since our *VetOffice* relation in the third normal form does not have any candidate key dependencies, we will refer to another example to illustrate BCNF. We consider the following form of the *Student* relation:

STUDENT (<u>StudentID</u>, <u>Major</u>, Advisor, Major-GPA)

Each student can have more than one major and must have exactly one advisor for each of his or her majors. Advisors can only advise in one major. There is also a GPA associated with each major that a student pursues. It is clear from the dependency diagram (see Figure 4.32 (A)) that the relation does not have any partial or functional dependencies and is already in the third normal form. However, there are still some anomalies:

- If an advisor leaves the school and is replaced by another advisor, this change must be made for all the students who have that advisor (update anomaly).
- We cannot add an advisor to a particular major until at least one student is assigned to that advisor (insertion anomaly).
- If an advisor has only one advisee, the advisor information is lost if the corresponding student is removed from the relation (deletion anomaly).

The *Student* relation has the following functional dependency for which the determinant is not a candidate key:

FD2: Advisor → Major

Therefore, the *Student* relation is not in the BCNF. To convert a relation into the BCNF, we decompose the relation into smaller relations based on the functional dependencies for which its determinant is not a candidate key. Specifically, we perform the following steps:

1. We identify those functional dependencies for which the determinant is not a candidate key. For each identified dependency, we create a new relation.
2. The determinant of the identified dependency forms the primary key of the new relation.
3. The attributes on the right side of the arrow in the identified dependency form other attributes of the new relation. These attributes are removed from the original relation (even though they are part of the primary key in the original relation).
4. We add the primary key of the new relation as a foreign key in the original relation. If required, we designate a set of attributes as a new primary key in the original relation.

Figure 4.32(b) depicts the BCNF for the *Student* relation. We create the new relation *Advisor* with the attribute *Advisor* as its primary key (assuming the *Advisor* attribute is the advisor's unique identification). The *Major* is the other attribute of the *Advisor* relation. Therefore, *Advisor* and *Major* are removed from the *Student* relation to form the new relation. The primary key of the new relation, *Advisor*, is added as a foreign key in the *Student* relation. The *StudentID* and *Advisor* together form a new primary key of the *Student* relation. This was required as *StudentID* is not unique in the *Student* relation as student can major in one or more areas.

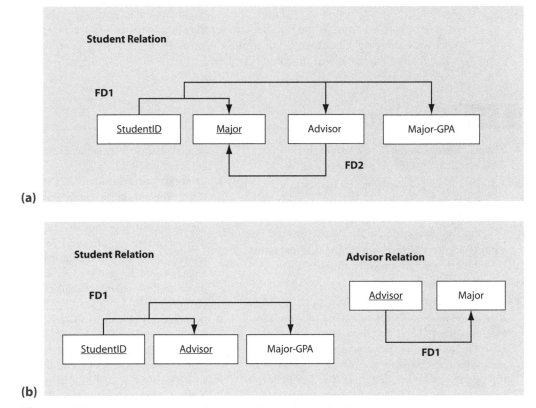

Figure 4.32 (a) *Student* relation before BCNF; (b) *Student* and *Advisor* relations in BCNF.

Definitions

A relation is said to be in the **first normal form** if each cell in the relation contains exactly one value.

A relation is said to be in the **second normal form** if it is already in the first normal form and has no partial functional dependencies.

A relation is said to be in the **third normal form** if it is already in the second normal form and has no transitive dependencies.

A relation is said to be in the **Boyce-Codd normal form** if it is already in the third normal form and if every determinant is a candidate key.

4.12   *In-Class Assignment*

In this in-class assignment, create a relational schema for a book store that wishes to keep information about the books, publishers, and customers using the following entities:

    a. BOOK: book name, author name, publication date, and price.
    b. PUBLISHER: publisher's name, address, and telephone number.
    c. CUSTOMER: customer's name, address, and reading preferences.

Develop an appropriate E-R diagram for the above entities and transform it to a relational schema showing all integrity constraints. Consider *Address* as a composite attribute and *ReadingPreferences* as a multi-valued attribute.

4.13   *Summary*

■ The relational data model consists of three components:

    a. Relational Data Structure: where data is organized.
    b. Data Manipulation: operations used to manipulate data stored in the data structure.
    c. Relational Data Integrity: rules that maintain the integrity of data when they are manipulated.

■ The main data structure that stores and organizes data in the relational data model is a relation, a two-dimensional grid that holds data about the object represented in the database. A column of a relation is referred to as an *attribute*, while a row is referred to as a *record*, or a *tuple*. The number of attributes in a relation is defined as a *degree*, and the number of records in a relation is defined as *cardinality*.

■ A *super key* is a set of one or more attributes that uniquely identifies each record in a relation. A *candidate key* is a super key with a minimum number of attributes. The *primary key* is a candidate key that has been selected to identify unique records in a relation. The *foreign key* is an attribute or a set of attributes of a relation that serves as a primary key of the same or other relation.

■ The *domain constraint* states that the values of an attribute must be from the same domain. *Entity constraints* ensure that every relation of a relational data model has a primary key and primary key cannot be NULL. A *referential integrity constraint* ensures that the foreign key values of a relation must come from the primary key values in the related relation; otherwise, the value of a foreign key must be NULL.

■ Relations with redundant data may cause inconsistency problems known as *anomalies*. *Deletion anomalies* occur when data has been removed from the database unintentionally. *Insertion anomalies* occur when we want to add a new record to the relation and not all of the information is available. *Update anomalies* occur when the DBMS must make multiple changes to reflect a single attribute change.

■ A *functional dependency* is a relationship among attributes. A *dependency diagram* is a pictorial representation of a functional dependency. A *partial dependency* is a functional dependency in which the non-primary key attributes functionally depend on a part of (but not all) the primary key. A *transitive dependency* is a functional dependency in which none of the attributes involves attributes of a primary key.

■ The term *normalization*, as defined by Codd, refers to a series of tests performed on relations that determines whether a given relation satisfies or violates the requirements of a *normal form*. A relation is said to be in the *first normal form* if each cell in the relation contains exactly one value. A relation is said to be in the *second normal form* if it is already in the first normal form and there are no partial functional dependencies. A relation is said to be in the *third normal form* if it is already in the second normal form and if it has no transitive dependencies. A relation is said to be in the *BCNF* if it is already in the third normal form and if every determinant is a candidate key.

4.14 *Exercises*

4.14.1 **Review Questions**

1. What are the three components of a relational data model? Explain each of the components.

2. Define the following terms using an example:
   a. Relation
   b. Primary key
   c. Composite key
   d. Foreign key
   How do they relate to each other?

3. What are the properties of a relation? Give an example of each property.

4. Explain the relation that exists between the following terms:
   a. Determinant, candidate key
   b. Candidate key, primary key
   c. Primary key, composite key
   d. Functional dependency, transitive dependency
   e. Normal form, normalization.

5. What is the minimal normal form that a relation must satisfy? Support the answer by citing an example.

6. What is the purpose of normalizing a relation?

7. What is the difference between the terms *relation* and *relational schema*? Support the answer with an example.

8. What are the principal integrity constraints of a relational data model? Explain why it is important to enforce these constraints.

9. The following table is part of a manufacturing company database. Transform it into a relation.

SUPPLIER

Supplier ID	Name	Address	Order No	Order Date
101	James Martin	Huston, TX	1453	Sept 23, 2002
			1454	Sept 30, 2002
			1455	Oct 10, 2002
103	Susan Lorenzo	Miami, FL	1456	Oct 20, 2002
			1457	Oct 25, 2002
150	Chris Davis	Chicago, IL	1458	Nov 2, 2002
			1459	Nov 13, 2002

10. Transform the following E-R diagrams into relations:

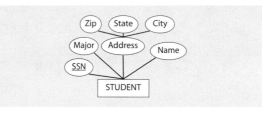

(a)

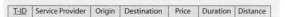

TRIP

T-ID	Service Provider	Origin	Destination	Price	Duration	Distance

(b)

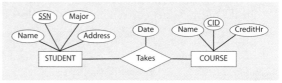

(c)

11. Answer the following questions:
    a. When and why do we normalize a relation?
    b. Provide an example of a relation that is not in the first normal form. Explain how this relation can be normalized.
    c. Provide an example of a relation that has partial functional dependencies. Explain how this relation can be normalized.
    d. Provide an example of a relation that has transitive dependencies. Explain how this relation can be normalized.

12. Answer the following questions:
    a. In what normal form is a relation that has no multi-valued attributes?
    b. In what normal form is a relation that has partial functional dependencies?
    c. In what normal form is a relation that has no partial functional or transitive dependencies?

13. The following table is part of a travel agency database. Normalize this relation.

TRIP

T-ID	Service Provider	Origin	Destination	Price	Duration	Distance

14. The American Tennis Association keeps a record of the tournaments organized as well as of the participants. The following is a part of their database. In what normal form is this relation? Transform the relation into a third normal form.

TOURNAMENT

T-ID	Name	Location	Date	Female-Winner	Male-Winner	Female-Time	Male-Time	Court	Court Type

4.14.2 Hands-On Exercises

1. The table below presents the *Patient* relation that is part of a hospital's database. Does this relation satisfy the integrity constraints? If not, name which constraint is not satisfied, explain why, and make the necessary corrections. If so, how does it satisfy them?

PATIENT

Patient ID	Name	Address	Birthday	Gender
10001	James Martin	Gainesville, FL	January 10, 1980	Male
10010	Joanna Bennett	Tampa, FL	10-9-1981	Female
12120	Jordan Johnson	Orlando, FL	12/12/65	Male
11278	Susan May	Jacksonville, FL	31 March 1974	Female

2. The following table presents the *Route-Bus* relation that is part of a bus company's database. Is *Route-Bus* a well-structured relation? If not, determine some of the anomalies that may result when a user attempts to update the table and transform this relation into a set of well-structured relations. If it is well structured, explain why.

ROUTE-BUS

Route ID	Bus ID	Bus Capacity	Origin	Destination
101	B10	40	Tampa, FL	Atlanta, GA
111	B21	60	Gainesville, FL	Chicago, IL
132	B22	60	Gainesville, FL	Miami, FL
451	B45	60	Orlando, FL	Cincinnati, OH

3. The table below presents the *Room* relation that is part of a university's database. Does this relation satisfy the integrity constraints? If not, name which constraint is not satisfied, explain why, and

make the necessary corrections. If so, how does it satisfy them?

ROOM

Room ID	Size	Equipment	EquipmentQuantity
BUS 220	Thirty	Computer	30
ENG 212	20	VCR	One
ECO 456	Forty	TV Set	One
BUS 330	20		
BUS 120	50	Computer	1
ENG 122	Twenty	Projector	1

4. The table below presents the *Professor* relation that is part of a university's database. Does this relation satisfy the integrity constraints? If not, name which constraint is not satisfied, explain why, and make the necessary corrections. If so, how does it satisfy them?

PROFESSOR

ProfID	Name	Department	College
1001	S. Doe	Industrial	Engineering
	A. Smith	Industrial	Engineering
1231	V. Don	Management	Business School
	S. Davis	Pharmacy	Pharmaceutics
1678	D. May	Fine Arts	Theater & Dance

5. The following table presents the *Patient-Dependents* relation that is part of a health insurance agency's database. Is *Patient-Dependent* a well-structured relation? If not, determine some of the anomalies that may result when a user attempts to update the table and transform it into a set of well-structured relations. If it is well structured, explain why.

PATIENT

Patient ID	Name	Dependent ID	Dependent	Gender
P101	J. Doug	D140	F. Doug	Male
		D141	A. Doug	Female
P212	M.	D231	S. Nathan	Female
		D232	G. Nathan	Female

6. Draw a relational schema for each of the following entities:

    a. The entity CUSTOMER has the following attributes: *CustomerID*, *Name*, and *Address*.

The attribute *Name* is a composite attribute consisting of *FirstName*, *LastName*, and *MiddleName*. The attribute *Address* is also a composite attribute consisting of *StreetName*, *City*, *State*, and *Zip*.

b. The entity PROFESSOR has the following attributes: *SSN*, *Name*, *Department*, *College*, and *CoursesTaught*. *CoursesTaught* is a multivalued attribute.

c. The entity DEPENDENT is part of the database of a health insurance company. Its attributes are *PolicyHolderID*, *PolicyHolderName*, *DependentName*, *Birthday*, and *Gender*. Note that DEPENDENT is a weak entity.

7. Draw a relational schema that represents the relational integrity constraints for each of the following binary relationships:

a. The College of Engineering keeps records of the departments and the corresponding department chairs in its database. The attributes of the entity DEPARTMENT are *Name* and *Address*. The attributes of the entity DEPARTMENTCHAIR are *SSN*, *Name*, and *Address*. Note that the relation between entity DEPARTMENT and entity DEPARTMENTCHAIR is a binary one-to-one (1:1) relationship.

b. A university department keeps record of its professors and courses offered. The attributes of the entity PROFESSOR are *SSN*, *Name*, and *Address*. The attributes of the entity COURSE are *IdentificationNumber* and *Name*. Note that the relation between the entity PROFESSOR and the entity COURSE is a binary many-to-many (M:N) relationship.

c. A college in a university keeps records of its students and departments. The attributes of the entity STUDENT are *SSN*, *Name*, *Address*, and *Department*. The attributes of the entity DEPARTMENT are *Name* and *Address*. Note that the relation between the entity STUDENT and the entity DEPARTMENT is a binary one-to-many (1:M) relationship.

8. The following are examples of associative entities. For each example, transform the E-R diagram into a relational schema, identify the primary key or keys and the foreign key or keys of each relation, and draw the relational integrity constraints.

a. A running club organizes a number of events during the year. In a database, the club

records information about the members and each race organized.

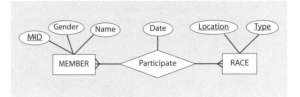

b. A library records information about their members as well as their books in a database.

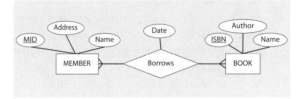

c. University stores information about their students and the courses offered in a database.

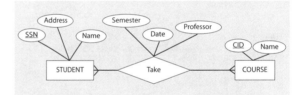

9. The following are examples of ternary relationships. For each example, transform the E-R diagram into a relational schema, identify the primary key or keys and the foreign key or keys of each relation, and draw the relational integrity constraints.

a. In the *Airline* database model presented in the Hands-On Exercise 6 in Chapter 3, the relationship between AIRLINE, ROUTE, and AIRPLANE is a ternary relationship.

b. In the *Coca-Cola* database presented in Hands-On Exercises 3 and 4 in Chapter 3, the relation between CUSTOMER, PRODUCT, and VEHICLE is a ternary relationship.

c. In the database of the academic institution presented in the Hands-On Exercise 12 in Chapter 3, the relation between TEACHER, COURSE, and CLASSROOM is a ternary relationship.

10. A university's medical school serves the students as well as the public as a medium-sized hospital. The hospital stores information about patients, such as name, address, date of visit, and doctor's name, in a database. The hospital does not charge the students for services and charges special rates if the patient is university faculty or staff. For the students, faculty, and staff, the hospital records the name of their department and their college. Note that the entity PATIENT has subtypes. Draw the E-R diagram of the entity PATIENT. Transform the diagram into a relational schema, and identify the primary key and the foreign key(s) of each relation.

11. An airline company keeps the information about flights and prices in the following table.

  a. Transform this table into a relation in the first normal form.

  b. Draw a relational schema and show the transitive dependencies. In what normal form is this relation?

  c. Transform the relation into a set of 3NF relations. Draw the relational schema of each 3NF relation.

FLIGHT

Flight	Origin	Dest.	Departure	Arrival	Duration	Cap.	Cabin	Price
1001	MCO	JAX	10am	11am	1hr	80	Coach	200
							Business	400
							First	600
			1pm	2pm			Coach	200
							Business	40
							First	600
1031	JAX	SAN	2pm	8pm	8hr	80	Coach	350
							Business	550
							First	700

12. A car rental company keeps information about cars and prices in the following table. The company offers different prices depending on the brand name of the car rented, its size, and the length of the rent period.

  a. Transform this table into a relation in the first normal form.

  b. Draw a relational schema and show the functional and transitive dependencies of this relation. In what normal form is this relation? Transform the relation into a set of 3NF relations and then into the BCNF.

CAR

Brand	Year	Inventory	Size	Duration	Price ($)
Chevrolet	2000	10	Subcompact	1 day	48.^{99}
		8	Compact		51.^{99}
		4	Full Size		61.^{99}
			Subcompact	2 days	97.^{98}
			Compact		103.^{98}
			Full Size		123.^{98}
Buick	2001	15	Full Size	2 days	125.^{98}
		22	Premium		133.^{96}

13. An on-line electronics shop sells CDs. The company keeps information about the products offered in the following table. For every CD sold, the company pays 30% of the price to the producer of the CD.

  a. Transform this table into a relation (named CD) in the first normal form. Illustrate the relation with sample data in the table.

  b. List the partial and transitive dependencies of the CD relation.

  c. Explain how the insert, delete, and modification anomalies would affect the CD relation.

  d. Transform the CD relation into the 3NF.

CD

ItemNo	Name	Singer	Songs	Producer	Address	Price $	Sales ($)	Amt Due
1001	CD1	Singer 1	Track 1	Producer 1	Dallas, TX	10	100	20
			Track 2					
			Track 3					
			Track 4					
1223	CD9	Singer 3	Track 1	Producer 8	Tampa, FL	12	156	23
			Track 2					
			Track 3					

14. In a manufacturing plant that uses a lot of equipment, planning for proper and timely maintenance is critical. Generally, spare parts are categorized into two groups: fast moving and slow moving parts. Fast moving spares are very often required, and slow moving spares are rarely required. The Hillside Company keeps a record of all the spares required for maintaining a particular type of equipment, as well as the number of spares received and used in the past, and a list of major forthcoming maintenances. The company also keeps a list of equipment, parts, and the vendors with the details of the spares that they supply. The following relationship exists between spares and vendors. A vendor may provide one or more spares, and a spare part may be provided by exactly one vendor.

a. Draw an EE-R diagram of this database.

b. Transform the EE-R diagram into a relational schema.

c. If the relation is not in the 3NF, transform the relation into a set of 3NF relations.

15. Central Lechera Asturiana (CLAS) Company is one of the largest distributors of dairy products in the north of Spain. It has 700 employees in its locations across the country, and it processes 1.3 million liters of milk every day. Its products are distributed through a network of 19 distributors situated throughout the country, each serving a specific area. Every distributor has a number of team leaders (sales promoters), each coordinating five to ten vendors who deal directly with the clients (between 5,000 and 15,000 depending on the distributor). These clients include small retailers, markets, and supermarkets. The company keeps a detailed database that includes information about each of the following:

- Customers: customer identification number, name, address, and location in latitude and longitude coordinates

- Employees: social security number, name, gender, birth date, address, starting date of working with the company, and education

- Distributors: distributor identification number, address, and name

- Vendors: vendor identification number, name, and address

- Team leaders: social security number, name, and address

- Products: product identification number, name, and price

The following system of relationships exists: a customer buys a product from a vendor. An employee may work for exactly one vendor, and a leader may work for exactly one distributor. Additionally, a distributor provides one or more products to the vendors, and each vendor receives milk from exactly one distributor.

a. Draw an E-R diagram of this database.

b. Transform the E-R diagram into a relational schema that shows the referential integrality constraints.

c. If the relation is not in the 3NF, transform the relation into a set of 3NF relations.

16. The University of North Carolina has roughly 450 student athletes. The university's sports club keeps the following information about each student: identification number, citizenship, college, major, scholarship code(s), special program, sport, tax status, and classification (for example, first year professional, graduate doctorate, graduate masters, exchange student, etc.).

Athletes may qualify for tuition, fees, room, board, books, insurance, and reimbursement of their application fees depending on their performance and financial situation. The full scholarship is defined as tuition, fees, room, board, and books. Typically, only a small number of athletes receive full scholarships. In general, athletes may receive any combination of tuition, fees, room, board, or books, with any combination of caps (such as fee reimbursements, books, and $500 per room).

The sports club keeps the following information about each vendor (the bookstore, the university cashier, off-campus housing, etc.): vendor identification number, address, telephone number, fax number, and account number.

The following scheme of relationships exists: an athlete may make one or more transactions with a vendor, and a vendor may make a transaction with one or more athletes. For each transaction, the date and the identification number of the transaction is recorded (consider the option of using an associate entity for transactions made between vendors and athletes.)

a. Draw an E-R diagram of this database.

b. Transform the E-R diagram into a relational schema.

c. If the relation is not in the 3NF, transform the relation into a set of 3NF relations.

d. Show, if any, the functional and transitive dependencies.

17. Consider the E-R diagram of the veterinary hospital database presented in the Hands-On Exercise 20 in Chapter 3.

a. Transform the E-R diagram into a relational schema that shows the referential integrity constraints.

b. For each relation, identify the primary key and the foreign key. Demonstrate if any of the primary keys is a composite key.

c. For each relation, draw the functional dependencies.

d. If any of the relations are not in the 3NF, transform them into the 3NF.

18. For each of the following relations, indicate the normal form of that relation. If the relation is not in the second normal form, decompose it into 2NF relations.

a. Note that the yield, price, and earnings of a particular crop differ from one year to the next.

CROP

Crop ID	Name	Classification	Date	Yield	Price

b. Note that the database keeps historical information about the running times of the participant for all the races he or she has run.

PARTICIPANT

SSN	Name	Address	Gender	Birthday	Race	Running Time	Date

c. The following relation is part of the database described in the Hands-On Exercise 14 in Chapter 3.

COACH-EMPLOYEE

SSN	Name	Address	Employee Name	Years of Employment

For each coach, the database keeps historical information about the name and number of years of employment with each employer. Note that the number of years of employment depends on the attributes *SSN* and *EmployerName*.

19. For each of the following relations, indicate its normal form. If the relation is not in the third normal form, decompose it into 3NF relations.

a. The following relation is part of the database described in Chapter 3 hands-on problem 4. Note that the distance to a particular customer is calculated based on the X and Y coordinates.

CUSTOMER

SSN	Name	Address	X-coord.	Y-coord.	Distance

b. The following relation is part of the database described in the Hands-On Exercise 8 in Chapter 3. Note that a customer's length of stay at the hotel depends only on the check-in date and check-out date.

CUSTOMER

SSN	Name	Address	Check In	Check Out	Length of Stay

c. The following relation is part of the database described in the Hands-On Exercise 9 in Chapter 3. *ID* is the primary key of the above relation. Note, however, that the attribute *ManagerID* is enough to identify the name of the manager of a particular zone.

ZONE

ID	Name	Address	#Agents	Manager ID	Manager Name

d. The following relation is part of the database described in the Hands-On Exercise 12 in Chapter 3. The primary keys are *SSN* and *CourseID*. For every teacher, the name and identification number of the courses taught are recorded. Note, however, that the course name depends on the course identification number only.

TEACHER-COURSE

SSN	Name	Address	Department	CourseID	Course Name	Date

e. The following relation is part of the database described in the Hands-On Exercise 12 in Chapter 3. For every course, the name and identification number of the teacher of the course as well as the room number and type are recorded. Note, however, that the teacher's name depends on the teacher's identification number only, and the room type depends on the room number only.

TEACHER-COURSE-ROOM

Course ID	Name	Teacher ID	Teacher Name	Room No	Room Type

20. In the following table, the city library keeps information about its members and the books they borrow.

    a. Is this table in the 1NF? If not, transform it into a relation in the 1NF.

    b. Are there partial functional dependencies in the relation created in part (a)? If so, show the partial functional dependencies of this relation.

    c. Are there transitive dependencies in the relation created in part (a)? If so, show the transitive dependencies of this relation.

    d. The relation created in part (a) is susceptible to anomalies. Provide examples of the insertion, deletion, and update anomalies.

    e. Transform the relation created in part (a) into a set of relations in the 2NF.

    f. Is the set of relations created in part (e) in the 3NF? If not, transform them into a set of relations in the 3NF.

MEMBER

ID	Name	Address	Phone	BookID	Location	Date
2301	James Martin	330 West	332-399-0952	7645	AF231	1/12/02
1341	Joanna Bennett	120 East	331-312-9047	7081	FG561	1/23/02
				9078	HJ782	2/2/02
				4522	OP987	2/20/02
3490	Jordan Johnson	89 North	345-135-3564	6572	UI876	2/21/02
				1323	FG123	2/26/02
				4577	KL234	3/21/02
6578	Suzan May	11 South	333-318-9812	5623	UO908	5/1/02

21. Read the Hands-On Exercise 16 in Chapter 3. In the following table, the Internet-based company JobSearch.com keeps information about companies and the students they hired.

    a. Convert this E-R diagram into a relational schema.

    b. Are there functional dependencies in the relation created in part (a)? If so, show the functional dependencies.

    c. Are there transitive dependencies in the relation created in part (a)? If so, show the transitive dependencies.

    d. The relation created in part (a) is susceptible to anomalies. Provide examples of the insertion and update anomalies.

    e. Transform the relation created in part (a) into a set of relations in the 2NF.

    f. Is the set of relations created in part (e) in the 3NF? If not, transform them into a set of

relations in the 3NF, and show the referential integrity constraints.

COMPANY-STUDENT

Date	Com. ID	Com. Name	Address	Phone	Student ID	Name	Profession
5/10/02	2211	J.M. Chemicals	110 West	445-199-6954	3129	A. Dave	Chemist
6/3/02					5634	M. Char	Chemist
6/12/02					2345	D. Brown	Chemist
7/4/02					8667	F. Dean	Accountant
7/24/02	3490	M.D. Consulting	234 North	445-136-8795	7644	J. Duncan	Mech. Eng.
8/10/02					4523	G. Horton	Mech. Eng.
8/13/02					9885	F. Monte	Civil Eng.
8/15/02	6578	Eat Smart	781 South	449-334-4519	1209	G. Dong	Chemist

22. The following are examples of ternary relationships. For each example, draw the E-R diagram, transform the E-R diagram into a relational schema, identify each relation's primary key(s) and foreign key(s), and draw the relational integrity constraints.

    a. In the *Traveling Agency* database model in the Hands-On Exercise 17 in Chapter 3, the relationship between BUS, ROUTE, and TRIP is a ternary relationship.

    b. In the *Memorabilia* database in the Hands-On Exercise 21 in Chapter 3, the relation between CUSTOMER, SUPPLIER, and PRODUCT is a ternary relationship.

    c. In the database of the academic institution in the Hands-On Exercise 12 in Chapter 3, the relation between PROFESSOR, COURSE, and CLASSROOM is a ternary relationship.

23. Review the Hands-On Exercise 22 in Chapter 3. In the following table, a bookstore keeps information about publishers and books.

    a. Is this table in the 1NF? If not, transform it into a relation in the 1NF.

    b. Are there functional dependencies in the relation created in part (a)? If so, show them.

    c. Are there transitive dependencies in the relation created in part (a)? If so, show them.

    d. The relation created in part (a) is susceptible to anomalies. Provide examples of the insertion, deletion, and update anomalies.

    e. Transform the relation created in part (a) into a set of relations in the 2NF.

    f. Is the set of relations created in part (e) in the 3NF? If not, transform it into a set of relations in the 3NF, draw a relational schema, and show the referential integrity constraints.

PUBLISHER

Pub. ID	Name	Address	Book ID	Book Subject	Pub. Date	Inventory
3421	Academic	129 West	12MA	Architecture	2/11/02	1,657
			78OP	Business	7/8/02	3,563
			45MK	Economics	7/14/02	2,431
			67MS	Accounting	8/10/02	890
9067	City	45 East	10FD	Biology	9/10/02	3,908

24. Medicare keeps information about its patients in the following table.

    a. Is this table in the 1NF? If not, transform it into a relation in the 1NF.

    b. Are there functional dependencies in the relation created in part (a)? If so, show them.

    c. Are there transitive dependencies in the relation created in part (a)? If so, show them.

    d. The relation created in part (a) is susceptible to anomalies. Provide examples of the insertion and update anomalies.

    e. Transform the relation created in part (a) into a set of relations in the 2NF.

    f. Is the set of relations created in part (e) in the 3NF? If not, transform it into a set of relations in the 3NF, draw a relational schema, and show the referential integrity constraints.

PATIENTS

Patient ID	Name	Address	Visit Date	Doctor ID	Doctor Name
P1209	J. Johns	134 West	3/3/02	D1256	A. Frank
			9/10/02	D1256	A. Frank
			10/8/02	D4523	D. Gomez
P1221	F. Brown	223 South	6/7/02	D6712	G. Kelly
P8912	K. Dong	45 East	9/12/02	D8917	M. Julius

25. Draw a relational schema that shows the relational integrity constraints for each of the following binary relationships:

    a. The Florida Tennis Association keeps records of the tennis clubs and their members. The attributes of the entity CLUB are *ID*, *Name*, and *Address*. The attributes of the entity MEMBER are *SSN*, *Name*, *Address*, *Birthday*, and *Gender*. Note that the relation between the entity CLUB and the entity MEMBER is a binary one-to-many (1:M) relationship.

    b. A university keeps records of the sports clubs and their members. The attributes of the entity CLUB are *ID*, *Name*, and *Address*. The

attributes of the entity MEMBER are *Name* and *Address*. Note that the relation between the entity MEMBER and the entity CLUB is a binary many-to-many (M:N) relationship.

    c. A university keeps records of each sports club and its coach. The attributes of the entity CLUB are *ID*, *Name*, and *Address*. The attributes of the entity COACH are *SSN*, *Name*, and *Address*. Note that the relation between the entity COACH and the entity CLUB is a binary one-to-one (1:1) relationship.

26. Consider the EE-R diagram of the *Great Marbles* database presented in the Hands-On Exercise 32 in Chapter 3.

    a. Transform the EE-R diagram into a relational schema that shows the referential integrity constraints.

    b. For each relation, identify the primary and foreign keys. Show if any of the primary keys is a composite key.

    c. For each relation, draw the functional dependencies.

    d. If any of the relations are not in the 3NF, transform them into a set of 3NF relations.

27. Consider the EE-R diagram of the financial institution database presented in the Hands-On Exercise 31 in Chapter 3.

    a. Transform the EE-R diagram into a relational schema that shows the referential integrity constraints.

    b. For each relation, identify the primary and foreign keys. Show if any of the primary keys is a composite key.

    c. For each relation, draw the functional dependencies.

    d. If any of the relations is not in the 3NF, transform them into a set of 3NF relations.

28. The following Flight-Airline relation is part of a travel agency's database. Note that the different airlines charge different prices for each trip.

    a. Are there functional dependencies in this relation? If so, show them.

    b. Are there transitive dependencies in this relation? If so, show them.

    c. The above relation is susceptible to anomalies. Provide examples of the insertion, deletion, and update anomalies.

    d. Is this relation in the 3NF? If not, transform the *Flight-Airline* relation into a set of 3NF relations, draw a relational schema for the 3NF relations, and show the referential integrity constraints.]

FLIGHT-AIRLINE

Flight ID	Airline ID	Name	Address	Origin	Destination	Distance	Price	Departure	Arrival

29. Consider the EE-R diagram of the *National Car Rental Agency* database introduced in the Hands-On Exercise 34 in Chapter 3.

   a. Transform the EE-R diagram into a relational schema that shows the referential integrity constraints.

   b. For each relation, identify the primary key and the foreign key. Show if any of the primary keys is a composite key.

   c. For each relation, draw the functional dependencies.

   d. If any of the relations is not in the 3NF, transform them into a set of 3NF relations.

30. Consider the EE-R diagram of the *Department* database presented in the Hands-On Exercise 35 in Chapter 3.

   a. Transform the EE-R diagram into a relational schema that shows the referential integrity constraints.

   b. For each relation, identify the primary and foreign keys. Determine if any of the primary keys is a composite key.

   c. For each relation, draw the functional dependencies.

   d. If any of the relations is not in the 3NF, transform them into a set of 3NF relations.

31. A steel manufacturing company keeps information about raw materials and its final products in a database. The following *Product-Raw Material* relation is part of this database. The company buys the raw materials from suppliers around the country, and the price paid depends on the type of the material and supplier. The company monitors the inventory levels as well. In this relation, the field *Rate* contains the quantity of raw materials needed to produce one pound of the final product.

   a. Are there functional dependencies in this relation? If so, show them.

   b. Are there transitive dependencies in this relation? If so, show them.

   c. The above relation is susceptible to anomalies. Provide examples of the insertion, deletion, and update anomalies.

   d. Is this relation in the 3NF? If not, transform the *Product-Raw Material* relation into a set of 3NF relations, draw a relational schema for the 3NF relations, and show the referential integrity constraints.

PRODUCT-RAW MATERIAL

RMID	PID	Rate	RM Inventory	Product Inventory	Supplier ID	Supplier Name	Supplier Address	Cost

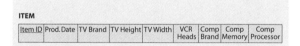

32. An electronics shop sells computers, TVs, and VCRs. The shop keeps a detailed database that keeps track of each item. The following is the *Item* relation of the electronic shop's database.

   a. Are there transitive dependencies in this relation? If so, show them.

   b. Is this relation in the 2NF? If not, transform the Item relation into a set of 2NF relations. Draw the referential integrity constraints.

   c. Is this relation in the 3NF? If not, transform it into a set of 3NF relations. Draw the referential integrity constraints.

ITEM

Item ID	Prod. Date	TV Brand	TV Height	TV Width	VCR Heads	Comp Brand	Comp Memory	Comp Processor

33. Consider the EE-R diagram of YXZ Company introduced in the Hands-On Exercise 37 in Chapter 3.

   a. Transform the EE-R diagram into a relational schema that shows the referential integrity constraints.

   b. For each relation, identify the primary and foreign keys. Show if any of the primary keys is a composite key.

   c. For each relation, draw the functional dependencies.

   d. If any of the relations is not in the 3NF, transform them into a set of 3NF relations.

PART TWO

Database Development with Microsoft Access

five Access Introduction: Touring Access

chapter OVERVIEW

135

5.1 *Introduction*

Microsoft Access is a *relational database management system* (DBMS), software that facilitates data definition, data creation, and data management. Examples of other well-known DBMS include Oracle, Microsoft SQL Server, IBM DB2, Informix, dBase, and FoxPro. We have chosen to work with the Access DBMS for several reasons. First, it is very popular in the business world as well as in the academia. While medium to small scale industries often use the Access DBMS to support their data management needs, Access is also enjoying considerable success as a pedagogical tool in academia. Second, the Access DBMS is fairly easy to learn and can be used in conjunction with many other Windows-based applications. Third, despite its simplicity, it provides many powerful features that can be found in commercial level database management systems. Finally, Access supports two industry standard query languages, *Structured Query Language* (SQL) and *Query By Example* (QBE). This provides a fairly straightforward way for Access users to adapt to other commercial DBMS with minimal effort.

Microsoft Access software provides its own development environment (Access's Database Window) to assist the database development process. The objective of this chapter is to make the reader comfortable with the Access development environment. We will accomplish this by touring the Access environment and introducing various features and design tools. We begin our discussion with the section on the architecture of Microsoft Access. We will then briefly discuss Access architecture components: tables, relationships, and queries, each in a separate section to follow. We will conclude the chapter with a section on getting Access help.

5.1.1 Topics

This chapter discusses the following topics:

- The architecture of Access.
- The development environment of Access.
- How to explore tables and relationships.
- How to explore queries.
- How to use Access help.

5.2 *The Architecture of Microsoft Access*

An Access database is a collection of working elements referred to as *data objects*. Tables, queries, forms, reports, relationships, toolbars, and almost all visible features in the Access window are examples of Access data objects. Access data objects facilitate creation, manipulation, and presentation of data and thus perform functions of a DBMS. Among these data objects, a few are designated as core data objects—those that are directly associated with data. Tables, queries, forms, and reports are Access's core data objects. These core data objects form a layered architecture of Microsoft Access are shown in Figure 5.1. The architecture is also referred to as *Access's data object model*.

The table is the foundation of Access architecture and is fundamental to the concept of relational databases. Access stores all its data in tables and core objects queries, forms, and reports, are directly or indirectly dependent on tables for data manipulation and presentation. A typical Access database has more than one table object that serve as a repository of data.

Query objects come next in the hierarchy of the architecture. The primary task of this layer is to retrieve data from Access tables and forward them up in the hierarchy for presentation.

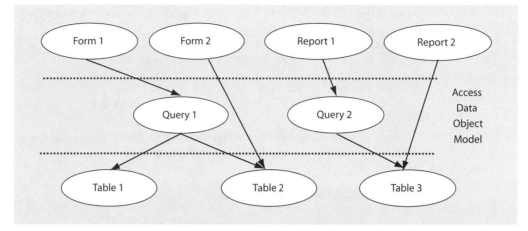

Figure 5.1 The architecture of Microsoft Access.

Queries can combine data or parts of data from multiple tables and thus provide users of the database a desired view of the data stored in individual tables. A typical Access database has several query objects; each is designed to give a particular view of data stored in the tables. The third and top layer of architecture is the presentation layer. The objects from this layer—forms and reports—are responsible for the data presentation. The raw data for presentation can either come directly from the tables or, more often, from the views provided by Access queries. We will not discuss the presentation layer objects in this book. Rather, we will use more sophisticated Visual Basic forms and crystal reports to present queried data to the user as discussed in Chapters 10–19.

5.3 *Access's Development Environment*

Developing an Access database entails building its data object model. A typical development process includes creating and defining Access tables and designing several queries based on the tables. The environment that assists this development process is called *Access's development environment*. This environment is simply an Access window and components that appear when we open Access. In this section we explore Access's development environment in depth. We begin our discussion with some of its supporting features such as the *Task Pane*, the *Database Window*, and the *Toolbar*.

In this chapter and throughout our discussion of Access, we will use an example of the university database that we have developed through Chapter 3 and Chapter 4. We request the reader to revisit the entity-relationship diagram in Figure 3.25 of Chapter 3 for the version of the university database that we will be referring to. The actual database file "University.ch5.1.mdb" can be found in the "HandsOn/Chapter5" folder on the book Web site. We will build this database as we continue to learn Access in subsequent chapters.

5.3.1 The Task Pane

The Task Pane appears as a panel-like structure on the right-hand side of the Access window (see Figure 5.2). The Task Pane reveals the most frequently accessed tasks and allows us to open and browse existing Access databases. We use the *Open* heading under the *Getting Started* profile to open the existing database files or to create a new database file. We can also choose other Task Pane profiles (default is *Getting Started*) from the drop-down list that appears when we click the profile name (see Figure 5.2). The *New File* profile allows us to create a new Access database file using existing data or using an existing file.

The Task Pane should appear automatically when we start Access. If it does not, we can easily open the Task Pane using the following How-to topic:

■ How-to: Open a Task Pane.
   1. Choose View | Toolbars | Customize from the main menu to open the *Customize* dialog box.
   2. Choose the *Task Pane* check box under the *Toolbars* tab (see Figure 5.2).
   3. Click *Close* to exit the dialog box and return to the Access window.

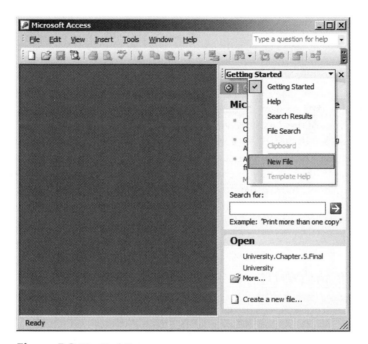

Figure 5.2 The Task Pane.

5.3.2 The Database Window

Let us now open the existing university database. We explore the Access data object model using this database. To open an existing database, we do one of the following:

■ Use the Task Pane; or alternately,
■ Choose File | Open from the main menu. Locate and select the "University.ch5.1.mdb" in the *Open* dialog box and click *Open*.

The Database Window for the university database should resemble the screen shot in Figure 5.3. We now briefly describe various components of this window.

The *Title Bar* at the top of the Database Window displays the name of the opened database. The *Object Bar* on the left-hand side of the Database Window lists the choices available for different types of data objects. For example, the Object Bar in Figure 5.3 lists Tables, Queries, Forms, Reports, and a few other data objects. The *Database View* makes up the remaining part of the Database Window, and it lists the tasks and objects available for each selection in the Object Bar. In Figure 5.3, for example, the Database View displays a list of all available tables because the table option has been selected in the Object Bar.

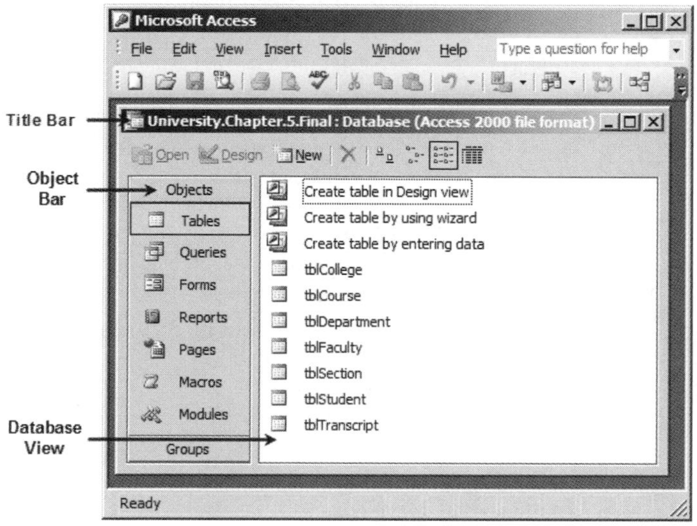

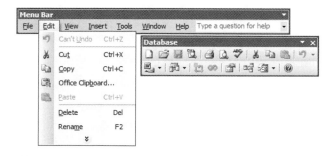

Figure 5.3 The Database Window.

5.3.3 Toolbars

Access offers more than a dozen built-in toolbars. We primarily discuss the two most frequently used: the *Menu* (or the main menu) and the *Database* toolbar. These toolbars are also the default toolbars that appear when the Database Window is opened.

The name of a toolbar can be viewed by dragging it out of its position (see Figure 5.4). We dock the toolbar to an edge of the Database Window by dragging it near an edge. We can also view and add other toolbars to the developing environment using these steps:

1. Choose View | Toolbars | Customize from the main menu to open the *Customize* dialog box.
2. Check the desired toolbar name under the *Toolbar* tab.

Many of the buttons on the *Database* toolbar are initially disabled. This is not a problem, though; once we select a data object in the Database View, most of these buttons become available. If we then place the mouse pointer over any one of these buttons, a *tool tip* that displays the name of a particular button appears. We cover some important buttons on *Menu* and *Database* toolbars in Table 5.1 and leave the task of exploring the remaining buttons to the reader.

Figure 5.4 The Access toolbars.

Table 5.1 A summary of the main menu and the database toolbars.

Toolbar	Option	Description
Main Menu or Menu Bar	File	Used to create, open, save, print, import, and export database files.
	Edit	Used to delete, rename, cut, copy, and paste operations with database objects.
	Insert	Used to insert new objects into a database.
	Tools	Used to access various design tools available.
	Windows	Used to customize the appearance of a window. The *hide item* and *unhide item* options can be used to conceal or reveal objects and windows.
	Help	Used to get Access help.
Database		Includes buttons for the most commonly used main menu functions like *new*, *open*, *copy*, *paste*, and *relationships*.

5.3.4   The Options Dialog for Global Options

Global options are the options that are accessible across all the database objects. Access offers many global options that allow us to customize databases. These global options are available through the customization window known as the *Options* dialog box (see Figure 5.5). To open the *Options* dialog box select Tools | Options from the main menu. Table 5.2 lists several of the most common options and provides a brief summary of their functions.

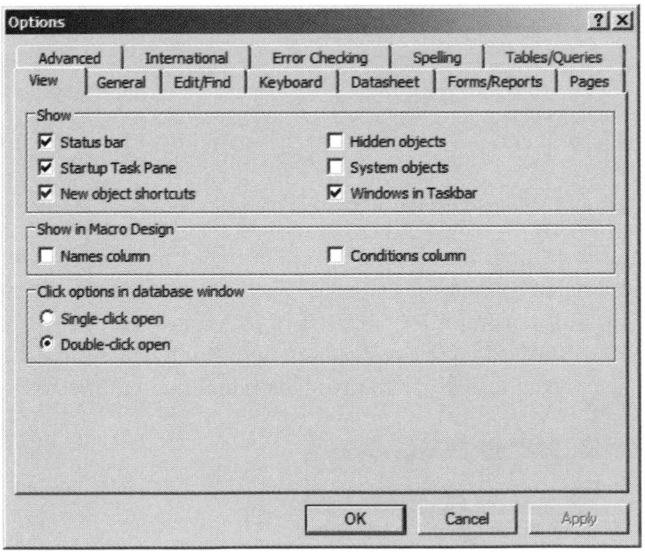

Figure 5.5 Options dialog box for global options.

Table 5.2 The summary of *Options* dialog box's global options.

Tab	Heading	Functionality
View	Show	Determines what to show. Click on the appropriate boxes in the list of options to customize the view.
	Click options…window	Specifies the way in which we can open objects.
General	Default database folder	Specifies the default path to the database.
Edit/Find	Confirm	Asks the user to confirm major changes. For example, the document delete option, if checked, prompts the user for confirmation before deletion.
Datasheet	All Headings	Used to alter the appearance of the Datasheet View.
Tables/Queries	Default field sizes	Controls the default text, the number size, the field type (set to text), and the auto index field name.

We now explore the tables, relationships, and queries objects in the following sections.

5.4 *Exploring Tables*

Access stores and relates its data in ***tables***. As mentioned in the Access architecture section, tables are essential to relational databases and all other database objects are directly or indirectly dependent on tables for their data manipulation and presentation. Each table holds the data about a particular subject. For example, in the university database, the student table (*tblStudent*) stores all of the relevant data about students including the social security number, name, date of birth, address, and email of each student.

Recall the entity-relationship (E-R) diagram from Chapter 3. If we draw similarities between an E-R diagram in Figure 3.25 and the university database, an entity in E-R diagram is the subject of a table, attributes of an entity are columns of the table, and the instances of entity type are rows of the table. These similarities are used to the great extent in Chapter 4 to transform an E-R diagram into a relational schema. The set of relations in the relational schema are used in Access table design. We explore table design in depth in Chapter 6.

A table in Access is presented as a two-dimensional grid. Each *data field*, or *column* of the grid, holds a piece of data about the subject of the table. For example, the column *FirstName* in the student table holds the first name of every student in the database. Each *row* or *record* or *tuple* of a grid represents a complete entry of the table subject. For example, the third row of the student table provides specific data about the student named Jonathan Carlson.

To view the list of available tables in the university database, choose the *Tables* option in the Object Bar. The Database View reveals the names of seven different tables (see Figure 5.6.). Note that there are three entries before the first table name in the Database View:

- ■ Create table in Design View
- ■ Create table by using wizard
- ■ Create table by entering data

These categories provide different ways to build new tables with Access. We explore these possibilities in Chapter 6.

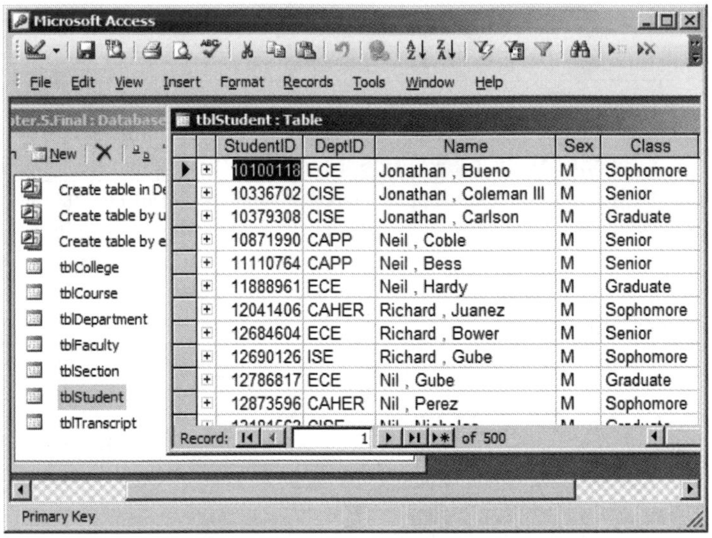

Figure 5.6 The student table: Datasheet View.

Access supports two types of views for its table. The first option, *Datasheet View*, allows non-specialists to view or modify a table through a user-friendly interface of a two-dimensional grid. All unnecessary design issues are hidden from the user in this view. *Design View*, the second option, creates an environment that allows database designers and developers to define and determine how tables will function. For example, using Design View we can specify the column names and data types.

5.4.1 Tables in Datasheet View

The Datasheet View option provides the simplest way to look at data. To open the student table of the university database, double-click *tblStudent* in the Database Window. The Datasheet View for this table should resemble Figure 5.6. This is a default view for tables. Datasheet View is commonly used to view, change, insert, or delete data from the tables.

The columns (fields) and rows (records) of the table form the axis of the two-dimensional datasheet grid. The navigation bar at the bottom of Datasheet View (see Figure 5.6) allows us to navigate through the grid. We can also move within or across the record by using either the *Tab* or *Up* and *Down* arrow keys.

5.4.2 Tables in Design View

Unlike Datasheet View, which is best used to alter data, Design View allows us to create or change the structure of the table. To open the Design View for the student table from its Datasheet View, use the *View* button located on the far left of the toolbar. The *View* button can be used to toggle between the Design View and the Datasheet View (see Figure 5.7). Also, if we right-click on *tblStudent* while in the Database Window, we can choose Design View from the right-click menu. The Design View and its components for *tblStudent* are depicted in Figure 5.7.

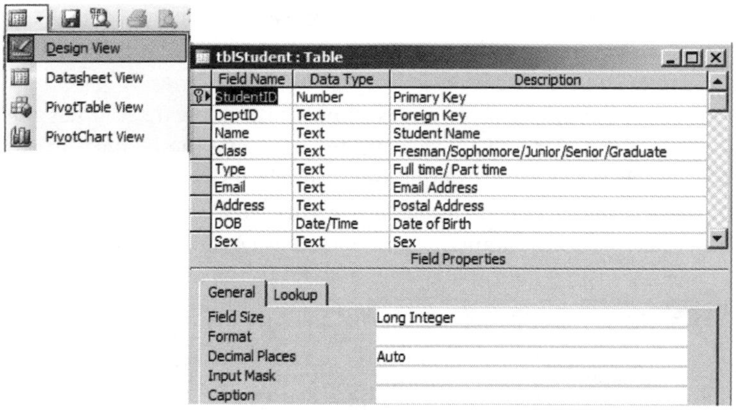

Figure 5.7 The student table: Design View.

The Design View consists of two distinct halves; the top half of the screen contains the *Design Grid*, while the bottom half provides the *Field Properties*. The Design Grid contains several rows and three columns. Each row of the Design Grid defines a column (data field) of the table. The first column of the Design Grid, *Field Name*, defines the name of the data field that serves as the title of the column in the Datasheet View. The second column of the Design Grid, *Data Type*, dictates the type of values that each data field can hold. For example, the data type for the *Name* field is *Text*, while the *SSN* field is expressed as *Number*. To observe the data type options available for each row, we use the drop-down menu that appears when we click anywhere in *Data Type* column. Finally, the *Description* column of the Design Grid allows us to provide a short description about each data field. This column is primarily for documentation purposes.

We can navigate across the columns of the Design Grid using the *Tab* or *Up* and *Down* keys. The shortcut menu and the toolbar buttons in the Design View allow us to add or delete design rows. We can also change the order of the data fields by first selecting and then dragging and dropping Design Grid rows at the desired location. One of the most important features of the Design Grid enables us to assign a data field(s) as a primary key of the table (see Chapter 6 for details about primary keys).

The bottom half of the Design View allows us to manipulate the data field properties for the selected data field from the top grid. These properties are helpful to govern what data can be entered into the field, to validate the entered data, and to manipulate the appearance of the Datasheet View. We will expand more on Access tables in Chapter 6.

5.5   *Relationships*

A ***relationship*** connects or relates two tables. As we have learned in Chapter 4, we must normalize the database schema so as to eliminate anomalies and data redundancies. The process of normalization generally splits a table into more than one table. Although normalization enables efficient data storage, it makes it difficult to query the fragmented data. For example, in the university database we have the student table and department table as a result of normalization. However, a user might ask a question related to these tables together: "how many students are enrolled in the Industrial Engineering department?" Before normalization, this question would have been answered using one table, but now that we have two tables we need to combine (join) these two tables to answer the question. *Combining* or *joining* two tables is like anti-normalization. We elaborate on joins in Chapters 8.

In order to join two or more tables, Access should know how these tables are related to each other. Access relationships accomplish this task by managing the relationships between tables. Its user-friendly interface allows us to define and maintain relationships. In fact, we can drag and drop tables and data fields to create relationships. Figure 5.8 illustrates the Relationship Window for the university database. See Chapter 7 for detailed discussion of relationships.

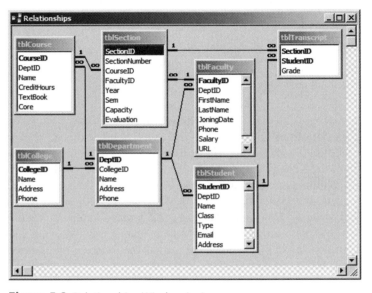

Figure 5.8 Relationships Window in Access.

5.6   *Exploring Queries*

A *query* is a question posed against database tables. For example, "how many students are enrolled in the Physics department?" This sample query then examines *tblStudent* and *tblDepartment* tables to answer the question. Queries, thus, process data stored in one or more database tables to derive meaningful information.

In effect, queries provide the desired view of data from one or more tables. In the previous example, the number of students in the Physics department is the desired view. The desired view can take many forms, including the following: a list of data rows (e.g., names and addresses of students); aggregate values such as sum, count, and average (e.g., average GPA for a college); and grouped lists (e.g., names and addresses of the faculty from the Chemistry department). Queries are very powerful tools and serve as the *epicenter* of any database management system. Access allows us to build up the queries using a *graphical query design grid* (Query-by-Example or QBE) and *SQL statements* (SQL).

In addition, Access supports many types of queries, such as select queries, update queries, action queries, crosstab queries, and parameter queries. Select queries allow us to select data from one or more tables while update queries allow us to update existing data. Action queries make it easy to perform actions such as inserting and deleting records from a database.

Access stores only the definition and properties of a given query and generates results when a user performs (executes) the query. The query does not store the query result anywhere in the database. Consider this example query; "how many students are enrolled in the Physics department?" The actual enrollment will be calculated based on the number of physics students in the student table at the time of query execution. The enrollment won't be stored in the database, only the definition of the query, tables to join and actions to perform will be stored.

To view the list of available queries for the university database, choose the *Queries* option from the Object Bar. The Database View displays the names of all the available queries. Before the first query, we should see two entries:

- Create query in Design View
- Create query by using wizard

Each of these options provides a way of building a new query in Access. Like tables, queries have a Datasheet View as well as a Design View. The Datasheet View displays the result of the query while the Design View assists in the query's design process. To open a query in Datasheet View, we double-click the query name in the Database View. Again, as with tables, Datasheet View is the default view for queries.

5.6.1 Queries in Datasheet View

If we open the *qryStudentInfo* in the Datasheet View (see Figure 5.9) we might be unable to tell the difference between this view and the Datasheet View of the student table. Datasheet View for tables and queries actually appears and operates in a similar manner. However, there are a few important differences between the two. First, in order to observe the results of a query in the Datasheet View, the user must first execute a query (i.e., double-click the query name in the Database Window). In other words, the data in the Datasheet View of a query is *generated* while that of tables is *stored* in the database. Second, we cannot always update data in the query's Datasheet View; our ability to update data in the query's Datasheet View is determined by the query design. In both the table's and query's Datasheet Views, however, we can use the *View* button on the toolbar to toggle between Datasheet View and Design View.

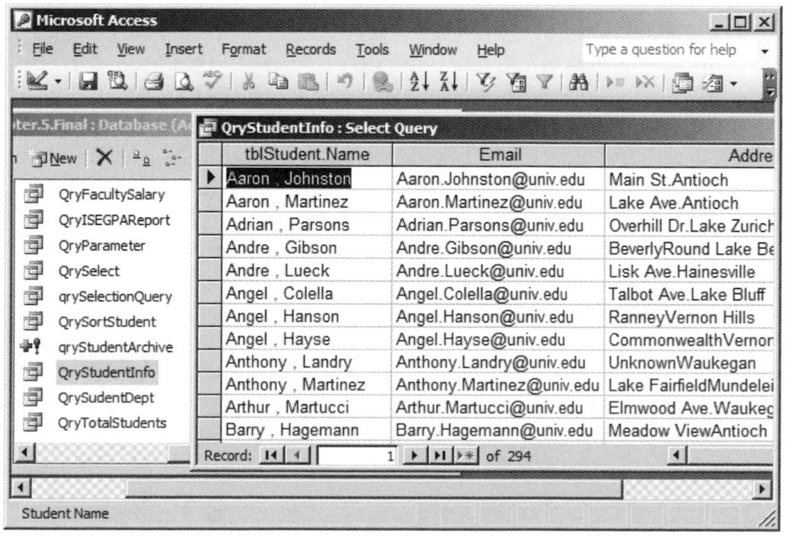

Figure 5.9 List of Access queries and a query in the Datasheet View.

5.6.2   Queries in Design View

We can use the query Design View to create and change the definition, structure, and design of a query. As with the table's Design View, the query's Design View screen is divided into halves (see Figure 5.10); the upper half is referred as the *Table Pane* and displays the field lists (column list) of the query tables. The lower half is referred as the *Design Grid*.

The Table Pane allows us to specify query tables. For example, consider the following student information query: "display the average grades and the contact information for each student in the College of Engineering." To answer this query we need *tblStudent*, *tblTranscript*, *tblDepartment*, and *tblCollege* tables. We specify or add these tables to the Table Pane to start the query design. To add tables we use the shortcut menu available in the Table Pane. Once we add the tables, Access automatically shows the list of columns and any relationships among added tables (see Figure 5.10).

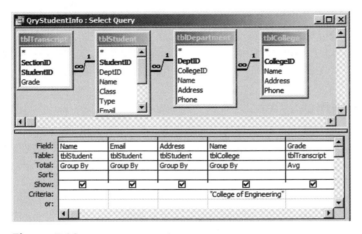

Figure 5.10 Access query in the Design View.

The lower half, the Design Grid, contains the information about the fields (or columns) that are included in the query. Thus, the fields in the Design Grid constitute the columns of the query output. We double-click the fields of interest in the Table Pane to add them to the Design Grid and thus include them in the query design. In addition to the fields, the Design Grid also displays the source table, the sorting criteria, and the selection criteria for each query column. The Design View allows us to choose whether or not a particular field should be visible in the query output using its *Show* row. Further, through simple drag-and-drop operations, we can change the size of columns in the Design Grid, move them around, and even alter the size of the Design Grid itself. We explore query design in Chapter 8.

5.7   *Getting Access Help*

As we may already know, recent business trends have compelled software companies to complement, if not replace, printed help manuals with online help. Consequently, a solid understanding of the online help system is essential for users interested in learning more about any new software package. In this section, we will illustrate how to use the Access online help system.

There are several ways to invoke online Access help including:

- Pressing the F1 function key
- Selecting Help | Microsoft Access Help from the main menu
- Clicking on the Microsoft Access Help icon on the toolbar

Each of these methods causes the Access help to appear on the right side of the Access window. The help features a *Table of Contents* and *Search Assistant* links. The *Table of Contents* lists all the help topics and their subtopics in a tree-like structure. The *Table of Contents* allows us to learn about Access's features and structure, simply by looking at a topic heading and then exploring its contents. The *Search Assistant* lists the help topics related to the keyword entered or question posed by us.

5.7.1 Getting Help on Compressing Database Size

Although we may be familiar with these help features while using other software, we will explore a help topic related to an important and useful Access feature: "compacting database files." As we work with Access database files, adding new data tables, images, and queries, we may find that the database files have grown too large. Fortunately, we can compress database files to improve storage efficiency.

Let us see how we can compact or compress an Access file. We use the Access help feature to find an answer to the following How-to topic.

- How-to: Compress database files.
    1. Open the Access help as described earlier.
    2. In the *Search for* text box, enter the question, "how do I compact a database?" Then, hit the *Start searching* button.
    3. The help displays several relevant topics. Select the *Compact and repair an Access file* option (see Figure 5.11).
    4. Read and follow the help topic description. The following line should appear on the instructions page: "On the *Tools* menu, point to *Database Utilities*, and then click *Compact and Repair Database.*"

Figure 5.11 Getting Access help to compact a database file.

5.8   *Summary*

- Microsoft Access is a *database management system* (DBMS). Examples of other well-known DBMS are Oracle, Microsoft SQL Server, IBM DB2, Informix, dBase, and FoxPro.

- An Access database is a collection of working elements referred to as *data objects*. The core Access data objects includes: tables, queries, forms, and reports. The *Access data object model* provides the architecture of core data objects.

- The Access *development environment* is a window under which all the Access data objects are put together to facilitate the process of development.

- Access stores and relates its data in a *table*. A table is a two-dimensional grid. A column of the grid is referred as a *data field* and a row is a *record* or *tuple*. Table's *Datasheet View* is the simplest way to look at data. We design tables in the *Design View*.

- *Relationships* link two tables. Access allows us to define and maintain relationships in a user-friendly interface.

- A *query* is a question posed against data tables. Queries provide the desired view of data from one or more tables. Queries are very powerful tools and are the epicenter of any DBMS. Access supports select queries, update queries, action queries, crosstab queries, and parameter queries.

5.9   *Exercises*

5.9.1 Review Questions

1. Explain the concept of a data object model. Provide examples of three different objects in Microsoft Access.

2. What do the columns and rows of a table represent?

3. What is the purpose of relationships in Access?

4. How do select queries differ from action queries?

5. Name two functions that the Task Pane can perform.

6. List three methods for creating a table.

7. Describe the difference between Datasheet View and Design View when viewing a table.

8. What is a way to create a primary key in Access? What view must we use to create it?

9. What are the similarities and differences between the Datasheet View of tables and queries?

10. Describe the Design View of a query.

CHAPTER

six *Access Tables: Building Data Foundations*

chapter OVERVIEW

6.1   *Introduction*

Table is the most fundamental and foundational element of a relational database. Microsoft Access stores and relates its data using tables. A table in Access is essentially a two-dimensional grid. Each column of the grid, also referred to as a *data field*, contains information about the subject of the table. For example, in the university database, the *Name* column of the student table features the student names. A row of the table grid, also referred to as a *record* or *tuple*, is the particular instance of the subject. In our example, a row represents a complete entry of a particular student. Figure 6.1 gives a snapshot of the student table, *tblStudent*, in the university database.

StudentID	DeptID	Name	Class	Type	Email
10100118	Electrical &	Jonathan , Bueno	Sophomore	Full Tim	Jonathan , Bueno@
10336702	Computer &	Jonathan , Colema	Senior	Full Tim	Jonathan , Coleman
10379308	Computer &	Jonathan , Carlson	Graduate	Full Tim	Jonathan , Carlson@
10871990	Center for th	Neil , Coble	Senior	Full Tim	Neil , Coble@univ.e
11110764	Center for th	Neil , Bess	Senior	Full Tim	Neil , Bess@univ.ec
11888961	Electrical &	Neil , Hardy	Graduate	Full Tim	Neil , Hardy@univ.e
12041406	Center for th	Richard , Juanez	Sophomore	Full Tim	Richard , Juanez@u
12684604	Electrical &	Richard , Bower	Senior	Full Tim	Richard , Bower@un
12690126	Industrial & S	Richard , Gube	Sophomore	Full Tim	Richard , Gube@un
12786817	Electrical &	Nil , Gube	Graduate	Full Tim	Nil , Gube@univ.edu
12873596	Center for th	Nil , Perez	Sophomore	Full Tim	Nil , Perez@univ.ed
13181563	Computer &	Nil , Nicholas	Graduate	Full Tim	Nil , Nicholas@univ.
13302908	Industrial & S	Vic , Blair	Freshman	Part Tim	Vic , Blair@univ.edu
13317811	Electrical &	Vic , Maloney	Freshman	Full Tim	Vic , Maloney@univ
13326952	Center for th	Vic , Leith	Junior	Part Tim	Vic , Leith@univ.edu

Record: 15 of 500

Figure 6.1 The student table of the university database.

Developing an Access database essentially starts with designing and creating Access tables. Recall the relational data model and normalization process we discussed in Chapter 4. A relational data model maps an E-R diagram into the list of relations and referential integrity constraints between the relations. We employ the list of relations of relational data modeling to design Access tables. For each relation, we create an Access table with the attributes of a relation forming columns of the table. The actual data forms the table rows. The most common methods used to build tables in Access include the following:

- Create table in the Datasheet View.
- Create table in the Design View.
- Create table by using *Table Wizard*.
- Create table by using *Import Wizard*.

Although the method we choose depends on personal preference and data location, we must start in the Database Window to use any of these options. When we click the *Tables* option in the Object Bar, the Database Window displays the first three options listed above. The fourth, *Import Wizard* option is available in the Database Window's right-click menu (see Figure 6.2). Alternatively, we can select the *Tables* option from the Object Bar and click the *New* button in the Database Window toolbar. This should open the *New Table* dialog box, which lists all the table building methods (see Figure 6.2).

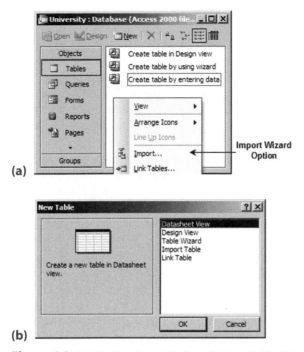

Figure 6.2 (a) The Database Window; (b) *New Table* dialog box.

6.1.1 Topics

This chapter discusses the following topics:

■ How to create tables in the Datasheet View.
■ How to create tables in the Design View.
■ How to use field types, field properties, and the *Lookup Wizard*.
■ How to define a primary key.
■ How to create tables by using *Import Wizard*.

6.2 *Hands-On Tutorial: Creating Access Tables in the Datasheet View*

Creating tables by entering data directly in the Datasheet View is one of the simplest and quickest ways to build new tables in Access. Using this method, we manually enter data to specify the number of columns and rows in the table. Access also allows us to modify column names by double-clicking on column headings.

We use this hands-on to build the *tblCollege* table of the university database. The college table stores information about different colleges in the university. For each college, we are interested in the following attributes: unique college identification, college name, its office address, and the phone number. This hands-on tutorial covers the following How-to topic:

- How-to: create tables in Datasheet View.
  1. Open the Microsoft Access using the *Start* menu.
  2. Choose File | New from the main menu to open the *New File* Task Pane on the right side of the Access window. Choose the *Blank database* option from the Task Pane to create a new Access database file named "University.Chapter.6.mdb."
  3. In the new database file, select the *Table* item in the Object Bar and choose the *Create table by entering data* option in the Database Window. A grid-like Datasheet View appears with the default name *Table1* on the title bar and the default column names *Field1*, *Field2*, and so forth.
  4. Enter the first record in the table as shown in Figure 6.3.
  5. Double-click the column heading to rename them (see Figure 6.3 for column names). Alternatively, right-click the column heading, and choose the *Rename Column* option from the short-cut menu.
  6. To complete the table design, enter the remaining records in the subsequent rows of the grid. The screen should now resemble Figure 6.3.
  7. Save the college table by choosing File | Save As from the main menu. Change the default name *Table1* to *tblCollege* in the *Save As* dialog box, and click *OK* to save.
  8. Access displays a warning if we do not define a primary key for a table. For now click *No* to ignore the warning. We will discuss defining a primary key later in this chapter.

	CollegeID	Name	Address	Phone
▶	CED	College of Education	140 Norman Hall	(352) 392-0798
	CFA	College of Fine Arts	245 Fine Arts Bldg	(352) 392-4767
	COE	College of Engineering	300 Weil Hall	(352) 392-6000
	COM	College of Medicine	189 Shands Bldg	(352) 392-4000

Record: 1 of 4

Figure 6.3 Creating the college table in Datasheet View.

Although creating tables in Datasheet View option is fairly simple and quick, this method has limitations. First, there is no simple way to define a primary key in Datasheet View. Second, we cannot specify any data validation rules in Datasheet View. For example, if we would like to store the *CollegeID* column as three-letter abbreviation, there is no way to enforce this rule in Datasheet View. Finally, we cannot specify column data types in Datasheet View. The data type of a column is indicative of the type of data that column will hold. *Text*, *Number*, and *Currency* are a few examples of column data types. The Datasheet View assigns a default data type to each column based on data entered into the columns. We cannot view or change auto selected column data types. In general, Datasheet View compromises flexibility for the sake of simplicity and, as such, serves as a good starting point for creating tables. However, to effectively design and create tables, we must use comprehensive and flexible tool like Design View.

6.3 *Hands-On Tutorial: Creating Access Tables in the Design View*

The Design View is a comprehensive, powerful, and flexible tool to create tables (see Figure 6.4). The table Design View is divided into two halves: the *Design Grid* (the upper half) and the *Field Properties* (the lower half). The Design Grid allows us to specify the field names, field data types, and descriptions of each field or column of the table. The Field Properties display the properties of each field or an entry in the Design Grid. We use properties of a data field to control the characteristics of the data entered in the table column. We begin with the following exercise to familiarize ourselves with the most basic features of the Design View.

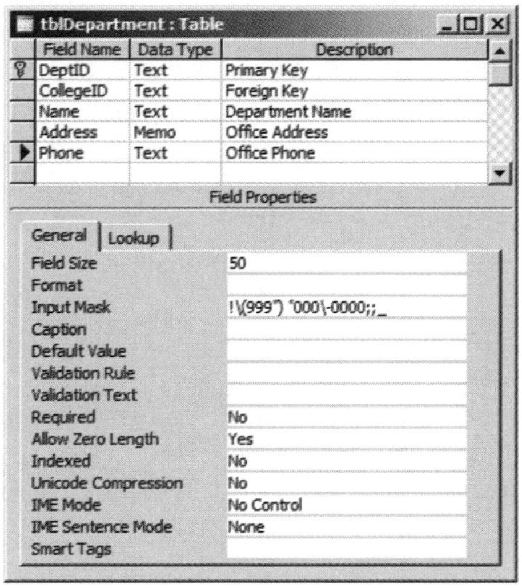

Figure 6.4 The department table in Design View.

In the following hands-on tutorial, we use the Design View to create the department table of the university database. The department table contains data about each department in the university, specifically, its name, office address and the phone number. Also, note that the *CollegeID* is a foreign key in the department table (see Section 4.3 for detailed discussion on primary key and foreign keys). This hands-on tutorial covers the following How-to topic:

- ■ How-to: create tables in Design View.
    1. Start in the Database Window with *Tables* option selected in the Object Bar. Double-click the *Create table in Design View* option in the Database Window to open the new table in Design View. Alternatively, select the similar option from the *New Table* dialog box.
    2. In the Design View, specify the fields of the department table on individual rows in the Design Grid (see Figure 6.4). The first column of the grid takes the name of the field; the second column takes the field type, which can be selected from the drop-down list of available data types; and the third column takes description of the field.

3. Select the *DeptID* row by clicking on the row selector (leftmost portion of the row). Right-click and choose the *Primary Key* option from the shortcut menu to assign *DeptID* as a primary key.

4. Save the table as *tblDepartment*.

We now explore few important components of Design View.

6.4 *Field Data Types*

Each field or column of a table is designed to contain a specific type of data. For example, the *Name* column in the student table contains student names; the *Salary* column in the faculty table contains salary numbers, and so forth. The type of data a column contains is referred to as field data type. Access offers ten different data types: *Text, Memo, Number, Date/Time, Currency, AutoNumber, Yes/No, OLE Object, Hyperlink,* and *Lookup*. The *Lookup* helps define the foreign key fields and is discussed in depth later in this chapter. Table 6.1 summarizes field data types.

Table 6.1 Access field data types.

Keyword	Description	Size
Text	Alphanumeric data. Examples include names and addresses.	Maximum 255 bytes
Memo	Long sentences and paragraphs. Examples include notes, comments, and descriptions.	Maximum 65,536 bytes
Number	Numeric data. Examples include age values, quantities, and unique IDs.	1,2,4 or 8 bytes (max. 16)
Date/Time	Dates and times. Examples include login time, birth date, starting date, and ending date.	8 bytes
Currency	Currency data. Examples include price, charges, salaries, and shipping cost.	8 bytes
Yes/No	Boolean (yes/no or true/false) data.	1 bit (1/8th byte)
OLE Objects	OLE objects from other Windows-based applications. Examples include Word files, pictures, and graphs.	Maximum 1 GB
Hyperlink	An alphanumeric string used as a hyperlink (elements that link to another place in the same or a different electronic document). Examples include Web addresses in the form of URL's.	Maximum 65,536 bytes
Lookup	Allows us to select data from another table. Generally used for foreign keys.	Same as the primary key to which foreign key refers.

Selecting a correct data type at the design stage can greatly affect the performance and functionality of a database and database application. While there are no fixed rules for selecting data types, storage space and application requirements influence the selection. The following text discusses the data type selection criteria for each of ten data types.

Text: The default data type, *Text*, is also the most common data type. Apart from storing the "text" data, the text data type also works for numerical data not used in calculations (e.g., phone numbers, zip codes, and any codes that begin with zeros). Access provides a default maximum of 50 bytes per data field that can be raised to 255 bytes.

Memo: This data type works best for storing large text data. Long sentences, notes, detailed descriptions, and paragraphs can be placed in fields with *Memo* data type. The *Memo* data type allows us to store 65,536 bytes, or approximately 18 pages of text, in a single field.

Number: Whenever we would like to perform arithmetic operations on numbers, we use the *Number* data type.

Date/Time: This data type stores valid dates, times, or combinations date and time formats. With Date/Time data type, we can perform calculations in standard units of time, such as seconds, minutes, hours, days, months, and years. We can use this data type to calculate the difference between two dates or to measure a period of elapsed time.

Currency: This data type stores currency data. We use this data type to store money values, float (double) and precise numbers. We can use fields with this data type in calculations, just like *Number* data type. The *Currency* data type provides a level of precision up to four decimal places.

AutoNumber: As the name suggests, this data type is specifically designed to automatically generate sequential numbers. It is mainly used for the primary key fields. Access allows a maximum of one AutoNumber data type field per table.

Yes/No: This data type is best suited for Boolean data. *Yes/No* stores logical "yes/no," "true/false," or "on/off" data. The *Yes/No* data type is the most compact data type and takes just one bit (1/8th of byte) of a storage space per entry. The data type is frequently used for "flag" fields such as *IsValid*, *IsOpen*, or *IsSelected*.

OLE Object: OLE stands for *Object Linking and Embedding*. This data type holds complex data from other Windows-based applications, such as Word, Excel, and PowerPoint. We can store text files, pictures, graphs, or sound and video files up to 1 GB with this data type.

Hyperlink: This data type stores hyperlinks—URL (*Uniform Resource Locator*) addresses that can link to other information or files. If the size of the database is a concern, we should use the *Hyperlink* data type to concisely point to the large data stored outside the database file.

Lookup: Foreign key fields are generally assigned a *Lookup* data type. Apart from that, fields with fixed and small numbers of input values are excellent candidates for *Lookup* data type. The examples fields include: ShippingMode (standard, 2-days, and overnight), Sex (male and female), and Shirt-Size (S, M, L, XL, and XXL).

6.5 *Field Properties*

The next step in designing tables is to customize the field properties. Every field has its own properties that control data storage, data format, and the data that can be entered into each column. We view the properties of a field in the *Field Properties* half of the Design View by selecting the field of interest in the Design Grid (see Figure 6.3). We now discuss a few important field properties.

Field Size.   We use this property to specify the length of text and numeric data types. The default field size for *Text* data type is 50 characters and can be raised to a maximum of 255 characters. For *Number* and *Currency* data type, we can choose any of the appropriate options from the drop-down menu. Table 6.2 lists the characteristics of number formats.

Table 6.2 Access field sizes for the *Number* data type.

Format	Size
Byte	Single-byte integer ranging from 0 to 255.
Integer	Two-byte integer ranging from –32,768 to 32,768.
Long Integer	Four-byte integer ranging from –2,147,438,648 to 2,147,438,648.
Single	Four-byte floating point number ranging from -3.4×10^{38} to 3.4×10^{38}.
Double	Eight-byte floating point number ranging from -1.797×10^{308} to 1.797×10^{308}.
ReplicationID	Sixteen-byte global unique identifier.

Format   The Format property allows us to control on-screen and printed data displays. This property can be used with all data types except *OLE Object* data type. The value of this property varies depending on data type as discussed below.

- *Number*, *Currency*, and *AutoNumber* data types, the value options are:

  General Number: default—no commas, no decimal places, no currency symbols.

  Currency: dollar symbol with two decimal places.

  Percentage: percentage symbol after two-decimal places.

  Scientific: number in scientific notation.

- The *Date/Time* data type has the following value options: default *General Date* (6/19/1999 5:34:23 PM), *Short Date* (6/19/99), *Long Time* (5:34:23 PM), and *Short Time* (17:34).
- The *Yes/No* data type has the following value options: *Yes/No* (default), *True/False*, and *On/Off*.

Input Mask   We use the Input Mask property to "mask" the user input. This feature restricts the input to a pre-defined format. This property is available for *Text*, *Number*, *Date/Time*, and *Currency* data types. The difference between the *Format* property and the *Input Mask* property is that the former controls "how data is displayed" to the user, while latter controls "how data is entered" by the user.

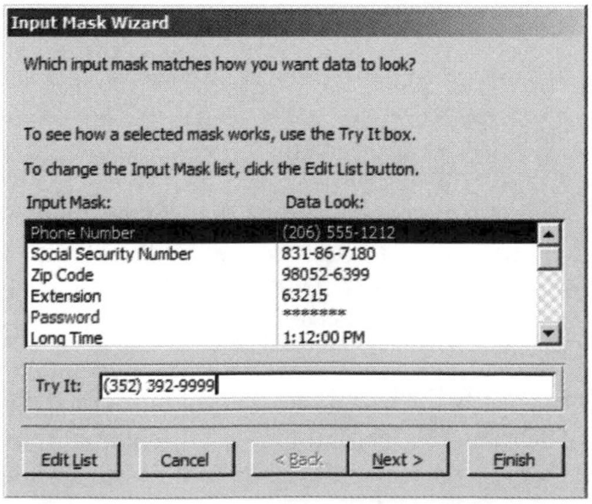

Figure 6.5 The *Input Mask Wizard* page 1: Selecting the mask.

The *Input Mask* property is typically used for fields such as phone numbers, social security numbers, and various fixed-format identification fields. The *Input Mask Wizard* assists us in setting-up the input mask through simple steps (see Figure 6.5).

Caption   The next available property in the list is *Caption*. *Caption* allows us to include more descriptive or logical field names. A caption becomes the column heading in the Datasheet View.

Required   The *Required* property indicates if the data *must be entered* for the column before a user can save the record. If the value of this property is set to *No*, the field can be kept empty while saving the record. The *Required* property can be used to enforce business rules. For example, we can use this property to make sure that students' email addresses be entered in all students' records.

Validation Rule and Validation Text   Another important field property is the *Validation Rule*. This property limits "what user can enter" into the tables. We specify the validation rule in the form of an expression. Newly entered data is then tested against the validation expression; failure to pass the test invalidates the data.

The *Validation Text* property goes hand-in-hand with the *Validation Rule* property. The value of the *Validation Text* property serves as an error message when the validation rule invalidates any data. If the *Validation Text* property value is empty, Access displays a default error message.

Indexed   While reading books, a reader may refer to the index of the book to search for specific subjects or sections. The book index is a list of *ordered key words*. An entry in the book index is a pointer (page number) in the book. In the similar context, an index in a database table is a list of *ordered field values* on which the index is built. An entry in the database index is a pointer (row number) in the table. For example, an index of a *Zip* field is a list of ordered zips in the table that points to the actual row in the table. Like the book index, the table index provides fast lookup if the searcher is using the field values on which the index is built. The *Indexed* property of a field indicates whether or not a field has been indexed.

By default, Access builds an index on primary key fields. We can index any of the table fields. The fields that are frequently used in database queries are good candidates to build an index on (see Chapter 8 for more on database queries). Though, indexes on appropriate table field give us a good query performance, with each additional index it imposes disk storage requirements. The detailed discussion of indexing and its tuning is beyond the scope of this book.

We now present three hands-on tutorials in the remainder of this section illustrating *Input Mask*, *Validation Rule*, and *Indexed* properties, respectively.

6.5.1   Hands-On Tutorial: Using Input Mask Wizard

In this hands-on tutorial, we will mask the phone number field in the department table. We will use the standard telephone number format: (xxx) xxx-xxxx (three-digit area code followed by seven-digit phone number). This tutorial covers the following How-to topic:

- How-to: use the *Input Mask* property and *Input Mask Wizard*.
  1. Open the *tblDepartment* table in the Design View, and click on the *Phone* field to view its field properties.

2. Locate and click on the *Input Mask* property under the *Field Properties*. Use the build button (...) to invoke the *Input Mask Wizard* (see Figure 6.6).

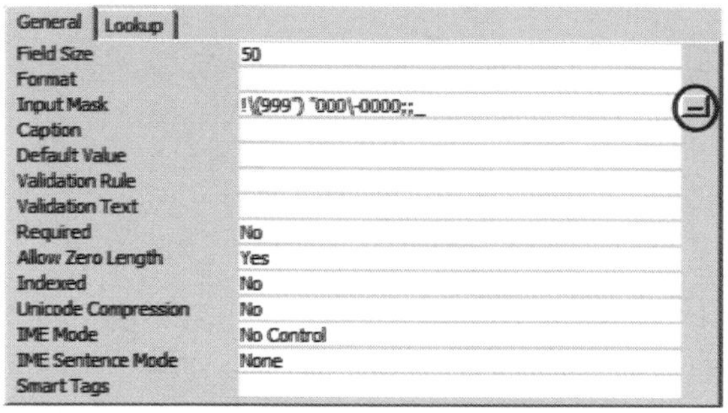

General	Lookup	
Field Size	50
Format	
Input Mask	!\(999") "000\-0000;;_
Caption	
Default Value	
Validation Rule	
Validation Text	
Required	No
Allow Zero Length	Yes
Indexed	No
Unicode Compression	No
IME Mode	No Control
IME Sentence Mode	None
Smart Tags	

Figure 6.6 Invoking the *Input Mask Wizard* from the *Field Properties*.

3. On the first page of the wizard (see Figure 6.5), select the *Phone Number* option under *Input Mask* list. Click inside the *Try It* text box at the bottom of the page to test the format.

The next two pages of the wizard allow us to modify the default format of selected mask. For example, we can change the placeholder character "#" of a phone number (see Figure 6.7).

4. Accept the default values for next two pages of the wizard and click *Finish* button to close the wizard. At this point, the Design View should resemble Figure 6.6. Try out input mask in the Datasheet View.

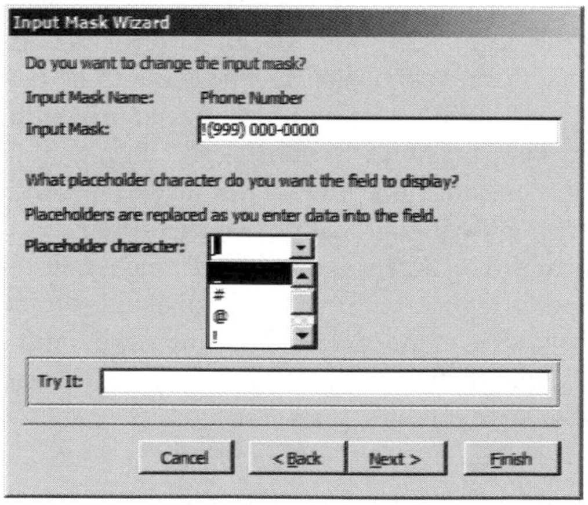

Input Mask Wizard

Do you want to change the input mask?

Input Mask Name: Phone Number

Input Mask: !(999) 000-0000

What placeholder character do you want the field to display?

Placeholders are replaced as you enter data into the field.

Placeholder character: _

Try It:

Cancel   < Back   Next >   Finish

Figure 6.7 The *Input Mask Wizard* page 2: Selecting the placeholder character.

6.5.2 Hands-On Tutorial: Using Validation Rule and Validation Text Properties

In this hands-on tutorial, we would like to validate the date entered by the user in the *DOB* (date of birth) field of the student table. This is to keep in line with the university's new policy to have students with age 16 and older. We use the *Validation Rule* and *Validation Text* properties of the *DOB* field to enforce this rule. This tutorial covers the following How-to topic:

■ How-to: use *Required*, *Validation Rules*, and *Validation Text* properties.
1. Open the student table in the Design View. Click on the *DOB* field to reveal its properties in the *Field Properties*.
2. Set the *Required* property to *Yes*. We thus force user to enter the *DOB* field value for each student record.
3. Next, set the *Validation Rule* and the *Validation Text* properties as shown below:
   ■ *Validation Rule*: > **Date()-(365*16)**
   ■ *Validation Text*: "Student age must be at least 16 or more!"
   Explanation: If the date entered is greater than today's date minus 365 × 16 days (i.e., 16 years), then Access should display an error message and invalidate the data (see Figure 6.8).
4. Save the changes made to the table, and verify the *Validation Rule* and *Validation Text* properties by entering erroneous data into the student table.

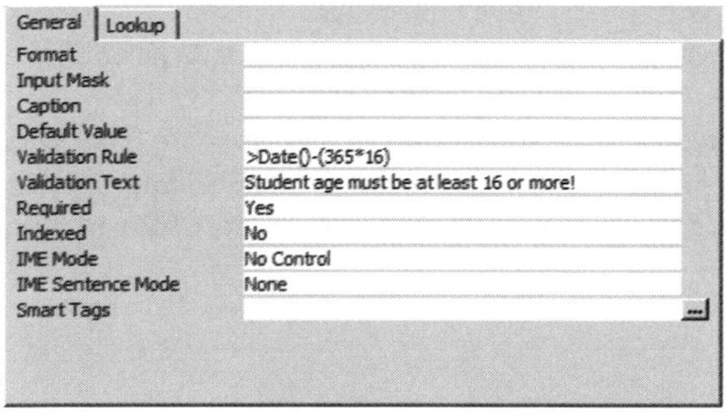

Figure 6.8 Using *Validation Rule* and *Validation Text* properties.

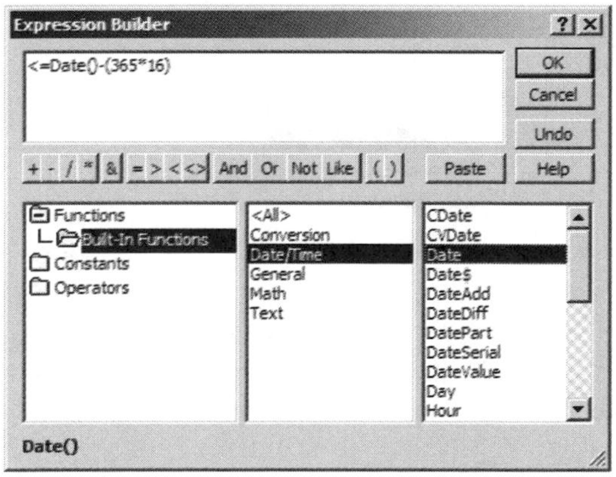

Figure 6.9 Working with the *Expression Builder*.

The validation rule expression can be constructed using the build button found at the end of the *Validation Rule* property entry. Click this button to open the *Expression Builder* dialog box. We can use existing object names and many built-in functions to build expressions.

When we try to save a table with a new validation rule, Access asks us if we would like to validate the existing data in the table. If we answer *No*, only new data entered or existing data when updated will be checked against the validation rule.

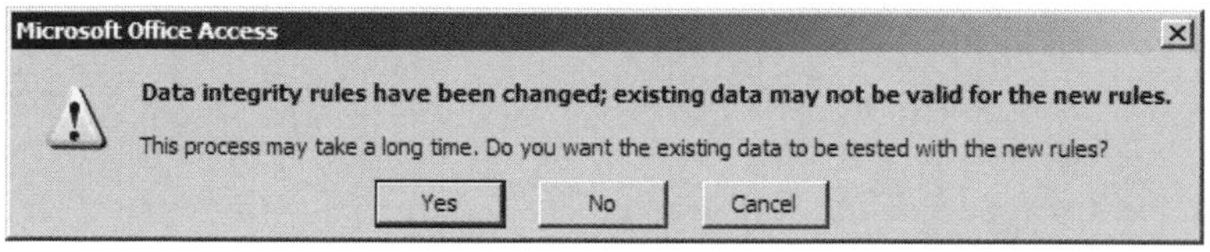

Figure 6.10 Prompt for testing the existing data for the new *validation rule*.

6.5.3 Hands-On Tutorial: Creating a Table Index

In this hands-on tutorial, we build an index on the *Class* field of the student table. This tutorial covers the following How-to topic:

- ■ How-to: create an index on a table field.
  1. Open the student table in the Design View and click on the *Class* field to view its field properties.
  2. Locate the *Indexed* property and change its value from *No* to *Yes*. There are two options available for selection: *Yes* (*Duplicates OK*) and *Yes* (*No Duplicates*). We select the former for primary key fields and later for non-primary key fields (see Figure 6.11).

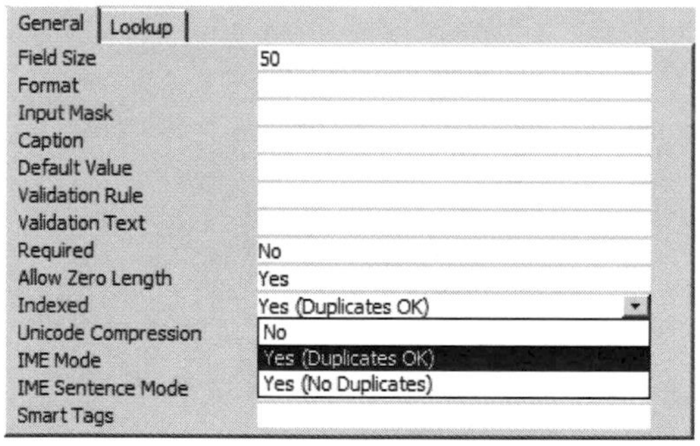

Figure 6.11 Setting-up an *Indexed* property to create table index.

Once the property is set to *Yes* for a selected field, Access builds an index on it. We can verify the creation of the *Class* field index by viewing a list of field indexes in the *Indexes* dialog box (see Figure 6.12). To open the *Indexes* dialog box, either click the *Indexes* button on the *Database* toolbar, or alternatively choose the View | Indexes option from the main menu.

We can use the *Indexes* dialog box to add multiple indexes to a table. We do so by first selecting the desired field from the drop-down menu in the second column (*Field Name*) of the dialog box. We then assign a logical name to the index in the first column (*Index Name*) and choose the sorting order for the indexed records in the *Sort Order* column.

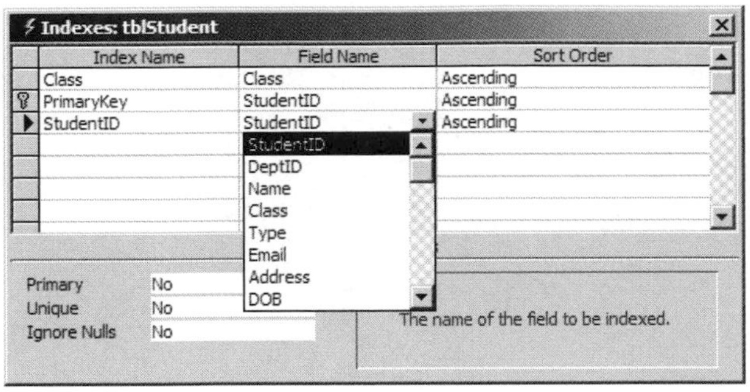

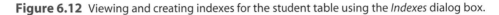

Figure 6.12 Viewing and creating indexes for the student table using the *Indexes* dialog box.

6.6 *The Lookup Wizard*

As the name suggests, *Lookup Wizard* helps us to "look-up" field values from columns of the same or other tables. It is a useful tool for foreign key fields. Creating a lookup for foreign key fields allows us to locate foreign key values from the primary key field. This helps avoid violations of referential integrity constraints (see Section 4.2.3) and also simplifies the data entry process. The *Lookup Wizard* appears as the tenth option in the data type drop-down list (see Figure 6.13). The *Lookup* properties for a field appear as a separate tab in the *Field Properties* half of the Design View. The following hands-on tutorial illustrates the use of *Lookup Wizard*.

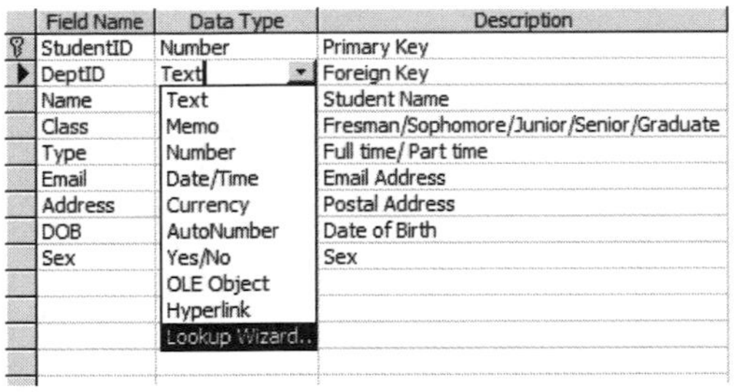

Figure 6.13 Setting-up the *Lookup* data type for the *DeptID* field.

6.6.1 Hands-On Tutorial: Using Lookup Wizard

In this hands-on tutorial, we create a lookup for the *DeptID* foreign key field in the student table. The lookup should be from the *DeptID* primary key field in the department table. We use *Lookup Wizard* to set up this lookup. This tutorial covers the following How-to topic:

- How-to: set-up lookup for table fields.
    1. Open the student table in the Design View and click on the *DeptID* field. Choose the *Lookup Wizard* option from the drop-down list of data types (see Figure 6.13). This should bring up the *Lookup Wizard*.
    2. Keep the default option of looking up values from an existing table and click *Next* (see Figure 6.14).

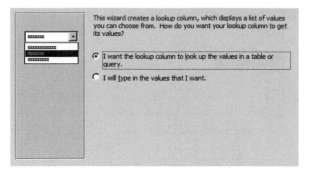

Figure 6.14 The *Lookup Wizard* page 1: Specifying the lookup source.

The *Lookup Wizard* provides two options on the first page. We can either look up values from a field of an existing table (for foreign keys), or we can enter a list of values to look up from (for simple data entry fields such as student class and type).

3. The wizard displays a list of existing tables to choose a Lookup table from on the next page. Select the department table and click *Next* (see Figure 6.15).

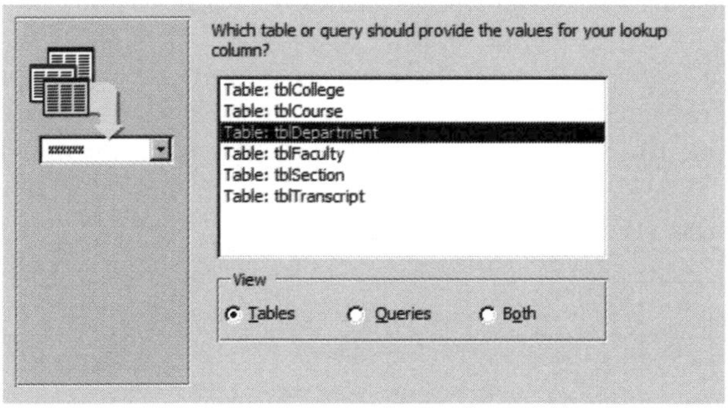

Figure 6.15 The *Lookup Wizard* page 2: Selecting a lookup table.

4. Select the *DeptID* and *Name* fields from the list of *Available Fields* to the list of *Selected Fields* (see Figure 6.16).

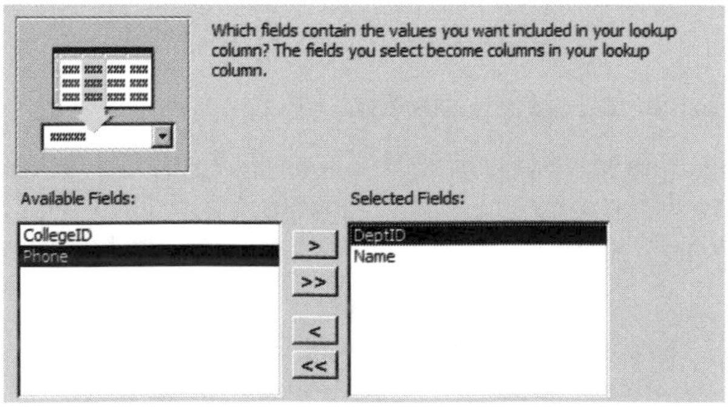

Figure 6.16 The *Lookup Wizard* page 3: Selecting a lookup field.

We choose two fields, one for the actual value (*DeptID*) and one for the display value (*Name*). When we look up for values of the *DeptID* field in the student table, we actually see the display value (name of the department). See Figure 6.18(a). However, when a lookup is performed (that is, a department name is selected), the actual value (*DeptID*) is stored in the *DeptID* field of the student table. Thus, the display value is only to ease the data selection on the user's part, but the actual field value is always stored in the database.

5. Accept the default sorting selection on the next page and click *Next*. We can optionally sort the lookup value display on the actual or display value field.

6. Accept the *Hide key column* check box selection and click *Finish* (see Figure 6.17).

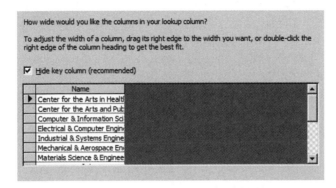

Figure 6.17 The *Lookup Wizard* page 4: Hiding the key column.

The Datasheet View of the student table with a lookup on the *DeptID* field is shown in Figure 6.18. Also note the Design View of the student table in the same figure. Under the *Lookup* tab in the *Field Properties*, we can see a *Combo Box* value has been assigned as a *Display Control* property. This is the control we will see for a lookup in the Datasheet View. Further, the *Row Source Type* property is set to *Table/Query* (corresponds to the selection on wizard's first page), and the *Row Source* property is set to a string representing an SQL query that actually brings the lookup value (see Chapter 9 for SQL queries).

Figure 6.18 (a) Lookup for *DeptID* field in the Datasheet View; (b) *Lookup* tab in the Design View.

6.6.2 The Lookup Tab

In this subsection, we discuss few important lookup properties on the *Lookup* tab of *Field Properties*.

Display Control: This property dictates the type of control that must be used to display the lookup values in the Datasheet View. The available options are *Combo Box*, *List Box*, and *Text Box*. The *Combo Box* and *List Box* are used to display foreign key field values, and the *Text Box* value is used for all other purposes.

Row Source Type and Row Source: We use the *Row Source Type* property to specify the source type of the lookup field. The *Row Source* property is used to specify the actual source to be used to retrieve the values. For example, for the row source type Table/Query, we have an SQL query as a row source.

Bound Column: The *Bound Column* property is used to specify the column that will provide the actual lookup values. In our example, we chose *DeptID* and *Name* as Lookup fields (the actual value and display value). Note that the *Bound Column* is set to 1, indicating the actual value should come from the *DeptID* field. In other words, the *Bound Column* property value distinguish selected fields as a value field and display field.

6.7   *Defining a Primary Key*

A primary key is the set of one or more fields that uniquely identifies a record. In other words, a primary key distinguishes one record from another. We discussed in Chapter 4 that each table in the relational database must have a primary key. In this section, we show how to specify the primary key of a table in Access.

In Access, assigning the primary key is simply a matter of a few mouse clicks. To assign a primary key, we do the following:

1. In the Design View, select the field(s) by clicking the row selector on the left-hand side of the *Field Name* column (press down the *Control* (Ctrl) key for multiple-field selection).
2. Click the *Primary Key* button on the *Database* toolbar, or alternatively right-click and select the *Primary Key* option from the shortcut menu (see Figure 6.19). We can also choose the Edit | Primary Key option from the main menu to achieve the same result.

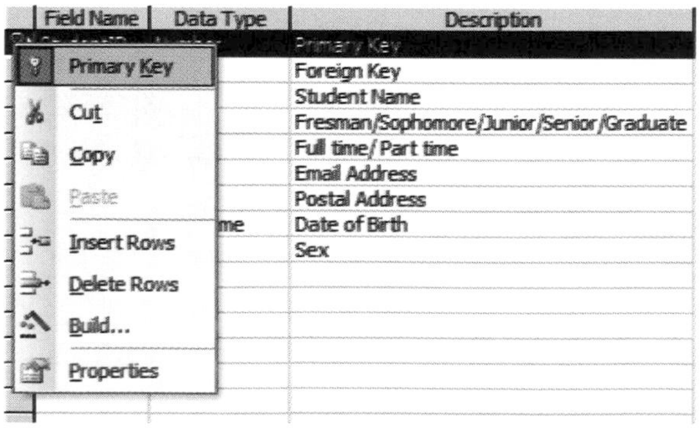

Figure 6.19 Defining a primary key in Design View.

Access displays a small "key symbol" on the row selector for the primary key field(s) to indicate that the key has now been defined. Access automatically acknowledges the definition of the primary key and will not allow keeping the primary key field(s) empty during the data entry process. Additionally, Access creates an index, called the *PrimaryKey* index, on primary key fields.

6.8 *Creating Access Tables by Using Import Wizard*

At times, we might have to create a table to suit data that we already have. We can use existing data to create and define a table in the Datasheet View as discussed earlier in this chapter. However, manually entering all the data (especially for large tables) in the Datasheet View might not always be feasible. The *Import Wizard* option allows us to import large amounts of existing data from external files, such as Excel or text files, directly into Access tables.

Following are the steps to create the section table of the university database using existing data in the Excel file.

1. To invoke the *Import Wizard*, right-click anywhere in the Database Window and select the *Import* option from the shortcut menu.
2. Access will first prompt us to select the external file to import. Select the "Course Table.xls" Excel file provided on the book Web site: www.dssbooks.com.
3. On the next page, Wizard displays the preview of the data. In case of an Excel file, it also prompts for selection of a worksheet within a file. Accept the default selection and click *Next*.
4. On the next page, we assign the first row in the Excel sheet as the column heading in the Access table.
5. We can either import the data to an existing table or create a new table for imported data. In this example, we import the course data to a new table (see Figure 6.20).
6. The next page allows us to modify field names, create indexes on fields, and decide to skip a column from importing (see Figure 6.21).
7. On the next page, we can specify the primary key of the table. We can choose from fields to be imported or let Access add a new ID field (see Figure 6.22).
8. On the last page, we name the new table.

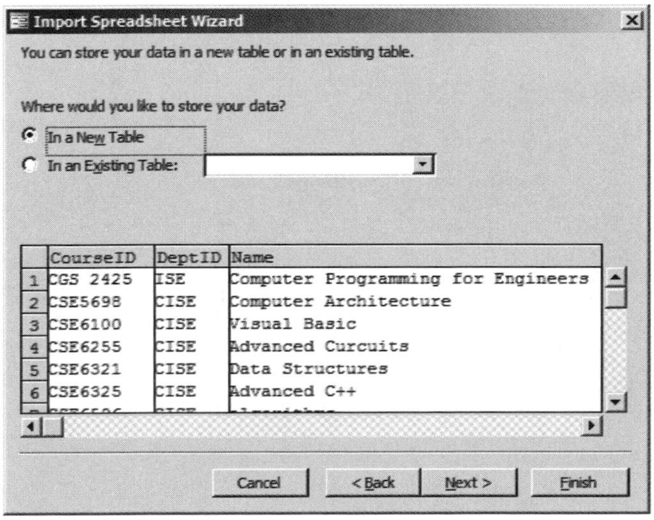

Figure 6.20 Creating Access tables by using *Import Wizard*.

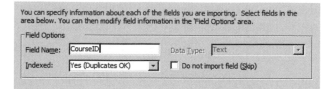

You can specify information about each of the fields you are importing. Select fields in the area below. You can then modify field information in the 'Field Options' area.

Field Options

Field Name: CourseID Data Type: Text

Indexed: Yes (Duplicates OK) ☐ Do not import field (Skip)

Figure 6.21 Selecting the fields to create in the *Import Wizard*.

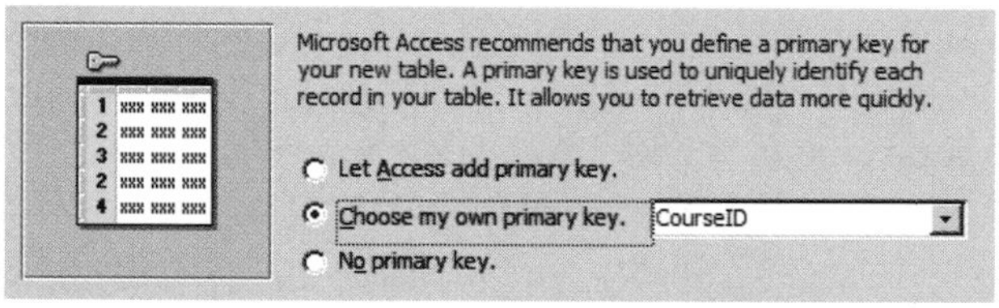

Microsoft Access recommends that you define a primary key for your new table. A primary key is used to uniquely identify each record in your table. It allows you to retrieve data more quickly.

○ Let Access add primary key.

◉ Choose my own primary key. CourseID

○ No primary key.

Figure 6.22 Defining a primary key in the *Import Wizard*.

6.9   *Working with Table Properties*

Like a table field, a table itself has its own properties that control the behavior and appearance of the table. To view the table properties, we first open the table in the Design View and then click the *Property* button on the toolbar. Alternatively, we can choose the View | Properties option from the main menu. The *Table Properties* dialog box for the student table is shown in Figure 6.23.

The first property, *Description*, is used to describe the table and its data. Next, the *Default View* property dictates which view should be used to open the table by default. The next available properties are *Validation Rule* and *Validation Text*. These properties are similar to the *Validation Rule* and *Validation Text* properties of a table field (see Section 6.5.2), but the former is applicable at the record level, while the latter is applicable at the field level.

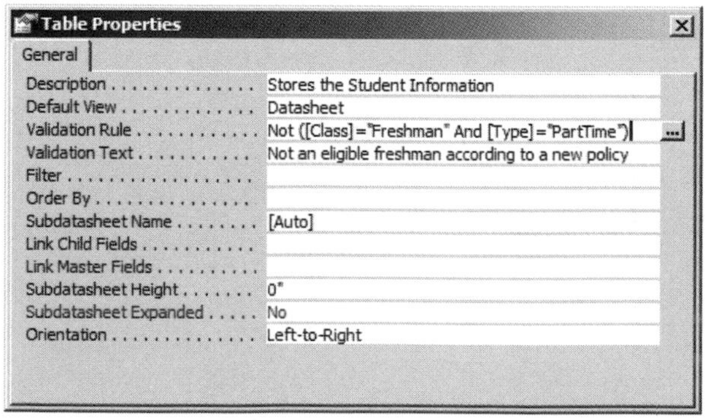

Table Properties

General

Description . . . . Stores the Student Information
Default View . . . . Datasheet
Validation Rule . . . . Not ([Class]="Freshman" And [Type]="PartTime")
Validation Text . . . . Not an eligible freshman according to a new policy
Filter . . . .
Order By . . . .
Subdatasheet Name . . . . [Auto]
Link Child Fields . . . .
Link Master Fields . . . .
Subdatasheet Height . . . . 0"
Subdatasheet Expanded . . . . . No
Orientation . . . . Left-to-Right

Figure 6.23 The *Table Properties* dialog box for the student table.

Table Validation Rule and Table Validation Text

The *Validation Rule* property validates the data entered into a row. Consider, for example, that a university has a new policy that no part-time freshman can be a student. We add this validation rule as an expression (see Figure 6.23). The validation rule for a table is checked when a new row is entered in the table. If the new row is not a valid row as per the validation rule, then the validation text is used to display an error message.

6.10 *In-Class Assignment*

The marketing department of a firm wants to create a database with detailed information about its customers. This will facilitate the process of designing strategies to identify potential customers for new products. Create a table that includes the following personal information about each customer: address, phone number, and email. Name this table as *tblCustomers*. Make the following modifications to the table to improve its functionality:

a. For each customer, the following information must be recorded: identification number, full name, address, zip code, phone number, and fax number. Make each of these fields required fields. Assign appropriate field as a primary key of the table.

b. Use the *Input Mask Wizard* to appropriately mask the phone number and fax number fields.

The department researchers are also interested in demographic characteristics of the customers, such as age and gender. They plan to scan the data in the database based on particular age ranges and gender.

c. Add additional fields for these characteristics. Set the default value of the field *Gender* to "M." The values to be entered in the *Age* field should be between 1 and 100. Display an error message for inappropriate age values.

d. Create indexes on the *Age* and *Gender* fields to facilitate an efficient search based on these fields.

6.11 *Summary*

- Tables are fundamental elements of a relational database and act as data foundation objects.
- Tables can be built using following options:
  a. Creating a table in Datasheet View.
  b. Creating a table in Design View.
  c. Creating a table by using *Table Wizard*.
  d. Creating a table by using *Import Wizard*.
- The field data type dictates what kind of data can reside in the field. Field properties control the behavior of a field and its data. The following are a few important field properties:

- *Format*: controls how to display data.
- *Input Mask*: controls how to input data.
- *Validation Rule*: controls what data can be stored.
- *Indexed*: allows setting an index on a field for searching.
- *Lookup Wizard*: allows looking up values from other fields.
- Table properties control the behavior of a table. We can use the validation rules to control how data is entered or modified at the record level.

6.12   *Exercises*

6.12.1   Review Questions

1. What is the purpose of assigning a data type to a field?

2. Describe the difference between the *Number* and the *AutoNumber* data types, and give an example of when to use each.

3. List the format options for the *Currency* data type.

4. Describe the difference between *Format*, *Input Mask*, and the *Validation Rule* properties.

5. What data type and format should be selected for the number -2.6×10^{30} in Access?

6. What is an index? When should we index a field?

7. Describe the advantages of creating a table in the Design View as compared to in the Datasheet View.

8. What are the benefits of using the *Lookup* properties to determine the values of a field?

9. What are the two ways by which the *Lookup Wizard* can display values in a table?

10. Why does Access not allow a primary key field to be empty when entering records into a table?

11. Suppose a database of driver's license information contains the following fields for each driver: birth date, height, eye color, gender, license number, address, and phone number. Which of these fields should be chosen as the primary key? Why?

12. How can we enforce mandatory data entry into a field?

13. What is the difference between a field *Validation Rule* property and a table *Validation Rule* property? Which type of rule allows us to satisfy conditions in multiple fields at once?

14. Refer to the review question 6 in Chapter 3. Create a list of tables necessary for this database. Identify the fields that should be included in each table.

6.12.2   Hands-On Exercises

NOTE: *The database files for these hands-on exercises are available at: www.dssbooks.com.*

1. Hospitals use databases to keep track of information about patients, doctors, medications, suppliers, and patient bills. The database *Hospital.mdb* consists of the following tables: *tblPatients*, *tblDoctors*, *tblMedicines*, *tblSuppliers*, and *tblBillInfo*. Use this database to answer the following questions.

Update *tblDoctor* to reflect this change:

   a. Dr. Peter Harper is leaving the hospital. Remove his record from the database.

   b. Dr. James Kramer is being hired by the Pediatrics department. Add him to the database.

   c. The hospital executives have examined the distribution of the doctors in different departments. They have come to the conclusion that instead of classifying the doctors based on the department they belong to, they should do the classification based on the doctors' specializations. The database should reflect this change. Change the *Department* field name to *Specialization*.

   d. To ensure that the assignment of duties is not biased, switch the primary key from *LastName* to *DoctorID*.

   e. In the the Datasheet View, move the *DoctorID* field in front of the *LastName* field.

   f. Add a new field with the address of each doctor.

Update *tblBillInfo* to reflect this change:

   g. A patient, Brian Ginger, visited Dr. Knight on 1/10/2002. Brian had a cold. Dr. Knight recommended that he take "Cold Reliever" for 3 days. Brian will have to pay $10.50 for the medicine.

Update *tblPatients* to reflect these changes:

   h. Add a new field to input the telephone number of each patient.

   i. Add a new field to input the name of a contact person for each patient.

   j. Olga Brown is a new patient. Her address is, "310 North Side." Her phone number is (440) 582-8134, and her contact person is Sandra Lee. Add her information in the database.

   k. Stacy Western changed her address recently to: "493 South Side." Make the update.

2. The owner of a campus textbook store has noticed that during the first weeks of classes, the customers are waiting in long lines to buy books. Concerned about losing business to other stores, the owner wants to perform a data analysis. From

this analysis, she is expecting to understand whether she should hire a few seasonal employees or reschedule the existing ones. The analysis includes collecting data about line length, the number of cashiers attending a customer, and the number of idle cashiers. She is planning to collect this data every hour for one week (e.g., the number of customers in the line at exactly 9 AM, 10 AM, 11 AM, etc.). She also wants to record the comments from customers waiting in line during the observations. Create a table in the Design View to record the results from these observations (Hint: we need four fields). Give appropriate names, data types, and descriptions to each field. Assign a primary key. Title the table *tblQueue*. Finally, make the following modifications to the table to improve the functionality:

a. The store is open from 9:00 AM to 6:00 PM seven days a week. Ensure that the times of day entered in the table fall into the store hours.

b. Enter several records of mock data into the table to test the modifications.

3. The manager of a manufacturing plant is about to place an order for new material handling equipment for the plant. Every year, he checks whether the equipment is in good working condition. Based on the observations, he decides which equipment to replace and which to keep for another year. Other factors that affect his decision are the cost of new equipment, the age of the current equipment, the equipment's useful life, the yearly maintenance cost, and the salvage value. However, no piece of equipment is kept longer than three years. The following material handling equipment is used in the plant: boom cranes, chain hoists, leveling jacks, electric winches, motorized trolleys, and forklifts. (Hint: Think of *Lookup Wizard*.) Open the database entitled *EquipmentOrder*. Create a new table called *tblEquipment* with all of the necessary information to assist the manager in making his decision. Choose appropriate names, data types, and descriptions for each field. Make the following modifications to the table to improve the functionality:

a. The cost of new equipment depends on the vendor from which the equipment is purchased. Use the *Lookup Wizard* to allow the user to look up the prices offered from the table *tblVendorPrices* when choosing a vendor

and setting the cost of new equipment. The user should be able to view all three fields (*Equipment*, *Vendor*, and *Price*) with their column headings in the lookup.

b. Test the modifications through examples.

4. A team of industrial engineers is designing a new workstation for the assembly of a product. The team plans to consider ergonomic factors in the design to minimize fatigue of the assembly personnel. To create the most ergonomically sophisticated design possible, the team decides to collect suggestions from the current assembly personnel. The team prepares a questionnaire for the assembly workers. It contains the following questions:

■ Do you prefer to gather all of the parts prior to assembly or one part at a time during assembly?

■ Do you prefer to use both hands during the assembly process?

■ Do you prefer to stand, sit, or alternate between the two?

■ During assembly, do you prefer to hold the product above the table or on the table?

Create a table in Access that allows the team to analyze each worker's motions and save it as *tblErgonomics*. Make the following modifications to the table to improve the functionality:

a. Create a primary key that uniquely identifies each record.

b. Using the *Lookup* properties, allow the user to select the data for each field from a list (with the exception of the primary key).

5. A bank requires a database to record the transactions made by its account holders. The following information is recorded during a transaction: a transaction identification number, the date and time, the account number, the name of the account holder, the social security number of the employee who performed the transaction, a short description, the amount of money deposited or withdrawn, and the service charge, if applicable. Create the table *tblBankTransactions* with appropriate fields. Make the following modifications to improve functionality:

a. Accounts are identified by a twelve-digit number with hyphens between every four digits. Create an input mask for the field that identifies the account so the entries fit this format.

b. The date and time of a transaction are recorded. Include a field for the date and a field for the time in the table. The format for the date should be *Medium Date* and the format for the time should be *Medium Time*.

c. There are three transaction types that can be performed: withdrawal, deposit, or service charge. Include a field that describes the type of transaction by allowing the user to choose from a list of the categories.

d. Withdrawals and charges must always be negative to indicate a decrease in the account balance. Similarly, deposits must always be positive to indicate an increase. Ensure that the entries into these fields fit these requirements. Display error messages if the requirements are not met.

6. The table created in the previous exercise is part of a larger database used by the bank. This database, *Bank.mdb*, stores information about the bank's accounts, account holders, and employees. Open the database *Bank.mdb* and make the following modifications to it:

a. Import the table *tblBankTransactions* into the bank database.

b. Each transaction involves some activities with one of the bank accounts. Therefore, the field *AccountID* is part of the table *tblBankTransactions*. Include *AccountID* in the table if it is not already done. Create an index for *AccountID*.

c. The field *ID* in the table *tblAccounts* is identified by a twelve-digit number with hyphens between every four digits. Create an input mask for the field that identifies the account so the entries fit this format.

d. Using the *Input Mask Wizard*, create input masks for telephone number, extension, and fax number fields in table *tblAccounts* and *tblEmployees*.

7. A quality assurance expert at a soft drink bottling plant has been assigned to develop a plan to reduce the number of defective bottles that the plant produces. To find the cause of the defects, she plans to analyze the effect of several factors associated with the bottling lines and the types of bottles being produced. The expert has randomly sampled sets of bottles from different bottling lines and counted the number of defective bottles in the sample. She keeps track of the bottling line number, the size of the sample, and the number

of nonconforming bottles. She then computes the fraction of nonconforming bottles. Open the table *tblDefects* in the database *Bottling.mdb* to view her results. Make the following modifications to *tblDefects*:

a. Check that her data has been entered correctly by verifying that the fraction of nonconformities equals the number of nonconforming units divided by the sample size. Correct the data in the *Fraction Nonconforming* field if it does not follow this guideline (of course, we have to use *Validation Rules* property).

b. To make her data readable, display the data in the *Fraction Nonconforming* field as a percentage with no decimal places.

c. The expert has collected 25 samples for each bottling line so that she can determine which line has the majority of the defects. She records in the table *tblDefects* the number of defects in each sample for each bottling line. Modify the primary key of *tblDefects* so it consists of both the line number and the sample number.

8. Horse racing is one of the most highly documented sports. There are thousands of pieces of data published on each upcoming race. This data is available to us, and we need to build a database to manage all of this information.

- For each horse, the following information is recorded: name, owner, age, height, weight, breed (Arabian, English, etc.), parents, a history of races attended, races won, and injuries.

- For each jockey, the following information is recorded: social security number, weight, height, age, the number of years he or she has been racing, race history, and major achievements.

- For each racetrack, the following information is recorded: name, address, type (dirt, turf, etc.), and distance.

- For each race, the following information is recorded: name, distance, the number of times a year it is held, its location, the first time it was organized, attendance, prize amount, and the winners of each race.

9. Open the database *HorseRace.mdb*. Create a new table in this database called *tblHorses* that stores the following information about each horse: name, owner's name, age, height, weight, breed, parents' names, past wins, and past injuries.

Make the following modifications to the table to improve functionality:

a. Define a primary key that uniquely identifies each horse.

b. Create appropriate captions for each field to make the table user-friendly.

c. Create an input mask for the height field that displays the height using feet-and-inches notation; e.g., 6′10″ denotes 6 feet and 10 inches.

d. Using the *Lookup Wizard*, look up the values for the breed field in *tblBreeds* so that the user may select from the list of breeds when entering data into the table.

e. For the Injuries field, enable the user to check whether or not the horse is currently injured.

f. For the history of races attended and races won, enable the user to write several paragraphs of information.

10. The *University.mdb* database includes information about the course timetable of an academic institution. Create the following database tables.

- For each course, the following information is recorded: an identification number, the name of the course, the name of the instructor, the number of periods each week it is taught, the number of students attending the course, and the name of the group of courses to which it belongs.

- For each teacher, the following information is recorded: his or her social security number, his or her name, the name of the department he or she works for, the area of specialization, and the yearly salary.

- For each class period, the following information is recorded: period number, starting time, and ending time.

- For each room, the following information is recorded: room number, room type (classroom, office, auditorium, or computer lab), and capacity.

11. Open *University.mdb* and review the existing tables. Make the following modifications to the tables to improve the functionality:

a. In *tblRooms*, allow the user to select the room type from a list of possible room types: classroom, office, computer lab, and auditorium.

b. The capacity of a room varies according to the room type. For now, however, limit the capacity of each room type to 150 persons.

c. Each department at the university is assigned a code that consists of three letters. For example, the Industrial and Systems Engineering department is assigned the code ISE. Create an input mask for the *Department* field in table *tblClasses* and *tblTeachers* that will allow only codes in this format to be entered.

d. The university should be able to quickly search the database for teachers in certain departments and certain salary ranges. Create indices in *tblTeachers* that make this function possible.

e. Create an input mask for the social security number of teachers and students in the appropriate tables.

f. Create a new table called *tblPeriods*. This table should maintain the information about the starting time and ending time of class periods.

g. Create a final table for this database called *tblAssignments*. This table should record the following information for each class offered in the university: class ID, social security number of the professor teaching the class, the days of the week the class meets, the time it meets, the social security numbers of the students attending the class, the classroom number, and the letter grade assigned to each student.

h. In *tblAssignments*, allow the user to select a grade from a list of possible letter grades (A, B+, B, C+, C, D, F, and S).

i. In *tblAssignments*, the user prefers to look up the starting and ending time when assigning the class time period. This information can be found in table *tblPeriods*. Allow the user to see the three columns of this table when making his or her selection.

12. Florida Bus Traveling Agency needs to computerize their reservation database systems. The corporation has 18 buses spread over 20 routes to various destinations in Florida. There are two types of buses: 10 regular buses with a seating capacity of 48, and 8 super deluxe buses with a seating capacity of 36.

- The buses travel certain routes. For each route, the following information is recorded: route identification number, name of the city of origin, name of the destination, and type of bus that is assigned on that route.

■ Customers usually book trips that do not necessarily have to correspond to bus routes. A trip starts in one of the cities that is visited by a route (not necessarily the city of the origin of the route) and ends in another city visited by that route (not necessarily the city of the destination of the route). For every trip that a customer books his or her ticket, the following information is recorded: trip identification number, city of origin, city of destination, departure time, and arrival time.

Open the database *BusTrips.mdb*. The database consists of the following tables: *tblBuses*, *tblTrip*, and *tblRoutes*.

a. Add a new table called *tblTransactions*. This table should have the following fields: *RouteID*, *TripID*, *BusID*, *Departure* (date and time), *Arrival* (date and time), *Bus Capacity*, *Reservations*, and *Available*?

Make the following updates to *tblTransactions*:

b. Format the fields *Departure* and *Arrival* to show the time and date (of departure and arrival) together in the same field.

c. The departure date and time should be no earlier than the present date and time.

d. Use *Lookup Wizard* to allow the user to look up the capacity of each bus from the table *tblBuses* when choosing the bus capacity. Note that the bus capacity depends on the *BusID*; therefore, the user should be able to see both fields *BusID* and Capacity from table *tblBuses* and choose the appropriate capacity.

e. The city of origin cannot be the same as the destination city.

f. The number of reserved seats should not exceed the bus capacity.

13. The annual Bolder Boulder is one of America's top 10 km races. The race is held each Memorial Day in Boulder, Colorado. This race attracts world-class runners as well as casual joggers. The race has grown to approximately 20,000 runners. The race is a point-to-point race beginning at the Bank of Boulder at the northeast corner of the city, winding throughout the city streets, and ending near the town center in the University of Colorado's football stadium.

The organizers record the following information for each race: the date of the race, the total number of runners registered for the race (on-line pre-registration is possible), the actual number of participants, the number of male runners, the number of female runners, the name of the male winner, the name of the female winner, the name of the male master (runner of more than 40 years of age) winner, and the name of the female master winner. In addition, the following information about each participant is recorded: social security number, name, birthday, gender, address, and certified personal record (PR) running times for a 10 km race. Create a new database called BoulderRace.mdb that contains all of the necessary tables for the database. Consider the following when preparing the tables:

a. The registration form for a race requires the following information: social security number, name, gender, birthday, and address. Note that this information is required and should not be omitted. Create a table called *tblRunners* that records the necessary information for each runner.

b. To improve the functionality of the table *tblRunners*, make the following updates: (i) create an input mask for the field *SSN*; (ii) format the field *Birthday* to *Short Date* type; (iii) set the default value for the field *Gender* to *M*.

c. Create a table entitled *tblRaceInfo* that contains the following information about a race: race ID, name, date, location, length, number of runners registered for the race, number of runners who finished the race, number of female runners, number of male runners, social security number and time of the overall female winner, social security number and the time of overall male winner.

d. To improve the functionality of table *tblRaceInfo*, make the following updates: (i) the number of female runners and the number of male runners should together total the actual number of participants in the race; (ii) create an input mask for the fields that contain the social security numbers of the male and female winners; (iii) format the field *Race Date* to *Medium Date* type.

e. Create a table *tblAgeGroups*. The runners are classified in an age group based on their age. The ages groups are created as follows: the first age group consists of runners up to 5 years old; the second age group consists of runners between 6 and 10 years old; the third age group consists of runners between 11 and 15 years old, and so on up to the 15th age group, which consists of runners 71 years old and up.

f. Create a table *tblResults*. This table should contain the following information: race ID, runner's social security number, age group, gender, and running time.

g. Use the *Lookup Wizard* to allow the user to look up the age group of a runner when entering the race results in the table *tblResults*. The user should be able to see both columns of the table *tblAgeGroup* (age group and age interval).

h. To select the winners, the organizers of the race must be able to search the table *tblResults* for the age, gender, and running time of each runner. Describe what the person responsible for this database should do in order to collect this information.

seven Relationships: Linking Access Tables

chapter OVERVIEW

7.1   *Introduction*

In Chapter 3, we defined relationship as an association between one or more entities. Consider, for example, an association between STUDENT and COURSE entities; in such a relationship, students register for courses and receive grades (an attribute of the relationship). In this chapter, we will discuss how to specify relationships in Access.

We categorized relationships based on cardinality (one-to-one, many-to-one, and many-to-many relationships) and based on degree (unary, binary, and ternary relationships) of a relationship. The *register* relationship in Figure 7.1 is a binary, many-to-many relationship.

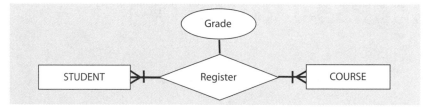

Figure 7.1 The STUDENT-COURSE relationship; student *register* for courses.

Using the mapping techniques from Chapter 4, we can easily convert the E-R diagram in Figure 7.1 into a relational schema of Figure 7.2(a). We then use Access's *Relationships Window* to specify relationships and referential integrity constraints between Access tables (see Figure 7.2(b)). The **Relationships Window** serves as a powerful graphical tool for defining relationships and is the subject matter of this chapter.

Topics   This chapter discusses the following topics:

■ How to define relationships in Relationships Window.
■ Types of relationships.
■ How to work with existing relationships.

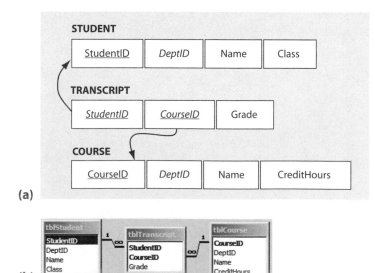

Figure 7.2 (a) The relational schema for STUDENT-COURSE relationship; (b) Access's Relationships Window for the relational schema in (a).

7.2 *Defining Relationships in the Relationships Window*

In Access, the Relationships Window defines relationships. This window features powerful graphical user interface tools that enable us to define, view, and edit relationships between Access tables. Specifically, these tools allow us to add and relate tables, to specify relationship types, to enforce referential integrity, and to specify the join types. We will explore these options in detail as we go through the chapter. The discussion on join types is deferred to Section 8.3.

A completely designed Relationships Window presents a list of all database tables with their field names. The window displays the primary key of each table in boldface (see Figure 7.3). The lines joining the common attributes of tables depict the relationships between those two tables. If the referential integrity constraint has been enforced for a relationship, then Access displays the type of relationship on an adjoining line. For example, in the case of a one-to-many relationship, the "one" side of the relationship shows the digit "1" and the "many" side of the relationship displays the "∞" symbol. Refer to the Relationships Window of the university database in Figure 7.3.

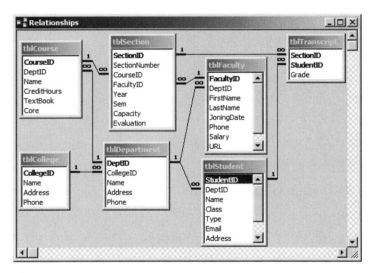

Figure 7.3 The Access Relationships Window.

We will now use the university database to illustrate the procedure of defining relationships. To better elucidate this procedure, we have divided it into several subsections. Our discussion includes: opening the Relationships Window; adding tables to the Relationships Window; exploring the *Relationships* toolbar and menus; drawing the relationships lines; enforcing referential integrity; and specifying types of relationships.

7.2.1 Opening the Relationships Window

To open the Relationships Window, do the following:

1. Open the university database file for this chapter.
2. From the active Database Window, click the *Relationships* button on the toolbar or choose the Tools | Relationships option from the main menu.

7.2.2   Adding Tables to Relationships Window

If we were opening the Relationships Window for the first time, we would see a *Show Table* dialog box (see Figure 7.4). We open the *Show Table* dialog box manually as follows:

■ Click the *Show Table* button on the toolbar (see Table 7.1),or
■ Select the Relationships | Show Table option from the main menu (see Figure 7.5).

The *Show Table* dialog box displays the list of all database tables. We add tables from the dialog box to the Relationships Window as follows:

1. Select the desired tables and click the *Add* button. For multiple selections, hold the *Shift* or *Control* (Ctrl) key while selecting the tables.
2. To return to the Relationships Window, click *Close* button.

Once added, tables are displayed in the form of field lists in the Relationships Window. Note that the primary key fields of each table appear in boldface (see Figure 7.3).

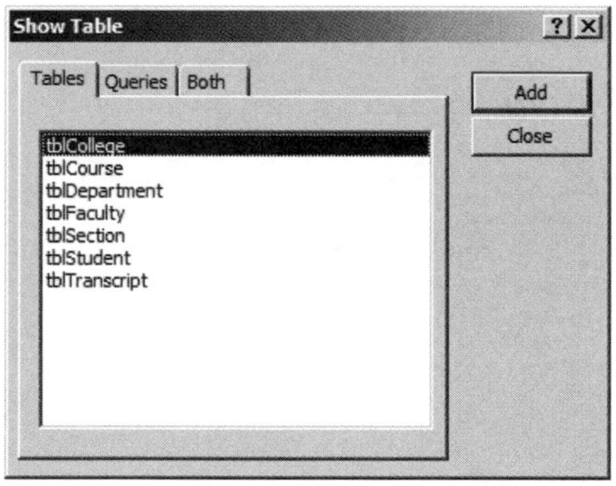

Figure 7.4 The *Show Table* dialog box.

7.2.3   Exploring *Relationships* Toolbar and Menu

The Relationships Window has a number of frequently used features accessible through toolbar buttons and the *Relationships* menu. These features assist us in working with the relationships. Table 7.1 lists and summarizes a few important features in the *Relationships* toolbar and menu.

Figure 7.5 The *Relationships* menu.

Table 7.1 Options in *Relationships* toolbar and menu.

Buttons	Name	Main Menu	Function
	Show Table	Relationships	Show Table	Opens the *Show Table* dialog box.
	Show Direct Relationships	Relationships	Show Direct	Displays the relationships for the selected table.
	Show All Relationships	Relationships	Show All	Displays all the relationships.
	Clear Layout	Edit	Clear Layout	Clears the layout by removing tables and relationships from the display. This does not alter relationship definitions.
—	—	Relationships	Hide Table	Temporarily hides the selected table.
—	—	Relationships	Edit Relationships	Opens the *Edit Relationships* dialog box for selected relationships.

7.2.4 Drawing a Relationship Line

In Access, drawing a line between two tables defines a relationship. The process of drawing a line can be divided into two sub tasks:

1. Deciding the common field from two tables to draw the line between the two fields, and
2. Drawing the line and enforcing referential integrity constraint.

To draw a line, we drag a common field from the field list of one table and drop it on the common field of another table. For example, to define the relationships between *tblStudent* and *tblTranscript* in the university database, we first decide the common field, *StudentID*. Note that *StudentID* is the primary key in the student table and the foreign key in the transcript table. In general, we choose fields from two tables for which there is a referential integrity arrow depicted in the relational schema. We then drag the *StudentID* field of the student table on *StudentID* field of the transcript table (see Figure 7.6). The direction of drag-and-drop is irrelevant to the relationship definition.

At this point, Access automatically opens the *Edit Relationships* dialog box. This dialog box is used to enforce the referential integrity constraint. We will discuss enforcing this constraint in the next subsection, for now click *OK* to create the relationship without editing it.

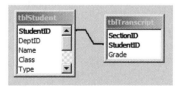

Figure 7.6 Drawing a relationships line.

7.2.5   Enforcing Referential Integrity

A *referential integrity constraint* ensures that the foreign key values of a relation must come from the primary key values of the related relation; otherwise, the value of a foreign key must be NULL (see Chapter 4 for details). The referential integrity constraint prevents the creation of *orphan records* in the tables and thus maintains the consistency between two tables that are connected by a primary key-foreign key relationship. If we refer to the table with primary key of the relation as *parent table* and the table with the foreign key of the relation as *child table*, an orphan record is the record for which there is no related parent record. For example, consider the One-to-Many relationship between the student and department tables. The primary key of the department table, *DeptID*, is the foreign key in the student table. A referential integrity constraint ensures that the value of the *DeptID* in the student table matches one of the departments in the department table or *DeptID* in the student table must be NULL. Thus, no records in the student table will have department assigned that does not exist in the department table, i.e., there will be no orphan records.

Fortunately, Access simplifies enforcement of a referential integrity constraint. We simply check the *Enforce Referential Integrity* check box in the *Edit Relationships* dialog box to enforce the constraint.

To enforce referential integrity, do the following:

1. Open the *Show Table* dialog box and add department table to the Relationships Window (note that we have already added the student table to the window).
2. Drag the *DeptID* field from one table to the *DeptID* field of the other table. This should open the *Edit Relationships* dialog box.
3. Check the *Enforce Referential Integrity* check box to enforce the constraint (see Figure 7.7).

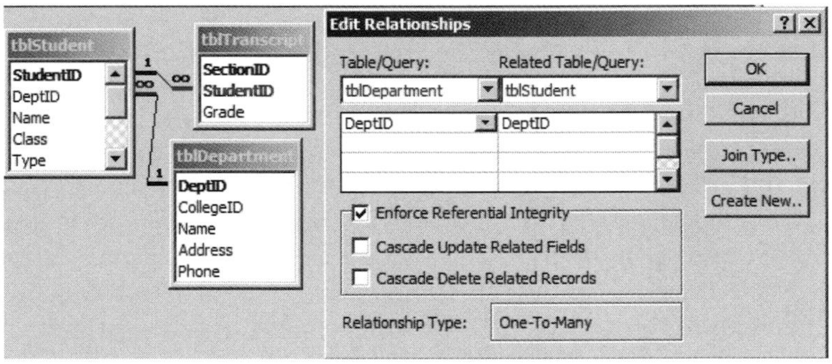

Figure 7.7 Enforcing referential integrity using *Edit Relationships* dialog box.

We will next consider another example of enforcing the referential integrity constraint in which relationships already exist among the tables. We drew a relationship line between *tblStudent* and *tblTranscripts* in the previous section but did not enforce the referential integrity constraint.

1. Open the *Edit Relationships* dialog box. To do so, either:
   ■ Select the relationship and right-click to choose the *Edit Relationships* option, or
   ■ Select the relationship and choose Relationships | Edit Relationships option from the main menu.
2. In the *Edit Relationships* dialog box, check *Enforce Referential Integrity* check box to enforce the constraint.

Before we leave this subsection, we would like to make two observations about the *Edit Relationships* dialog box:

Observation 1: The type of a relationship for the tables under consideration is automatically detected and is displayed at the bottom of the *Edit Relationships* dialog box. Also, after enforcing the constraint for a relationship, notice that the "1" and "∞" symbols indicating a relationship type are displayed in the Relationship Window.

Observation 2: As we check the constraint enforcement option in the *Edit Relationships* dialog box, two other options related to cascade updates and cascade deletes become available. We will discuss these two options in detail in the next subsection.

7.2.6 Cascade Updates and Cascade Deletes

Access simplifies enforcement of the referential integrity constraint. However, following are the few conditions that must hold *before* the enforcement of referential integrity:

Rule 1: The common field on "one" side of the relationship must be a primary key field or must have a unique index. If we try to enforce referential integrity between, for example, the *Name* field in *tblDepartment* and the *Name* field in *tblFaculty*, Access will display an error message.

Rule 2: If we are planning to enforce the referential integrity constraint, then we have to have the same data type for linking fields. The *AutoNumber* and *Number* data types constitute the only exceptions, provided that their field size property is set to *ReplicationID*.

Rule 3: When enforcing the constraint, the existing data in the tables cannot violate referential integrity constraint. For example, while enforcing the referential integrity between *tblStudent* and *tblDepartment*, no existing student can have a *DeptID* not listed in *tblDepartment*.

Following are the few conditions that must hold *after* the enforcement of referential integrity:

Rule 4: Once the referential integrity constraint is in place, we cannot delete a record from the parent table if a record exists in the child table with the same key value. For example, once the department table (the parent table) and the student table (the child table) are linked and the constraint is enforced, we cannot delete a department from *tblDepartment* as long as a student in *tblStudent* belongs to that department.

Rule 5: Similarly, once the constraint is enforced, we cannot update the common field from the parent table if corresponding records exist in the child table. For example, we cannot update the *DeptID* in *tblDepartment* as long as a student in the student table belongs to that department.

Maintaining the last two conditions related to the referential integrity can be tedious. Consider, for example, if we have to update the *DeptID* for Industrial Engineering from "ISE" to "ISENG" in the department table. Now to obey the *Rule 5* to maintain the referential integrity constraint, we must first update the *DeptID* field in the student table for all the students that belong to Industrial Engineering. That is, we update the *DeptID* field in the student table from "ISE" to "ISENG." We can then update the "ISE" record in the department table as required. In general, it is tedious to manually maintain *Rule 4* and *5* pertaining to deleting and updating records with the referential integrity constraint. Access makes this job easy with the *cascade update* and *cascade deletes* check boxes in the *Edit Relationships* dialog box.

Cascade Delete Related Records   When we enforce the referential integrity constraints in the *Edit Relationships* dialog box, the *Cascade Delete Related Fields* option becomes available. We check this box to allow cascade deletes. If we delete a record with a unique field in the parent table, Access automatically deletes the related records in the child table. For example, if we decide to remove a particular college from *tblCollege*, Access automatically deletes all of the related department records from *tblDepartment*. The cascade delete, as the name suggest, *cascades* the effect and will also remove the student and faculty records associated with the deleted college.

Once we check *Cascade Delete Related Records* option, we have to be very cautious whenever we delete records. If we have not properly examined the relationship, we could mistakenly delete a large amount of useful data.

Cascade Update Related Fields   When we enforce the referential integrity constraints in the *Edit Relationships* dialog box, the *Cascade Update Related Fields* option becomes available. We check this box to allow the cascade updates. Thus, if we update a unique field in the parent table, Access automatically updates the related records in the child table. For example, if we decide to update all the student identification numbers, i.e., the *StudentID* field in *tblStudent* (the parent table) from a eight-digit number to a nine-digit numbers by appending a digit 9, the related records in *tblTranscript* (the child table) are automatically updated to reflect this change. If we update the *DeptID* in the department table, then not only the related records in the student tables will be updated, but because of cascade updates, records from section and faculty tables will also automatically get updated.

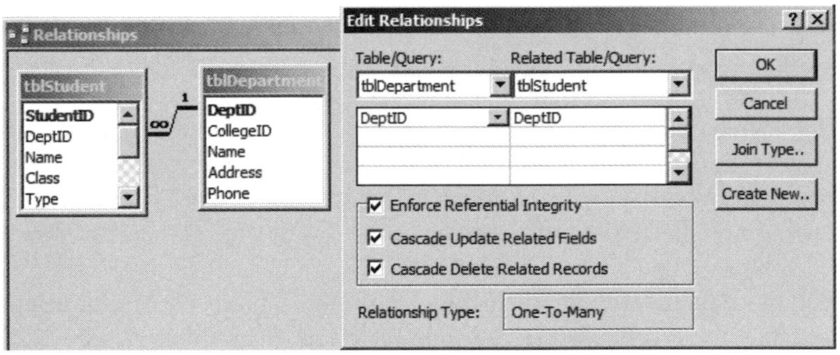

Figure 7.8 Enforcing cascade updates and cascade deletes.

7.2.7   Saving a Layout of Relationships Window

Access automatically saves relationship lines that have been added to the Relationships Window. However, Access does not automatically preserve its layout. Therefore, we must manually save it after it has been created or altered. Saving the layout preserves the orientation of the field lists and so preserves the readable view of the Relationships Window. To save the layout, do either of the following:

- Choose the File | Save option from the main menu, or
- Press the shortcut keys Ctrl+S on the keyboard.

7.3   *Types of Relationships*

Three types of relationships can exist among database tables (also see Chapter 3):

1. One-to-Many or Many-to-One (most common): In a one-to-many relationship, a record in *Table A* can have many matching records in *Table B*, but a record in *Table B* has exactly one matching record in *Table A*.

2. Many-to-Many: A many-to-many relationship consists of two one-to-many relationships, one from *Table A* to *Table B* and one from *Table B* to *Table A*.

3. One-to-One: In a one-to-one relationship, a record in *Table A* has exactly one matching record in *Table B*, and a record in *Table B* has exactly one matching record in *Table A*.

We have seen in Chapter 3 that the entity-relationship data model determines the types of a relationship and depicts it on an E-R diagram using "|" and "<" symbols. When Access automatically detects the relationship types, it refers to the following predefined rules for an assignment:

- If the common field in the parent table is the primary key or has a unique index and the corresponding field in the child table is a foreign key, then Access establishes a One-to-Many relationship between these two tables.
- If a common field from both the tables is the primary key or has a unique index, then Access establishes a One-to-One relationship between these two tables.
- If none of the common fields is a primary key or has a unique index, then Access establishes an indeterminate relationship between these two tables. We cannot enforce referential integrity constraints for such relationships.

In Access, we never need to depict a Many-to-Many relationship type. This is because the normalization process or the process of transforming an E-R diagram into a relational schema (see Chapter 4) is guaranteed to break a Many-to-Many relationship into two—One-to-Many —relationships, and we use the output of relational data modeling, a relational schema, to design Access tables.

7.4 *Hands-On Tutorial: Defining Relationships in Access*

So far in this chapter, we have linked the *tblStudent*, *tblDepartment*, and *tblTranscript* tables of the university database. The objective of this hands-on tutorial is to complete the remaining relationships and to summarize the procedure of defining relationships. This section covers the following How-to topic:

- How-to: define relationships in Access.
  1. Open the university database and open the Relationships Window by choosing the Tools | Relationships option from the main menu.
  2. Right-click anywhere in the window and choose the *Show Table* option from the shortcut menu. This should open the *Show Table* dialog box.
  3. Use the *Show Table* dialog box to make sure that all of the tables from the university database are visible in the Relationships Window. Click *Close* button to return to the Relationships Window.
  4. Relate the *tblCollege* and *tblDepartment* tables. Select the *CollegeID* field from *tblCollege*; drag and drop it on the *CollegeID* field in *tblDepartment*. This should open the *Edit Relationships* dialog box.
  5. Use the *Edit Relationships* dialog box to enforce the referential integrity, cascade updates related fields, and cascade deletes related records by checking appropriate check boxes.

Complete relationships for the university database by repeating Steps 4 and 5 for *tblCourse* and *tblSection*, *tblSection* and *tblFaculty*, *tblFaculty* and *tblDepartment*, and *tblTranscript* and *tblSection*.

7.5 *Working with Existing Relationships*

Because data and data constraints can change, we may also want to modify the existing relationships in our databases. These modifications can entail adding tables to or removing tables from the Relationships Window. Additionally, we can modify the relationships or remove relationships from specific tables. We use the Relationships Window to make these modifications. Before opening the Relationships Window to institute changes, we must be sure to close any open tables in the Database Window. This prevents any discrepancy between what we see in the table Design View and what exists in the Relationships Window.

7.5.1 Adding, Removing, and Hiding Tables in Relationships Window

We add database tables to the Relationships Window using the *Show Table* dialog box (see Section 7.2.2). If we would like to remove a table from the Relationships Window, we select the table and press *Delete* on the keyboard. Note that removing a table from the Relationships Window does not remove it from the database. It only affects the layout of the Relationships Window. Additionally, removing a table from the Relationships Window does not even remove the relationships associated with that table. If we again add these removed tables, Access automatically restored and displays the relationships.

We can also hide tables in the Relationships Window for clearer presentation. To hide a table, select the table and choose the Relationships | Hide Table option from the main menu. To unhide the hidden tables, choose the Relationships | Show Table option from the main menu, and select the desired table(s) from the *Tables* tab to unhide.

7.5.2 Modifying and Deleting Relationships

Relationship lines are not permanent. We can edit or remove these lines as we build our database.

Editing Relationships

1. First, open the Relationships Window. If necessary, unhide/add the missing tables or rearrange the existing tables for a clearer view.
2. Locate and double-click on the relationship line that we would like to edit. This should bring up the *Edit Relationships* dialog box.
3. Make the desired changes in this dialog box to edit the relationship.

Deleting Relationships

1. Open the Relationships Window; locate and select the relationship we would like to delete.
2. Press *Delete* on the keyboard, or select the Edit | Delete option from the main menu.
3. Click *Yes* when Access seeks confirmation before permanently deleting the relationship.

To make editing and deleting changes effective, we must save the relationships layout before closing the Relationships Window.

7.6   *In-Class Assignment*

The purpose of this assignment is to reinforce topics discussed pertaining to Access relationships. Open the *University.mdb* database from "Chapter7" folder on book Web site. Examine *tblStudent*, *tblCourse*, *tblStudentCourse*, *tblInstructor*, *tblInstructorCourse*, and *tblRoom*. Answer the following questions:

1. What is the relationship between the table *tblStudent* and *tblCourse*? Why?
2. Open the Relationships Window and show all tables. Create relationships between the *tblStudent* and *tblCourses* tables. Enforce the referential integrity.
3. What types of relationships exist between *tblStudent*, *tblCourse*, and *tblStudentCourse*? Add these relationships in the Relationships Window.
4. Edit relationships so that when student information is changed, the changes are automatically reflected in all related tables.

7.7   *Summary*

- A relationship is an association between tables.
- The graphical interface known as the Relationships Window allows us to create, view, and edit relationships.
- Referential integrity constraint is a constraint on data that prevents the creation of orphan records in tables.
- When enabled, the *Cascade Update* and *Delete* options can update or delete records from the child table that are related to records in the parent table that have been updated or deleted, respectively.
- Relationship types are denoted by the symbols "1" and "∞."

7.8   *Exercises*

7.8.1 Review Questions

1. Define a relationship.
2. Compare the types of relationships that can exist in an Access.
3. What type of relationship would a field in a table of students have with a field in the faculty table? Explain why.
4. How do we construct a many-to-many relationship in Access?
5. What functionalities does the Relationships Window in Access provide?
6. How does selecting to *Show Direct Relationships* from the *Relationships* toolbar differ from selecting to *Show All Relationships*?
7. What constraint does referential integrity impose? What is an orphan record?
8. Explain the conditions that must be satisfied for enforcing referential integrity.
9. When is it not necessary to enforce referential integrity? When is it not possible?
10. What is the only instance in which different data types are linked with a relationship that enforces referential integrity?
11. How can we identify a primary key in the Relationships Window?
12. How do we draw the relationship line between two tables? What does this line tell Access about the two fields it connects?
13. What does checking *Cascade Delete Related Fields* in the *Edit Relationships* dialog box allow us to do?

7.8.2 Hands-On Exercises

NOTE: *The database files for these hands-on exercises are available at: www.dssbooks.com.*

1. Open the Relationships Window for *HorseRace.mdb*. Examine the relationship between the two tables.

   a. What fields does the relationship line connect?

   b. Edit the relationship so that if we were to change the name of a breed of a certain *BreedID*, the breed names of the horses of that breed would automatically change.

   c. What type of relationship is the one shown between the tables?

2. Open the Relationships Window for *Bank.mdb* and show all of the tables in the database. Form relationships between the following fields in these tables:

   ■ *AccountID* in *tblAccounts* and *AccountID* in *tblBankTransactions*

   ■ *AccountHolderID* in *tblAccountHolders* and *AccountHolderID* in *tblAccounts*

   ■ *EmployeeID* in *tblEmployees* and *EmployeeID* in *tblAccounts*

   a. Enforce referential integrity on all the relationships.

   b. What type of relationship did we form between *tblBankTransactions* and *tblAccounts*? Which table is the parent table?

   c. What type of relationship did we form between *tblEmployees* and *tblAccounts*? Which table is the child table?

   d. Edit the relationships to meet the following requirements: *(i)* if an account holder is deleted from the database, the account belonging to that account holder is also deleted, and *(ii)* if an account is modified, the transactions associated with that account are also modified.

3. Open the Relationships Window for *Hospital.mdb* and show all of the tables in the database. Create relationships between the tables. Enforce referential integrity on all the relationships that we create.

   a. How many relationships did we create? What types of relationships are they?

   b. Which tables are parent tables? Which are child tables? Which are both?

   c. Edit the relationships so that any modification to the information regarding a patient, doctor, supplier, or medicine is reflected in corresponding records.

   d. Edit the relationships so that *Cascade Delete Related Fields* is checked for all relationships. What will happen to a patient's billing information if that patient's doctor is deleted from the database?

4. Consider the table *tblErgonomics*. Each employee gives his or her preferences on how to assemble a product. Relate the *tblEmployees* to *tblErgonomics*.

   a. What type of relationship is appropriate for associating these two tables? Why?

   b. Open the Relationships Window and enforce referential integrity on the relationship we created. Is the type of relationship formed the same as our answer to part (a)?

5. Think of an example in which two entities share a many-to-many relationship. Create a database that depicts this relationship. Be sure to identify a primary key for each of our tables.

6. Open the database *Hotel.mdb* and answer the following questions:

   a. The field *CustomerID* exists in both *tblFoodBills* and *tblBooking*. Should we set a relationship between these two tables through *CustomerID*? Why or why not?

   b. Add the table *tblBilling* to the Relationships Window.

   c. Create a relationship between the *BillingID* fields in *tblBilling* and *tblBooking*, and enforce referential integrity on the relationship. What type of relationship did we create?

   d. Create and enforce referential integrity on all remaining relationships.

7. Consider the *Bottling.mdb* database. As mentioned, the samples that the quality assurance expert took came from one of many bottling lines with different characteristics.

   a. What relationships will we consider for this database?

   b. Enforce the referential integrity constraint for all relationships. What are the different types of relationships we created?

   c. For which relationships will we consider enforcing cascade updates and deletes?

8. A shipping company uses a database to track packages, mailing rates, and deliveries. Open the

Packages.mdb database, and examine the existing tables.

   a. Open the table *tblPackages*. Observe values for the *ShipmentType* field in *tblRates*.

   b. What relationship exists between *tblPackages* and *tblRates*? How do we relate this type to the observation from part (a)?

   c. What type of relationship should exist between *tblPackages* and *tblCertified*? Why? Create this relationship and enforce referential integrity.

9. A corporation's information technology department is comparing software packages of a new type of software needed for company-wide use. The corporation is considering three software packages: SimpleSoft, OfficeEase, and Quickware. The corporation asked each IT employee to use each type of software for a trial period of two weeks and then to rank the three packages on a scale of one to three at the end of the trial period. The corporation based rankings on three categories: user-friendliness, ease of learning, and variety of features. Open the database *Software.mdb*, and examine the existing tables.

   a. What types of relationships should exist between the tables? Explain why.

   b. Create the relationships and enforce referential integrity.

   c. If a user or package is removed from the study, the associated rankings should also be removed. If the department decides to evaluate a fourth package, users must rank this package also. If the department hires new employees, their names are added to the database for future reference, but they are not asked to participate in the study. Edit the relationships to reflect these policies.

10. An airline uses a database to keep track of its flights, customers, reservations, prices, and cancellations. Open the database *Airline.mdb* and examine the existing tables.

   a. Which tables should share a one-to-one relationship? Explain why.

   b. Create the one-to-one relationship and enforce referential integrity. Edit the relationship so that any modification or deletion in one table is reflected in the other table.

   c. Create all remaining possible relationships between tables with common fields. Are there any many-to-many relationships? If so, to what tables do they relate?

   d. Enforce referential integrity on each remaining relationship so that any deletion from or modification to a parent table is reflected in the child table.

eight Queries: Building Application Foundations

chapter OVERVIEW

8.1 *Introduction*

In Chapter 6 and 7, we have seen how database tables are designed around the set of relations of a relational schema. This design approach guaranteed us efficient data storage eliminating most of the data anomalies and data redundancies. While efficient database storage is essential for database performance, a *unified view of data* is an important factor for database utilization. Most business people like to see *only the required* information *at a glance*. For example, "a list of students from College of Engineering who have taken and finished computer related courses with grade point of 4.0," is a unified view of interest for an IT recruiting personnel. A database stores its data into multiple tables and multiple columns, whereas a user may be interested in only a set of columns from one or more tables as in the case of an IT recruiting personnel.

In this chapter, we introduce database queries, which enable us to present a unified view of data from database tables. A ***database query*** is a question posed against database tables and the answer or *query result* is a unified view of data that the user wants to see. The query result can be a single number (Aggregate queries) or a record set (Select queries) from one or more database tables. For example, consider following "Student Enrollment" query on the student table of the university database: "What is the total student enrollment in the Industrial Engineering department?" The query result in this case is a single number; the number of students from Industrial Engineering department. The count aggregation is used to compute this query result. Consider another example, "Contact List" query: "List the contact information of all the students from College of Engineering." The query result in this case is a record set; a list of students that satisfies the selection criteria. Further, a query may unify data from a single table or multiple tables. For example, the "Student Enrollment" query only involves the student table, whereas the "Contact List" query requires data from the student, department, and college table to provide the desired view. Finally, a query should be viewed as *a set of instructions*, which when executed, operates on database tables to output the query result. A query itself does not store any data or query results. It must be executed every time to see the results.

Access allows us to build (design) queries using a graphical query grid (Query-by-Example or QBE) and by writing SQL statements. We explore the first option extensively in this chapter and discuss SQL statements in Chapter 9. In Access, query results are shown in the Datasheet View (like tables in Chapter 6). Access queries can be broadly classified into three function-based categories (see Figure 8.1):

- ■ Select queries.
- ■ Special purpose queries (Crosstab, Parameter, and Make-Table queries).
- ■ Action queries (Update, Append, and Delete queries).

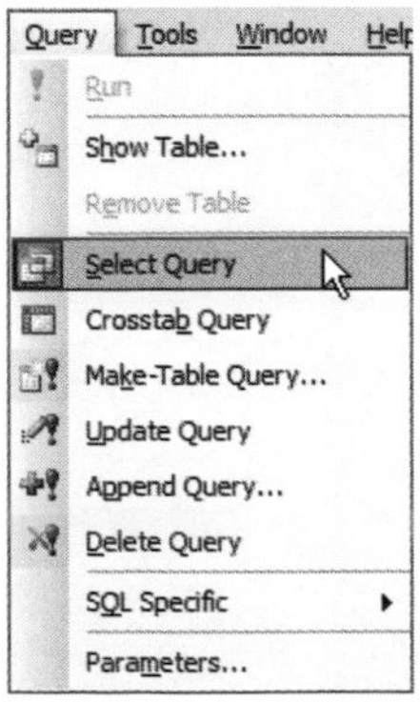

Figure 8.1 The Access query types.

8.1.1 Topics

This chapter discusses the following topics:

- How to create Select queries.
- Queries with multiple tables.
- How to use *Total* row for GroupBy operation.
- Adding calculated fields to the query design.
- How to create Parameter queries.
- How to create Crosstab queries.
- How to create Action queries.

Summary

A **query** is a question posed against database tables.

Access queries can be broadly classified into three function-based categories: (1) **Select** Queries; (2) **Special Purpose** Queries (Crosstab, Parameter, and Make-Table queries); and (3) **Action** Queries (Update, Append, and Delete queries).

8.2 *Working with Select Queries*

Select queries are the most common types of queries used in database applications. If we refer to a set of records as a *recordset*, a Select query is a database query that performs Projection, Selection, and/or Sorting operations on an input recordset to *extract* an output recordset of some interest.

We first define Projection, Selection, and Sorting operations. Each operation takes an input recordset and performs a specific operation to give an output recordset.

Projection Projection is a vertical slicing of an input recordset. Projection is used to display one or more selected fields of a table. For example, a projection over the student table (input recordset) may display only the *Name*, *Email*, and *DOB* fields (output recordset) rather than displaying all student table columns (see Figure 8.2).

Name	Email	DOB
Jonathan , Bueno	Jonathan , Bueno@univ.	5/12/1974
Jonathan , Coleman I	Jonathan , Coleman III@	11/21/1980
Jonathan , Carlson	Jonathan , Carlson@univ	3/17/1978
Neil , Coble	Neil , Coble@univ.edu	4/11/1976
Neil , Bess	Neil , Bess@univ.edu	9/9/1983
Neil , Hardy	Neil , Hardy@univ.edu	9/14/1976
Richard , Juanez	Richard , Juanez@univ.e	2/15/1984
Richard , Bower	Richard , Bower@univ.ec	9/12/1980
Richard , Gube	Richard , Gube@univ.edi	7/16/1972
Nil , Gube	Nil , Gube@univ.edu	8/2/1976

Figure 8.2 The Projection operation.

Selection

Selection is a horizontal slicing of an input recordset. Selection is used to select one or more records (or rows) that satisfy specified selection criteria. For example, a selection over the student table (input recordset) may display only full time (Type = "Full Time") student (output recordset) records rather than displaying all student records (see Figure 8.3).

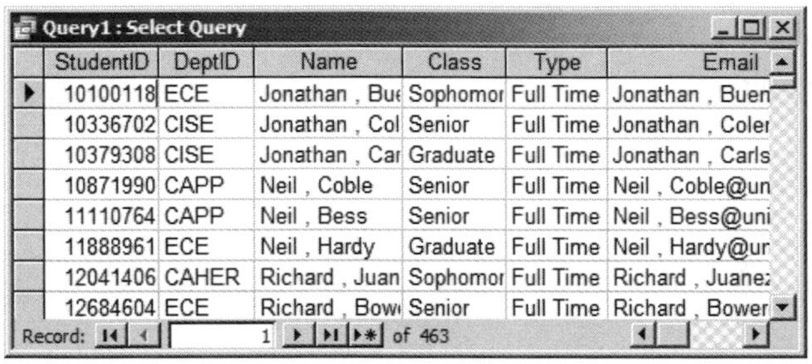

StudentID	DeptID	Name	Class	Type	Email
10100118	ECE	Jonathan , Bue	Sophomor	Full Time	Jonathan , Buen
10336702	CISE	Jonathan , Col	Senior	Full Time	Jonathan , Coler
10379308	CISE	Jonathan , Car	Graduate	Full Time	Jonathan , Carls
10871990	CAPP	Neil , Coble	Senior	Full Time	Neil , Coble@un
11110764	CAPP	Neil , Bess	Senior	Full Time	Neil , Bess@uni
11888961	ECE	Neil , Hardy	Graduate	Full Time	Neil , Hardy@ur
12041406	CAHER	Richard , Juan	Sophomor	Full Time	Richard , Juanez
12684604	ECE	Richard , Bow	Senior	Full Time	Richard , Bower

Figure 8.3 The Selection operation.

Sorting

Sorting provides an ordered sequence of an input recordset. For example, Figure 8.4 displays a list of students sorted in ascending order of *StudentIDs* (output recordset).

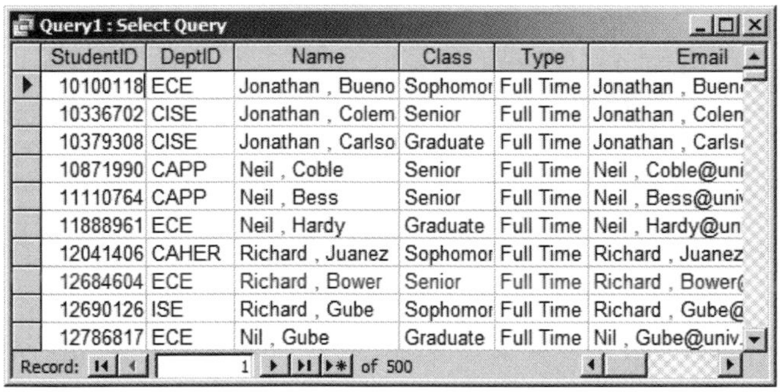

StudentID	DeptID	Name	Class	Type	Email
10100118	ECE	Jonathan , Bueno	Sophomor	Full Time	Jonathan , Buen
10336702	CISE	Jonathan , Colem	Senior	Full Time	Jonathan , Colen
10379308	CISE	Jonathan , Carlso	Graduate	Full Time	Jonathan , Carls
10871990	CAPP	Neil , Coble	Senior	Full Time	Neil , Coble@uni
11110764	CAPP	Neil , Bess	Senior	Full Time	Neil , Bess@uni
11888961	ECE	Neil , Hardy	Graduate	Full Time	Neil , Hardy@un
12041406	CAHER	Richard , Juanez	Sophomor	Full Time	Richard , Juanez
12684604	ECE	Richard , Bower	Senior	Full Time	Richard , Bower(
12690126	ISE	Richard , Gube	Sophomor	Full Time	Richard , Gube@
12786817	ECE	Nil , Gube	Graduate	Full Time	Nil , Gube@univ.

Figure 8.4 The Sorting operation.

We now discuss how to create a Select query in Access environment. We first introduce Access's query Design View and then show how we can perform Projection, Selection, and Sorting operations in the Design View to build a Select query.

8.2.1 Creating a Query in the Design View

We can use a variety of methods to create Access queries. The Design View and Simple Query Wizard are the two most frequently used options for creating queries. In this section, we explore the Design View option in detail. We leave the Simple Query Wizard option for the readers to explore.

To create a new query using Design View, we follow these steps:

1. Select the *Queries* option in the Objects Bar that is on the left-hand side in the Database Window. This should display the two popular options for creating a new query (see Figure 8.5).

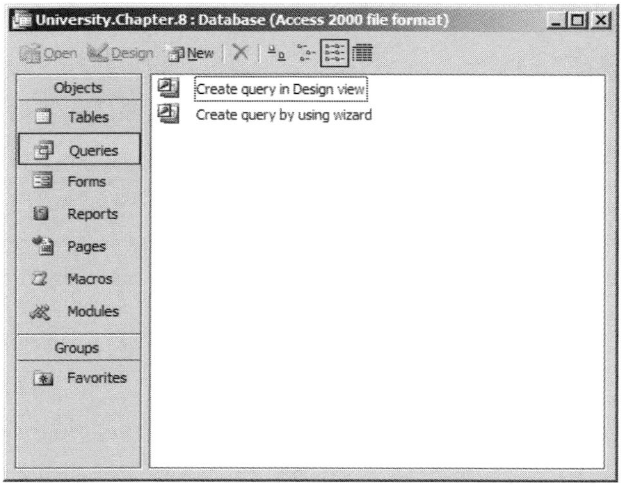

Figure 8.5 "Create query" options in Database View.

2. Double-click on the *Create query in Design View* option. Alternatively, use the *New* button on the Database Window toolbar to first invoke the *New Query* dialog box (see Figure 8.6) and then select the *Design View* option. Either method should open a new query in the Design View.

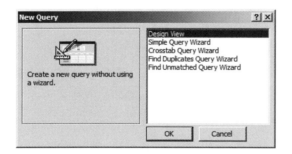

Figure 8.6 *New Query* dialog box.

The query Design View (see Figure 8.7) is divided into two halves. The upper half, called a Table Pane, displays all the fields from the desired query tables. The lower half, the Design Grid, holds the table fields on which we would like to perform Projection, Selection, and/or Sorting operations.

We now illustrate the process of developing a Select query. We consider following example query: "*list the students' information (StudentID, Name, and Email) for all full time, freshman students sorted in descending order of their names.*" The query design involves the following steps: (1) projecting student identification number, name, and email columns (the Projection operation); (2) selecting only full time, freshman students (the Selection operation); and (3) sorting selected records in descending order of student names (the Sorting operation). The following subsections demonstrate these steps.

8.2.2   Projecting Student's Contact Information

We design our example query using the Design View. The database used in this chapter can be found in the Chapter 8 folder on the book Web site.

    1. Open the university database and create a new query in the Design View.

When we open a new query in the Design View, the *Show Table* dialog box appears automatically. We use this dialog box to add tables to the Table Pane. We can also invoke the *Show Table* dialog box by choosing the Query | Show Tables option from the main menu. Alternatively, we can right-click anywhere in the Table Pane and select *Show Table* from the shortcut menu to open the *Show Table* dialog box (see Figure 8.7). The *Show Table* dialog box lists all of the available database tables.

    2. Select the table *tblStudent* and click the *Add* button to add it to the query design.
    3. Click *Close* to exit the *Show Table* dialog box.

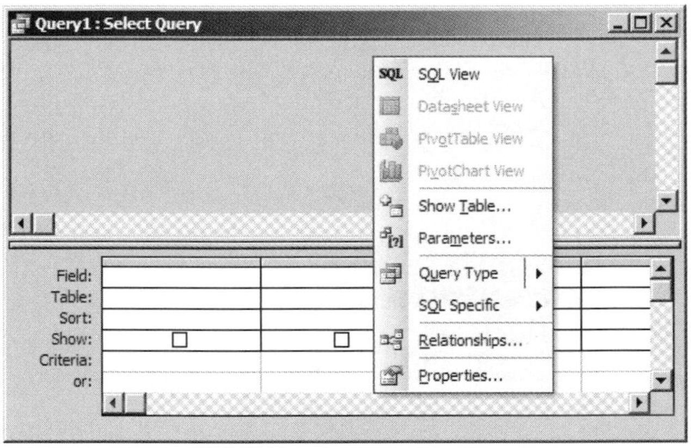

Figure 8.7 The query Design View.

The student tables appear in the Table Pane as a list of table fields. Once we have added the table to the query design, we can add fields from the field list to the Design Grid.

    4. Add the *StudentID*, *Name*, and *Email* fields from the Table Pane to the Design Grid (see Figure 8.8). To add these fields, either double-click them or select, drag, and drop individual fields from the field list to the next available column in the Design Grid.

To add more than one field at a time to the Design Grid, use the *Shift* key (contiguous selection) or *Ctrl* key (non-contiguous selection). To select all the fields in the list, double-click the title bar of the field list or add an asterisk (*) sign from the field list to the Design Grid. Once we have added the desired fields, the first row (the *Field* row) of the Design Grid displays the name of the field that has been added to the query design and the second row (the *Table* row) displays the source table name.

Interestingly enough, adding fields to the Design Grid from the Table Pane constitutes a Projection operation. If we save and run the query (see Section 8.2.3) designed in Figure 8.8, we see that only three columns of the student table are displayed. Thus, adding fields to the Table Pane performs vertical slicing and displays only columns of interest rather than displaying all columns in the Table Pane.

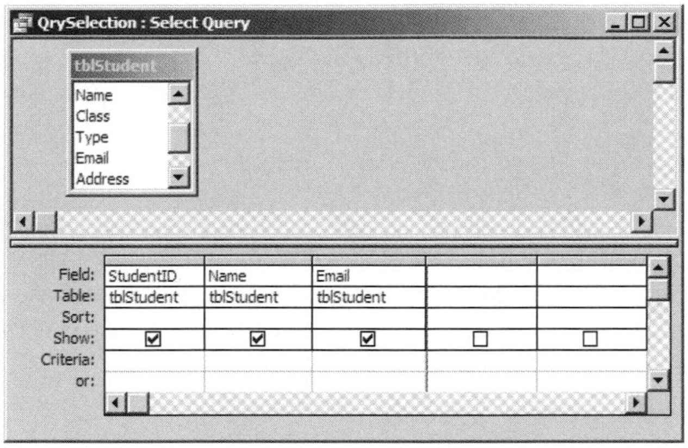

Figure 8.8 Projecting fields of the student table.

8.2.3　Saving and Executing a Query

To save a query design and the layout of the Design View, we choose File | Save from the main menu or click on the *Save* button on the toolbar. To run a query and to view the query result, we choose Query | Run from the main menu, or click on the *Run* button on the toolbar. The Datasheet View displays the query result.

> **5.** Save this query as "QrySelection" and run the query to verify the Projection operation.

8.2.4　Selecting, Freshman and Full Time Students

The Selection operation is the extraction of records that satisfy specific selection criteria. Typically, selection criteria are arithmetic and/or logical expressions applied to one or more table columns. We use the *Criteria* row of the Design Grid to specify the selection criteria. For example, continuing with the query described in Section 8.2.1, we must select full time, freshman students. The selection criteria here are based on the *Class* and *Type* columns of the student table. The selection criteria can be written as: Class = "Freshman" and Type = "Full Time." We specify these criteria under *Class* and *Type* columns in the Criteria row (see Figure 8.9).

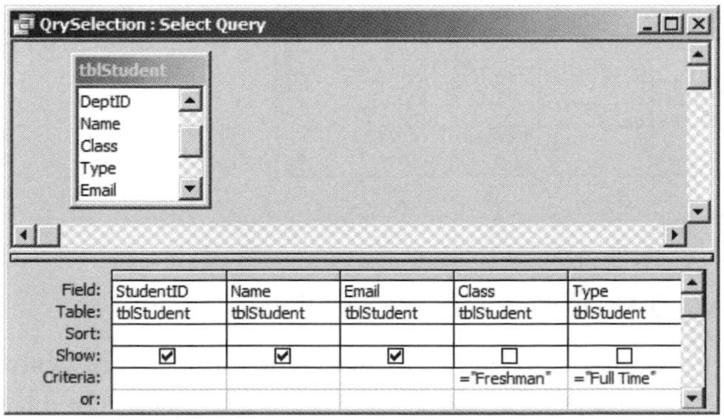

Figure 8.9 Selecting rows of the student table.

6. Add =“Freshman” criterion for the *Class* column and =“Full Time” criterion for the *Type* column under *Criteria* row of the Design Grid.
7. Uncheck the check boxes in the *Show* row for the *Class* and *Type* columns (see Figure 8.9).
8. Save and run the query to verify Selection operation.

The *Show* row of the Design Grid allows us to include non-projecting columns in the query design. That is, when the check box in the *Show* row of a column is unchecked, that column in the Design Grid is not projected in the query result. However, we can still use the column in query design to specify selection criteria and for other operations discussed later in the chapter.

8.2.5 Sorting Student's Records

When we run a query, the records in the query result are displayed in the same order in which they appear in the table. We can sort the output records on any output column by assigning a sort order in the query design. For example, continuing with our example query, we would like to sort selected student records in descending order of their names, whereas they appear by default in ascending order of *StudentID* in the table. To sort on a particular column, we choose the desired sorting order using the drop-down list in the *Sort* row of the corresponding column.

9. Choose the "descending" order using the drop-down list in the Sort row of the Name column (see Figure 8.10).
10. Save and run the query to verify Selection operation.

Combining the Projection, Selection, and Sorting operations required by our example query, the query Design View should resemble Figure 8.10. The query output is depicted in Figure 8.11.

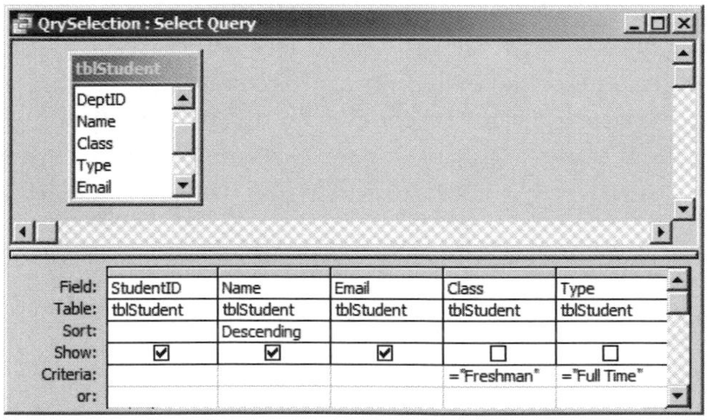

Figure 8.10 Sorting student records in descending order by student names.

8.2.6 Moving or Removing Fields and Tables in Design View

Notice that the order of the columns in the Design Grid is the order of the columns in the query result as well. We may want to move the columns in the Design Grid to have the desired ordering of columns in the query result. The Datasheet View follows the sequence of the columns in the Design Grid from left to right. To move the columns in the Design Grid, we select the entire column and drag it to the desired location. To remove a column from the Design Grid, we select the entire column and hit the *Delete* button on the keyboard.

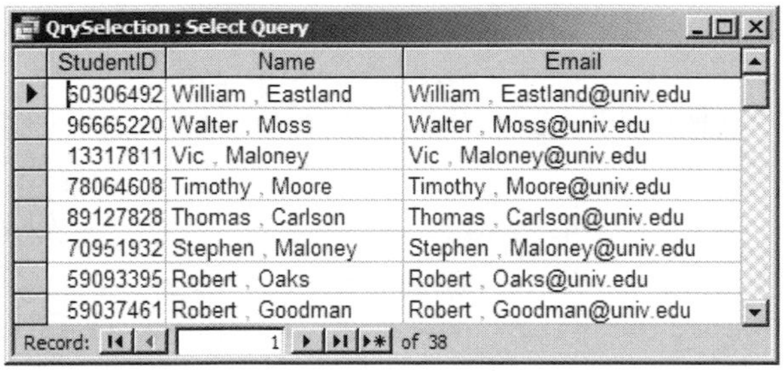
QrySelection : Select Query

StudentID	Name	Email
60306492	William . Eastland	William . Eastland@univ.edu
96665220	Walter . Moss	Walter . Moss@univ.edu
13317811	Vic . Maloney	Vic . Maloney@univ.edu
78064608	Timothy . Moore	Timothy . Moore@univ.edu
89127828	Thomas . Carlson	Thomas . Carlson@univ.edu
70951932	Stephen . Maloney	Stephen . Maloney@univ.edu
59093395	Robert . Oaks	Robert . Oaks@univ.edu
59037461	Robert . Goodman	Robert . Goodman@univ.edu

Record: 1 of 38

Figure 8.11 The output of the example Select query.

To remove a table from the Table Pane, we first select the table by clicking on the table list and then remove it by hitting the *Delete* button on the keyboard. Alternatively, we can right-click on the table and select the *Remove Table* option from the shortcut menu. Note that removing the table list from the Table Pane also removes the corresponding columns of that table from the Design Grid. Removing tables or columns from the Design Grid does not affect tables or its columns.

8.2.7 Exploring Query Toolbar and Menus

It is important to familiarize ourselves with the various features available in the Design View. Table 8.1 summarizes some of the useful toolbar and main menu options.

Table 8.1 Menu and toolbar options in the Design View.

Picture	Name	Functionality	Main Menu	Short-cut Menu
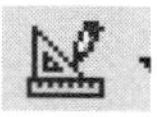	Design View	Switches to the Design View	View | Design View	Table Pane | Design View
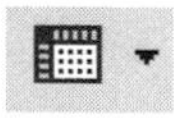	Query Type	Provides options to choose query type	Query | {Query Type Name}	Table Pane | Query Type | {Query Type Name}
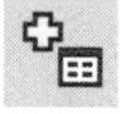	Show Table	Opens the *Show Table* dialog box to add tables/queries	Query | Show Table	Table Pane | Show Table
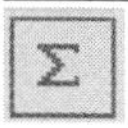	Totals	Adds *Total* row to the Design Grid for total queries	View | Totals	—
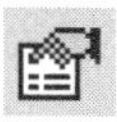	Properties	Opens the *Query Properties* window	View | Properties	Design Grid | Properties
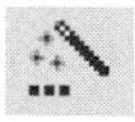	Build	Opens the *Expression Builder* dialog box	—	*Criteria* row | Build

8.3 *Queries with Multiple Tables (The Join Operation)*

Recall from Chapter 4 that we normalize database relations (or tables) to remove anomalies and thus reduce data redundancies. Almost all forms of normalization decompose a larger relation into two smaller relations. While relation decomposition is the key for anomaly removal, many database applications required a unified view of the data. For example, the normalization process will decompose the larger *StudentDepartment* relation into two smaller relations—the student relation and the department relation. This decomposition avoids duplicating department information for each student who belongs to the department (refer to Section 4.8 for more explanation). On the other hand, a database application may require viewing student records along with the departmental information (see Figure 8.12). The Join operation reconciles the situation.

Queries can systematically join multiple tables to create a unified view of the fragmented data. In Access, we perform a Join operation by adding multiple tables to the Table Pane. Consider an example in which we add the student and department tables to the Table Pane. Access automatically tries to compute a join of these two tables (see Figure 8.12).

The Join operation can be combined with the Projection, Selection, and Sorting operations to create more complex queries. We first consider a hands-on tutorial illustrating the Join operation and Projection operation and discuss how Access joins two tables.

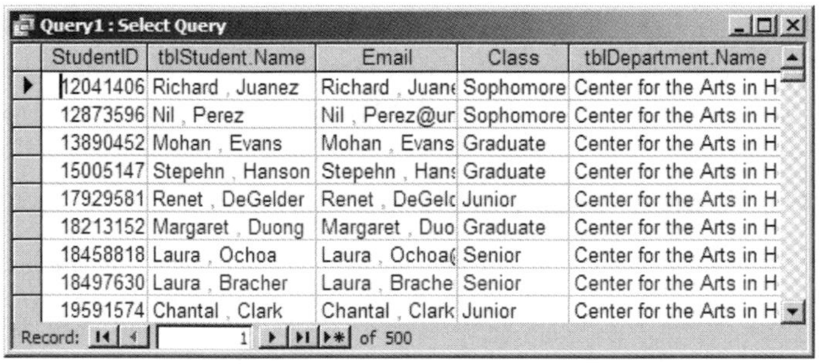
Query1 : Select Query

StudentID	tblStudent.Name	Email	Class	tblDepartment.Name
12041406	Richard , Juanez	Richard , Juane	Sophomore	Center for the Arts in H
12873596	Nil , Perez	Nil , Perez@ur	Sophomore	Center for the Arts in H
13890452	Mohan , Evans	Mohan , Evans	Graduate	Center for the Arts in H
15005147	Stepehn , Hanson	Stepehn , Hans	Graduate	Center for the Arts in H
17929581	Renet , DeGelder	Renet , DeGelc	Junior	Center for the Arts in H
18213152	Margaret , Duong	Margaret , Duo	Graduate	Center for the Arts in H
18458818	Laura , Ochoa	Laura , Ochoa(	Senior	Center for the Arts in H
18497630	Laura , Bracher	Laura , Brache	Senior	Center for the Arts in H
19591574	Chantal , Clark	Chantal , Clark	Junior	Center for the Arts in H

Record: 1 of 500

Figure 8.12 The Join operation.

8.3.1 Hands-On Tutorial: Working with Join Queries

In this tutorial, we provide steps necessary to create a query with multiple tables. The query statement is as follows: "List the student information (StudentID and Name) and name of their departments (not the *DeptID*). This hands-on tutorial discusses the following How-to topic:

- How-to: design a query that involves multiple tables.
  1. Open the university database and start with the new query in the Design View. Use the *Show Table* dialog box to add the *tblStudent* and *tblDepartment* to the Table Pane (see Figure 8.13(a)).

(a)

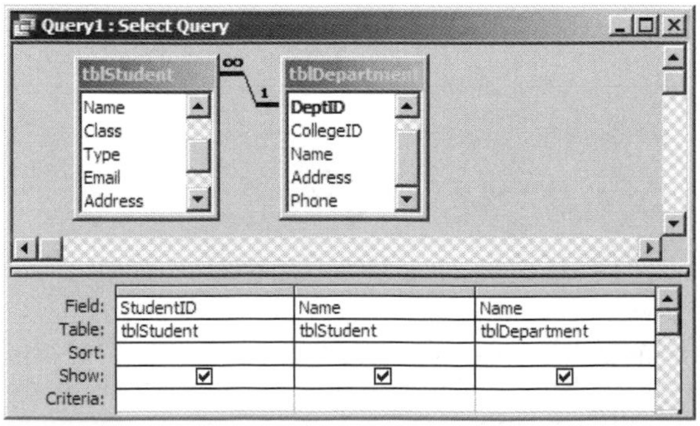

(continues)

Figure 8.13 (a) Joining student and department tables in the Design View; (b) The join result in the Datasheet View.

Query1 : Select Query

StudentID	tblStudent.Name	tblDepartment.Name
12041406	Richard , Juanez	Center for the Arts in Healthcare
12873596	Nil , Perez	Center for the Arts in Healthcare
13890452	Mohan , Evans	Center for the Arts in Healthcare
15005147	Stepehn , Hanson	Center for the Arts in Healthcare
17929581	Renet , DeGelder	Center for the Arts in Healthcare
18213152	Margaret , Duong	Center for the Arts in Healthcare
18458818	Laura , Ochoa	Center for the Arts in Healthcare
18497630	Laura , Bracher	Center for the Arts in Healthcare
19591574	Chantal , Clark	Center for the Arts in Healthcare

Record: 1 of 500

(b)

Figure 8.13 (*continued*)

2. Add the required fields from their respective tables to the Design Grid. For details, see Figure 8.13(a).
3. Save the query as "QryJoinQuery" and run it.

8.3.2 The Join Operation

The Join operation unlike Projection, Selection, or Sorting operations takes two distinct recordsets as an input and produces a single output recordset, referred as the *join result.* The join result features all the columns from two input recordsets. Further, each record from the first input recordset is joined with all the records from the second input recordset. Whether each joined record qualifies in the join result is then determined by a *join condition* (like a selection criteria).

If two join tables are related to each other and are added to the Table Pane to join, Access automatically displays the relationship between these tables (one that is defined in the Relationships Window). For such related tables, Access applies the default join condition; the values of the foreign key must match the value of the primary key. For example, the student and department tables are related to each other through a common column, *DeptID*. When we add these two tables to the Table Pane, Access uses the join condition *tblStudent.DeptID=tblDepartment.DeptID* to perform the Join operation. In other words, only those records from the student table will appear in the join result for which *DeptID* value matches with the *DeptID* in the department table (verify the fact in the query result, Figure 8.13(b)). The join based on equality condition of primary key-foreign key columns are also referred as *inner join*. Thus, in the inner join only those records from both the tables that satisfy the primary key-foreign key conditions are included in the join result.

The other type of join is *outer join*. Imagine that there are few new students in the university for which the department information is not included in the student table (i.e. *tblStudent.DeptID* is NULL). With the inner join condition on *DeptID* (*tblDepartment.DeptID* = *tblStudent.DeptID*), the join result will not feature new students. However, this might not be desirable. We would like to see a list of all the students even if they are not assigned to a particular department. In other words, we would like to include all the records from the student table and only those records from the department table in which joined fields are equal. A similar scenario can be imagined in which we would like to include all the records from the department table and only those records from the student table in which joined fields are equal. Thus, we would like to include all the records from one table and only those records from the other table in which joined fields are equal. These types of join are popularly known as *outer join*. Depending on which table is included completely in the join result, the outer joins are referred to as *left outer join* or *right outer join*.

Though, inner join is the default join type in Access, we can view and alter join types using the *Join Properties* dialog box (see Figure 8.14). In Access, to invoke the *Join Properties* dialog box, right-click the relationship line in the Table Pane and choose *Properties* from the shortcut menu. In this dialog box, we can choose one out of three join options (1) inner join (2) left outer join and (3) right outer join.

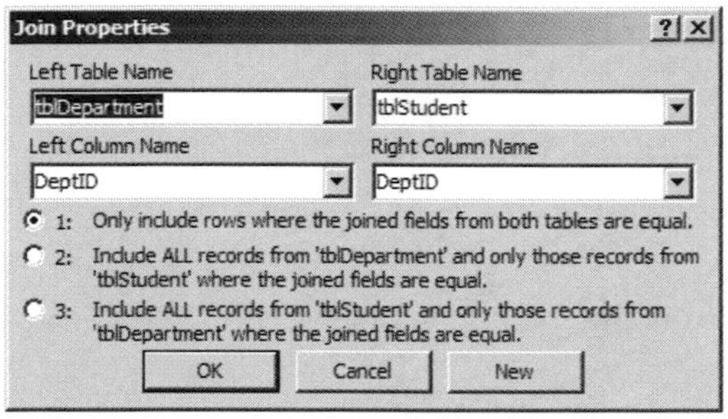

Figure 8.14 Selecting a join type in *Join Properties* dialog box.

If the two tables added to the Table Pane to join are not related to each other, no join condition is used in the Join operation. In the absence of any join condition, each record from the first input recordset is joined with all the records from the second input recordset. This all-to-all join is also known as the *Cartesian product*. The number of rows in the Cartesian product is exactly the product of rows from the first and second input recordsets. However, providing a join condition, i.e., joining related tables, is common in the queries used in a decision support system. Join conditions allow us to choose records of specific interest from a large Cartesian product.

If we add more than two tables to the Table Pane, Access performs join of two tables at-a-time, and the join result of two tables is then joined with the next table. The order of multiple join is decided by how these tables are related to each other. For example, if we add the college, department, and student tables to the Table Pane, Access will first join the college and the department tables, and then the result is joined with the student table. Access, automatically picks the join order if we add all the related tables in the Table Pane.

8.4   *Working with Operators*

In Access, we have an option to use different operators in the query design. The most commonly used operators are the comparison operators, such as > and =, the logical operators, such as AND, OR, and NOT, the BETWEEN operator, and the LIKE operator. We now discuss these operators in detail.

8.4.1 The Comparison Operators

We use comparison operators to select a specific group of records from a table. For example, if we have to find all courses with 3.0 credit hours or more, or a list of sections offered in the year 2002, we must write an expression that defines the criteria using a combination of comparison operators and field values, such as `CreditHours > 3.0 OR Year = 2002`. When we run the query, only the records with values satisfying the specified criteria are selected for further processing.

8.4.2 The Logical Conditions

When we use more than one condition in a query to obtain the desired result, we need logical operators such as AND, OR, and NOT, to combine multiple criteria. For example, to find a list of faculty members who earn more than $70,000 and less than $100,000, we must specify the following criteria for the salary field: `Salary > 70000 AND Salary < 100000`. Consider another example in which we use the Student table to list all the students who are in their first two years of college. The criterion for this query is: `Class= "Sophomore" OR Class= "Freshman."` We use the quotation marks ("") to specify a text value in the criteria expression.

We can also use the logical operators to impose conditions on two different fields. For example, the criteria to list all full-time sophomore students from the Computer Science (CISE) department read: `Class = "Sophomore" AND Type = "Full Time" AND tbl Department.Name = "CISE."`

Access automatically applies the AND operator across the fields when we specify the criteria in the criteria row of the Design Grid. Access offers separate rows for the OR operator that are located below the *Criteria* row (see Section 8.5 for an illustrated example).

8.4.3 The BETWEEN Operator

We use the BETWEEN operator along with the logical AND operator to specify an inclusive range between two values. We can use this operator with a text, numeric, or date field. For example, we can use this operator to list all the faculty members who have joined the university `BETWEEN #1/1/95# AND #1/1/2002#` or list all the faculty members who earn `BETWEEN 70,000 AND 100,000`.

8.4.4 The LIKE Operator and Wildcard Character

The LIKE operator finds groups of potentially related items. It is often used with the wildcard character, the asterisk (*). In the university database, we could use this operator to find all the courses with the word "computer" in their titles. We type `LIKE "*Computer*"` to express this query. We can think of the asterisk as a wildcard that can have any value when compared with the database field values. Thus, the asterisk can also be used to find records with patterns, such as all course titles that begin with the word "Applied" with the criteria `LIKE "Applied*."`

8.4.5 Working with Dates

We use the pound sign (#) to represent the date data type. The simplest form of an expression with dates is `<= #1/1/2001#`, i.e., everything on and before January 1, 2001. In addition to the basic arithmetic and logical operators discussed so far, Access has many built-in functions to handle dates and times data types (refer to Section 8.7.3 for additional details).

8.5 *Hands-On Tutorial: A Select Query with Join of Multiple Tables*

In this tutorial, we provide the steps necessary to create a fairly complex query for the university database. This example illustrates the use of the Projection, Selection, Sorting, and Join operations. This tutorial also summarizes the query design process. The query statement is as follows:

"List the contact information (name, email, and address) for all Industrial Engineering (ISE) students who have taken any computer- or database-related courses in the last six years and earned a grade point average of 3.5 or better in these courses. Sort the list in descending order of student's letter grade."

Query Tables: To answer this query, we need the student table (to project student contact information), the transcript table (to select and sort by grades), the section table (to select by year criteria), and the course table (to select by course name).

This tutorial covers the following How-to topic:

■ How-to: write a complex query with the Projection, Selection, Sorting, and Join operations.

1. If necessary, open the university database and start with the new query in the Design View. Use the *Show Table* dialog box to add the required four tables to the Table Pane. Make sure that the relationship lines between all related tables are in place in the Table Pane.

2. Add the required fields from their respective tables to the Design Grid. For details, see Figure 8.15.

It is always advisable to partially build the query and view the partial output as we add fields, selection criteria, and sorting. At this point, save the query as "qrySelection-Query," and run the query to review its output.

3. Now, we specify various selection criteria. First, add the criteria >= 3.5 for the *Grade* column. This will filter out all students with grades below 3.5 in the target courses. Next, specify the expression ="ISE" for the *DeptID* field. This will keep only ISE students in the result set. Save and run the query to verify the design so far.

4. Then, assign the expression >Year (Now ())-6 in the *Year* field.

The above expression uses two Access built-in functions, *Year ()* and *Now ()*. The *Now* function returns the current date; when passed to the *Year* function, it returns the year of the current date. For example, if *Now* returns 1/1/2007, then *Year* returns 2007. We then specify the criteria limiting our output to only those records in which the year value exceeds 2007 – 6 = year 2001. This operation keeps only those students who have taken these courses in the last six years.

5. Place the final expression Like "*computer*" Or Like "*database*" in the course name field. This expression lists only those course titles that contain the word "computer" or "database."

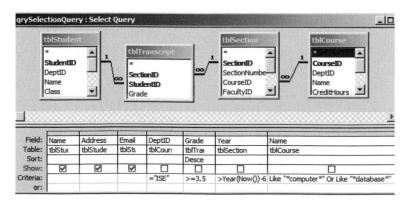

Figure 8.15 A Select query design with multiple tables.

6. Next, use the *Sort* row to specify descending order for the *Grade* column.
7. Since we are only interested in projecting the student contact information, use the *Show* row to display only the Name, Address, and Email columns. Uncheck all other columns in the *Show* row.
8. Save and run the query.

8.6   *Using Total Row (The GroupBy Operation)*

The GroupBy operation puts together records based on some similarity criteria and treats them as one unit or a group. For example, the student table includes the information about students' departments (i.e., *DeptID*). We can put together all the students with the *same DeptID* into a single group. Thus, we will have multiple groups within the student table, one for each department in the department table. GroupBy is an important operation and extensively used to furnish data summaries. For example, once we group student records by department, we can count the number of records in each group and can easily display the summary of number of students enrolled in each department. In general, the GroupBy operation allows us to apply aggregate functions to the set of records. Consider another example in which we group the records from the transcript table for each student with students' grade point averages. We now illustrate the GroupBy operation with two hands-on tutorials. In the first example, we consider a simple GroupBy, and in the second example, we illustrate GroupBy using the Where clause in the *Total* row.

8.6.1   Hands-On Tutorial: Using the Total Row

In this tutorial, we will walk through a procedure of creating *Totals* (or GroupBy) queries in Access. We use a simple example in which we have to determine the total number of students in each department. This tutorial covers the following How-to topic:

■ How-to: create a *Totals* (or GroupBy) query.
1. Open the university database and start with a new query in the Design View. Use the *Show Table* dialog box to add the student and department tables.
2. Add the student ID and department name fields to the Design Grid.
3. Now, designate this query as a *Totals* query by either choosing the View | Totals option from the main menu or by clicking on the *Totals* button on the toolbar. A *Total* row with a default value of *Group By* will appear in the Design Grid.
4. Click in the *Total* row under the *StudentID* column, and select the *Count* option from the drop-down list of aggregate functions (see Figure 8.16).
5. Save and run the query for the result shown in Figure 8.17.

The aggregation fields (like StudentID in this example) are named as *<aggregation> Of<field name>* by default in the Datasheet View. In our example, the StudentID field is named as "CountOfStudentID" in the Datasheet View. We rename fields in the Design Grid to give them more meaningful names using ":" operator as discussed in the next step.

6. In Figure 8.16 rename the StudentID count column as "TotalStudents: StudentID" (see Figure 8.17).

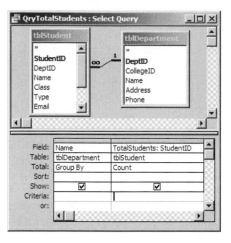

Figure 8.16 Grouping student records by department in the Design View.

Name	TotalStudents
Center for the Arts and Public Policy	114
Center for the Arts in Healthcare Research and Education	92
Computer & Information Science & Engineering	116
Electrical & Computer Engineering	88
Industrial & Systems Engineering	90

Record: 5 of 5

Figure 8.17 The output of GroupBy operation.

It is also worth mentioning here that once we have grouped similar records, we cannot access individual records from that group. Consider the example in this hands-on tutorial. Once we group students from the same department together, we cannot access individual student records to find a student's email or home address. Instead, we have to consider the group of students as a single unit and operate on that unit as such, i.e., apply aggregate functions on the whole unit.

8.6.2 Hands-On Tutorial: Using the Total Row with the Where Clause

Consider another example of the GroupBy operation along with the Selection operation. The query statement is as follows: "List the course information for those courses whose average evaluation was better than 80 points in the last 5 years." This tutorial covers the following How-to topic:

- How-to: create a *Total* query using the *Where* clause in the *Total* row.
  1. Open the university database and start with a new query in the Design View. Use the *Show Table* dialog box to add the course and section tables.
  2. Add the *Name* field from the course table and the *Evaluation* and *Year* fields from the section table to the Design Grid. The *Total* query starts with the join of the course and section tables.
  3. Now, designate this query as a *Total* query by either choosing the View | Totals option from the main menu or by clicking on the *Totals* button on the toolbar. A *Total* row with a default value of *Group By* will appear in the Design Grid.
  4. Click on the *Total* row under the *Evaluation* column, and select the *Average* option from the drop-down list of aggregate functions.

Since we join the course and section tables, each course record is joined with multiple section records from section table where it is course's section. When we apply Group By operation to the join result, we group all the sections for a given course name. We also apply the average aggregate function on evaluation field. This gives us the average evaluation of each course (i.e., each group).

5. We add a selection criteria using the *Where* option under the *Year* column. The expression > `Year (Now ())`-5 selects only those sections for GroupBy operation which were offered in last 5 years. Note that the criteria specified using the *Where* clause will be applied to individual records of the section table prior to the GroupBy operation.

6. We then specify the selection criteria for a group of records. The expression > 80 under the *Evaluation* column specifies that only those groups for which the average evaluation is greater than 80 are selected. Since this criterion is not listed under the *Where* clause in the *Total* row, by default it is applied to groups rather than individual records of the section table.

7. Remove the check in the *Show* row for the *Year* column. We are only interested in displaying the course name and its average evaluation. In fact, we cannot display columns with the *Where* clause in the *Total* row. This is because there is no *single value* computed for groups to display. For example, we do not compute aggregate year for each course; it is just used for the selection prior to GroupBy.

8. Save the query as "QryCourseEvaluation" and run it. Figure 8.18 displays the Design View details and the output snapshot for the above query.

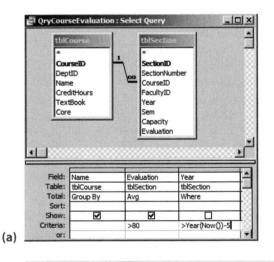

(a)

(b)

Figure 8.18 (a) Using the *Total* row with the Where clause; (b) The query output.

Summary

A **Select query** selects or extracts data from one or more existing tables and displays the selection in the Datasheet View.

Select query operations: *Projection* is a vertical slicing of a recordset. *Selection* is a horizontal slicing of a recordset. *Sorting* provides an ordered sequence of a recordset. *Join* is a vertical merging of two tables. While the *GroupBy* operation places similar records together and treats them as one unit or group.

8.7 *Creating Calculated Fields*

Recall the definition of *derived attributes* from Chapter 3. Derived attributes are the attributes that are calculated using other attributes of the relation. *Age* attribute is an excellent example of a derived attribute, which is calculated using the current date and the *DateOfBirth* attribute. Also recall from Chapter 4 that derived attributes are not included as a part of the relational schema (and hence in the database) when converted from an E-R diagram. Thus, we must calculate values of derived attributes when required by an application or end user. Access queries allow us to create calculated fields as a part of the query design. Consider another example of a derived attribute in the university database, GPA (grade point average) of a student. GPA is derived from students' credit hours (*CreditHours* field) and letter grades (*Grades* field). In this section, we deal with this example in depth to illustrate calculated fields in Access.

In Access, calculated fields are expressed as a new field in separate columns of the query Design Grid. Instead of adding a column from the Table Pane, we write an expression in the Design Grid that, when evaluated, gives the value of the field. Since derived field expressions involve other fields, the existing field names are enclosed in square brackets ([ ]) to distinguish them from other entries in the expression. For example, for the *Age* attribute expression, we enter `Age: Now()-[DateOfBirth]`. The *DateOfBirth* is the existing field and is enclosed in the square brackets. The *Now* is Access's built-in function that returns the current date. Also note that we named the derived field using the renaming operator ":," as discussed before.

8.7.1 Hands-On Tutorial: Creating Calculated Fields

In this tutorial, we illustrate creating calculated fields in Access with an example of students' Grade Point Average (GPA) calculation. Note that GPA is calculated by first summing the product of the grade point and corresponding credit hours and then averaging it over the total number of credit hours earned. That is, if a student has two 3-credit hour courses with a grade point of 3.5 in each and two more 3-credit hour courses with a grade point of 4 in each, we determine the GPA by evaluating the following equation: `(3 * 3.5) + (3 * 3.5) + (3 * 4) + (3 * 4) / 12 = 3.75`.

This tutorial covers the following How-to topic:

■ How-to: create the calculated fields in Access queries.

    1. Open the university database and start with a new query in the Design View. Use the *Show Table* dialog box to add required tables to the Table Pane (see Figure 8.19).

2. Add the student *Name*, *StudentID*, and *CreditHours* fields to the Design Grid. We will add other fields using expressions.

3. Make this query a *Total* query by clicking on the *Total* button on the toolbar and selecting the *Sum* aggregate function in the *Total* row of the *CreditHours* column. This action evaluates the total number of credit hours for each student. Rename this column as `TC:CreditHours`.

4. Now, add a calculated field to the Design Grid. The field features the product of the *CreditHours* and *Grade* fields summed over all the courses for each student. The expression for the column looks like `TG: [CreditHours]*[Grade]`, where *TG* is the name of the new column. Choose the *Sum* aggregate in the *Total* row to evaluate the sum of the product of credit hours and grades for a student.

5. Finally, add one more calculated field, `GPA: [TG]/ [TC]`, to the Design Grid to complete the query. The GPA is calculated by taking the ratio of total grade to total credits. We assign an *Expression* option in the *Total* row for this column (see Figure 8.19).

Note that we could have used the following single expression to replace the three columns TC, TG, and GPA with one GPA column: `GPA: Sum ([CreditHours]*[Grade])/Sum ([CreditHours])`.

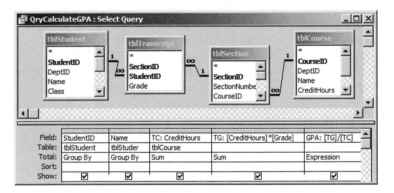

Figure 8.19 Creating calculated fields for GPA calculations.

8.7.2 Calculated Fields with Strings

We can also perform string operations on fields. Consider an example of an expression using strings—`Name: [FirstName] & " " & [LastName]`—to obtain the full name by combining the first name and the last name. The ampersand (&) operator combines the string values from FirstName, LastName, and an empty string (white space). The query in Figure 8.22 displays the full names of all the faculty members.

8.7.3 Expression Builder

Developing complicated expressions for calculated fields or even for selection criteria requires tedious work and remembering field names. The Access's *Expression Builder* dialog box simplifies the process by allowing us to select and add existing fields and built-in functions to an expression. To invoke the *Expression Builder* dialog box, we click the *Build* button on the toolbar or right-click in the *Criteria* row of the Design Grid and choose the *Build* option from the shortcut menu. An *Expression Builder* dialog box then appears (see Figure 8.20).

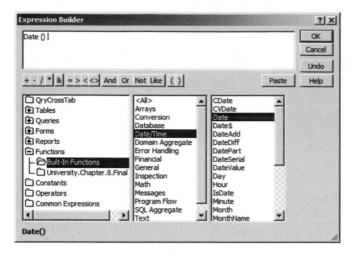

Figure 8.20 The *Expression Builder* dialog box.

We build our expressions in the upper pane of the window. The lower pane of the window is divided into three panels. The left-most panel displays the list of tables, queries, and built-in functions in a collapsible tree structure. The middle panel and right-most panel provide additional details about the items displayed in the left-most panel. For example, if we select the *Built-In Functions* option from the left-most panel, we see a list of function categories in the middle panel. If we select the *Date/Time* category, we see the list of functions, such as *Date* and *Year*, in the right-most panel. We can double-click on function names in the right-most panel to add them to the top pane as we build expressions.

8.8   *Parameter Queries*

While discussing the Selection operation, we gave an example of a selection criteria, DeptID = "ISE." The criteria when applied to the student table outputs students only from the "ISE" department. These selection criteria are *static* in the sense that we write them at the query design time, and they remain fixed for each query execution. What if the user is now interested in viewing a list of students from the "CISE" department? We have no option but to change the query design and modify the selection criteria to DeptID = "CISE." Access allows dynamic assignment of criteria values in the Parameter queries. A *Parameter query* is the query that prompts for parameter values and dynamically assigns user-entered values in the selection criteria to run the query. In the above example, a Parameter query (where *DeptID* is a parameter) will ask for a department name, and the user-entered value ("ISE," "CISE," or something else) is assigned to the DeptID = selection criteria at run time to output students from the desired department. Every time the query is executed, users may enter different parameter values for the desired result.

We create a Parameter query in the same manner we create a Select query. We specify one or more parameters of the query in the selection criteria using square brackets ([ ]). Thus, the criterion for previous examples looks like DeptID = [ ]. If we would like to prompt the user with an appropriate message to enter parameter values, we can enclose the message in the square brackets. For example, we can write DeptID = [Please Enter Department Name] (see Figure 8.21).

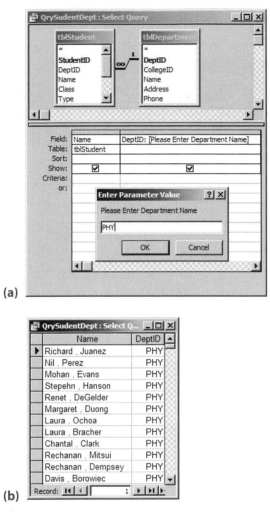

(a)

(b)

Figure 8.21 (a) The Parameter query in the Design View; (b) The query output.

8.8.1 Hands-On Tutorial: Working with Parameter Queries

In this tutorial, we create a Parameter query with multiple parameters. Our Parameter query should display a list of faculty members who have joined a particular college within a specified date range. Thus, our parameters are college name, starting date, and ending date. We need the tblCollege, tblDepartment, and tblFaculty tables for this query. This tutorial covers the following How-to topic:

- How-to: work with the Parameter queries.
  1. Open the university database for a new query in the Design View. Add the college, department, and faculty tables to the Table Pane.
  2. Add fields to the Design Grid as shown in Figure 8.22. Note that the *Name* field is a concatenation of the *FirstName* and *LastName* fields.
  3. Specify the criteria with parameters. Enter the [Enter the College] parameter under the criteria row for the *CollegeID* column. Also, assign the Between [Starting Date] And [Ending Date] criteria under the *JoiningDate* column.

4. Save and run the query. Enter the appropriate parameter test values (COE, 1/1/1995, 1/1/2000) when prompted.

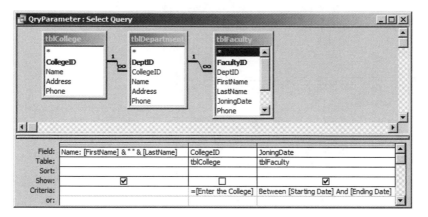

Figure 8.22 The Parameter query with multiple parameters.

8.9 *Crosstab Queries*

We use the Crosstab queries to group and summarize the information and display it in a spreadsheet format. Crosstab queries create less repetition of information in the Datasheet View, making it easier to read and analyze the selected field data. We need three fields to create a Crosstab query: the *row-heading field*, values of which are used in the row headings of the datasheet, the *column-heading field*, values of which are used in the column heading of the datasheet, and the *Value field*, values of which are used in cells of a datasheet. In Figure 8.23, the *DeptID* is the row-heading field, and various *DeptID* values are used as row headings (the first column values). The *Class* field is the column-heading field. There is a column for each distinct class in the *Class* field, and the value of the field is used as the column heading. The *StudentID* is the value field that is counted to display the number of students for a given class (column) and in the given department (row). For example, there are 23 "Junior" students in the "ISE" department.

DeptID	TotalStudents	Freshman	Graduate	Junior	Senior	Sophomore
CAHER	92	5	38	23	15	11
CAPP	114	12	30	34	28	10
CISE	116	11	39	25	24	17
ECE	88	9	33	13	15	18
ISE	90	6	28	23	18	15

Record: ◄◄ ◄ 5 ► ►► ►* of 5

Figure 8.23 Output of a Crosstab query.

It is not difficult to see that the Crosstab query is a special type of the Total query that features the addition of a column heading. A Crosstab query can have *exactly one* field designated as a column heading and *at least one* field designated as a row heading and value type. In the following hands-on tutorial, we consider another Crosstab query example.

8.9.1 Hands-On Tutorial: Working with Crosstab Queries

The Crosstab query, we will develop in this tutorial, is stated as follows: for all the courses in the Computer Science department, we would like to display the total student enrollment in the Fall, Spring, and Summer semesters. For this query, we must use the course names as the row heading, the *Sem* field from tblSection as the column heading, and *StudentID* as the value field (see Figure 8.24). This tutorial covers the following How-to topic:

- ■ How-to: work with Crosstab queries.
  1. Open the university database with the new query, and add the course, section, and transcript tables to the Table Pane.
  2. Add the *CourseID*, *Name*, and *DeptID* fields from the course table, the *StudentID* field from the transcript table, and the *Sem* field from the section table.
  3. Change the type of query from the default Select query to the Crosstab query by choosing the Query | Crosstab Query item from the main menu. An empty *Crosstab* row and a *Total* row with the value "Group By" should appear (a Crosstab query is a special Total query).
  4. Select the *Row Heading* option for the *CourseID* and *Name* columns in the *Crosstab* row. Note that we define more than one row heading to display both course number and name. The Crosstab query must have at least one row heading, and can have as many of them as required by the query design.
  5. Select the *Column Heading* option for the *Sem* field. The Crosstab query must have exactly one column heading.
  6. Select the *Value* option for the *StudentID* field. Also choose the *Count* function in the *Total* row for the *StudentID* column. The *Count* function counts the number of students for each row and column intersection (i.e., each semester and course).
  7. We specify the department selection criteria under *DeptID* column. As in Total queries, any selection criteria that are applied to individual records before grouping must appear under the *Where* option in the *Total* row. Use the criteria =`"CISE"` in the criteria row for the *DeptID* column. We choose no option for this column in the *Crosstab* row as we don't want to display this column in the query result (see Figure 8.24).
  8. Save and then run the query to produce the result shown in Figure 8.25.

Summary

A **Parameter query** prompts user for criteria values when the query is executed. The input values are then used in the selection criteria to run the query.

We use **Crosstab queries** to group and summarize information and display it in a spreadsheet format. Crosstab queries create less repetition of information in the datasheet, making it easier to read and analyze the selected field data.

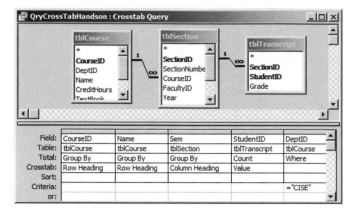

Figure 8.24 The Crosstab query (students per semester per course) in the Design View.

CourseID	Name	Fall	Spring	Summer
CSE5698	Computer Architecture	145	147	116
CSE6100	Visual Basic	146	148	59
CSE6255	Advanced Curcuits	149	148	90
CSE6321	Data Structures	145	146	88
CSE6325	Advanced C++	139	148	58
CSE6596	algorithms	144	143	145
CSE6710	Curcuits	146	147	86
CSE6781	DBMS	146	146	87

Record: 1 of 8

Figure 8.25 The output of the Crosstab query (students per semester per course).

8.10 *Action Queries*

All of the queries that we have created thus far have been variations of Select queries. These queries only display the data, but do not actually change the data in the tables. However, Access queries are not restricted only to data retrieval; they can also perform actions such as updating field values, deleting records, and appending records. Queries that can alter data by performing actions are called *Action queries*. The primary advantage of Action queries is that they allow us to modify a large number of records without having to write any special programs. Access provides three different types of Action queries:

Update Queries: modifies the values of one or more fields in the table.

Delete Queries: uses criteria to delete one or more records from the table.

Append Queries: appends one or more records to an existing table.

A Select query returns the query result as a recordset (set of one or more records) that can be further processed. On the other hand, an Action query does not return any recordset; rather, it performs actions to alter tables. This is why we cannot use Action queries as data sources for further processing or for presenting data on forms or reports; rather, they are used to perform actions on tables.

8.10.1 How to Set Action Query Types

To design an Action query (irrespective of its type), we begin with the query's Design View. As mentioned before, to open the Design View, we double-click on the *Create Query in the Design View* option in the Database Window. This opens the Design View with the default type Select queries. To change the query type, we select the desired query type from the *Query* menu under the main menu, which is only visible in the Design View, as shown in Figure 8.1. Alternatively, we can right-click anywhere in the Table Pane and choose Query Type | <desired query type> from the shortcut menu.

8.11 *Update Queries*

An *Update query* is an Action query that can change field values in an existing table. For example, we can use an Update query to raise the salary of all faculty members by increasing (updating) the *Salary* field of the faculty table by 5%. Figure 8.26 illustrates the effect of the Update query on the *Salary* field.

Update queries primarily update existing values in the database fields. These updates occur mainly because of changes in business policies or changes in data values over time. For example, a policy decision may result in salary increases. Updates of textbooks, department phone numbers, or student class/type values are examples of changes that may require using update queries.

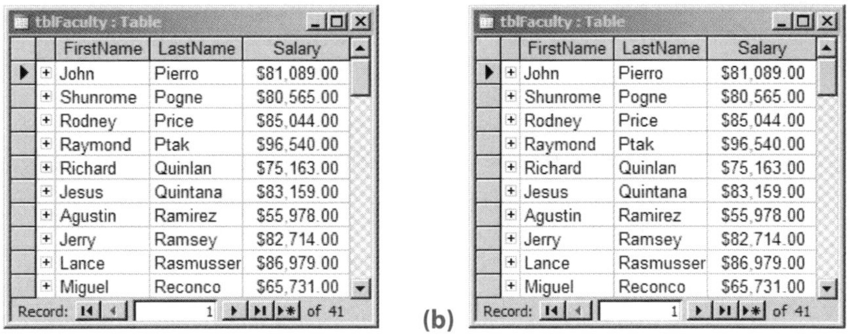

(a)

tblFaculty : Table

FirstName	LastName	Salary
John	Pierro	$81,089.00
Shunrome	Pogne	$80,565.00
Rodney	Price	$85,044.00
Raymond	Ptak	$96,540.00
Richard	Quinlan	$75,163.00
Jesus	Quintana	$83,159.00
Agustin	Ramirez	$55,978.00
Jerry	Ramsey	$82,714.00
Lance	Rasmusser	$86,979.00
Miguel	Reconco	$65,731.00

Record: 1 of 41

(b)

tblFaculty : Table

FirstName	LastName	Salary
John	Pierro	$81,089.00
Shunrome	Pogne	$80,565.00
Rodney	Price	$85,044.00
Raymond	Ptak	$96,540.00
Richard	Quinlan	$75,163.00
Jesus	Quintana	$83,159.00
Agustin	Ramirez	$55,978.00
Jerry	Ramsey	$82,714.00
Lance	Rasmusser	$86,979.00
Miguel	Reconco	$65,731.00

Record: 1 of 41

Figure 8.26 (a) Faculty table before update; (b) The effects of an Update query (5% salary raise) on faculty table.

Update queries thus can update a large number of records in a table at once. If we do not want to update all the records in the table, we can select the records we would like to update by specifying update criteria (similar to selection criteria seen before). Reconsider the above example; now, we only want to raise the salary for faculty members who joined the university before 1995 and have a salary of less than $70,000. Figure 8.27 depicts the Update query in the Design View with update expressions using *JoiningDate* and *Salary* fields. An Update query does not require all the fields from the table in the Design Grid. We only add the fields that we want to update and the fields involving update criteria.

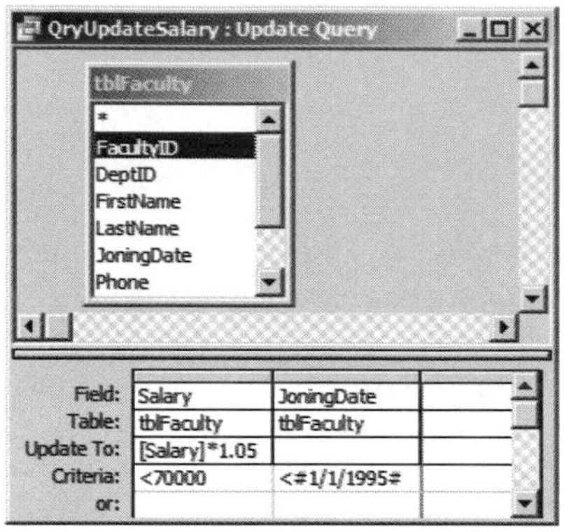

(a)

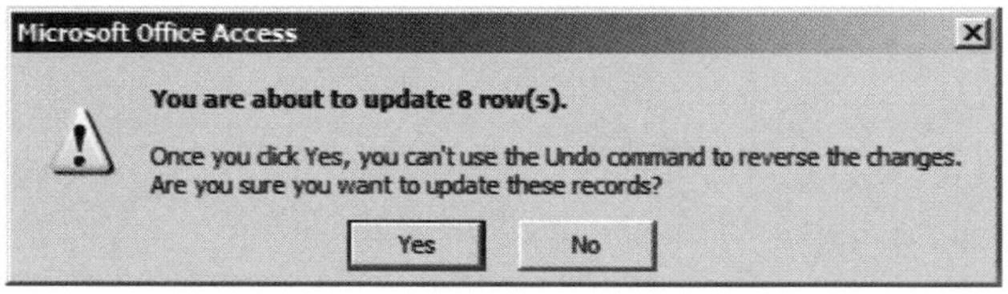

(b)

Figure 8.27 (a) The Update query in the Design View; (b) Access' update warning.

8.11.1 Hands-On Tutorial: Working with an Update Query

In this tutorial, we will build an Update query. The query updates the *Salary* field in the faculty table for those faculty members who joined the university before 1995 and have a salary less than $70,000 (see Figure 8.27). This tutorial covers the following How-to topic:

■ How-to: work with Update queries.

1. Open the university database and begin with a new query in the Design View. Use the *Show Table* dialog box to add the faculty table to the query design.

2. Change the query type from the default Select query to the Update query. Use the query menu or right-click anywhere in the Table Pane, and choose the Update query type. An *Update To* row should appear in the Design Grid.

We use *Update To* row to specify the "*update to*" value or "*update expression*" for a field. We can update more than one field by specifying values/expressions in *Update To* row in respective columns.

3. Add the *Salary* and *JoiningDate* fields from the table list to the Design Grid. In the *Salary* field, enter the expression [Salary]*1.05 under the *Update To* row.

4. In the *JoiningDate* field, specify the following criteria for all dates prior to 1995: < #1/1/1995#. Then, enter < 70,000 criteria in the *Criteria* row of the *Salary* field.

5. Save the query as "QrySalaryUpdates" and run it using the *Run* button on the toolbar. Or, choose Query | Run from the main menu. Access flashes a warning message prompting the number of rows it is updating (see Figure 8.27). Accept the action and verify the updates in the faculty table.

8.11.2 How to Preview Records That the Action Query Alters

When we run Action queries, the changes made to the database tables are irreversible. For example, once we update fields or delete records (see next section), we cannot go back to the previous state of the table. This makes it important that we preview the exact changes that will occur due to an Action query before executing such queries. Fortunately, Access allows us to preview the records that an Action query is about to change. We must always remember to preview the records before actually running the query so that we do not unintentionally change or lose important information.

After designing the Action query in the Design View, we preview the query action in the Datasheet View. To preview, click the *View* button on the toolbar at the top left corner of the Database Window. This button opens the query in the Datasheet View with records that the Action query will alter. For example, the preview of our salary Update query (see Figure 8.28) displays eight records with the salary column. The preview only shows the *Salary* field, as all other fields, such as *JoiningDate* and *Name*, remain unaffected.

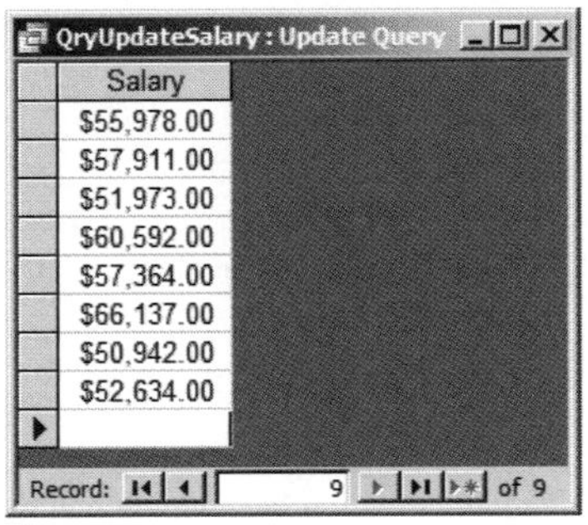

Figure 8.28 Preview of an Update query in the Datasheet View.

8.11.3 How Cascade Updates Work with Update Queries

What happens when we update the primary key of a table that is a foreign key in some other table and vice versa? In the first case, Access allows us to update the primary key value, and if the Cascade Updates option is selected for the primary key-foreign key relationship (see Chapter 7), then Access automatically updates the foreign key value to maintain referential integrity. For example, suppose we want to append the digit "0" to all existing 8-digit student identification numbers. The Update query depicted in Figure 8.29 not only updates all the records in the student table, but also automatically updates all the StudentIDs in the transcript table as well.

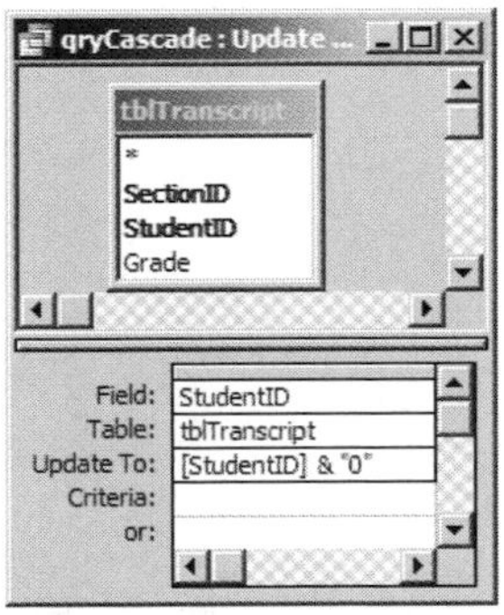

Figure 8.29 A query illustrating the cascade updates (Design View).

In the second case, when we update the foreign key of a table, Access warns us for referential integrity constraint violations. If we continue with this update, we leave data in an inconsistent state, as the Cascade Update option does not update the primary key values for the changes in the foreign key. For example, if we try updating the *StudentID* field in the transcript table first, Access displays a warning similar to the one shown in Figure 8.30.

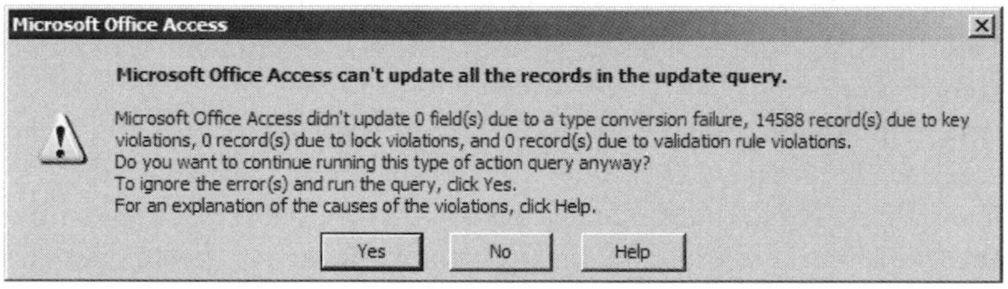

Figure 8.30 The Cascade Update error.

8.12   *Delete Queries*

A *Delete query* is an Action query that deletes records from existing tables. For example, we can use a Delete query to remove course sections that are at least five years old from the section table. Delete queries allow us to delete specific groups of records by applying deletion criteria to the appropriate fields. Figure 8.31 depicts the Design View for a Delete query.

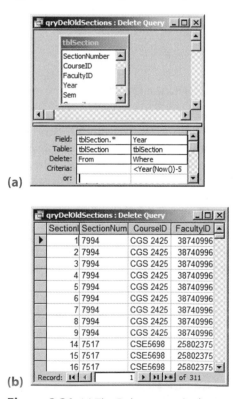

(a)

(b)

Figure 8.31   (a) The Delete query in the Design View; (b) Preview of the Delete query displaying records to be deleted.

We must add all fields or "*" in the Design Grid to delete records (i.e., delete from). We may also add additional individual columns to specify deletion criteria (i.e., delete where). In the following hands-on tutorial, we will work with another example of a Delete query.

8.12.1   Hands-On Tutorial: Building a Delete Query

In this tutorial, we build a Delete query. This query is shown in Figure 8.32. We would like to delete the Industrial Engineering student records for those students who have recently graduated (i.e., say all of the senior class). This tutorial covers the following How-to topic:

- How-to: work with Delete queries.
  1. Open the university database and start with the new query in the Design View. Use the *Show Table* dialog box to add the student and department tables to the query design.
  2. Change the query type from the default Select query to the Delete query. A *Delete* row should appear in the Design Grid.

The *Delete* row has two options to select from: *Where* and *From*. As discussed before, the *Where* option is used for criteria fields, and the *From* option specifies the group of columns under consideration for deletion.

  3. Add the *Class* and *DeptID* fields from the student and department lists, respectively, to the Design Grid. Access automatically selects the *Where* option in the *Delete* row for these fields.
  4. Now, add all fields from the student tables by adding an asterisk (*) to the Design Grid. Access selects the *From* option for this field, indicating that all columns of student records will be deleted.
  5. Specify the criteria for the *Class* field as = "Senior" and for *DeptID* field as = "ISE" under the criteria row.
  6. Save the query as "qryDelStudents." Preview the deleting records using the *View* button on the toolbar, and then run the query for deletion. Verify the action in the student table.

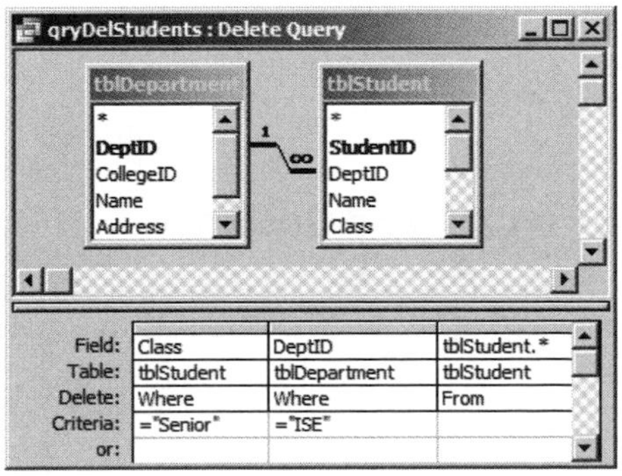

Figure 8.32 The Delete query in the Design View.

8.12.2   Caution with the Cascade Delete Option

As with cascade updates, Access performs cascade deletes when the Delete query removes records that contain primary key values. Consider the example from the previous hands-on tutorial. If we have the Cascade delete option selected for the relationships between the student and transcript tables, we would have inadvertently deleted student records from the transcript table as well. Such an operation could cause problems for graduates attempting to order transcripts. Indeed, Cascade deletes often increase the danger of massive data loss and should be used with caution.

8.13   *Append Queries*

An *Append query* is an Action query that copies records from one or more tables and adds them at the end of another table. In other words, it appends records from one or more tables or a Select query result to an existing table. For example, we can retrieve the contact information and the date of birth of students in the College of Engineering and append them to a temporary table in the database for further processing. The Append query first selects the desired students (as in the Select query with selection criteria) and then appends the resulting data set at the end of a specified temporary table. Figure 8.33 provides the Design View of the Append query. The following hands-on tutorial describes the steps for designing this query.

Append queries also help us to quickly populate tables through bulk inserts. For example, if new student records are available in a temporary table, we can run an Append query to easily move these records from the temporary table to the student table.

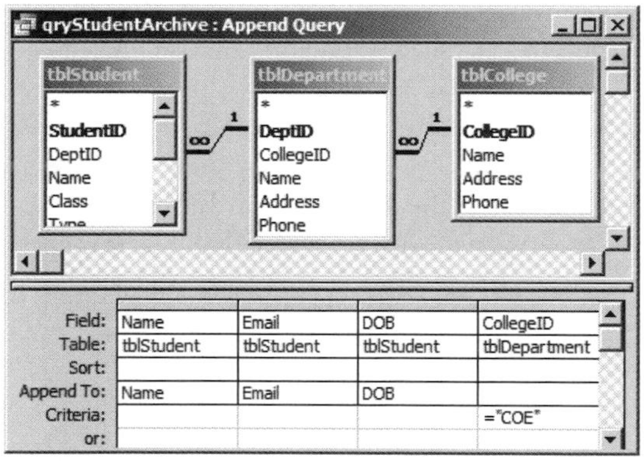

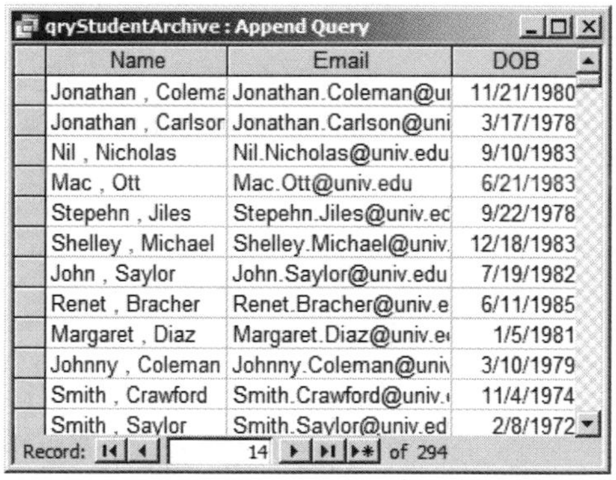

Figure 8.33 (a) The Append query in the Design View; (b) Preview of the Append query.

8.13.1   Hands-On Tutorial: Building an Append Query

Consider the example of an Append query discussed before. We would like to select the contact information and birthdates for all students in the College of Engineering and append them to a temporary table, *tblStudentArchive*, in the database for further processing. This tutorial covers the following How-to topic:

- ■ How-to: work with Append queries.
   1. Open the university database and start with the new query in the Design View. Use the *Show Table* dialog box to add the student, department, and college tables to the query design.

2. Change the query type from the default Select query to the Append query. An Append dialog box (Figure 8.34) should appear asking what table records should be appended to. Select the *tblStudentArchive* table from the drop-down list and click *OK* button.

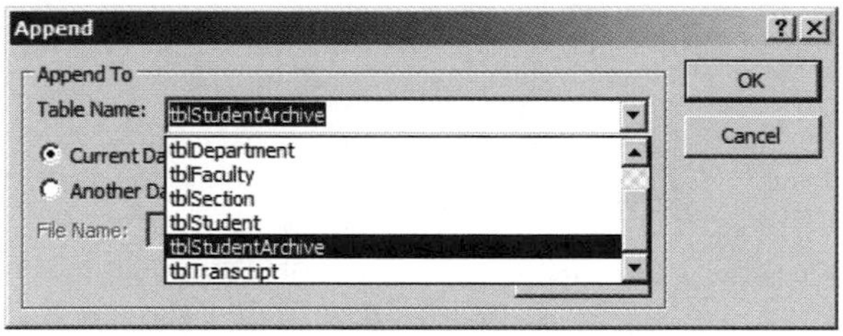

Figure 8.34 The *Append* dialog box.

3. An *Append To* row appears in the Design Grid. Add all the required fields and the selection criteria as shown in Figure 8.33(a).

4. Save the query as "QryStudentArchive." Preview the records selected to append to the archive table and run the query. Verify the action in the archive table.

Summary

Queries that can alter data by performing actions are aptly called **Action queries**. There are three types of Action queries we studied, (1) **Update Queries:** modifies the values of one or more fields in the table; (2) **Delete Queries:** uses criteria to delete one or more records from the table; and (3) **Append Queries:** appends one or more records to an existing table.

8.14 *In-Class Assignment*

In this in-class assignment, we ask to create two simple queries. Consider the *Bottling.mdb* database, the database of a soft drink bottling plant. The database manager has observed several defects of the bottles produced. An expert is going to query the database of observations to try to pinpoint potential sources of defects. The quality expert wants to investigate whether there is a relationship between bottle characteristics (such as material and size) and the number of defects.

- Create a query that, for each type of material and bottle size, calculates the sum of the fraction of nonconforming bottles (the fraction is the ratio of the number of defective bottles to the total number of bottles). Title the query, "QryMaterials." Are there any trends?
- Create a query that, for each type of drink, displays the sum of the fraction of nonconforming bottles. Title the query, "QryDrinkType." Are there any trends?

8.15 *Summary*

- A *query* is a question posed against database tables.
- Access allows us to build queries using a graphical query grid (Query-by-Example or QBE) and by writing SQL statements.
- Access queries can be broadly classified into three function-based categories:
  a. Select Queries
  b. Special Purpose Queries (Crosstab, Parameter, and Make-Table queries)
  c. Action Queries (Update, Append, and Delete queries)
- Select queries are the most common type of query used in database applications. A Select query selects or extracts data from one or more existing tables and displays the selection in the Datasheet View.
- **Query Operations:** *Projection* is a vertical slicing of a recordset. *Selection* is a horizontal slicing of a recordset. *Sorting* provides an ordered sequence of a recordset. *Join* is a vertical merging of two tables. While the *GroupBy* operation places similar records together and treats them as one unit or group.
- A Parameter query prompts user for criteria values when the query is executed. The input values are then used in the selection criteria to run the query.
- We use Crosstab queries to group and summarize information and display it in a spreadsheet format. Crosstab queries create less repetition of information in the datasheet, making it easier to read and analyze the selected field data.
- Access queries are not restricted to only data retrieval and can also perform actions such as updating field values, deleting records, and appending records. Queries that can alter data by performing actions are aptly called *Action queries*.
  a. Update Queries: modifies the values of one or more fields in the table.
  b. Delete Queries: uses criteria to delete one or more records from the table.
  c. Append Queries: appends one or more records to an existing table.

8.16 *Exercises*

8.16.1 Review Questions

1. What is the purpose of a query in databases?
2. Briefly describe the three categories of Access queries.
3. How can we add all of the fields from a table to a query at once?
4. How can we include a field in a query without displaying it in the Design View?
5. Write a criterion that returns only those records in which the *Title* field ends in "Analyst." Where in a query's Design View would we put this expression?
6. Write a date criterion that returns only those records in which the expiry date is after the current year.
7. When writing an expression, how can we specify which table a certain field is from when the same field name is used in different tables?
8. How can we concatenate two strings in an expression?
9. Which total row option should we select if we wish to return only records with a unique value in a particular column? Which option should we select if we wish to multiply the values in two different fields?
10. What type of query groups data both horizontally and vertically? What must this type of query consist of?
11. Why is it important to spell field names in brackets correctly when writing expressions?
12. What is a parameter? What is a Parameter query?
13. How can we prompt the user for a parameter?
14. Where can we specify the parameters for a query?
15. True or False: The parameter names we enter in the *Query Parameters* dialog box must match exactly the parameter text in the Design View.
16. What are the types of Action queries? Briefly describe each.
17. How do Action queries differ from Select queries? Which type of query requires confirmation from the designer before the query is executed?

18. How can we change from one Action query type to another?

19. True or False: For both, Update and Delete queries, we can select just the particular fields we want to perform an action on.

20. What types of Action queries perform archive operations?

21. How can we delete records from related tables when referential integrity has been enforced without using the *Cascade Delete Related Fields* option?

8.16.2 Hands-On Exercises

NOTE: *The database files for these hands-on exercises are available at: www.dssbooks.com.*

1. Bottling Database: Consider the *Bottling* database, the database of a soft drink bottling plant. The database manager has observed several defects of the bottles produced. An expert is going to query the database of observations to try to pinpoint potential sources of defects. Use the database *Bottling.mdb* to create the following queries:

a. First, the expert wants to examine if any particular characteristic of the bottling line is the source of the defects. If one of these characteristics is found to be a likely cause of the defects, she will then determine which lines have this characteristic.

- She begins by examining the possibility that there is a correlation between the fraction of nonconforming bottles in a sample and whether or not an inspection has been performed on the line. Create a Select query that displays this information. Title the query, "QryInspectors." Sort the query so that samples with a large fraction of nonconforming bottles are displayed first. Are there any trends?

- The expert investigates for a possible correlation between the fraction of nonconforming bottles and the number of attendants working in the line. Create a query that displays this information. Title the query, "QryAttendants." Sort the query so that samples with a large fraction of nonconforming bottles are displayed first. Are there any trends?

- Based on the results of QryInspectors and QryAttendants, the quality expert has concluded that lines without inspectors and lines with fewer than three attendants have larger fractions of nonconforming bottles. Create a query that displays the line number of the lines that have these two characteristics. Title the query, "QryDefectiveLines."

b. The quality expert wants to determine the total number of defective bottles produced by each line. Create a query that will determine the total number of nonconforming bottles for each line. Title this query, "QryTotalDefects."

c. When the expert first started collecting samples, she had not perfected her sampling technique. So, she has decided to disregard the results of her first six samples and gather new samples for lines one and two.

- Create a query that will delete the first six samples from *tblDefects*. Title the query, "QryDeleteSamples."

- The expert's results in the second sampling from lines one and two can be found in the table *tblNewSamples*. Create a query that will append the contents of this table to *tblDefects*. Save this query as, "QryAppSamples."

d. Create a query that prompts the expert for a type of drink and the size (in number of fluid ounces) of the bottle. The query should return *only* the types of materials that bottles with these characteristics are made of. Title this query, "QryAvailMatl." Test this query by identifying the types of materials used to produce 22-ounce bottles of cola.

e. The quality expert wants to complete her study by developing a single query summarizing her results. Create a Crosstab query that will display all the factors that she determined to be most likely to cause defective bottles. The rows should consist of the number of attendants, materials, and inspection factors. The columns should be the different varieties of drinks that the plant bottles. The intersections of the rows and columns should compute the average fraction of nonconforming bottles corresponding to the four factors. Save the query as, "QrySummary." Which cell has the largest average fraction of nonconforming bottles?

2. **Airline Reservation System**: Consider the database *Airline.mdb*. Create the following queries for the *Airline* database:

   a. Table *tblReservations* contains data about the ticket reservations. Customers book tickets for the particular flight that services their desired route at the time they want to fly. Design a query to identify the first five flights sorted by the highest number of reservations recorded. Title the query, "QryMaxTkts."

   b. The airline provides special offers to frequent fliers. A frequent flier is a customer who has booked at least three tickets in the past year. Design a query that will provide a list to identify the frequent fliers. Title the query, "QryFrequentFliers." Arrange the results in descending order of the number of tickets purchased.

   c. Create a query to update the information about the customer Margaret Peacock in *tblCustomers*. The fields *CustomerID* and *City* should become "C020" and "Jacksonville," respectively. Title this query, "QryUpdCustomer." Notice the cascaded updates that occur because of this modification.

   d. The airline company is facing budget problems. Therefore, they decide to cancel the flight that is doing the least amount of business. Design a Delete query to delete the flight record that has the least number of seats in it. Title this query, "QryDelFlight." Notice the cascaded deletes that occur. (*Hint*: Use another sub query "SubQryDelFlight" to obtain the required information first.)

   e. The customer with the customer identification number "C004" scheduled to fly on "6/20/2002" on flight number "4" decides to cancel his ticket. Create a query to append a record in the *tblCancellation* table for this operation. Use $50 as the fine amount and the current date as the cancellation date. Title the query, "QryAppCancel."

   f. Prepare a summary report showing, for each flight, the total amount of money earned from the Economy, Business, and Club classes. Design a Crosstab query that lists the flight numbers as row headings and the seat classes (Economy/Business/Club) as column headings. Each cell must contain the total earnings from a class of seats in a particular flight. Title

   the query, "QryCrosstabBusiness." Arrange the results in increasing order of flight number.

   g. To better cater to customer tastes, the airline looks for trends in meal purchases when planning future meals. Create a Crosstab query that lists the flight number and class of seats for each flight as row headings and the meal preferences as column headings. Each cell should contain the total number of passengers for the corresponding flight who have indicated a particular meal preference. Title the query, "QryCrosstabMeals." Arrange the results in ascending order of flight numbers.

   h. The airline provides the names of high-spending customers to certain retailers for marketing purposes. Create a query that identifies the customers, who have spent between $500 and $1000 on airline tickets since Feb. 1, 2002. Title the query, "QryRange."

   i. Design a query that finds all the customers living in the state of Florida (FL) whose first names begin with "Re." Title this query, "QryReCustomers."

   j. Create a query that lists customers' information (*CustomerID* and *Name*) along with the average amount of money they spend on tickets. Title this query, "QryAvgPayment."

   k. Canceling tickets is generally considered an unfavorable practice, and the airline wishes to identify customers who have done so. Design a query to identify the customers who have cancelled tickets at least once. Title the query, "QryCancels."

   l. Design a query that displays the number of seats available and the cost per seat of a requested flight. The flight number and seat class should be the input from the user. Title this query, "QryFlightParameter."

3. **Hospital Database**: Open the database *Hospital.mdb*. Create the following queries for the *Hospital* database:

   a. Table *tblPatients* contains data about patients, including their identification numbers, names, diagnoses, and consulting doctors. *tblBillInfo* contains the billing information for these patients. Using these tables, design a query to identify the patients who have spent between $100 and $250 on medicine starting January 1, 2002. Title the query, "QryPatient-

Expenses." Arrange the results in alphabetical order by the patients' last name.

b. A doctor examines a patient if his or her specialization is related to the patient's illness. Create a query that identifies all the doctors eligible to treat a particular disease. The name of the disease should be entered as a parameter. This query should facilitate the process of assigning a doctor to a patient. Title the query, "QryDoctorAssignment."

c. The hospital is organizing the annual Employee Recognition dinner, which honors the hard work of the doctors and nurses. An award will be handed out to the most popular doctor of the hospital. A doctor is the most popular if he or she had the highest number of patient visits in the last year. Create a query that identifies the five most popular doctors, including their ID numbers, first names, and last names. Title this query, "QryPopularDoctors."

d. The hospital classifies cancer and heart disease as life-threatening diseases. Create a query that lists the names of the patients who suffer from such diseases and the name of the attending doctor. Title the query, "QryDiseases." Arrange the results in alphabetical order by last name and first name of the patient.

e. A 5% late fee is charged to patients who pay their bills after the due date. Design a query to increase the bill amount by 5% for all the patients who bought Hiperlax, Daily +, or Bone Friend and have not paid their bills on time (i.e., the pay date is after the current date). Title the query, "QryLateFee."

f. A new format for the identification number of the heart specialists has been designed. The heart specialists' identification code now begins with "DH," followed by the current two-digit code. Create a query to perform this modification. Title it, "QryDoctorID." Notice the cascaded updates that occur.

g. Dr. Franklin is diagnosed with hemophilia. Create a query that adds him to the patients table and assigns him to the doctor identified as "D005." Title the query, "QryNewPatient."

h. Design a query that identifies patients who bought their medication from the hospital's pharmacy either before January 1, 2002 or

after May 1, 2002. Do not display the bill date in the query results. Title this query, "QryMedicineDate."

i. The hospital would like to know the initials of all the patients suffering from cancer or liver problems. Design a query to perform this task. Title the query, "QryPatientInitials."

j. Design a Parameter query that obtains a region from the user and then displays information about the suppliers operating in that region. Title this query, "QryRegion-Parameter."

k. Patients pay their bills using various modes of payment, including cash, check, and credit card. Design a Crosstab query that displays the name of the patients as row headings and the various payment modes as column headings. A cell in this table should present the total amount of money a patient spent in a particular payment mode. Title this query, "QryCrosstabPayment."

l. Design a query that displays the following details for each supplier: identification number, name, and the medicines they supply. Title this query, "QrySupplierMeds." (*Hint*: Use an outer join.)

m. Several patients have outstanding bills. Create a query that identifies the patients whose outstanding bills exceed $35. Title this query, "QryOutstandingBills."

4. Post Office Database: The database *Packages.mdb* used by a shipping company is actually part of a larger database used by the post office. Open the database *Post Office.mdb* to view the entire database. Review the existing tables and relationships in this database and create the following queries:

a. The shipping costs for a package depend on its weight and the mailing rate per ounce. There is also an additional one-time cost for certified mail packages. Queries can be used to calculate the shipping costs of a package based on its particular characteristics.

■ Build a query that computes the shipping cost of all standard packages that weigh more than one ounce. Save this query as, "QryStdCost."

■ Build a query that computes the shipping cost of a piece of first class mail that is certified and weighs less than one ounce. Save this query as, "QryFirstClassCost."

b. A regional manager of the post office wants to identify the location of the handler of a particular piece of mail. Use the Query Wizard to create a query that displays, for every package in the database, the full name of the handler and the location of the post office that he or she is assigned to. Sort the records alphabetically by post office location. Title this query, "QryHandlerLocation."

c. Customers send packages by certified mail so that they can check whether or not their packages have been received. Create a query that prompts a customer for the identification number of a certified package and returns the delivery status of that package. Title the query, "QryStatusRequest."

d. The post office keeps count of all the letters sent in the current year. Create a query that shows these letters, and title the query, "QryCurrentLetters."

e. The post office accountants must determine the total amount of postage owed by the customers so that they can record it as accounts receivable in their books. Create a query that totals the amount owed by all the customers and returns only that value. Title this query, "QryAcctsReceivable."

f. A package sent to the zip code "32608" is missing. The post office manager wants to contact the offices that serve this zip code to ask for details about the missing package. Create a query that returns the office code and location of all offices servicing the zip code "32608." Title this query, "QryMissingZip."

g. At the end of each year, the post office tabulates all successful certified shipments for the year. A shipment is considered successful if the package has been sent or received. Create a query that returns all the records of certified packages that either were received in the year 2002 or were sent and are en route to their destinations. Title this query, "QryCertifiedSuccess."

h. The package with the identification number "8" has been received. Create a query that updates the (certified delivery) status of this package. Title the query, "QryNewStatus."

i. The manager of the post office wants to determine which mail routes are the busiest. Create a Crosstab query that calculates the number of packages sent from a particular return address to a particular destination address. The cells should contain the total number of packages sent from the address of that row to the address of that column. Title this query, "QryCrossRoutes."

5. Distribution Center Database: A furniture manufacturer has distribution centers in different regions of the country. These centers supply retailers with products to sell. The manufacturer maintains a database of information about the distribution centers, retailers, products, and shipments. Open the database *Furniture.mdb* and examine the existing tables and relationships. Create the following queries:

a. The managers at the manufacturing plant need a list of the origins and destinations of all shipments to be made. Create a Select query that will display this information. To ensure that the list is easy to read, display location names, not identification numbers. Also, include the distance between the locations for each route. Title the query, "QryShipmentRoutes."

b. When a truck leaves a distribution center, it is important to know the total value of the goods that the truck is carrying. Create a query that calculates the total cost of goods per shipment. Name the calculated value, *ShippingCost*. Save the query as, "QryShipmentCosts."

c. Create a query that prompts the user for a distribution center identification number and returns a list of all the retailers that the center serves. Also, include information about the type and amount of product being shipped to the retailers selected in the query. Title the query, "QryRetailerList."

d. Furniture Warehouse in Knoxville, TN is going out of business. Remove this retailer and all of its related records from the database. Title this query, "QryRemoveRetailer."

e. The nationwide retailer Rooms Express is expanding into the Southeast region. Table *tblNewStores* contains information about these new locations. Add the records from *tblNewStores* to *tblRetailers* using a query. Title it, "QryAddRetailers."

f. The manufacturer wants to determine which retailers have the highest sales. Assume that the quantity sold by the retailer is equal to the quantity shipped to a retailer.

- Create a query that determines for each location the list of the retailers ordered by the quantity sold starting from the retailer having maximum sales. Title this query, "QrySellsMost."

- Most of the retailers have multiple locations. Create a query that determines which retailer sells the most in all of its locations combined. Title this query, "QrySellsMost-Total." Which retailer has the highest sales overall?

g. The distribution center manager for the Southeast region is preparing the delivery schedule for the next sixty days. Create a query that shows all the shipments that must be made in the Northeast region during the next sixty days. Title this query, "QryShipmentDates." (Note: To test the query, we may need to revise the dates in *tblShipments* so they include dates that are within sixty days from the present.)

h. The manufacturer has decided to reduce the price of all products by 15% to clear out old inventory and to make room for new furniture designs. Create a query that modifies the price of the products to reflect this change. Title this query, "QryNewPrices."

i. New trucks have been purchased and are going to be allotted to the distribution centers based on their needs. Create a query that determines for each distribution center the average number of miles traveled by each truck. Title this query, "QryNewTrucks."

j. Customers in some locations have complained about the quality of the furniture. Complaints about the Hunter Collection were received in the Northeast region, and complaints about beds (in general) were received in the Southeast region. Create a query that displays how many beds and how many products of the Hunter Collection were shipped in these regions. Save this query as, "QryBadFurniture."

6. Schools Database: The database *Schools.mdb* maintains information about the instructors, courses, and students of a private high school.

Examine the existing tables and relationships in this database. Create the following queries:

a. The school is now offering higher salaries in an attempt to attract qualified instructors. Design a query that identifies the instructors hired during or after the year 2000 who have salaries higher than the average salary level. Save this query as, "QryInstructorSalary." (*Hint*: Create a sub query titled, "SubQryInstructorSalary" to obtain the necessary information first.)

b. The school will be offering short courses during the summer. It is preferable to have the most experienced instructors teach these courses. Create a query that shows for each instructor how many times he or she has taught a particular course. Title this query, "QryMaxTaught."

c. The school presents awards to the best students. Design a query that lists a student's information along with the average percentage that the student earned in his or her classes. Arrange the results in descending order by average percentage score. Title this query, "QryStudentAverages."

d. A faculty committee has decided to change Macroeconomics to an undergraduate course worth 4 credit hours (instead of 3). The course identification number has also been changed to CM06. Design an Update query that performs this operation. Save the query as, "QryUpdCourse." Notice the cascaded updates that occur.

e. One of the just hired instructors decided not to take the job after all. Design a query that deletes the record of this instructor. Save the query as, "QryDelInstructor." Notice the other cascaded deletes that occur. (*Hint*: Create a sub query titled, "SubQryDelInstructor" to get the required information first.)

f. Design a Crosstab query that displays the identification numbers and names of all the courses offered as row headings and the semester when they were offered as column headings. The number of students enrolled in each course during each semester should be displayed in the individual cells. Title this query, "QryCrosstab."

g. Instructors are paid based on years of experience and the number of courses they have taught so far. Design a query that identifies instructors who have taught more than one course and whose salary is between $45,000 and $65,000. Title this query, "QrySalaryRange."

h. The records of some students with similar last names have accidentally been mixed together. Design a query to resolve this problem by displaying information about all the students whose last names begin with "Jo." Label this query, "QryLikeName."

i. Students may enroll in school during the spring or fall semesters. Design a query that displays the name of all the students currently enrolled and the number of days each student has attended school so far. Title this query, "QryCalculateDays."

j. Students needing assistance in a particular subject should determine which instructors can help them with that subject. Design a query that prompts the user for a course identification number and returns the names of all the instructors who have taught that course. Save this query as, "QryCourseParameter."

k. Design a query that lists the title and name of all the school's instructors along with their identification numbers and the student feedback for the courses they taught. Some instructors may not have taught a course, but they should be included in this list. Title the query, "QryInstructorInfo."

l. Student Michael Frank has decided to drop out of school. Design a query that adds relevant parts of his current record to the table *tblLeaveNonGraduating*, which includes the information about all the students who left school without graduating. Save this query as, "QryMoveToLeave."

7. Restaurant Database: A restaurant uses a database to maintain information about its managers, servers, bartenders, cooks, and very important customers (VIPs). The database is also used to create the employees' work schedules. The database is updated every week with the new schedules. Open the database *Restaurant.mdb*, and view the existing tables and relationships. Create the following queries for the database:

a. Managers' salaries depend on the number of employees supervised. Create a query that calculates the number of cooks, bartenders,

and servers that each manager supervises. Title this query, "QryManagersTeam" (create separate queries for each).

b. Servers use the database to find out their schedules for the week. Create a query that prompts a server for his or her identification number and displays that server's schedule for the week. Title this query, "QryServerSchedule."

c. At least one server must be working from 6 p.m. to close every day of the week in order to help clean the restaurant (the restaurant is not open on Sundays.) In the servers' current schedule, there is no one scheduled to work from 6 p.m. to close on Tuesdays and Saturdays. Create a query that updates the schedule of a server (say, the server with *ServerID* 3) in such a way that in addition to his or her current working hours, the server is working Tuesday and Saturday nights. Call this query, "QryClose."

d. To become a bartender, an employee must have first worked as a server for at least two years. Design a query that displays the names and start dates of all the servers who are eligible to become bartenders. Title this query, "QryEligibleServers."

e. The restaurant calls its VIPs on their birthdays to see if they would like to reserve a table. Design a query that displays the names of all the VIPs with birthdays in the current month. Title this query, "QryVIPBirthdays."

f. The restaurant management has heard a rumor that a food critic will be dining at the restaurant either on Wednesday, Thursday, or Friday. Create a query that returns the names of the cooks who will be working on these three days. Title this query, "QryFoodCritic."

g. The server Heather Phillips is about to become a bartender. Revise her records in the database by doing the following:

- Create a query that will move her current record from *tblServers* to *tblBartenders*. Title this query, "QryNewBartender."

- Once the Append query *QryNewBartender* is executed, create a query that removes her old record from *tblServers*. Title this query, "QryRemoveServer."

- Now that she is a bartender, Heather Phillips has a new manager and a new schedule. Create a query that modifies her record in *tblBartenders* so that her manager is Jerry Simmons and her shifts for Tuesday, Wednesday, Friday, and Saturday are 7–2, 7–2, 9–close, and 5–8, respectively. Title this query, "QryNewSchedule."

h. The owner of the restaurant wants to compare the wages paid to her employees with other restaurants. To do so, she should compute the average wage for each type of employee (servers, bartenders, and cooks) as well as the overall (for all employees) average wage. Create a query to complete this task. Title this query, "QryAvgWages."

i. The managers want to design the schedules so that cooks who close one night do not have to work the early shift the next day. Create a query that displays the schedules of cooks who have at least one shift from 5–close followed by a shift from 10–6 the next day. Title this query, "QryCookSchedule."

8. Menu Database: A restaurant uses the database *Menu.mdb* to keep track of the menu items being offered and the ingredients used. Open this database and examine the existing tables and relationships. Create the following queries:

a. Design a query that calculates the cost of each ingredient for the amount indicated in the recipes. Note that prices are given per pound and that amounts are given in ounces. Save this query as, "QryTotalCost."

b. A customer has allergic reactions to fish and large quantities of mushrooms. Create a query that lists the name of the menu items that contain fish or more than 4 oz of mushrooms. Title this query, "QryAllergies."

c. The chef needs to compile a list of dishes that will not be offered this week because the ingredients are not available. Design a query that lists the name of unavailable ingredients together with the dishes that use them. The ingredient and dish names should be the only fields displayed. Title this query, "QryNotAvailable."

d. The customers at Table # 2 have finished their meals and are ready for the bill. Create a query that calculates the total bill amount for Table # 2. The query should display only this amount. Save the query as, "QryBillAmt."

e. A 15% gratuity is added to the bills of parties larger than five. Calculate the bill amount for the parties of this size. Title this query, "QryLargeParty."

f. The chef needs a copy of the recipe for Chicken à la King. Design a query that creates a new table called *tblChickenRecipe* that shows the ingredients and corresponding amounts needed to prepare this dish. Title the query, "QryMakeRecipe."

g. The restaurant's management wants to get an idea of which meals are the most popular. Create a Crosstab query that displays the total amount of money each table spends on each menu item. Save the query as, "QryCrosstabMeals."

h. The price of beef has risen by 10%. Create a query that will increase the prices of all dishes containing beef by 10%. Title this query, "QryPriceChange."

i. The information in the database is used to create receipts for customers. Design a query that prompts a server for the number of a table and the date. Then, it should return the names and prices of the menu items that that table ordered. Do not display the table number on the receipt. Save this query as, "QryReceipt."

j. The manager wants to determine which menu items are infrequently ordered. Using queries, list all the items that were ordered just once. Title this query, "QryUnpreferredItems." (*Hint*: First determine how many times each menu item was ordered using a sub query titled, "QryNumberOrdered.")

9. MegaBucks Bank Database: The MegaBucks Bank has just converted all its records about customers, accounts, loans, and transactions to a database called *MegaBucks.mdb*. Open this file and view its tables and relationships. Develop the following queries:

a. Design a query that identifies all the customers whose current balance is between $500 and $1,500. Call this query, "QryCustomerBalance."

b. The transaction table maintains records of daily deposits and withdrawals occurring in the bank. Design a query that displays, for each account with at least one withdrawal during the year 2002, the account number, the social security number of the account holder, and the total amount withdrawn. Arrange the results in descending order of amount withdrawn. Title this query, "QryWithdrawal."

c. Design a query that changes the account number of the person whose social security number is 314-65-4648 to 234222. Increase the amount of interest earned in all of his or her accounts by 3%. Note the cascaded revisions that occur. Title this query, "QryModifyAcct."

d. Design a query that creates a new table called *tblCustomerLoan*. The new table should contain the name, account, and loan information of all customers whose loans have not yet been closed. Call this query, "QryMakeCustomerLoan."

e. Design a query that lists information about each customer along with the amount of loans each has received. Title this query, "QryLoanAmts."

f. The account holder with social security number 314-65-4648 has decided to open a Christmas club account with a starting balance of $100. He wants to start the account today and close it in 3 months. Design a query that adds this account to the Accounts table. Title this query, "QryNewAccount."

g. Design a Crosstab query that displays the first and last name of customers as row headings and the various account types available as column headings. Each cell should contain the current balance a customer has in each of the accounts. Arrange the results alphabetically by last name then first name. Save this query as, "QryCrosstabBalance."

h. Design a Crosstab query that displays the account number and account type as row headings and the transaction types as column headings. The total amount of money involved in transactions of a certain type and for a certain account number since January 1, 2002 should be displayed in the cells. Title this query, "QryCrosstabTran."

i. The bank needs to prepare a monthly report of certain accounts. Create a query that identifies customers from Austin with last names ending in "et" who have active accounts. Title this query, "QryAustinCustomers."

j. The bank reports information about all currently active loans. Create a query that dis-

plays the *AcctNo*, *TypeID*, and *CloseDate* fields of the table *tblLoans* as well as the amount yet to be paid for all currently active loans. Use the long date format for the *CloseDate* field. Save this query as, "QryLoanCalculate."

k. Customers often forget their account numbers, and the bank tellers must look up the numbers for them. Create a query that prompts the user for the customer's social security number and then displays the corresponding first name, last name, and number of the account. Title this query, "QryCustomerAccount."

10. Hotel Database: Consider the database *Hotel.mdb*. Continue improving the functionalities of this database by creating the following queries:

a. The hotel management has decided to give a free vacation to the first 5% of customers who have the highest number of bookings during the last two years. Design a query to identify these customers. Title this query, "QryMaxCustomers."

b. Customers who keep pets in their hotel room must pay a fine. Create a query that lists information about the customers who kept (or are keeping) pets in their room, including the total fine they had (or have) to pay. Arrange the results in descending order of total fine paid. Title this query, "QryFines."

c. The customer with the booking identification number 27 has decided to vacate his room on 6/16/2003. He has no fines and no food bills. The customer has to pay for the room only. Create a query to insert the billing records into the billing table. Save this query as, "QryAppBill."

d. Design a query that revises the identification number and first name of the customer with the last name "Peacock" who lives in the state of Florida (FL). The identification number and first name should be changed to "C020" and "Nancy," respectively. Title the query, "QryChangeCustomer." Notice the cascaded updates that occur.

e. The hotel managers have noticed that the more expensive items on the menu are not selling. Create a query that lists the most expensive food items in the table *tblFood*. Title this query, "QryExpensiveFood." (*Hint*: Create a sub query titled, "SubQry-

ExpensiveFood" to obtain the required information from *tblFood*.)

f. The managers of the hotel require a report of the most preferred room types by the customers. Design a Crosstab query that displays the identification number and last name of customers as row headings and the various room types as column headings. The number of times each customer has booked a room of a certain type should appear in the cells. Arrange the results in alphabetical order by the customers' last names. Title this query, "QryCrosstabBooking."

g. Hotel management is researching customers who spend within certain price ranges. Design a query that identifies all customers who have spent between $1000 and $2000 on rooms since March 1, 2002. Call this query, "QrySpendRange."

h. Create a query that displays the name and number of bookings for customers who have made more than one booking and who have a first name that begins with "La." Save this query as, "QryLaNames."

i. Design a query that prompts the user for the first and last name of a customer and displays the total amount spent so far by that customer on hotel rooms. Title this query, "QryCustomerSpending."

j. For the customers who purchased food in the hotel, display their names, identification numbers, and total food bills. Make sure not to include in this list the customers who did not purchase food. Save this query as, "QryCustomerFood."

k. Some of the menu items are sold more frequently than others. Design a query that displays the identification number, name, and quantity sold for each type of food on the menu. Sort the items based on the total sales. Title this query, "QryFoodSales."

CHAPTER
nine
SQL: Creating and Processing RDBs

chapter OVERVIEW

9.1   *Introduction*

In Chapter 8, we discussed how to use the graphical query design grid to query Access tables. The Access GUI helped us design a query with a few mouse clicks. However, these clicks automatically produced a query written in a standard query language known as SQL (pronounced as "sequel") or *Structured Query Language*. The SQL query was visible to us through the query's SQL View. As we could switch to the query's Design View or Datasheet View, we could have also switched to SQL View using the option from the *View* drop-down list on the *Query* toolbar. In this chapter, we focus on understanding SQL.

SQL is a complete and widely used relational database (RDB) query language. SQL allows us to query relational databases to create, manipulate, and control database objects. For example, we can use SQL to create tables, select data from one or more tables, add or delete rows from existing tables, update data fields, and more. IBM originally developed SQL for its Relational Database Management Systems project, DB2, in the late 1970s. Soon after that, SQL became the industry standard. The knowledge of SQL gives us an ability to write queries even from outside the Access environment. We will explore this ability in the database application development parts (part III and IV) of this book.

The SQL language is modeled on a series of simple English phrases referred as SQL *statements*. Although, SQL is a complete database language, it is not a complete programming language like Visual Basic, C/C++, or Java. Unlike standard programming languages, SQL cannot support any arbitrary development of logical sequences. It can only operate in database context. However, we can embed SQL statements (*embedded SQL*) into general purpose programming languages. Because of this capability, developers often use SQL in conjunction with programming languages to create database applications. Thus, this chapter builds the SQL background for topics to be discussed in Parts III and IV of the book.

9.1.1   Topics

This chapter discusses the following topics:

- Types of SQL statements.
- DDL SQL statements such as CREATE, DROP, and DELETE.
- DML SQL statements such as SELECT, INSERT, DELETE, and UPDATE.

9.2   *Types of SQL Statements*

We divide SQL statements into four categories based on the database operations they perform:

- Data Definition Language (DDL) statements
- Data Manipulation Language (DML) statements
- Data Control Language (DCL) statements
- Database Stored Procedure Language (DSPL) statements

The *Data Definition Language* (*DDL*) statements are used to define data in the database by creating, altering, and destroying database objects. For example, CREATE TABLE statements create database tables, while DROP TABLE statements delete database tables. We discuss important DDL statements early in this chapter. The second type, *Data Manipulation Language* (*DML*) statements, consists of the core SQL statements used to manipulate (i.e., select, insert, update, and delete) data in the database tables. For example, the INSERT and SELECT statements insert a new row and select rows from a table, respectively. We provide a detailed discussion of DML statements in the remaining sections of this chapter.

The next category, *Data Control Language* (*DCL*) statements, configures and controls the database permissions, roles, and referential integrity controls. For example, GRANT ACCESS and REVOKE SQL statements allow or deny a user's read or write access privileges to a database table. Finally, the *Database Stored Procedure Language* (*DSPL*) statements are used for triggers, event handlers, and stored procedures in transaction processing. The detailed analysis of DCL and DSPL statements is beyond the scope of this book; we recommend the reader to refer to SQL reference books for DCL and DSPL.

9.3 *The Data Definition Language (DDL)*

DDL statements define the structure of the data in a database. These statements allow users to create, alter, and drop database objects such as tables and indexes. In Chapters 6 and 7, we learned how to create database tables, define a primary key for a table, create table indexes, and relate tables using Access GUI. DDL statements can perform those visual steps to create tables, keys, indexes, and relationships. In this section, we focus on CREATE, DROP, and ALTER DDL statements for database tables. We also illustrate how to define a primary key and an index on a database table. Before we proceed, however, we would like to briefly review a few key concepts.

Tables   A *table* is a two-dimensional grid that serves as the most fundamental element of a relational database. A database management system stores and relates its data in tables. Each column of the table, an *attribute*, contains information about the subject of the table. Each row of the table, referred to as a *record* or tuple, is a particular instance of a subject.

Primary Key   A *primary key* is an attribute or minimal set of attributes that uniquely identifies each tuple within the table.

Foreign Key   A *foreign key* is an attribute or a set of attributes in a table that acts as a primary key to the same or another table in the database.

Indexes   A reader of a textbook may refer to book index to search for specific subjects or sections. The book index is the ordered list of topics with a pointer to page numbers on which that topic can be found. Similarly, a database *index* is the ordered list of indexing attributes with a pointer to table rows where the actual record can be found. For example, an index of the *Zip* attribute is the ordered list of zip codes with pointers to table rows in which we can find the zip code value. Indexes allow fast searching through database tables when searched by indexing attribute.

9.3.1 The CREATE Statement

CREATE statements, as the name suggests, create database objects. For example, the CREATE TABLE statement creates a table and defines its columns. We can also use a CREATE TABLE statement to define primary and foreign keys for a new table. We use the CREATE INDEX statement to create an index on a table attribute.

Syntax:

```
CREATE TABLE [Table Name]
            ({<Column name> <Data type> <Constraint>}, {} . . .)
CONSTRAINT  {<Key Name> <key Type> (Field1, Field2 . . .)},
            {} . . .;
```

Query:

Create a new table, *tblDepartment*, to store department information. Store the department identification number, name, address, and phone number for all the departments in the university database.

SQL Statement:

```
CREATE TABLE tblDepartment
            (DeptID     VARCHAR2 (10)      NOT NULL,
            Name        VARCHAR2 (50)             ,
            Address     VARCHAR2 (200)            ,
            Phone       NUMBER (30)        DEFAULT 0,
            CollegeID   VARCHAR2 (3)              )
CONSTRAINT  DeptPK      PRIMARY KEY (DeptID)
            DeptFK FOREIGN KEY (CollegeID) REFERENCES tblCollege (CollegeID);
```

Explanation:

The CREATE TABLE statement first takes the name of the new table to create. It then takes the list of column names, their data types, and any column constraints. We can compare these lines of SQL statement with the process of designing a table in Access's Design View. Providing the table name in the SQL statement is like saving the table in Access GUI. Providing the list of column names and data types is like inserting column names and choosing the data type from the drop-down list in the table's Design View. The column constraints in the SQL statements are like setting the field properties in the Design View.

The CREATE TABLE statement then takes table constraints to define primary and foreign keys. The primary key statement is the equivalent of assigning a field as a primary key in the table's Design View. The foreign key statement is like drawing a relationship line between two tables (given after the REFERENCES keyword) in the Relationship Window of Access (refer to Chapter 7).

The VARCHAR2 data type in the SQL statement is the equivalent of the *text* data type in the Access environment. The input parameter of VARCHAR2 indicates the space allocated for the field value. This value performs the same role as the *Field Size* property of the text data in table's Design View. Table 9.1 lists a few column constraints that can be used with the CREATE TABLE SQL statement.

Create Index Example:

Create an index (named *tblDeptAddressIndx*) on the *Address* field of the department table.

```
CREATE INDEX    tblDeptAddressIndx
ON              tblDepartment (Address);
```

Table 9.1 SQL field constraints.

Constraints	Meaning	MS Access Equivalent
NOT NULL	Cannot be null.	Required.
NULL	Set to null.	Allow Zero Length.
UNIQUE	Should be unique.	–
DEFAULT VALUE	Set the default value.	Default Value.
CHECK (Condition)	Check for the condition.	Validation Rule.

9.3.2 The DROP Statement

The DROP statement removes database objects. DROP TABLE, for example, removes a table from a database. By removing the table, we delete all its data, columns, field constraints, table constraints (primary key and foreign keys), and indexes associated with the table. We can also use the DROP INDEX statement to remove only an index. Note that in order to remove only a column, we would use the ALTER statement (see Section 9.3.3). The DROP statement drops an entire database object such as a table or an index.

Syntax:

```
DROP TABLE [Table Name];
DROP INDEX [Index Name];
```

Query:

Remove the department table, its data, columns, and indexes.

SQL Statement:

```
DROP TABLE tblDepartment;
```

Index Drop Example:

Remove only the index on the *Address* field of the department table.

```
DROP INDEX    tblDeptAddressIndx;
```

9.3.3 The ALTER Statement

ALTER statements, predictably, alter existing database objects. For example, ALTER TABLE can change the existing table definition. These changes may include, but are not limited to, the addition or deletion of columns and table constraints or the revision of data types and field constraints.

Syntax:

```
ALTER TABLE       [Table Name]
ADD COLUMN        [<Column name> <Data type> <Constraint>]
ADD CONSTRAINT    [<Key Name> <key Type> (Field1, Field2 ...)];

ALTER TABLE       [Table Name]
DROP COLUMN       [Column name]
DROP CONSTRAINT   [Key Name];
```

Query:

Add a field for the department chairperson to the department table. Make this field a foreign key in the faculty table.

SQL Statement:

```
ALTER TABLE    tblDepartment
ADD COLUMN    Chair    NUMBER (10)
ADD CONSTRAINT DeptFK2 FOREIGN KEY (Chair) REFERENCES tblFaculty(FacultyID);
```

Removing Columns and Constraints Example:

For illustration, let us drop the newly created field and constraint.

```
ALTER TABLE        tblDepartment
DROP COLUMN        Chair
DROP CONSTRAINT    DeptFK2;
```

Summary

Data Definition Language (DDL) statements **CREATE**, **DROP**, and **ALTER** are used to create, drop, and alter database objects such as tables and indexes.

9.4 The Data Manipulation Language (DML)

Data Manipulation Language (DML) statements form the core and are the most often used SQL statements. The manipulation involves selection, insertion, updates, and deletion operations and the SELECT, INSERT, UPDATE, and DELETE statements are used to perform these operations, respectively. The SELECT statement is by far the most used DML statement and is studied in great detail in this chapter as well. The DML statements have equivalent Access query types, which we have seen in Chapter 8. The Access Select queries are SELECT SQL statements, the Access action queries, Append query Delete query and Update query, are INSERT, DELETE, and UPDATE SQL statements, respectively. We now deal with all these DML statements in separate sections to follow.

9.5 The SELECT Statement

SELECT statements are by far the most frequently used SQL statements. While we can employ these statements for a variety of purposes, we discuss them in the context of the following basic query operations: Projection, Join, Selection, Sorting, and GroupBy (also see Chapter 8).

9.5.1 Projection: The SELECT Clause

The basic SELECT statement presented below projects the selected table columns as a query output. The statement features two clauses, the SELECT clause and the FROM clause. We use the

SELECT clause to specify the columns of query output. The FROM clause is used to list the tables involved in the query design to select columns *from* (discussed in Section 9.5.3).

Syntax:

```
SELECT    [Field name (s)]
FROM      [Table name];
```

Query:

Project the student name, email, address, and phone fields from the student table.

SQL Statement (QrySelectClause):

```
SELECT Name, Email, Address, Phone
FROM   tblStudent;
```

An Example: projecting all columns of a table:

We use the asterisk (*) to select all the columns without individually listing them in the SELECT clause. The following SQL code selects all the columns of student table.

```
SELECT * FROM tblStudent;
```

9.5.2 Hands-On Tutorial: Running DML Statements in the Access Environment

Before we discuss DML statements further, we would like to illustrate how to run and test SQL statements in the Access environment using a hands-on tutorial. This tutorial covers the following How-to topic:

■ How-to: write, execute, and test SQL statements in the Access environment.
1. Click the *Create Query in Design View* option in the Database Window. This should open a new query in the Design View.
2. Click the *Close* button in the *Show Table* dialog box without adding any tables. This should automatically open the SQL View. To open the SQL View manually, locate the *View* button at the top left-hand corner of the toolbar, and select the *SQL View* option (refer to Figure 9.1). Alternatively, choose the View | SQL View option from the main menu.
3. Write the SQL statement and choose the *Run* (!) button on the toolbar to execute the query (refer to Figure 9.1). Alternatively, choose the Query | Run option from the main menu.

9.5.3 Join: The FROM Clause

Join, a powerful and frequently used operation, systematically draws data from multiple tables in order to provide a unified view of data in individual tables. We join tables in SQL by specifying table names (separated by commas) in the FROM clause.

Syntax:

```
SELECT    [Field name (s)]
FROM      [Table1, Table 2, Table 3 . . .];
```

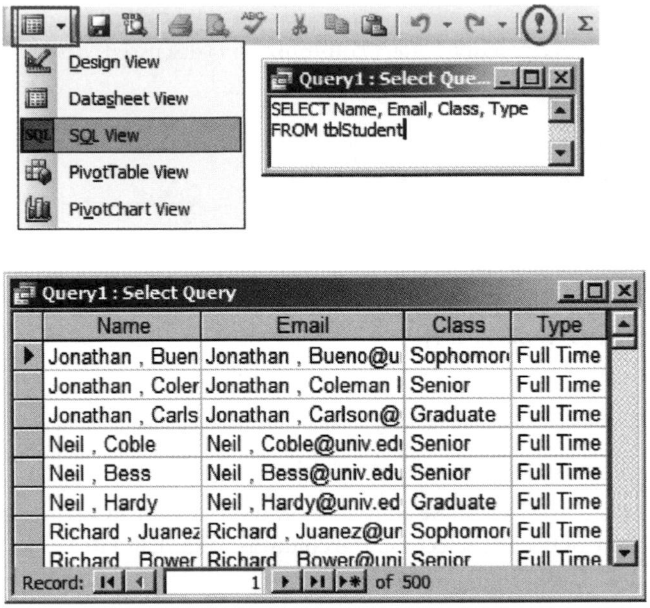

Figure 9.1 (a) Running DML SQL statements in the Access environment; (b) Query output.

Query:

Select the contact information and department name for faculty members.

SQL Statement (QryJoinQuery):

```
SELECT    Name, Email, Address, Phone, Name
FROM      tblFaculty, tblDepartment;
```

The tables listed in the FROM clause are joined, and the attributes listed in the SELECT clause are projected from the joined tables.

Renaming Query Tables and Fields Using the Keyword "AS"

In the previous example, the SELECT clause has two *Name* fields, one for the faculty name and one for the department name. However, this is a conflict of names as SQL doesn't know which name refers to which table or which one to output first in the display order. To resolve conflicts we identify columns by prefixing tables' names:

```
SELECT    tblFaculty.Name, Email, Address, Phone, tblDepartment.Name
FROM      tblFaculty, tblDepartment;
```

Sometimes, table names might be long and complex. Prefixing them for multiple fields in the SELECT clause might render the SQL statement cluttered and difficult to read. This is where we could use the keyword **AS** to temporarily rename tables or fields.

```
SELECT    Fac.Name, Email, Address, Phone, Dept.Name
FROM      tblFaculty AS Fac, tblDepartment AS Dept;
```

9.5.4 Selection: The WHERE Clause

If we execute the join query in the previous subsection, we notice that each faculty record is joined with all the records from the department table. However, we are interested in displaying the name of the department the faculty member belongs to. The tables in the FROM clause are joined to output the Cartesian product (also see Section 8.3.2). In the Cartesian product, each record from the first table is joined with all the records from the second table. What we would like to do is to join a faculty record to the record in the department table where the *DeptID* of the faculty record is same as the *DeptID* in the department table. Recall that these types of joins are referred to as *inner joins*. Inner joins can be viewed as a selection of specific records from the Cartesian product. To specify the selection condition of an inner join, we use the WHERE clause. Particularly, we equate the primary key and foreign key values in the WHERE clause (QryWhereClause2):

```
SELECT   Fac.Name, Email, Address, Phone, Dept.Name
FROM     tblFaculty AS Fac, tblDepartment AS Dept
WHERE    Fac.DeptID = Dept.DeptID;
```

The WHERE clause is an optional clause of the SELECT statement and is used to specify any selection criterion.

Syntax:

```
SELECT   [Field Name (s)]
FROM     [Table Name (s)]
WHERE    [Criteria];
```

Query:

Select the contact information and department name of the faculty members who joined the university after 1995 and whose salary exceeds $75,000.

SQL Statement (QryWhereClause3):

```
SELECT   Fac.Name, Email, Address, Phone, Dept.Name
FROM     tblFaculty AS Fac, tblDepartment AS Dept
WHERE    (Fac.DeptID = Dept.DeptID) AND (Salary > 75000)
         AND (JoiningDate > #31/12/1995#);
```

Explanation:

The above query selects the faculty information from an inner join of the faculty and department tables (the first criterion in the WHERE clause). The output is then filtered based on the salary and the joining date criterion specified in the WHERE clause.

The expressions in the WHERE clause can include a combination of one or more of the following operators:

Arithmetic Operators	*=, <, <=, >, >=*
Clause Operators	*BETWEEN, LIKE, IN*
Logical Operators	*AND, OR, NOT*

Using the BETWEEN Clause Operator

The BETWEEN clause operator is used in conjunction with the logical AND operator to specify the range of values.

Query:

Select the contact information and department name of the faculty members whose salary is between $65,000 and $75,000 and who joined the university after 1995.

SQL Statement (QryBetweenClause):

```
SELECT   Fac.Name, Email, Address, Phone, Dept.Name
FROM     tblFaculty AS Fac, tblDepartment AS Dept
WHERE    (Fac.DeptID = Dept.DeptID) AND (Salary BETWEEN 65000
         AND 75000) AND (JoiningDate > #31/12/1995#);
```

Using the LIKE Clause Operator

The LIKE clause is widely applied in search criteria; often with wildcard characters (also see Section 8.4.4).

Query:

List the contact information for all the industrial engineering students who have taken computer- or database-related courses.

SQL Statement (QryLIKEClause):

```
SELECT   T1.Name, Email, Address, Phone
FROM     tblStudent AS T1, tblTranscript AS T2, tblSection AS T3, tblCourse AS T4
WHERE    (T1.StudentID = T2.StudentID) AND (T2.SectionID = T3.SectionID)
         AND (T3.CourseID = T4.CourseID) AND (T1.DeptID = "ISE")
         AND ((T4.Name LIKE "*Computer*") OR (T4.Name LIKE "*Database*"));
```

Explanation:

The above SQL query is based on the four tables (renamed as T1–T4). The first three AND criteria in the WHERE clause designate the join condition for the inner join. The next AND criterion selects students from the ISE department. Finally, the LIKE clause selects students who have taken courses, *tblCourse.Name*, with the words "computer" or "database" in the course name.

Using the Keyword DISTINCT

If we execute the previous query, we observe that the number of resulting rows exceeds the number of students in the Industrial Engineering department. This happens because students have taken one or more computer- or database-related courses. For each course taken that satisfies query criteria, a student record is produced. Thus, we observe the same student record for each course the student has taken, whereas we would just like to see the *distinct* student records that satisfy the query criteria. We can obtain distinct records using the keyword DISTICNT in the SELECT clause. See an example query under the IN clause operator heading next.

Using the IN Clause Operator

The IN clause is often used for nested or sub queries. It specifies the inner query to look *in*. We rewrite the LIKE clause example query to illustrate the IN clause.

Query:

List the contact information for all the distinct industrial engineering students who have taken computer- or database-related courses.

SQL Statement (QryInClause):

```
SELECT Name, Email, Address, Phone
FROM   tblStudent
WHERE  (DeptID = ISE)
       AND (StudentID IN
               (SELECT DISTINCT StudentID FROM tblTranscript WHERE SectionID IN
                 (SELECT SectionID FROM tblSection WHERE CourseID IN
                   (SELECT   CourseID
                     FROM   tblCourse
                     WHERE  (Name LIKE "*Computer*") OR (Name LIKE "*Database*")
       ) ) ) );
```

Explanation:

The above SQL query has three nested queries linked using the IN clause. The innermost query selects all the computer- or database-related courses. The next outer query selects all the sections for the courses selected in its inner query. The next outer query then selects the *distinct* students who have registered for the sections selected in its inner query. Finally, the outermost query selects the industrial engineering students from the students selected in its inner query.

9.5.5 Sorting: The ORDER BY Clause

When we execute a query, the output records appear in the order they were in the table. We can use the ORDER BY clause to sort the output records based on one or more attributes in ascending (ASC) or descending (DESC) order.

Syntax:

```
SELECT   [Field Name (s)]
FROM     [Table Name (s)]
WHERE    [Criteria]
ORDER BY [Field name (s)] <ASC, DESC>;
```

Query:

Select the contact information and department name of the faculty members whose salary is between $65,000 and $75,000. List the output, first in ascending order of their joining date and then in descending order of their salary.

SQL Statement (QryOrderByClause):

```
SELECT   Fac.Name, Email, Address, Phone, Dept.Name
FROM     tblFaculty AS Fac, tblDepartment AS Dept
WHERE    (Fac.DeptID = Dept.DeptID) AND (Salary BETWEEN 65000 AND 75000)
ORDER BY JoiningDate ASC, Salary DESC;
```

9.5.6   Grouping: The GROUP BY Clause

A grouping operation combines similar records and treats them as a single unit or group. For a detailed discussion of grouping operations and aggregate functions, refer to Section 8.6.

Syntax:

```
SELECT     [Field Name (s)]
FROM       [Table Name (s)]
WHERE      [Criteria]
GROUP BY   [Field name (s)];
```

Query:

Count the number of students in each department in the department table.

SQL Statement (QryGroupByClause):

```
SELECT     Dept.Name, COUNT (Std.StudentID) AS TotalStudents
FROM       tblStudent AS Std, tblDepartment AS Dept
WHERE      Std.DeptID = Dept.DeptID
GROUP BY   Dept.Name;
```

Explanation:

In the above SQL query, we perform an inner join on the student and department tables. We group the records of the join result based on the department name. All the student records from the same department are grouped and treated as a single unit and counted.

We can use aggregate functions such as MIN, MAX, SUM, AVG, and COUNT to process a group of records.

> *MIN, MAX —Provides the minimum or maximum value.*
> *SUM, AVG—Calculates the sum or average value.*
> *COUNT   —Finds the count of records.*

We use the following syntax for these functions:

```
[Function Name] [Field name] AS <Rename>
```

Note that with GROUP BY clause in place, the fields in the SELECT clause either appear with aggregate function or they are used in the GROUP BY clause. For example, in the above query, the *Name* field is used in the GROUP BY clause and the other field in the SELECT clause, *StudentID*, is used with the aggregate function. The fields that don't appear in the GROUP BY clause and are listed in the SELECT clause must be aggregated so as to give a single value per unit grouped by the GROUP BY clause. The field in the GROUP BY clause can appear in the SELECT clause without aggregate function as it already has a single value per unit grouped by the GROUP BY clause.

Using the HAVING Clause

The HAVING clause is always used with the GROUP BY clause to specify the filtering criteria for group values. This clause is similar to the WHERE clause we have seen before. The HAVING clause is to the GROUP BY clause as the WHERE clause is to the SELECT clause.

Syntax:

```
SELECT     [Field Name (s)]
FROM       [Table Name (s)]
WHERE      [Criteria]
GROUP BY   [Field name (s)]
HAVING     [Criteria];
```

Query:

List the departments in the College of Engineering that have enrollments of 100 or more students.

SQL Statement (QryHavingClause):

```
SELECT     Dept.Name, COUNT (Std.StudentID) AS TotalStudents
FROM       tblStudent AS Std, tblDepartment AS Dept
WHERE      (Std.DeptID = Dept.DeptID) AND (Dept.CollegeID = "COE")
GROUP BY   Dept.Name
HAVING     (COUNT (Std.StudentID)) > 100;
```

Explanation:

In this SQL statement, as before, we group students from the same department into one group. For each group, we count the number of students as *TotalStudents*. We only retain and output groups *having* a count of students more than 100. Note that the college selection criterion is used to filter join records even before using the grouping operation.

Summary

A **SELECT** clause can have those fields without aggregate functions that are grouped in the **GROUP BY** clause.

A **HAVING** clause can have those fields that either appear in the **GROUP BY** clause or are used with aggregate functions in the **SELECT** clause.

Summary

Structure of the **SELECT** Statement:

Mandatory {
```
SELECT
FROM
```

```
WHERE
GROUP BY      } Optional, but must appear in this order
HAVING
ORDER BY
```

9.6   *The INSERT Statement*

INSERT statements are DML statements that insert one or more records into database tables.

Syntax:

```
INSERT INTO  [Table Name]
             ([Column1, Column2, Column3 . . .])
VALUES       ([Value1, Value2, Value3 . . .]);
```

Query:

Insert information about the new department, "Digital Institute," into the department table.

SQL Statement (QryInsert):

```
INSERT INTO  tblDepartment
             (DeptID, Name, Address, Phone, CollegeID)
VALUES       ("DGI," "Digital Institute," "303FAB UFL 32611," 3921044, "CFA");
```

Explanation:

The above example inserts a single record into the department table. The INSERT statement assigns items from the VALUES list for each corresponding column in the INSERT INTO list. In the previous SQL statement, for example, the *DGI* value is added for the *DeptID* column, and *CFA* is assigned for the *CollegeID* field. In addition to the correct sequence of fields and their values, another important aspect of INSERT statements is the data types of the field values. It is our responsibility to know and obey the data types. The *DeptID*, *Name*, *Address*, and *CollegeID* fields have VARCHAR (string) data types, and thus their values are embedded in quotation mark to indicate string type, while a *Phone* is a number data type and requires a numeric value.

More INSERT Statement Examples:

- We can skip assigning data values for one or more non-primary key fields. Consider, for example, a new entry into the department table. The new department's address and phone number are unknown when we are entering the data.

```
INSERT INTO  tblDepartment
             (DeptID, Name, Phone, CollegeID)
VALUES       ("BIE," "Bio Informatics Eng," NULL, "COE");
```

- We can also insert multiple records into a table with a single INSERT statement. We do so in conjunction with a sub query. We insert the result of a sub query into a table as follows:

```
INSERT INTO  tblDepartment
             (DeptID, Name, Address, Phone, CollegeID)
             SELECT DeptID1, Name1, Address1, Phone1, CollegeID1
             FROM tblDownload WHERE CollegeID1 = "COE";
```

The field names in the SELECT statements are renamed for clarity; however, the number of fields and their data types should match the INSERT INTO list.

9.7 *The DELETE Statement*

DELETE statements are DML statements that delete one or more records from database tables. We can specify the deletion criteria using a WHERE clause to select the records to delete.

Syntax:

```
DELETE FROM  [Table Name]
WHERE        [Criteria];
```

Query (QryDelete):

Delete all last year (senior) industrial engineering students.

SQL Statement:

```
DELETE  *
FROM    tblStudent
WHERE   Class = "Senior" AND DeptID = "ISE";
```

Another DELETE Statement Example:

We can delete records in conjunction with a sub query. The above student example can be rewritten in a sub query format as follows:

```
DELETE  *
FROM    tblStudent
WHERE   StudentID IN
        (SELECT StudentID FROM tblStudent
        WHERE Class = "Senior" AND DeptID = "ISE");
```

9.8 *The UPDATE Statement*

UPDATE statements are DML statements that update one or more rows of a table. We can specify the update criteria using a WHERE clause to select the records to update.

Syntax:

```
UPDATE  [Table Name]
SET     [Column1 = Value1, Column2 = Value2 . . .]
WHERE   [Criteria];
```

Query:

Raise the salary field in the faculty table by 5% for all the faculty members who joined the university before 1995 and who earn less than $70,000.

SQL Statement (QryUpdate):

```
UPDATE  tblFaculty
SET     Salary = Salary * 1.05
WHERE   JoiningDate < #1/1/1995# AND Salary < 70000;
```

Another UPDATE Statement Example:

We can update records in conjunction with a sub query. The above salary example can be rewritten in a sub query format as follows:

```
UPDATE    tblFaculty
SET       Salary = Salary * 1.05
WHERE     FacultyID IN
          (SELECT FacultyID FROM tblFaculty
          WHERE JoiningDate < #1/1/1995# AND Salary < 70000);
```

Summary

CREATE, **ALTER**, and **DROP** statements are used to create, update, and delete database objects such as tables and indexes. **INSERT**, **UPDATE**, and **DELETE** statements are used to create, update, and delete records within tables.

INSERT statements insert one or multiple records into database tables. **DELETE** statements delete one or more records from database tables. **UPDATE** statements update one or more rows of database tables.

9.9   Summary

- Based on their database operations, we divide SQL statements into four categories. The first category, *Data Definition Language* (*DDL*) statements, is used to create, drop, and alter database objects such as tables and indexes. The second category, *Manipulation Language* (*DML*) statements, is used to manipulate (i.e., select, insert, update, and delete) data in database tables. The third category, *Data Control Language* (*DCL*) statements, configures and controls the database permissions, roles, and referential integrity controls. The fourth category, *Database Stored Procedure Language* (*DSPL*) statements, is used for triggers, event handlers, and stored procedures in transaction processing.
- The SELECT statement features two clauses: the SELECT clause to specify the columns of query output and the FROM clause to list the tables involved in the query design to select columns *from*.
- We use the ORDER BY clause to sort the output records based on one or more attributes in ascending (ASC) or descending (DESC) order.
- We obtain distinct records using the keyword DISTINCT in the SELECT clause.

- A SELECT clause can have those fields without aggregate functions that are grouped in the GROUP BY clause.
- A HAVING clause can have those fields that either appear in the GROUP BY clause or are used with aggregate functions in the SELECT clause.

Structure of the **SELECT** Statement:

```
Mandatory {  SELECT
             FROM

             WHERE
             GROUP BY     Optional, but must
             HAVING       appear in this order
             ORDER BY
```

- CREATE, DROP, and ALTER statements are used to create, delete, and update database objects such as tables and indexes. INSERT, DELETE, and UPDATE statements are used to create, delete, and update records within tables.

- INSERT statements insert one or multiple records into database tables.
- DELETE statements delete one or more records from database tables. We specify the deletion criteria using a WHERE clause to select the records to delete.

- UPDATE statements update one or more rows of database tables. We specify the update criteria using a WHERE clause to select the records to update.

9.10 *In-Class Assignment*

Write SQL statements for the following queries based on the university database.

- Query 1: Create a new faculty table, *tblFaculty*. Assume appropriate fields and their data types, including a primary key field. The table must have a *DeptID* as a foreign key referring to the department table, *tblDepartment*. Also, create an index on the primary key of the faculty table.

- Query 2: Display the number of faculty members working for each department in the department table.
- Query 3: Delete all those faculty members who have been at the university for 15 years (use *JoiningDate* fields) and who are earning less than $50,000 (use *Salary* field).

9.11 *Exercises*

9.11.1 Review Questions

1. What is "SQL" an acronym for?
2. SQL commands can be divided into three major groups. What are these groups? Provide an example of each.
3. The following is an SQL statement that intends to display the identification number, price, and names of products (from *tblProduct*) that cost more than $100:

   ```
   SELECT ProductID, Name, Price
   FROM tblProduct
   WHERE Price LIKE 100;
   ```

   Is this statement correct? If not, write the correct statement.
4. The following SQL statement displays the total sales for each product sold in a retail store.

   ```
   SELECT ProductID, Price, SUM (Sales) AS
   TotalSales
   FROM tblProduct
   GROUP BY ProductID;
   ```

   Is this statement correct? If not, correct the statement.

5. Explain what the following statement displays.

   ```
   SELECT BookID, SUM (Sales) AS Total
   FROM tblBook
   GROUP BY BookID
   HAVING SUM (Sales) >= 50;
   ```

6. Explain what the following statement displays.

   ```
   SELECT T1.BookName, SUM (Sales) AS TotalSales
   FROM tblBook AS T1, tblTransactions AS T2
   WHERE T1.BookID = T2.BookID
   GROUP BY T1.BookName;
   ```

7. What does the following statement do?

   ```
   UPDATE tblProduct
   SET Price = 250
   WHERE Name LIKE "*TV Set*";
   ```

8. What does the following statement do?

   ```
   SELECT COUNT (Price)  AS TotalItems,
          MIN (Price)    AS MinPrice,
          MAX (Price)    AS MaxPrice,
          AVG (Price)    AS AvgPrice
   FROM tblProduct
   WHERE Name LIKE "*Dinning table*";
   ```

9. Is the following statement correct? If not, give the correct statement and explain what the statement does.

```
SELECT ISBN, Price, SUM (InStock) AS
TotalStock,
MAX (Price) AS MaxPrice, AVG (Price) AS
AvgPrice
FROM   tblBooks
GROUP BY ISBN;
```

10. Is the following statement correct? If not, give the correct statement and explain what the statement does.

```
SELECT AccountNo, SUM (TransactionAmt) AS
Balance,
FROM tblTransactions
GROUP BY AccountNo
WHERE SUM (TransactionAmt) < 50;
```

11. Answer the following questions about the statement below:

　a. What does the statement do?

　b. Why do we use `T1.FlightID` instead of `FlightID`?

　c. Why do we use `SUM (Sales) AS TotalSales` instead of `SUM (Sales)`?

　d. What does the `GROUP BY` clause do?

```
SELECT T1.FlightID, SUM (Sales) AS
TotalSales
FROM tblFlights AS T1, tblReservations AS T2
WHERE T1.FlightID = T2.FlightID
GROUP BY T1.FlightID;
```

12. What does the following statement do?

```
INSERT INTO tblReservations
(TicketNo, CustomerID, FlightID, Class,
BookingDate, TravelDate, NoInfants,
MealPref, PaymentMode, PaymentAmt)
VALUES (134, "C312," "F786," "Economy,"
2/5/2002, 6/8/2002, 0, "vegetarian,"
"Mastercard," 239.99);
```

13. Is the following SQL statement correct? If not, fix it.

```
INSERT INTO tblCustomers
(CustomerID, CustomerName, Address, City,
State, Zip)
VALUES (214, "James Silver," 121 Main
Street, Athens, Georgia, 77123);
```

14. Is the following statement correct? If not, explain why and provide the correct statement.

```
SELECT CategoryID, SUM (InStock) AS
TotalStock,
```

```
MAX (Price) AS MaxPrice, AVG (Price) AS
AvgPrice
FROM tblProduct
GROUP BY CategoryID
WHERE SUM (InStock) >= 50;
```

15. Is the following statement correct? If not, explain why and provide the correct statement.

```
SELECT T1.CustomerID, T1.CustomerName,
T2.Destination
FROM tblCustomers AS T1, tblReservations AS
T2
B>GROUP BY T2.Destination
WHERE T1.CustomerID = T2.CustomerID;
```

16. The table *tblVendor* contains information about vendors along with an identification number, *VendorID*, for each. Is the following statement correct? If not, explain.

```
ALTER TABLE tblVendor
DROP COLUMN VendorID;
```

9.11.2 Hands-On Exercises

NOTE: *The database files for these hands-on exercises are available at: www.dssbooks.com.*

1. Write an SQL statement that displays the name and author of science fiction books in *tblBook*. Order the books in ascending order by price.

2. The student table consists of the following fields: SSN, name, address, and department. The following fields are listed in tblDepartment: department name, college, and address. Write an SQL statement that lists the names and addresses of students enrolled in the College of Engineering. A bookstore keeps information about books in *tblBook*. Write an SQL statement that displays the names of the textbooks that cost more than $50 but less than $100.

3. A supermarket keeps historical data about products sold in *tblSales*. This table consists of the following fields: product identification number, product name, quantity sold, price per unit, and purchase date. Write an SQL statement that displays the total amount of money the store made on January 10, 2002.

4. The student table consists of the following fields: *SSN*, *Name*, *Address*, *Department*, and *College*. Write an SQL statement that finds the names and addresses of students enrolled in the "Management" department.

5. Using *tblStudents*, the International Student Center at a university maintains the following information about each international student: social security number, name, address, and nationality.

 a. Write an SQL statement that finds the names and addresses of students from India.

 b. Write an SQL statement that finds the names and addresses of students from India, China, and Russia.

6. Write an SQL statement that allows the secretary of a middle school to update the address of Greg Brown in *tblStudent* to "456 Metropark Road, Dallas, TX 23411."

7. Sandy is working with Safe Travel, an airline company. Write an SQL statement that allows her to do the following:

 a. Delete a reservation from *tblReservations* when a customer cancels his or her reservation.

 b. Update information about flights in *tblFlights* when the city of departure or destination changes.

 c. Insert information about a new customer in *tblCustomers*.

8. An elementary school maintains information about students, teachers, classes offered, and school activities. Write the SQL statements needed in order to build a database for the school. Identify field names, primary keys, foreign keys, and the data type for each field.

9. GetWell Hospital stores information about doctors, patients, medicines, etc. in its database. The database consists of the following tables:

 ■ *tblDoctors* contains the following fields: *DoctorID*, *LastName*, *FirstName*, *Specialization*, and *OfficeNR*.

 ■ *tblPatients* contains the following fields: *PatientID*, *LastName*, *FirstName*, *Disease*, and *DoctorID*.

 ■ *tblSuppliers* contains the following fields: *SupplierID*, *CompanyName*, *Address*, and *Region*.

 ■ *tblMedicines* contains the following fields: *MedicineID*, *MedicineName*, *SupplierID*, and *SideEffect*.

 ■ *tblTransactions* contains the following fields: *BillID*, *BillDate*, *PayDate*, *PatientID*, *MedicineID*, *Description*, *BillAmount*, and *PayMode*.

Write the SQL statements that enable a doctor or a nurse to find the following information:

 a. The names of the patients who were diagnosed with liver failure.

 b. A list of all of Dr. Jones' patients.

 c. The names of the patients who visited the hospital more than 10 times in the last two months.

 d. The names of the suppliers and the medicines they offer.

 e. The names of the suppliers located in the Southwest region.

 f. The names of all the patients who visited the hospital last month and their expenses.

 g. The names of the doctors who specialize in pathology.

10. A manufacturer of plastic and glass bottles maintains information about the different types of bottles produced, production lines, etc. The database consists of the following tables:

 ■ *tblBottles* contains the following fields: *BottleTypeID*, *DrinkType* (for example: Water, Cola etc.), *FluidOunces*, and *Material*.

 ■ *tblLines* contains the following fields: *LineNo*, *BottleTypeID*, *NoAttendants*, *Inspection*, *EquiAge*, and *ZoneNo*.

 ■ *tblDefects* contains the following fields: *SampleNo*, *LineNo*, *SampleSize*, *NoNonConfirming*, and *FractionNonConfirming*.

Write the SQL statements that enable a production manager to find the following information:

 a. The names of the drinks that come in glass bottles.

 b. The bottle types that hold up to 16 ounces of liquid.

 c. The bottle type IDs produced in production line #1.

 d. The production line that has the highest number of defects.

 e. The production lines that have equipment more than seven years old.

11. The geography department in a university maintains information about students, courses, and

instructors. The database consists of the following tables:

- *tblCourses* consists of these fields: *CourseID*, *Name*, *Category* (classroom or distance learning), *Level* (undergraduate or graduate), and *Credit*.
- *tblInstructors* consists of these fields: *InstructorID*, *LastName*, *FirstName*, *Title*, *ResearchArea*, *HireDate*, *Salary*, *StreetAddress*, *City*, *State*, and *Zip*.
- *tblStudents consists of these fields:* StudentID, LastName, FirstName, Category, EnrollDate, CreditsEarned, StreetAddress, City, State, Zip, *and* PhoneNo.
- *tblStudentCourse* consists of these fields: *StudentID*, *CourseID*, *Semester*, *Year*, and *Grade*.
- *tblInstructorCourse* consists of these fields: *CourseID*, *Semester*, and *Year*.

Write the SQL statements that enable the department secretary to find the following information:

a. The names of the students who have a grade point average of 4.0.
b. The names of the students who took World Geography.
c. The names of the courses taught by Professor Johns.
d. The names of the courses offered in Fall 2001.
e. The names of the students enrolled in the department in Fall 2002.
f. The names of the professors who are interested in U.S. geography.

12. A restaurant in Dallas maintains information about its tables, food, reservations, etc. in a database. The database includes the following tables:

- *tblTables* consists of two fields. One displays the table number, and the other displays the number of guests that can be accommodated at each table.
- *tblMenuItems* consists of the following fields: *MenuItemNo*, *ItemName*, and *Price*.
- *tblOrders* consists of the following fields: *OrderNo*, *TableNo*, and *MenuItemNo*.
- *tblRecipes* consists of the following fields: *ReceipNo*, *MenuItemNo*, *IngredientNo*, *Date*, and *Amount*.
- *tblIngredients* consists of the following fields: *IngredientNo*, *IngredientName*, *PricePerPound*, and *Availability*.

Write the SQL statements that enable the restaurant manager to determine the following information:

a. The total amount of money received on August 2002.
b. The tables (indicated by table numbers) that can accommodate at least six guests.
c. The ingredients those are not available.
d. The most popular items on the menu.
e. The menu items that contain ingredient #10.
f. The most expensive ingredients.

13. The central office of FG Post Office is located in Ocala, Florida. The post office serves customers in Florida and Georgia and maintains information about packages, customers, offices, rates, etc. in a database. The database consists of the following tables:

- *tblCustomers* contains the following fields: *CustomerID*, *ReturnAddress*, *TotalAmtOwed*, and *PaymentType*.
- *tblOffices* contains the following fields: *OfficeCode*, *Location*, *Manager*, and *ZipCodesServiced*.
- *tblPackages* contains the following fields: *PackageID*, *CustomerID*, *HandlerID*, *PackageType*, *Destination*, *DatePostmarked*, *ShipmentType*, *PackageWt*, and *Certified*.
- *tblRates* contains the following fields: *ShipmentType*, *FirstOunceRate*, *RateAfterFirst*, and *CertificationRate*.
- *tblHandlers* contains the following fields: *HandlerID*, *OfficeCode*, *LastName*, *FirstName*, *Title*, and *Supervisor*.
- *tblCertified* contains the following fields: *PackageID*, *PackageStatus*, and *DateReceived*.

Write the SQL statements that enable a post office manager to determine the following information:

a. The total amount of money that the post office has received so far.
b. A list of certified mail that has been received in the year 2004.
c. The packages (indicated by ID numbers) that are postmarked February 12, 2002.
d. A list all first class packages. For each package, display the package ID number, the package weight, and the shipping cost.
e. The names of the handlers located in Florida.
f. The codes and names of the managers in Illinois.

g. A list of the codes and the locations of the post offices that serve any of Gainesville's zip codes. (Management wants to know if service covers all the zip codes in Gainesville, Florida. The first three digits of zip codes in Gainesville are 326.)

14. A product manger prepares a report on inventory and sales at the end of each month. *tblTransactions* maintains historical information about the quantity produced and sold and the price for each final product. In order to prepare the report, the manager follows these steps:

  a. Select *ProductName*, *QuantityProduced*, *QuantitySold*, and *Price* from *tblTransactions*.

  b. Calculate the inventory level at the end of the month for each product.

  c. Identify which product has the maximum inventory level.

  d. Calculate the total amount of sales for each product.

  e. Identify which product sold the most.

  f. Identify which product sold the least.

Write an SQL statement that enables the manager to prepare the report.

15. An airline company maintains information about customers, reservations, flights, cancellations, and prices. The following tables contain this information.

  ■ *tblCustomers*: customer identification number, name, and address.

  ■ *tblReservations*: ticket number, customer identification number, flight number, flight class, booking date, travel date, number of infants traveling, meal preferences, payment method, and payment amount.

  ■ *tblFlights*: flight number, type of aircraft, city of origin, city of destination, total number of seats, travel time, and frequency of flight.

  ■ *tblCancellations*: ticket number, cancellation date, and fine amount.

  ■ *tblSeatCosts*: flight number, flight class, price, and seats available.

Write the SQL commands that enable a flight manager to prepare the following queries.

  a. "qryTotPayment" should display the following information for each customer: customer identification number, customer name, and total amount of money spent.

  b. "qryReCustomers" should determine the identification number and the name of the customers whose first name begins with "Re" (for example: Rene, Regina, etc.).

  c. "qryCancels" should display the identification number and the name of the customers who canceled their tickets.

  d. "qryFrequentFliers" should find the name and identification number of customers who flew at least three times in the last year and then order them in descending order.

  e. "qryMaxTkts" should determine the flight number and the type of aircraft that has the maximum number of reservations.

  f. "qryRange" should find the name and identification number of the customers who have paid more than $500 but less than $1,000 for airplane tickets.

16. Quality Furniture produces furniture and distributes it nationwide. The company maintains information about distribution centers, retail stores, products, and shipments in a database, which consists of the following tables:

  ■ *tblDistCenters* contains the following information about each distribution center: identification number, region, and address.

  ■ *tblProducts* contains the following information about each product: identification number, name, description, and unit cost.

  ■ *tblRetailers* contains the following information about each retailer: identification number, identification number of the distribution center from which the retail store receives shipments, address, and name.

  ■ *tblShipments* contains the following information about each shipment: identification number, identification number of the distribution center, identification number of the retailer, product identification number, quantity shipped, distance from the distribution center to the retailer, and delivery date.

Write the SQL commands to perform the following:

  a. Find the name and location of all retail stores that sell dining room tables.

  b. Management is considering buying new trucks to improve delivery. In order to help management decide on the number of trucks to buy and the manner of distribution, determine the average number of miles traveled per day for each distribution center.

c. Display the name and address of the retail stores that made at least $100,000 in sales last week. Do not include any sales figures or items sold in the database design.

d. Management estimates that for each shipment, the company pays an average of $5 per mile traveled. Display the total transportation costs for each shipment.

e. Display the names of the retailers that will receive a shipment on January 12, 2007.

17. A hotel in Miami maintains information about customers, rooms, booking, etc. in a database. The database includes the following tables:

- *tblCustomers* includes these fields: *CustomerID, FirstName, LastName, Address, City, State,* and *Zip.*

- *tblRoomTypes* includes these fields: *TypeID, Name, DailyRent,* and *AvailableRooms.*

- *tblBooking* includes these fields: *BookingID, CustomerID, RoomType, RoomNo,* and *InDate.*

- *tblBilling* includes these fields: *BookingID, OutDate, Fines,* and *TotalAmt.*

- *tblFood* includes these fields: *FoodID, Name,* and *Cost.*

- *tblFoodBills* includes these fields: *ReceiptNo, Date, CustomerID, FoodID, Quantity,* and *Amount.*

Build the following queries to assist management with everyday decisions.

a. "qryCustomerFood" presents the total amount of money spent on food by each customer. The query includes these fields: *CustomerID, FirstName, LastName,* and *SumOfAmt.*

b. "qryRoomAvailable" lists rooms that are available. Include *RoomType* and *DailyRent* for each room.

c. "qryCustomerSpendings" presents the total amount of money due from customers whose first names begin with "Jo."

d. "qryFindCustomer presents the *InDate, OutDate,* and *RoomNo* for customers who live in Florida.

e. "qryMaxBooking" lists the names of customers who have visited the hotel at least three times.

f. "qrySpendRange" lists the names of customers who have spent at least $1,200.

g. "qryLaNames" lists the names, arrival dates, and departure dates for customers whose last names begin with "La."

18. A small bank in Ocala, Florida maintains information about customers, accounts, transactions, etc. in a database. The database contains these tables:

- *tblCustomers* includes these fields: *SSN, First-Name, LastName, Address, City, State,* and *Zip.*

- *tblAccounts* includes these fields: *AcctNo, TypeID, SSN, StartDate, CloseDate, Current-Balance,* and *TotalInterest.*

- *tblLoans* includes these fields: *LoanID, AcctNo, AcctTypeID, LoanAmt, InterestRate, Monthly-Payment, StartDate,* and *CloseDate.*

- *tblAcctTypes* includes these fields: *TypeID, Name, Description,* and *InterestRate.*

- *tblTransactions* includes these fields: *TrnID, TrnDate, TrnType, AcctNo, TypeID,* and *TrnAmt.*

Write the SQL statements that do the following:

a. List customers who do not live in Ocala but who have an account with the bank.

b. List the names and social security numbers of those customers who opened an account after January 2002.

c. Add a new customer to the database. Note that a new customer has to deposit at least $50 to open an account.

d. List the names and social security numbers of the customers who made at least one withdrawal in the last two months.

e. List the names and social security numbers of customers whose loan is due in December 2002.

f. List the names and social security numbers of customers who never took out a loan from the bank.

g. List the names and social security numbers of customers who pay more than $1,000 per month in interest.

h. Find the current balance for customers who have taken out a loan from the bank in all the accounts. Display the names and social security numbers of these customers.

19. A small restaurant maintains information about its employees in a database. The database includes these tables:

- *tblBartenders* includes these fields: *BartenderID, LastName, FirstName, StartDate, ManagerID, Wage, MonShift, TuesShift, WedShift, ThursShift, FriShift,* and *SatShift.*

- *tblCooks* includes these fields: *CookID, LastName, FirstName, StartDate, ManagerID, Wage, MonShift, TuesShift, WedShift, ThursShift, FriShift,* and *SatShift.*

- *tblManagers* includes these fields: *ManagerID, LastName, FirstName, StartDate, Salary, MonShift, TuesShift, WedShift, ThursShift, FriShift,* and *SatShift.*

- *tblServers* includes these fields: *ServerID, LastName, FirstName, StartDate, ManagerID, Wage, MonShift, TuesShift, WedShift, ThursShift, FriShift,* and *SatShift.*

Write the SQL statements that perform the following functions:

a. Calculate the average wages of the bartenders, cooks, and servers.

b. List the three most experienced servers in the restaurant.

c. Calculate how many bartenders each manager supervises.

d. Present the schedule of the servers who began working last year.

e. Add a new server to *tblServers.*

f. Update the "Monday schedule" of the bartender whose last name is Thomas.

20. Mark works in a shop that sells electronic products. The shop maintains information about each product in a database. Mark realized that a customer's decision about buying a product depends on its price and brand name. Write an SQL statement that lists the TV sets in ascending order by price. Also, list the brand name of each product.

21. Enjoy Reading is a small bookstore in Denver, Colorado. They maintain information about their books, publishers, and customers in a database. Write SQL statements that do the following:

a. Add a new customer to *tblCustomers.*

b. Create *tblTransactions.*

c. Add a new book to *tblBooks.*

d. Update the address of a publisher.

e. Add a new transaction to *tblTransactions.*

PART THREE

Windows Application Development with VB .NET

chapter **OVERVIEW**

10.1   *Introduction*

Knowledge of database design and development alone won't suffice to meet today's business needs. There is a need for an additional tool that can present processed data effectively and efficiently to the user. Presenting the data in a legitimate format is as important as processing it. A presentation tool not only broadens perception of information, but also enhances the efficiency of data editing, processing, and printing operations. A *database application* allows us to achieve these goals. Database applications are computer programs that allow users to manipulate the data in a DBMS through a user-friendly interface (refer to Section 2.4 for a detailed discussion of database applications). With this in mind, we present various tools and technologies to build database applications in this part of the book.

A database application can be *Windows based* (for a single user) or can be *Web based* (for multiple users). Both Windows and Web-based database applications can be developed using *Visual Basic .NET* (VB .NET) programming language. We introduce VB .NET programming language in Chapters 11–13; discuss Windows-based database application development in Chapters 14–16, and present Web-based database application development in Chapters 17–19. However, before getting into the details of VB .NET language and database application development, we devote this chapter to the exploration of *Visual Studio* environment, an **I**ntegrated **D**evelopment **E**nvironment (IDE), to develop, debug, and deploy various applications. The goal of this chapter is to make readers familiar with the development environment, its windows, available features and tools, and to walk through a very simple Windows application (without involving databases). The subsequent Chapters, 11–19, are developed around the Visual Studio environment.

10.1.1   Topics:

This chapter discusses the following topics:

- Visual Studio IDE.
- Various IDE windows and their functionalities.
- Running Windows applications.
- Writing code in IDE.

10.2   *Exploring Visual Studio IDE*

Visual Studio is Microsoft's development tool for Windows-based and Web-based applications. The Visual Studio package includes component-based development tools such as Visual Basic, Visual C++, Visual C#, J#, and other supporting technologies that facilitate the process of design, development, debugging, and deployment of applications. The *Integrated Development Environment* (IDE)—a powerful and sophisticated tool with a wealth of features for application development—integrates and manages development tools under one single window or environment. In this chapter, we will focus on IDE features and support for the Visual Basic language.

10.2.1   Getting Started with a Visual Basic Application

We use the Window's *Start* menu to launch Visual Studio. On start up, Visual Studio displays the tabbed Start Page (see Figure 10.1). The Start Page shows the list of a few recent projects in the area, *Recent Projects*. We often use Start Page to open existing projects and to create new projects using quick links under the Recent Projects list.

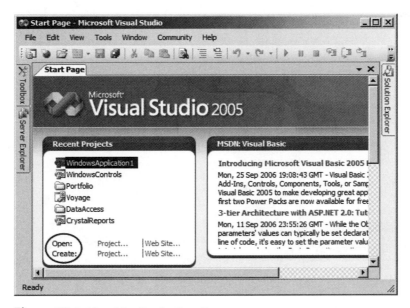

Figure 10.1 Visual Studio, the Start Page.

To open an existing project, do one of the following:

- Click the name of the project from the list of Recent Projects (if available)
- Choose File | Open Project option from the main menu

To create a new project, do the following:

- Choose File | New Project from the main menu

We now start developing our first Windows application. As we walk through this development process, we illustrate various features of Visual Studio IDE. The application we are going to develop is fairly simple and straightforward. This single-form Windows application greets the user by displaying a welcome message, "Welcome to the World of Programming!" accompanied by a graphic image. We will later extend this application to change the displayed message to read, "Welcome to the VB .NET!" when the user clicks on the image.

- How-to: create a new Visual Basic Windows application.
    1. From the Start Page, click Create | Project. This opens the *New Project* dialog box. Select the *Visual Basic* option under the *Projects* types, and then choose the *Windows Application* icon under the *Templates* area. Name the project "FirstProgram" and click *OK* (see Figure 10.2).

At this point, the screen should resemble Figure 10.3. The IDE displays the project name as the title of a familiar Windows environment with menus and toolbars. The main component of the IDE is the *Design Window*. The Design Window contains a gray, rectangular, grid-like structure called *Windows Form* (or simply a *form*) with the default name Form1.vb [Design]. A Windows form is the basic construction element of any Windows application. A Windows application is a series of one or more forms simulating application flow. All other components of the IDE assist in developing applications around these forms. Other important tools in the IDE are *Menus and Toolbars*. We discuss the Design Window, Menus, and Toolbar in the remainder of this section.

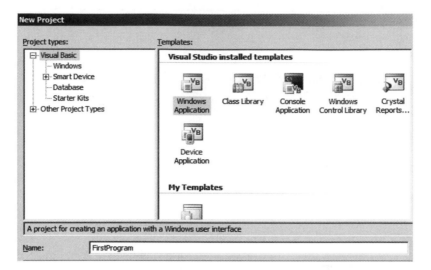

Figure 10.2 Creating a new Windows application; the *New Project* dialog box.

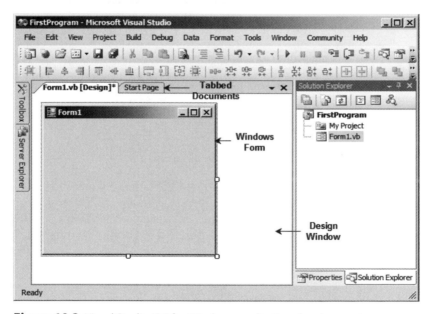

Figure 10.3 Visual Studio IDE for Windows application development.

The Design Window   The Design Window consists of tabbed documents. Each form is displayed as a separate tab in the window with its name displayed on the top. In our example, the second tab contains the Form1.vb [Design]. To access any of the open documents, we simply click on its tab. We can also move tabs around to reorder the documents. The Tab system saves a lot of space and allows easy access to multiple documents. The Active tab is always positioned in front of all other tabs and is displayed with a boldface name.

The Main Menu and Toolbar   Figure 10.4 features an enhanced view of the standard toolbar and main menu. See Table 10.1 for a summary of the features available through the toolbar and menu.

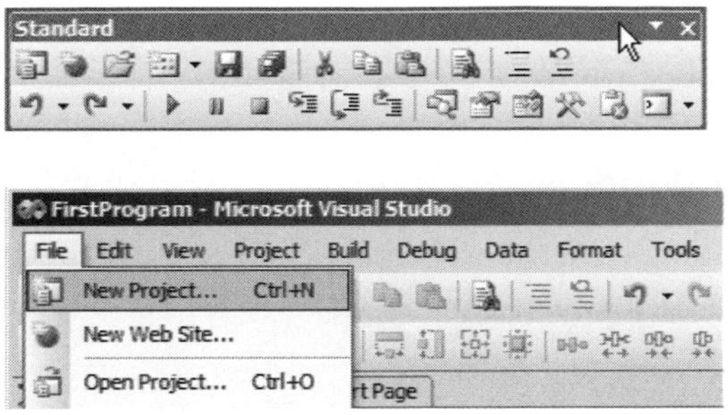

Figure 10.4 (a) Visual Studio toolbar; (b) Visual Studio main menu.

Table 10.1 Essential Menu and Toolbar options.

Main Menu:	
File	Creates, Opens, Saves, and Closes projects.
View	Allows us to quickly open various IDE windows.
Project	Facilitates addition of new items to the current project.
Build	Compiles, builds, and runs the project.
Debug	Allows us to debug the current project.
Tools	Used to configure Visual Studio IDE.
Toolbar:	
Solution Explorer	Opens the Solution Explorer Window.
Property Window	Opens the Property Window.
ToolBox	Opens the ToolBox.

10.3   *Visual Studio IDE Windows*

Visual Studio IDE consists of various windows that assist in the application development process. The following are important windows we will be covering in this chapter:

- The Solution Explorer
- The ToolBox
- The Property Window
- The Server Explorer

These windows can do the following:

- Be moved around the design window and docked along the edges of the Visual Studio Window.
- Be set to auto-hide. When auto-hide is enabled (using the small pin icon on these windows), the corresponding IDE window automatically appears hidden along an edge of the Visual Studio Window. If we place the mouse pointer on them, they appear in the IDE. This feature balances the design space and the availability of IDE tools.

Most of the IDE windows are accessible from the *View* menu and toolbar buttons. We will now explore a few important IDE windows.

10.3.1 The Solution Explorer Window

The Solution Explorer Window gives us a *hierarchical view* of all the files that belong to the current project. Figure 10.5 depicts the Solution Explorer Window for our newly created project.

Figure 10.5 The Solution Explorer Window for the FirstProgram application.

The Solution Explorer provides access to all the files and components of the project. We can select any file from the Solution Explorer and choose the *Open* option from the right click menu to view the contents of the file. If we right-click the project name in the Solution Explorer, we get a rich list with various options that allow us to add new items to the project and build and run the project.

10.3.2 The ToolBox

The ToolBox contains a set of reusable components called controls. The ToolBox is a tool gazette for our application. The controls in the ToolBox assist us in *Visual Programming*, a programming paradigm in which we add visual components to build applications without writing much code. The ToolBox groups the controls together and arranges them by group name. We click on tabs in the ToolBox to view controls from different groups (see Figure 10.6). The groups we will often use are All Windows Forms, Common Controls, Data, and Crystal Reports. The *All Windows Forms* group consists of controls used to customize forms in the Windows application, while the Data group features controls that assist in database connectivity. The ToolBox is depicted in Figure 10.6.

■ How-to: add a Windows control from the ToolBox on the Windows form.

To add any Windows control on a form, use the following procedure:

1. First, click the desired control in the ToolBox. Then, place the mouse pointer on the form at the desired control position.
2. Drag the pointer to designate the desired size of the control (See Figure 10.7).

Before we proceed to the other windows, we would like to define the term *object*. We use this term in a very general sense, designating an object as any element that can be named and has some specific purpose. Using this definition, we must refer to Windows forms, ToolBox controls, Toolbars, and the Main Menu as objects because all of these elements serve some specific purpose and have names.

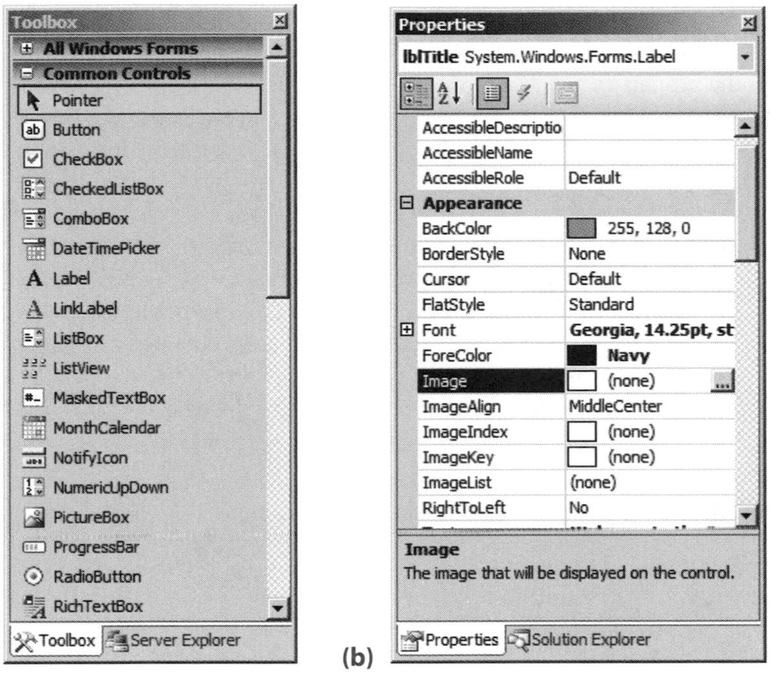

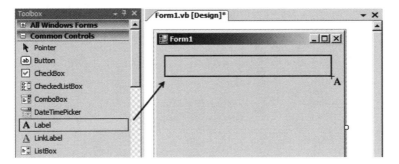

Figure 10.6 (a) The ToolBox; (b) Properties of a Label control in Property Window.

Figure 10.7 Adding a Control object to the form.

10.3.3 The Properties Window

Properties are attributes of an object. For example, the name of a form serves as its property, and the size and color of a control object constitute its properties. We manipulate the appearance and behavior of an object by manipulating its properties.

The Property Window (shown in Figure 10.6(b)) displays a list of properties for a selected object. If the Property Window is not in place, we can invoke it by using the Properties button on the toolbar or by choosing the View | Properties Window option from the main menu. Figure 10.6(b) shows the Properties Window for the Label control. (We will add such a control to our example form shortly.) The top box in the Property Window shows the name of the selected object. In our case, this is a System.Windows.Forms.Label. We request you not to worry about the meaning of this long string for now; it simply means that we have selected a Label control.

The Properties Window arranges object properties in the alphabetical order or sorts them by categories. The left column of a property indicates the property name, while the right column shows the property value. We can see a short description for a selected property in the status bar of the window.

Now since we are familiar with some IDE windows, let us continue building our FirstProgram application from Section 10.2.1.

2. Use the procedure shown in Figure 10.7 to add the *Label* control to Form1.
3. Change the Label control properties as described in Table 10.2.
4. Change the *Text Align*, *Fore Color*, and *Font* properties as shown in Figure 10.8. Use the drop-down button to select the property values for *Text Align* and *Fore Color*, and use the ellipsis button at the end of the property value to open the *Font* dialog box. Set the *Font*, *Font Style*, and *Size* values in this dialog box.

Table 10.2 Properties and property values for various objects of the FirstProgram application.

Object	Property Name	Property Value
Label Control	Name	lblTitle
	Text	Welcome to the World of Programming
	Text Align	Middle Center
	Fore Color	Navy
	Font	Georgia, Bold, 14
Form1	Text	First Form
	BackColor	255,128,0 (Orange)
PictureBox	Cursor	Hand
	Image	System.Drawing.Bitmap—(Saved as Bitmap image under the Drawing Name Space.) Locate the image using Built button.
	Name	imgSample

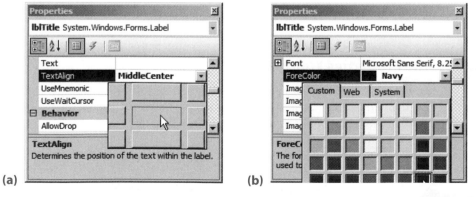

(a)   (b)

(continues)

Figure 10.8 Setting Label control's (a) Text Alignment; (b) Text Fore Color; (c) Text Font; and (d) Text Size properties.

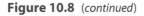

(c)   **(d)**

Figure 10.8 (*continued*)

5. Select the form itself so that we can view its properties. Change its properties as described in Table 10.2.
6. Add the *PictureBox* control to the form at the location shown in Figure 10.9(a). We use the PictureBox to add graphics to the form. Select and manipulate the PictureBox properties using the guidelines shown in Table 10.2 (also see Figure 10.10).

We have almost completed our first application. However, in order to view the output, we must run the application.

(a)   **(b)**

Figure 10.9 (a) Adding PictureBox control on the form; (b) Manipulating form's properties in the Property Window.

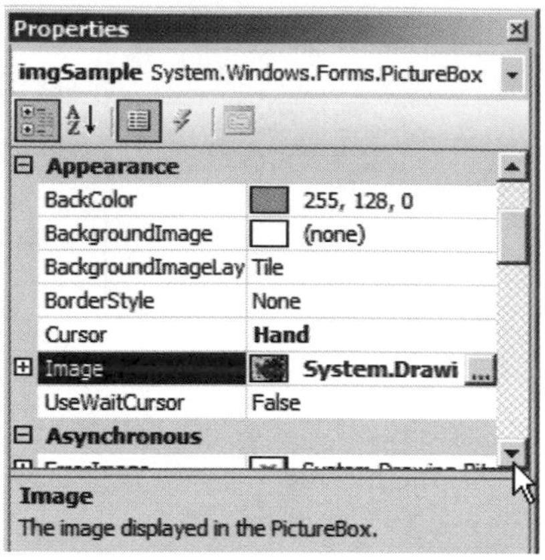

Figure 10.10 Properties of a PictureBox controls.

10.3.4   Running an Application

Visual Studio compiles and runs an application to produce its output.

■ How-to: run an application.

To run an application, use one of the following steps:
■ From the main menu, choose Debug | Start Without Debugging (see Figure 10.11)
■ Press Ctrl + F5 from the keyboard

The resulting window shows the form in its final running version (without the Design Grid); we refer to this as a running form.

7. Run the application (see Figure 10.12). Close the running form to return to the Design Window.

We explore a few more Visual Studio IDE Windows to conclude this section.

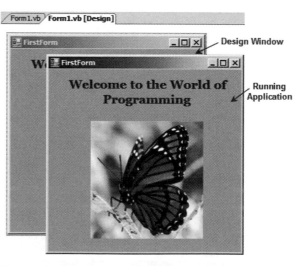

Figure 10.11 Running an application using the debug menu.

Figure 10.12 The running FirstProgram application.

10.3.5 The Server Explorer Window

The Server Explorer Window gives access to the available servers (see Figure 10.13). A server is a piece of software that provides some service. For example, the Access database is a server that provides database-related services. We will focus on the Server Explorer Window when we examine database connectivity in Chapter 14. We will use the Server Explorer to simply drag and drop an Access database table into the Windows form. The powerful Server Explorer creates the database connection and all other objects required to display database tables on Windows forms.

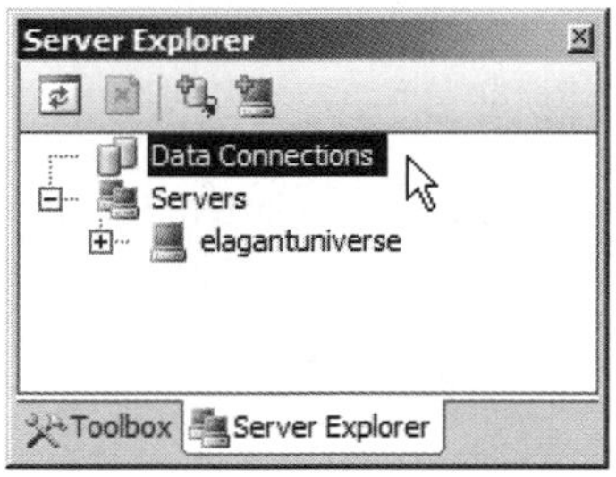

Figure 10.13 The Server Explorer Window.

10.3.6 The Help Menu and Dynamic Help Window

Visual Studio has an excellent online help feature that provides assistance to developers. The *Help* menu shown in Figure 10.14 has four main menus: (1) *Contents* displays a series of articles that are categorized by topic; (2) *Index* displays help topics organized alphabetically; (3) *Search* finds and displays help topics based on the search keyword; and (4) the *Dynamic Help* menu option opens up the Dynamic Help Window and offers a list of help topics specifically tailored to the user's current tasks and needs in the IDE.

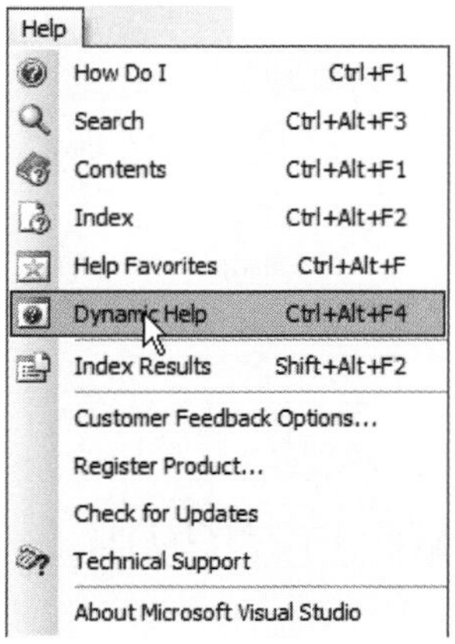

Figure 10.14 The *Help* menu.

10.4 *Object-Naming Conventions*

In this section, we formalize some of the object-naming conventions that we will be using in this book. While programming, we use the object's name to refer to the object. We must follow some naming conventions in order to manage an application that features an increasing number of objects. The following list highlights a few of these conventions:

- Naming should be logical.
- Names should start with a capital letter. While names can include any number of digits, they cannot start with a digit.
- Every object name should have a prefix (three lower case letters) indicating the type of object. See Table 10.3 for examples of some the common prefixes. While there are no specific prefix rules, the prefixes chosen should remain consistent throughout the development process.

Table 10.3 Naming standards.

Object	Prefix	Example	Object	Prefix	Example
Label	lbl	lblTitle	TextBox	txt	txtFirstName
PictureBox	img	imgSample	ComboBox	cmb	cmbCustomerID
CheckBox	chk	chkSex	CommandButton	cmd	cmdSubmitOrder

10.4.1 The File Extensions

When we browse the application folder, we see a number of files with file extensions that we have not previously encountered. Table 10.4 provides a brief summary of the most common file extensions used by a Visual Basic application.

Table 10.4 A few commonly encountered file extensions.

File Type	Extension	File Type	Extension
Solution	.sln	Text File	.txt
Project	.vbproj	Bitmap File	.bmp
Form, Code File	.vb	Resource File	.resx

10.5 *A Look at the VB .NET's Code Window*

The Code Window is Visual Basic's programming environment. IDE opens the Code Window under a new tab named after the associated form; in our example, "Form1.vb" (see Figure 10.15). In order to open the Code Window, double-click anywhere on the form. In the Code Window, locate the default class, *Form1*. Class *Form1*, named after the form name, encloses the entire code for the form. Each class begins with `Public Class <Class Name>` and ends with the key words `End Class`.

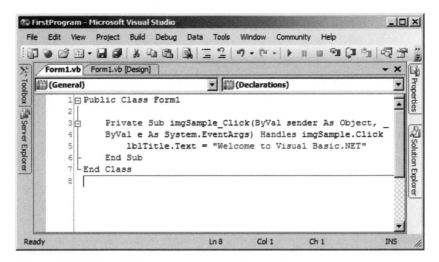

Figure 10.15 The Code Window.

We will now go back to extend our hands-on tutorial. We are going to add a functionality that allows the user to click on the butterfly picture. Once the user clicks on this picture, the form title changes to display the message "Welcome to Visual Basic .NET!"

Unlike other programming languages, the Visual Basic program's control flow is designed around a user's actions. For example, in our sample application, we first display to the user a text heading and an image. When the user clicks the image, we change the text heading. There are two actions involved here. The first non-obvious action is the loading of the form, and the second obvious action is the click on the image. These actions trigger Visual Basic *events*. For example, the user's click on the image triggers the *Click* event of a PictureBox control. We associate Visual Basic code with an event that gets executed when that event is triggered. For example, we will associate a code to change the text of the Label control with the *Click* event of the Picture-Box. Thus, when the user clicks the image, the *Click* event will be triggered, and a text heading change code will be executed. This process is referred to as *Event-Driven Programming*. The *Click* event in our example triggers a dynamic manipulation of the *Text* property of the Label control.

Visual Basic provides a rich set of events associated with each Windows control. Each control has one event designated as its default event. For example, the default event of the Form control is the *Load* event; the default event of the Button control is the *Click* event, and so on. To view the code associated with the default event of a control, we simply double-click the control in the Design Window. For example, if we double-click the Form control itself, the code associated with the *Load* event appears. This code *handles* the default event of the form object.

■ How-to: open the Code Window

To open a code window and the code associated with a particular control's event, do one of the following:
- Double-click the control in the Design Window.
- Locate the object in the Solution Explorer, and click on the *View Code* button in the Solution Explorer toolbar.
- Select the Object and choose View | Code from the main menu or Press F7 on the keyboard.

8. Open the Code Window for the PictureBox control, "imgSample," and associate the following code with its *Click* event (see Figure 10.16).

9. Run the application and verify the output by clicking on the image (see Figure 10.20).

```
1 ⊟ Public Class Form1
2
3 ⊟     Private Sub imgSample_Click(ByVal sender As Object, _
4         ByVal e As System.EventArgs) Handles imgSample.Click
5             lblTitle.Text = "Welcome to Visual Basic.NET"
6 └       End Sub
7 └ End Class
```

Figure 10.16   Code for the *Click* event of the PictureBox control.

10.5.1   Understanding the Code

The keyword Sub marks the beginning of an event subroutine. The name of an event subroutine is always a combination of the control name and the type of the event. For example, imgSample_ Click is the event subroutine for handling the *Click* event of the "imgSample" PictureBox. Each subroutine has a fixed syntax. It begins with Private Sub <name> and ends with the END Sub keyword. We clarify and develop terminologies of Method/Event and Subroutine/Function in Chapter 12.

Visual Basic automatically executes the code inside the event subroutine every time the event is triggered. We therefore include the code that assigns the value "Welcome to Visual Basic .NET!" to the *Text* property of the Label control (line 5). Note that the value assigned to the *Text* property of the Label control in the Design Window is still "Welcome to the Programming World!" and will be assigned to the Label control when we start the application. It is only when a user clicks the image that the Label control's *Text* property will gets its new value. Thus, the property manipulation in the Code Window is visible only at the **run-time** (i.e., in the output when the application is running), whereas the property manipulation in the Property Window is visible at the **design-time** as well as at run-time until changed.

10.5.2   Additional Features of the Code Window

The Code Window makes it easy to add an event other than a default event for an object. The top portion of the Code Window has two drop-down boxes. The left box lists the available objects while the right box lists all possible methods and events for the object selected in the left box. Figure 10.17 depicts one such insertion.

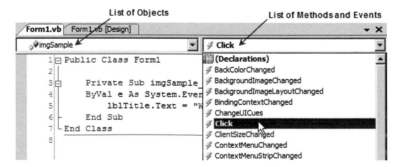

Figure 10.17   Class and Method selection in the Code Window.

IDE provides online help to assist the code-writing process in two different forms. First, when we use the "dot" (.) operator immediately after an object name, the IDE displays a list of properties and methods associated with that object. We refer to this list as *IntelliSense*, because it automatically prompts appropriate properties and methods that we can use with the current object. Second, when a property or method for an object has been selected, IDE displays a *Code Tip* with the exact syntax (command structure) of a selected method/event. See Figure 10.18 for an example.

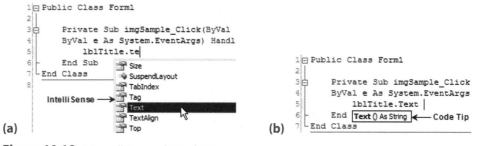

Figure 10.18 (a) IntelliSense; (b) Code Tip.

10.5.3 Saving the Work

Each unsaved tab in the IDE that shows an asterisk (*) indicates that the document has not been saved or the saved version does not include recent changes. Once we save the document, the asterisk disappears. To save our work, we do one of the following:

- Choose the File | Save Project or File | Save All option from the main menu.
- Click on the *Save active tab file* or *Save all files* button on the toolbar (refer to Figure 10.19).

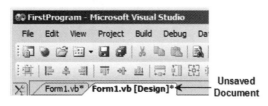

Figure 10.19 Saving the work.

10.6 *The Object Browser*

There are many ways like Properties Window and IntelliSense in which we can view the list of existing classes, properties, and methods of various Windows controls. Object Browser is one such Window that allows us to quickly access information about various objects. The Object Browser appears as a separate tab in the IDE window and lists all possible classes, built-in objects, and more in its left pane. Once an object has been selected from this list, the Object Browser displays a list of methods and events associated with the selected object in the right pane. *The Object Browser thus serves as a dictionary of .NET objects.*

To open an Object Browser, choose the View | Object Browser item from the main menu or click the *Object Browser* icon on the toolbar. The Object Browser Window is depicted in Figure 10.21. The Object Browser toolbar (shown in Figure 10.21) provides functions for navigating, sorting, and searching through object lists.

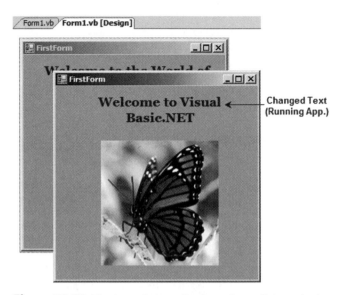

Figure 10.20 Final running application: after a click on the image.

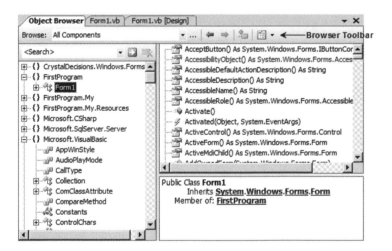

Figure 10.21 Object Browser Window.

10.7 *In-Class Assignment*

This in-class assignment further extends the application developed in this chapter. The simple extension is as follows: we would like to close the form (running application) on the click of the *Close* button.

10.8 *Summary*

- Visual Studio .NET integrates its development tools under one environment known as Integrated Development Environment (IDE). The IDE is a powerful tool that provides a wealth of features for the application development process.
- The Design Window is the part of the IDE that allows the user to graphically manipulate the design of a form and other controls.
- Visual Studio .NET IDE is made up of various windows that assist in the process of application development.
  - **a.** The Solution Explorer Window displays a hierarchical view of the solution.
  - **b.** The ToolBox is the container for reusable components called controls.
  - **c.** The Properties Window displays the property list for a selected object.
  - **d.** The Server Explorer Window provides access to the available servers.
  - **e.** The Dynamic Help Window provides a list of help topics related to the current content of the IDE.
- The Object Browser is a dictionary of .NET objects.

10.9 *Exercises*

10.9.1 Review Exercises

1. How would we go about making our database more adaptable to handle the challenges of today's business environment?
2. Describe some features of Visual Studio .NET.
3. List and explain various methods used to open old and new projects.
4. What is the importance of tabbed documents in the Design Window?
5. What are the IDE windows? Discuss a few IDE windows and their functions.
6. What is a Solution Explorer and what are its functions?
7. Explain the concept of Visual Programming. How do we manipulate objects in Visual Programming?
8. Discuss the "Auto-Hide" feature available in Visual Studio. How can it be controlled?
9. Describe how to add a control to a Form.
10. What are objects?
11. Highlight the significance of a Properties Window.
12. Explain important features that provide online help to application developers.
13. Explain the significance of the Object Browser in Visual Studio.
14. Discuss the concept of Event-Driven programming and explain how it differs from the classical way of programming. Also, discuss the differences in the program flow between the two programming paradigms.
15. We discussed the concepts of design-time properties and run-time properties. Discuss the difference between these two concepts.

10.9.2 Hands-On Exercises

1. Displaying the "Hello World" message is the first exercise in almost all programming language books. In this exercise we develop a Windows application that displays this message to the user when the form is loaded. We also add a Button control to the form. When user clicks this button we would like to display a message, "Hello World Again!" to the user. Develop this application and name it as "HelloWorld." Use a Label control to display messages on the form.
2. The "PersonalInfo" application lets users enter the personal information (Name, Address, Email, and Phone) using TextBoxes on a Windows form. When user completes the data entry, they click a "Submit" button. We would like to display user's input information back to the user for confirmation on click of the Submit button. Use Label controls to display the information to the user for confirmation. Also associated with each input TextBox add a Label control showing the name of the information field the user is supposed to enter. For example, for the TextBox that

is supposed to input user's name, add a Label control with text "Name."

3. In this exercise we extend the "PersonalInfo" application developed in the Hands-On Exercise 2. When the application is running and the form is loaded, we would like to show some default values in all the TextBoxes. Write a VB .NET code to assign reasonable values to each input TextBox on the form load. Is there another way we can do the same exercise?

4. *OptiSoft*, a firm specializing in optimization research software, has asked us to create a project that will attract potential clients to their site. We must create a project that will welcome clients to OptiSoft. OptiSoft has already specified some of the characteristics for this project. The control objects to be added are given in the table below along with their required properties. Create a project to suit the requirements of OptiSoft. A click on the image should cause the text in the Label to change to "Thank you for visiting Opti-Soft." Customize this project to achieve this effect (refer to the table below).

Object	Property Name	Property Value
Label	Name	lblIntro
	Text	Welcome to OptiSoft
	Text Align	Middle Center
	Fore Color	DarkOrchid
	Font	Arial, Bold, 14
Form1	Text	OptiSof
	BackColor	Turquoise
	PictureBox Cursor	Hand
	Image	System.Drawing.Bitmap

5. *Atlantic* is a small airline that offers service only between Orlando and New York. They have a limited number of aircraft, which offer services only three times a day. Design a project that indicates arrival and departure times from the Orlando airport when a user clicks on the text indicating the time of day.

Morning (A-D)	7:30am	9:00am
Afternoon (A-D)	1:00pm	2:30pm
Evening (A-D)	7:00pm	8:30pm

6. *Connect* is a new wireless provider that is trying to attract a large number of customers. It introduced a set of subscription plans. The table below shows the monthly cost and the minutes available in each plan. To attract new customers, Connect also introduced a number of free gifts for new subscribers. The table below describes the gift that is provided to new subscribers of each plan.

Plan Description	Minutes Per Month	Monthly Fees	Gift
Basic Plan	250	$20	Two Months Free
Family Plan	500	$30	Two Months Free
Business Plan	1000	$40	Free Mobile

Our task is to design a desktop application that lists the available plans. Once users click a certain plan, they can view all the details shown in the previous table. By default, we should display the Family plan details on start up. (Showing the table grid is not important.)

7. "RunAway" is a fun VB .NET application. The application when running, first displays an image (doesn't matter which) on the top-left corner of the form. When we move the mouse over the image, the image moves to the top-right corner of the form. If we now move the mouse over the image, it moves to the bottom-right corner. Next time to the bottom-left corner, and then back to the top-left corner. This clock-wise cycle continues as we keep moving the mouse over the image. We build this application using *Visible* property and *MouseEnter* event of the PictureBox control. (*Hint*: Add the same image in all four corners. Make image visible and invisible on the form load and mouse enter events).

eleven
Visual Basic .NET Programming Language

chapter OVERVIEW

11.1   *Introduction*

In the previous chapter, we introduced a development environment for Visual Basic applications—Visual Studio IDE. In this chapter, we present the Visual Basic programming language and illustrate its features and constructs using Visual Studio IDE. We will first define a few key terms related to programming languages. A **computer program** is a sequence of precise, unambiguous, and detailed *instructions* on how to complete a task, written in a language that can be interpreted by a computer. A language used to express these instructions is referred as a **programming language**. *Visual Basic* is an example of one such programming language (other examples include C, C++, and Java). Computer programs written in the Visual Basic programming language form the backbone of Visual Basic applications.

Computer programs in the Visual Basic language use a sequence of *Visual Basic statements* similar to sentences in English. Each Visual Basic statement has a specific structure described using the syntax of a programming language. In this sense, the syntax of a programming language parallels the grammatical rules that govern English and determines the combinations of keywords, variables, and constants that are allowable in a programming language. Visual Basic statements are grouped into subroutines, functions, and modules to enhance the readability and flow of logic of an application (see Chapter 12).

11.1.1   Topics

This chapter discusses the following topics:

- Visual Basic data types and statements.
- User input and output.
- Visual Basic control structures (If-Then-Else, Do-While, and For-Next loops).
- Array data type.
- Code debugging.

11.2   *Visual Basic Statements*

The Visual Basic (VB) programming language is a sequence of instructions used to communicate with the computer. A complete instruction written in the VB language is known as a **Visual Basic statement**. The rules and regulations that govern the composition of VB statements are known as **language syntax**. A VB statement contains one or more of the following elements:

Keywords: Reserved words of the language. Programmers can use them but cannot modify their meaning.

Variables: Containers for values.

Constants: Special variables with fixed values.

Operators: Symbols used to perform arithmetic and logical operations on operands.

Operands: Numerical or String values that may be parts of expressions.

Expressions: Combination of one or more of the above terms that yields a value.

11.2.1   Keywords

Keywords are the reserved words of a programming language. Keywords convey the same specific meaning every time they are used in the program. They are reserved in the sense that a programmer can use them but cannot modify their meaning. Let us take a look at the first VB code we discussed in the previous chapter, shown in Figure 11.1.

```
1  Public Class Form1
2
3      Private Sub imgSample_Click(ByVal sender As Object, _
4      ByVal e As System.EventArgs) Handles imgSample.Click
5          lblTitle.Text = "Welcome to Visual Basic.NET"
6      End Sub
7  End Class
```

Figure 11.1 Visual Basic code example.

In this example, words such as `Public`, `Private`, `Class`, `Sub`, `As`, `Text` and `End` are Visual Basic keywords. The keyword `Sub` conveys that we are about to start a subroutine; while the keyword `End Sub` marks the end of a subroutine (we will formally define the term *subroutine* in Chapter 12). The keywords `Public` and `Private` indicate the access type of a subroutine. There are hundreds of other keywords in the language, but we do not have to know them all in order to begin writing programs. Table 11.1 features some of the most frequently used keywords. The meanings of keywords and their usage will become clearer as we move through the structure of the language.

Table 11.1 Visual Basic keywords.

Boolean	Class	Do	EOF	For	Loop	Null
ByRef	Const	Double	End	Function		ReDim
ByVal	Date	Else	Exit	If	Mod	True
Case	Dim	ElseIf	False	InputBox	Month	With

11.2.2 Variables

A variable is a temporary name given to a memory location. When writing a program, we need to store, manipulate, and reuse intermediate data values. Variables can temporarily store values and thus act like containers for values.

We use the keyword `Dim` to declare variables in Visual Basic. This keyword allocates or reserves the space for values to be stored in. We must name and declare variables before we can use them. We also have to tell Visual Basic in advance the kind of data we want to store in the variable. Special data-type keywords are used for this purpose. The space reserved for a variable depends on the type of the variable. Finally, we (optionally) initialize the variables in a declaration statement with an initial value, as shown in the following example. The syntax for the variable declaration statement is as follows:

```
Dim <Variable Name> As <Data Type> [= <Initial Values (s) >]
```

Examples of Variable Declarations:

```
Dim TemperatureF As Integer = 1
Dim Weather As String = "Cold"
Dim Comments As String
```

A variable name in Visual Basic can be as long as 255 characters and may contain both letters and digits; however, a variable name cannot begin with a digit. A variable name can neither contain spaces, commas, and punctuation marks, nor can it be the same as any keyword. It is always advisable to use descriptive names for variables. For example, the name *TemperatureF* implies that the variable will hold a temperature value expressed in Fahrenheit.

11.2.3   Constants

A constant is a special type of variable whose value is not allowed to change once it has been assigned. Constants in Visual Basic are declared using the keyword `Const`. The syntax for constant declaration is similar to that of variable declaration:

```
Const <Constant Name> As <Data Type> = <Final Values>
```

Examples of Constants:

```
Const factor As Integer = 32
Const PI As Integer = 3.14
```

In the above examples, the values of constants *factor* and *PI* are set to 32 and 3.14, respectively. These values cannot be changed in the program. That is, a statement like `PI = 10` would result in an error.

Visual Basic features two kinds of statements: ***declaration*** statements and ***executable*** statements. A declaration statement names and creates variables, determines their types, and assigns some initial values. An executable statement, on the other hand, performs an action that generates an output and can be stored in declared variables. The two statements from the previous code lines are declaration statements, while lines 9 and 11 from Figure 11.3 are examples of executable statements.

Before we go into the greater detail about language structure, we will introduce the *Input-Box* and *MessageBox* statements. We will extensively use these statements to build examples for other topics. InputBox and MessageBox are the easiest ways of taking inputs from the user and displaying outputs back to the user, respectively.

11.3   *InputBox and MessageBox*

InputBox is a function that helps us obtain data from a user using a dialog box. The InputBox function returns a value entered by the user that we may store in a variable for further manipulation. On the other hand, the **MessageBox** is a function that takes a value as an input parameter and displays it to the user in a dialog box (we will formally define the term *function* in Chapter 12).

InputBox Function:

The InputBox function prompts an input dialog box and waits for the user input. When the user clicks the *OK* button on the input dialog box, the function returns the input value.

Syntax for InputBox:

```
Variable x = InputBox (Prompt, Title, Default Response, X-Pos, Y-Pos)
```

MessageBox Function:

The MessageBox function is used to display a message to the user in an output dialog box.

Syntax for MessageBox:

```
MessageBox.Show (Message, Title, Type, Icon)
```

11.3.1   Hands-On Tutorial: User Input/Output

In this hands-on tutorial, we build a simple *Temperature Calculator* that will convert temperature values measured in Fahrenheit to Celsius. We prompt the user to enter the temperature in Fahrenheit unit, and then we convert and display the temperature in Celsius unit to the user. This hands-on tutorial covers the following How-to topic:

■ How-to: use Visual Basic InputBox and MessageBox functions.
  1. Create a new Visual Basic project, "VisualBasicIntro."
  2. To the default form ("Form 1"), add a new Button control. Set the *Text* property of the button to "Temperature Conversion" and name it, "cmdConvert." Use the GroupBox control with no text value around the Button control (see Figure 11.2).
  3. Double-click the Button control to open the Code Window with the *cmdConvert _Click* subroutine.
  4. Declare the variables *TemperatureC* and *TemperatureF* as Integers, and write conversion logic as shown in Figure 11.3.
  5. Save and run the application to view the output shown in Figure 11.4.

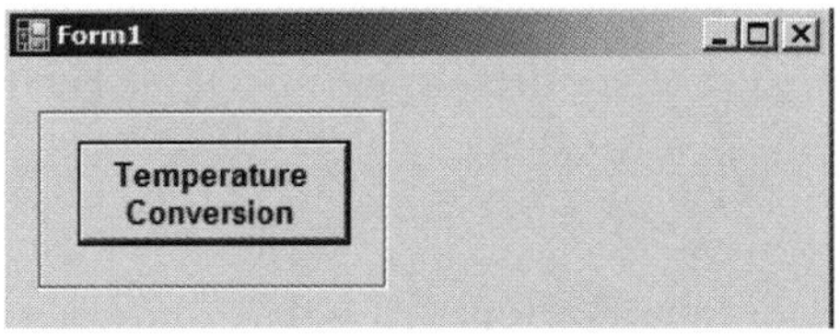

Figure 11.2 User input/output: Design Window.

```
3   Private Sub cmdConvert_Click(ByVal sender As System.Object, _
4   ByVal e As System.EventArgs) Handles cmdConvert.Click
5       'Variable declarations
6       Dim TemperatureF As Integer
7       Dim TemperatureC As Integer
8       'User input
9       TemperatureF = InputBox("Enter the Temp In F", "Input Temp", 59)
10      'Intermediate processing
11      TemperatureC = (TemperatureF - 32) * 5 / 7
12      'User output
13      MessageBox.Show("The Temperature in C is : = " & TemperatureC, _
14                      "Converted Temp", MessageBoxButtons.OKCancel)
15  End Sub
```

Figure 11.3 User input/output: Code Window.

Figure 11.3 Explained:

In lines 6–7, we use declaration statements to declare the integer variables *TemperatureF* and *TemperatureC*. Line 9 uses the InputBox function to take temperature input in Fahrenheit units from the user. In line 11, we perform temperature conversion to the Celsius unit. The MessageBox function invoked in lines 13–14 displays the converted temperature value to the user.

In the IDE, if a Visual Basic statement is too long to fit on one line and must span over multiple lines (line 3–4), we add an underscore (_) at the end of the line. The underscore indicates that the line has not yet ended.

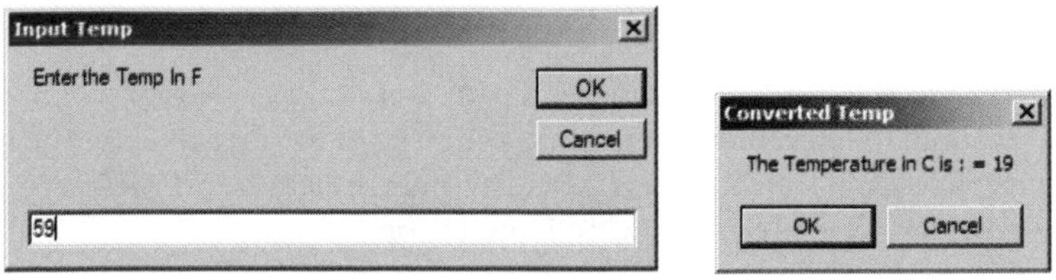

Figure 11.4 User input/output: Application output.

11.3.2   The InputBox Function

We now detail the InputBox syntax:

```
Variable x = InputBox (Prompt, Title, Default Response, X-Pos, Y-Pos)
```

> *Prompt*: A string that appears as a text inside the dialog box that prompts the user for input. In our hands-on tutorial, the Prompt is "Enter the Temp In F" (see Figure 11.4).
>
> *Title*: A string that appears as text in the title bar of the dialog box. The title of the InputBox in our hands-on tutorial is "Input Temp" (see Figure 11.4).
>
> *Default*: The default value of the InputBox. This value is displayed when the dialog box is shown to the user. In our hands-on tutorial, the default value is 59 (see Figure 11.3, line 9).
>
> *X-Pos, Y-Pos*: Integer values for X and Y co-ordinates for positioning the dialog box on the screen.

The only required input parameter for InputBox function is the Prompt; all other parameters are optional, as illustrated by the following examples:

```
InputBox ("Enter Your Age", "Age Calculator", , 100,100)—No default value
InputBox ("Enter Your Age", ,25)—No Title and No X-Pos and Y-Pos
InputBox ("Only Prompt")
```

11.3.3   The MessageBox

We now describe the MessageBox syntax:

```
MessageBox.Show (Message, Title, Type, Icon)
```

> *Message*: The text to display. It may be a string, integer, variable, or some combination (concatenation) of these. In our hands-on tutorial, the Message is, "The temperature in C is:" (see Figure 11.4).
>
> *Title*: A string that appears as a text in the title bar of the dialog box. In our hands-on tutorial, the Title is "Converted Temp" (see Figure 11.4).
>
> *Type*: The Type of MessageBox (see Table 11.2 for available options).
>
> *Icon*: Icon for the MessageBox (see Table 11.2 for available options).

Some examples of the MessageBox are shown next

```
MessageBox.Show("Your Age is :=" & Age, "Age Calculator", _
    MessageBoxButtons.OK, MessageBoxIcon.Information)
MessageBox.Show("Your Age is :=" & Age, "Age Calculator")
MessageBox.Show("Your Age is :=" & Age)
```

Table 11.2 MessageBox buttons and icons.

Option		Description
MessageBoxButtons.AbortRetryIgnore		Allows user to abort, retry, or ignore the running operation.
MessageBoxButtons.OKCancel		Allows user to either continue or cancel the operation.
MessageBoxButtons.YesNoCancel		Allows user to respond in yes or no format or select cancel to exit.
MessageBoxIcon.Warning	⚠	Shows an exclamation mark on the dialog box. Used to indicate caution.
MessageBoxIcon.Information	ⓘ	Shows an information mark on the dialog box.
MessageBoxIcon.Error	✖	Shows an error mark on the dialog box.
MessageBoxIcon.Question	?	Shows a question mark on the dialog box.

11.3.4 Visual Basic's Online Help

The Visual Studio IDE assists us in the process of application development in several ways, making it an interactive process. While we are writing code, the IDE provides online tips on the syntax of statements. This is helpful, making it unnecessary for programmers to memorize all of the syntax and rules. Refer to Figure 11.5 for *tool tips* on the syntax of the InputBox function.

Another excellent feature of the IDE is *IntelliSense*. As we write a code, the Visual Studio IDE intelligently displays only the relevant methods or options. As we type the keyword "MessageBox" (see Figure 11.6), IntelliSense displays available methods pertaining to a MessageBox. See Figure 11.7 for another example.

```
'User input
TemperatureF = InputBox("Enter the Temp In F", "Input Temp", 59)
'Intermediate p Public Function InputBox(Prompt As String, [Title As String = ""], [DefaultResponse As String = ""]
TemperatureC =  Integer = -1]) As String
```

Figure 11.5 An example of online tool tip.

```
12        'User output
13            MessageBox.Show("The Temper
14                              Equals
15    - End Sub            ReferenceEquals
16                          Show
17
18                     Common      All
```

Figure 11.6 The MessageBox IntelliSense.

```
8          'User input
9              TemperatureF = InputBox("Enter    MessageBoxButtons.AbortRetryIgnore
10         'Intermediate processing           MessageBoxButtons.OK
11             TemperatureC = (TemperatureF -   MessageBoxButtons.OKCancel
12         'User output                        MessageBoxButtons.RetryCancel
13             MessageBox.Show("The Temperatur  MessageBoxButtons.YesNo
14                    "Converted Temp", MessageBoxButtons)  MessageBoxButtons.YesNoCancel
```

Figure 11.7 MessageBox button and icon options.

11.3.5 Adding Comments to Visual Basic Code

We should notice the code lines 5, 8, 10, and 12 of Figure 11.3. These are Visual Basic comments. Visual Basic allows us to write useful explanatory comments along with the code lines. The comment is a text line that begins with a single quote or apostrophe (') character. We can either comment out the entire line by putting a single quote at the beginning of the line, or we can partially comment out the line by placing the single quote in the column where we want to start the comment. Comments are ignored while the program is executing. Some examples of comments are as follows:

```
'This entire line is a now a VB comment.
Dim TemperatureF As Integer    'Variable Holds the Temp in F
```

11.4 *Visual Basic Data Types*

When we declare new variables, we must specify its data type. A variable data type indicates the kind of data that will be stored in the variable. Visual Basic supports several data types, including *Integer*, *Double*, *String*, *Char*, and *Boolean*. Table 11.3 summarizes these types.

Table 11.3 Visual Basic data types.

Data Type	Size	Range
Integer	4 Bytes	–2,147,483,648 to 2,147,483,648
Long	8 Bytes	~ -9.2×10^{18} to 9.2×10^{18}
Double	8 Bytes	~ -1.79×10^{308} to 1.79×10^{308}
String	Variable	0 to 2 Billion Characters
Char	2 Bytes	0 to 65535
Boolean	2 Bytes	True or False
Date	8 Bytes	January 1, 0001 to December 31, 9999
Object	4 Bytes	Anything that can be stored as a Object

Some examples of data type declaration include the following:

```
Dim AtomicNumber As Byte
Dim AtomicWeight As Single
Dim IsRadioactive As Boolean
Dim CityName As String
Dim Population As Integer
Dim SquareMiles >As Double
```

11.4.1 Checking and Converting Data Types

Two common operations, checking existing data types and converting to other data types, are associated with data types. Visual Basic provides excellent support for data type manipulations with its dozens of built-in functions. The checking functions listed below are also known as logical functions, as they check for a particular data type and return a logical *True* or *False* value.

IsNumeric ()	Returns True if numeric value; False otherwise.
IsDate ()	Returns True if date value; False otherwise.
IsArray ()	Returns True if an Array; False otherwise.
IsError ()	Returns True if an Error; False otherwise.

Some of the data type conversion functions are as follows:

CInt	Converts to the Integer data type.
CLng	Converts to the Long data type.
CDbl	Converts to the Double data type.
CStr	Converts to the String data type.
CBool	Converts to the Boolean data type.
CDate	Converts to the Date data type.
CObj	Converts to the Object data type.

There is a generic function, CType (ConvertMe, toThis), for data type conversions, which takes the values to convert (ConvertMe) and a target data type (toThis) as input parameters and returns the converted value.

11.4.2 Hands-On Tutorial: Data Type Conversion

In this Hands-on tutorial, we consider an example illustrating usage of data type conversion functions. We will calculate the area and perimeter of a circle with and without the aid of data type conversion functions. This Hands-on tutorial covers the following How-to topic:

- How-to: use data type conversion functions.
    1. Continue with the "VisualBasicIntro" project and "Form1" from the "Temperature Conversion" hands-on tutorial. Add a "cmdDataTypeConvert" command button, and change the *Text* property to "Data Type Conversion" (see Figure 11.8). Use the GroupBox control with no text value around the Button control.
    2. Associate the code in Figure 11.9 with the newly added command button.
    3. Press Ctrl+F5 to run and test the application.

Figure 11.8 Data type conversion example: Design Window.

```
17   Private Sub cmdDataTypeConvert_Click(ByVal sender As System.Object, _
18   ByVal e As System.EventArgs) Handles cmdDataTypeConvert.Click
19       'Variable declarations
20       Dim PI As Double = Math.PI
21       Dim r As Double
22
23       'Take the radius from the user
24       r = InputBox("Enter the radius", "Input Radius")
25       'Area with and without data type conversion & Output
26       MessageBox.Show("Area =  " & (PI * r * r), _
27                       "Area without conversion")
28       MessageBox.Show("Area =  " & (CInt(PI) * CInt(r) * CInt(r)), _
29                       "Area with conversion")
30   End Sub
```

Figure 11.9 Data type conversion example: Code Window.

Figure 11.9 Explained:

Lines 20–21 are used to declare required variables. In line 20, we use the built-in Math function, Math.PI to assign value to the variable *PI*. Lines 26–27 calculate and display the area of the circle. Lines 28–29 do the same task, but all the variables are converted to the *Integer* type during the evaluation of the area expression. Thus, the double value of *PI*, 3.14, will get converted, and integer value 3 will be used for calculation. Though artificial, the conversions are performed for illustrative purpose. The difference in the results of these two calculations is shown in Figure 11.10.

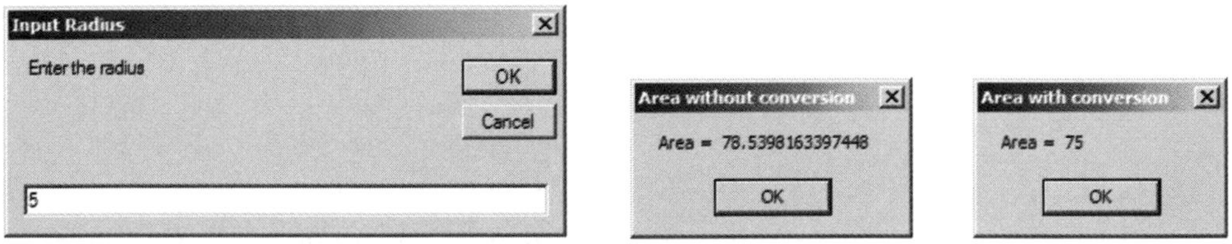

Figure 11.10 Data type conversion example: Application output.

11.4.3   Hands-On Tutorial: Data Type Checking

In this Hands-on tutorial, we consider an example illustrating the usage of data type checking functions. The example will check whether the user input is a number or not and appropriate message is displayed. This Hands-on tutorial covers the following How-to topic:

- How-to: use data type checking functions.
  1. Continue with the Form1 from the previous Hands-on tutorial. This time add a "cmdDataTypeChk" command button; change its Text property to "Data Type Checking" (see Figure 11.11).
  2. Associate the code in Figure 11.12 with the *cmdDataTypeChk_Click* event.
  3. Save and run the application. Application output is shown in Figure 11.11.

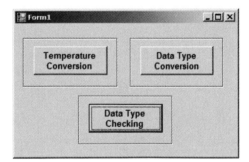

Figure 11.11 Data type checking example: Design view.

```
32    Private Sub cmdDataTypeChk_Click(ByVal sender As System.Object, _
33    ByVal e As System.EventArgs) Handles cmdDataTypeChk.Click
34        'Illustrating data type checking
35        MessageBox.Show("Was Input a Number? :" & IsNumeric(InputBox( _
36              "Enter the Number", "Type Check")), "Test Result")
37    End Sub
```

Figure 11.12 Data type checking example: Code Window.

Figure 11.12 Explained:

Line 35 of the code illustrates the use of the data type checking function, *IsNumeric*. The InputBox takes input from the user and passes it to the *IsNumeric* function. The *True* or *False* output of the *IsNumeric* function is then displayed using the MessageBox function.

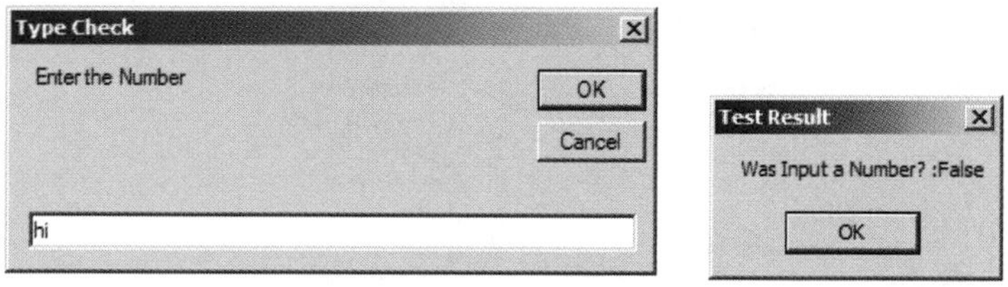

Figure 11.13 Data type checking example: Output Window.

11.5 *Adding Windows Forms and Setting a Start-up Form*

Before we discuss further details of the Visual Basic programming language, we discuss how we can add multiple Windows forms to the project and choose a particular form as a start-up form. A Visual Basic application typically consists of multiple forms, which, when compiled and run, begin with a form designated as a start-up form. When we created new projects in Visual Studio, we always had one default form, Form 1. Since there was only one form, it was by default set as the start-up form of the application.

To add a Windows form to the existing project:

1. Choose Project | Add Windows Form option from the main menu. Alternatively, right-click the project title in the Solution Explorer, and choose Add | Add Windows Form option from the short-cut menu (see Figure 11.14). Any of these options should lead us to the *Add New Item* dialog box.
2. In the *Add New Item* dialog box, select *Windows Form* icon in the template area on the right side of the window; accept the default form name and click *Add* button to add a new form to the application (see Figure 11.15).

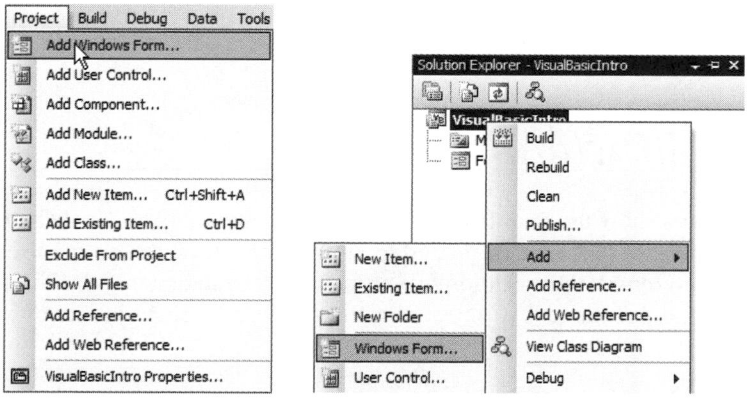

Figure 11.14 Selecting the *Add Windows Form* option.

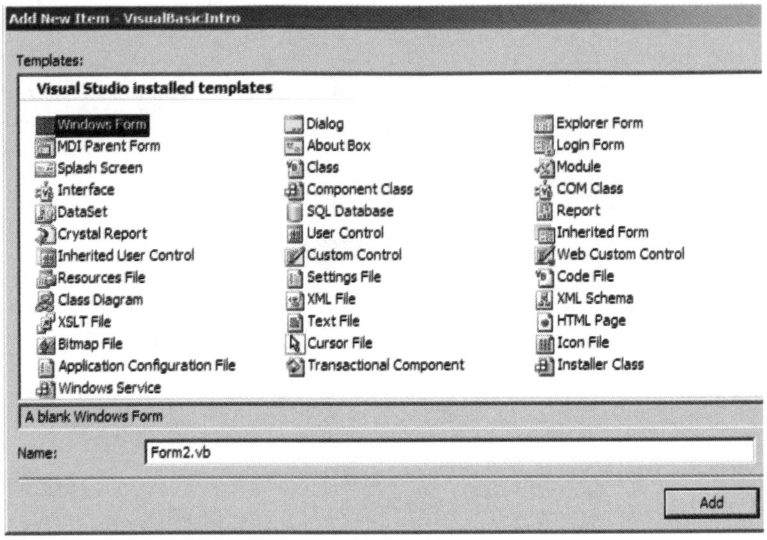

Figure 11.15 Adding a new Windows form.

To set the start-up form:

1. Choose Project | <Project Title> Properties option from the main menu. Alternatively, right-click the project title in the Solution Explorer, and choose the *Properties* item from the shortcut menu. This should open the *Properties* page as shown in Figure 11.16.
2. Select the desired startup form from the "Startup form" drop down list. Press Ctrl+S to save the settings.

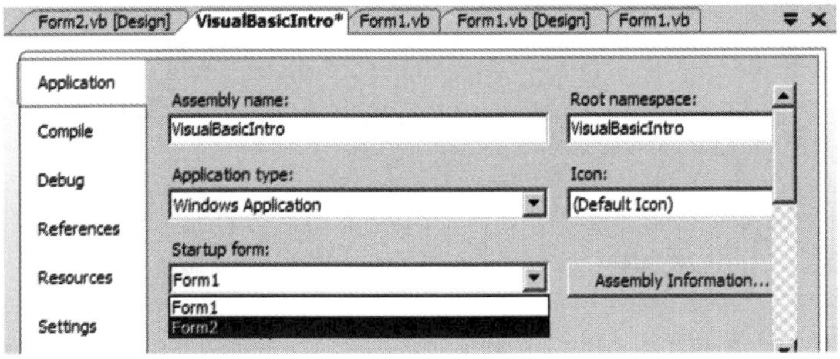

Figure 11.16 Setting up the startup form.

11.6   *Control Structures*

Control structures allow us to control the flow of program execution. By default, a program is executed sequentially from left to right and top to bottom. However, we can use control structure statements to *control* the execution of a program. These statements allow us to skip over or loop a given section of the code. Control structures can be classified into two categories based on their behavior:

■ Decision Structures
■ Loop Structures

Decision structures allow us to test conditions. Depending on the results of the test, we can either execute or skip lines of code. Visual Basic supports decision structures such as If-Then-Else and Select-Case. Loop structures allow us to execute one or more lines of code repetitively. Visual Basic supports loop structures such as Do-Loop, For-Next, and For Each-Next. We explore these structures in subsequent subsections.

11.6.1   Using If-Then Structure

We use an If-Then structure to execute one or more statements conditionally. The syntax for this structure is as follows:

Syntax for If-Then

```
If (<condition>) Then
    Body of If
End If
```

The *condition* is an expression that evaluates to a Boolean *True* or *False* value. If the condition is *True*, Visual Basic executes all statements in the structure body.

Examples:

```
'Check whether the input number is greater than 100
If (x > 100) Then
    MessageBox.Show("The Input Number is greater than 100")
End If

'Check whether Num is zero
If (Num = 0) Then
    Factorial = 1
End If
```

If-Then-Else

The `Else` statement allows us to specify the action to be performed if the *condition* of the `If` statement is not satisfied. The syntax for the `Else` statement is as follows:

Syntax for If-Then-Else

```
If (<condition>) Then
    Body of If
Else
    Body of Else
End If
```

Examples:

```
'Check whether the input is an even or odd number
If (x Mod 2) = 0 Then
    MessageBox.Show(x &  "is an even number")
Else
    MessageBox.Show(x &  "is an odd number")
End If
```

Note that the `Else` statement is an optional statement. In absence of this statement, Visual Basic continues to execute the program right after the If-Then structure. Refer to Figure 11.17 for a logical flow chart of the If-Then-Else structure.

If-Then-ElseIf-Else

We can also write a nested If statement to apply multi-level selections using an If-Then-ElseIf-Else statement. The syntax for this structure is as follows:

Syntax for If-Then-ElseIf-Else

```
If (<condition1>) Then
    Body of If1
ElseIf (<condition2>) Then
    Body of If2
.
.
Else
    Body of Else
End If
```

The body of the first If block will be executed if the first condition (condition1) evaluates to *True*. If not, the second condition (condition2) is checked. If it evaluates to *True*, the body of the second If block will be executed, and so forth. If none of the conditions evaluates to *True*, the body of the Else statement will get executed. If the body of the If statement or any ElseIf statement gets executed, the rest of the ElseIf and Else statements will be skipped.

Examples:

```
'Compare the input numbers
If (a > b) Then
    MessageBox.Show("The First Number is greater than Second Number")
ElseIf (b > a) Then
    MessageBox.Show("The Second Number is greater than First Number")
Else
    MessageBox.Show("Both Input Numbers are Equal")
End If
```

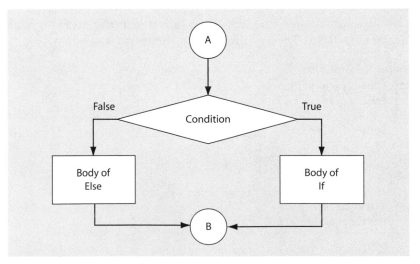

Figure 11.17 If-Then-Else structure's logical flow chart.

Before we illustrate the If-Then-Else structure using a hands-on tutorial example, we introduce the RadioButton control. We will use the RadioButton control to illustrate various control structures that follow.

11.6.2   The RadioButton Control

RadioButton controls force their users to select from a set of two or more mutually exclusive choices. Consider the example of shipping modes. Assume that we have three options: Standard Shipping, Second Day Air, and Next Day Air. The user can select only one of these (mutually exclusive) options. The selection of the Standard Shipping option is depicted in Figure 11.18.

Consider another example of RadioButton controls. We again have three options: Bachelor of Science (BS), Master of Science (MS), and Doctor of Philosophy (PhD). User can select only one of these mutually exclusive options to indicate her highest degree. A Form with three radio buttons for BS, MS, and PhD degrees is shown in Figure 11.19. We will use this example to illustrate the If-Then-Else control structure.

The *Checked* property of a RadioButton control is set to *True* when a button is selected and *False* otherwise. Table 11.4 describes some of the often-used properties and events of a RadioButton control.

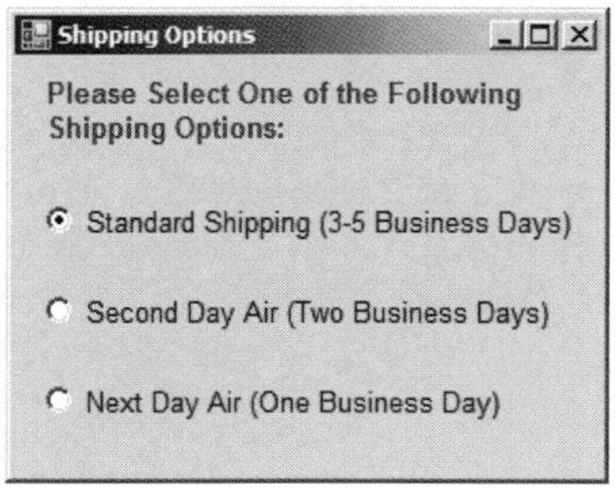

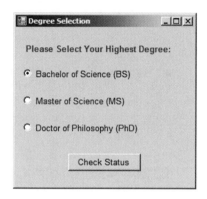

Figure 11.18 RadioButton control example: shipping mode option selection.

Figure 11.19 RadioButton control example: degree selection.

Table 11.4 Radio Button properties and events.

Name	Description
Checked	Sets/gets a value indicating whether the radio button is checked.
Image	Sets/gets a checkbox image.
CheckedChanged	Occurs when the *Checked* property changes.

11.6.3   Hands-On Tutorial: Using If-Then-Else Structure

The following steps are based on the RadioButton control example shown in Figure 11.19. On the click of the *Check Status* button, we would like to display to the user her selection. This hands-on tutorial covers the following How-to topics:

- How-to: use the properties of a RadioButton control.
- How-to: use the If-Then-Else control structure.
    1. Design the *Form 2* added in Section 11.5 as shown in Figure 11.19. Make *Form 2* the start-up form. Name the three RadioButton controls as: *radBS*, *radMS* and *radPhD*, and name the Button control as *cmdCheckStatus*.
    2. Associate the code in Figure 11.20 with the command button's *Click* event.

3. Save, run, and test the application.

```
 3   Private Sub cmdCheckStatus_Click(ByVal sender As System.Object, _
 4   ByVal e As System.EventArgs) Handles cmdCheckStatus.Click
 5       Dim status As String
 6       If radBS.Checked Then
 7           status = "Undergraduate Student"
 8       ElseIf radMS.Checked Then
 9           status = "Graduate Student"
10       ElseIf radPHD.Checked Then
11           status = "PhD Student"
12       Else
13           status = "Not a Student!"
14       End If
15       MessageBox.Show("Your status is: " & status, "Status")
16   End Sub
```

Figure 11.20 The Code Window illustrating If-Then-Else structure.

Figure 11.20 Explained:

In lines 6–14, we check the degree that is selected by the user using the *Checked* property of a RadioButton control. If a radio button is selected, the *Checked* property returns *True*, and thus the appropriate If or ElseIf clause will be satisfied. If none of the options are selected, then the body of the *Else* statement will be executed. The body of the If, ElseIf, and Else statements assigns the appropriate string value to the *status* variable. In line 15, we display the *status* variable using a MessageBox. If a *Bachelor of Science* radio button is selected, the output shown in Figure 11.21 should be displayed.

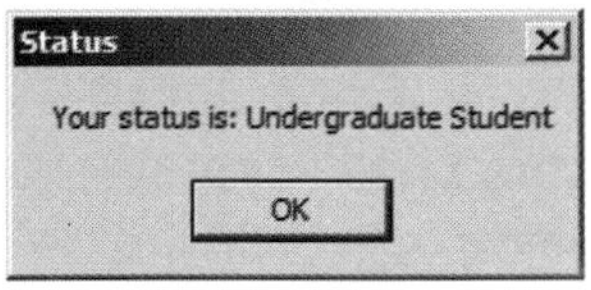

Figure 11.21 Degree selection application output.

11.6.4   Using Select-Case Structures

The Select-Case structure offers an alternative to the If-Then-Else structure. It selectively executes one among multiple "cases." Although, a Select-Case structure is conceptually very similar to the If-Then-Else structure, it enhances the code readability when there are several possibilities to consider. A Select-Case structure works with a single test expression that is evaluated once at the beginning. The result of evaluation is compared with the values of each Case clause in the structure. If there is a match, the block of statements associated with that case are executed. If more than one Case clause matches the test expression, only the statement block associated with the first matching case gets executed. If there is no match, the body of the Else clause gets executed. Figure 11.22 provides a logical flow chart of the Select-Case structure.

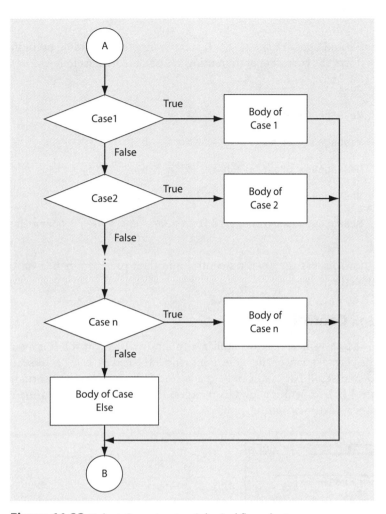

Figure 11.22 Select-Case structure's logical flow chart.

Syntax for Select-Case Structure

```
Select Case <TestExpression>

Case <Expression 1>
   Body of Case1
Case <Expression 2>
   Body of Case2
     .
     .
Case <Expression n>
   Body of Case n
Case Else
   Body of Case Else
End Select
```

Examples:

Numbers *a* and *b* and operator *op* (+, –, *, /) are user inputs. Depending upon the input operator, we can perform the correct operation using a Case statement as follows:

```
Select Case op
    Case +
        MessageBox.Show("a + b =" & (a + b))
    Case -
        MessageBox.Show("a - b =" & (a - b))
    Case *
        MessageBox.Show("a * b =" & (a * b))
    Case /
        MessageBox.Show("a / b =" & (a / b))
    Case Else
        MessageBox.Show("Enter only (+ OR - OR * OR /) Operators")
End Select
```

We will now discuss the TextBox control and then present a hands-on tutorial on the Select-Case structure.

11.6.5 The TextBox Control

Every Windows user is in some way familiar with the TextBox control. It is a box-shaped control that can display text data or allow the user to input the text data. A TextBox control can have multiple lines and scroll bars and can be made read-only. The most important property of a TextBox control is *Text*, which allows us to access the text value of a TextBox control. Figure 11.23 illustrates a TextBox control.

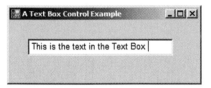

Figure 11.23 An example of a TextBox control.

11.6.6 Hands-On Tutorial: Working with Select-Case Structure

We develop a small application using the Select-Case structure that displays the number of days in a month, given 3-letter month abbreviations. The user will input the month abbreviation using a TextBox control and will click a command button to view the number of days in the specified month. This hands-on tutorial covers the following How-to topics:

■ How-to: use the properties of a TextBox control.
■ How-to: use the Select-Case control structure.
   1. Add a new form, *Form3*, to the *VisualBasicIntro* project and set *Form3* as the start-up form. Add a TextBox named *txtMonthAbbr* and a command button, *cmdCheckDays*.
   2. Design the form as shown in Figure 11.24.
   3. Use the code shown in Figure 11.25 for the *Click* event of the command button. Save, run, and test the application.

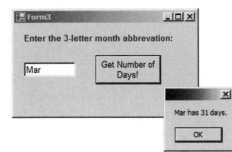

Figure 11.24 Hands-on tutorial for the Select-Case structure: design and output.

```
3  Private Sub cmdCheckDays_Click(ByVal sender As System.Object, _
4  ByVal e As System.EventArgs) Handles cmdCheckDays.Click
5      Dim MonthAbbr As String
6      Dim DaysInMonth As Integer
7      MonthAbbr = txtMonthAbbr.Text
8      Select Case MonthAbbr
9          Case "Jan", "Mar", "May", "Jul", "Aug", "Oct", "Dec"
10             DaysInMonth = 31
11         Case "Apr", "Jun", "Sep", "Nov"
12             DaysInMonth = 30
13         Case "Feb"
14             DaysInMonth = 28
15         Case Else
16             MessageBox.Show(MonthAbbr & " is invalid abbreviation")
17     End Select
18     MessageBox.Show(MonthAbbr & " has " & DaysInMonth & " days.")
19 End Sub
```

Figure 11.25 Hands-on tutorial for the Select-Case structure: Code Window.

Figure 11.25 Explained:

In line 7, we get the month abbreviation entered by the user in the *txtMonthAbbr* TextBox control. Depending on the value of the abbreviation (line 8), we assign the number of days of the corresponding month (lines 9–14). Note that the Case clauses in lines 9 and 11 have more than one value for comparison. The Else clause (line 15) is used to display an error message to the user. Finally, in line 18, a MessageBox displays the appropriate number of days for specified month.

11.6.7 Using Do-Loop Structures

In this section, we describe the various loop structure used to execute a block of statements multiple times. We discuss four types of a Do-Loop structure: Do-Loop-While, Do-While-Loop, Do-Loop-Until, and Do-Until-Loop. All these variants evaluate a Boolean condition to determine whether or not to continue the execution of the loop. They can be categorized as following:

1. When the Boolean condition is checked:
    - ■ Prior to loop execution: Do-While-Loop and Do-Until-Loop
    - ■ After the loop execution: Do-Loop-While and Do-Loop-Until
2. How the Boolean condition is interpreted:
    - ■ Continue loop execution while the condition is true, stop once it is false: Do-While-Loop and Do-Loop-While
    - ■ Continue loop execution until the condition is false, stop once it is true: Do-Until-Loop and Do-Loop-Until

We now present syntaxes and examples of these four types of Do-Loops. Figure 11.26 depicts logical flow charts of the **Do-Loop-While** and **Do-While-Loop structures**. We use the example of factorial value calculation to illustrate all four structures.

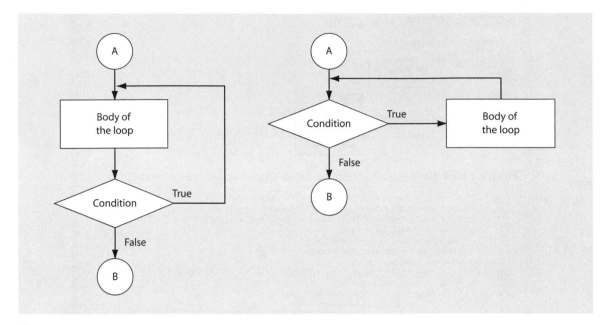

Figure 11.26 Do-Loop-While and Do-While-Loop logical flow chart.

1. Syntax for Do-Loop-While Structure

```
Do
     Body of the loop
Loop While (<condition>)
```

Example:

The following example finds the factorial of a number using Do-Loop-While structure.

```
'Finding Factorial of a Number
Dim Fact As Double = 1
Dim i As Integer = 0
Dim Num As Integer = InputBox("Enter a Number")
Do
    i = i + 1
    Fact = Fact * i
Loop While (Num > i)
MessageBox.Show("Factorial of " & Num & " = " & Fact)
```

2. Syntax for Do-While-Loop Structure

```
Do While (<condition>)
     Body of the loop
Loop
```

Example:

The following example finds the factorial of a number using Do-While-Loop structure.

```
Do While (Num > i)
    i = i + 1
    Fact = Fact * i
Loop
MessageBox.Show("Factorial of " & Num & " = " & Fact)
```

3. Syntax for the Do-Loop-Until Structure

```
Do
     Body of the loop
Loop Until (<condition>)
```

Example:

The following example finds the factorial of a number using Do-Loop-Until structure.

```
Do
    i = i + 1
    Fact = Fact * i
Loop Until (Num <= i)
MessageBox.Show("Factorial of " & Num & " = " & Fact)
```

4. Syntax for Do-Until-Loop Structure

```
Do Until (<condition>)
     Body of the loop
Loop
```

Example:

The following example finds the factorial of a number using Do-Until-Loop structure.

```
Do Until (Num <= i)
    i = i + 1
    Fact = Fact * i
Loop
MessageBox.Show("Factorial of " & Num & " = " & Fact)
```

11.6.8 Hands-On Tutorial: Working with Do-Loop Structures

In this section, we develop an application using Do-Loop structures. We ask user to input any two numbers a and b such that a < b. We also ask user for the third input number c such that c > 0. We then sum all the numbers in a series: a, a+c, a+2c, a+3c, . . . , b. We can think of this series as all the numbers from a to b in step of c units. The sum is displayed to the user as the output of an application. This hands-on tutorial covers the following How-to topic:

- ■ How-to: use the Do-Loop control structure.
    1. Add a new form (*Form4*) to the existing project. Set the *Form4* as a startup form.
    2. Add three TextBox controls named *txtFirstNum*, *txtSecondNum* and *txtSumStep*. Also add a Button control named *cmdSum*. Manipulate these controls as shown in Figure 11.28.
    3. Use the code of Figure 11.28 for the *Click* event of the *cmdSum* Button control.
    4. Save, run, and test the application (see Figure 11.27).

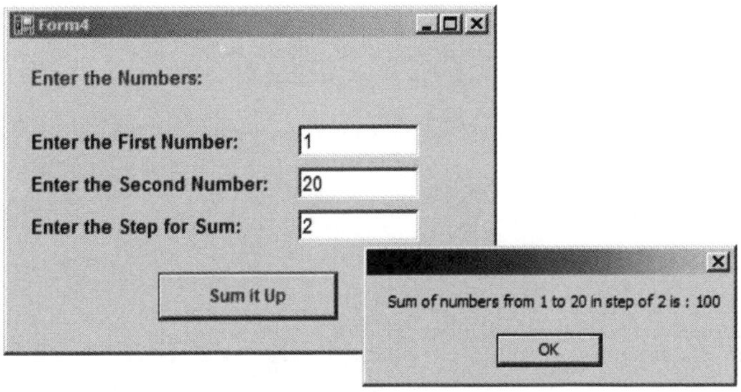

Figure 11.27 Sum using Do-Loop-While structure: Design Window and Output.

```
 3    Private Sub cmdSum_Click(ByVal sender As System.Object, _
 4    ByVal e As System.EventArgs) Handles cmdSum.Click
 5        Dim Count As Integer = 0
 6        Dim Sum As Integer = 0
 7        Dim Num1 As Integer = CInt(txtFirstNum.Text)
 8        Dim Num2 As Integer = CInt(txtSecondNum.Text)
 9        Dim Num3 As Integer = CInt(txtSumStep.Text)
10        If Num1 > Num2 Then
11            MessageBox.Show("Invalid Starting and Ending Numbers")
12        ElseIf Num3 <= 0 Then
13            MessageBox.Show("Invalid Step Number")
14        Else
15            Count = Num1
16            Do
17                Sum = Sum + Count
18                Count = Count + Num3
19            Loop While (Count <= Num2)
20            MessageBox.Show("Sum of numbers from " & Num1 & _
21            " to " & Num2 & " in step of " & Num3 & " is : " & Sum)
22        End If
23    End Sub
```

Figure 11.28 Sum using Do-Loop-While structure: Code Window.

Figure 11.28 Explained:

In lines 7–9, we assign user inputs to the local variables. The If and ElseIf statements in line 10 and 12 are used to check two constraints on input numbers as described in the application description. Lines 16–19 illustrate Do-Loop-While structure. We accumulate the *Sum* of *Count*, which is incremented by *Num3* in each execution of the loop. The loop is executed while *Count* is less than or equal to *Num2* (line 19). Finally, the result is displayed in the MessageBox in lines 20–21.

Figure 11.29 to Figure 11.31 illustrate the piece of code written using Do-While-Loop, Do-Until-Loop, and Do-Loop-Until to perform the same task.

```
13            Count = Num1
14            Do While (Count <= Num2)
15                Sum = Sum + Count
16                Count = Count + Num3
17            Loop
18            MessageBox.Show("Sum of numbers from " & Num1 & _
19            " to " & Num2 & " in step of " & Num3 & " is : " & Sum)
```

Figure 11.29 Sum using Do-While-Loop Structure: Code Window.

```
33            Count = Num1
34            Do Until (Count > Num2)
35                Sum = Sum + Count
36                Count = Count + Num3
37            Loop
38            MessageBox.Show("Sum of numbers from " & Num1 & _
39            " to " & Num2 & " in step of " & Num3 & " is : " & Sum)
```

Figure 11.30 Sum using Do-Until-Loop Structure: Code Window.

```
53            Count = Num1
54            Do
55                Sum = Sum + Count
56                Count = Count + Num3
57            Loop Until (Count > Num2)
58            MessageBox.Show("Sum of numbers from " & Num1 & _
59            " to " & Num2 & " in step of " & Num3 & " is : " & Sum)
```

Figure 11.31 Sum using Do-Loop-Until Structure: Code Window.

11.6.9 Using For-Next Structures

The Do-Loop structures works well when we do not know how many times we must execute the loop statements. For-Next is an alternative when we know the specific number of times we want to execute the loop. Figure 11.32 shows a logical flow chart for the For-Next loop structure.

Syntax for For-Next

```
For <counter = Start Value> To <End Value> [Step <Increment Value>]
    Body of the For Loop
Next
```

Example:

```
'Finding Factorial of a Number
Fact = 1
Num = InputBox("Enter a Number")

For i = 1 To Num
    Fact = Fact * i
Next
```

In the syntax, the *Increment Value* of the *Step* can be a non-zero positive or negative number. If the *Step* is positive, the *Start Value* must be less than or equal to the *End Value*; if *Step* is negative, the *Start Value* must be greater than or equal to the *End Value*. The default *Increment Value* is 1.

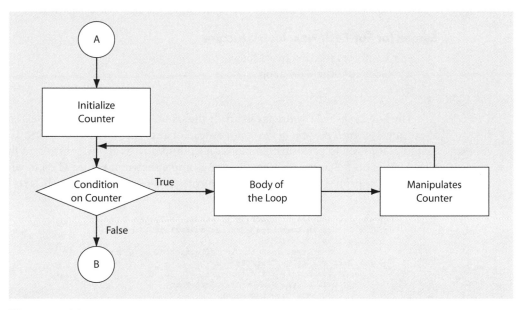

Figure 11.32 For-Next structure's logical flow chart.

11.6.10 Hands-On Tutorial: Working with For-Next Loop Structure

We will reuse the example of the Do-Loop structure from previous hands-on tutorial to illustrate the For-Next loop structure. This hands-on tutorial covers the following How-to topic:

■ How-to: use the For-Next control structure.
   1. Add a new form, *Form5*, to the existing project. Set the *Form5* as a startup form. Set up this form and form controls as in Form4 (see Figure 11.27).

2. Use the code of Figure 11.33 for the *Click* event of the command button. The code uses the For-Next loop in lines 15–17 instead of the Do-Loop structures used in the previous hands-on tutorial.

3. Save, run, and test the application.

```
3    Private Sub cmdSum_Click(ByVal sender As System.Object, _
4    ByVal e As System.EventArgs) Handles cmdSum.Click
5        Dim Count As Integer = 0
6        Dim Sum As Integer = 0
7        Dim Num1 As Integer = CInt(txtFirstNum.Text)
8        Dim Num2 As Integer = CInt(txtSecondNum.Text)
9        Dim Num3 As Integer = CInt(txtSumStep.Text)
10       If Num1 > Num2 Then
11           MessageBox.Show("Invalid Starting and Ending Numbers")
12       ElseIf Num3 <= 0 Then
13           MessageBox.Show("Invalid Step Number")
14       Else
15           For Count = Num1 To Num2 Step Num3
16               Sum = Sum + Count
17           Next Count
18           MessageBox.Show("Sum of numbers from " & Num1 & _
19           " to " & Num2 & " in step of " & Num3 & " is : " & Sum)
20       End If
21   End Sub
```

Figure 11.33 Sum using For-Next loop structure: Code Window.

We now discuss a variation of For-Next loop structure, For-Each-Next.

Syntax for For-Each-Next loop structure

```
For Each <element> In <Group>
    Body of the For loop
Next
```

The For-Each-Next syntax is essentially the same as the For-Next syntax except that the loop is executed *for each element of the group* instead of a specific number of times. This is especially helpful if we need to perform operations on a group such as all the controls on the form, all the CheckBoxes on the form, etc. Consider the example shown in Figure 11.34 in which we change the *BackColor* property of each TextBox control to *Navy* using the For-Each-Next loop structure.

```
3    Private Sub cmdForEach_Click(ByVal sender As System.Object, _
4    ByVal e As System.EventArgs) Handles cmdForEach.Click
5        Dim ctl As Control
6        'For each control in Controls collection of THIS form DO
7        For Each ctl In Me.Controls
8            'If its a Text Box control
9            If ctl.GetType.Name = "TextBox" Then
10               'Change its back color
11               ctl.BackColor = Color.Navy
12           End If
13       Next
14   End Sub
```

Figure 11.34 Manipulating group of TextBox controls using the For-Each-Next loop structure.

Figure 11.34 Explained:

Line 5 declares a variable *ctl* of type Control. For each *ctl* on the form (group of controls: `Me.Controls`), the lines 9–12 are executed. If the control type is the *TextBox* (line 9), we manipulate its *BackColor* property and set it to *Navy* color (line 11).

11.6.11 Using Exit Statement

The Exit statement allows us to end the execution of a loop, subroutine, or function. When Visual Basic encounters an Exit statement, it exits the structure specified by its parameter.

Syntax for Exit

```
Exit <What?>
```

Examples

```
Exit Sub
Exit Select
Exit Do
Exit For
Exit Function
```

Code examples in Figure 11.35 and Figure 11.36 illustrate the use of an Exit statement. The code in the Figure 11.35 is the code for the Select-Case structure example in Figure 11.25. In line 17, we have added the Exit Sub statement. Thus, if the user entered an incorrect month abbreviation, we would exit the subroutine and avoid displaying an empty message to the user in line 19. The example in Figure 11.36 uses an Exit statement to stop the execution of a Do-Loop structure. Note that the Exit statement in line 30 is used in place of a While or Until keywords that are usually used to terminate a Do-Loop structure.

```
3   Private Sub cmdCheckDays_Click(ByVal sender As System.Object, _
4   ByVal e As System.EventArgs) Handles cmdCheckDays.Click
5       Dim MonthAbbr As String
6       Dim DaysInMonth As Integer
7       MonthAbbr = txtMonthAbbr.Text
8       Select Case MonthAbbr
9           Case "Jan", "Mar", "May", "Jul", "Aug", "Oct", "Dec"
10              DaysInMonth = 31
11          Case "Apr", "Jun", "Sep", "Nov"
12              DaysInMonth = 30
13          Case "Feb"
14              DaysInMonth = 28
15          Case Else
16              MessageBox.Show(MonthAbbr & " is invalid abbreviation")
17              Exit Sub
18      End Select
19      MessageBox.Show(MonthAbbr & " has " & DaysInMonth & " days.")
20  End Sub
```

Figure 11.35 An example of Exit Sub statement.

```
22  Private Sub cmdExitDo_Click(ByVal sender As System.Object, _
23  ByVal e As System.EventArgs) Handles cmdExitDo.Click
24      Dim count As Integer = 1
25      Dim found As Boolean = False
26      'We simulate DO-LOOP's termination condition using "Exit Do"
27      Do
28          If found Then
29              MessageBox.Show("Count has reached 10")
30              Exit Do
31          End If
32          count = count + 1
33          If count = 10 Then found = True
34      Loop
35  End Sub
```

Figure 11.36 An example of Exit Do statement.

11.7   *Arithmetic, Logical, and String Operators*

Operators operate on one or more *operands* to produce an output value. There are three types of operators we will study in this section: arithmetic, logical, and string operators. We summarize arithmetic and logical operators in Table 11.5 and Table 11.6, respectively. We discuss a few important Math functions and string operators in two separate subsections.

11.7.1   Using Math Functions

Table 11.7 summarizes some of the functions associated with the `Math` collection.
We illustrate the use of *Pow* and *Sqrt* math functions with an example of Pythagoras' Theorem. In this example, we calculate the length of the hypotenuse of a right-angled triangle, given the length of its other two sides. In algebraic terms, $c^2 = a^2 + b^2$, where c is the hypotenuse, while

Table 11.5 Arithmetic operators (in order of precedence).

Operator	Meaning	Example
*, /	Multiplication and division	**x * y**. Multiply *x* with *y*
+, –	Addition and subtraction	**x + y**. Add *x* to *y*
^	Exponential	**x ^ y**. *x* to the power of *y*
Mod	Modulo	**x Mod y**. *x* Modulo *y*
*=, /=	Multiplication/division followed by assignment	**x *= y**. *x* = *x* * *y*
+=, –=	Addition/subtraction followed by assignment	**x += y**. *x* = *x* + *y*
=, <>	Equal to, Not equal to	**x <> y**. *x* is not equal to *y*
>, <	Greater than, less than	**x > y**. *x* is greater than *y*
>=, <=	Greater than or equal to, Less than or equal to	**x >= y**. *x* is greater than or equal to *y*

Table 11.6 Logical operators.

Operator	Meaning	Example
And	Logical And two operands	**X And Y**. If both X and Y are true, return true; otherwise, return false.
Not	Reverse the logical value of a operand	**Not X**. If X is true, then return false and vice versa.
Or	Logical Or two operands	**X Or Y**. If either X or Y is true, return true; otherwise, return false.
Xor	Logical Exclusive Or two operands	**A Xor B**. If A is true OR B is true, return true (Exclusive). If both A and B have the same value (true/false), return false.

Table 11.7 Important math functions.

Function	Meaning	Example
Abs	Returns the absolute value of a specified number	**Math.Abs(-20.5)**. Returns 20.5
Sin, Tan, Cos	Returns the Sine, tangent and Cosine value of the angle, respectively	**Math.Sin(90)**. Returns 1 **Math.Tan(0)**. Returns 0 **Math.Cos(0)**. Returns 0.
Min, Max	Returns the smaller and greater of the given two numbers, respectively	**Math.Min(4, 10)**. Returns 4 **Math.Max(0, 100)**. Returns 100
Log, Log10	Log Returns the natural logarithm and Log10 returns base 10 logarithm of the specified number	**Math.Log(4000.0)**. Returns 8.29404964010203 (4000 is given as a double value) **Math.Log10(4000.0)**. Returns 3.60205999132796
Floor	Returns the greatest integer less than or equal to its numeric argument	**Math.Floor(2.56)**. Returns 2 as a result
Ceiling	Returns the smallest integer greater than or equal to its numeric argument	**Math.Ceiling(2.56)**. Returns 3 as a result
Sqrt	Returns the square root of the specified number	**Math.Sqrt(36)**. Returns 6 as a result.
Pow	Returns the specified number raised to the specified power	**Math.Pow(2, 3)**. Returns 8 as a result.
Round	Returns the value of the integer nearest to the given number	**Math.Round(10.89)**. Returns 11as a result.

a and b are the sides of the triangle. In Figure 11.37, line 8 calculates the squares of a and b using the *Pow* function. Line 9 finds the square root of the sum of the squares using the *Sqrt* function.

```
3    Private Sub cmdPythagoras_Click(ByVal sender As System.Object, _
4    ByVal e As System.EventArgs) Handles cmdPythagoras.Click
5        Dim a, b, c As Double
6        a = InputBox("Enter A value", "Input")
7        b = InputBox("Enter B value", "Input")
8        c = Math.Pow(a, 2) + Math.Pow(b, 2)
9        c = Math.Sqrt(c)
10       MessageBox.Show("Hypotenuse C = " & c & ", give side a = " _
11       & a & " and b = " & b, "Pythagoras Theorem")
12   End Sub
```

Figure 11.37 Pythagoras' Theorem example: Code Window.

11.7.2 Handling Strings

Working with the string data type is an important aspect of application development process. VB .NET has tremendous support for string manipulation. We can perform a variety of operations on strings, several of which are listed below:

- Change the string case
- Get part of the string
- Concatenate two strings

- Compare two strings
- Search a string

Table 11.8 summarizes the VB .NET functions for these string operations. The hands-on tutorial in Section 11.7.3 illustrates the usage of these functions.

Table 11.8 String operators.

What To Do	How
Concatenate two strings	&, +, String.Concat
Compare two strings	String.CompareTo(*CompareMe*), String.Equals(*CompareMe*)
Copy String	=, String.Copy(*CopyFrom*)
Change Case	UCase, LCase, String.ToUpper
Length	Len, String.Length
Substring	String.Substring(*StartPos*, *Length*)
String Search	String.IndexOf(*SearchString*)
Trim Spaces	LTrim, RTrim, String.Trim

11.7.3 Hands-On Tutorial: String Operations

In this hands-on tutorial, we will illustrate various string operations. The section covers the following How-to topic:

- How-to: use string *Concat*, *Compare*, *Substring*, *IndexOf*, and *Length* functions.
    1. Add a form, Form6, to the current project and set it as the start-up form.
    2. Design the form as shown in Figure 11.38.
    3. Each of the GroupBox control in Figure 11.38 illustrates a string operation.
    4. Use Code Window1 (see Figure 11.40) and Code Window2 (see Figure 11.41) to assign code for each of the four command buttons.
    5. Save, run, and test the application (see Figure 11.39).

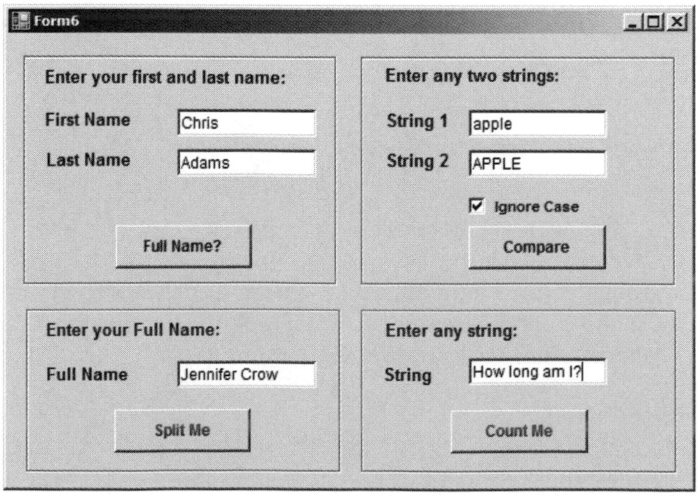

Figure 11.38 Illustrating string operators: the form in Design Window.

String concatenation code:

To illustrate the string concatenation operation, we ask the user for first name and last name strings and put them together using the *Concat* function and output the full name on the click of the command button. The *Concat* function is used in line 6 of Code Window1. The first name, a white space, and the last name are three arguments of the *Concat* function. The output is shown in the first output window of Figure 11.39.

String comparison code:

The string comparison operation is illustrated by comparing two user input strings. We also give an option of *case insensitive* comparison by providing a CheckBox control. If the check box is checked, we ignore the case while doing the comparison and opposite when it is not checked. Line 12 features the *Compare* function. The function takes three arguments, two strings to compare and a Boolean value for case-sensitive comparison. The value of the Boolean input parameter is set to the value of the *Checked* property of the CheckBox control and reflects user's selection while using the *Compare* function (see Figure 11.39).

Substring operation:

We illustrate the *Substring* operation by splitting the user-given full name. A *Substring* function takes the starting and ending index in the string as its input arguments and returns the substring that falls within these indexes. For example, if we use *Substring* with arguments 0 and 5 on our sample input "Chris Adams," we obtain the string "Chris."

We use the *IndexOf* function to find the index of the white space in the full name and obtain a substring before the space (i.e., first name) and a substring after the space (i.e., last name). Line 24 features the *IndexOf* function with a white space as its input argument (see Figure 11.41). The function returns the index of the first occurrence of a space in the string. The index of the space is then used as an argument to the *Substring* function. In line 25, the *Substring* function is used with the argument "0" and the index of the white space to obtain the first name. In line 26, however, we specify only one index to obtain the last name. If the *Substring* function is called with only one argument, the argument is taken as the starting index, and a substring is returned from the starting index till end of the string.

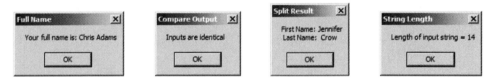

Figure 11.39 Illustrating string operators: application output.

```
 3   Private Sub cmdConcat_Click(ByVal sender As System.Object, _
 4   ByVal e As System.EventArgs) Handles cmdConcat.Click
 5       Dim fullName As String
 6       fullName = String.Concat(txtfName.text, " ", txtlName.text)
 7       MessageBox.Show("Your full name is: " & fullName, "Full Name")
 8   End Sub
 9
10   Private Sub cmdCompare_Click(ByVal sender As System.Object, _
11   ByVal e As System.EventArgs) Handles cmdCompare.Click
12       If String.Compare(txtS1.Text, txtS2.Text, chkCase.Checked) Then
13           MessageBox.Show("Inputs are not the same", "Compare Output")
14       Else
15           MessageBox.Show("Inputs are identical", "Compare Output")
16       End If
17   End Sub
```

Figure 11.40 Illustrating string operators: Code Window1.

```
19    Private Sub cmdSubString_Click(ByVal sender As System.Object, _
20    ByVal e As System.EventArgs) Handles cmdSubString.Click
21        Dim whiteIndex As Integer
22        Dim fname, lname, fullName As String
23        fullName = txtFullName.Text
24        whiteIndex = fullName.IndexOf(" ")
25        fname = fullName.Substring(0, whiteIndex)
26        lname = fullName.Substring(whiteIndex)
27        MessageBox.Show("First Name: " & fname & vbLf _
28        & " Last Name: " & lname, "Split Result")
29    End Sub
30
31    Private Sub cmdLength_Click(ByVal sender As System.Object, _
32    ByVal e As System.EventArgs) Handles cmdLength.Click
33        Dim inputStr As String = txtString.Text
34        MessageBox.Show("Length of input string = " _
35        & inputStr.Length, "String Length")
36    End Sub
```

Figure 11.41 Illustrating string operators: Code Window2.

String length:

Line 35 illustrates the use of the *Length* function. The function returns the total length of the string (see Figure 11.41).

11.8 *Arrays*

An array is a basic data structure that allows us to refer to multiple variables by the same name. We can index into an array to point at a particular variable. All the variables (or elements) in an array have the same data type. Arrays, like any other variables, must be declared before they can be used. We use variable declaration keyword `Dim` to declare arrays as well.

Array Declaration Syntax:

```
Dim <Array Name> As ([<Array Size>-1]) <Data Type>
```

Examples:

```
Dim IntArray (4) As Integer    '5 elements
Dim DobArray (14) As Date      '15 elements
Dim LongArray (49) As Long     '50 elements
```

The above statements declare arrays. In the first line, we create an array of five elements of the *Integer* data type. Each *Integer* variable is then accessed using its index (see section 11.9.3 for more on the uses of arrays). Figure 11.42 depicts an instance of an *IntArray*.

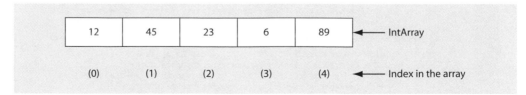

Figure 11.42 An example of an integer array.

11.8.1 Hands-On Tutorial: Working with Arrays

In this hands-on tutorial, we will demonstrate how to declare and use arrays in VB .NET. We declare an array of size five and ask user for array elements using an InputBox. The array contents are then displayed to the user in a MessageBox. This section covers the following How-to topic:

- How-to: declare and use arrays.
   1. Add a new form (*Form7*) to the existing *VisualBasicIntro* project. Set *Form7* as the start-up form.
   2. Design the form as shown in Figure 11.43. Name the command button as, *cmdPopulateArray*. Set its *Text* property to "Populate Me."
   3. For the *Click* event of the command button *cmdPopulateArray*, write the code shown in Figure 11.44.
   4. Save, run, and test the application.

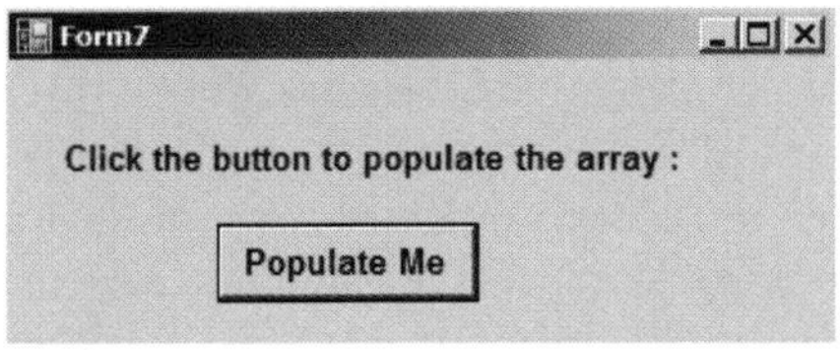

Figure 11.43 An array example: Design Window.

```
3  Private Sub cmdPopulateArray_Click(ByVal sender As System.Object, _
4  ByVal e As System.EventArgs) Handles cmdPopulateArray.Click
5
6      Dim output As String
7      Dim Arr(4) As String
8      Dim i As Integer
9      For i = 0 To 4
10         Arr(i) = InputBox("Enter " & i & _
11         " element of the Array", "User Input")
12     Next i
13     output = "You have entered the following array" & vbLf
14
15     For i = 0 To 4
16         output &= Arr(i) & vbLf
17     Next i
18     MessageBox.Show(output, "Array Display")
19  End Sub
```

Figure 11.44 An array example: Code Window.

Figure 11.44 Explained:

We declare a string array of five elements in line 7. In lines 9–12, we ask the user to enter the values for the elements of the array using an InputBox. In line 16, we concatenate values of the array elements into a string variable. We use the Visual Basic line-feed character (*vbLf*) to output each array element on a new line. Line 18 displays the output string in a MessageBox (see Figure 11.45).

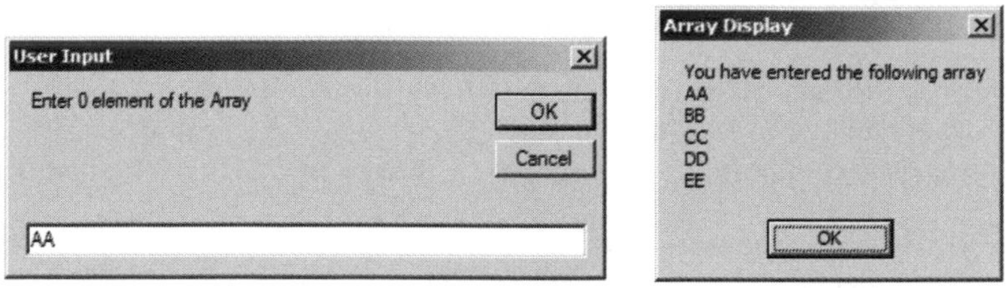

Figure 11.45 Array example: Output Window.

We next describe the ListBox control, which is used in the further discussion on Arrays.

11.8.2 The ListBox Control

The ListBox control presents a *list* of choices to the user. By default, the choices are displayed vertically in a single column. Figure 11.46(a) shows an example of the ListBox control. The user can select one or more choices from the list and the user selection can be accessed using *SelectedItem* or *SelectedItems* properties of a ListBox control. Table 11.9 describes few important properties, methods, and events of a ListBox control.

The **SelectedIndex** property is set to an index of the selected item (or the index of the first selected item for multiple selections). For example, if the first list item is selected, the property is set to zero. If no item is selected, the *SelectedIndex* property is set to –1. Another property re-

Table 11.9 Properties, methods and events of a ListBox control.

Name	Description
ColumnWidth	Gets/sets the column width for the multi-column list.
Items	Gets/sets collection of all the items.
MultiColumn	If set to true, makes a multi-column list.
ScrollAlwaysVisible	Indicates if the scroll bar should always be visible in the list.
SelectedIndex	Gets/sets the index of a currently selected item.
SelectedIndices	Gives the collection of indices of selected items.
SelectedItem	Gets/sets the currently selected item.
SelectedItems	Gives the collection of all the selected items.
SelectionMode	Gets/sets the mode of selection.
Sorted	If set to true, alphabetically sorts the items in the list.
Text	Gets the selected text.
ClearSelection	Sets SelectedIndex = –1; it clears any selection.
GetSelected	Returns true if the indicated item is selected.
SetSelected	Selects the indicated item.
Items.Clear	Clears all the items in the list.
Items.RemoveAt(i)	Removes the item with index i.
SelectedIndexChanged	Occurs when the *SelectIndex* property, or selection, changes.

lated to selection is **SelectedItem**, which is very similar to *SelectedIndex* but returns the item it-self rather than its index. Finally, we can access all items in the list using the *Items* collection. For example, to determine the number of items in a list, we use **Items.Count**; to add an item to or delete an item from the list we use an **Items.Add** method and an **Items.Remove** method, respectively.

11.8.3   Adding Items to a List Box

We can add items to a list at design time using Properties Window or at run time in the VB .NET code. To add items at the design time, locate the *Items* property in the Property Window and click the build button in the property row to open the **String Collection Editor**. The editor allows us to enter item values to the list. To add items in the code, we employ the ListBox control's **Items.Add** method (see Figure 11.46(b)).

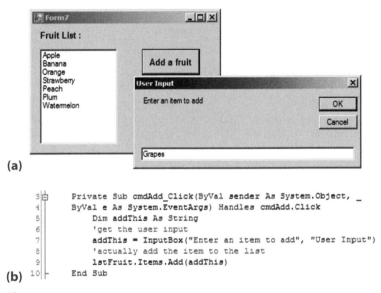

(a)

```
 3    Private Sub cmdAdd_Click(ByVal sender As System.Object, _
 4    ByVal e As System.EventArgs) Handles cmdAdd.Click
 5        Dim addThis As String
 6        'get the user input
 7        addThis = InputBox("Enter an item to add", "User Input")
 8        'actually add the item to the list
 9        lstFruit.Items.Add(addThis)
10    End Sub
```

(b)

Figure 11.46 (a) An example of a ListBox control; (b) Adding items to a ListBox control.

11.8.4   Hands-On Tutorial: Displaying Array in a ListBox Control

We reconsider an example of the integer array presented in Section 11.8.1. In this hands-on tutorial, however, we display the array contents in a ListBox control instead of a MessageBox. This hands-on tutorial covers the following How-to topic:

■ How-to: add elements to a ListBox control
  1. Add a new form (*Form8*) to the existing *VisualBasicIntro* project. Set *Form8* as the start-up form.
  2. Add a ListBox and Button controls as shown in Figure 11.47. Name the Button control as "cmdArray" and the ListBox control as "lstArray." Set the *Text* property of the ListBox control to "Populate Me."
  3. Associate the code in Figure 11.48 with the *Click* event of the *cmdArray* command button.
  4. Save and run the application by pressing Ctrl+F5.

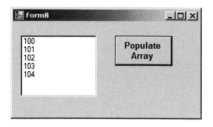

Figure 11.47 Displaying array in a ListBox control: Design Window.

```
 3    Private Sub cmdArray_Click(ByVal sender As System.Object, _
 4    ByVal e As System.EventArgs) Handles cmdArray.Click
 5
 6        Dim Arr(4) As Integer
 7        Dim i As Integer
 8        'get the array elements
 9        For i = 0 To 4
10            Arr(i) = InputBox("Enter " & i & _
11            " element of the Array", "User Input")
12        Next i
13        'add the array to the list box item collection
14        For i = 0 To 4
15            lstArray.Items.Add(Arr(i))
16        Next i
17    End Sub
```

Figure 11.48 Displaying array in a ListBox control: Code Window.

Figure 11.48 Explained:

In line 6, we declare an integer array *Arr* of size 5. In lines 9–12, we ask the user to enter the values for the elements of the array using an InputBox. In lines 14–16, we add the array elements to the *Items* collection of the ListBox control.

11.9 *Multi-Dimensional Arrays*

The arrays introduced in Section 11.8 are also referred to as one-dimensional arrays as they store data about one subject (or dimension). For example, the one-dimensional array in Figure 11.42 can be used to store student's grades for five different courses; one course per array element. The "course grade" is the only dimension we are storing in this case. If we wish to store grades for these five courses for four different students we must declare four one-dimensional arrays; or we can add an additional dimension—"students"—to one-dimensional array, "students." Arrays with two or more dimensions are referred to as multi-dimensional arrays. A two-dimensional array can be visualized as a grid with rows of the grid that represent one of the dimensions and the columns that represent the other (see Figure 11.49). The syntax for multi-dimension arrays in Visual Basic is given below.

Multi-dimensional Array Declaration Syntax:

```
Dim <Array Name> ([<1st D Size>]),... ([<nth D Size>]) As <Data Type>
```

Examples:

A two-dimensional student array can be declared as follows:

```
Dim Students (3, 4) As Double    '4 rows and 5 columns
```

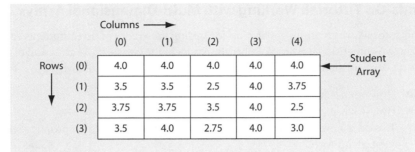

Figure 11.49 An example of the two-dimensional array.

11.9.1 Using Loop Structures to Populate and Read Multi-Dimensional Arrays

We can efficiently process a multi-dimensional array by using nested For-Next loops. For example, the code shown in Figure 11.50 initializes every element in the *Student* array in two nested For-Next loops (lines 9–14). The code then displays the two-dimensional array contents to the user in a MessageBox using two nested For-Next loops (lines 16–21).

```
5       Dim i, j As Integer
6       Dim output As String = "Student grades " & vbLf
7       Dim Student(3, 4) As Double
8       'get the array elements
9       For i = 0 To 3
10          For j = 0 To 4
11              Student(i, j) = InputBox("Enter student " & i & _
12                  "'s grade in subject " & j, "User Input")
13          Next j
14      Next i
15      'add the array to the output string
16      For i = 0 To 3
17          For j = 0 To 4
18              output &= Student(i, j) & vbTab
19          Next j
20          output &= vbLf
21      Next i
22
23      MessageBox.Show(output, "Student Grades")
24  End Sub
```

Figure 11.50 Using For-Next loop structure to populate and read two-dimensional array: Code Window.

Figure 11.51 Displaying a two-dimensional array in the DataGridView control: Design Window.

11.9.2 Hands-On Tutorial: Working with Multi-Dimensional Arrays

In this tutorial, we create an application for storing the grades of three students for three courses using a two-dimensional array. We store the grades in the *Grades* (2, 2) array and display the grades using a DataGridView control. This hands-on tutorial covers the following How-to topics:

- How-to: use multidimensional arrays.
- How-to: use DataGridView control.
    1. Add a new form (*Form9*) to the existing *VisualBasicIntro* project. Set *Form9* as the start-up form.
    2. Drag and drop a DataGridView control from the Toolbox on *Form9*. The DataGrid-View control is present under the *Data* category in the Toolbox. Name the Data-GridView control as *dgvArray*.
    3. Also add a Button control named *cmdMultDArray* to form and set its *Text* property to "Enter Grades" (see Figure 11.51).
    4. Associate the code shown in Figure 11.52 with the *Click* event of the command button.

```
3   Private Sub cmdMultDArray_Click(ByVal sender As System.Object, _
4   ByVal e As System.EventArgs) Handles cmdMultDArray.Click
5       'Store and display grades using multi dimentional array
6       Dim Grades(2, 2) As Integer
7       Dim Rows As Integer
8       Dim Cols As Integer
9       'Insert appropriate columns and rows to DataGridView
10      For Cols = 0 To 2
11          dgvArray.Columns.Add("Col " & Cols, "Course " & Cols)
12      Next
13      For Rows = 0 To 2
14          dgvArray.Rows.Add()
15      Next
16      'get user input for student grades
17      For Rows = 0 To 2
18          For Cols = 0 To 2
19              Grades(Rows, Cols) = CInt(InputBox("Enter Course " & _
20                                  Cols & " Grade for Student " & Rows))
21          Next
22      Next
23      'Populate DataGridView cells
24      For Rows = 0 To 2
25          For Cols = 0 To 2
26              dgvArray.Rows(Rows).Cells(Cols).Value = _
27              Grades(Rows, Cols)
28          Next
29      Next
30  End Sub
```

Figure 11.52 Displaying a two-dimensional array in the DataGridView control: Code Window

Figure 11.52 Explained:

In line 6, we declare a two-dimensional integer array *Grades* (2, 2) to hold the grades of three students for three courses. In lines 10–15, we add three columns and three rows to the grid view to display the grades. We use *Columns* and *Rows* collection of the DataGridView controls and call their respective *Add* methods to setup the grid. The user is then asked to enter student's grades using an InputBox in two nested For-Next loops (lines 17–22). The grades are stored in the *Grades* (2, 2) array in lines 19–20. In lines 24–29, we populate the DataGridView cells using the values stored in the *Grades* (2, 2) array.

11.10 *Dynamic Arrays*

Visual Basic features two types of arrays: a *static* array whose size always remains the same, and a *dynamic* array whose size can be changed at runtime. In Section 11.8 and 11.9, we presented static arrays. We knew the size of the array while declaring them. Dynamic arrays are useful in the situation when we do not know the exact number of elements to be stored in an array. Visual Basic lets us assign or change the array size at runtime using the ReDim (re-declare) keyword.

Re-declaration Syntax:

```
ReDim <Array Name> (<Array Size>)
```

Figure 11.53 and Figure 11.54 present an example of one-dimensional dynamic arrays.

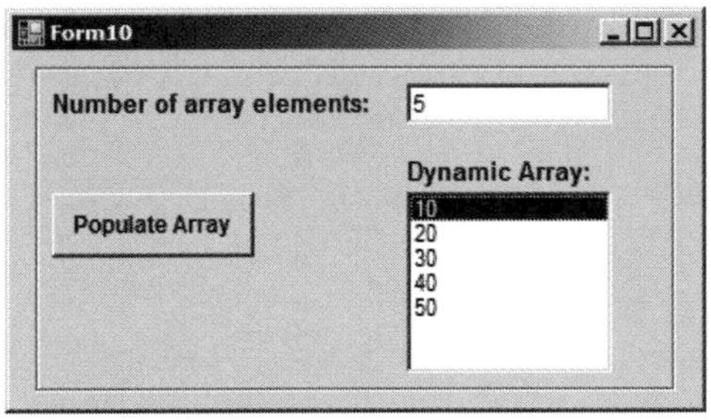

Figure 11.53 An example of dynamic arrays: Form Design.

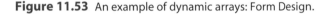

```
3    Private Sub cmdDynamic_Click(ByVal sender As System.Object, _
4    ByVal e As System.EventArgs) Handles cmdDynamic.Click
5        Dim Arr() As Integer
6        Dim i As Integer
7        Dim NoElements As Integer
8        NoElements = txtNoElements.Text
9        NoElements -= 1
10       ReDim Arr(NoElements)
11       For i = 0 To NoElements
12           Arr(i) = CInt(InputBox("Enter No. " & i))
13       Next
14       For i = 0 To NoElements
15           lstDynamicArray.Items.Add(Arr(i))
16       Next
17   End Sub
```

Figure 11.54 An example of dynamic arrays: Code Window.

Figure 11.54 Explained:

We declare an integer array *Arr* in line 5. However, we do not mention the size of the array. The array size is obtained from the TextBox control on the form in line 8. The array is re-declared in line 10 with known size of the array. We use an InputBox within a For-Next loop to allow the user to enter the values for the array elements (lines 11–13). Array contents are added to the List-Box in lines 14–16.

11.11 *Code Debugging*

There are two kinds of errors that can occur in a program: syntax errors and logical (semantic) errors. The process of finding and fixing syntax and logical errors is known as ***debugging***.

11.11.1 Syntax Errors

Syntax errors occur because of incorrect syntax use or human errors. For example, suppose that we ended the If structure without the keyword End If. Since the syntax of the *If* structure requires the End If keyword to end the structure, this results in a syntax error. Dealing with syntax errors is relatively easy. We can always refer to the help section or some other reference for the correct syntax. In addition, Visual Studio .NET also assists us in detecting syntax errors as we write the code.

Visual Studio .NET underlines the construct where there is a syntax error. For example, in Figure 11.55 we forgot to add the second Next keyword for the outer For-Next loop structure. The tool tip at the location of the syntax error provides the description of the error.

```
16      'For' must end with a matching 'Next'. dent grades
17      For Rows = 0 To 2
18          For Cols = 0 To 2
19              Grades(Rows, Cols) = CInt(InputBox("Enter Course " & _
20                              Cols & " Grade for Student " & Rows))
21          Next
22
```

Figure 11.55 Syntax error in the outer For-Next loop structure.

11.11.2 Logical Errors

Logical errors arise due to flaws in the logical reasoning of an application design. Detecting and handling logical errors can be very challenging. Consider the example of the dynamic arrays code shown in Figure 11.54 and the same program as written in Figure 11.56.

In this code, we have introduced logical errors in lines 11 and 14. Suppose that a user enters values of "5" for *NoElements*. We re-define the array in line 10 with *Arr(5-1)*; that is, this array will have 5 elements that are indexed from 0 to 4. In lines 11 and 14, the For-Next loop iterates from index 0 to *NoElements* (i.e., from 0 to 5). This is an error because there is no element at index "5" in the array. Since this program is syntactically correct, Visual Studio does not show

```
3       Private Sub cmdDynamic_Click(ByVal sender As System.Object, _
4       ByVal e As System.EventArgs) Handles cmdDynamic.Click
5           Dim Arr() As Integer
6           Dim i As Integer
7           Dim NoElements As Integer
8           NoElements = txtNoElements.Text
9
10          ReDim Arr(NoElements - 1)
11          For i = 0 To NoElements
12              Arr(i) = CInt(InputBox("Enter No. " & i))
13          Next
14          For i = 0 To NoElements
15              lstDynamicArray.Items.Add(Arr(i))
16          Next
17      End Sub
```

Figure 11.56 Dynamic array code with logical errors.

any error lines. These errors are revealed when program is executed. The code in Figure 11.56 produces a run-time exception when executed (see Figure 11.57).

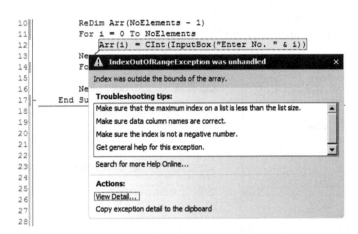

Figure 11.57 Logical error: run-time error message for IndexOutOfRange exception.

In this section, we describe the method to debug logical errors. In the following subsections, we present topics that will help us to execute code line by line and also watch the values assigned to variables in the code to help us locate the logical errors. For example, if we execute the code from the previous example and watch for the value of variable *i* and the array, we would see that the variable *i* has been assigned incorrect value 5 in line 11 and 14.

11.11.3 Using Breakpoints

Breakpoints are an excellent tool available in Visual Studio that helps us to debug logical errors. With breakpoints, we can specify a line in the code where we want to break the execution of a program. The program execution is paused at the breakpoint and we can observe the values of various variables at that point in time. If everything is found as expected, we can continue executing the program until we hit the next breakpoint. We can include multiple breakpoints in the code.

To add a breakpoint, we click in the selector area of the code line. This adds a red dot in the selector area and also highlights the breakpoint line with red background (see Figure 11.58). To remove a breakpoint, click the red dot in the selector area of the line. Breakpoints offer many interesting features that are accessible on the shortcut menu of a breakpoint (see Figure 11.58). We

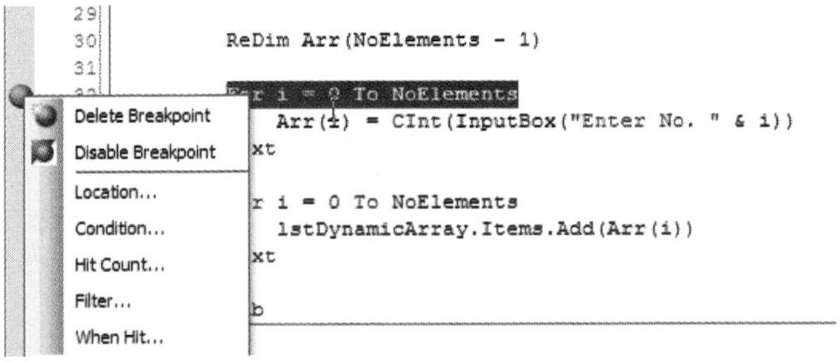

Figure 11.58 Adding breakpoints to the code.

can break on a breakpoint conditionally. For instance, in the previous example, we would like to break the program execution only if the variable i's value is greater than the size of the array (see Figure 11.59). We can also skip a breakpoint based on how many times it was hit (see Figure 11.59). This feature is useful to debug loop structures in which we may like to skip breakpoints within a loop structure for certain loop iterations.

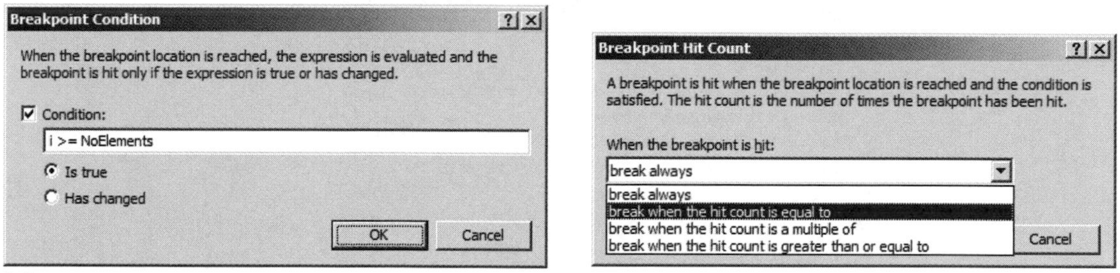

(a)   **(b)**

Figure 11.59 Specifying (a) breakpoint condition; and (2) breakpoint hit count.

11.11.4   Using the Watch Window

Another important debugging feature in Visual Studio is the Watch window. We use this feature to *watch* the values of different variables during the execution of a program. Every time we break (or pause) the execution using a breakpoint, we can watch the values of variables in the Watch Window. To open a Watch Window, we must be in debug mode. That is we must execute the program Debug | Start Debugging or F5 option from the main menu. In the debugging mode, we can open a Watch Window by choosing Debug | Windows | Watch | Watch1 option from the main menu (Figure 11.60). We can open as many as four Watch Windows at a time. In a Watch Window, we can add the names of the variables we would like to watch and the corresponding values are displayed in the *Value* column. For instance, we can add the array name *Arr* to view its contents as shown in Figure 11.61.

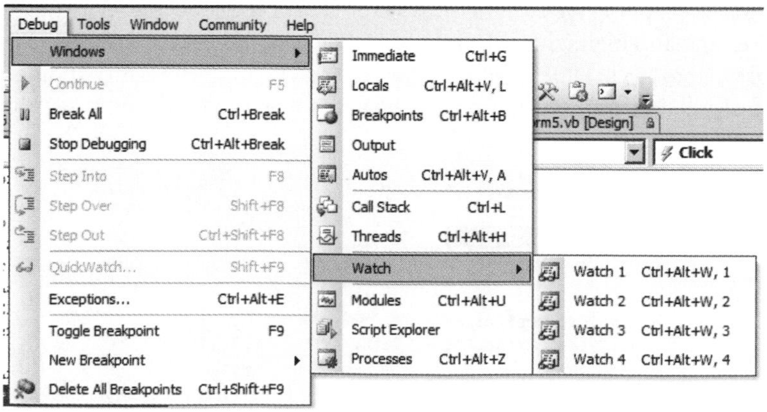

Figure 11.60 Opening a Watch Window.

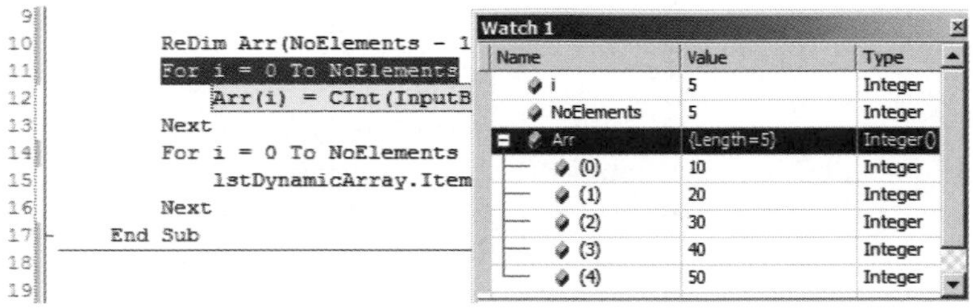

Figure 11.61 Adding variables to the Watch Window.

11.11.5 Using Debug Toolbar and Menu

As we break program execution and watch variables, we can *step over* or *step into* a procedure (see Chapter 12) using options available in the *Debug* toolbar or *Debug* menu (Figure 11.62). Table 11.10 summarizes these options.

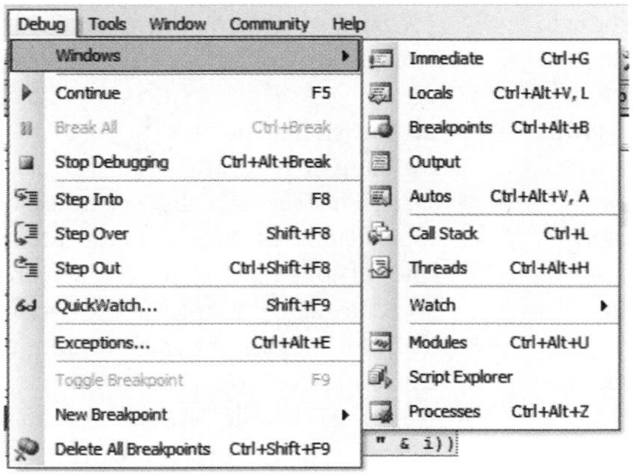

Figure 11.62 The *Debug* menu.

Table 11.10 *Debug* menu options.

Option		Description
Continue		Continues the execution until next break point.
Stop Debugging		Stops the execution. Gets us out of debugging mode.
Step Into		Steps into a *procedure*. If the current line of the program is not a procedure call, we move to the next line of the code.
Step Over		Executes the procedure without stepping into it. The procedure will be executed and we move to the next code line. Again, if the current line is not a procedure call, we move to the next line of the code.
Step Out		Executing remaining statements of the procedure and gets out of the procedure.

11.12   *In-Class Assignment*

Create a Windows application that will compute the sum of squares of a series of numbers, given a starting number (SN), ending number (EN), and a step value (SV). For example, given SN = 1, EN = 5, and SV = 1, the series is 1, 2, 3, 4, and 5, and the sum of squares is $1 + 2 + 9 + 16 + 25$ = 53. Use either a Do-While loop or a For-Next loop to compute the sum, and display it in a MessageBox to the user. Also display a series and square values in two ListBox controls.

Use a "double" variable to hold the sum of squares. Also, if the value entered for EN is larger than 100,000, we exit the program without computing the sum.

11.13   *Summary*

- A **computer program** is a sequence of precise, unambiguous, and detailed instructions on how to complete a task, written in a language that can be interpreted by a computer. A language used to express these instructions is referred as a **programming language**.
- A complete instruction written in Visual Basic language is known as a **Visual Basic statement**. The rules and regulations that govern the composition of VB statements are known as **language syntax**.
- A Visual Basic statement contains one or more of the following elements:
  - **a.** Keywords: Reserved words for Visual Basic's use.
  - **b.** Variables: Containers for values; temporary names given to memory locations.
  - **c.** Constants: Special variables with fixed values.
  - **d.** Operators: Symbols used to perform arithmetic and logical operations on operands.
  - **e.** Operands: Numerical or string values to operate on.
- We use the keyword `Dim` to declare a variable in Visual Basic. The type of a variable (*data type*) indicates the kind of data that will be stored in the variable.
- **InputBox** is a function that helps us obtain data from a user using a dialog box. **MessageBox** is a function that takes a value as an input parameter and displays it to the user in a dialog box.

- Control structures allow us to control the flow of program execution. Control structures consist of two categories, that are based on the behavior they create:
  - **a.** Decision Structures
  - **b.** Loop Structures
- Decision structures allow us to test conditions and loop structures allow us to execute one or more lines of code repetitively. If-Then and Select-Case structures are examples of the decision structure. The Do-Loops and For-Next loops are examples of the loop structures.
- An array is a basic data structure that allows us to refer to multiple variables by the same name.
- An array is a basic data structure in Visual Basic that allows us to refer to multiple variables by the same name. Visual Basic features two types of arrays: a *static* array whose size always remains the same, and a *dynamic* array whose size can be changed at run-time.
- There are two kinds of errors that can occur in a program: syntax errors and logical (semantic) errors. The process of finding and fixing syntax and logical errors is known as *debugging*. Syntax errors occur because of incorrect syntax use or human errors. Logical errors arise due to flaws in the logical reasoning of an application design. Detecting and handling logical errors can be very challenging. However, Visual Studio provides features like breakpoints and Watch Windows to help detect logical errors.

11.14   *Exercises*

11.14.1 Review Questions

1. Explain the difference(s) between an InputBox and a MessageBox.

2. Suppose the user enters "123" in a TextBox. How will you determine if this is an integer data type? If user input is not an integer data type, how will you convert it to an integer?

3. What is the difference between the Do-Loop-While and Do-While-Loop structures? Give an example that illustrates this difference.

4. What control structure is ideal when we know the exact number of times we want to execute a loop? Give the syntax of this structure.

5. Which control structure we can use to set the *Visible* property to False for all the Label controls on a form?

6. There is an application that has to check if only one of two light bulbs is "on." Which logical operator can accomplish this task?

7. A person at the cash counter of a gift shop has run out of coins for giving change. He decides to give the customers the next highest dollar bill as change. Which math function can he apply to do this computation?

8. Which string functions will you use to perform these operations?
   a. Find out if the string "line" appears in the word "headlines."
   b. Remove the spaces from the string " Padded String."

9. What are the two types of arrays provided by Visual Basic? What is the difference between them?

10. What is the function of *SelectIndexChanged* event of the ListBox control?

11. When are multidimensional arrays useful? Give an example.

12. How do you resize an array at run-time?

13. What are the different kinds of errors in a program? Which of these are easier to detect and handle?

14. What is a run-time exception? What is the most common bug while dealing with arrays that leads to run-time exceptions?

15. What are the different tools provided by Visual Basic for debugging running programs?

11.14.2 Hands-On Exercises

1. Create a greetings application that takes in the user name through an InputBox prompt "Enter your name" and displays a message "Hello <user name>! Welcome to my application."

2. Design an application that helps the user count her change. Use separate InputBox prompts to input the number of quarters, dimes, nickels and pennies the user has. Store these values as integers, and then compute the dollar value using the following formula:

   Dollars = (0.25*quarters) + (0.10*dimes) + (0.05*nickels) + (0.01*pennies)

   Store the dollar value as a double, and display it to the user in a MessageBox.

3. Bryce has decided to keep track of his monthly expenses. He has classified his expenses into the following categories: rent, food, gas, clothing, entertainment, and other. Create a form that has labels denoting each expense category and corresponding text boxes for his inputs. Add a command button "Total Expenses" to the form. When Bryce clicks this button, the click event should evaluate the sum and average of all the expense categories and display it in a Message-Box. The average is calculated as a floating point number (double data type).

4. **CheckMultiple:** Write an application to check if a given number is a multiple of 3. Create a form and add a command button "Find If Multiple." On the click of this button, the user should be prompted to provide an input number. The code should then check if the input is a multiple of 3. If yes, display a message, "The given number is a multiple of 3"; otherwise, display, "The given number is not a multiple of 3. (Hint: Use the "Mod" operator.)

5. Identify and correct the errors in each of the following codes:
   a. We want to calculate the total sales of a retail shop for the year 2002. The SalesArr maintains the information about the monthly sales.

```
Dim totalSales as Integer = 0
Dim ind as Integer = 0
Dim SalesArr(11) as Integer
While ind < 12
  totalSales += SalesArr[ind]
End While
```

b. The following code calculates the average monthly sales (AvgSales) for the year 2002, given the monthly sales (SalesArr).

```
Dim totalSales as Integer = 0
Dim AvgSales as Integer = 0
Dim ind as Integer
Dim SalesArr(11) as Integer
For ind 1 To 12
  totalSales += SalesArr[ind]
End For
AvgSales = totalSales/12
```

c. The following code prints the monthly sales in a MessageBox.

```
Dim ind As Integer = 1
Dim SalesArr(11) as Integer
Do While ind < 12
  MessageBox.Show(SalesArr[ind])
End While
```

d. The following code prints the monthly sales in a MessageBox.

```
Dim ind As Integer = 0
Dim SalesArr(11) as Integer
   Do Until ind > 1
MessageBox.Show(SalesArr[ind])
ind += 1
   Loop
```

6. Create a billing-related application that totals the price of articles bought at a store. Provide Input-Box prompts for the billing clerk to enter the price of each article. Keep adding the price values in a Do-Loop-While till the clerk enters a value of zero for price. At that point, exit from the loop and display the total value of articles purchased in a MessageBox.

7. Hours of Operation: Create an application that will display the hours of operation of a museum based on the day of the week. Create a form and add RadioButton controls for the days of the week (Mon., Tue., Wed., Thu., Fri., Sat., Sun.) and a "Get hours" command button. When the user selects a radio button and clicks on "Get hours," the application should display the hours based on the following timetable:

a. Mon., Tue., Wed.: 9 a.m.–5 p.m.

b. Thu., Fri.: 9 a.m.–6 p.m.

c. Sat.: 11 a.m.–5 p.m.

d. Sun.: 11.30 a.m.–2.30 p.m.

Use a Select-Case structure to get the appropriate time, and display it using a MessageBox.

8. Timezones: Create an application that takes the current GMT time value in hours and minutes as an input and display the user's current time in her time zone. Create a form and add TextBox controls for GMT time value inputs and a Check-Box control to indicate whether it is AM or PM time. Add RadioButton controls for the following zones: Eastern, Central, Mountain and Pacific. Finally, add a Button control "Display My Time." The output time based on the user's time zone is calculated as follows:

a. Eastern: GMT – 5 hours

b. Mountain: GMT – 6 hours

c. Central: GMT – 7 hours

d. Pacific: GMT – 8 hours

For instance, if the user inputs 2 hours 30 minutes PM, and selects an Eastern zone, the application should display time 9 hours and 30 minutes AM. Use either the Select-Case or If-Then-Else control structure. Use MessageBox for output display.

9. GenerateMultiples: Create an application that will generate the multiples of a given number between 10 and 20. The maximum multiplier value required is 100. Create a form and add a TextBox control and a Button control "Generate Multiples." Get the user input for the number *n*, whose multiples have to be generated, using a TextBox control. When the user clicks "Generate Multiples," we calculate multipliers of *n* less than 100 (for instance, for n = 11, there are 100/11 = 9 multiples, 11, 22, 33,..., 99). Create an array to hold the multipliers. Use a Do-Loop-While structure to generate the multipliers and add them to the array. In the end, display all the multipliers stored in the array in a MessageBox. Repeat the exercise using Do-While-Loop, Do-Until-Loop, Do-Loop-Until, and For-Next loop structures.

10. A university professor uses the following algorithm to decide on the final letter grade for each student in her class. During the semester, she gave five homework questions, four quizzes, two midterm exams, and a final exam. All the assignments are graded on a scale from 1 to 100. The five homework assignments count for 20% (4% each) of the final grade; the quizzes count for 20% (5% each) of the final grade; each midterm counts for 20% of the final grade; and the final exam counts for 20% of the final grade. The following letter grades are assigned based on the final grade value:

■ Grade > 90% : A

- Grade between 80% and 90% : B+
- Grade between 70% and 80% : B
- Grade between 60% and 70%: C+
- Grade between 50% and 60%: C
- Grade < 50%: F

Create a form with the following controls:

- TextBox controls to take the professor's input for the following fields: Student Name, grade values for each homework, quiz, midterm, and final exam.
- Command button "Calculate Final Grade."

On click of the command button, display the final letter grade for the student.

11. **Interest Calculation:** Use TextBox controls to take user input for principal amount, interest rate, and duration (number of years). Let the user choose between Simple and Compound interest options using RadioButton controls. Given principal p, rate r and duration n, calculate the interest as follows:

   a. Simple interest = $p \times n \times r$

   b. Compound interest = $p (1 + r)^n$

   Display the interest to the user in a Label control on the form.

12. Design an application to compute the volume of various geometric shapes, such as cube, sphere, cylinder and cone. Let the user select the desired shape using a RadioButton control. Get the appropriate input dimensions from the user and use a Select-Case statement to compute the volume of various shapes:

   a. Cube: a^3, where "a" is the side of the cube

   b. Sphere: $(4/3) \times Pi \times r^3$, where "$r$" is the radius of the sphere

   c. Cylinder: $Pi \times r^2 \times h$, where "r" is the radius of the circular base and "h" is the height of the cylinder

   d. Cone: $(1/3) \times Pi \times r^2 \times h$, where "$r$" is the radius of the circular base and "h" is the height of the cylinder

13. A year is a leap year if it is divisible by 4 but not by 100. However, years divisible by 400 are leap years. Create an application that displays all leap years within a user-defined year's range. Use a Do-Loop to iterate over every year in the given range. Test the leap year condition and add the leap years to a ListBox control for display.

14. Create an application that will manage the records of monthly sales for a retail store. Create a form and add two Button controls "Enter Monthly Sales Data" and "Report Annual Sales." Also add a ListBox control. When the user clicks on "Enter Monthly Sales Data" button, the code should obtain user input for the year and monthly sales amount for each month using InputBox. Use an array to store the monthly sales amounts. Once the amounts for all the months have been entered, display it to the user using the ListBox control. When the user clicks on the "Report Annual Sales" button, the code should report the following through a MessageBox:

   - The total sales for the given year
   - The average sales for the given year

15. Martino is a professional runner who is getting ready to run the Disney marathon, which takes place in the first week of January. Create an application that will track Martino's weekly training routine. He runs a certain number of miles every day. Create a form with command buttons "Start Week" and "End Week." Add TextBox controls for taking the number of miles run and time it took for every day of the week as the user inputs. Add appropriate Label controls to indicate the values to be entered. When the user clicks on "Start Week," he should be prompted to enter Martino's weight at the start of the week. All the text boxes should also be cleared. After the inputs for all the days of the week have been provided, the user clicks on the "End Week" button. The user should then be prompted to enter Martino's weight at the end of the week. Also, the associated code should report the total number of miles run during the week, the average speed, and the percentage increase or decrease in Martino's weight. Use a multidimensional array to store the number of miles and time for each run. Use a For-Next loop to compute the total number of miles and average speed (Average Speed = Total Number of miles/Total time).

16. In mathematics, a perfect number is defined as an integer that is the sum of its proper positive divisors, that is, the sum of the positive divisors not including the number. An example of a perfect number is 6, because 1, 2 and 3 are its proper positive divisors and $1 + 2 + 3 = 6$. Write a program to generate all the perfect numbers less than a given user input number. Use a Do-While

or For-Next loop. (Search online for an algorithm to determine a perfect number.)

17. The following is a classical problem in probability: Compare the probability of getting a total of 9 with the probability getting a total of 10 when three fair dice are tossed once.

The probability of getting a total of 9 is $25/6^3 = 0.1157$. Where 6^3 is the total number of outcomes from this experiment, and 25 is the number of outcomes that give the sum of 9 [e.g., (1, 2, 6) or (1, 3, 5), etc]. The probability of getting a total of 10 is $27/6^3 = 0.125$.

We want to simulate the experiment of rolling three dice using Visual Basic in order to prove that the probability of getting a total of 9 is 0.1157 and the probability of getting a total of 10 is 0.125.

Write a Visual Basic code that does the following (use methods in the System.Random class for random number generation.):

Step 1: Set *Count* = 0, *CountFor9* = 0, *CountFor10* = 0, *Sum* = 0

Step 2: Generate three random numbers (integers) from 1 to 6. Say Rnd1, Rnd2 and Rnd3.

Step 3:
- Set *Sum* = *Rnd1* + *Rnd2* + *Rnd3*
- *Count++*
- If *Sum* = 9 Then *CountFor9* ++
- If *Sum* = 10 Them *CountFor10++*
- If *Count* < 1000 Then GoTo **Step2**

Step 4: Report:
- Probability of a total of 9 is = CountFor9/1000
- Probability of a total of 10 is = CountFor10/1000

18. Create an application that finds repeating alphabets in a string. Let the user input the string. Create an integer array of size 26 and initialize each element to zero. Use a For-Next loop to iterate over each letter in the input string and increment the count of the corresponding array element. Finally, make a pass over the entire array, and output the alphabets that have a count greater than one. (*Hint:* Use ASC function.)

19. In this application, let us create multiplication tables for numbers up to 10. Create a multidimensional array and store the product of the (i, j) element at position (i, j). Provide two TextBox controls for the user to input two numbers between 0 and 10. Retrieve the corresponding product from the array, and display it to the user.

20. For a chemistry project, create an application that will take in the names of chemicals and display them in a ListBox control. Store the names using a dynamic array initialized to the user-specified number of chemicals. Display the specified number of input boxes to take in user input. Finally, display all the names in a ListBox control.

21. Create an application to display "State" information to the user. First, get the number of States, State names, and a State short description. Store this information in two dynamic arrays. Display the State names in a ListBox control. Whenever a user clicks on a State name, display the description of the selected State in a Label control.

22. Java Hot is a coffee shop located on a university campus. The shop sells coffee as well as light snacks (bagels, cookies, and chips). At the end of the month, the manager calculates the shop's total expenses as well as the revenues. Other than the purchasing cost of the products sold, monthly expenses of the shop are rent and the salary for two employees. The following is the pseudo-code that the manager uses to calculate the monthly profits:
- Enter the quantity purchased and cost and selling price per coffee.
- Enter the quantity purchased and unit cost and selling price of each type of snack.
- Enter the amount of money paid on rent and wages.
- Calculate the total profits as the difference between the total amount of money received from sales and the amount of money spent.

Write the Visual Basic code that calculates the monthly profits.

CHAPTER

twelve Objects and Procedures

chapter OVERVIEW

12.1   *Introduction*

We defined a Visual Basic statement as a complete instruction written in the Visual Basic programming language. We also defined Visual Basic program as a set of Visual Basic statements. Most of the programs that solve real-world problems are compilation of hundreds and thousands of Visual Basic statements. Experience has shown that the best way to develop and maintain large programs is to construct them from small and manageable blocks of statements. Visual Basic language features the *procedure* construct to facilitate design, development, and maintenance of large programs. *Procedures* allow us to group a block of statements that perform a specific small task; and a typical program contains multiple procedures to solve a fairly complex problem.

Software reusability and avoiding duplicate development efforts are essential to effective and efficient implementation of large programs. In this paradigm, a program is developed as a collection of reusable pieces referred to as modules. VB .NET standard *modules* typically contain one or more procedures and perform a specific task. VB .NET also features *class modules* to help develop reusable modules. A VB .NET class module can be thought of as a blueprint for a task, and VB .NET *objects* can be thought of as actual instances of a class. We design program modules around classes and objects. This programming methodology is known as *object-oriented programming*. VB .NET is a complete object-oriented programming language and supports many features to exercise principles of object-oriented programming. The detailed discussion of these principles is however beyond the scope of this book.

12.1.1   Topics

This chapter discusses the following topics:

- Procedures and their types (Subroutine, Function, Event, Property procedures).
- How to pass parameters to procedures: Pass-by-Value and Pass-By-Reference.
- How to declare and use Modules in VB .NET.
- VB .NET Classes.
- How to navigate through Windows forms.
- How to handle run-time exceptions using Try-Catch-Finally structure.

12.2   *Procedures*

A *procedure* is a block of *Visual Basic statements* that accomplishes a specific task. Figure 12.1 shows two sample procedures.

```
17  Private Sub cmdDataTypeConvert_Click(ByVal sender As System.Object, _
18  ByVal e As System.EventArgs) Handles cmdDataTypeConvert.Click
19      'Variable declarations
20      Dim PI As Double = Math.PI
21      Dim r As Double
22
23      'Take the radius from the user
24      r = InputBox("Enter the radius", "Input Radius")
25      'Area with and without data type conversion & Output
26      MessageBox.Show("Area =  " & (PI * r * r), _
27                      "Area without conversion")
28      MessageBox.Show("Area =  " & (CInt(PI) * CInt(r) * CInt(r)), _
29                      "Area with conversion")
30  End Sub
```

```
32   Private Sub cmdDataTypeChk_Click(ByVal sender As System.Object, _
33   ByVal e As System.EventArgs) Handles cmdDataTypeChk.Click
34       'Illustrating data type checking
35       MessageBox.Show("Was Input a Number? :" & IsNumeric(InputBox( _
36                   "Enter the Number", "Type Check")), "Test Result")
37   End Sub
```

Figure 12.1 Examples of procedures.

These examples are from the previous chapter. Lines 17–30 show the *cmdConvert_Click* procedure, which converts a temperature in Fahrenheit to a temperature in Celsius, whereas lines 32–37 show the *cmdDataTypeChk_Click* procedure, which checks the user input for numeric data-type.

It is a common engineering practice to break up a complex task into multiple, simpler subtasks. We solve each of these sub-tasks and put the solutions together to solve the bigger task. This methodology is popularly known as the *Divide and Conquer* principle. Procedures are based on this principle. We divide a large and complex programming task into smaller sub-tasks by writing multiple procedures, each designed to perform a specific task. These procedures together help us to achieve the bigger goal. This concept is termed as *modular programming*.

There are two important things we should be able to do with procedures: (1) declare procedures, and (2) call or invoke procedures. We declare procedures by grouping related Visual Basic statements and enclosing the group between a procedure declaration statement and an end statement (see lines 17, 30, 32, and 37 in Figure 12.1). The main purposes of declaring a procedure is to mark its starting and ending statements and to name the procedure. We call/invoke a procedure by its name. Calling a procedure executes the statements enclosed by the procedure. Consider the following example of a *Multiply* procedure and a procedure call.

Example:

```
Sub Multiply (a As Integer, b As Integer)
     MessageBox.Show (a*b)
End Sub
```

Procedure Call:

```
Multiply (10, 20)
```

A procedure call can be placed anywhere in the code, even within another procedure. For example, a *Factorial* procedure (one that computes the factorial of a number) would call the *Multiply* procedure several times in order to compute the factorial value.

Often, procedures take one or more parameters as inputs. The statements inside a procedure operate on values of these *input parameters*. For example, the *Multiply* procedure takes two input parameters of type *Integer*, *a* and *b*. In the procedure body, it multiplies these values before showing the result to the user. We pass input parameter values to the procedure in a procedure call. In the above example, 10 and 20 are the input parameters that are multiplied in the *Multiply* procedure.

12.2.1   Why Use Procedures?

- *Ease of programming*: Modular programming makes it easier to accomplish large and complex tasks.
- *Division of labor*: Breaking up a huge task into smaller sub-tasks facilitates the division of labor in a team development environment.

■ *Code reusability*: We can reuse the procedures developed for one task while writing a code for another task. For example, the *Multiply* procedure can be called by the *Factorial* procedure as well as by the *Square* procedure.

12.2.2 Types of Procedures

There are four types of procedures in Visual Basic:

- **Subroutine procedure** is a procedure that executes the statements specified in the body of the procedure. However, the procedure does not return any value to the caller.
- **Event procedure** is the *special subroutine procedure* that automatically gets invoked in response to a specific event triggered by the user's actions.
- **Function procedure** is the procedure that executes the statements specified in the procedure body and returns a value to the caller.
- **Property procedure** is the procedure that contains two sub-procedures in it, a *Get* function procedure and a *Set* subroutine procedure.

We will discuss subroutine procedures and function procedures in depth in the following sections. We cover property procedures in the later section of this chapter. Event procedures are explained in depth in Chapter 13.

12.3 *Subroutine Procedures*

A subroutine procedure is a block of Visual Basic statements enclosed by the `Sub` and `End Sub` statements. The syntax for a subroutine procedure is given below.

Subroutine Procedure Declaration Syntax:

```
Sub <Subroutine Name> (Comma separated input parameter list)
      Body of the subroutine
End Sub
```

Figure 12.2 shows an example of a subroutine procedure that computes the factorial of a number that is passed as an input parameter to it.

```
3    Sub Fact(Num As Integer)
4        Dim Result As Double, i As Integer
5
6        Result = 1
7        For i = 1 To Num
8            Result = Result * i
9        Next
10       MessageBox.Show("Result = " & Result, _
11       "Factorial of given number")
12
13    End Sub
```

Figure 12.2 An example of a subroutine procedure.

In this example, we declare the *Fact* subroutine procedure in line 3 with an integer input parameter *Num*. The factorial is computed by code in lines 6–9, and the end of the subroutine procedure is marked in line 13. Note that the *Fact* subroutine procedure does not return any value. (As discussed later, we use the Return statement to return a value from a function procedure.)

12.3.1 Hands-On Tutorial: Working with Subroutine Procedures

In this hands-on tutorial, we will create an application that displays a Fibonacci series of n terms, where n is the user-specified non-zero integer value. The first few terms of the Fibonacci series are as follows:

0, 1, 1, 2, 3, 5, 8, 13, 21 . . .

The first two terms in the Fibonacci series are 0 and 1. All the subsequent terms of the series are derived by adding two previous terms. More formally, if we denote the ith term of the series by T_i, then we have the following:

$$T_0 = 0, \quad T_1 = 1, \quad T_i = T_{i-1} + T_{i-2} \text{ for all } i > 1$$

This hands-on tutorial covers the following How-to topic:

- How-to: write a subroutine procedure.
  1. Create a new Windows application named "ProceduresObjects."
  2. Design the default form, *Form1*, as shown in Figure 12.3. Add a TextBox control named "txtNoElements." Users will enter the desired number of terms in the Fibonacci series (n) using this TextBox control. This value will serve as an input parameter for the subroutine procedure that will generate the series.
  3. Add a Button control named "cmdTestSub" and a ListBox control named "lstFibSeries."
  4. Create a subroutine procedure, *FibSeriesSub*, which generates the Fibonacci series of n terms, where n is the user-defined input parameter (see Figure 12.4 (a)).
  5. Call the *FibSeriesSub* subroutine procedure from the code for the *Click* event of the *cmdTestSub* command button (see Figure 12.4 (b)).

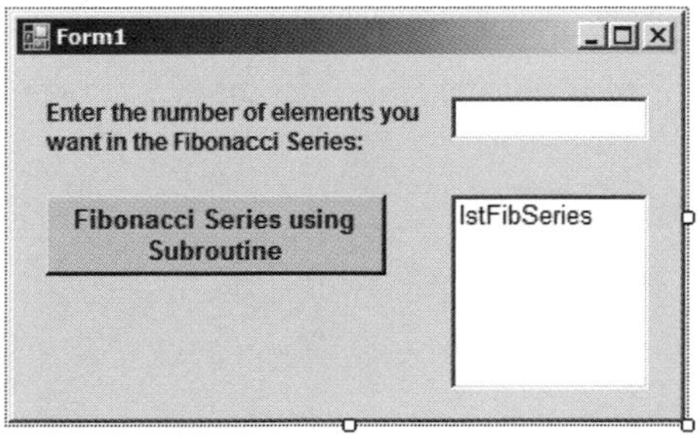

Figure 12.3 Subroutine procedure for Fibonacci series: Design Window.

```
20   Public Sub FibSeriesSub(ByVal n As Integer)
21       Dim a, b, c, i As Integer
22
23       'Initialize First two elements in the series
24       a = 0
25       b = 1
26       'Add first two elements
27       lstFibSeries.Items.Add(a)
28       lstFibSeries.Items.Add(b)
29       For i = 2 To n - 1
30           'Next Fibonacci Num
31           c = a + b
32           'Add element
33           lstFibSeries.Items.Add(c)
34           'Reassignment
35           a = b
36           b = c
37
38       Next
39   End Sub
```
(a)

```
3    Private Sub cmdTestSub_Click(ByVal sender As System.Object, _
4    ByVal e As System.EventArgs) Handles cmdTestSub.Click
5
6        Dim num As Integer
7        'Number of Fibonacci numbers to be generated
8        num = CInt(txtNoElements.Text)
9        If num < 2 Then
10           MessageBox.Show("Enter number greater than 2")
11           Exit Sub
12       End If
13       'clear the items in the list box
14       lstFibSeries.Items.Clear()
15       'Subroutine Call
16       FibSeriesSub(num)
17
18   End Sub
```
(b)

Figure 12.4 Subroutine procedure for Fibonacci series: Code Window.

Figure 12.4 Explained:

Figure 12.4 (b): The procedure *cmdTestSub_Click* accepts user input for the desired number of terms in the Fibonacci series. If the input number (*num*) is not less than two, we call the *FibSeriesSub* subroutine procedure in line 16 and pass *num* as its input parameter.

Figure 12.4 (a): The *FibSeriesSub* subroutine procedure takes a number n as an input parameter (line 20). We initialize the first two numbers in the series (lines 24–25). In lines 27–28, we add the first two Fibonacci numbers to the display list (*lstFibSeries*). We generate the remaining numbers in the series iteratively in lines 29–38.

The application output with first six terms of the Fibonacci series is shown in Figure 12.5.

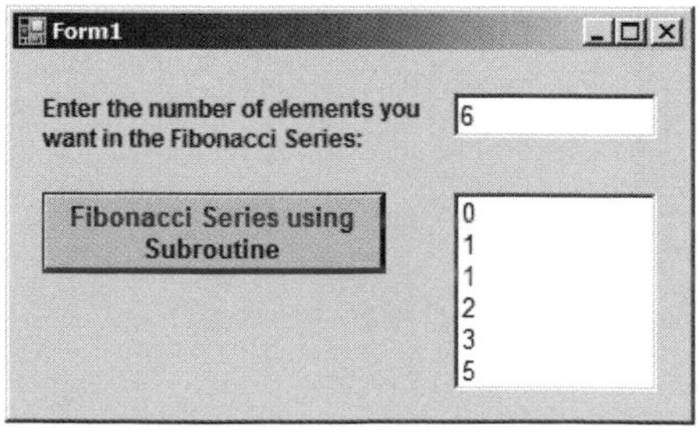

Figure 12.5 Subroutine procedure for Fibonacci series: Application Window.

12.4 *Function Procedures*

Function procedures are like subroutine procedures except that a function procedure must return a value to the caller.

Function Procedure Declaration Syntax:

```
Function <Name> (Comma separated argument list) As <ReturnDataType>
    Body of the Function
    Return <Value>
End Function
```

Figure 12.6 illustrates the usage of a function procedure to reverse the digits of a positive integer. For example, the application given an input integer like "12345" outputs the integer "54321." The function procedure *ReverseDigits* takes an integer number to reverse as an input parameter in line 3 and returns the reversed number in line 13. The code lines 9–12 compute the reversed number.

```
3   Public Function ReverseDigits(ByVal n As Integer) As Integer
4       Dim RevNum As Integer
5
6       'Initialize reverse num
7       RevNum = 0
8
9       Do While (n > 0)
10          RevNum = RevNum * 10 + n Mod 10
11          n = n / 10
12      Loop
13      Return RevNum
14  End Function
```

Figure 12.6 A function procedure example: reverse digits.

The two main differences between a subroutine procedure and a function procedure are: (i) in the procedure declaration where we specify the data type of the return value (see line 3); and (ii) that the Return statement in the body of the function procedure returns a value (see line 13). Return statement is the last statement "executed" in the function procedure. When Return is encountered, the program control along with the return value is automatically transferred to the caller.

Similar to a subroutine procedure, we call/invoke a function procedure by referring to it by its name and pass any input parameters that the function procedure may take. Figure 12.7 illustrates a call to the ReverseDigits function procedure (line 29). The input parameter for a function procedure is taken from a user via an InputBox. If the input number is a positive number, we call the *ReverseDigits* function procedure in line 29. The returned value from a function procedure is assigned to the variable *Num*, which is displayed using a MessageBox in line 31.

```
17    Private Sub cmdRevDigit_Click(ByVal sender As System.Object, _
18    ByVal e As System.EventArgs) Handles cmdRevDigit.Click
19        Dim Num As Integer
20
21        'User Input
22        Num = CInt(InputBox("Enter a Positive Integer"))
23        If Num < 0 Then
24            MessageBox.Show("Invalid Input Number")
25            Exit Sub
26        End If
27
28        'Function Call
29        Num = ReverseDigits(Num)
30
31        MessageBox.Show("Reversed digits = " & Num, _
32        "Digits Reversed")
33    End Sub
```

Figure 12.7 Reverse digits subroutine procedure call.

12.4.1 Hands-On Tutorial: Working with Function Procedures

In this hands-on tutorial, we consider the example of generating the Fibonacci series described in Section 12.3.1. However, we use function procedures rather than subroutine procedures to perform the task. This hands-on tutorial covers the following How-to topic:

■ How-to: write a function procedure.
  1. Add a command button, *cmdTestFunction*, to *Form1* of the *ProceduresObjects* application (see Figure 12.8).
  2. Associate the code shown in Figure 12.9(b) with the Click event of the *cmdTestFunction* button.
  3. Write a function procedure called *Fibseries* as shown in Figure 12.9(a).

When the user clicks on the *cmdTestFunction* button, we generate the Fibonacci series with the number of terms specified in the TextBox control and display it to the user in the ListBox control.

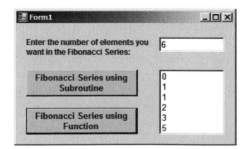

Figure 12.8 Function procedure example for Fibonacci series.

```
74  Public Function FibSeries(ByVal x As Integer, _
75  ByVal y As Integer) As Integer
76
77      Dim res As Integer
78      'Next Fib Number
79      res = x + y
80      Return res
81
82  End Function
```

(a)

```
41  Private Sub cmdTestFunction_Click(ByVal sender As System.Object, _
42  ByVal e As System.EventArgs) Handles cmdTestFunction.Click
43
44      Dim a, b, c, i, num As Integer
45
46      'Number of Fibonacci numbers to be generated
47      num = CInt(txtNoElements.Text)
48      If num < 2 Then
49          MessageBox.Show("Enter number greater than 2")
50          Exit Sub
51      End If
52
53      'clear the items in the list box
54      lstFibSeries.Items.Clear()
55      'Initialize First two elements in the series
56      a = 0
57      b = 1
58      'Add First two elements
59      lstFibSeries.Items.Add(a)
60      lstFibSeries.Items.Add(b)
61
62      For i = 2 To num - 1
63          'Function call
64          c = FibSeries(a, b)
65          'Add element
66          lstFibSeries.Items.Add(c)
67          'Reassignment
68          a = b
69          b = c
70      Next
71  End Sub
```

(b)

Figure 12.9 Function procedure example for Fibonacci series: Code Window.

Figure 12.9 Explained:

As in Figure 12.4, we initialize the first two terms of the series and add them to the ListBox control (lines 56–60). The For-Next loop (62–70) iteratively calls the *FibSeries* function procedure in line 64. The return value of the function procedure is then added to the ListBox control for the user display (line 66). The function procedure takes two terms of the Fibonacci series and returns the next number of the series by adding its two input parameters (line 79).

The main differences between this function procedure example and the example in Figure 12.4 with the subroutine procedure are as follows. The initialization of the first two terms and their addition to the ListBox was handled by a subroutine procedure in the previous hands-on tutorial. In the function procedure hands-on tutorial, the *FibSeries* function procedure is a light-weight function procedure in the sense it only implements the logic of computing the next term of the Fibonacci series. All other application logic is outside the function procedure. This is possible because a function procedure can return a value to the caller, unlike subroutine procedures. The output window is identical to Figure 12.8.

12.4.2   Pass-By-Value and Pass-By-Reference

We call the subroutine procedures and function procedures by passing input parameters. This can be accomplished in two different ways:

- Pass–By–Value   (or Call by Value)
- Pass–By–Reference   (or Call by Reference)

Pass-By-Value

We can pass input parameters *by value* using the `ByVal` keyword (default option). In the Pass-By-Value option, the caller procedure (one with the procedure call) makes a copy of input parameters before passing them to the callee procedure (one with the procedure declaration). Thus, the callee procedure cannot modify the contents of the parameters as viewed by the caller procedure. Even if the callee procedure operates on arguments and modifies them, the parameter variables in the caller procedure remain unchanged when the control returns to the caller.

Pass-By-Reference

We can pass input parameters *by reference* using the `ByRef` keyword. In the Pass-By-Reference option, the callee procedure can modify the input parameters as viewed by the caller procedure. The caller passes the pointer or memory location of the input parameter to the callee. So, if the callee operates on input parameters, the memory value of the passed variable gets overwritten; therefore, when the control returns to the caller procedure, the argument variable has its new value.

We implemented the Fibonacci series example using the Pass-By-Value option in both the subroutine procedure hands-on tutorial (see Figure 12.4(a), line 20) and in the function procedure hands-on tutorial (see Figure 12.9(a), line 74). We now illustrate the function procedure in Figure 12.9(a) with the Pass-By-Reference option in Figure 12.10(a).

The function procedure *FibSeries* takes its input parameters *by reference* (line 116). We not only calculate the next term of the series by adding two input parameters (line 121), but also update the variables that store values for the last two terms of the series. In lines 123 and 124, we update the input parameters, *x* and *y*, with the last two terms of the series. Since these parameters are passed by *reference*, the variables *a* and *b* in line 109 reflects the change. The next call to the function procedure uses these updated values. As a result, we are not required to explicitly update these variables in the *Click* event code as in Figure 12.9, lines 68–69.

```
116    Public Function FibSeries(ByRef x As Integer, _
117    ByRef y As Integer) As Integer
118
119        Dim res As Integer
120        'Next Fib Number
121        res = x + y
122        'Reassignment
123        x = y
124        y = res
125        Return res
126
(a) 127    End Function
```

(continues)

Figure 12.10 An example of Pass-By-Reference: Code Window.

```
86    Private Sub cmdTestFunction_Click(ByVal sender As _
87    System.Object, ByVal e As System.EventArgs) _
88    Handles cmdTestFunction.Click
89        Dim a, b, c, i, no As Integer
90
91        'Number of Fibonacci numbers to be generated
92        no = CInt(txtNoElements.Text)
93        If no < 2 Then
94            MessageBox.Show("Enter number greater than 2")
95            Exit Sub
96        End If
97
98        'clear the items in the list box
99        lstFibSeries.Items.Clear()
100       'Initialize First two elements in the series
101       a = 0
102       b = 1
103       'Add First two elements
104       lstFibSeries.Items.Add(a)
105       lstFibSeries.Items.Add(b)
106
107       For i = 2 To no - 1
108           'Function call
109           c = FibSeries(a, b)
110           'Add element
111           lstFibSeries.Items.Add(c)
112       Next
113   End Sub
```

(b)

Figure 12.10 (*continued*)

12.5   *Visual Basic Modules*

Visual Basic code is stored in a module: a standard module or a class module. An application by default consists of a single *form class* module. For all the forms we have created so far, we have written our code inside a form class module. As our applications grow bigger and more sophisticated, we add more form class modules. Eventually, the program might consist of a common code that we execute several times. Instead of duplicating this common code in every form class module, we can create a separate standard module that contains procedures with common code. Over time, we can build up a library of modules containing shared procedures.

A standard module (or simply, *module*) can contain any number of declaration statements and procedures. Modules are containers for procedures and declarations commonly accessed by other modules within the application.

The syntax for the standard module is as follows:

```
Module <Module Name>
     Body of the module
End Module
```

Class modules form the foundation of object-oriented programming in Visual Basic. We can write code, which can include its own customized properties and methods, in class modules to create new objects. We will discuss class modules in the following section.

12.5.1 Hands-On Tutorial: Working with Visual Basic Modules

We continue with our Fibonacci series example in this hands-on tutorial as well. We will create a Fibonacci module that will create the Fibonacci series of a desired number of terms and will display it to the user in the specified ListBox control. This hands-on tutorial covers the following How-to topic:

- How-to: write a re-usable standard Visual Basic module.
  1. Add another form (*Form2*) to the *ProceduresObjects* application and establish it as the start-up form.
  2. Design the form as shown in Figure 12.11. This form is similar to the one used in the previous hands-on tutorial.
  3. Associate the code of Figure 12.13 with the *Click* event of the command button.
  4. Add a new module to the project, by choosing Project | Add Module from the main menu (See Figure 12.12). An *Add New Item* dialog box should appear. Name the module "FibonacciModule," and click *Open* button to add the module. The new module appears as a separate tab in the Design Window.
  5. Use the code in Figure 12.14 for the module code. Save and run the application.

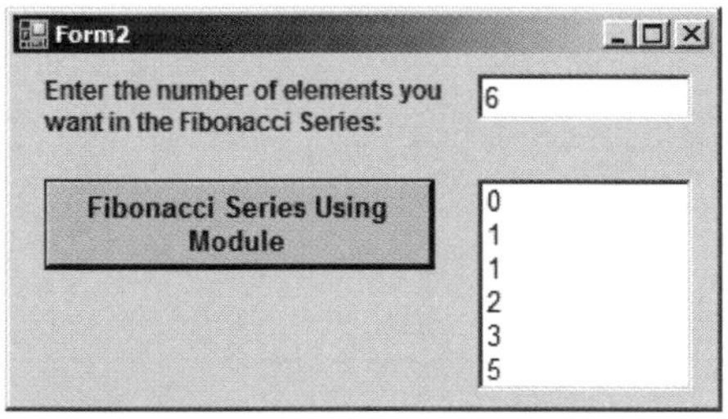

Figure 12.11 Fibonacci series module example: Design Window.

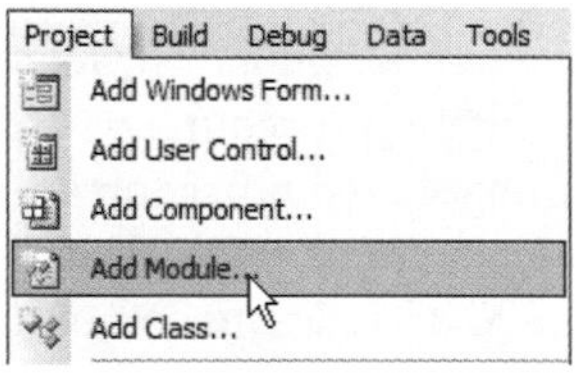

Figure 12.12 Adding a new standard module.

Figure 12.13 Explained:

The main difference between this code and the subroutine procedure hands-on tutorial code is line 16. Instead of calling a subroutine procedure or a function procedure that is part of the same form, we now call a subroutine procedure that is defined in the *FibonacciModule* module (Figure 12.14). The module initializes the initial terms of the series, generates all next terms, and puts them in the ListBox control that is passed to it (by reference) as an input parameter (line 5, Figure 12.14).

```
3      Private Sub cmdTestModule_Click(ByVal sender As _
4      System.Object, ByVal e As System.EventArgs) _
5      Handles cmdTestModule.Click
6          Dim no As Integer
7
8          'Number of Fibonacci numbers to be generated
9          no = CInt(txtNoElements.Text)
10         If no < 2 Then
11             MessageBox.Show("Enter number greater than 2")
12             Exit Sub
13         End If
14
15         'Subroutine Call from Module- FibonacciModule
16         FibonacciModule.FibSeriesSub(no, lstFibSeries)
17
18     End Sub
```

Figure 12.13 Fibonacci series module example: Code Window for subroutine procedure.

```
1  Module FibonacciModule
2      Public a As Integer
3      Public b As Integer
4
5      Public Sub FibSeriesSub(ByVal n As Integer, _
6      ByRef lstFibSeriesMod As ListBox)
7          Dim c, i As Integer
8          'Initialize First two elements in the series
9          a = 0
10         b = 1
11
12         'clear the items in the list box
13         lstFibSeriesMod.Items.Clear()
14
15         'Add first two elements
16         lstFibSeriesMod.Items.Add(a)
17         lstFibSeriesMod.Items.Add(b)
18         For i = 2 To n - 1
19             'Next Fibonacci Num
20             c = a + b
21             'Add element
22             lstFibSeriesMod.Items.Add(c)
23             'Reassignment
24             a = b
25             b = c
26         Next
27     End Sub
28  End Module
```

Figure 12.14 Fibonacci series module example: Code Window for module.

Figure 12.14 Explained:

We declare the standard module *FibonacciModule* in line 1. We declare *a* and *b* as module level variables (lines 2–3). These variables are accessible to all the procedures of this module. As before, these variables are used to hold the preceding two terms of the Fibonacci series. We then define a subroutine procedure *FibSeriesSub* (line 5). The subroutine procedure takes two input parameters: the number of desired terms of the series to generate, and a ListBox control to display the series. Note that list box *lstFibSeriesMod* is passed by reference. This is essential, as we would like to add the terms of the series to the same ListBox control that is passed by the caller procedure. In other words, we would like to manipulate the ListBox control that is part of the caller procedure. The subroutine procedure *FibSeriesSub* (lines 5–27) generates the Fibonacci Series as described in section 12.3.1.

12.6   *Visual Basic Classes*

Classes are symbolic representations of objects. They describe the properties, methods, and events that make up objects in the same way that a blueprint describes the components and structure of a building. Like blueprints, classes define the structure of an object. Just as a single blueprint can be used to create multiple buildings, a single class can be used to create as many objects as necessary. A blueprint defines which parts of a building are accessible to people who use the building. Similarly, classes control user access to object items through encapsulation (not discussed in this book). Classes in Visual Basic can be added a class modules; their syntax looks like this:

```
Class <Class Name>
     Body of the Class
End Class
```

Classes can also be viewed as user-defined data types. Like the system data types, *Integer* (holds integer values) and *String* (holds string values), classes can hold specific user data. For example, a *Student* class can hold information about a student. A class typically has one or more *data members* and one or more *methods*. The data members are the variables declared in a class. For example, the *StudentName* as a string and *SSN* as an integer are members of the *Student* class. The procedures of a class are its methods. For example, the function procedure that returns the full name of a student and the function procedure that returns the age of a student are class methods.

We now create the *Student* class in the following subsections. The *Student* class defines the structure that holds data for a university student. It also supports methods for a few common operations on student records.

12.6.1   Adding Class Modules to a Project

1. To add a new class to an existing project, choose Project | Add Class option from the main menu. Alternatively, right-click on the project title in the Solution Explorer, and choose Add | Add Class from the shortcut menu.
2. Either of these options will lead to the *Add New Item* dialog box. Name the new class as "Student," and click *OK* button to add a new class tab in the Design Window.
3. Use the code in Figure 12.15 to add class data members.

```
1  Public Class Student
2      Dim StudentID As Integer
3      Dim FName As String
4      Dim LName As String
5      Dim DOB As Date
6      Dim GPA As Double
7  End Class
```

Figure 12.15 *Student* class data members.

12.6.2   Adding Class Methods

To add methods to a class, we write procedures inside a class declaration. The *Student* class with its methods is shown in Figure 12.16.

```
1   Public Class Student
2       Dim StudentID As Integer
3       Dim FName As String
4       Dim LName As String
5       Dim DOB As Date
6       Dim GPA As Double
7
8       'Function that returns student's name
9       Public Function Name() As String
10          Return FName & " " & LName
11      End Function
12
13      'Function that returns student's age
14      Public Function Age() As Integer
15          Dim currAge As Integer
16          currAge = DateDiff(DateInterval.Year, DOB, Now.Date)
17          Return currAge
18      End Function
19
20      'Subroutine that sets student's GPA
21      Public Sub SetGPA(ByVal grade As Double)
22          GPA = grade
23      End Sub
24
25  End Class
```

Figure 12.16 Student class methods

Figure 12.16 Explained:

Lines 2–6 declare the class data members. When the class is instantiated (i.e., an object of the class is created), each instance (an object) has space allocated for these members. In other words, each class instance is a student object holding the following fields: *StudentID*, *FName*, *LName*, *DOB*, and *GPA*. The data members of the *Student* class are manipulated using its methods. The method *Name* (lines 9–11) is a function procedure that returns the student's full name as the concatenation of the first and last name. Similarly, the function procedure *Age* in lines 14–18 calculates and returns a student's age using *DOB* (date of birth) data member. Note that the class methods can have their own variables. However, these variables are not class data members, but the local variables are created only when we call the methods. The third method (lines 21–23) is a subroutine procedure that receives a GPA score as an input parameter (grade) and assigns it to the GPA data member of the class.

12.6.3   Constructor of a Class

A constructor is a special method of a class that creates a new object of the class (initiates data members) when called. In most cases, the constructor also populates the data members of the object. The syntax for a class constructor is as follows:

```
Public Sub New (Argument list)
    Body — Initialization
End Sub
```

To define a class constructor, we create a subroutine procedure *New*. The arguments of the constructor (if any) can be used to populate the class data members. We can have multiple constructors with different input parameters. For example, one of the constructors of the *Student* class may take all five data members as arguments, while another constructor may take only *Name* and *DOB* as arguments. We can also have an empty constructor that takes no arguments. All constructors share the same name, *New*. The appropriate constructor method is called based on the number and type of arguments that are passed to the constructor call. Refer to Figure 12.17 for the *Student* class with two constructors. The first constructor assigns the input parameter values to the data members, while the second constructor assigns default values for *StudentID*, *DOB* and *GPA*.

```
 8    'Class constructor 1
 9    Public Sub New(ByVal id As Integer, ByVal fn As String, _
10    ByVal ln As String, ByVal bdate As Date, _
11    ByVal grade As Double)
12        StudentID = id
13        FName = fn
14        LName = ln
15        DOB = bdate
16        GPA = grade
17    End Sub
18    'Class constructor 2
19    Public Sub New(ByVal fn As String, ByVal ln As String)
20        StudentID = 100
21        FName = fn
22        LName = ln
23        DOB = System.DateTime.Now
24        GPA = 0
25    End Sub
```

Figure 12.17 The constructors for the *Student* class.

12.6.4   Instance of a Class

Objects are instances of a class. A class object is created by calling its constructor, New. The *Student* class can be instantiated as expressed below.

```
Dim student1 As New Student ("John," "Doe")
Dim student2 As New Student (111, "Chris," "Doe," "1/1/1978," 4.0)
```

The first statement calls a constructor with two string arguments. Hence, constructor 2 (Figure 12.17) is called. The *student1* object has a valid first and last name, and other data members are assigned default values. The *student2* object is created using constructor1, which populates all the data members with valid values. We now use this class and its methods using these objects. Figure 12.18 illustrates the use of the class methods *Name* and *Age* to display the name and age of newly created objects (student1 and student2) of the *Student* class.

The output of the code appears in Figure 12.19. The age is calculated as the number of years between the current date and the date of birth (*DOB*). The first MessageBox prints the age as zero, as the default value of the date of birth for *student1* is set to today. The correct age (suppose the current year is 2006) is displayed for *student2*, as we have populated the *DOB* data member using the constructor.

```
 3    Private Sub cmdClass_Click(ByVal sender As System.Object, _
 4    ByVal e As System.EventArgs) Handles cmdClass.Click
 5        Dim student1 As New Student("John", "Doe")
 6        Dim student2 As New Student(111, "Chris", "Doe", _
 7        "1/1/1978", 4.0)
 8
 9        MessageBox.Show(student1.Name & " is " & _
10        student1.Age & " years old")
11        MessageBox.Show(student2.Name & " is " & _
12        student2.Age & " years old")
13    End Sub
```

Figure 12.18 Instantiating the *Student* class: Code Window.

Figure 12.19 Using methods of the Student class: application output.

12.6.5 Property Procedures

We mentioned that the properties of an object control its appearance and behavior. The object properties are, in fact, special procedures that *set* and *get* data members of a class.

Property procedures are blocks of code declared within property definitions. Visual Basic offers two types of property procedures: *get* (to get the property value) and *set* (to assign a value to the property). Consider an example of the *BirthDate* property for the *Student* class in Figure 12.20.

```
27    'Birthdate property
28    Public Property BirthDate() As Date
29        Get 'Get block
30            Return DOB
31        End Get
32        Set(ByVal input As Date) 'Set block
33            DOB = input
34        End Set
35    End Property
```

Figure 12.20 The *BirthDate* property of the *Student* class.

Figure 12.20 Explained:

The code begins with the declaration of the property in line 28. Lines 29–31 and 32–34 define the *Get* and *Set* procedures, respectively. The *Get* block returns the date value (line 30), while the *Set* block assigns the date input parameter to the *DOB* data member (line 33).

Using Properties

We use a property by its name. When a property name is used with the equal (=) assignment operator, it automatically calls the *Set* block of the property. If we use the property name in an expression, it automatically calls the *Get* block of the property. Consider the following example for the usage of the *BirthDate* property.

```
Dim Student3 As New Student ("John," "Adams")    ' New Object
Student3.BirthDate = "1/1/1978"                  ' Calls the Set Block
MessageBox.Show (Student3.BirthDate)             ' Calls the Get Block
```

12.7 *Navigating Through Application Forms*

Windows forms are special class modules. In this section, we learn how to use these class modules to navigate through a multi-form application by opening a new form and closing the existing form.

To open or close a form:

We first create an instance of a form object using its empty constructor. We then use its *Open* method to open the form or the *Close* method to close it:

```
Dim testForm As New <FormName>
testForm.Open()
testForm.Close()
```

If we are already working inside a form class and want to close the current form, we make a use of self-reference rather than creating a new instance. The keyword Me is used for self-referencing as follows:

```
Me.Close()      'Closes the current form
```

12.8   *Exception Handling*

In Chapter 11, we introduced two types of errors: syntax errors and logical errors. We also introduced various debugging techniques to help eliminate these types of errors. However, errors can also occur at runtime and may stem from user input. These errors cannot be debugged at the design time but can be *anticipated* while writing the code. Runtime errors, also known as *exceptions*, can be dealt with by *exception handling*, the technique of anticipating exceptions and accordingly manipulating the code to provide user-friendly error messages. Consider the following part of a simple code used to divide two numbers entered by the user.

```
 2     Private Sub cmdDivision_Click(ByVal sender _
 3     As System.Object, ByVal e As System.EventArgs) _
 4     Handles cmdDivision.Click
 5         Dim X As Integer
 6         Dim Y As Integer
 7         Dim Result As Integer
 8
 9         X = CInt(InputBox("Enter X Value", "User Input"))
10         Y = CInt(InputBox("Enter Y Value", "User Input"))
11         Result = X / Y
12         MessageBox.Show("Result = " & Result, _
13         "Result of Division")
14
15     End Sub
```

Figure 12.21 Division subroutine procedure without exception handling.

Syntactically, this code is error free. It does not contain any logical errors, either. However, when the program runs, it could be erroneous if the user enters a value *zero* for variable *Y*. Division by zero at line 10 results in a runtime error, and Visual studio provides the following error message (in the debug mode):

Figure 12.22 Division subroutine procedure: runtime error due to an overflow exception.

Visual Basic offers two approaches for exception handling: *unstructured exception handling* and *structured exception handling*. We will focus on the object-oriented structured exception handling approach in this chapter. The unstructured exception handling is almost obsolete from the Visual Basic language.

Structured exception handling is a very common technique that is supported by almost all existing object-oriented programming languages. It employs the `Try-Catch` structure to handle exceptions. The basic idea of this structure is very straightforward. We write our code inside a *Try* block (indicating that we are *trying* to execute this piece of the code). If something goes wrong and there is an exception, the program control automatically goes to the *Catch* block (indicating that we anticipated this exception and were able to *catch* it). If there are no errors, the *Try* block terminates normally, and the program control never enters the *Catch* block.

12.8.1   Using a Try-Catch Block

We use the keywords `Try` and `End Try` to specify the *Try* block. A `Catch` statement must appear inside the *Try* block to catch exceptions that might occur. If the *Try* block throws an exception, the *Catch* block catches the exception. The syntax of the `Catch` statement is as follows:

```
Catch <name> As <Exception Type>
    Body of the Catch Block
```

When an exception is caught, the program control executes the body of the *Catch* block, which typically contains user-friendly error messages. Figure 12.23 depicts the working of a Try-Catch structure.

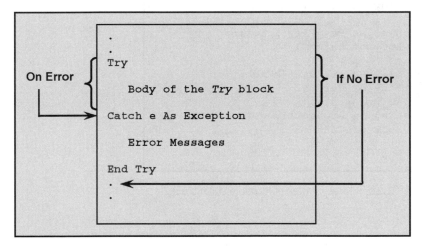

Figure 12.23 The Try-Catch structure.

When an error object *e* is thrown by the *Try* block, the *Catch* block catches it as the type *Exception*. We can further employ exception object *e* to print a user-friendly error message, as illustrated in the example of Figure 12.24. The figure shows a modified division subroutine example with a Try-Catch block to handle the exception caused by the division by zero. Now, if the user enters a zero value for variable *Y* value, then an exception is caught in line 31, and an error message is displayed in line 32. The statements that can cause an exception are included inside the *Try* block (lines 25–29).

```
17   Private Sub cmdWithExcep_Click(ByVal sender _
18      As System.Object, ByVal e As System.EventArgs) _
19      Handles cmdWithExcep.Click
20         Dim X As Integer
21         Dim Y As Integer
22         Dim Result As Integer
23
24         Try
25            X = CInt(InputBox("Enter X Value", "User Input"))
26            Y = CInt(InputBox("Enter Y Value", "User Input"))
27            Result = X / Y
28            MessageBox.Show("Result = " & Result, _
29            "Result of Division")
30
31         Catch ex As Exception
32            MessageBox.Show _
33            ("Division by Zero Exception, re-enter Y value")
34         End Try
35
36   End Sub
```

Figure 12.24 A Try-Catch example for division subroutine procedure: Code Window.

12.8.2 Using Multiple Catch Statements

Every *Try* block requires at least one *Catch* block. However, inside the *Try* block, we can incorporate as many *Catch* blocks for different exceptions as we need. The following is the logical representation of multiple *Catch* blocks.

```
Try
      Body of Try Block

Catch e1 As OverFlowException
    Body of Catch 1

Catch e2 As ArithmeticException
    Body of Catch 2

Catch e3 As ArgumentException
    Body of Catch 3

End Try
```

Figure 12.25 Representation of multiple *Catch* blocks.

12.8.3 Hands-On Tutorial: Using the Try-Catch Block for Exception Handling

Let us consider an example of an array in which we will add elements to a dynamic array and display the array contents to the user in a ListBox control. This hands-on tutorial covers the following How-to topic:

■ How-to: write a Try-Catch block for exception handling.
  1. Add a form (*Form3*) to the *ProceduresObjects* application and design it as shown in Figure 12.26. Add two Button controls: *cmdInitArray* (Initialize Array) and *cmdAddElements* (Add Elements). Add four Label controls (two are not visible in the

figure) to display the capacity and size of the array. Add a ListBox control, *lstArray* to display the array contents.

2. Declare a dynamic array *Arr* and *arrSize* variables outside any procedure so that they can be accessible to the entire form class.

3. Associate the code in Figure 12.27 with the *cmdInitArray* command button.

4. Associate the code in Figure 12.29 with the *cmdAddElements* button. We explain this code in the following subsection.

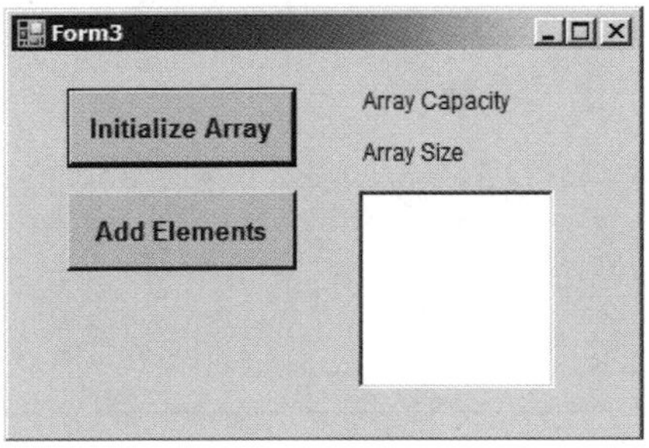

Figure 12.26 A multiple *Catch* blocks example: Design Window.

```
5    Private Sub cmdInitArray_Click(ByVal sender As _
6    System.Object, ByVal e As System.EventArgs) _
7    Handles cmdInitArray.Click
8
9        Dim n As Integer
10
11       'User Input: Number of elements in the array
12       Try
13           n = InputBox("Enter the array capacity")
14           lblArrCap.Text = n
15           ReDim Arr(n - 1)
16           arrSize = 0
17           lstArray.Items.Clear()
18
19       Catch ex1 As InvalidCastException
20           MessageBox.Show("Incorrect Array Capacity", _
21           "Exception Caught")
22       Catch ex2 As Exception
23           MessageBox.Show(ex2.Message, _
24           "Exception Caught")
25       End Try
26
27   End Sub
```

Figure 12.27 A multiple *Catch* blocks example: Code Window.

Figure 12.27 Explained:

A user enters the capacity of the array (the maximum number of elements that an array can hold) in line 13. This input is stored in a variable *n*. We assign the value stored in *n* to one of the Label control (*lblArrCap*) in line 14 for user display. We re-declare the dynamic array with its highest index initialized to (*n–1*) in line 15 (this will create an array with *n* elements, indexed from *0* to *n–1*). We handle the exceptions in lines 19–25. If a user inputs an invalid number such as a string or symbols as an array capacity, InvalidCastException is raised (as the input cannot be *cast* to an integer value). A second *Catch* block is introduced to handle any other general exceptions (*ex2*) in the code.

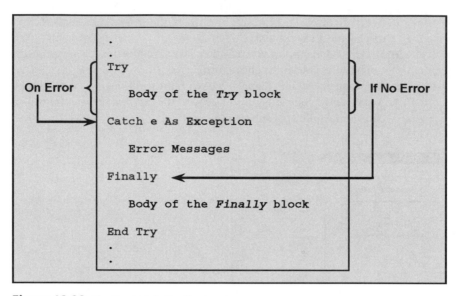

Figure 12.28 The Try-Catch-Finally structure.

12.8.4 Using the Finally Statement

The Finally statement appears after all the *Catch* blocks. If the *Finally* block is present, it is always executed, whether or not the *Try* block throws an error or the control goes inside the *Catch* block(s). The logical diagram of a simple Try-Catch-Finally is shown in Figure 12.28.

We explain the code for the *cmdAddElements* button from the previous hands-on tutorial. The code in Figure 12.29 shows the usage of a Try-Catch-Finally block.

```
29    Private Sub cmdAddElements_Click(ByVal sender As System.Object, _
30    ByVal e As System.EventArgs) Handles cmdAddElements.Click
31        Dim i, n As Integer
32        Try
33            'Array Size
34            n = InputBox("Enter Array Size", "Array Size")
35            lblArrSize.Text = n
36            For i = 0 To n - 1
37                Arr(arrSize + i) = InputBox("Enter No. " & (i + 1))
38                lstArray.Items.Add(Arr(arrSize + i))
39            Next
40            arrSize += n
41            lblArrSize.Text = arrSize
42
43        Catch ex1 As InvalidCastException
44            MessageBox.Show("Incorrect Number", "Exception  Caught")
45        Catch ex2 As IndexOutOfRangeException
46            MessageBox.Show("Array Size must be less than capacity", _
47            "Exception  Caught")
48        Catch ex3 As Exception
49            MessageBox.Show(ex3.Message)
50        Finally
51            MessageBox.Show("Array Size = " & n, "Array Size")
52            Beep()
53        End Try
54    End Sub
```

Figure 12.29 The Try-Catch-Finally example for division subroutine procedure: Code Window.

Figure 12.29 Explained:

The size of the array (line 34) is the number of elements the user wants to add to the array. If a user enters a negative number for the array size or array element, an InvalidCastException is caught in line 43, and an error message is displayed in line 44. Another constraint is that the array size has to be less than or equal to the array capacity, as the array can hold only as many items as specified by its capacity. If the user enters an array size greater than the capacity, an In-dexOutOfRangeException is generated and the *Catch* block in line 45 catches it. An appropriate error message is displayed in line 46. Any other exception in the code will be caught using the *Catch* statement in line 48. In the *Finally* block, we display the size of the array to the user and generate a beep. The statements in the *Finally* block are executed in all cases. The output of this application is shown in Figure 12.30. We see that an exception is generated when we try to enter the third element of an array whose capacity is 2.

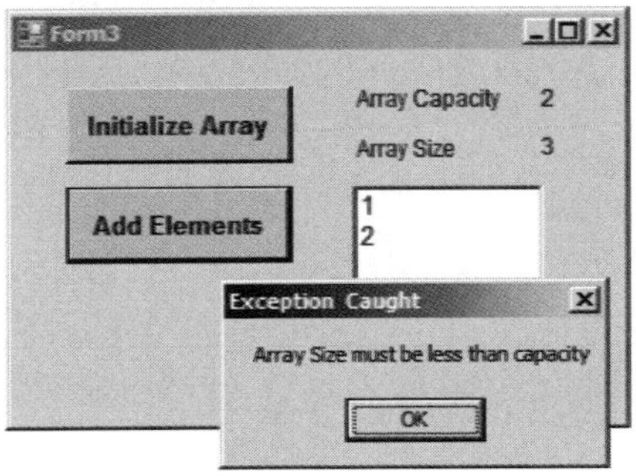

Figure 12.30 The Try-Catch-Finally example: Form Design and application output.

12.9 *In-Class Assignment*

A geometric progression is a sequence in which each term (except the first term) is derived by multiplying the preceding term by a non-zero constant referred as a common ratio. A geometric series is formed by a succession of terms in a geometric progression. Let the first term be a and the common ratio be r, then the general form of a geometric progression is as follows: a, ar, ar², ar³, . . .

Develop a Visual Basic module to generate a geometric series. The module should support a procedure *GenerateGP* that takes a, r, number of desired terms n and a ListBox control as input parameters. The procedure should generate n terms of the series and populate the ListBox control. Test the module code from an application form. Also add exception-handling code as necessary.

12.10 *Summary*

- A *procedure* is a block *of Visual Basic statements* that accomplishes a specific task. A ***procedure call*** consists of a call to a procedure by its name and a list of input argument values.
- There are four types of procedures in Visual Basic.

a. Subroutine procedures: These execute statements specified in the body of the subroutine procedure but do not return any value to the caller procedure.

b. Event procedures: These are like subroutine procedures except that they are executed in response to an event triggered by a user action.

c. Function procedures: These execute statements specified in the function procedure body and return a value to the caller procedure.

d. Property procedures: These are the procedures that contain two sub-procedures, a Get function procedure and a Set subroutine procedure.

■ Visual Basic code is stored in modules: a standard module or a class module. A standard module (or simply, *module*) can contain any number of declaration statements and procedures. Modules are containers for procedures and declarations commonly accessed by other modules within the application.

■ *Classes* are symbolic representations of objects. They describe the properties, methods, and events that make up objects in the same way that a blue-print describes the components and structure of a building.

■ Runtime errors, also known as **exceptions**, can be dealt with through **exception handling**, the technique of anticipating exceptions and accordingly manipulating the code to provide friendly error messages.

■ The keywords `Try` and `EndTry` are used to specify a *Try* block. A `Catch` statement must be used inside the *Try* block to catch and handle the exceptions that might occur. Every *Try* block requires at least one **Catch** block. However, we can incorporate as many *Catch* blocks inside a *Try* block as needed for handling different exceptions. The `Finally` statement appears after all the *Catch* blocks. If the `Finally` statement is present, it is always executed, whether or not the *Try* block throws an error.

12.11 *Exercises*

12.11.1 Review Questions

1. Are the following statements true? Correct those that aren't.
   a. A subroutine procedure must be terminated with the `End Sub` statement.
   b. A function procedure must be terminated with the `End Function` statement.
   c. There should be exactly one return statement in the body of a function procedure.

2. Explain the difference(s) between a function procedure and a subroutine procedure.

3. Answer the following:
   a. We call a subroutine procedure and function procedure by passing parameters to them. What are the two methods by which we can pass parameters to a procedure?
   b. What is the keyword that indicates the choice of Pass-By-Value of the arguments in a procedure?
   c. What is the keyword that indicates the choice of Pass-By-Reference of the arguments in a procedure?
   d. What is the difference between the Pass-By-Value and Pass-By-Reference methods?

4. What is a module? What are the advantages of using a module?

5. Answer the following:
   a. What is a class?
   b. What is the keyword that instantiates an object of a class?
   c. What is a constructor?

6. What is a property procedure?

7. How will you close the current form from within itself?

8. What are the constructs in Visual Basic for structured exception handling? Give the syntax.

9. What is the purpose of the *Catch* block? What does it typically contain?

10. Under what conditions is the *Finally* block executed?

12.11.2 Hands-On Exercises

1. Find the errors in each of the following pieces of code and correct them:

```
Function Profit(ByVal Revenues As Integer, _
ByVal Expenses As Integer) As Integer
    Dim profit As Integer
    Profit = Revenues - Expenses
End Function

Sub Profit()
    Dim p As Integer
```

```
        Dim r As Integer 1000
        Dim e As Integer 330
        p = r - e
        Return p
End Sub

Sub Profit(ByVal Revenues, ByVal Expenses)
        Dim p As Integer
        Dim r As Integer 1000
        Dim e As Integer 330
        p = r - e
End Sub
```

2. **CheckPrime:** An integer *n* is called a prime number if the only positive integers that divide *n* are 1 and itself. Write a function procedure, *CheckPrime*(), that takes in an integer *n* and returns *True* if *n* is prime; *False* otherwise. Create a form that has a TextBox control for user input and a command button "Check if prime." Write code for the *Click* event of the command button that will call *CheckPrime*() with *n* as a parameter. If *CheckPrime*() returns *True*, display, "n is a prime number." Otherwise, display, "n is a composite number." Note that it is sufficient to check divisors up to the square root of *n*.

2. **Triangles:** Create an application that will ask a user for the length of three sides of a triangle and determines the type of the triangle. Create a form with TextBox controls for user input (lengths of the sides of the triangle). Add a command button, "Triangle Type," to the form. Write a subroutine procedure to handle the *Click* event of this button. This subroutine procedure should first call a *ValidateInput*() function procedure that checks the following:

   a. All three length values are greater than zero
   b. The sum of the lengths of any two sides is greater than the third side

   If (a) or (b) is not satisfied, display a message box saying, "Invalid length values," and clear all the text boxes. If both conditions are satisfied, call a function procedure, *TriangleType*(), that determines the type of triangle based on the following criteria and displays an appropriate message:

   a. All three sides are of equal length: Equilateral
   b. Only two sides are equal: Isosceles
   c. All three sides are of different lengths: Scalene

4. Recall the application we developed in Hands-On Exercise 14 in Chapter 11 to manage the annual sales for a retail store. We add some more functionality to this application using function proce-

dures. Add two command buttons, "Minimum Sales Month" and "Maximum Sales Month," that, when clicked, report the month when the sales amount was the maximum and the month when it was the minimum, respectively.

   Use an array to store the monthly sales amounts. Write two function procedures for finding the months when the sales were minimum and maximum. Each function procedure should take the array as an input parameter and return the index of the minimum (or maximum) values.

5. **Swap Integers:** In this exercise, we write a subroutine procedure to swap the values of two given integers. Create a form and add two TextBox controls with labels "X" and "Y." Add two Button controls, "Swap by value" and "Swap by reference." After entering the values for X and Y, the user clicks on either button. We call following function procedure to swap these input values. The new values of X and Y are displayed in the TextBox controls to the user. The following are the function procedures associated with the two buttons:

   a. Swap-By-Value: The associated code calls a function `SwapValue(ByVal X as Integer, ByVal Y as Integer)` to interchange the values of X and Y.

   b. Swap-By-Reference: The associated code calls a function `SwapReferece(ByRef X as Integer, ByRef Y as Integer)` to interchange the values of X and Y.

   Compare the values in the TextBox controls after calling a Swap-By-Value and Swap-By-Reference. Explain the difference.

6. **Automobile:** A driver who has several trips planned would like to estimate the total driving cost. Create an application called *TripEstimator* to help this driver. Use the TextBox controls for the following user inputs: Current odometer reading (miles driven so far), odometer reading during the last oil change, reading when the tires were last replaced, average gas price, average miles per gallon, and total distance to travel. Add command buttons "Analyze Cost" and "Analyze distance," and write subroutine procedures to handle their *Click* events. The "Analyze Cost" subroutine procedure should do the following:

   a. Call an *OilChange*() function procedure that adds $20 to the "cost so far" for every 2000 miles driven. The function procedure should return the new "cost so far."

b. Call a *TireChange*() function procedure that adds $200 to the "cost so far" for every 10,000 miles driven. The function procedure should return the "cost so far."

c. Call a *GasPrice*() function procedure that calculates and returns the cost of gas needed.

d. The "Analyze Cost" subroutine procedure should sum the "cost so far" and the value returned by the *GasPrice*() function procedure and display the total cost to the user.

7. Random Number Generation: Create an application that enables users to obtain a specified number of random integers within a specified range. Write a subroutine procedure that will ask the user to input the total number of random integers to be generated and the low and high values of the range. The code should compute and display the random values to the user. Write the following subroutine procedures to modularize the code:

a. The *InputData*() subroutine procedure gets the user input for the total number of random numbers, range values (low and high), and the mean and standard deviation of the distribution.

b. The *RandomIntegers*() subroutine procedure generates and displays the random integers. Use the methods in the `System.Random` class for random number generation. Use the following pseudo code for computing a random integer within the specified range:

```
RandomInteger = (HighValue – LowValue +
1) * RandomNumber + LowValue
```

where *HighValue* and *LowValue* are the end points of the range, respectively, and *Random-Number* is the random number generated using the methods of the `System.Random` class.

c. The *Main*() subroutine procedure calls the other subroutine procedures to complete the application flow.

8. Write a Visual Basic code to define a VB Class called *Book*. The Class holds the following variables that are needed to describe a *Book* object: ISBN, title, author, publication date, and price. Include property procedures for Title, Author, Price and PublicationDate data members. Also include the following function procedures:

a. *RecentPublication*() that returns *True* if the publication date is within one year of the current date.

b. *PriceCategory*() that returns a string that indicates the category of the price as follows:

   i) "Economy": If price < 100

   ii) "Medium": If price is between 100 and 300

   iii) "Expensive": If price > 300

9. Overflow Exception Handling: Create an application to multiply two large integers X and Y (X and Y can both have values larger than 1 million). Get the values for X and Y from the user at runtime. Write the code that will compute the product of these two variables, X and Y, and store it in another integer, *Product*. If the user inputs a value of 1,000,000 for both X and Y, the product is too large to be stored in an integer data type. Instead, we want to provide a user-friendly message to the user. Use a Try-Catch block to catch the overflow exception and display the message "Product is too large to handle. Enter smaller values for X and Y."

10. Bubble Sort: Bubble Sort is a simple technique for sorting a list of items. The procedure repeatedly goes through the list to be sorted, compares two items at a time, and swaps those that are not in the sorted order. Let us create an application called "BubbleSort." There are two parts to this application.

a. Add a Visual Basic module, *BubbleSortModule*, to the application. Write a subroutine procedure, *BubbleSortSub*, as part of *BubbleSortModule*. *BubbleSortSub* takes in the following parameters: an array of integers by value, a ListBox control by reference, and a Label control by reference. *BubbleSortSub* should sort the given integer array, set the Label control's *Text* property to "Sorted List," clear the ListBox control, and add the integers in sorted order to it. Refer online help for the exact Bubble Sort algorithm.

b. Add a start up form to the application and add the following controls to it: a ListBox, Label, and two Button controls, "Input list" and "Sort." When the user clicks on "Input List," command button, the subroutine procedure that handles the *Click* event should first get the list of integers to sort from the user. It should then add these elements to the ListBox and store them in an array. The Label control should now display, "Un-sorted list" title to the ListBox control. When the user clicks on "Sort," the *Click* event should call the *BubbleSortSub*.

11. **Time Format Conversion:** Write a subroutine procedure that converts a given time duration in seconds to the hh:mm::ss format, where "hh" denotes hours, "mm" denotes minutes and "ss" denotes seconds. Create a form with a TextBox control for user input. On click of a "Convert time" button, call the subroutine procedure that performs the conversion and displays the formatted time in a Label control.

12. **Base conversion:** Write a function procedure to convert a number in decimal system to a user-specified base number system. Create a form with a TextBox control for the user to input the decimal number and provide RadioButton controls for each of the following options: Binary, Octal, and Hexadecimal. When the user clicks on a "Convert" button, call a subroutine procedure that uses a Select-Case structure to determine the right function procedure to be called, based on the user selection. Write separate function procedures for each conversion: decimal number to binary, decimal number to octal and decimal number to hexadecimal. The function procedure should return the converted number as a string to the subroutine procedure.

13. **Shipping Cost Calculator:** In this application, we will create a self-service application that computes and displays the total shipping cost of a shipment to the user. Create a form and provide appropriate controls for the user to input the following details: sender's name, receiver's name, start address, destination address, approximate distance, number of packages. Also provide the user the following shipping options: standard, two-day, and overnight. Initialize a dynamic array to the user-specified number of packages and prompt the user to enter the weight of each package. Compute the total cost of shipping using the following information:

    a. Weight up to 20 lb: $22

    b. Weight above 20 lb but less than 60 lb: $45

    c. Weight above 60 lb but less than 100 lb: $70

    d. Weight above 100 lb: display an error message saying "Cannot be shipped by self-service option"

For a package to be shipped by the two-day option, add $30 to the standard shipping cost. Similarly, for overnight shipping, add $80 to the standard shipping cost. Also, add cost based on distance as follows:

a. Distance greater than 1000 miles but less than 5000 miles: add $20

b. Distance greater than 5000 miles: add $50

Create a new form to display a confirmation to the user. Display all the user-entered information in Label controls and display the shipping cost of each package. Also, display the total cost of shipment. When the user clicks on the "Done" command button on the first form, call a subroutine procedure that will perform all the shipping cost calculations and navigate the user to the new confirmation form.

14. In this exercise, we will write a function procedure to find and return the *greatest common divisor* (GCD) of two nonnegative integers by applying the binary GCD algorithm defined by the following rules:

    a. GCD (0, v) = v, because everything divides zero, and v is the largest number that divides v. Similarly, GCD (u, 0) = u and GCD (0, 0) is not defined.

    b. If u and v are both even, then GCD (u, v) = 2·GCD (u/2, v/2), because 2 is a common divisor.

    c. If u is even and v is odd, then GCD (u, v) = GCD (u/2, v), because 2 is not a common divisor. Similarly, if u is odd and v is even, then GCD (u, v) = GCD (u, v/2).

    d. If u and v are both odd, and u = v, then GCD (u, v) = GCD ((u-v)/2, v). If both are odd and u < v, then GCD (u, v) = GCD (u, (v-u)/2).

    e. Repeat steps *(ii)–(iv)* until u = v, or u = 0. Write a *GCD (u, v)* as a function procedure. You will be calling this function procedure within itself based on the cases in step *(ii)* to *(iv)*. Procedures that feature procedure calls to themselves are also referred to as *recursive procedures*. The case *(i)* serves as a base case of the recursion and is tested at the beginning of the function procedure.

15. Write a Visual Basic program for a class called "Tree." A tree object can be described by the

following properties: name, type (coniferous/deciduous), height, region (tropical/ temperate/ arctic). Include the *Get* and *Set* property procedures to get and set values for these properties. Also include the following function procedures:

a. *OptimalClimate*( ), which returns a string that indicates the climatic condition of the region where the tree grows as follows:

   i) "Hot": if region is Tropical

   ii) "Moderate": if region is Temperate

   iii) "Cold": if region is Arctic

b. *GrowthTendency*( ), which returns a string that indicates the growing tendency of the tree as follows:

   i) "Tall": if tree height is greater than 100 feet

   ii) "Medium": if tree height is between 40–100 feet

   iii) "Short": if tree height is between 7–40 feet

   iv) "Dwarf": if tree height is less than 7 feet

chapter OVERVIEW

13.1   *Introduction*

The *user interface* is perhaps the most important part of an application. To users, it is the application or, at least, the most visible part of an application. Users probably are not aware of, and may not care about, the code that is executed behind the scenes. Therefore, it is important that we keep potential users in mind when we design applications. No matter how much time and effort we put into programming, the usability of an application depends on its interface. A well-designed user interface separates the user from the underlying technology, making it straightforward to perform intended tasks. A brilliantly coded application is useless without a *practical* user interface.

In Visual Studio, we build user interfaces with the aid of forms and controls. An application generally consists of a *multiple-document interface* (MDI), in which several forms are linked with navigation functionalities. Each form includes several controls for user interactions, input, and output. Visual Basic code is associated with each form and control in a code-behind form file. These code files allow us to complement interface requirements with our programming.

Controls play an integral role in the construction of an application's user interface. They are at the heart of all Windows-based applications as well as Web-based applications (see Chapter 18). Controls allow us to acquire user input and to display output. We have already introduced Button, RadioButton, and TextBox controls in previous chapters. We will explore these controls in more depth and introduce more controls in this chapter. The controls discussed in this chapter include the following: Label, TextBox, CheckBox, RadioButton, Button, ListBox, ComboBox, CheckedListBox, DateTimePicker, and TreeView.

13.1.1   Topics

This chapter discusses the following topics:

- Controls summary and their common properties, methods, and events.
- How to use the Label and LinkLabel controls.
- Properties, Methods, and Events of the TextBox control and how to use these to validate user inputs.
- Properties, Methods, and Events of the Button control.
- How to use the CheckBox control and its properties, methods, and events.
- How to use the ListBox and multi-select ListBox control for displaying choices to the user.
- How to use the ComboBox control for displaying choices to the user.
- An overview of CheckedListBox, DateTimePicker, and TreeView controls.

13.2   *The Controls*

We introduced the Toolbox (Figure 13.1) in Chapter 10 as a gazette of Visual Basic controls. We first summarize some of the key controls we will be discussing throughout this chapter. We present a list of these controls in Table 13.1.

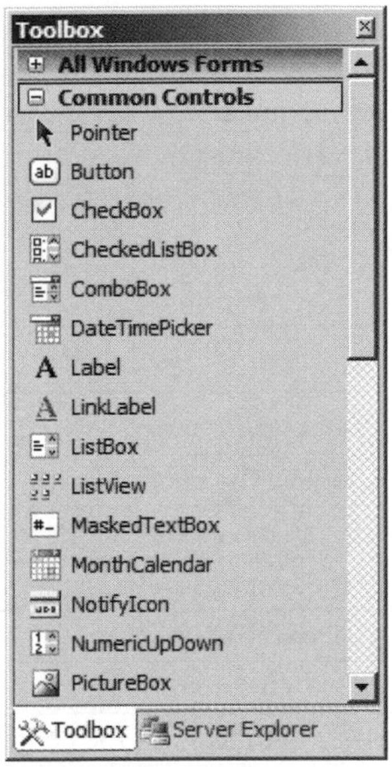

Figure 13.1 The Toolbox.

Table 13.1 A summary of controls and their functions.

Name	Image	Description	Function
Label	 A	Displays read-only text.	Display text
TextBox	|ab|	Provides an area to display, edit, or enter text.	Edit text
CheckBox	 ☑	Displays a yes/no CheckBox with its label. Allows multiple selections.	Set value
Radio Button	◉	Displays an on/off button, which is used for a single selection from multiple choices.	Set value
ListBox		Displays a single column list of items for single/ multiple selection.	Selection from list
ComboBox		Displays a drop-down list of items (combines the TextBox and ListBox).	Selection from list
CheckedListBox		Displays a scrollable list of items, each accompanied by a CheckBox.	Set value and Selection from list
TreeView		Displays a hierarchical collection of node objects, which can consist of text with optional CheckBoxes.	Selection from list
DateTimePicker		Displays a graphical calendar to allow the selection of a date or a time.	Set Date

All the controls in the Toolbox have their own properties, methods, and events, which define their appearance and behavior. However, there are some properties, methods, and events that are common across these controls. Here are some of the noteworthy properties (Table 13.2), methods (Table 13.3), and events (Table 13.4) that are common to all the controls.

We now explore controls summarized in Table 13.1 in subsequent sections.

Table 13.2 Control class's properties.

Property	Description
BackColor	Set/view the background color of the control.
BackgroundImage	Set/view the background image of the control.
Cursor	Set/view the cursor display when the mouse points to the control.
Font	Set/view the font face, size, and emphasis.
ForeColor	Set/view the foreground color of the control.
Text	Set/view the text associated with the control.
Enabled	Set/view the value indicating whether or not the control is enabled.
TabIndex	Set/view the tab order of this control in a given group.
Visible	Set/view the value indicating whether or not the control is visible.
Name	Set/view the name of the control.
Location	Set/view the coordinates of the upper left-hand corner of the control.
Width	Set/view the width of the control.
Height	Set/view the height of the control.

Table 13.3 Control class's methods.

Method	Description
Hide	Hides the control.
Select	Activates the control.
Show	Displays the control by setting its visible property to True.
ToString	Returns a string that represents the current control.
SendToBack	Sends the control to the back of the stacking order.
SendToFront	Sends the control to the front of the stacking order.

Table 13.4 Control class's events.

Event	Description
BackColorChanged	Occurs when the BackColor property value is changed.
Click	Occurs when the control is clicked.
DoubleClick	Occurs when the control is double-clicked.
FontChanged	Occurs when the Font property value is changed.
VisibleChanged	Occurs when the Visible property value is changed.
KeyPress	Occurs when a key is pressed while the control is focused.

13.3 *The Label and LinkLabel Controls*

A Label control displays information to the user. The text of the Label control is read-only, in the sense that a user cannot change or delete it. We generally use labels to convey the meanings of other controls, to display calculated information to the user, and to display titles and headings. For example, a Label control is used with the TextBox control to indicate that it displays a student's email address. Figure 13.2 illustrates an example in which a label is used to display a form heading ("Student Login Page"). Table 13.5 summarizes the properties and events of the Label control.

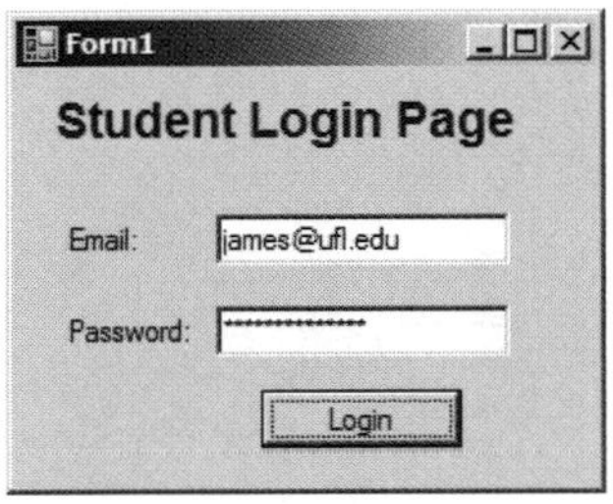

Figure 13.2 An example of a Label control.

Table 13.5 Label control: Properties and events.

Name	Description
AutoSize	If the value is set to *True*, makes the size of the control increase or decrease automatically to fit the text.
Font	Uses the *Build* button to change the font face and the size of the text in the control.
ForeColor	Assigns fore color to the control.
TextAlign	Aligns label text.
Click	Occurs when the Label control is clicked.
DoubleClick	Occurs when the Label control is double-clicked.

We can also use labels as navigation links. In fact, Visual Basic features a control called Link-Label for this purpose. Using LinkLabel, we can link to other forms and Web pages. Table 13.6 presents some of the useful properties and events of the LinkLabel control.

Table 13.6 LinkLabel control: Properties and events.

Name	Description
ActiveLinkColor	Set/view the color of the active (when we put the mouse pointer on it) link.
LinkBehavior	Set/view a value that indicates the behavior of a link.
LinkColor	Set/view the color of a normal link.
LinkVisited	Set/view a value indicating whether the link has been visited or not.
VistedLinkColor	Set/view the color for a visited link.
LinkClicked	Occurs when the link is clicked.

13.3.1   Using LinkLabel for Navigation

In this section, we illustrate usage of a LinkLabel control. We first use the control to open the Industrial Engineering Web site at the University of Florida and then to close the form (see Figure 13.3). This section covers the following How-to topic:

- ■   How-to: use LinkLabel for navigation.

```
3   Private Sub LinkLabel1_LinkClicked(ByVal sender As System.Object, _
4   ByVal e As System.Windows.Forms.LinkLabelLinkClickedEventArgs) _
5   Handles LinkLabel1.LinkClicked
6       LinkLabel1.LinkVisited = True    'Set Visited to True
7       'System Process will open the default browser
8       System.Diagnostics.Process.Start("http://www.ise.ufl.edu/")
9   End Sub
10
11  Private Sub LinkLabel2_LinkClicked(ByVal sender As System.Object, _
12  ByVal e As System.Windows.Forms.LinkLabelLinkClickedEventArgs) _
13  Handles LinkLabel2.LinkClicked
14      Me.Close()
15  End Sub
```

Figure 13.3   Navigating using a LinkLabel control.

Figure 13.3 Explained:

We use the LinkClicked method to associate our navigation code. On *LinkLabel1*'s click, we open the Industrial Engineering Web site in line 8. A default Web browser (such as Internet Explorer or Firefox) will open when the user clicks on this link. In line 6, we mark that the link was visited. On *LinkLabel2*'s click, we close the current form (Me) in line 14.

13.4   *The TextBox Control: In Depth*

We have used a TextBox control in almost every form we created so far. In this section, we will explore this control and go over its properties, methods, and events in depth. Table 13.7 presents some noteworthy properties, methods, and events of the control.

13.4.1   Hands-On Tutorial: Validating TextBox Control's Input

Using TextBox control's properties, methods, and events, we can validate the input into a control at runtime. Consider a situation in which a TextBox is designed to input social security numbers. In order to ensure that a user enters only numbers (any letters or special characters are invalid), we write the following application. This hands-on tutorial covers the following How-to topic:

- ■   How-to: validate input in a TextBox control.
    Follow these steps to build the described application:
    1. Create a new project named *WindowsControl*.
    2. Add a TextBox control, *txtVerify*, and a Label control to the *Form1* (refer to Figure 13.4).
    3. Open the Code Window and select the *txtVerify* control in the top-left drop-down list and select the *KeyPress* event from the top-right drop-down list.
    4. Associate the code shown in Figure 13.5 with the *KeyPress* event of the TextBox.

Table 13.7 TextBox control: Properties, methods, and events.

Name	Description	Value	Example
Multiline	If set to True, allows for a maximum of 60 lines in the box.	True/False	I am a default, simple Text Box I am a Multiline TextBox. My Multiline Property is set to True. Also my Word-Wrap property is set to true, you can see that by looking at me.
Word-Wrap	If multiline and word-wrap are both set to True, the control will wrap the lines.	True/False	I am a Multiline TextBox. My Multiline & Word-Wrap Properties are set to True.
ScrollBars	Indicates which scroll bars to show.	Horizontal/ Vertical/Both	
TextAlign	Indicates how the text should be aligned.	Left/ Right/ Center	
ReadOnly	If set to True, makes the TextBox read-only. The user can view and/or copy the text, but cannot edit or paste it.	True/False	
Enable	If set to False, disables the TextBox. It grays both the control and text, indicating that the control is inaccessible.	True/False	I am a Read-Only Text Box My Enable Property is set to False *************************
Password Char	Masks the text with a string of special characters.	Any special Char value: * #	
Clear	Clears the text from the TextBox.	–	
Select	Selects the text in the control.	–	
SelectAll	Selects all the text in the TextBox.	–	
Click	Occurs when the TextBox is clicked.	–	

Figure 13.4 TextBox control input validation: Output.

```
 3    Private Sub txtVerify_KeyPress(ByVal sender As Object, _
 4      ByVal e As System.Windows.Forms.KeyPressEventArgs) _
 5      Handles txtVerify.KeyPress
 6        If Not Char.IsDigit(e.KeyChar) Then
 7            MessageBox.Show(e.KeyChar & _
 8            " is invalid. Please enter a numeric value" _
 9            , "Error Msg", MessageBoxButtons.OK, _
10            MessageBoxIcon.Error)
11            e.Handled = True
12        End If
13    End Sub
```

Figure 13.5 TextBox control input validation: Code Window.

Figure 13.5 Explained:

The *txtVerify_KeyPress* event is invoked for every key selection performed to enter the text in the TextBox. The event takes every input character as an object *e*. The *KeyChar* property of a character is used to access the character value entered by a user. In line 6, the *IsDigit* method returns *True* if its argument is a digit (0–9) and *False* otherwise. If the character entered by the user in the SSN TextBox control is anything other than a number (i.e., letter or special character), the program control enters the body of the If statement and displays the error message that appears in lines 7–10. Figure 13.4 shows the error message displayed when the user enters the invalid character 'r.' In line 11, we set the *Handled* property to *True*, which indicates that Visual Basic will remove the erroneous character from the TextBox. If we don't set the *Handled* property to *True*, the application provides an error message but does not prevent the user from entering the wrong character.

13.5 *The Button Control*

We have used the command button in almost every form that we have created so far. In this section, we explore more properties, methods, and events of the Button control. Table 13.8 presents a few important properties and events for the control.

Table 13.8 Button control: Properties and events.

Name	Description	Example
Text	Sets the button caption.	Button1.Text = "Close Me"
Font	Sets/views the font of the button caption. Uses the Build button to set the font style and size.	
ForeColor	Sets/gets the color for the caption text.	Button1.ForeColor = Color.Yellow
BackColor	Sets/gets the value of the color of the button background.	Button1.BackColor = Color.Blue
TextAlign	Sets/gets the value associated with text alignment.	Button1.TextAlign = Center
Image	Sets/gets the background image for the button.	Button1.Image = Image.FromFile ("c:\gator.jpg")
Size	Sets/gets the button size.	Button1.Size = New Size (200,20)
Location	Sets/gets the location and X and Y coordinates of a button.	Button1.Location = New Location (200,200)
Visible	If set to False, hides a button.	Button1.Visible = False
Enabled	If set to False, disables a button.	Button1.Enabled = False
Click	Occurs when a button is clicked.	

13.6   *The CheckBox Control*

The CheckBox control is one of the common controls that is used to provide different options to the user. CheckBox controls are used to gather multiple choices from the user, unlike the RadioButton controls (discussed in Chapter 11). If a CheckBox has been selected, a check sign appears in the box. We can toggle between selecting and de-selecting a CheckBox control by simply clicking on it. The CheckBox control is used to obtain True/False or Yes/No answer from the user. For example, in Figure 13.6, we have selected multiple hobbies, namely, Reading, Swimming, and Hiking, by checking the respective boxes.

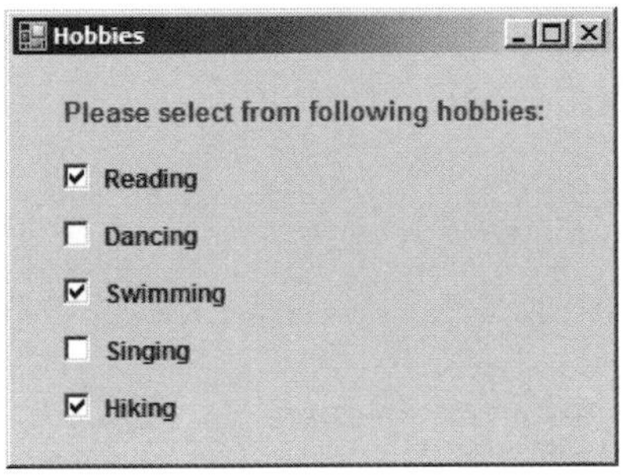

Figure 13.6 An example of a CheckBox control.

Next, we take a look at the properties and events of a CheckBox control (Table 13.9). The *Checked* property, one of the most important properties of the CheckBox control, returns *True* or *False* to indicate whether or not the control has been selected. Another important property, *CheckState*, returns a *CheckState* value of *Checked* or *Unchecked*. If we set the *ThreeState* property to *True*, *CheckState* also returns the state, *intermediate*. In the intermediate state, the check mark in the box is displayed in a gray shade, unlike the usual black color.

Table 13.9 CheckBox control: Properties and events.

Name	Description	Value
Checked	Sets/gets a value indicating if a CheckBox has been checked.	True/False
CheckState	Sets/gets the state of the CheckBox.	0/1/2
Image	Sets/gets the CheckBox image.	Image URL
ThreeState	If set to True, designates a three-state CheckBox.	True/False
CheckedChanged	Occurs when the Checked property changes.	
CheckStateChanged	Occurs when the CheckState property changes.	

13.6.1   Hands-On Tutorial: Getting and Setting a Checkbox's State

Let us use the CheckBox control to create a small application that allows users select their favorite fruits. This hands-on tutorial covers the following How-to topic:

- How-to: get and set the state of a CheckBox control.
    1. Add a new form (*Form2*) to the *WindowsControls* project created during the previous hands-on tutorial. Set the new form as the project's start-up form.

2. Add three CheckBox controls to *Form2*. Name them *chk1*, *chk2*, and *chk3*. Add two command buttons to the form as shown in Figure 13.7.

3. Use the Figure 13.8 code to complete the application. Run and test the application (see Figure 13.9).

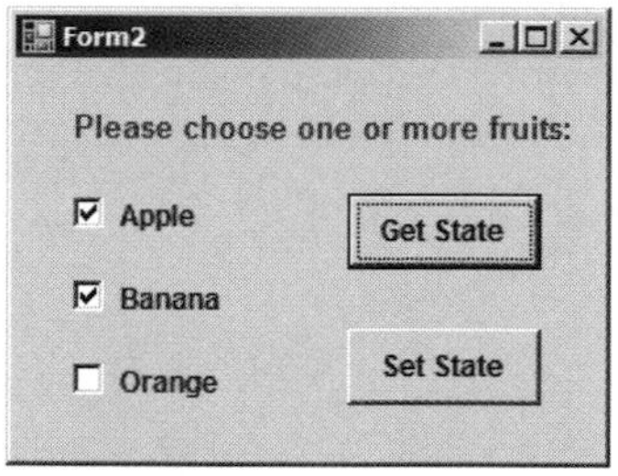

Figure 13.7 Using a CheckBox control: Design Window.

```
3    Private Sub cmdGetState_Click(ByVal sender As System.Object, _
4    ByVal e As System.EventArgs) Handles cmdGetState.Click
5        Dim states As String = ""
6        If (chk1.Checked) Then states &= " Apple "
7        If (chk2.Checked) Then states &= " Banana "
8        If (chk3.Checked) Then states &= " Orange "
9        MessageBox.Show("Selected fruits are: " & states)
10   End Sub
11
12   Private Sub cmdSetState_Click(ByVal sender As System.Object, _
13   ByVal e As System.EventArgs) Handles cmdSetState.Click
14       chk1.Checked = True
15   End Sub
```

Figure 13.8 Using a CheckBox control: Code Window.

Figure 13.8 Explained:

We first explain the code for the *Get State* button. In line 6, we verify whether the first Check-Box control is selected or not using its *Checked* property. If it is checked (indicated by a value of True), we update our string variable *states* by concatenating the fruit associated with the first CheckBox. Similarly, we verify the second and third CheckBoxes in lines 7–8. Finally, in line 9 we display the selected fruits to the user using the concatenated *states* string. When the user clicks on the *Set State* button, the code in line 14 checks the first CheckBox by *setting* its *Checked* property to *True*. Hence, the user sees Apple box selected.

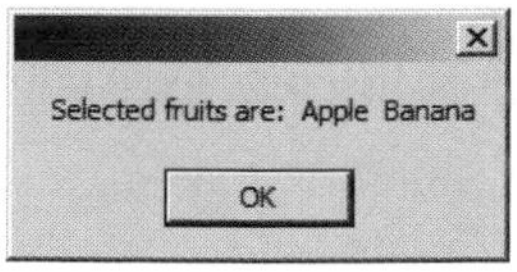

Figure 13.9 Using a CheckBox control: Output.

13.7 *The ListBox Control: In Depth*

The ListBox control goes beyond the CheckBox or RadioButton controls to present a list of choices to the user. The user can select one or more choices from the ListBox control displayed as a vertical column. We can also display a list with vertical and horizontal scroll bars. If the total number of items exceeds the number that can be displayed, scroll bars are automatically added to the ListBox control. The noteworthy properties, methods, and events of the control are listed in Table 13.10.

Probably the most important property of a ListBox is the *SelectedIndex*. This property returns an integer value for the index of the selected item (or the first selected item for multiple selections) of a ListBox. If the first item in the list is selected, then the index value zero is returned. If none of the items are selected, then −1 is returned. We can set the value of *SelectedIndex* property to −1 to void any selection. Another important property related to selection is *SelectedItem*. This property is very similar to the *SelectedIndex* property, but it returns the item itself rather than an integer index. Finally, we can access all items in the list using the *Items* Collection. For example, to determine the total number of items in a list, we use the *Items.Count* property. To add an item to or delete an item from the list, we use an *Items.Add* method and an *Items.Remove* method, respectively.

Table 13.10 ListBox control: Properties, methods, and events.

Name	Description
ColumnWidth	Gets/sets the column width for the multi-column list.
DisplayMember	Shows the item property that displays the list. By default, the ToString method displays the item's string.
ItemHeight	Gets/sets height of the item in the list.
Items	Gets/sets collection of all the items.
MultiColumn	If set to true, makes a multi-column list.
ScrollAlwaysVisible	Indicates whether the scroll bar should always be visible in the list.
SelectedIndex	Gets/sets the index of a currently selected item.
SelectedIndices	Gives the collection of indices of selected items.
SelectedItem	Gets/sets the currently selected item.
SelectedItems	Gives the collection of all the selected items.
SelectionMode	Gets/sets the mode of selection.
Sorted	If set to True, alphabetically sorts the items in the list.
Text	Gets the selected text.
ClearSelection	Sets SelectedIndex = −1; it clears any selection.
GetSelected	Returns True if the indicated item is selected.
SetSelected	Selects the indicated item.
Items.Clear	Clears all the items in the list.
Items.RemoveAt(i)	Removes the item with index *i*.
SelectedIndexChanged	Occurs when the SelectedIndex property, or selection, changes.

13.7.1   Sorting a ListBox Control

The *Sorted* property alphabetically arranges items in a ListBox. The application is illustrated in Figure 13.10. We can see that the fruit list is sorted alphabetically in an ascending order by setting the list's *Sorted* property to *True*. Once *Sorted* is set to *True*, even when we add a new fruit item, the list will place the new entry at an appropriate location to maintain the sorted order.

<table>
<tr><td>

Sorting List Box

Fruit List:

Apple
Banana
Orange
Peach
Plum
Strawberry
Blueberry
Raspberry
Cranberry

[Add a Fruit]

[Sort the List]

</td><td>

```
Private Sub cmdSort_Click(ByVal _
sender As System.Object, _
ByVal e As System.EventArgs) _
Handles cmdSort.Click
    lstFruit.Sorted = True
End Sub
```

</td></tr>
</table>

Figure 13.10 Sorting items in a ListBox control.

13.7.2   The Multi-Select ListBox Control

ListBoxes allow the user to select more than one item at a time if we choose the *MultiSimple* option for the *SelectionMode* property (see Figure 13.11(a)). Once multiple selections have been enabled, we can use the *SelectedItems* and *SelectedIndices* to access all the selected items in the list. The For-Each-Next loop can loop over all selected items to individually select item text and indices. Figure 13.12 illustrates this application. The application output is shown in Figure 13.11(b) and (c).

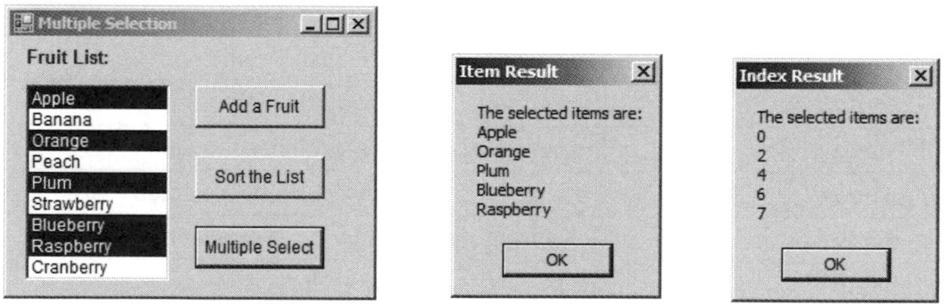

<table>
<tr><td>

Multiple Selection

Fruit List:

Apple
Banana
Orange
Peach
Plum
Strawberry
Blueberry
Raspberry
Cranberry

[Add a Fruit]

[Sort the List]

[Multiple Select]

</td><td>

Item Result

The selected items are:
Apple
Orange
Plum
Blueberry
Raspberry

[OK]

</td><td>

Index Result

The selected items are:
0
2
4
6
7

[OK]

</td></tr>
<tr><td>**(a)**</td><td>**(b)**</td><td>**(c)**</td></tr>
</table>

Figure 13.11 Multi-Select ListBox control: Output.

```
 3      Private Sub cmdMult_Click(ByVal sender As System.Object, _
 4      ByVal e As System.EventArgs) Handles cmdMult.Click
 5          Dim item As String    'to get item text
 6          Dim index As Integer 'to get item index
 7          Dim output As String 'to output result
 8          'First get item text for selected items
 9          output = "The selected items are: " & vbLf
10          For Each item In lstFruit.SelectedItems
11              output &= item & vbLf
12          Next
13          MessageBox.Show(output, "Item Result")
```

Figure 13.12 Multi-Select ListBox control: Code Window.

```
14        'Now get selected item indices
15        output = "The selected items are: " & vbLf
16        For Each index In lstFruit.SelectedIndices
17            output &= index & vbLf
18        Next
19        MessageBox.Show(output, "Index Result")
20    End Sub
```

Figure 13.12 (*continued*)

13.8 ■ *The ComboBox Control*

Like the ListBox, the ComboBox control presents a list of choices to the user. However, this control displays the choices in a drop-down box rather than as a list. A ComboBox allows the user to select an item either by typing text into the drop-down box or by selecting it from the list. Therefore, a ComboBox can be viewed as a combination of TextBox and ListBox controls, and hence the name. In fact, a ComboBox appears as a TextBox until its drop-down list is expanded, when it appears as a ListBox. It should not be surprising that most of the properties, methods, and events of the ComboBox are those of the TextBox and ListBox controls.

Most of these properties, methods, and events have already been discussed in Sections 13.4 and 13.7. Let us create an application that illustrates the usage of the ComboBox control.

Table 13.11 ComboBox control: Properties, methods, and events.

Name	Description
DropDownStyle	Manages appearance and functionality. The Simple option makes a Combo Box a TextBox, while DropDownList makes it a ListBox. Drop Down is the default ComboBox option.
DisplayMember	Determines which property of the item displays the list. By default, the ToString method displays the string of an item.
ItemHeight	Gets/sets the height of an item in the list.
Items	Gets the collection of all items.
MaxDropDownItems	Maximum number of entries to be displayed in the list.
SelectedIndex	Gets/sets the index of a currently selected item.
SelectedItem	Gets/sets the currently selected item.
SelectedText	Gets the selected text from the TextBox part of a control.
Sorted	If set to True, sorts the items in the list alphabetically.
GetItemText	Gets the text of the selected item.
Select	Selects the range of the text.
SelectedAll	Selects all the text in the TextBox of the ComboBox.
Items.Clear	Clears all the items in the list.
Items.RemoveAt(i)	Removes an item with index *i*.
SelectedIndexChanged	Occurs when the *SelectedIndex* property, or selection, changes.
DropDown	Occurs when the drop-down portion of the control is shown.

13.8.1 Hands-On Tutorial: Using a ComboBox Control

Figure 13.13 presents an application that illustrates some of the properties, methods, and events of the ComboBox control. As in the ListBox control hands-on tutorial, we build the fruit list and let the user add new items, sort existing items, and additionally remove one or more items from the ComboBox control. We also illustrate the *SelectedIndexChanged* event of the ComboBox. Every time the user selects a different item from the list, we display the selected fruit and its index in the TextBox control. This hands-on tutorial covers the following How-to topic:

- How-to: use a ComboBox control.
    1. Add a new form (*Form3*) to the *WindowsControls* project. Set *Form3* as the project's start-up form.
    2. Set up Form3 as shown in Figure 13.13. Name the ComboBox "cmbFruits," the TextBox "txtFruits," and four buttons "cmdAdd," "cmdSort," "cmdRemove," "cmdClear."
    3. Access the *Items* property of the *cmbFruits* ComboBox in the Property Window. Launch the *String Collection Editor* and add a few fruit name strings to start with.
    4. Use the Figure 13.14 code to complete the application.

Figure 13.13 A ComboBox control application: Design Window.

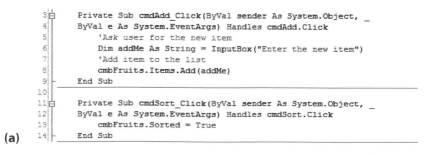

```
 3    Private Sub cmdAdd_Click(ByVal sender As System.Object, _
 4    ByVal e As System.EventArgs) Handles cmdAdd.Click
 5        'Ask user for the new item
 6        Dim addMe As String = InputBox("Enter the new item")
 7        'Add item to the list
 8        cmbFruits.Items.Add(addMe)
 9    End Sub
10
11    Private Sub cmdSort_Click(ByVal sender As System.Object, _
12    ByVal e As System.EventArgs) Handles cmdSort.Click
13        cmbFruits.Sorted = True
14    End Sub
```

(a)

(continues)

Figure 13.14 A ComboBox control application: Code Window.

```
16   Private Sub cmdRemove_Click(ByVal sender As System.Object, _
17        ByVal e As System.EventArgs) Handles cmdRemove.Click
18        'Ask user for index of an item to remove
19        Dim idx As Integer = InputBox("Which index to remove?")
20        'Validate entered index
21        If idx < 0 Or idx > cmbFruits.Items.Count - 1 Then
22            MessageBox.Show("Enter a valid index!", "Error Msg")
23        Else
24            cmbFruits.Items.RemoveAt(idx)
25        End If
26   End Sub
27
28   Private Sub cmdClear_Click(ByVal sender As System.Object, _
29        ByVal e As System.EventArgs) Handles cmdClear.Click
30        cmbFruits.Items.Clear()
31   End Sub
```
(b)

```
32
33   Private Sub cmbFruits_SelectedIndexChanged(ByVal sender As _
34        System.Object, ByVal e As System.EventArgs) _
35   Handles cmbFruits.SelectedIndexChanged
36        txtFruits.Text = "You selected " & cmbFruits.SelectedItem _
37                       & ". Index: " & cmbFruits.SelectedIndex
38   End Sub
```
(c)

Figure 13.14 (*continued*)

Figure 13.14 Explained:

The *cmdAdd_Click* subroutine calls the *Add* method of the *Items* collection to add user-entered fruit strings to the ComboBox list in line 8. The *cmdSort_Click* subroutine sets the *Sorted* property of the ComboBox control to *True* to sort the fruit list (line 13). As in the case of the ListBox, the ComboBox list will now be kept sorted even when new items are added. The *cmdRemove_Click* subroutine calls the *RemoveAt* method of the *Items* collection of a ComboBox control to remove items at an index specified by the user (line 24). We also validate the index entered by the user in line 21. If the input index is –1 or greater than the index of the last item in the list, we display an error message in line 22. The *cmdClear_Click* subroutine deletes all the existing items from the list using the *Clear* method of the *Items* collection (line 30). Whenever the user selects an item in the ComboBox, the *SelectedIndexChanged* event is triggered. It displays the selected item and its index in the TextBox (*txtFruits*), using the *SelectedItem* and *SeletecdIndex* methods (lines 36–37).

13.9 *The CheckedListBox Control*

The CheckedListBox can be thought of as a combination of a CheckBox control and a ListBox control, and hence the name. The CheckedListBox control can also be viewed as an extension of the ListBox control. It does almost everything that a ListBox does and additionally displays a CheckBox control next to each item of the list (refer to Figure 13.15). However, there is difference between these two. The CheckedListBox has two distinct states: item checked and item selected. We can select an item by clicking on it and check an item by putting a checkmark in its CheckBox control. We can check more than one item by default, whereas we can only select one item at a time, unless we set the CheckedListBox control's *SelectionMode* property to *MultiSimple*. We list some of the properties, methods, and events of the CheckedListBox control in Table 13.12.

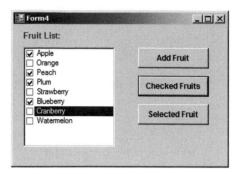

Figure 13.15 An example of a CheckedListBox control.

Table 13.12 CheckedListBox control: Properties, methods, and events.

Name	Description
CheckedIndices	Collection of indices of the checked items in the CheckedListBox.
CheckedItems	Collection of checked items in the CheckedListBox.
SelectedItems	Collection of selected items in the MultiSimple CheckedListBox.
SelectedItem	Selected item for a One select CheckedListBox.
SelectionMode	Gets or sets a value specifying the selection mode.
ThreeDCheckBoxes	Gets or sets a value indicating whether the CheckBoxes display Flat or Normal in appearance. (True if the CheckBox has a flat appearance; False otherwise). Default is false.
GetItemChecked(i)	Returns a value indicating whether an item at index *i* is checked.
GetItemCheckState(i)	Returns a value indicating the check state of the item with index *i*.
SetItemChecked(i, value)	Sets the item at the index *i* to value (True or False). True to set the item as checked; False otherwise.
SetItemCheckState(i, value)	Sets the checked state of the item at the index *i* to value.
OnItemCheck	Occurs when the checked state of an item changes.

13.9.1   Hands-On Tutorial: CheckedListBox Control

We will create a small application that illustrates some of the properties, methods, and events of the CheckedListBox control. We use the same example of ListBox or ComboBox control, a fruit list. We mainly focus on understanding the difference between check and select states of the control. This hands-on tutorial covers the following How-to topic:

■ How-to: use a CheckedListBox control.
    1. Add another form (*Form4*) to the project *WindowsControls* and set it up as the start-up form.
    2. Design *Form4* as shown in Figure 13.15. Name the CheckedListBox "clbFruits." Name the command buttons appropriately.

3. Associate the code in Figure 13.16 with the *Checked Fruits* and *Selected Fruit* command buttons.
4. Save and run the application.
5. While testing, check and select the fruits shown in Figure 13.15. Selected fruit is highlighted in blue, and checked fruits have a checkmark next to them. Compare the output with Figure 13.17.

```
11    Private Sub cmdChecked_Click(ByVal sender As _
12    System.Object, ByVal e As System.EventArgs) _
13    Handles cmdChecked.Click
14        Dim output As String = ""
15        Dim i As Integer
16        output = "You have checked the following items:" _
17        & vbLf
18        For i = 0 To ClbFruits.CheckedItems.Count - 1
19            output &= _
20            ClbFruits.CheckedItems.Item(i).ToString & vbLf
21        Next
22        MessageBox.Show(output, "Checked Fruits")
23    End Sub
24
25    Private Sub cmdSelected_Click(ByVal sender As _
26    System.Object, ByVal e As System.EventArgs) _
27    Handles cmdSelected.Click
28        Dim output As String = ""
29        output = "You have selected the following item:" _
30        & vbLf
31        output &= ClbFruits.SelectedItem.ToString
32        MessageBox.Show(output, "Selected Fruit")
33    End Sub
```

Figure 13.16 A CheckedListBox control example: Code Window.

Figure 13.16 Explained:

The *Selected* subroutine is fairly straightforward. We append the selected fruit text to our output string in line 31. The *SelectedItem* property is used in conjunction with its *ToString* method. Since the items in the list are themselves strings, use of *ToString* is optional. However, when we deal with items other than strings, we may have to use the *ToString* method to extract string data from a selected item. Next is the *Checked* subroutine. Since a user can check more than one item in the list, we use the *CheckedItems* collection to access all of the checked items. In lines 18–21, we loop over all the checked items. We make use of the *CheckedItems* collection's count property to constrain the loop. We access each item in line 20 using the indexed Item property of the collection. The text associated with an item is extracted using the *ToString* method and appended to the output string.

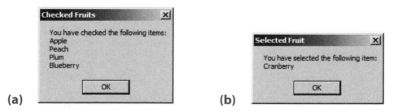

(a)   **(b)**

Figure 13.17 A CheckedListBox control Example: Output.

13.10 *The DateTimePicker Control*

The DateTimePicker control is a ComboBox of date and time items. It allows the user to select a single item from a list of dates or times (Figure 13.18). The control reveals the date in the text form and features a calendar grid in the drop-down list. The *MaxDate* and *MinDate* properties of the control determine the range of dates and the times shown. The *Value* property of the control contains today's date and the current time. Some of the important properties and events of the DateTimePicker control are listed in Table 13.13.

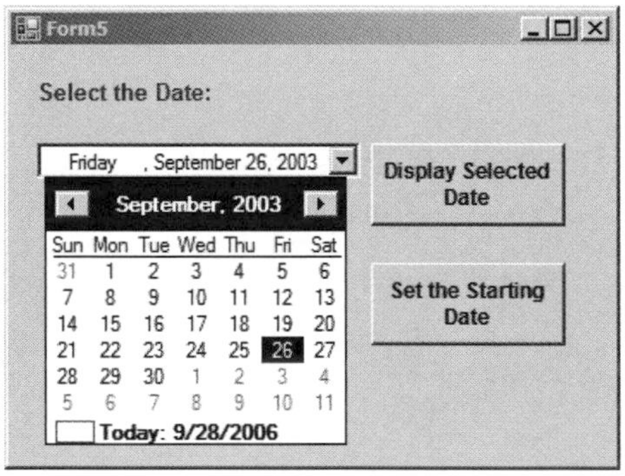

Figure 13.18 An example of a DateTimePicker control.

Table 13.13 DateTimePicker control: Properties and events.

Name	Description
CalendarFont	Gets/sets the font style applied to the calendar.
CalendarForeColor	Gets/sets the foreground color of the calendar.
CalendarMonthBackground	Gets/sets the background color of the calendar month.
CalendarTitleBackColor	Gets/sets the background color of the calendar title.
CalendarTitleForeColor	Gets/sets the foreground color of the calendar title.
MaxDate	Gets/sets the maximum date and time that can be selected in the control.
MinDate	Gets/sets the minimum date and time that can be selected in the control.
PreferredHeight	Gets/sets the preferred height of the control.
ShowUpDown	Gets or sets a value indicating whether an up-down control is used to adjust the date/time value.
Text	Gets or sets the text associated with this control.
Value	Gets or sets the date/time value assigned to the control.
CloseUp	Occurs when the drop-down calendar is dismissed and disappears.
DropDown	Occurs when the drop-down calendar is shown.
ValueChanged	Occurs when the Value property changes.

13.10.1 Hands-On Tutorial: DateTimePicker Control

Let us build a small application that illustrates some of the properties and events of the Date-TimePicker. Using this hands-on tutorial, a user should be able to see the selected date and set a new starting date or minimum display date of the calendar. This hands-on tutorial covers the following How-to topic:

- How-to: use a DateTimePicker control.
  1. Add a new form (*Form5*) to the existing project and set it up as the start-up form.
  2. Add a DateTimePicker control and name it "dtpDate." Add two command buttons with text values *Display Selected Date* and *Set the Starting Date*. Name these command buttons "cmdSelected" and "cmdSetStart," respectively. Place the controls on the form as shown in Figure 13.18.
  3. Use the code in Figure 13.19 to complete the application.
  4. Save, run, and test the application as shown in Figure 13.20.

```
4    Private Sub cmdSelected_Click(ByVal sender As System.Object, _
5    ByVal e As System.EventArgs) Handles cmdSelected.Click
6        MessageBox.Show("You selected " & dtpDate.Value.Date, _
7        "Date Selection", MessageBoxButtons.OK, _
8        MessageBoxIcon.Information)
9    End Sub
10
11   Private Sub cmdSetStart_Click(ByVal sender As System.Object, _
12   ByVal e As System.EventArgs) Handles cmdSetStart.Click
13       Dim startDate As String
14       Try
15           startDate = InputBox("Enter starting date as MM/DD/YYYY")
16           dtpDate.MinDate = Convert.ToDateTime(startDate)
17       Catch ex As Exception
18           MessageBox.Show("Enter valid date format!", "Error Msg")
19       End Try
20   End Sub
```

Figure 13.19 A DateTimePicker control example: Code Window.

Figure 13.19 Explained:

The Selected subroutine displays the selected date in the MessageBox. The *Value* property of the DateTimePicker control gives us access to the selected date (line 6). We use the *Value's Date* property to separate the date from the time string. The *Set Starting Date* subroutine asks the user to enter the desired starting date in a specific format (line 15). The *Value* of the DateTimePicker control is then set to the user entered date (line 16). However, the property expects the assigned value to be a *Date* type. So, we first convert the string date to the required format using a *Convert.ToDateTime* call. If the conversion fails because of erroneous input, an exception will be caught (line 17), and an appropriate error message will be displayed to the user in line 18.

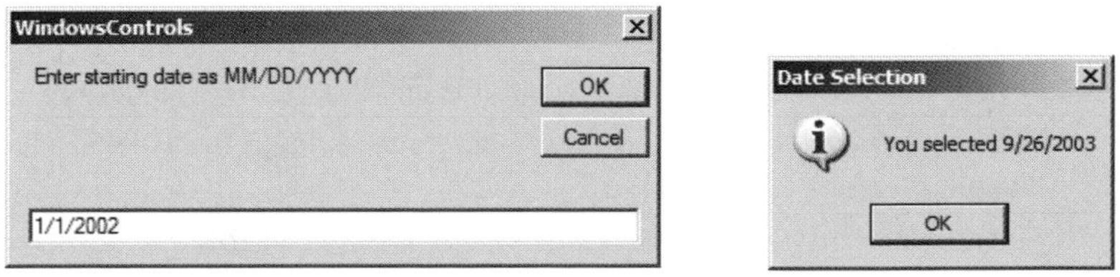

Figure 13.20 A DateTimePicker control example: Output.

13.11 *The TreeView Control*

The TreeView control displays a hierarchy of nodes in a manner similar to the display of files and folders in the Solution Explorer or in the Windows Explorer we often use. A parent node can be expanded to display its child nodes, which recursively serves as a parent of other nodes, and so forth. If the *CheckBoxes* property is set to *True*, the TreeView control displays a CheckBox control next to each node. We can also use the *Nodes* and *SelectedNodes* properties to programmatically select or clear nodes. We will further discuss this control in the case studies part of the book. Some of the noteworthy properties, methods, and events of the TreeView control are listed in Table 13.14.

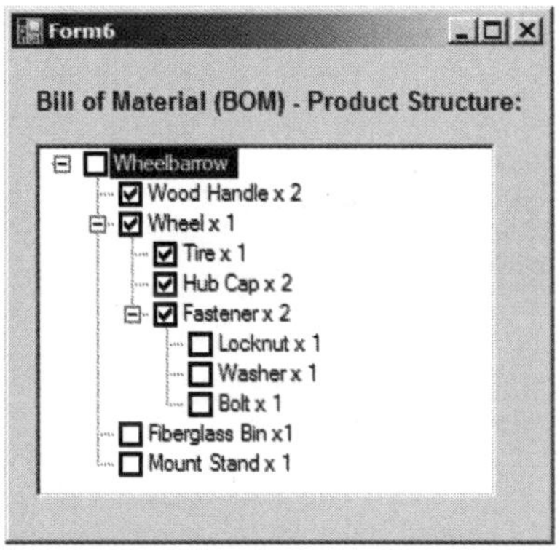

Figure 13.21 An example of TreeView control.

Table 13.14 TreeView control: Properties, methods, and events.

Name	Description
CheckBoxes	Gets/sets a value indicating whether CheckBox controls are displayed next to the tree nodes. The default is *False*.
Nodes	Gets the collection of tree nodes that are assigned to the TreeView control.
Scrollable	Gets/sets a value indicating whether the TreeView control displays scroll bars when they are needed.
SelectedImageIndex	Gets/sets the image list index value of the image that is displayed when a tree node is selected.
SelectedNode	Gets/sets the tree node that is currently selected in the TreeView control.
ShowLines	Gets/sets a value indicating whether lines are drawn between tree nodes in the TreeView control. The default is *True*.
ShowPlusMinus	Gets/sets a value indicating whether plus-sign (+) and minus-sign (-) buttons are displayed next to tree nodes that contain child tree nodes. The default is *True*.
Sorted	Gets or sets a value indicating whether the tree nodes in the TreeView are sorted. The default is *False*.
TopNode	Gets the first fully visible tree node in the TreeView control.
VisibleCount	Gets the number of tree nodes that can be fully visible in the TreeView control.

Table 13.14 (*continued*)

Name	Description
CollapseAll	Collapses all the tree nodes.
EndUpdate	Enables the redrawing of the TreeView.
ExpandAll	Expands all the tree nodes.
GetNodeCount	Retrieves the number of tree nodes, optionally including those in all subtrees, assigned to the TreeView control.
AfterCheck	Occurs after the tree node CheckBox control is checked.
AfterCollapse	Occurs after the tree node is collapsed.
AfterExpand	Occurs after the tree node is expanded.

13.12 *Arranging Controls on a Form*

When we add multiple controls to the form surface, we might want to align them, size them equally, or adjust the spacing between controls consistently. These adjustments are essential to enhance the appearance of a graphical user interface. In this section, we will provide quick tips for efficiently arranging multiple controls on a form.

We can adjust the following features of controls by selecting them together:

- **a)** Width and height
- **b)** Horizontal and vertical spacing
- **c)** Left-center-right alignments
- **d)** Common properties

For items (a)–(c), we use the *Layout* toolbar with all the controls selected (refer to Figure 13.22). To open the Layout toolbar choose View | Toolbar | Layout option from the main menu. The various buttons on the *Layout* toolbar allow us to arrange controls on the form surface. For item (d) above, with multiple selections, the Properties Window automatically displays the common properties for selected controls. For example, we can select a Button, TextBox, and ComboBox control and alter their *Text*, *BackColor*, and *ForeColor* properties all at once.

Finally, we can also copy single or multiple controls and paste them on the same or different form to copy their layout, names, and formatting. Copy does not export the code behind the control.

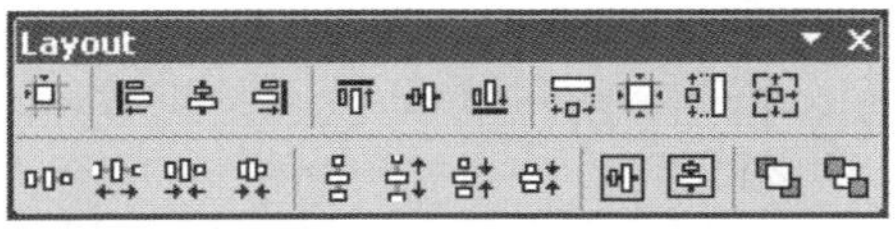

Figure 13.22 The Layout toolbar.

13.13 *The Start-up Object*

So far we have seen how to set up a Windows form as a start-up object of an application. In this section, we explore other available options.

13.13.1 Starting an Application without a Start-up Form

The Properties Window of a project allows us to specify a project's start-up form. However, with this functionality, we can assign a particular form as a start-up form. Every time a user runs an application, a start-up form will appear first. However, there may be situations when we would like to display different forms at the start-up depending on the type of user. In this case, instead of picking any one form as a start-up form, we would like to choose the *Main* method as a starting method in the project's Properties Window. The Main method (for which we have to write the code) now becomes a starting object instead of a form and is executed first whenever the user runs the application.

The code in Figure 13.23 illustrates how to apply the Main method to open different forms based on user status (line 6). Line 7 opens the *Welcome* form for the normal users, while in line 9 we open the *Password* form for the administrative users.

```
1  Module ForMain
2      Sub Main()
3          'Check the status
4          Dim status As String = SeeWhoIsGotIn()
5          'Show start-up form based on the status.
6          If status = "Normal" Then
7              frmWelcome.Show()
8          Else
9              frmPassword.Show()
10         End If
11     End Sub
```

Figure 13.23 An example of a Main procedure.

Note that the Main procedure must be a subroutine procedure, and it cannot be a part of any form class. We must write it as a part of a standard module. The following list summarizes the steps necessary to run an application using the Main procedure:

1. Add a standard module to the existing project.
2. Write the Main subroutine procedure to perform the desired task.
3. Open the Properties Window for a project (Project | Property) and set the start-up object to Main.

13.13.2 Displaying a Splash Screen at the Start-up

Displaying a splash screen at the start-up adds an attractive appearance to an application. It also buys time to load large elements, such as database values or images. A splash screen is a form that usually displays the name of the application, the copyright details, a simple image, and perhaps some additional information. For example, the screen that is displayed when we start the Visual Studio is a splash screen. It is important to keep the splash screen simple; otherwise, its load time could defeat its purpose. We could use the Main subroutine discussed in the previous section to first display the splash form and then to display the next desired form. A splash form typically has a code for time delay of a few seconds.

13.14   *In-Class Assignment*

In this in-class assignment, we aim at developing a greeting card application. The application assists the creation of customized birthday greeting cards. The user will select the various parameters of the card, such as background color, font type, size and fore color, and border style. The user will also provide the text for the greeting. The application provides these options and their values to select from using various Windows controls. Once the user has selected her likings, the greeting card is developed. The self-explanatory application snapshot is shown in Figure 13.24. The greeting card itself is a Panel control. The background color and border selection applies to the panel. The text inside the Panel control is a Label control, and the image is displayed using the PictureBox control (use *Image* property). Use the *Visible* property of a PictureBox control to implement the logic of the *Add the default picture* CheckBox.

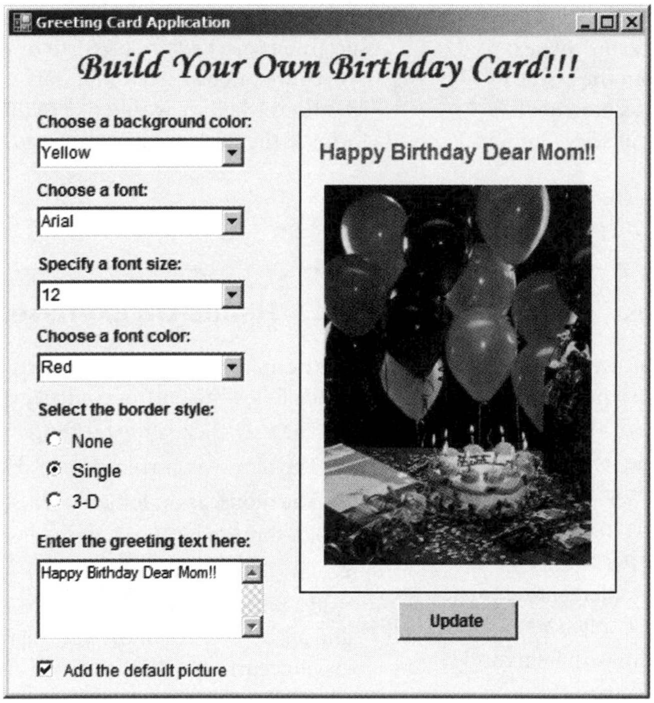

Figure 13.24 The greeting card application.

13.15   *Summary*

■ The *user interface* is perhaps the most important part of an application. To users, it is the application or, at least, the most visible part of an application. *Controls* play an important role in the construction of an application's user interface.

■ *Label* controls display information. The text of the Label control is read-only in the sense that a user cannot change or delete it. We use labels to convey the meaning of other controls, display calculated information to a user, and display titles and headings.

■ The *CheckBox* control is one of the common controls that is used to provide different options to a user. If a box has been selected, a check sign appears in the checkbox. We can toggle between selecting and deselecting a checkbox by simply clicking on it. CheckBox is used to obtain true/false or yes/no options from a user.

■ The *ListBox* control goes beyond the CheckBox and RadioButton controls to present a list of choices to the user. Users can select one or more choices from the ListBox control.

■ Like ListBox, the *ComboBox* control presents a list of choices to the user. However, this control displays the choices in a drop-down box rather than in a list. A ComboBox control allows the user to select an item either by typing text into the drop-down box or by selecting it from the list. Therefore, a ComboBox can be viewed as a combination of the TextBox and ListBox features.

■ A *CheckedListBox* can be viewed as a combination of the CheckBox and ListBox. The control does almost everything that a ListBox control does and additionally displays a CheckBox control next to the items of the list. It differs from the ListBox control in that it has two distinct states: item checked and item selected. We can select an item by clicking on it and check an item by putting a check mark in its CheckBox control.

■ The DateTimePicker control is a ComboBox of date and time items. It allows the user to select a single item from a list of dates or times. The control reveals the date in the text form and features a calendar grid in the drop-down list.

■ The TreeView control displays a hierarchy of nodes in a manner similar to the display of files and folders in the Solution Explorer or even in the Windows Explorer we often use. A parent node can be expanded to display its child nodes, which recursively serves as a parent of other nodes, and so forth.

■ The Properties Window of a project allows us to specify a project's start-up form or object. A Main procedure can be used as the start-up object in situations when we would like to display different forms at the start-up depending on the user type.

13.16   *Exercises*

13.16.1 Review Questions

1. At the beginning of this chapter, we mentioned that the user interface is perhaps the most important part of an application. Why?

2. One of the properties applicable to all the controls is *Visible*. What is its purpose?

3. One of the properties applicable to all the controls is *Enabled*. What is its purpose?

4. Which is the ideal control for implementing each of the following requirements? Explain why.

   a. A restaurant provides a menu with items and the user can pick any three dishes.

   b. An airline company has hundreds of destinations that a client can choose from.

   c. On a certain form, the user should specify whether he or she is married or not.

5. For the CheckBox control, what is the difference between the following two properties: *Checked* and *CheckState*?

6. Assume that we want to use the DateTimePicker control to allow the user to enter a specific date. We do not want to allow the user to enter dates before 1/1/2000. How can we achieve this?

7. What are the benefits of a splash (or intro) screen?

13.16.2 Hands-On Exercises

1. Create an application that reports the occurrence of the following button control events:

   a. The user clicked the button.

   b. The mouse is currently over the button.

   c. The mouse is no longer over the button.

   d. The button has focus now.

   e. The button lost focus.

   Add a button control, "Try Different Events," and a label control to display the message of an event occurring with the button control. To test the last listed event, we remove focus from the button by using the Tab key.

2. Create an application that modifies the properties of the container form through various controls. The interface should look like the figure at the end of this exercise. The application functionalities are as follows.

   a. As the user changes the text in the TextBox, we should modify the title of the form. (*Hint*: Use the *TextChanged* event of the TextBox control.)

   b. As the user checks the background color CheckBoxes, we should modify the background color of the form. If the user selects more than one color, the background color should be set as a combination of the selected colors. For instance, for the currently shown form, both green and blue are selected and so the background color is cyan. (*Hint*: Use the *CheckedChange* event of a CheckBox control, and use colors in their number codes.)

c. The rectangle is the default shape. Whenever the user selects either of the shapes, the form should reflect the selection. (*Hint*: Use `Me.Width` and/or `Me.Height`.)

d. Finally, provide the functionality for the three buttons as suggested by their captions. (*Hint*: Use `Me.WindowState`.)

3. A certain restaurant offers three different meals (Combo1, Combo2, and Combo3). The client has three different choices for the meal size (Small, Medium, and Large). Create a simple application that looks like the provided figure. Once the user clicks the *ViewOrder* button, you should display the meal type and its size to the user.

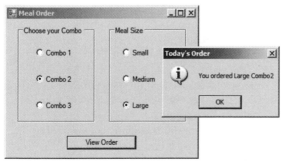

4. Most applications that require a secure login ask the user to create a username and a password. In this exercise, we will create such an application. Create a form with controls as shown in the

figure. The TextBox controls take in user inputs, namely, user name and password. Since the password is sensitive data, we need to make sure that the user does not mistype it. So, we will ask the user to re-enter it for confirmation. After entering the data, the user must click the *Submit* button. Code associated with the *Submit* button should validate the user input by checking the following:

a. That the user entered all the required information (i.e., all three TextBox controls are non-empty).

b. That the username is at least 8 characters in length.

c. That the text in the Password field is identical to that in the Verify Password field.

The application should prompt the user in case of any errors. If the data is valid, a simple message indicating such should be displayed. The code associated with the *Reset* button should clear all the TextBox controls.

5. A university's Computer Science and Engineering department is collecting information about its students' areas of interests. Create an application that can be used as an interface for the task. Design a form that has controls for taking in user input for the following fields for each student: Name, Student number (must be 8 digits), Date of birth, Level of study (undergraduate, master's student, or PhD student), Gender, and Areas of interest.

Each control should be appropriate for the type of information it is collecting. Once the student clicks the *Submit* button, the application should check for any missing or invalid data. Invalid data may result from one of the following:

a. The student number is not 8 characters in length.

b. The student did not select a level of study.

c. The student did not choose any area of interest.

In reality, once a valid data is submitted, we will populate a database with the students' interests, and we can use this data to create a number of different reports. We will cover those topics in the following chapters. For the purpose of this exercise, simply issue a message to the student indicating that the data was valid. See the following figure.

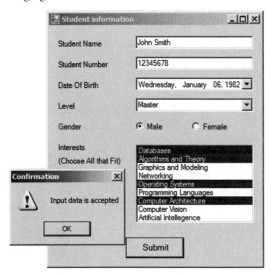

6. In this application, we will divide a form into four square areas and then report the position of the mouse within the form. Follow these guidelines:

a. Set the Form Size property to 400,400.

b. Divide the form into 4 equal squares, each of size 100,100.

c. Whenever the mouse enters a certain quarter, the number of that quarter should be viewed within the quarter itself.

d. Whenever the mouse leaves the current quarter, the quarter should be blanked.

(*Hint*: Use four labels, each of size 100,100, to fill the form, and then add the *MouseEnter* and *MouseLeave* events to each of the label controls. The label text should reflect the number of the current quarter (assume 1, 2, 3, 4 clockwise) when the mouse enters it and should be cleared during the *MouseLeave* event.)

7. Your friend Beth throws a lot of parties. She observed that her parties are getting too large, so she decided to divide each party into two groups. Create an application to help Beth with this job. You should follow the interface as it appears in the following figure.

Beth should be able to select people from the group to the left and then add them to either Group A or Group B. She should also be able to remove people from a specific group and send them back to the group on the left. The groups on the left and right can be implemented as List-Box controls. Whenever a button to move a selected item is clicked, write code in the click event that will add the item to the destination ListBox and remove it from the source ListBox. Do not worry about entering our data to the original group; for now use any random names provided at design time.

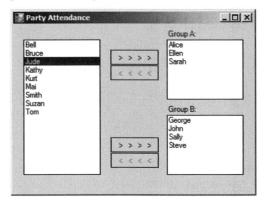

8. In this exercise, we will implement the TicTacToe game. The game starts by the players entering their names. Once one of the players wins, a message box will announce the winner. The player can play the game again and again. Note that we are assuming that both of the users are using the same machine. Follow the interface in the next figure.

(*Hints*: Use 9 Label controls for the TicTac-Toe board. Use the *Click* event of these Label controls to call a custom subroutine, say *handle_click*. The *handle_click* procedure does two tasks: (i) marks the label with either "x" or "o" based on who is playing (use simple toggling), and (ii) checks all the Labels for the winner. In other words, each invocation of the Label click indicates a player's move. Using an array to keep track of marking may further simplify programming logic.)

9. In this exercise we create a simple, scale-down version of a calculator. The Calculator application supports the addition, subtraction, multiplication, division, and square root functions. On click of 0–9 numbered buttons, append clicked number in the TextBox control. Once user clicks any of the function buttons, store the current TextBox control value in a temporary variable. If user then clicks the "sqrt" function button, display the output in the TextBox control. If user clicks any of the binary operator buttons, start appending for the second input number until user clicks the "=" button. Display the operation result on a click of the "=" button. The "CE" button clears the TextBox control as well as any temporary variables used.

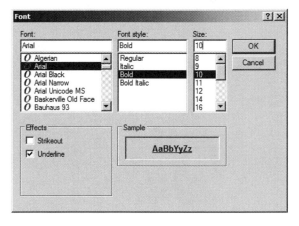

10. In this exercise we extend the Calculator application developed in the previous exercise. We add essential error handling code to the application. The Calculator code should do following error handling:

a. Ensure that the TextBox control inputs are always digits between 0–9.

b. User enters exactly two operands for a binary operator and one operand for a "sqrt" function.

c. All input operands should be an integer.

d. If the operation output is larger or smaller than what a *double* data type can handle, display an error message.

11. In this exercise we will develop Window's *Font* dialog box. Many of us must have used this dialog box in various Windows applications. In this exercise, we will only operate within this dialog box and show the sample text in the "Sample" TextBox as user selected font, font style, size, and effect. We will not actually change font setting outside this dialog box. Also, you may not add all font and size options in your application. Three font and size options each are enough for this exercise.

fourteen Database Connectivity with ADO .NET

chapter OVERVIEW

14.1 *Introduction*

We have learned how to work with various Windows controls and how to add them on application forms to build a graphics user interface, or GUI (see Chapters 11 and 13). These controls are more appealing when used to display and manipulate data residing in the databases. Recall from Chapter 2 that applications with such functionalities are referred to as *Database Applications*. A database application is a computer programs that allow users to manipulate data in a DBMS through a user-friendly interface.

Chapter 2 outlined several examples of database applications. We reiterate those examples here: online shopping at Amazon.Com, printing driving directions at Mapquest.com, and accessing transcripts and payment information through a university portal. In all these examples, a GUI is developed around the database, and users are allowed to view and potentially modify the data. In this chapter we learn how to develop a database application with MS Access databases in the Visual Studio environment. The applications developed in this chapter will be stand-alone Windows applications. (Web-enabled database applications, refer to Chapter 19.)

14.1.1 Topics

This chapter discusses the following topics:

- How to create a simple database application.
- How to display data on a form in a Windows application.
- How to bind data to Windows controls.
- How to display related tables on a form in a Windows application.
- How to create a search forms in a Windows application.
- How to create a lookup table.

14.2 *Database Applications Overview*

In this section, we first provide an overview of the database application development process. The details of database application development are discussed in subsequent sections of this chapter, in Chapter 15, and in Chapter 16.

Different database applications may have different requirements and needs. Based on the needs they meet, we can classify database applications into the following three categories:

1. **Display-oriented applications:** These database applications primarily display data retrieved from a relational database on forms or Web pages. Some examples of this category include a newspaper Web site, a portal to view student transcript and grades, Mapquest for driving directions, and an interface for employees to view their payment details. In all these examples, the application is mainly designed to fetch data from the database.

2. **Transaction-oriented applications:** These database applications may involve frequent transfer of data to and from database. For examples of this category, consider shopping at Amazon.com, a portal for university faculty to enter student grades, and a data-entry form for office secretaries. In all these examples, the application is designed for both fetching data from the database and saving updated data back into the database.

3. **Communication-oriented applications:** These database applications may also need to communicate with other applications or processes. For example, a database application might first send data from the database to specialized optimization software (e.g.,

Ciplex, MS Excel) or even to a C++ program to solve a problem. It may then store the results back in the database. Another example of this is integrating a database application with tools such as Crystal Reports and Map Point to develop professional interfaces and charts for business-oriented and geographic applications.

In this chapter, we deal with the database applications from the first category. Chapter 15 includes the topics that are relevant to the category 2 applications. Chapter 16 considers the topics related to incorporating Crystal Reports into a database application (category 3). The Case Studies part (Part V) illustrates various applications that are a combination of one or more of these three categories.

A VB .NET database application involves connectivity between a database and a graphical user interface (GUI). This is achieved through ADO .NET (ActiveX Data Objects .NET). *ADO .NET* is a collection of objects (classes) that are designed to support data access and manipulation. *Connection* object, *TableAdapter* object, and *DataSet* object are some examples of ADO .NET objects. The detailed ADO .NET architecture is discussed in Section 15.2. The ADO .NET architecture forms the basis of VB .NET database applications. The overall task of developing database applications can be divided into several top-level processes:

1. Connecting to the database—*Connection* object
2. Fetching data using database queries—*TableAdapter* object
3. Temporarily storing the result somewhere—*DataSet* object
4. Displaying data on Windows forms—Data binding
5. Editing data in the application
6. Saving updated data back in the database

The following diagram illustrates these processes. We deal with the first four processes in this chapter and defer the last two for the next chapter.

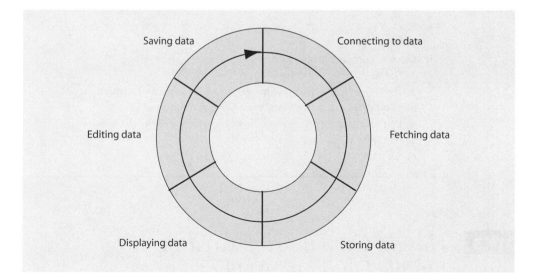

Figure 14.1 Data cycle for a database application.

1. Connecting to the database

We need to establish a two-way communication channel between the database and our application to fetch and save data from and to the database. An ADO .NET *Connection object* assists us in building this bridge. Visual Studio provides several tools included in the Server Explorer

Window and the Data Sources Window to assist us in creating and configuring *Connection* objects (see Section 15.3 for more details about a *Connection* object).

2. Fetching data by querying database tables

The next thing we need is the ability to bring data into our application. We might also be interested in a particular format or sorting order of the data brought from the database. ADO .NET's *TableAdapter object* can execute database queries and bring filtered and sorted data into our application. Visual Studio provides tools such as the *TableAdapter Configuration Wizard* and the *TableAdapter Query Configuration Wizard* that help us easily create and configure *TableAdapter* objects. (Refer to Sections 15.4–15.6 for more details about a *TableAdapter* object.)

3. Temporarily storing the result somewhere

Once the desired data is available to the application, we must temporarily store it where it can be accessed by Windows forms. The *DataSet* object is an in-memory data repository that stores and manages queried data for our application. The Windows controls *bind* to the *DataSets* and rely on them for their data. Visual Studio provides central places to manage all the *DataSets* for our application. These are the *Data Sources Window* and the *DataSet Designer*. (Refer to Section 15.8 for more details on *DataSet* objects.)

4. Displaying data on Windows forms

After bringing data to *DataSets*, we would like to display it on Windows forms for users to view and edit. Visual Studio provides tools such as the Data Sources Window and the Properties Window to achieve this. Hands-on tutorials in this chapter will walk us through this process.

Summary

- **ADO .NET** is the collection of objects (classes) that are designed to support data access and data manipulation.
- Top-level processes of a database application development:
  1. Connect to the database using a *Connection* object.
  2. Bring data using database queries using a *TableAdapter* object.
  3. Temporarily store the results in a *DataSet* object.
  4. Display the data on Windows forms by binding Windows controls to *DataSets*.
  5. Edit data in the application.
  6. Save data back to the database.

14.3 *Hands-On Tutorial: Creating a Simple Database Application*

In this hands-on tutorial, we walk through the process of creating a simple database application that displays the contents of the student table (University database) on a Windows form in a

DataGridView control. The section illustrates essentials of database connectivity and features various easy-to-use tools of Visual Studio. We divide this task into different steps.

Create the Project

1. In Visual Studio, choose the File | New Project option from the main menu. This opens the *New Project* dialog box.
2. In the *New Project* dialog box, make sure to select the *Windows Application* icon in the *Templates* area.
3. Name the project "DatabaseConnectivity" and click *OK*.

Create a Data Source

Create a Data Source   This step creates a *Data Source* based on the tables in the University database. It is a good practice to create one data source per application, with all the tables we need for that application. Of course, we can always add and remove tables if required during the design process. (Refer to Section 15.5 for details on adding tables to existing *Data Source*.) In this step, we add the student, department, transcript, and faculty tables to our data source. We illustrate the *Data Source Configuration Wizard* and the Data Sources Window through this exercise. Specifically, this step covers the following How-to topics.

- How-to: open the *Data Sources* Window.
- How-to: add a *Data Source* to the application.
- How-to: connect to an Access database from Visual Studio.
- How-to: use the *Data Source Configuration Wizard*.

To create a *Data Source*, do following:

4. Choose the Data | Show Data Sources option from the main menu (see Figure 14.2).
5. In the Data Sources Window, click *Add New Data Source* to start the *Data Source Configuration Wizard* (see Figure 14.3).

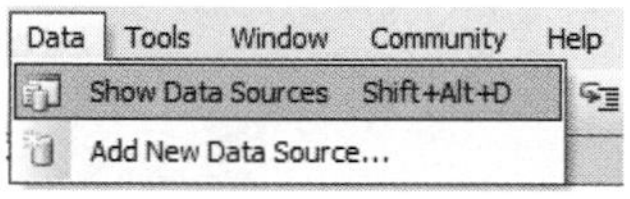

Figure 14.2 Opening the Data Sources Window.

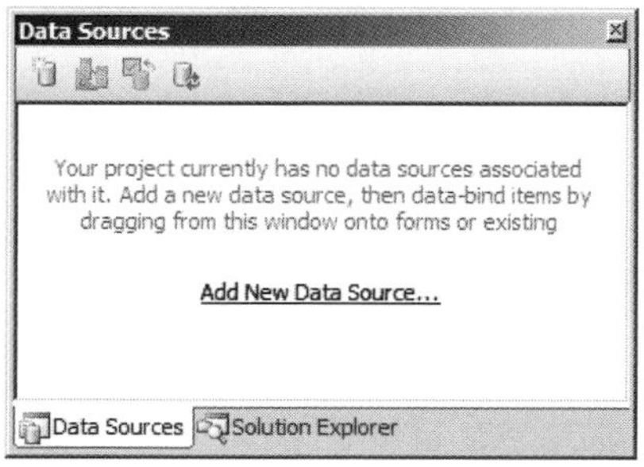

Figure 14.3 Invoking the *Data Sources Configuration Wizard*.

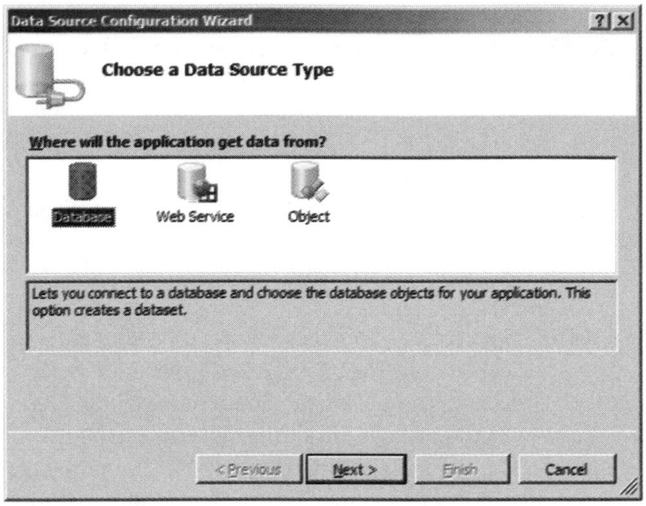

Figure 14.4 Choosing a *Data Source* type, step 1.

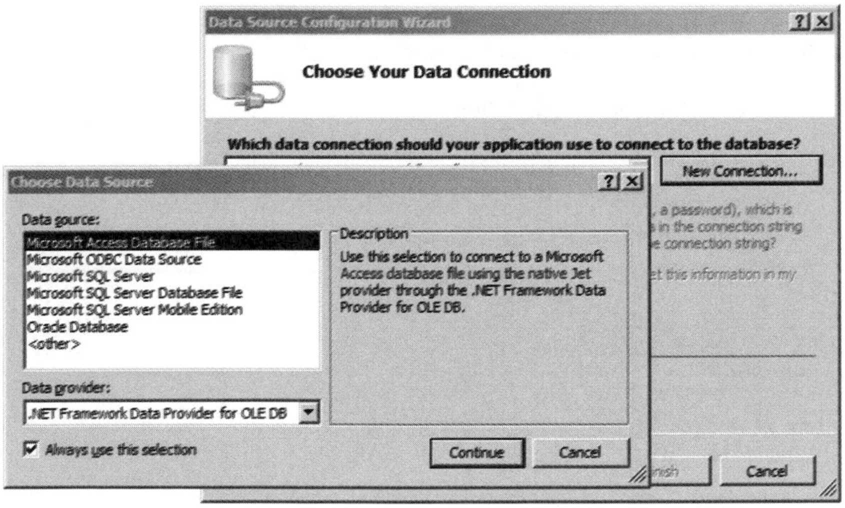

Figure 14.5 Specifying data connection, step 2.

6. Select the *Database* icon on the *Choose a Data Source Type* page of the Wizard (see Figure 14.4). Click *Next*.

7. On the *Choose Your Data Connection* page, click *New Connection* to open the *Choose Data Source* dialog box (see Figure 14.5).

8. Select the *Microsoft Access Database File* in the *Data Source* list box. The *Data provider* drop-down list should automatically show ".NET Framework Data Provider for OLE DB." Click on *Continue*.

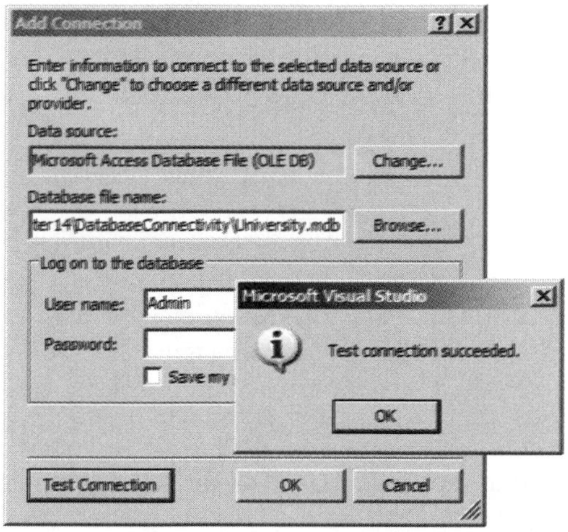

Figure 14.6 Creating the database connection, step 3.

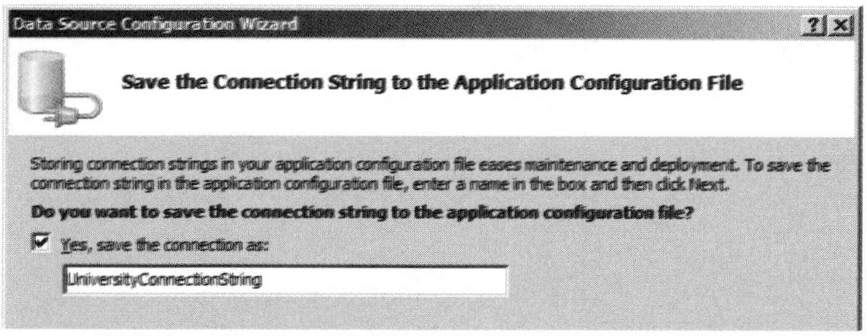

Figure 14.7 Saving the *Connection* string, step 5.

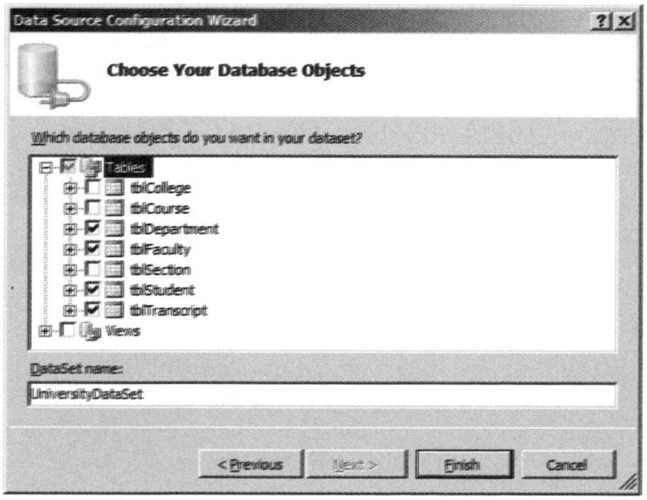

Figure 14.8 Selecting database tables for a *Data Source*, step 6.

9. In the *Add Connection* dialog box that opens, browse for and select the University database file (the files for this chapter are available on the book Web site). Click *Test Connection* to verify the connection to the University database. Click *OK* (see Figure 14.6).

10. Visual Studio will ask if we would like to copy the database to the current project folder. Click *Yes* to copy the database. Click *Next*.

11. On the *Save the Connection String to the Application Configuration File* page, make sure to save the connection string with its default name. It is a good practice to save the connection string, which can be then modified from the configuration file if we decide to alter the location of the project (see Figure 14.7). Click *Next*.

12. Expand the *Tables* node on the *Choose your Database Objects* page, and select the student, department, transcript, and faculty tables. Click *Finish* (see Figure 14.8).

The *UniversityDataSet* is added to the application, and all the selected tables appear in the Data Sources Window (see Figure 14.9). The Data Sources Window serves as a common place for all the data-related objects. We will explore its features as we proceed into the chapter.

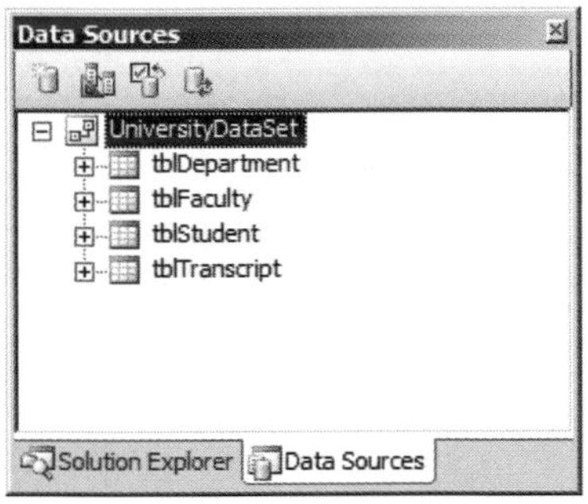

Figure 14.9 The Data Sources Window with *Data Sources*.

Referring back to the top-level processes of database application development, we have followed the first process thus far, creating a connection to the database. Through the *Data Source Configuration Wizard*, we have established a connection between our application and the University database. We also have the *Data Sources* we will use in the rest of the chapter.

Add a DataGridView Control to Display the Student Table   In this step, we continue the database application development process and bring the data from the student table, store it in a *DataSet*, and then display it on *Form1*. Interestingly, we will perform all three of these processes on one mouse click. This step covers the following How-to topics:

- How-to: display data in a DataGridView control.
- How-to: use ToolStrip control for navigation.

13. In the Data Sources Window, locate and drag the student table onto *Form1*. This should create the data-bind DataGridView control along with a ToolStrip at the top of the form. The ToolStrip provides navigational controls (move to previous, next, first or last record) and controls for adding/deleting records and saving data (see Figure 14.10).

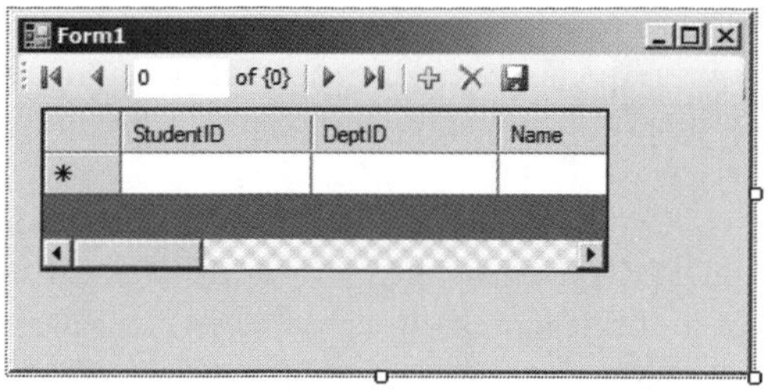

Figure 14.10 Drag-and-Drop to create data-bind DataGridView control.

This drag-and-drop also generated a *UniversityDataSet*, *TblStudentTableAdapter*, *TblStudent BindingSource*, and *TblStudentBindingNavigator* objects in the Component tray (see Figure 14.11).

Figure 14.11 Snapshot of the Component tray after adding the student table.

Test the Application

14. Press Ctrl + F5 to run the application.

15. Test the ToolStrip functionality by navigating through the student records. We can also navigate through student records using the DataGridView control alone (see Figure 14.12).

16. Alter values in the DataGridView control, and click on the *Save* button in the Tool-Strip. This allows us to modify the data in the DataGridView. (We discuss database updates in the next chapter.)

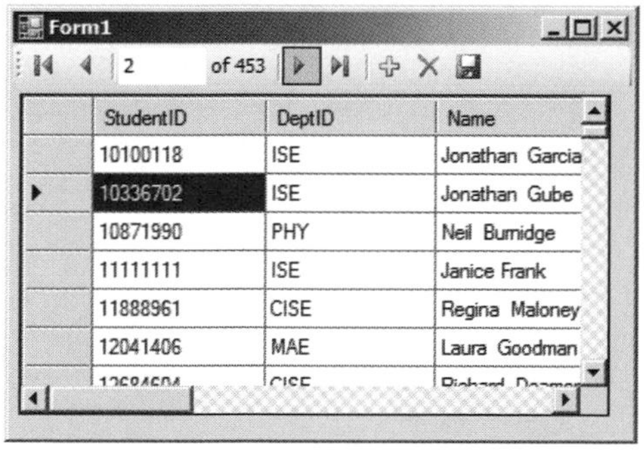

Figure 14.12 Running an application with DataGridView and ToolStrip controls.

Property Window Review (DataGridView Control) During the step in which we dragged and dropped the student table from the Data Sources Windows, the drag-and-drop not only created a DataGridView control, *TableAdapter*, *DataSet*, and other related objects, but also configured them to enable us to run the application. In this step, we review these auto-set properties to better understand the application development process.

A query, **SELECT * FROM** tblStudent, is auto generated in the *TblStudentTableAdapter* object. (Refer to Section 15.4 for how to view queries in a *TableAdapter*.) The code for the

Form1_Load event is auto-generated (reviewed in the next step). This code executes the SQL query at runtime and brings the result into the *UniversityDataSet*. The DataGridView control is already auto-configured and bound to the *DataSet* using the *TblStudentBindingSource*. To verify this binding, do the following:

17. Click the smart tag on the DataGridView control to view its Tasks list. Find that the *DataSource* property is set to the *TblStudentBindingSource* (see Figure 14.13).

Also notice that the *Enable Adding*, *Enable Editing*, and *Enable Deleting* options are checked. These options forced three buttons on the ToolStrip control to allow the user to add new records, save existing records, and delete records from the DataGridView control.

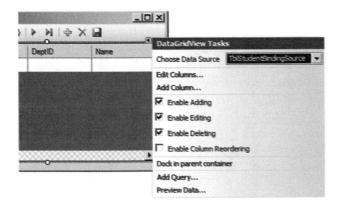

Figure 14.13 Tasks list of a DataGridView control.

Code Review

In this final step, we review the auto-generated code that was created when we dragged the student table from the Data Sources Window. This step covers the following How-to topic:

■ How-to: fill a *DataTable* with data.

18. Double click anywhere on the form to open the code behind the form.

Figure 14.14 shows the code that handles the *Form1_Load* event. In Line 19, the *Fill* method of the *TblStudentTableAdapter* is called with the table to be populated as its input parameter. This subroutine executes a *Select* SQL query to fill the *UniversityDataSet*'s *tblStudent* data table with student records. (To read more about *DataSet* architecture and *DataTables*, refer to Section 15.8.)

```
14    Private Sub Form1_Load(ByVal sender As System.Object, _
15    ByVal e As System.EventArgs) Handles MyBase.Load
16        'TODO: This line of code loads data into the
17        'UniversityDataSet.tblStudent' table. You can move,
18        'or remove it, as needed.
19        Me.TblStudentTableAdapter.Fill _
20        (Me.UniversityDataSet.tblStudent)
21
22    End Sub
```

Figure 14.14 The *Form1_Load* event populating the student *DataTable*

14.4 *Auto-Generated Objects in the Component Tray*

We saw that four objects—a *TableAdapter*, *DataSet*, *BindingSource*, and *BindingNavigator*—got added to the Component tray when we dragged the student table node from the Data Sources Window onto *Form1*. In this section, we briefly discuss these objects.

TableAdapter Object A *TableAdapter* object is the host for SQL queries. Corresponding to each query, it has a *Fill* method. The specified *Fill* method executes an SQL query and fills either a *DataSet* or *DataTable* object. For example, the *TblStudentTableAdapter* has a single SQL query and a default *Fill* method. The *TblStudentTableAdapter* executes the Select SQL query and fills the *tblStudent* data table of *UniversityDataSet* (for detailed architecture and functionalities of a *TableAdapter* object, refer to Sections 15.4–15.6.)

DataSet Object A *DataSet* acts as an in-memory data repository. In other words, *DataSets* are simply in-memory relational databases. A *DataSet*, like a relational database, can have any number of *DataTables*. Its *DataTables* are populated using a *TableAdapter*, by means of results of SQL queries. For example, *UniversityDataSet* has *tblStudent*, *tblDepartment*, *tblFaculty*, and *tblTranscript* DataTables storing query results related to these tables (for detailed architecture of a *DataSet* object, refer to Section 15.6.)

BindingSource Object A *BindingSource* object is also a part of the ADO .NET collection. It is designed to simplify the process of binding Windows controls to a database. It is essentially a wrapper that, on one hand, allows controls to bind to it and, on the other hand, communicates with the DataSets (see Figure 14.15). *BindingSource* is the mediator between a Windows control (for example, the DataGridView control) and a *DataSet* (for example, the *UniversityDataSet*). For instance, *TblStudentDataGridView*'s *DataSource* property is set to the *TblStudentBindingSource*. Further, the *DataSources* property of *TblStudentBindingSource* is set to *UniversityDataSet*, and its *DataMember* property is set to *tblStudent*. Thus, the student DataGridView gets its data from *TblStudentBindingSource*, and *TblStudentBindingSource* gets that data from *tblStudent* data table inside the *UniversityDataSet*.

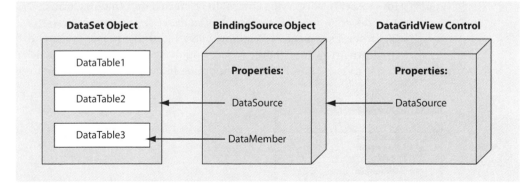

Figure 14.15 *BindingSource* object—work diagram.

BindingNavigator Object A *BindingNavigator* object is also a part of the ADO .NET suite. It is the navigation and data manipulation GUI for data-bind controls. A *BindingNavigator* control enables users to navigate through and manipulate data on Windows forms with the help of a ToolStrip control.

14.5 *Hands-On Tutorial: Displaying Data in Individual Windows Controls*

In the previous hands-on tutorial, we displayed the student table of University database in the DataGridView control. In this section, we again display the student table, but this time, each column of the student table will be displayed in an individual control on *Form1*. This means that, unlike the DataGridView control, the user will be able to view one student record at a time and must use the ToolStrip's navigation feature in order to browse through student records. Figure 14.16 shows an illustration displaying a student record at a time on a Windows form.

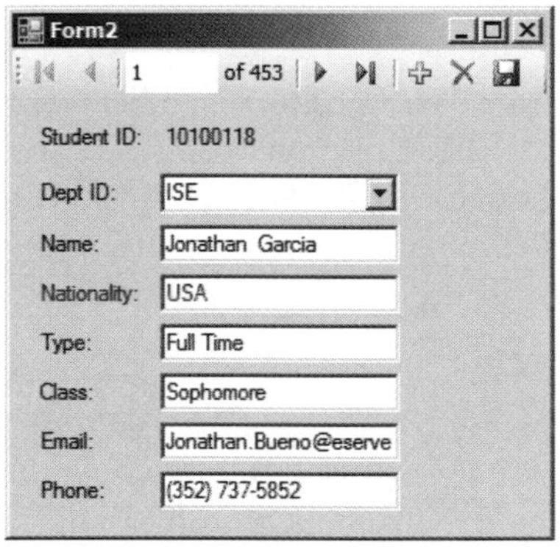

Figure 14.16 Student table displayed in a record at a time fashion.

Setting the Controls to be Created   In this step, we use the Data Sources Window to set the displaying controls for each column or field of the student table. This step covers the following How-to topics:

- How-to: display data in individual Windows controls.
- How-to: set the displaying control to be created on Windows forms.
    1. Add a new form (*Form2*) to the *DatabaseConnectivity* application.
    2. In the Data Sources Window, select the student table node, and click the drop-down arrow to select the *Details* option (see Figure 14.17). The default is the Data-GridView control (we saw this option in the previous hands-on tutorial).

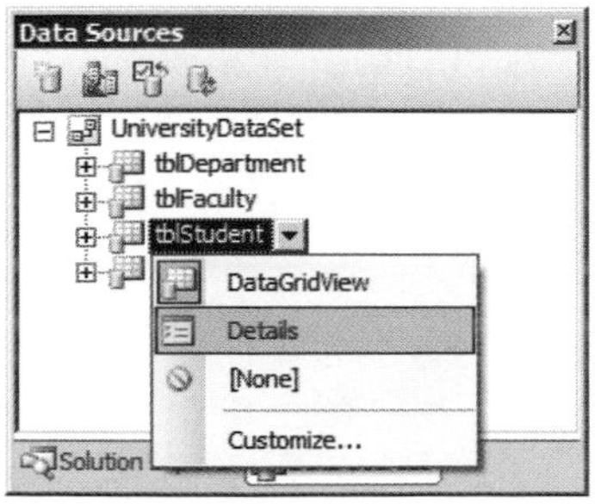

Figure 14.17 Selecting the *Details* option for a table display.

3. Expand the *tblStudent* node in the Data Sources Window. We now see individual columns of the student table. For each column, use its drop-down arrow to set the displaying control (see Figure 14.18).

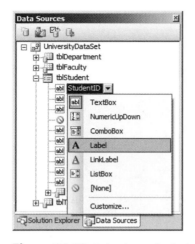

Figure 14.18 Selecting a displaying control for individual columns of a table.

4. Choose the controls for all the columns as shown in Figure 14.19. Note that if we choose the option *None* for a column, that column will not be displayed on the form.

5. Now drag the *tblStudent* node from the Data Sources Window onto *Form2* to create individual data-bind controls for each selected column. These controls are accompanied by an appropriately titled Label control on the form, as shown in Figure 14.20. Alternatively, we can also drag-and-drop individual columns onto the form to achieve the same result.

Note that Visual Studio did not create any new *TableAdapter*, *DataSet*, or *BindingSource* objects for *Form2*. Instead, it efficiently utilized the existing objects (from previous hands-on tutorial) in the Component tray.

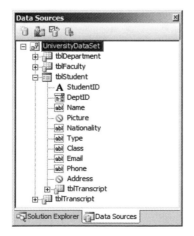

Figure 14.19 Individual displaying controls for the columns of the student table.

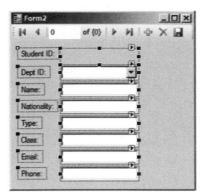

Figure 14.20 Individual controls shown in form's Design View.

Test the Application

6. Set *Form2* as the start-up form (use Project menu to open the application property tab). Press Ctrl + F5 to run the application. The first record displayed is shown in Figure 14.16.
7. Use the ToolStrip on top of the form to navigate through the student records. Edit the value of any field of a student record, and click on the *Save* button to test its functionality.

Property Window Review (Windows Controls)   As in the previous hands-on tutorial, we review some of the auto-set properties that enabled successful execution of our application.

8. Select the TextBox control for the *Name* field, and navigate to its *DataBindings* property in the Property Window (see Figure 14.21).

Note that the *Text* property of the *Name* TextBox is associated with the *Name* column from the *TblStudentBindingSource*. This is how we are able to view the data from the *Name* column of the student table in the TextBox control on the form. This association is called *Data binding*.

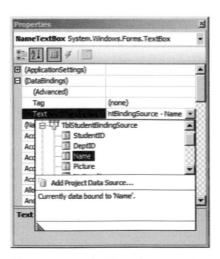

Figure 14.21 Data binding properties for the *Name* column's TextBox

Summary

- **Data binding** is an association between properties of Windows controls and BindingSource Objects.
- Displaying data on a Windows form:
  1. Add a Data Source using the Data Source Configuration Wizard.
  2. Choose the table node to be displayed from the Data Sources Window. Use the drop-down arrow to select either the DataGridView or Details option. For Details options, collapse the table node. For each column under the head node, choose its display control type from the drop-down list.
  3. Drag-and-drop the table node on the form to create a DataGridView control or individual selected controls, a ToolStrip control, and related objects in the Component tray.

14.6 *Hands-On Tutorial: Binding Data to Existing Controls*

We know that if we drag-and-drop a column from the Data Sources Window, it creates the pre-assigned data-bind displaying control for that column. We can also drag a column from the Data Sources Window onto existing controls (controls that are already on a form) at any time during the development process to bind an existing control to a column. If a control is already data-bind to a column, its data binding is reset to the column that was dragged onto it most recently. In this hands-on tutorial, we display the student picture on the Windows form. We add a PictureBox control to the form and then bind to the *Picture* column from the student table.

Add a PictureBox Control to the Form

1. Continue with the Windows form created in the previous hands-on tutorial. Drag-and-drop a PictureBox control from the *Common Controls* tab of the Toolbox onto the right of the existing controls on *Form2* (see Figure 14.22).
2. Verify that the *Image* property of the PictureBox control has the default value *None*.

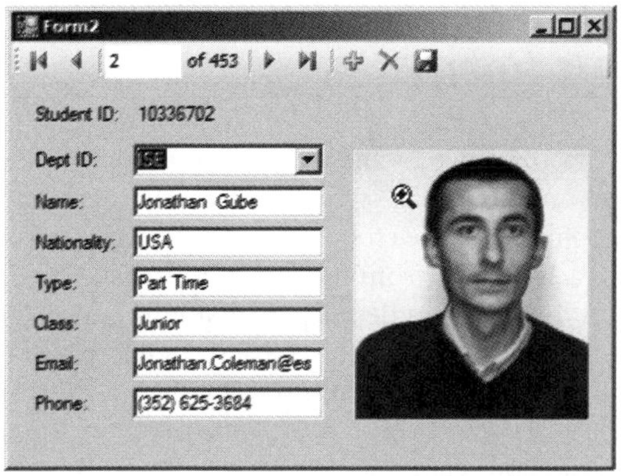

Figure 14.22 Running application with data-bind PictureBox control.

Associate *Picture* Column from the Student Table   This step covers the following How-to topics:

- How-to: bind data to existing controls.
- How-to: display pictures from the database on Windows forms.
    3. Drag-and-drop the *Picture* column under the student table node from the Data Sources Window onto the PictureBox control.

Test the Application

4. Press Ctrl + F5 to run the application. Test the data binding for PictureBox by navigating through student records using the ToolStrip (Figure 14.22).

Property Window Review (PictureBox)

5. Now reopen the Property Window for the PictureBox control and review its *Image* property. It is now associated with the *Picture* column from the *TblStudentBindingSource* (Figure 14.23).

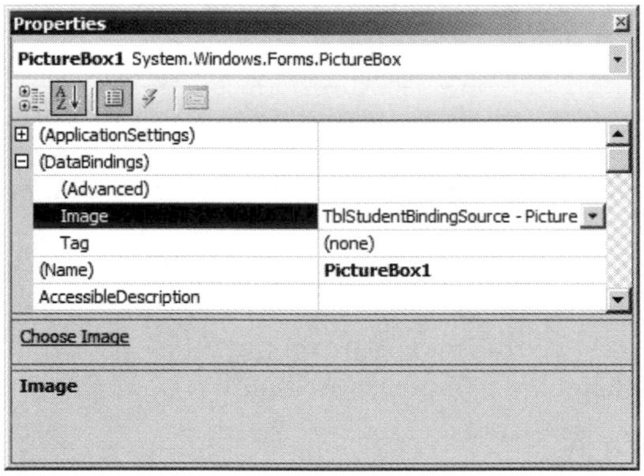

Figure 14.23 Data-bind *Image* property for the PictureBox control.

14.7 *Hands-On Tutorial: Displaying Related Data on a Windows Form*

Until now, we have displayed data from a single table on a form. In many scenarios, we may want to work with data that comes from more than one table and, often, with data from related tables. For example, as we display columns of the student table, we might also want to display course and grades information for each student from the transcript table. Thus, as we navigate through the student records, we not only see a student's personal information but also see her transcript. The relationship between the student and the transcript table is also termed *parent-child relationship*. The student table is a parent and the transcript table is a child. In other words, the student table owns a primary key, *StudentID*, which is a foreign key in the transcript table (refer to Chapters 4 and 6 for discussion on relational keys).

Add the Related Transcript Table to the Form In this step, we add the transcript table to *Form2* to create a parent-child relationship. This step covers the following How-to topic:

■ How-to: display related data in a database application.

To create a DataGridView control that displays the transcript (child records) for each student (parent record), do the following:

1. In the Data Sources Window, expand the student table node and select the last node, the transcript table node (see Figure 14.24), which itself is expandable, and drag-and-drop it onto the bottom of *Form2*.

Warning: If we drag the transcript table directly under the *UniversityDataSet*, we will not be establishing a parent-child relationship, but will rather be simply adding another un-linked table on the form. Note that a new DataGridView control, the *TblTranscriptBindingSource*, and the *TblTranscriptTableAdapter* are added to the Component tray (see Figure 14.25).

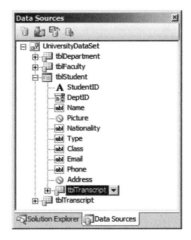

Figure 14.24 Adding related tables from the Data Sources Window.

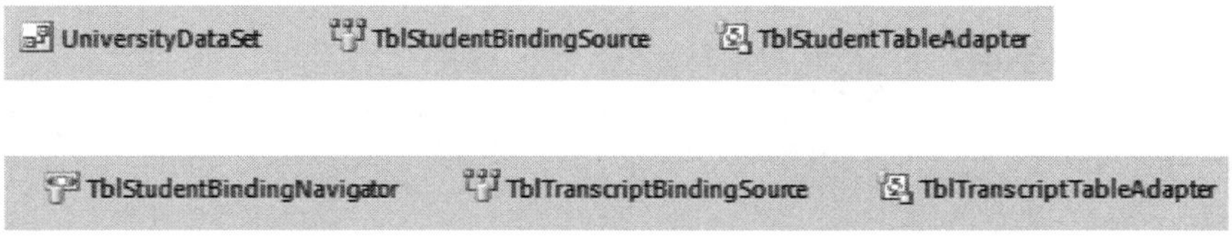

Figure 14.25 Component Tray after adding related transcript table.

Edit the Transcript DataGridView In this step, we edit the DataGridView for the related transcript table on the form. Specifically, we show how to edit columns of a DataGridView control by removing an unwanted *StudentID* column. We also show how to modify a DataGridView's properties to enhance its appearance. We assign different back color and fore color to alternating rows of the grid (see Figure 14.30). This step covers the following How-to topics:

- How-to: edit the columns of a DataGridView control.
- How-to: enhance the appearance of a DataGridView control.
    2. Select the transcript DataGridView and click its smart tag to view the Tasks list. Select the *Edit Column* option from the list (see Figure 14.26). This should open the *Edit Columns* dialog box.
    3. Select the *StudentID* column and click *Remove* to delete the column (see Figure 14.27). In general, we can use the *Edit Columns* dialog box to edit properties of existing columns, such as column heading, width, and more.
    4. Now select the DataGridView and navigate to the Property Window.
    5. Select the *AlternatingRowsDefaultCellStyle* property and click the *Build* button (. . .) to edit alternating cell style (see Figure 14.28).
    6. Choose the *BackColor* and *ForeColor* properties in the *CellStyle Builder* dialog box as shown in Figure 14.29.

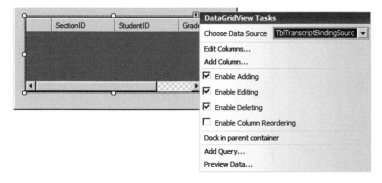

Figure 14.26 Invoking DataGridView's *Edit Columns* dialog box.

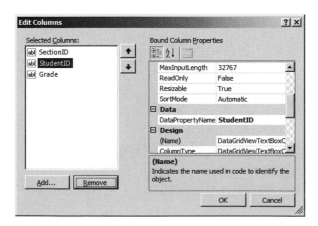

Figure 14.27 Removing *StudentID* column from the DataGridView control.

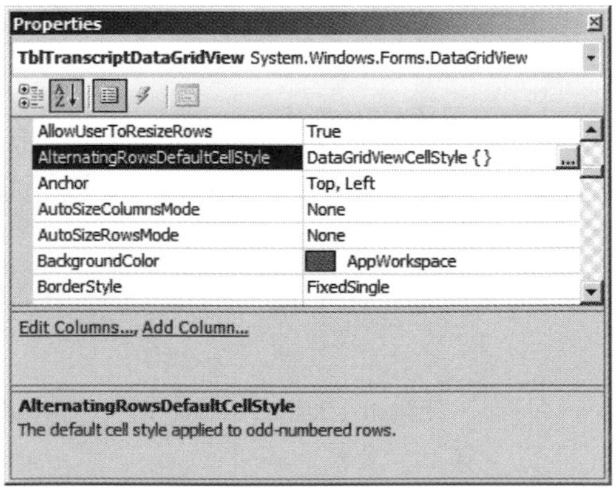

Figure 14.28 Styling alternate rows of a DataGridView control.

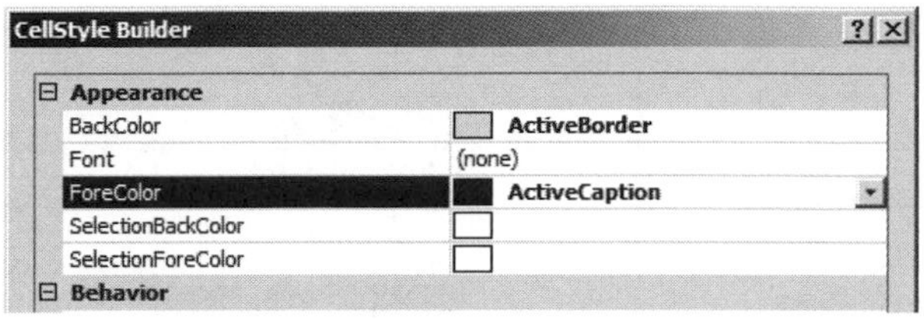

Figure 14.29 Setting *BackColor* and *ForeColor* properties for alternating rows.

Test the Application

7. Press Ctrl + F5 to run the application. Test the parent-child relationship by navigating through student records using the ToolStrip (see Figure 14.30).

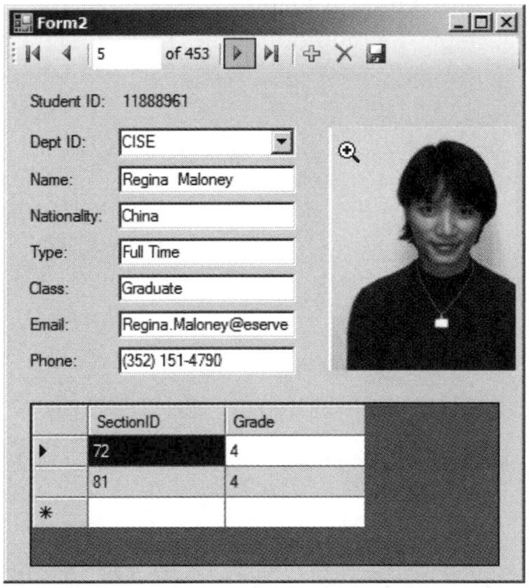

Figure 14.30 Running application with parent-child relationship.

Property Window Review (Foreign Key Linkage)

When we dragged the related transcript table on *Form2*, the parent-child relationship was established automatically. We now look into properties of *BindingSource* objects to review this establishment.

8. Select the *TblStudentBindingSource* object (parent) from the Component tray and open the Property Window. Note that the *DataSource* property of this object is set to the *UniversityDataSet*, and the *DataMember* property is set to the *tblStudent* data table (see Figure 14.31).

9. Now select the *TblTranscriptBindingSource* object (child) from the Component tray and open the Property Window. Note that the *DataSource* property of this object is set to the *TblStudentBindingSource* (the parent table's *BindingSource*) rather than to the *UniversityDataSet*. The *DataMember* property is set to *tblStudenttblTranscript*, which is the name of the *Data Relation* object that relates parent and child tables (see Figure 14.32).

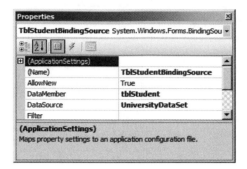

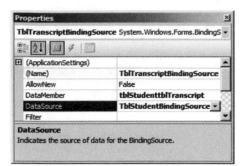

Figure 14.31 *DataSource* property of parent *BindingSource*.

Figure 14.32 *DataSource* property of child *BindingSource*.

Code Review (Figure 14.33) Since we added one more table on the form, Visual Studio added one more line of code (similar to the code shown in Figure 14.14) to execute the appropriate SQL query and fill the *tblTranscript* data table. The additional lines (17–18) in the following code snippet are self-explanatory.

```
13  Private Sub Form2_Load(ByVal sender As System.Object, _
14  ByVal e As System.EventArgs) Handles MyBase.Load
15      'TODO: This line of code loads data into the
16      'UniversityDataSet.tblTranscript' table.
17      Me.TblTranscriptTableAdapter.Fill _
18      (Me.UniversityDataSet.tblTranscript)
19      'TODO: This line of code loads data into the
20      'UniversityDataSet.tblStudent' table.
21      Me.TblStudentTableAdapter.Fill _
22      (Me.UniversityDataSet.tblStudent)
23  End Sub
```

Figure 14.33 Code for *Form2_Load* event populating the transcript and student tables.

Summary

- The meaning of the data binding properties of any control is as follows:
  - **Data Source:** Who (or which *DataSet*) is providing the data?
  - **Data Member:** Which member (a *column* or *table*) of the *Data Source* is providing the data?
- Displaying related records on a form is achieved by setting the *DataSource* property of the child *BindingSource* to the parent *BindingSource* (not the child table) and setting the *Data Member* property of the child *BindingSource* to the *DataRelation* that ties the parent and child tables together.

14.8 DataGridView Control

DataGridView control is one of the most used data controls. We use DataGridView to do the following: (i) Display data, (ii) Format data, (iii) Sort data, (iv) Update and delete data, and (v) Select and navigate through data records.

In this section, we cover some of the important properties of a DataGridView control, including data binding and sorting operation related properties.

14.8.1   DataGridView Tasks

The smart tag of a DataGridView control shows some of its important properties. Using this menu, we can quickly access the *DataSource* property of the control and choose an appropriate source from the drop-down list. We can also access or add a new column to DataGridView's column collection. The tasks list also allows us to perform enable or disable edit, delete, and insertion operations by simply selecting or deselecting the corresponding check boxes (see Figure 14.13 and Figure 14.26).

14.8.2   Sorting with a DataGridView

DataGridView offers a simple way to view the data in different sorting orders. When we click any column heading in the grid, a small triangular icon appears in the column, indicating its sorting order. Clicking the column heading one more time flips the sorting order (see Figure 14.34). Thus, we can sort the data in the grid based on any column in either ascending or descending order.

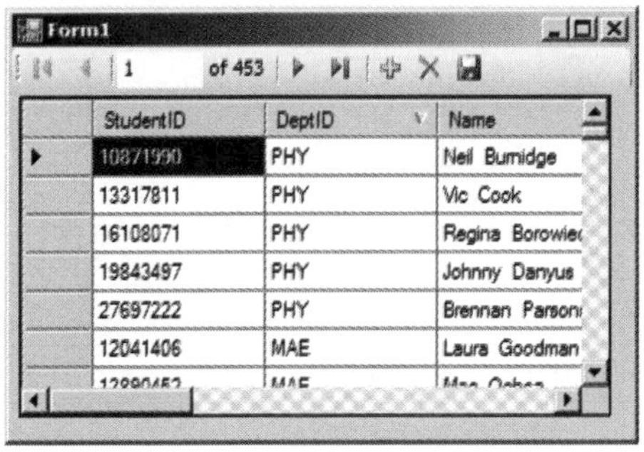

Figure 14.34 Sorting data by *DeptID* column in descending order.

14.8.3   Data Binding

Binding data to the DataGridView control is intuitive and straightforward. We specify the source of the data by setting DataGridView's *DataSource* property to a *BindingSource*. For example, the *DataSource* property of the *TblStudentDataGridView* is set to the *TblStudentDataBindingSource* (see Figure 14.35). If the data source we are binding the grid with has multiple tables, we set the *DataMember* property of the DataGridView to a specific table. If a *TableAdapter* has multiple queries, we set the *DataMember* property to indicate the source query (see Section 14.9 for an example).

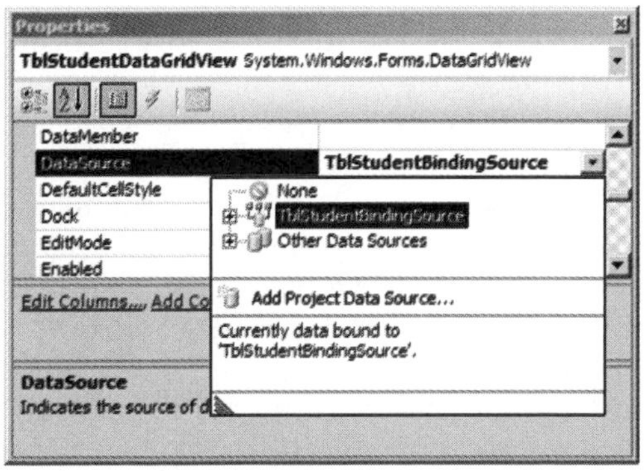

Figure 14.35 *DataSource* and *DataMember* properties of a DataGridView control.

14.8.4 DataGridView Control Properties

In this section, we tabulate a few essential properties of a DataGridView control.

Table 14.1 Essential properties of a DataGridView control.

Name	Description
BackColor	Gets or sets the background color for the control.
BackgroundColor	Gets or sets the background color of the grid.
ColumnCount	Gets or sets the number of columns displayed in the grid.
Columns	Gets a collection that contains all the columns in the control.
CurrentCell	Gets or sets the currently active cell.
CurrentRow	Gets the row containing the current cell.
DataMember	Gets or sets the name of the table in the data source for which the grid is displaying data.
DataSource	Gets or sets the data source for which the grid is displaying data.
Font	Gets or sets the font of the text displayed by the grid.
ForeColor	Gets or sets the foreground color of the grid.
Item	Gets or sets the cell located at the intersection of the specified row and column.
Name	Gets or sets the name of the control.
ReadOnly	Gets a value indicating whether the user can edit a cell's data.
RowCount	Gets or sets the number of rows displayed in the grid.
Rows	Gets a collection that contains all the rows in the grid.
Visible	Gets or sets a value indicating whether the control is displayed.
Width	Gets or sets the width of the control.

14.9 *Hands-On Tutorial: Creating a Search Form*

Often we are not interested in the entire table or entire join of one or more tables. Rather, we prefer to display only the data that satisfies some specified criteria. For example, instead of displaying all the student records from the University database, we might find it desirable to filter the student records based on some criteria (for example, students from a particular department) and display only the resulting records. In this scenario, a user enters information (a department name) into a form, and then a query is executed with the user's input as a parameter. Thus, only the data that satisfies the criteria value entered by the user is fetched and displayed on a form.

A query that takes in some criteria as parameters and retrieves records that satisfy the criteria is termed a *parameterized query*. Such queries are very similar to parameter queries we have seen in Chapter 8. The only difference between the two is that, in the MS Access environment, we used square brackets ([ ]) to indicate parameters, while in Visual Studio we will use a question mark (?) to indicate the same. Parameterized queries help to improve the efficiency of database applications. Instead of bringing the entire table into memory, we fetch only the portion of the data that interests us, making our application fast and efficient.

In this section, we filter the existing view of the student record in the DataGridView by a user-specified department (see running application in Figure 14.44).

Adding a Parameterized Query to the TableAdapter   In this step, we demonstrate how to create (or add) a parameter query to a *TableAdapter*. We make use of the existing *TblStudent-TableAdapter* in the *DatabaseConnectivity* application and add a new parameterized query to it. We also show how ToolStrip gets added for a parameter query to accept query parameters from the user. This step covers the following How-to topics:

- How-to: add multiple queries to a TableAdapter.
- How-to: create an SQL statement that returns rows.
- How-to: create parameterized queries in TableAdapter.
- How-to: create a ToolStrip for parameterized queries.

To add a parameterized query to a TableAdapter, do the following:

1. Add a form (*Form3*) to the *DatabaseConnectivity* application.
2. Drag and drop *tblStudent* from the DataSources Window to the form. This creates a DataGridView control (*TblStudentDataGridView*) as we saw in Figure 14.10.
3. Select the DataGridView control, and choose the *Add Query* option from the Tasks list of the DataGridView control (see Figure 14.36).

Alternatively, we can also add a query to a *TableAdapter* by first selecting an adapter object from the Component tray and then choosing the *Add Query* option from its Tasks list as shown in Figure 14.37.

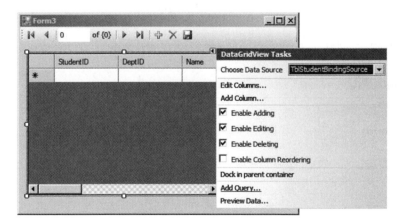

Figure 14.36 Adding a query to a *TableAdapter* through data bound DataGridView.

Figure 14.37 Adding a query to a *TableAdapter* using its Tasks list.

4. This opens the *Search Criteria Builder* dialog box. Name the new parameter query "FillByDept." Enter the SQL query as shown in Figure 14.38 in the *Query Text* area to construct a parameterized query.

5. Click the *Query Builder* button at the bottom of the *Search Criteria Builder* dialog box.

6. We can see the SQL query we specified in the text area in the *Query Builder*. Also, notice that the *Filter* column in the second pane shows a "=?" for the *DeptID* row. Click the *Execute Query* button to test the query (see Figure 14.39).

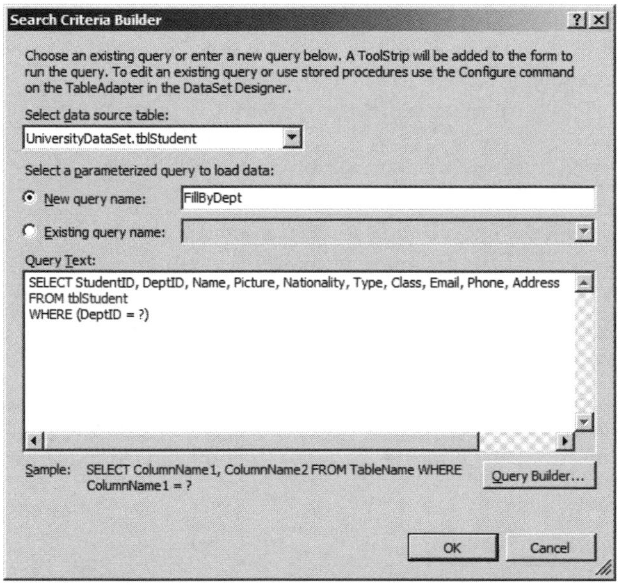

Figure 14.38 Adding queries in *Search Criteria Builder* dialog box.

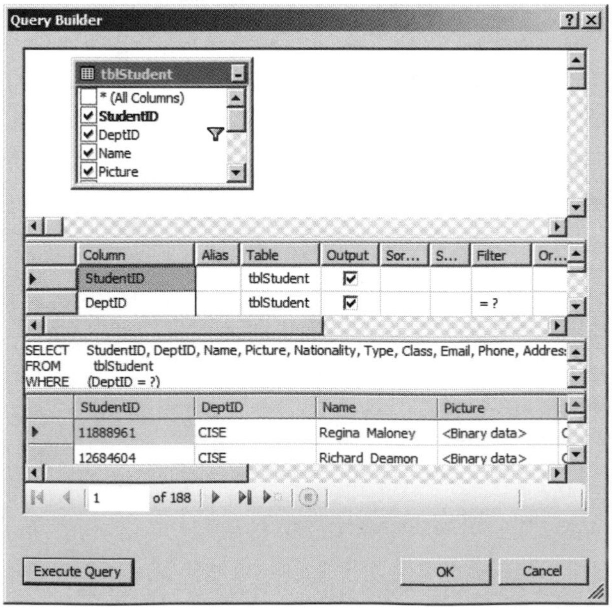

Figure 14.39 Working with the *Query Builder* to design SQL queries.

7. A *Query Parameters* dialog box opens. To test the query execution, we need to enter a sample value for the parameter specified by the "?" symbol in the WHERE clause (in this case, the *DeptID*). Test the query with the example "CISE" value and click *OK* (see Figure 14.40).

8. Preview the results of the query in the *Query Builder* itself. Notice that all the records that are displayed have *CISE* as the *DeptID*. Click *OK*.

9. We have now added a parameterized query, *FillByDept*, to the *TblStudent-TableAdapter*. This automatically creates the ToolStrip control for *DeptID* input at the top of *Form3* (see Figure 14.41). We can also see that a ToolStrip control has been added to the Component tray.

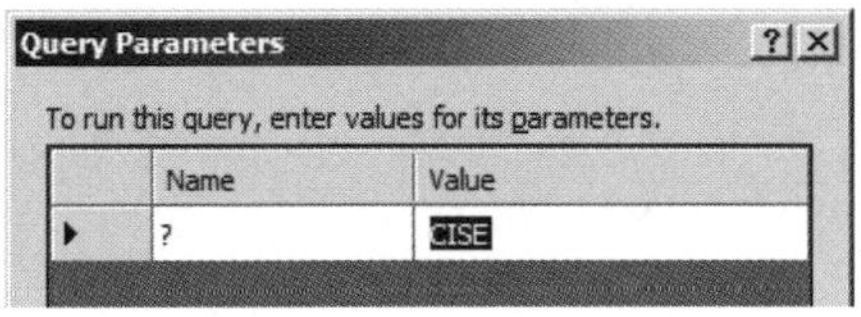

Figure 14.40 Assigning a sample value to a query parameter.

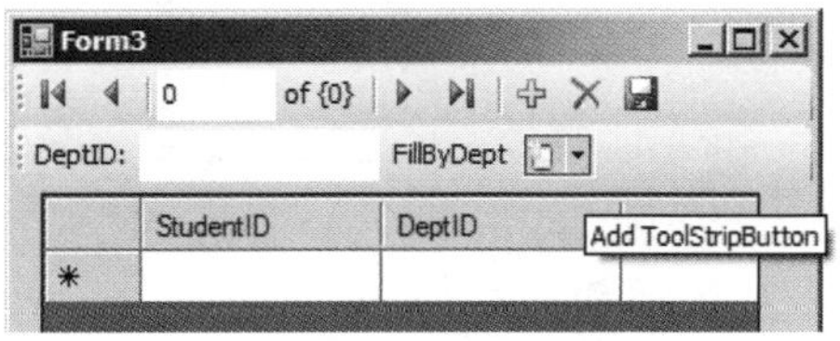

Figure 14.41 A ToolStrip control for a parameterized query.

Preview Data for Newly Added Query   We saw that we can preview query results in the *Query Builder*. Outside the *Query Builder*, we can use the *Preview Data* option from a Data-GridView's tasks list to preview the results. This step covers the following How-to topic:

■ How-to: preview query results outside the *Query Builder*.

10. Use the DataGridView's smart tag to view its Tasks list, and choose the *Preview Data* option from the list.

11. In the *Preview Data* dialog box, first choose the query we want to execute. In this step, we choose the query *FillByDept* from the drop-down list as shown in Figure 14.42.

12. Then provide the testing parameter for the query as "CISE" and click *Preview*. The dialog box resembles Figure 14.43.

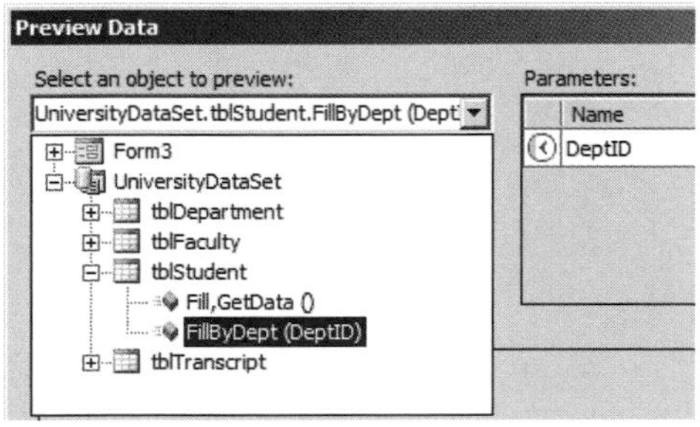

Figure 14.42 Selecting query in the *Preview Data* dialog box.

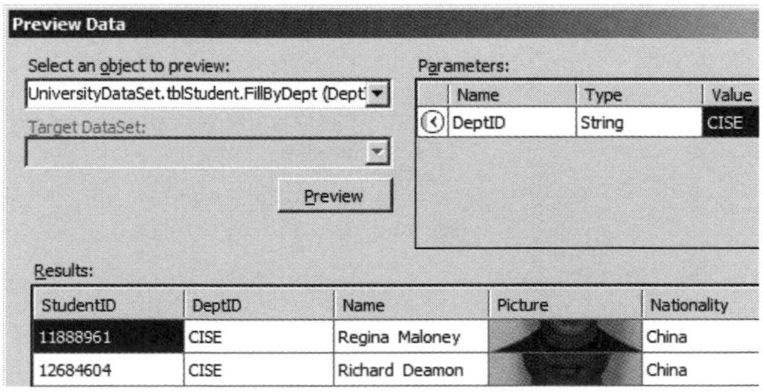

Figure 14.43 The *Preview Data* dialog box in action.

Test the Application

> **13.** Set *Form3* as the start-up form of the application, and press Ctrl + F5 to run the application. Test the search or filtering functionality by entering different *DeptID*s in the *FillByDept* ToolStrip.

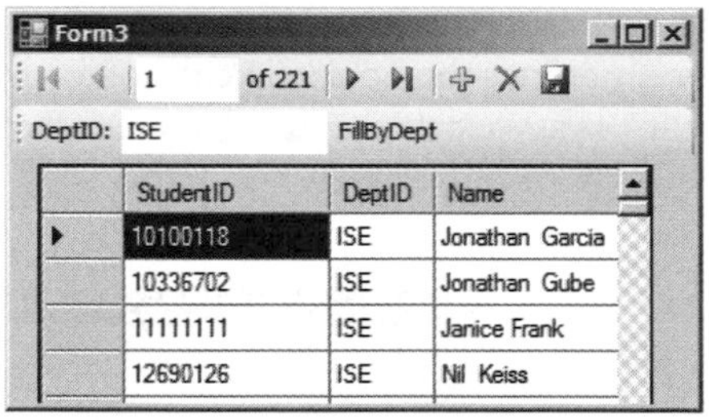

Figure 14.44 Running *Form3* with the search functionality.

Code Review   This step covers the following How-to topic:

■ How-to: execute an SQL statement with parameters.

> **14.** Open the Code Window for *Form3* either by double-clicking on the form or by double-clicking the ToolStrip.

As expected, the Visual Studio auto-generated the *Click* event for the button on the ToolStrip control (see Figure 14.45). Line 28 executes the *FillByDept* query of the *TblStudentTableAdapter* and fills the *tblStudent* data table of the *UniversityDataSet*. The text value of the *DeptIDToolStripTextBox* is the query parameter, and it is given as input parameter to the *FillByDept* method. This causes the method to fetch the records of the students who belong to the department indicated by the *DeptID*, and passes as the method argument.

```
23    Private Sub FillByDeptToolStripButton_Click _
24    (ByVal sender As System.Object, _
25    ByVal e As System.EventArgs) _
26    Handles FillByDeptToolStripButton.Click
27        Try
28            Me.TblStudentTableAdapter.FillByDept _
29            (Me.UniversityDataSet.tblStudent, _
30            DeptIDToolStripTextBox.Text)
31        Catch ex As System.Exception
32            System.Windows.Forms.MessageBox.Show _
33            (ex.Message)
34        End Try
35
36    End Sub
```

Figure 14.45 Executing parameterized SQL statements.

14.10 *The Query Builder*

We used the *Query Builder* dialog box in the previous section to help us build SQL queries. The *Query Builder* is a *Query-By-Example* type dialog box similar to MS Access' query Design View. We can create or edit existing queries using the *Query Builder* in the same manner we did Access queries in Chapter 8.

The *Query Builder* dialog box is divided into four horizontal segments (see Figure 14.39). The top segment, *Table Pane*, displays and allows the addition or deletion of *DataTables* and their relationships. *Table Pane* holds the tables involved in the query (similar to the Access query Design View's Table Pane). We can check attributes from various tables in the Table Pane to move them to the second segment, *Design Grid*, which is similar to the Access query Design View's Design Grid. We can specify the sorting order, filter criteria, group by, and output value for the fields in the Design Grid.

The third segment of the dialog box, the *SQL View*, displays the SQL statement as we build the query in the Design Grid. We can alternatively write SQL queries as described in Chapter 9, and other segments automatically reflect the query design. The fourth segment displays a preview of the query output. Once we design the query, we can execute and preview query results by clicking *Execute Query* at the bottom-left of the dialog box.

14.11 *Hands-On Tutorial: Creating a Lookup Table*

Lookup operations are familiar to us. Recall from Chapter 6 the properties of MS Access table objects. In a table's Design View, we can use *Lookup Wizard* to lookup values for a column from other tables. For example, consider the *DeptID* field in the student table. When displaying the student table on *Form2*, in record at a time fashion, we used a ComboBox control to display the *DeptID* (see Figure 14.16). As we navigate through student records, only the current student's department is displayed. Hence, the user of the form does not know what other departments exist in the university. Having a list of all the available departments on the form might be handy for a person doing data entry when he or she has to associate a department for a new student. One way to support this functionality is to build the lookup table for the *DeptID* column on the form. Note that *DeptID* is a foreign key in the student table, and we will lookup its values in the department table, where it is a primary key. This concept is called the *lookup table*.

When presenting a list of departments, we may want to display the actual department name, as opposed to the *DeptID*. At the same time, we may want to keep *DeptID* as the value of the selection in the ComboBox control. For example, it is desirable to use the name "Industrial Engineering" while displaying to the user and use the *DeptID* value "ISE" when the *ComboBox. SelectedValue* is used. We achieve this using the data binding properties (*DisplayMember* and *ValueMember*) of a ComboBox control as discussed below.

Link the Department Table   In this step, we link the department table node from the Data Sources Window to the *DeptID* ComboBox control already present on *Form2*. This step covers the following How-to topic:

■ How-to: create a lookup table.

   1. Drag *tblDepartment* from the Data Sources Window directly onto the *DeptID* ComboBox control on Form2.

2. Note that the *DataSource* property of the *DeptID* ComboBox control is set to *TblDe-partmentBindingSource*. Two objects, *TblDepartmentBindingSource* and *TblDepart-mentTableAdapter*, are added to the Component tray (see Figure 14.46).

3. Set the *DisplayMember* property of the *DeptID* ComboBox control to *Name* and ver-ify that the *ValueMemeber* property is set to the *DeptID* column. The new Compo-nent tray objects will query and bring the names of the departments as a list into the *DeptID* ComboBox control.

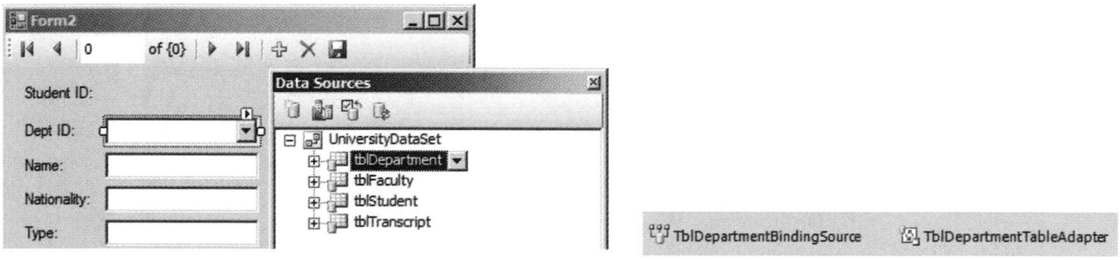

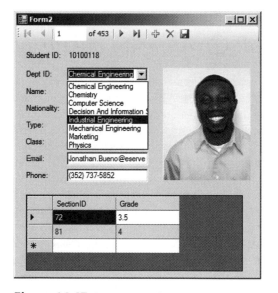

Figure 14.46 Creating a department lookup table.

Figure 14.47 Running application with a lookup table.

Test the Application

4. Set *Form2* as the start-up form, and press Ctrl + F5 to run the application (see Fig-ure 14.47).

5. Navigate through the student records to note that the ComboBox still displays the department to which the student belongs. If we use the drop-down arrow on the ComboBox, we also see the list of all the departments in the University database.

Property Window Review (ComboBox Control)   When we dragged the department table node from the Data Sources Window onto the *DeptID* ComboBox control, it assigned appropriate values for various properties of the ComboBox control to give us lookup table functionality. We review those properties in this step.

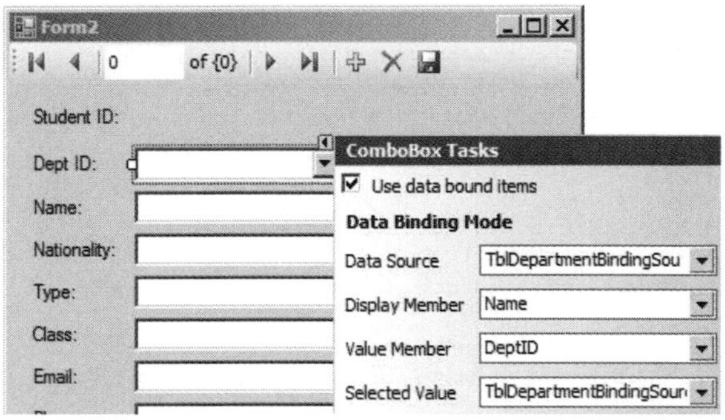

Figure 14.48 Tasks for ComboBox with a lookup table.

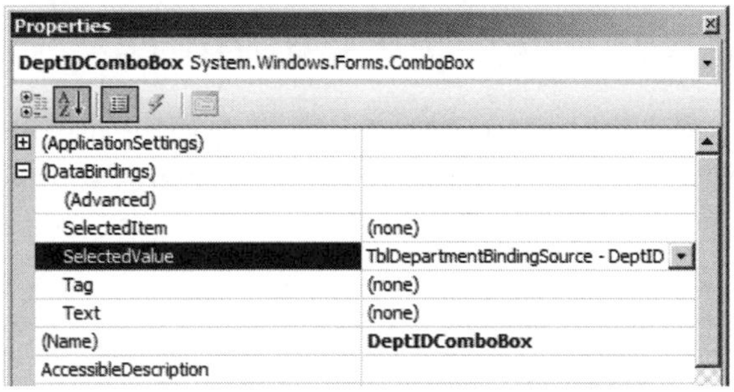

Figure 14.49 Property Window for *DeptID* ComboBox control.

> **6.** Open the tasks list for the *DeptID* ComboBox control (see Figure 14.48).

Note that the *DataSource* property of a ComboBox control is set to *TblDepartmentBindingSource*, the *DisplayMember* property (the field that gets displayed to the user) is set to the department's *Name* column, and the *ValueMember* property (the field that gives value to the ComboBox control) is set to the *DeptID* column.

If the ComboBox control is now associated with the department table, then how does it still display the department name that student belongs to when we navigate through student records?

> **7.** Open the Property Window for *DeptID* ComboBox control and locate its *Data Binding* section.

Note that the *SelectedValue* property of the ComboBox control is set to the *DeptID* column from the *TblStudentBindingSource* (see Figure 14.49). This enables selection of the appropriate department for the student as we navigate (refer to Section 14.12 for details of ComboBox control's data binding properties).

Code Review   The auto generated code for the lookup table is very simple. The only additions to the code in Figure 14.50 are lines 25–26, the call to the *Fill* method of *TblDepartmentTableAdapter*.

```
13      Private Sub Form2_Load(ByVal sender As System.Object, _
14      ByVal e As System.EventArgs) Handles MyBase.Load
15          'TODO: This line of code loads data into the
16          'UniversityDataSet.tblDepartment' table.
17          Me.TblDepartmentTableAdapter.Fill _
18          (Me.UniversityDataSet.tblDepartment)
19          'TODO: This line of code loads data into the
20          'UniversityDataSet.tblTranscript' table.
21          Me.TblTranscriptTableAdapter.Fill _
22          (Me.UniversityDataSet.tblTranscript)
23          'TODO: This line of code loads data into the
24          'UniversityDataSet.tblStudent' table.
25          Me.TblStudentTableAdapter.Fill _
26          (Me.UniversityDataSet.tblStudent)
27      End Sub
```

Figure 14.50 Code for *Form2_Load* event showing *Fill* method for lookup table.

14.12   *Data Binding Properties of a ComboBox Control*

The four main data binding properties of a ComboBox control we discussed in the previous hands-on tutorial are *DataSource*, *DisplayMember*, *ValueMember*, and *SelectedValue*. In this section, we tabulate more details about these properties.

Table 14.2 Data binding properties of a ComboBox control.

Data Source	Set it to the *BindingSource* object that will provide data for the ComboBox. Unlike DataGridView, *BindingSource* for ComboBox should contain a single table (simple binding).
Display Member	Set it to the field from the data source of a ComboBox that should be displayed to the user.
Value Member	Set it to the field from the data source from which the ComboBox should get its value. This value can be accessed in code through the property ComboBox.SelectedValue.
Selected Value	The value of a selection in the ComboBox. This property can be bound to any field in the project's *DataSet* as long as its value matches one or more values from the ComboBox's *ValueMember*. For example, we have the department table as the data source of the ComboBox with *DeptID* as the *ValueMember*. The *SelectedValue* property is set to the *DeptID* from the student table.

14.13   *In-Class Assignment*

In this section, we give an in-class assignment that is an extension of the student form we have developed in this chapter. Specifically, we work with the faculty table of the University database in the same manner we worked with the student table. However, we extend the application to illustrate how queries with multiple parameters are handled.

Develop an application that displays the list of faculty from the University database, both on DataGridView control and on individual controls. Show a faculty picture in the PictureBox control. Further, add a lookup table for the *DeptID* in an individual control on the form. Finally, add search functionality to the form to display only those faculty records for which the salary is greater than the user-entered salary value and the department is the department specified by the user. (*Hint*: Add a parameter query to the *TableAdapter* with two parameters.)

14.14 *Summary*

- The database applications can be roughly divided into three types: display-oriented, transaction-oriented, and communication-oriented applications.
- The database application development process can be summarized into the following steps, (i) Connect to the database using a *Connection* object, (ii) Fetch data using database queries in the *TableAdapter* object, (iii) Temporarily store the results in a *DataSet* object, (iv) Display data on a Windows form by binding Windows controls to *DataSet*, (v) Edit data in the application, (vi) Save data back in the database.
- We walked through the process of building a simple database application displaying the student table fields on the DataGridView control. We reviewed the auto-generated code and auto-set properties by Visual Studio.

- We also showed how the same data and columns can be displayed in individual controls on a form. We then extended this application to bind the PictureBox to the picture column of the student table.
- We further enhanced the application by adding a related transcript table to the form to display the courses and grades for each student record as we navigate through them.
- We have added a search or filter function to the form that displays only those student records belonging to the department specified by us in the ToolStrip.
- Finally, we have added a lookup table for the department field of the student table, which allows us to list all the department names via a drop-down list.

14.15 *Exercises*

14.15.1 Review Questions

1. What is ADO .NET?
2. What are database applications? How we can categorize them based on what they do with the data?
3. What are different top-level processes involved in a typical database application? Explain.
4. Summarize the steps we need to perform to show the database table on a form in a DataGridView control.
5. How can we individually choose the displaying controls for each column of a database table? How can we then display those controls on a form?
6. What are different controls and objects that are auto-created when we drag-and-drop tables from the Data Sources Window on a form?
7. How can we show the image field from the database table on a Windows form?
8. What are steps to display the related information on a form?
9. Write a short note on functionalities and properties of a DataGridView control.
10. Summarize the steps for creating search forms in our application.
11. What is the functionality of the *Query Builder* dialog box?
12. Explain how a lookup table works and when we would like to build such a table.
13. What are the steps to create a lookup table?
14. What are important data binding properties of a ComboBox control?

14.15.2 Hands-On Exercises

NOTE: *The database files for these hands-on exercises are available at: www.dssbooks.com.*

1. A hospital requires the creation of a single-form application to access their database and view doctor-wise listing of patient records. Use a Data-GridView control to list the first and last names of doctors. Use a related DataGridView control to display the details of the patient's (first name, last name, and disease) treated by the doctor currently selected in the first, doctor's DataGrid-View control. You need not provide any other functionality (use the *Hospital* database).

2. Megabucks, a banking company, is trying to automate its system, and it is currently hiring. You have applied for the position of database developer. In order to test your skills, they want you to create a simple database application that accesses their database and displays their customer records one at a time. It is sufficient to display the following information for each record (use the *Megabucks* database):

   a. First and last name

   b. Address

   c. Account number, current balance and total interest

3. A furniture company has a number of distribution centers. Each center is responsible for providing the required supplies for a number of retailers. The company keeps records of all the shipments made to the retailers through the different distribution centers. You are asked to design a single-form application that displays the following information about all the shipments made through the distribution centers (use the *Furniture* database).

   a. Product name, description, and price (sort price by ascending order).

   b. Number of items in each shipment and delivery date (sort delivery dates by descending order).

4. You are working on a project that implements a system to help people view information about a collection of books. Create a simple application that has a single form. Once the application starts up, the user should be able to view the following information about all the books available in the system (use the *Books* database).

   a. Title.

   b. Author's first and last name

   c. Publisher's name

   Provide a search feature based on publisher's name so that people can view books published by a specific publisher.

5. You have been asked to create a simple application that allows a user to view information about the instructors and offered courses at a certain university. The application should have a single form that contains two buttons, "View Course details" and "View Instructor Details." On the click of the "View Course Details" button and "View Instructor Details" button, the application should display the course details and instructor details, respectively (use the *School* database). Follow these steps:

   a. Create a *SchoolsApp* application. Add a Data-GridView control and two command buttons to Form1.

   b. Create a *DataSet* that has both the *Courses* and *Instructors* tables.

   c. Create two *Binding Sources* and set their data source to the above *DataSet*. Set their corresponding data members to the courses table and the instructors table, respectively.

   d. Write code in the *Click* event of each command button to set the *DataSource* property of the DataGridView control to the appropriate *Binding Source* created in the previous step.

6. Unlimited Airlines has asked you to create a simple application with the features listed below (use the *Airline* database).

   a. The user must be able to choose a certain flight from a list of all available flights.

   b. The system should be able to display all the customer reservations and preferences for a specific flight.

   Follow these steps:

   a. Create an *Airlines* application and add the *Flight* and *Reservations* tables to *Form1*.

   b. Create a DataGridView control for each table.

   c. Add a new parameterized query, *FillByFlightNo* that has the *FlightNo* as a parameter through the Tasks list of the DataGrid-View associated with the *Reservations* table.

7. You have access to a survey that displays the amount of money collected at a number of theaters on different dates (use the *Movies* database).

Design an application that displays the following information:

a. Movie title and category

b. Theater's name and city

c. The show date and the amount of money collected on that day

You also should provide a functionality to display the same information but for a specific date.

8. You have a database that contains information about a collection of movies and their actors. Your task is to implement a simple application that displays this information. It should allow the user the flexibility to view information about a single movie, a single actor, or all the movies and their actors. For each of the previous cases, view only the actors' first and last names and the movie titles (use the *Movies* database).

9. The Chilton hotel keeps track of all its operations in a database. Open the "Hotel" database and help its manager to create the following application. The manager is thinking of attracting customers from the state of Florida. As one marketing strategy, he decided to send discounted package deals to all the customers from Florida who had been to his hotel before. Create an application to list all Florida customers.

10. In this exercise we will extend the application developed in the previous exercise. Since the hotel manager liked your work, he asked you to create a form that can display customers from

any particular state that he would like to see. Also, now the manager is interested in knowing the booking details of these customers. Add related information from *tblBooking* on the same form for the manager to view.

11. Open the "Post Office" database and review the existing tables and relationships in this database and create the following form. The post office accountants must determine the total amount of postage owed by the customers so that they can record it as accounts receivable in their books. Create a form that shows all the details for the customers who have a total amount owed greater than $10.

12. A package sent to the zip code "32608" is missing. The post office manager wants to contact the offices that serve this zip code to ask for details about the missing package. Create a form that returns the office details of all offices servicing a particular zip code that user is interested in. Test the application with zip code "32608" (use "Post Office" database).

13. At the end of each year, the post office tabulates all successful certified shipments for the year. A shipment is considered successful if the package has been sent or received. Create a form that displays all the records of certified packages that either were received in the year 2002 or were sent and are en route to their destinations (use "Post Office" database).

chapter OVERVIEW

15.1   *Introduction*

In the previous chapter, we discussed basic database connectivity topics. Specifically, we introduced the Data Sources Window and demonstrated how to display information on Windows forms, how to display related information, and how to build search forms and lookup tables. These basic topics are adequate to develop simple database applications. However, real life database applications are seldom simple. Fortunately, Visual Studio provides a rich set of tools to develop professional applications efficiently. In this chapter, we discuss advance database connectivity topics that should assist us in developing some complex database applications.

15.1.1   Topics

This chapter discusses the following topics:

- ADO .NET architecture and its benefits
- Displaying data on a form with two or more parameters
- Displaying data from join of two or more tables on a Windows form
- Displaying data on a Windows form using existing MS Access query
- How to pass data between Windows forms within an application
- How to filter and sort data using a *Binding Source*
- How to insert, edit, save, and delete data in a Windows application

15.2   *ADO .NET Architecture*

Recall from Chapter 14 that ADO .NET (ActiveX Data Objects .NET) is the collection of objects that are designed to support data access and data manipulation. We have created and applied most of the functionally important ADO .NET objects in the previous chapter. When we used the *Data Source Configuration Wizard* to create a Data Source, it also created a *Connection* object for us. When we dragged and dropped tables from the Data Sources Window, it automatically created and configured a *DataAdapter* and *DataSet* object. We will discuss these objects in depth in this chapter. In order to understand how these objects interact, we shall first provide an overview of the ADO .NET architecture.

Database connectivity involves the following entities:

- Database—Stores data on the hard drive (disk)
- Connection—Connects to the database
- DataAdapter—Hosts SQL queries and executes them against the database
- DataSet—Stores data in main memory
- Form—Displays data to the user

These entities interact with one another in the following manner (also see Figure 15.1):

From Database to Windows Forms

1. A *Connection* object opens a live connection to the database.
2. A *DataAdapter* object executes Select SQL queries against the connected database.
3. The *DataAdapter* object further *fills* a *DataSet* object with query results. The *DataSet* stores the results in the main memory.

4. *DataSets* are associated with various Windows controls on a form. This association is referred as *Data Binding*. Data binding makes it possible for the query results in the *DataSet* to be displayed on a form for the user.

From Windows Forms to Database

1. If a user edits the data in Windows controls, the updates are propagated to the *DataSet* object.
2. The *DataAdapter* object then propagates the updates from the *DataSet* object to the connected database by executing Update SQL statements.

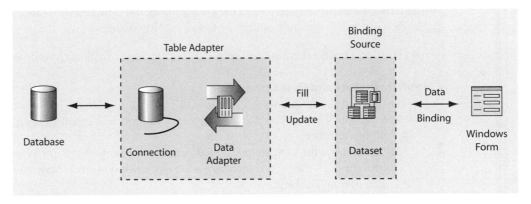

Figure 15.1 ADO .NET architecture.

Now, let us analyze these objects and their interaction in context of the database application we have developed in the previous chapter. When we created a Data Source using the *Data Source Configuration Wizard*, Visual Studio created a *Connection* object that connects to the University database. As we selected the tables of interest on the wizard's last page, Visual Studio configured default *DataAdapters* for each of the selected tables. When we dragged and dropped the student table from the Data Sources Window, Visual Studio added a *Dataset*—UniversityDataSet—objects on the form. Also, two more objects are added to the Component tray: the *tblStudentTableAdapter* and the *tblStudentDataBinding* objects. The *TableAdapter* and *BindingSource* objects are also part of the ADO .NET suite.

The *TableAdapter* object is comprised of a *Connection* and *DataAdapter* objects (see Figure 15.1). The *BindingSource* object is comprises of a *DataSet* object. *TableAdapter* and *BindingSource* objects can be thought as wrapper objects, designed to simplify the process of binding controls to a database. We explore the *Connection* object, various functionalities of a *TableAdapter*, and detailed architecture of a *DataSet* in this chapter.

15.3 *A Database Connection*

Creating a database connection is like opening a unique session with the database. Once opened, we can access contents of the database using the connection object. There are two ways to create a database connection in Visual Studio.

1. Using the *Data Source Configuration Wizard*
2. Using the Server Explorer Window

So far, we have used the *Data Source Configuration Wizard* to create a connection. On the second page of this Wizard, we either created a new connection or used an existing connection string (see section 14.3). The Server Explorer Window also supports creation of a new connection or displays the list of tables and views for an existing connected database.

15.3.1   Hands-On Tutorial: Creating a Connection Using the Server Explorer Window

In this section, we walk through the process of creating a database connection using the Server Explorer Window. We then create a Data Source using the *Data Source Configuration Wizard*. We also differentiate between the tables in the Data Sources Window and the table list in the Server Explorer Window. This section covers the following How-to topic:

■ How-to: create a database connection using the Server Explorer Window.

Create the Project and Data Connection

1. Create a new Windows Application with the name, *AdvanceDBConnectivity*.
2. Select the View | Server Explorer option from the main menu to open the Server Explorer Window.
3. Either select the *Connect to Database* icon on the Server Explorer Window's toolbar, or right-click the *Data Connection* node in the window and choose the *Add Connection* option (see Figure 15.2).

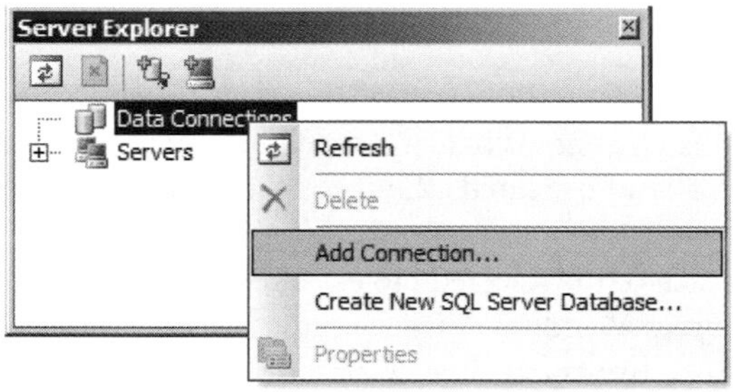

Figure 15.2 Adding a connection in the Server Explorer Window.

4. If the *Choose Data Source* dialog box opens, select the *Microsoft Access Database File* option and click *Continue*. Otherwise, we should directly see the *Add Connection* dialog box. Browse for the University database and select the same. Test the connection and click *OK* (see Figure 15.3).

   Note that the new database connection we have created is now a part of the *Data Connections* node of the Server Explorer window.
5. Collapse the *Tables* node and *Views* node to explore the list of tables and queries from the University database (see Figure 15.4).

   We now create a Data Source using the *Data Source Configuration Wizard*.

Figure 15.3 The *Add Connection* dialog box.

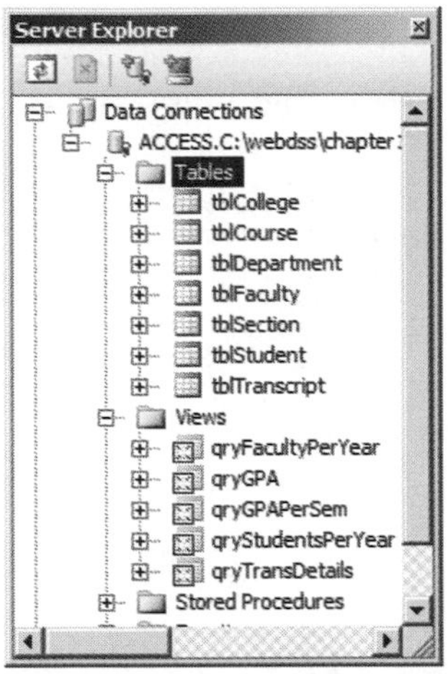

Figure 15.4 Server Explorer Window with the list of tables and views from the University Database.

Create the Data Source

6. Choose the Data | Show Data Sources option from the main menu.

7. In the Data Sources Window, click *Add New Data Source* to start the *Data Source Configuration Wizard*.

8. Select the *Database* icon on the *Choose a Data Source Type* page, and then click *Next*.

9. On the *Choose your Data Connection* page, accept the University database connection we have created in the previous step and click *Next* (see Figure 15.5).

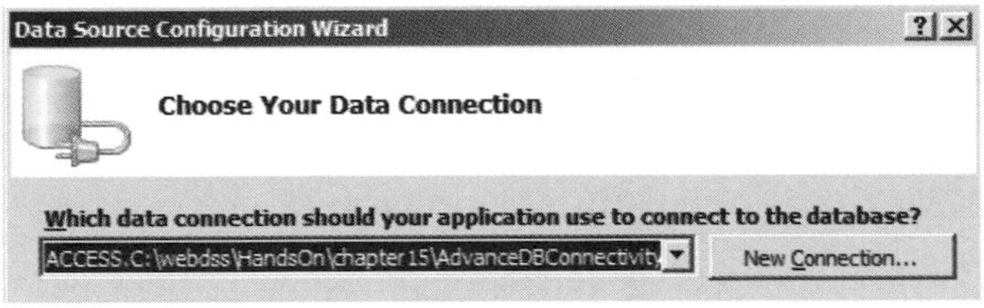

Figure 15.5 Accepting Connection created in the Server Explorer Window.

10. When enquired, copy the database to the current project folder. Click *Next*.

11. On the next page of the Wizard—*Save the Connection String to the Application Configuration File*—save the connection with the default name (*UniversityConnectionString*). Click *Next*.

12. Expand the *Tables* node on the *Choose Your Database Objects* page, and select all the tables except the college table (see Figure 15.6) and click *Finish*. The Data Sources Window now displays the University*DataSet* with the selected tables (see Figure 15.7).

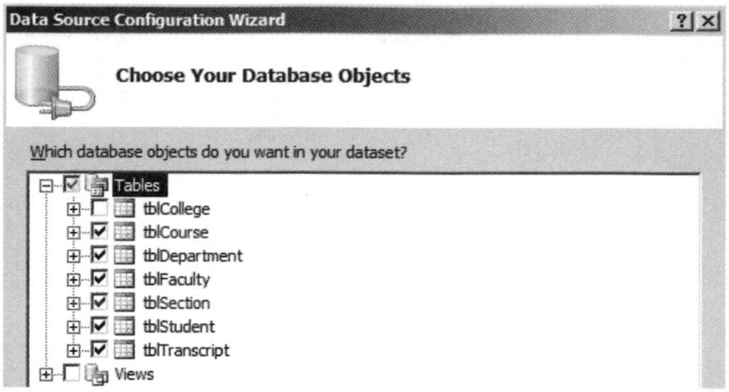

Figure 15.6 Selecting tables for a Data Source.

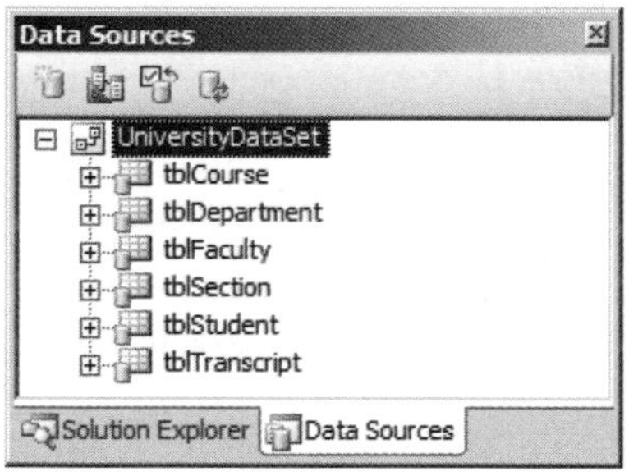

Figure 15.7 A View of Data Sources Window.

Note that a Data Source hosts only those tables that we believe are useful for our application (see Figure 15.7), whereas the list of tables in the Server Explorer Window gives us a view of all the tables that are present in the database (see Figure 15.4).

15.3.2 Properties and Methods of a Connection Object

In this section, we briefly discuss some important properties and methods of a *Connection* object. There are two important properties related to the *Connection* objects.

- ■ *Name:* the name given to a *Connection* object.
- ■ *Connection String:* the string that stores the information required to connect to the database. A typical *ConnectionString* property resembles the following string:

```
Provider=Microsoft.Jet.OLEDB.4.0;Data
Source=|DataDirectory|\University.mdb
```

The *Provider* attribute shows the type of the database (Jet Engine for MS Access database) whereas the *Data Source* attribute of the *Connection String* stores the physical path of the database file.

There are two primary methods available for a *Connection* object.

- ■ *Open:* This method makes use of the information in the *ConnectionString* to locate the database and opens a unique session to work with it.

- ***Close:*** This method shuts the connection down. Closing connections is essential because most databases support only a limited number of open connections.

When we use a *TableAdapter* (to be discussed later), it maintains the *Connection* object for us and opens and closes the connection as per the applications need, making application development easier, faster, and less error-prone.

15.4 *Hands-On Tutorial: Displaying Data on a Form with Multiple Parameters*

In the previous chapter, we created and added parameterized SQL queries to a *TableAdapter*. Visual Studio added the ToolStrip control to accept the parameter values from the user and then executed a query with those input values. In this section, we extend that application to include multiple input parameters. We also use this example to illustrate how to add queries to an existing *TableAdapter* using the *DataSet Designer* and the *TableAdapter Configuration Wizard*.

The application we develop is based on the faculty table. The two parameters are the faculty's department and salary, which are input by the user. We display the faculty members, who belong to the user-specified department and whose salary is at least as much as specified by the user. We continue with the *AdavanceDBConnectivity* project created in the previous section.

Create a DataGridView Control to Display the Faculty Table

1. In the Data Sources Window, locate and drag the faculty table onto *Form1*. This creates the data bound DataGridView control, a ToolStrip control, and related objects in the Component tray.

   Next, we add the parameterized query to the auto generated *TblFacultyTableAdapter*. Recall that we have discussed how to add a query to a *TableAdapter* using either the Tasks list of a DataGridView control or the right-click menu of a *TableAdapter* object in the Component tray. We now show how to achieve the same effect by using the *DataSet Designer*, which is an important component of the Visual Studio environment. It is a common interface to manipulate the *DataSets* and *TableAdapters* associated with our application.

Open the DataSet Designer for UniversityDataSet   This step covers the following How-to topic:

- How-to: open a *DataSet* in the *DataSet Designer*.
2. Right-click *TblFacultyTableAdapter* from the Component tray and choose *Edit Queries in DataSet Designer* option (see Figure 15.8). This should open the *DataSet Designer* tab.

Figure 15.8 Invoking the *DataSet Designer* to edit queries.

There are other alternatives to directly open the *DataSet Designer*. We can either double-click the *DataSet* (.xsd) file from the Solution Explorer Window or click the *Edit DataSet with Designer* icon from the Data Sources Window (see Figure 15.9).

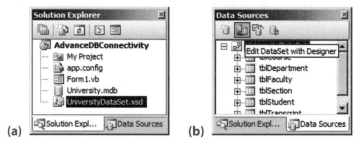

(a)   **(b)**

Figure 15.9 Opening the *DataSet Designer*.

Add a Parameter Query to *TblFacultyTableAdapter* in the *DataSet Designer*   We now edit the *TblFacultyTableAdapter* to add a parameterized query. This step covers following How-to topics:

- How-to: review and configure an existing query in a TableAdapter.
- How-to: add parameterized queries to a TableAdapter in the DataSet Designer.
- How-to: add multiple queries to a TableAdapter.
- How-to: create an SQL statement that returns rows.
- How-to: create a parameterized query with multiple parameters.

Note that, the DataSet Designer displays all the default *DataSets* and *TableAdapters* for our application. These default *DataSets* and *TableAdapters* were created when we generated a Data Source using the *Data Source Configuration Wizard* and selected tables of interest on its last page. Figure 15.10 shows the faculty table in the *DataSet Designer*.

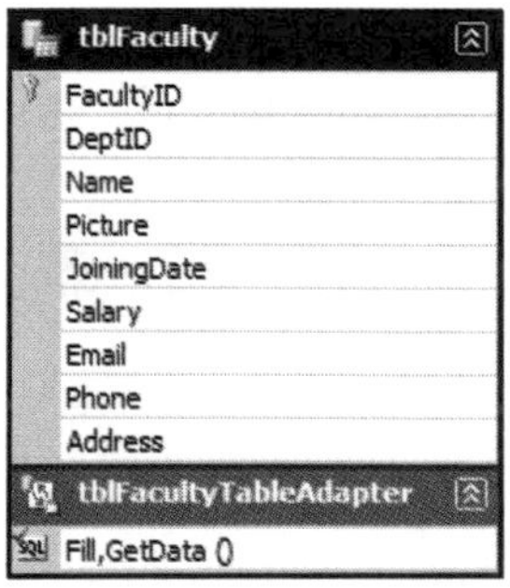

Figure 15.10 Faculty table in the *DataSet Designer*.

Further, note that for each *TableAdapter* there are two default methods available: *Fill* and *GetData*. The *Fill* method executes the SELECT * query to get all the records from the database into a *DataTable*. The *GetData* method executes the Update query to propagate changes in the *DataTable* back to the database. To review existing queries in a *TableAdapter*, do the following:

3. Select the *TblFacultyTableAdapter* in the *DataSet Designer* and right-click "*Fill, Get-Data ()*" text and choose the *Configure* option (see Figure 15.11). This should open the *TableAdapter Configuration Wizard*.

Figure 15.11 Review and configure existing queries in a *TableAdapter*.

In the *TableAdapter Configuration Wizard*, we have the Select query based on the faculty table. We can modify the existing query by either editing the SQL statement or using familiar *Query Builder* dialog box (see Figure 15.12).

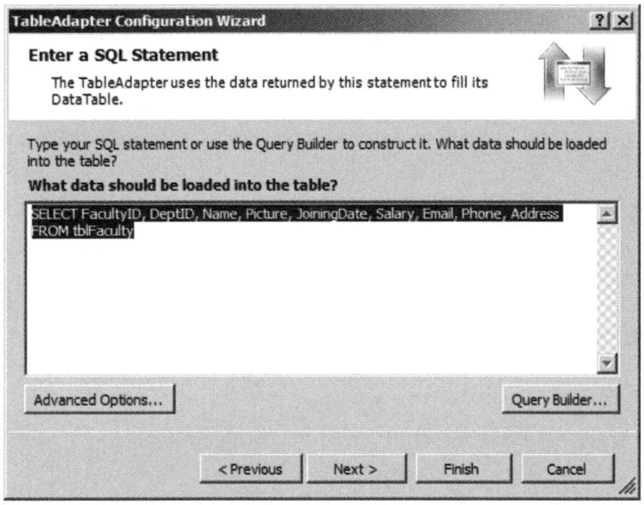

Figure 15.12 Edit existing query using *TableAdapter Configuration Wizard*.

Figure 15.13 Adding a query to a *TableAdapter*.

We now demonstrate how to add a new query to the *TblFacultyTableAdapter*.

4. Select the *TblFacultyTableAdapter* in the *DataSet Designer* and right-click to choose the *Add Query* option (see Figure 15.13). This should also open the *TableAdapter Query Configuration Wizard*.

5. On the first page of the wizard (*Choose a Command Type*), choose the way by which we wish to access the database. Accept the *Use SQL statements* option and click *Next* (see Figure 15.14).

6. On the next page (*Choose a Query Type*), we select the type of SQL query we wish to generate. The options are: SELECT query that returns a set of rows, SELECT query that returns aggregate values, UPDATE query, DELETE query and INSERT query. We need the parameterized query to retrieve the set of faculty records that satisfy two user-specified criteria. So, choose the first option (*SELECT which returns rows*) and click *Next* (see Figure 15.15).

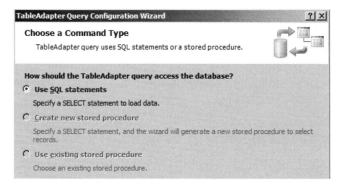

Figure 15.14 Choosing a command type in *TableAdapter Query Configuration Wizard*.

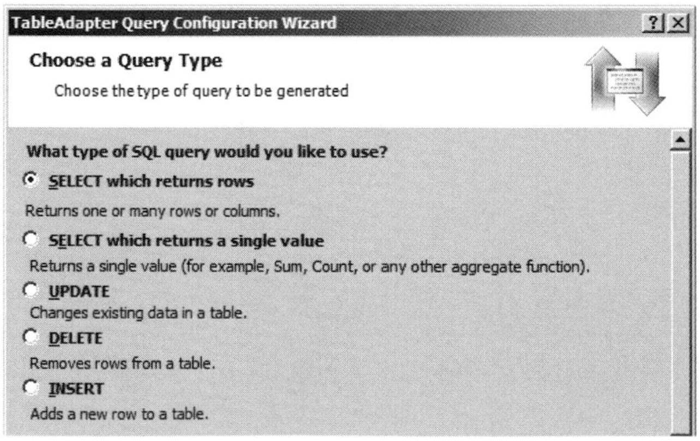

Figure 15.15 Choosing the query type in *TableAdapter Query Configuration Wizard*.

7. The next page (*Specify an SQL SELECT statement*) is similar to the one where we reviewed the process of editing an existing query. To create a new query, either enter the SQL statement on this page, or use the *Query Builder* dialog box. Note the *DeptID* and *Salary* parameters in Figure 15.16.

8. Finally, name the *Fill a DataTable* and *Return a DataTable* methods as shown in Figure 15.17 and click *Finish*.

The faculty *TableAdapter* now resembles Figure 15.18 with its additional methods.

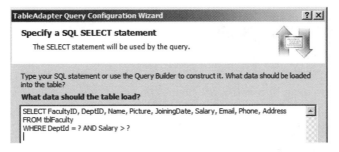

TableAdapter Query Configuration Wizard   ? X

Specify a SQL SELECT statement
  The SELECT statement will be used by the query.

Type your SQL statement or use the Query Builder to construct it. What data should be loaded into the table?

What data should the table load?

```
SELECT FacultyID, DeptID, Name, Picture, JoiningDate, Salary, Email, Phone, Address
FROM tblFaculty
WHERE DeptId = ? AND Salary > ?
|
```

Figure 15.16 Writing a SQL query in *TableAdapter Query Configuration Wizard*.

TableAdapter Query Configuration Wizard   ? X

Choose Methods to Generate
  The TableAdapter methods load and save data between your
  application and the database.

Which methods do you want to add to the TableAdapter?

☑ **Fill a DataTable**

Creates a method that takes a DataTable or DataSet as a parameter and executes the SQL
statement or SELECT stored procedure entered on the previous page.

Method name: FillByDeptSal

☑ **Return a DataTable**

Creates a method that returns a new DataTable filled with the results of the SQL statement
or SELECT stored procedure entered on the previous page.

Method name: GetDataByDeptSal

Figure 15.17 Choose and name the methods to be added to the *TableAdapter*.

tblFacultyTableAdapter

Fill,GetData ()

FillByDeptSal,GetDataByDeptSal (DeptID, Salary)

Figure 15.18 Faculty *TableAdapter* with parameterized query.

Add Existing Query to *TblStudentAdapter* in the Component Tray   If we analyze the *Form1* design again, we don't see any ToolStrips added for parameters of this query. Recall that in the previous chapter, when we added the parameterized query to the *TableAdapter*, it auto-created a ToolStrip for us. In order to create a ToolStrip with parameter inputs, we add the newly created query to the *TableAdapter* which is present in the Component tray. This step covers the following How-to topic:

■ How-to: create a ToolStrip for parameterized queries.

9. Select and right-click the *TblFacultyTableAdapter* from the Component tray (see Figure 15.19). Choose *Add Query* option to open the *Search Criteria Builder* dialog box.

10. In the *Search Criteria Builder* dialog box, choose the *Existing query name* option. Then, choose the *FillByDeptSal* method we created in the previous step from the drop-down list (see Figure 15.20). Thus, we make use of the query previously created in the *DataSet Designer*.

11. Click *OK* to create two TextBox controls for user input in the ToolStrip.

Figure 15.19 Adding a query to a *TableAdapter* in the Component tray.

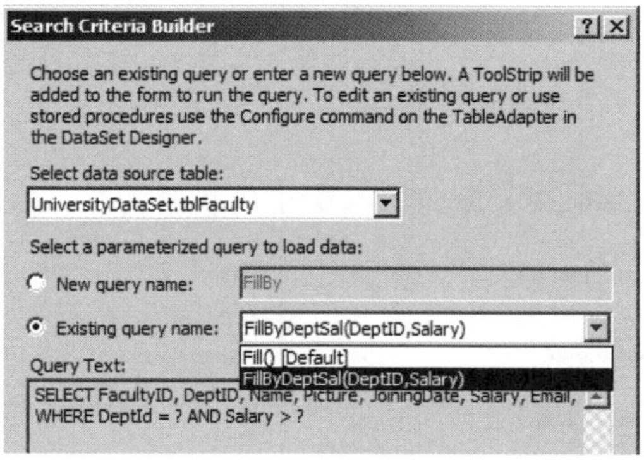

Figure 15.20 Assigning a query to a TableAdapter in the *Search Criteria Builder* dialog box.

Test the Application

12. Press Ctrl + F5 to run and test the application. Enter values for the department and salary parameters through the TextBox controls on the ToolStrip and check if all the records satisfy the specified criteria. In Figure 15.21, note that all the records that are retrieved have *DeptID = ISE* and *Salary > 70000*.

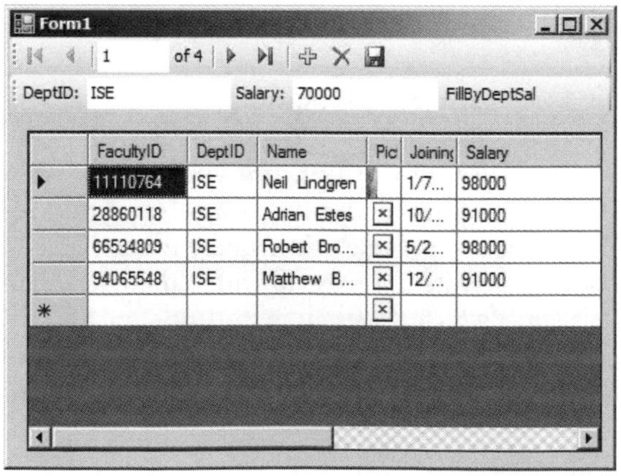

Figure 15.21 Running application with two input parameters.

Code Review

This step covers the following How-to topic:

- How-to: execute an SQL statement with multiple parameters.

In Chapter 14, we have reviewed the code for a single parameter query and saw how a parameter value gets assigned in the code. If there is more than one parameter, their values also get assigned in a similar manner as seen in lines 21–25 of Figure 15.22.

```
17    Private Sub FillByDeptSalToolStripButton_Click(ByVal _
18    sender As System.Object, ByVal e As System.EventArgs) _
19    Handles FillByDeptSalToolStripButton.Click
20        Try
21            Me.TblFacultyTableAdapter.FillByDeptSal _
22            (Me.UniversityDataSet.tblFaculty, _
23            DeptIDToolStripTextBox.Text, _
24            New System.Nullable(Of Decimal) _
25            (CType(SalaryToolStripTextBox.Text, Decimal)))
26        Catch ex As System.Exception
27            System.Windows.Forms.MessageBox.Show(ex.Message)
28        End Try
29
30    End Sub
```

Figure 15.22 Code review for the multiple parameter query.

15.5 *Hands-On Tutorial: Displaying Data on a Form from Join of Multiple Tables*

So far we have created queries involving only a single table. However, it is very common that applications require combining data from multiple tables. In this hands-on tutorial, we see how to display data resulting from the join of two or more tables from the University database. Specifically, we develop a Windows form that displays all the students in a particular department (a user-specified parameter) who have a grade of 4.0 in at least one of their courses. Note that this is a very simple application, but still involves join of student and transcript tables, illustrating the fact that almost all complex queries are likely to have join of two or more tables.

Initially, we add a new *TableAdapter* to our application and specify its multi-table query. We will then use the Data Sources Window to drag-and-drop this new table on the Windows form.

Add a New *TableAdapter* to the Application   This step covers following How-to topics:

- How-to: create a new *TableAdapter*.
- How-to: create a new *DataTable*.
    1. Add a new form (*Form2*) to the *AdvanceDBConnectivity* application.
    2. Open the *DataSet Designer*. Right-click anywhere in the designer window and choose the Add | TableAdapter option (see Figure 15.23). This should open the familiar *TableAdapter Configuration Wizard*.
    3. On Choose Your Data Connection page, accept the selected University database connection string (see Figure 15.24). Click Next.

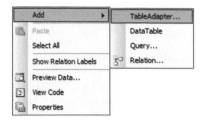

Figure 15.23 Adding a new *TableAdapter* to the application.

TableAdapter Configuration Wizard	? X
Choose Your Data Connection	
Specify the connection string required to connect to the database.	

Which data connection should your application use to connect to the database?

UniversityConnectionString (MySettings) ▼ | New Connection... |

Figure 15.24 Specifying connection for a new *TableAdapter*.

4. On the *Choose a Command Type* page, check *Use SQL statements* option (default) and click *Next*.
5. On the *Enter a SQL Statement* page, click on the *QueryBuilder* button. In the *Add Table* dialog box that opens, select the student and transcript tables (press *Ctrl* key while selecting multiple tables) and click *Add* (see Figure 15.25).
6. Note that the two selected tables appear in the table pane of the *Query Builder* dialog box (see Figure 15.26). Click *Close* on the *Add Table* dialog box.
7. Select the fields to be displayed from the student and transcript tables, namely, *StudentID*, *DeptID*, and *Name* from student table and *Grade* field from the transcript table. Notice that the corresponding SQL Select query (performing the join of the two tables) is automatically built in the SQL pane as we select the fields.
8. Now add the DISTINCT keyword after the SELECT keyword in the SQL pane, in order to retrieve only the unique student records (in case the student has 4.0 grade in more than one course, the DISTINCT keyword ensures that the student's record is retrieved only once).
9. Also add the query parameters (*DeptID* and *Grade*) in the WHERE clause as shown in Figure 15.26.

Add Table	? X
Tables	Views

tblCollege
tblCourse
tblDepartment
tblFaculty
tblSection
tblStudent
tblTranscript

Figure 15.25 Adding query tables in the *Query Builder* dialog box.

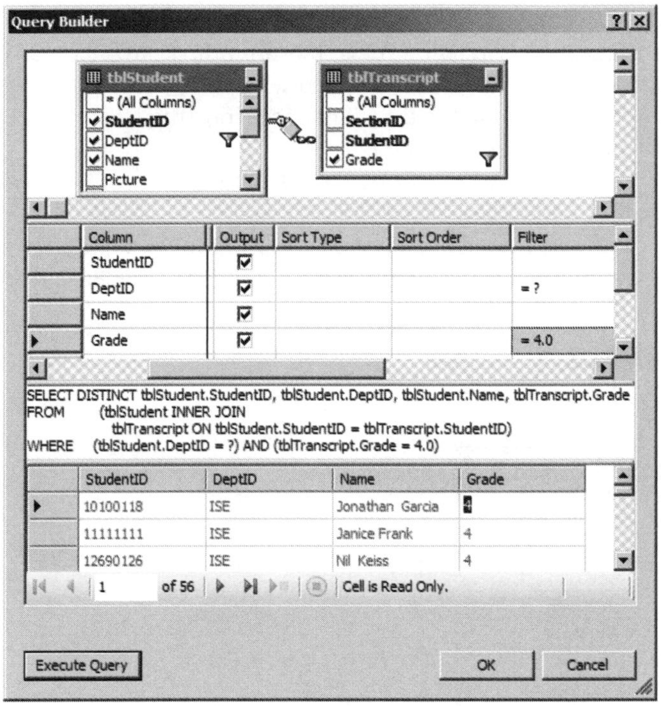

Figure 15.26 *Query Builder* dialog box showing the query design.

> **10.** Click *OK* on the *Query Builder* dialog box. Click *Next* on the *Table Adapter Configuration Wizard*, accept the default method names *Fill* and *GetData*, and click *Finish*. This adds a new data table, *DataTable1*, and a new table adapter, *DataTable1Table Adapter*, in the *DataSet Designer* as shown in Figure 15.27. Note that *DataTable1* is also added to the Data Sources Window along with the other database tables (see Figure 15.28).

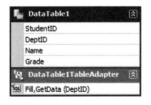

Figure 15.27 Newly added *TableAdapter* in the *DataSet Designer*.

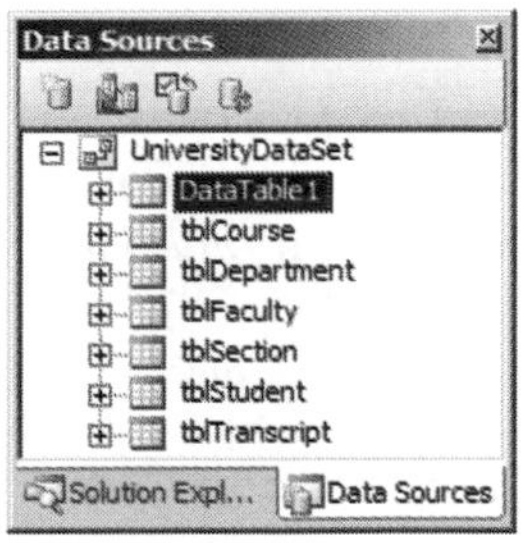

Figure 15.28 Data Sources Window with the new data table, *DataTable1*.

Create a DataGridView Control to Display the *DataTable1*

11. From the Data Sources Window, drag-and-drop the *DataTable1* table on *Form2* to create a DataGridView control. As expected, a ToolStrip, the *DataTable1TableAdapter*, and other objects get added to the Component tray (the *UniversityDataSet* is reused from the *Form1*'s Component tray).

Test the Application

12. Set *Form2* as the start-up object. Press Ctrl + F5 to run the application. Test the application by entering different department IDs through the ToolStrip (see Figure 15.29).

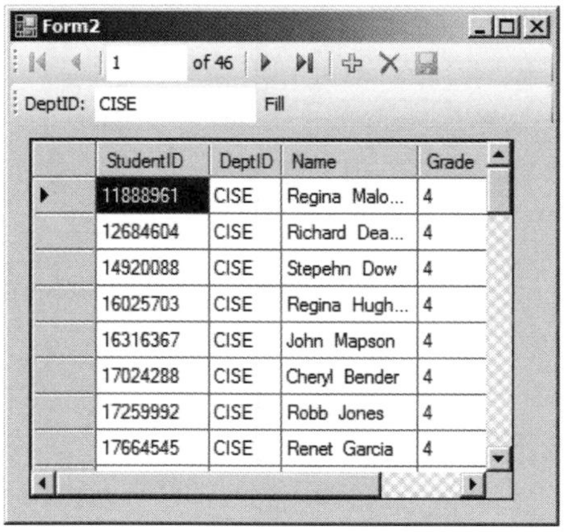

Figure 15.29 Data from the join of two tables.

15.6 *Hands-On Tutorial: Displaying Data Using Existing MS Access Query*

In Chapter 8, we learnt how to build queries in MS Access environment. We also extensively developed many complicated Select queries. We can make use of existing Access queries to create *DataTables* and include them in the Data Sources Window. In this section, we make use of the existing Access query, *qryGPA*, to display the Grade Point Average (GPA) for the students in the University database.

Add Access Query to the Existing Data Source This step covers following How-to topic:

■ How-to: add an existing Access table or query to the Data Sources Window.

1. Add a *Form3* to the *AdvanceDBConnectivity* application.
2. In the Data Sources Window, click the *Configure DataSet with Wizard* icon (see Figure 15.30). This should open the *Choose DataSet Editor* dialog box.
3. Choose the *Continue with wizard* option to open a familiar *Data Source Configuration* wizard (see Figure 15.31).
4. On the last page of the Wizard, *Choose Your Database Objects*, collapse the *Views* node and choose *qryGPA*, and click *Finish* (see Figure 15.32). This adds the *qryGPA* as a *DataTable* in the Data Sources Window (see Figure 15.33).

Figure 15.30 Using Data Sources Window to invoke the *Dataset Configuration* wizard.

Figure 15.31 Invoking *Data Sources Configuration Wizard*.

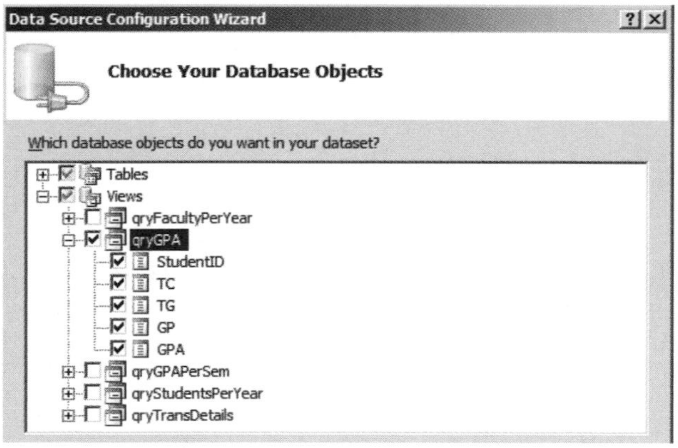

Figure 15.32 Choosing the *qryGPA* query from available queries.

Figure 15.33 Access query as a *DataTable* in the Data Sources Window.

Create a DataGridView Control to Display the GPA

5. From the Data Sources Window, drag-and-drop the *qryGPA* data table on *Form3* to create a DataGridView control. As expected, the *QryGPATableAdapter*, a *BindingSource* and *BindingNavigator* are added to the Component tray (the *UniversityDataSet* is reused from the *Form1*'s Component tray).

Test the Application

6. Set *Form3* as the start-up object. Press Ctrl + F5 to run the application. Navigate through the student records and notice that the calculated GPA is displayed in column 5 (see Figure 15.34).

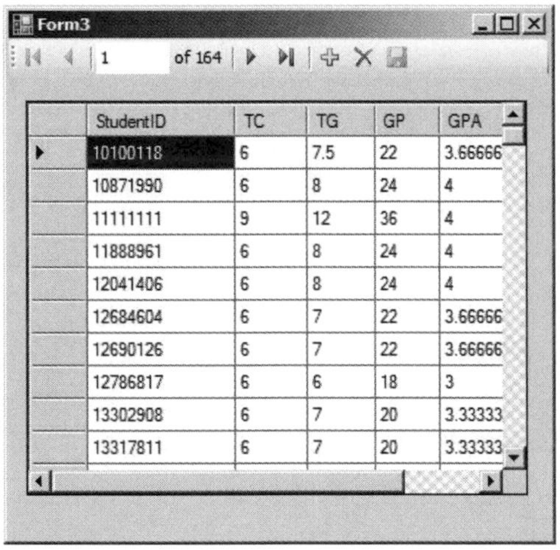

Figure 15.34 Running application with student GPAs.

15.7 *Hands-On Tutorial: Passing Data between Forms in a Windows Application*

We now discuss how to provide additional functionality to a Windows application to support complex and real life functionalities. In this hands-on tutorial, we illustrate how to pass data from one Windows Form to another. For example, consider that we have displayed faculty information in a DataGridView on a form. As user goes through these records, one might be interested in looking at the list of courses taught by a faculty member. Of course, we can add another data grid to display related information, but this is not always a feasible solution for the following two reasons:

■ The space available on a form is limited and hence we cannot display everything on one form.
■ The related query may not be a simple, single table query. It might possibly be a complex query that cannot be created by simply dragging a related table onto a form.

We reconcile by displaying linked information on a pop-up form. In our example, as a user browses through faculty records, we can provide the ability to view courses taught by a faculty in a pop-up form that opens when user double-clicks the faculty record in the DataGridView. To support this, we need the ability to pass information about the faculty, whose courses the user is interested in, to the pop-up form. In other words, we need to pass the *FacultyID* for the double-clicked record from the first (faculty) form to the second (course) form. Thus, on the course form, we can use the *FacultyID* from the faculty form to execute the parameter query to retrieve related course information. Figure 15.35 explains the application flow.

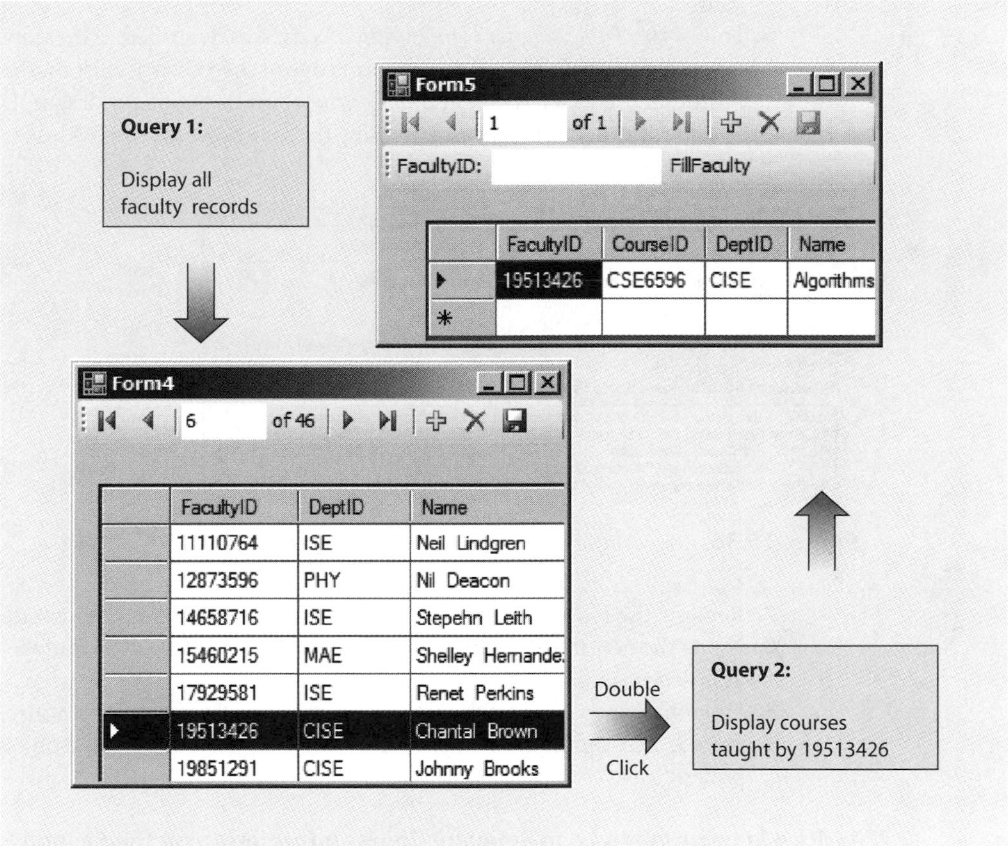

Figure 15.35 Application flow: Passing data between two Windows forms.

This section covers following How-to topic:

■ How-to: pass data between two Windows forms.

Create the First (Faculty) Form   The first form simply displays all the records from the faculty table. This should be very straightforward and is achieved from the following steps:

1. Add *Form4* to the *AdvanceDBConnectivity* application.
2. Drag-and-drop the faculty table from the Data Sources Window on *Form4*. This should create the faculty DataGridView and related objects in the Component tray.

Create the Second (Course) Form   Second form is based on the parameter query that joins the *tblFaculty* and *tblCourses* tables from the University database.

3. Add *Form5* to the same application.
4. Switch to the *DataSet Designer* (double-click on the *UniversityDataSet.xsd* file in the Solution Explorer).
5. Right-click in the designer window to add a new *TableAdapter* to the existing data source.
6. Follow the *TableAdapter Configuration Wizard* as described in the previous hands-on tutorial. On the *Enter a SQL Statement* page of the Wizard, click on the *Query Builder* button and add *tblSection* and *tblCourse* tables to the query design. Design the SQL statement shown in Figure 15.36 using the *Query Builder* dialog box.

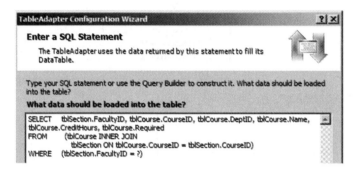

Figure 15.36 Course information query for the course form.

7. Rename the *Fill* method as *FillFaculty* before finishing the *Configuration Wizard*.
8. Name the new table adapter as *qryFacultyCoursesTableAdapter* and the new data table as *qryFacultyCourses*.
9. Drag-and-drop the *qryFacultyCourses* data table from the Data Sources Window on *Form5*. This should create the courses DataGridView and related objects in the Component tray.

Write a Subroutine to Load Relevant Course Information on the Second Form

10. In the *Form5.vb* file, write a new subroutine *LoadCourses* as shown in Figure 15.37, which takes in the *FacultyID* as an argument and passes it as a parameter to the *Fill-Faculty* method (this code is similar to the auto-generated code associated with the ToolStrip button's *Click* event).

```
12   Public Sub LoadCourses(ByVal FacultyID As Integer)
13       QryFacultyCoursesTableAdapter.FillFaculty _
14   (Me.UniversityDataSet.qryFacultyCourses, FacultyID)
15
16   End Sub
```

Figure 15.37 Subroutine to load course information for a given *FacultyID*.

Write the Code for the *DoubleClick* Event for the Faculty Form

11. In the faculty form (*Form4.vb*), we write the code for DataGridView's *DoubleClick* event. Select the *TblFacultyDataGridView* from the left drop-down list and its *Double Click* event from the right drop-down list at the top of the Code Window. Associate the code in Figure 15.38 with this event.

Figure 15.38 Explained:

In lines 23–24, we get the value of the selected *FacultyID* from the *SelectedRow* property of a DataGridView control. We create an instance of the course form (line 27) and then call its *Load-Courses* subroutine with the *FacultyID* value (line 28).

Test the Application

12. Set *Form4* as the application's start-up object. Press Ctrl + F5 to run the application. Test the application by double-clicking any faculty record from the DataGridView and viewing the related course data (see Figure 15.39).

```
16   Private Sub TblFacultyDataGridView_DoubleClick _
17   (ByVal sender As Object, ByVal e As System.EventArgs) _
18   Handles TblFacultyDataGridView.DoubleClick
19
20        'Get the selected Faculty ID
21        Dim facultyID As Integer
22
23        facultyID = _
24        TblFacultyDataGridView.SelectedCells(0).Value
25
26        'Load an instance of the second form (Form5)
27        Dim CourseForm As New Form5
28        CourseForm.LoadCourses(facultyID)
29        CourseForm.Show()
30   End Sub
```

Figure 15.38 *DoubleClick* event of a DataGridView for the faculty form.

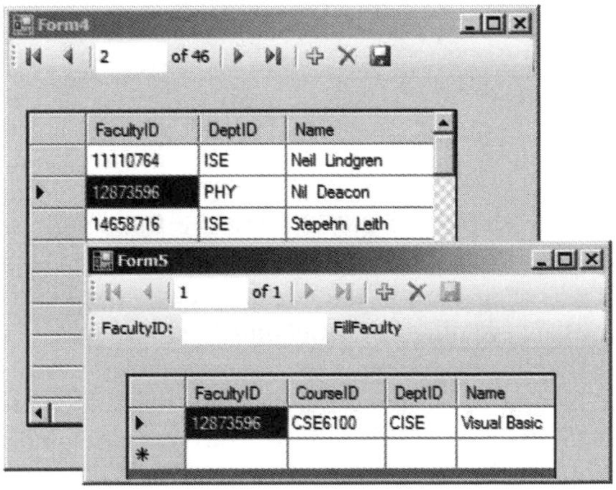

Figure 15.39 Running application showing related information displayed on the course form.

15.8 *DataSets*

A *DataSet* is an in-memory relational database.

- As relational databases have tables, *DataSets* also have *DataTables*.
- As database tables have rows and columns, dataset's *DataTables* also have *DataRows* and *DataColumns*.
- As database tables are related to each other through relationships, *DataTables* are linked together through *DataRelations* object.

Figure 15.40 illustrates the structure of a *DataSet* object with three *DataTables*.

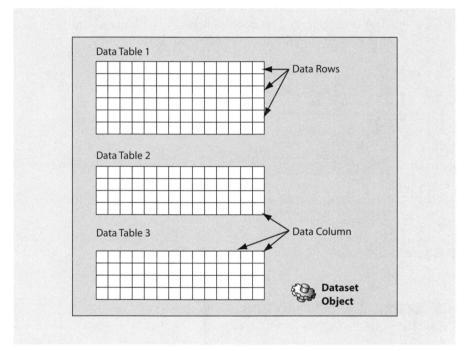

Figure 15.40 The architecture of a *DataSet* object.

Previously, we have created the *UniversityDataSet* using the *Data Sources Configuration Wizard*. The tables in the Data Sources Window are essentially the *DataTables* in the *UniversityDataSet* (see Figure 15.33). If we collapse any of these table nodes, we see the list of columns in that *DataTable*. These columns are essentially *DataColumns*.

For an application, a *TableAdapter* object queries the database tables and fills the *DataSet*'s *DataTables* with query results. The controls on Windows forms are data-bind to the *DataTables*. Once an adapter fills the *DataTables*, the user can view the data through data-bind controls on the Windows form. This allows user to see the data even after the database is disconnected. *DataSets* thus act as a cache (temporary storage) for an application.

We now discuss several How-to topics illustrating features of *DataSet* object. In all these topics, we use the *tblStudent* data table in the *UniversityDataSet* as an example.

How-to: Create a *DataSet* and Add a *DataTable*   We can add a *DataSet* to an application using the *Data Source Configuration Wizard* (see Section 14.3). We can add a *DataTable* to a *DataSet* using the *Data Sources Configuration Wizard* (see Section 15.5).

How-to: Add a *DataRow to a DataTable*   In order to add a new record into a *DataTable*, we first create a new *DataRow* and then add a new row to the *Rows* collection of a *DataTable*. Figure 15.41 shows the code that adds a new *DataRow* to the *tblStudent* data table.

```
 5    'declare a new data row
 6    Dim NewStudentRow As UniversityDataSet.tblStudentRow
 7    NewStudentRow = _
 8    UniversityDataSet.tblStudent.NewtblStudentRow
 9
10    'populate its columns (fields)
11    NewStudentRow.StudentID = 88888888
12    NewStudentRow.Name = "James Adams"
13    NewStudentRow.Email = "James@university.edu"
14    'we can populate its other columns here
15    'add the new row to the Student DataTable
16    UniversityDataSet.tblStudent.Rows.Add(NewStudentRow)
```

Figure 15.41 Adding a *DataRow* to a *DataTable*.

We "declare" a *NewStudentRow* (a *DataRow* object) of type *UniversityDataSet.tblStudentRow* (line 6). A new data row "instance" of type *tblStudentRow* is "created" using *NewtblStudentRow* property in line 8. This new instance is assigned to the *NewStudentRow* (line 7). Once instantiated, we assign values to the *DataColumns* of the *NewStudentRow* (lines 11–13). Finally, we add the *NewStudentRow* to the *Rows* collection of the *tblStudent* (a *DataTable* object) of the *University-DataSet* (a *DataSet* object)

How-to: Edit a *DataRow in a DataTable*   In order to edit an existing row in a *DataTable*, we should first locate the *DataRow*, and then update its one or more columns. The DataTable's *FindBy<PrimaryKey>* method can be used to find a *DataRow*. For example, we can search the student *DataTable* using its *FindByStudentID* method (line 26) and then update its *Email* data column (line 28) as shown in Figure 15.42.

```
22    Dim StudentRow As UniversityDataSet.tblStudentRow
23
24    'search for and locate the row of interest
25    StudentRow = _
26    UniversityDataSet.tblStudent.FindByStudentID(88888888)
27    'edit the row
28    StudentRow.Email = "James.Adams@university.edu"
```

Figure 15.42 Editing a *DataRow* in a *DataTable*.

If we know the row index (the row number) of a record to update, we can directly manipulate the *DataRow* as shown in Figure 15.43.

```
30    'edit the row of interest using row index (1)
31    UniversityDataSet.tblStudent(1).Email = _
32    "James.Adams@university.edu"
```

Figure 15.43 Editing a *DataRow* in a *DataTable* using a row index.

How-to: Delete a *DataRow* in a *DataTable*   We can make use of the *Delete* method of a *DataRow* to delete a row. Again, we must find the row before we can delete it. Figure 15.44 and Figure 15.45 illustrates a *DataRow* deletion for two different search strategies.

```
39        Dim StudentRow As UniversityDataSet.tblStudentRow
40        'search for and locate the row of interest
41        StudentRow = _
42        UniversityDataSet.tblStudent.FindByStudentID(88888888)
43        'delete the row
44        StudentRow.Delete()
```

Figure 15.44 Deleting a *DataRow* in a *DataTable*.

```
46        'delete the row of interest using row index (1)
47        UniversityDataSet.tblStudent.Rows(1).Delete()
```

Figure 15.45 Deleting a *DataRow* from a *DataTable* using a row index.

How-to: Commit Changes in a *DataSet*   The changes to *DataSet* are like changes in the Word or Excel document. We must save the changes to update the *Dataset*. Initially, we check if the *DataSet* has been changed (line 55) and then use its *AcceptChanges* method to commit insertions, edits, and deletions (line 57) as shown in Figure 15.46.

```
54        'check if there are any changes
55        If UniversityDataSet.HasChanges Then
56            'commit the changes
57            UniversityDataSet.tblStudent.AcceptChanges()
58        End If
```

Figure 15.46 Committing the changes in a *DataSet*.

How-to: Filter and Sort Data Using a *BindingSource* Object   We can filter data by using the *Filter* property of a *BindingSource*. In line 66 of Figure 15.47, the filter expression "Name LIKE 'John %'" is used by the *TblStudentBindingSource* to retrieve records of all the students whose first name is John.

In order to sort the data, we set the *Sort* property of the *BindingSource* to the column name on which we want to sort the data. *Sort* property supports *DESC* and *ASC* (Descending and Ascending order respectively) sort ordering. In line 69 of Figure 15.47, we set the *Sort* property to the *DeptID* column.

```
65        'Get the records of students whose first name is John
66        TblStudentBindingSource.Filter = "Name LIKE 'John %'"
67
68        'Sort students in ascending order of Department IDs
69        TblStudentBindingSource.Sort = "DeptID ASC"
```

Figure 15.47 Filtering and sorting data using the properties of a BindingSource object.

15.9 *Inserts, Updates, and Deletes in a Windows Application*

Until now, we have mainly focused on one directional data flow—from a database to Windows forms. We queried data using *TableAdapters* and cached it in *DataTables* (or *DataSets*). *Binding Sources* allowed us to display a *DataTable*'s contents on a form. However, a real-life application is seldom complete without the other direction of data flow—from Windows forms to a database. It is vital for an application to enable users to insert new data and edit, update, or delete existing data and then propagate those changes to the database. In this section, we illustrate how to make use of ADO .NET objects to propagate changes made by the user on Windows Forms back into the database.

In general, we exploit the *BindingSource* and *TableAdapter* objects for this propagation. Since *DataSets* are our in-memory data repositories, we use them to temporarily store changes made by the user. We then rely on Update queries of a *TableAdapter* to propagate the changes to the database. Thus, updating databases, by means of *DataSets*, can be viewed as a two-stage propagating process (see Figure 15.48).

In the previous section, we dealt with the *DataSet* object and learnt how to add, edit or delete a row(s) from a *DataSet*. We also saw how to commit changes to a *DataSet*. In this section, we concentrate on how to propagate the committed records from the *DataSets* to the database. Before proceeding further, we shall review some of the important *DataSet* preliminaries.

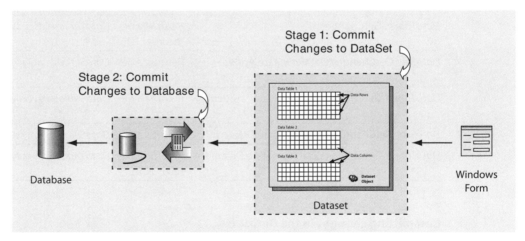

Figure 15.48 Two-Stage database update propagation process.

15.9.1 DataSet Preliminaries

Maintaining information about changes:

As a user makes changes in data-bind controls, the *DataSets* are automatically updated with the changes. The *DataRow* object keeps track of these changes and can be accessed using its properties (see Table 15.1).

Table 15.1 *DataRow* states.

DataRow State	Description
Added	The row that has been added to the *Rows* collection.
Deleted	The row that has been deleted.
Modified	A column of the row that has been changed.
Unchanged	Whether the row has been changed since the last call to *AcceptChanges*.

Retrieving changed rows:

It is also important that we are able to retrieve the changes made by a user. This feature is suitable for two reasons (i) we can easily review the changes made by a user and possibly validate those changes before committing them to a database, and (ii) we can efficiently handle and work with only the changed portion of the *DataSet* rather than the entire *DataSet*. We can retrieve changes either at the *DataSet* level or at *DataTable* level as shown in Table 15.2.

Table 15.2 Getting changes from a *DataSet* and *DataTable*.

Usage Example	Description
DataSet1.GetChanges()	Returns a new *DataSet* with only changed records.
DataTable1.GetChanges()	Returns a new *DataTable* with only changed records.
DataSet1.GetChanges(DataRowState.Added)	Returns a new *DataSet* with only newly added records.
DataTable1.GetChanges(DataRowState.Added)	Returns a new *DataTable* with only newly added records.
DataSet1.GetChanges(DataRowState.Deleted)	Returns a new *DataSet* with only deleted records.
DataTable1.GetChanges(DataRowState.Deleted)	Returns a new *DataTable* with only deleted records.

Committing changes in the *DataSet*:

Finally, we describe how to commit changes in the *DataSet* at: the *DataRow* level, the *DataTable* level, and the *DataSet* level in Table 15.3.

Table 15.3 Committing changes in a *DataRow*, or *DataTable*, or *DataSet*.

Methods	Results
DataRow.AcceptChanges()	Changes are committed only on the specific row
DataTable.AcceptChanges()	Changes are committed on all rows in a specific table
DataSet.AcceptChanges()	Changes are committed on all rows in all the tables of the DataSet

15.9.2 Hands-On Tutorial: Updating (Saving) Changes to the Database

We have come across the *Save* functionality before. Every time we dragged a *DataTable* on a Windows form, it automatically created a ToolStrip control for us with *Save*, *Delete*, and *Add* buttons (see Figure 15.21). A ToolStrip can be thus used to propagate changes made on the form to the database. In this section, we review and modify the code behind the ToolStrip's *Save* button. This section covers following How-to topic:

- How-to: save or update changes to the database by means of a *DataSet*.

Build the Application

1. Add a form (*Form6*) to the *AdvanceDBConnectivity* application.
2. Drag-and-drop the student *DataTable* on the form from the Data Sources Window. This creates a ToolStrip, a DataGridView control, and related objects in the Component tray.
3. Double-click the *Save* button on the ToolStrip to open the Code Window.
4. Use the code of Figure 15.49 to complete the *TblStudentBindingNavigatorSaveItem_Click* event.

```
3   Private Sub TblStudentBindingNavigatorSaveItem_Click _
4   (ByVal sender As System.Object, _
5   ByVal e As System.EventArgs) _
6   Handles TblStudentBindingNavigatorSaveItem.Click
7       SaveToDatabase()
8       MessageBox.Show("Database update succeeded")
9   End Sub
10
11  Private Sub SaveToDatabase()
12      Try
13          Me.Validate()
14          Me.TblStudentBindingSource.EndEdit()
15          Me.TblStudentTableAdapter.Update _
16          (Me.UniversityDataSet.tblStudent)
17      Catch ex As Exception
18          MessageBox.Show("Database update failed!")
19      End Try
20  End Sub
```

Figure 15.49 Saving changes to the database.

Figure 15.49 Explained:

We have replaced the auto-generated code of *Save* button's *Click* event with a call to the *Save-ToDatabase* subroutine (line 7). We wrote the *SaveToDatabase* subroutine to perform the same task as the auto-generated code. We will be using this subroutine in the following hands-on tutorial as well. The *SaveToDatabase* (lines 11–20) code is the same as the default code except that we have added a Try-Catch block for exception handling. The essential lines to analyze are lines 13–16. In line 13, a call to the in-built *Validate* method validates and saves the changes to the *DataSet* (stage 1). The call to the *EndEdit* method in line 14 makes the *DataSet* ready for propagation. In line 15, a call to *Update* method of the *TableAdapter* executes the Update SQL command to propagate the changes to the database (stage 2).

Test the Application

5. Set *Form6* as the start-up object of the application. Press Ctrl+F5 to run the application. Test the application by changing values in the DataGridView and by saving the changes using the ToolStrip's *Save* button.

15.9.3   Hands-On Tutorial: Inserting and Deleting Records in the Database

Although the ToolStrip has button controls to insert and delete records from the database, we will build our own insert and delete buttons to perform the same operations. This is important to comprehend the process of database updates as the auto-created ToolStrip buttons are of little use in related or multiple table scenarios (see the hands-on tutorial in Section 15.10). This section covers following How-to topics:

■ How-to: insert a row in a database table.
■ How-to: delete a row from a database table.

Build the Application

1. Add two command buttons named *cmdInsert* and *cmdDelete* to *Form6*, as shown in Figure 15.50.

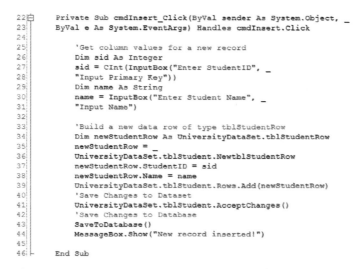

Figure 15.50 *Form6* with command buttons to insert and delete records from a database table.

2. Replace the *Click* event code of the *cmdInsert* button with the code shown in Figure 15.51. Similarly, replace the *Click* event code of the *cmdDelete* button with the code shown in Figure 15.52.

```
22   Private Sub cmdInsert_Click(ByVal sender As System.Object, _
23   ByVal e As System.EventArgs) Handles cmdInsert.Click
24
25       'Get column values for a new record
26       Dim sid As Integer
27       sid = CInt(InputBox("Enter StudentID", _
28       "Input Primary Key"))
29       Dim name As String
30       name = InputBox("Enter Student Name", _
31       "Input Name")
32
33       'Build a new data row of type tblStudentRow
34       Dim newStudentRow As UniversityDataSet.tblStudentRow
35       newStudentRow = _
36       UniversityDataSet.tblStudent.NewtblStudentRow
37       newStudentRow.StudentID = sid
38       newStudentRow.Name = name
39       UniversityDataSet.tblStudent.Rows.Add(newStudentRow)
40       'Save Changes to Dataset
41       UniversityDataSet.tblStudent.AcceptChanges()
42       'Save Changes to Database
43       SaveToDatabase()
44       MessageBox.Show("New record inserted!")
45
46   End Sub
```

Figure 15.51 Inserting a row in a database table.

Insert Button Code Explanation

In the two-stage update-propagation model (see Figure 15.48), initially we insert a row to the *tblStudent* data table of the *UniversityDataSet* and then update the student table in the database.

Stage 1: Insert a new *DataRow* in the *DataSet* (Lines 26–41)

In lines 26–31, we first request the user to input values of Student ID and student name for a new row (remaining columns are kept empty for brevity). Next (lines 34–38), we create a new *DataRow* of type tblStudentRow and assign the input values to its *StudentID* and *Name* data columns. We then add and accept the newly created row to the *tblStudent* data table (lines 39–41).

Stage 2: Commit changes to the database table (Line 43)

We call the custom subroutine *SaveToDatabase* (see Figure 15.49) to update the database with the changed *DataSet*.

```
48      Private Sub cmdDelete_Click(ByVal sender As System.Object, _
49      ByVal e As System.EventArgs) Handles cmdDelete.Click
50
51          Try
52              'find out which student's record to delete
53              Dim sid As Integer
54              sid = CInt(InputBox("Enter StudentID", "Primary Key"))
55
56              'Get the data row to be deleted
57              Dim studentRow As UniversityDataSet.tblStudentRow
58              studentRow = _
59              UniversityDataSet.tblStudent.FindByStudentID(sid)
60              Dim name As String = studentRow.Name
61              studentRow.Delete()
62              'OR USE:
63              'UniversityDataSet.tblStudent.Rows.Remove(studentRow)
64
65              'Save Changes to Dataset
66              UniversityDataSet.tblStudent.AcceptChanges()
67              'Save Changes to Database
68              SaveToDatabase()
69              MessageBox.Show("Deleted Record: " & name)
70          Catch ex As Exception
71              MessageBox.Show("Record deletion failed!!")
72          End Try
73
74      End Sub
```

Figure 15.52 Deleting a row from a database table.

Delete Button Code Explanation   The delete operation is also performed in two stages; first, delete the row from the *DataSet* and then update the changed *DataSet* to the database. We have also added a Try-Catch block for exception handling. It is recommended to add exception handling mechanisms when updating databases in order to avoid undesired effects on persistent data.

Stage 1: Delete specified *DataRow* from the *DataSet* (Lines 53–66)

In lines 53–54, we get the value of a primary key (StudentID) of the record to be deleted. Then, we locate the record by calling the *FindBy<PrimaryKey>* method of the student *DataTable* (line 59). We then delete the row from the *DataTable* (line 61).

Stage 2: Commit changes to the database table (Line 68)

We call our custom subroutine *SaveToDatabase* (see Figure 15.49) to update the database with the changed *DataSet*.

Test the Application

6. Ensure that *Form6* is set as the start-up form and press Ctrl+F5 to run the application.

7. Click the *Insert* button and insert the record [99999999, "James Adams"] (see Figure 15.53).

8. Now click the *Delete* button and delete the record inserted in previous step, by giving the *StudentID* 99999999 as input. Figure 15.54 shows the name value of the deleted student record.

(a)   **(b)**

Figure 15.53 Running application: adding a new record to the database.

Figure 15.54 Running application: MessageBox showing the record deleted from the database.

15.10 *Hands-On Tutorial: Updating Changes to Multiple Tables in the Database*

The previous section illustrates how to propagate updates to a single database table. A common application scenario provides related data or data from a join of multiple tables displayed on a form. In this case also, assumingly, we face the need to send the updated data back to the database.

When we added the student table to *Form6* from the Data Sources window, the code to save data was automatically added to the *Click* event of the ToolStrip's *Save* button. Any additional tables added to the form require code to update changes to the database. We illustrate how to add this code to save updates to multiple database tables. In this hands-on tutorial, we walk through the process of adding the related transcript table to the *Form6* (in addition to the already existing student DataGridView control) and illustrate how to save the updated transcript data back to the database.

One naive approach is to call the Update methods for both the tables, successively. However, this might cause referential integrity errors. For example, consider a scenario wherein we delete a student record and then call the update method to update the grades for the same student. When we try to save the updated grade information, it causes a referential integrity violation; the foreign key (*StudentID*) in the transcript table does not have the corresponding primary key entry in the student table. In order to avoid such violations, we manually save the data in a "proper order." This section covers the following How-to topics:

■ How-to: save updated data from more than one database table.
■ How-to: get changes from the *DataSet*.

Build the Application

1. Drag the related transcript table (under the student node) from the Data Sources Window on *Form6*. This adds the transcript DataGridView control and related objects in the Component tray.
2. Add a command button named *cmdSave* to the form.
3. Replace the *Click* event of the *Save* button with code shown in Figure 15.55

(a)

```
76  Private Sub cmdSave_Click(ByVal sender As System.Object, _
77  ByVal e As System.EventArgs) Handles cmdSave.Click
78      'Stop current edits
79      Me.Validate()
80      Me.TblStudentBindingSource.EndEdit()
81      Me.TblTranscriptBindingSource.EndEdit()
82      'Declare the data tables
83      Dim deletedGrades As _
84      UniversityDataSet.tblTranscriptDataTable
85      Dim newGrades As _
86      UniversityDataSet.tblTranscriptDataTable
87      Dim modifiedGrades As _
88      UniversityDataSet.tblTranscriptDataTable
89
90      'Populate our sets
91      deletedGrades = UniversityDataSet.tblTranscript. _
92      GetChanges(Data.DataRowState.Deleted)
93      newGrades = UniversityDataSet.tblTranscript. _
94      GetChanges(Data.DataRowState.Added)
95      modifiedGrades = UniversityDataSet.tblTranscript. _
96      GetChanges(Data.DataRowState.Modified)
```

(b)

```
97
98      Try
99          ' Remove deleted grades from the transcript table
100         If Not deletedGrades Is Nothing Then
101             TblTranscriptTableAdapter.Update(deletedGrades)
102         End If
103
104         ' Update the student table
105         TblStudentTableAdapter.Update _
106         (UniversityDataSet.tblStudent)
107
108         ' Add new grades to the transcript table.
109         If Not newGrades Is Nothing Then
110             TblTranscriptTableAdapter.Update(newGrades)
111         End If
112
113         ' Update all modified grades.
114         If Not modifiedGrades Is Nothing Then
115             TblTranscriptTableAdapter.Update(modifiedGrades)
116         End If
117
118         UniversityDataSet.AcceptChanges()
119         MessageBox.Show("Updated Multiple Tables!!")
```

(c)

```
120
121     Catch ex As Exception
122         MessageBox.Show("Update failed")
123
124     Finally
125         If Not deletedGrades Is Nothing Then
126             deletedGrades.Dispose()
127         End If
128
129         If Not newGrades Is Nothing Then
130             newGrades.Dispose()
131         End If
132
133         If Not modifiedGrades Is Nothing Then
134             modifiedGrades.Dispose()
135         End If
136     End Try
137
138  End Sub
```

Figure 15.55 Updating multiple database tables in an application.

Save Button Code Explanation   The code performs the following tasks:

- All delete operations of child (or related) table(s)
- All update operations of parent table
- All insert and update operations of child (or related) tables(s)

In order to perform these tasks we must get the set of records that we need to insert, modify, and delete, separately for each table. This is done through lines (79–96). Refer preliminaries from Section 15.9 for an elaborate explanation.

For each set, we check for non-empty changed records and perform above listed tasks (lines 98–116). Finally, we accept all the changes in the *DataSet* (line 118). Note that, we *should not* call the *AcceptChanges* method right after we call *EndEdit* on both *BindingSources* (line 80–81). This is necessary since we must extract all changes before accepting those changes. The **Finally** block disposes of temporary *DataSets* (lines 124–136). It is a good practice to dispose large temporary sets. This de-allocates the memory assigned for the sets and renders to improve the running performance of the application.

Test the Application

4. Press Ctrl+F5 to run the application.
5. Change values in both the data grids and click *Save*. Figure 15.56 shows the running application in which the record with StudentID 10100118 is updated in both data grids (*DeptID* is changed to *CISE* and the *Grade* changed to *3.6*). The MessageBox indicates that these changes were successfully stored to the database.

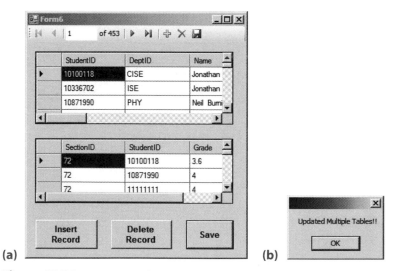

(a)   **(b)**

Figure 15.56 Running application: updating multiple tables in the database.

15.11 *In-Class Assignment*

In this section, we provide an in-class assignment that includes one or more advanced features we have studied in this chapter.

We will build an application with two forms. The first form should display the output of Query1. Query1 is given below. It has two parameters, *College name* and *Course name*:

- **Query 1:** List all the courses from the University database, in which the course belongs to *College name* and has a name in which *LIKE Course name*.

  Show the Query 1 output on a DataGridView on *Form1*. When a user double clicks any course entry in the DataGridView, we should open the second form that displays the output of the following query:

- **Query 2:** List all the sections that belong to the course selected on the first form and have capacity of at least 40 students.

15.12 *Summary*

- ADO .NET (ActiveX Data Objects .NET) is the collection of objects that are designed to support data access and data manipulation.
- Database connectivity involves the following entities: database—stores data on the hard drive (disk), connection—connects to the database, adapter—hosts SQL queries and executes them against the database, dataset—stores data in the main memory, form—displays data to the user.
- The ADO .NET objects interact with each other for Windows forms to database data transfer as follows: (i) a *Connection* object opens a live connection to the database; (ii) an *adapter* object executes SQL queries against the connected database; (iii) an *adapter* object further *fills* the *DataSet* object with query results. *DataSet* stores the result in the main memory.
- The ADO .NET objects interact with each other for Windows forms to database data transfer as follows: (i) if a user edits the data in the Windows controls, the updates are propagated to the *DataSets*; (ii) the *adapter* then propagates the updates from the *DataSets* to the connected database using its set of Update SQL statements.

- Creating a database connection is like opening a unique session with the database. Once opened, we can access contents of the database using the *Connection* object.
- We considered some advanced topics in displaying data on Windows forms. The topics were (i) how to display data from a query with multiple parameters, (ii) how to display data from a join of two or more tables, (iii) how to make use of existing MS Access queries to display data on forms, (iv) how to pass data between two Windows forms.
- A *DataSet* is essentially, an in-memory relational database. A DataSet may contain one or more *DataTables* and each *DataTable* can have multiple *DataRows* and *DataColumns*. *DataSets* act as a cache for a Windows application.
- We considered topics like how to insert, update, and delete rows from the database with the two-stage updates strategy. Finally, to conclude the chapter, we showed how to handle propagation of changes to the database for related or multiple tables.

15.13   *Exercises*

15.13.1 Review Questions

1. Which ADO .NET objects are involved in the propagation of updates from a Windows form to the database?

2. What are the functions of an *adapter* object?

3. What are the two ways of creating a database connection in Visual Studio? What are the two primary methods associated with a *Connection* object?

4. How does the *TableAdapter* object simplify the process of maintaining a database connection?

5. What is the difference between the tables listed in the Data Sources Window against those listed in the Server Explorer Window?

6. What are the two default methods associated with a *TableAdapter* object? Describe their functionality.

7. How do we add a *TableAdapter* to an application?

8. How do we add a query to a *TableAdapter* involving join of two or more tables?

9. What is the use of the DISTINCT keyword in SQL?

10. Can we make use of MS Access query in Visual Studio environment? How?

11. What are the steps to pass data from one form to the other form in an application?

12. Compare a *DataSet* and a database.

13. How do we add *DataTables* to the existing *DataSet*?

14. What are the stages in a two-stage update propagation process? Which ADO .NET objects are involved in this process?

15. How will we commit changes in a *DataSet* at different levels (*DataRow*, *DataTable*, and *DataSet*)?

16. What is a referential integrity violation? How does it occur? Provide an example.

17. Where should we dispose large data sets or tables we create within a function? Why should we dispose these objects?

15.13.2 Hands-On Exercises

NOTE: *The database files for these hands-on exercises are available at: www.dssbooks.com.*

1. Using the "Airline" database, create a form that allows the user to select a city of origin from a drop-down list. Use this selection to populate a second drop-down list from which the user can select a destination city. Finally, use both of these to display a list of available flights traveling between those two cities in a DataGridView control.

2. Using the "Post Office" database, create a form that allows the user to enter a ZIP code into a TextBox control and then displays the information for those post offices. Use this information to display a list showing all the addresses for packages sent from those post offices. Finally, allow the user to select an address and show all the package information in a grid, for the packages sent from that address. (*Hint:* The list of zip codes serviced by a particular branch is stored as a string.)

3. Using the "Movies" database, create a form that allows a user to select a state from a drop-down list. With this information, populate a second drop-down list that allows the user to select a city from those available in the selected state. Display a list of movie theaters in that city and allow the user to select one. Finally, display the appropriate movie data for that theater in a pop-up form.

4. Using the "Hotel" database, create a form that allows the user to select a room type from a drop-down list. The name of the room type should be displayed, but the value member stored should be the *TypeID*. Add two DateTimePicker controls to allow the user to select a beginning and ending date and display all the customers who have that room type reserved between those two dates.

5. Using the "Hospital" database, create a parent/child form that allows the user to select a doctor's name from a drop-down list and then displays all the patients assigned to the selected doctor.

6. Using the "Library" database, create a parent/child form that allows the user to select a member ID and displays all books checked out by that member.

7. Using the "Furniture" database, create a parent/child form that allows the user to select a product from a drop-down list (with the name displayed and the number as the value) and

displays a grid indicating every shipment that contains that product.

8. Using the "Airline" database, create an application that displays the customer contact information and ticket information. The application should allow the user to insert, delete or update any of the information. Add a *Save* button to the form. On click of the *Save* button, the application should save changes to the *Customer* and *Reservation* tables.

9. Using the "Megabucks" database, create an application that displays the details of all customers who have certain expected minimum current balance and those who currently have a loan from the bank. Perform a join of the *Accounts*, *Loans* and *Customer* tables to extract the required information and display the retrieved customer details in a DataGridView control.

10. Using the "Schools" database, design an application that lists all the students who have been enrolled for more than 2 years and have not passed all courses they had enrolled for.

11. In a restaurant, the chef needs to compile a list of dishes that will not be offered this week because the ingredients are not available. Design an application that lists the name of unavailable ingredients together with the dishes that use them (use the "Menu" database).

12. A hotel is researching customers whose expenditure is between a certain desired price range. Design an application that identifies all customers who have spent between $1,000 and $2,000 on rooms since March 1st, 2002 (use the "Hotel" database).

13. Create an application for a post office that provides a clerk the facility to select a particular customer from a drop-down list and view all the package information for that user in a grid view. Also, compute and display the cost of shipping each package according to the shipment type, package weight, and shipping rate (*Hint*: join *tblPackages* and *tblRates*). Sort the packages in an ascending order by package weight (use the "Post Office" database).

14. Create an application that displays the list of students who have earned about 60% in a user-specified course. Allow the user to select a specific course from a drop-down list of courses. Also, whenever the user clicks on a specific student ID, display the details of that student in a pop-up form (use the "Schools" database).

15. Using the "Bottling" database, create an application that displays the details of lines in which the equipment age is at most 2 years. Whenever the user clicks on a particular line, display the details of the associated bottle in a pop-up form.

16. Create an application for a hospital that allows the user to select a patient name from a drop-down list and displays the patient's bill information in a pop-up form (use the "Hospital" database).

17. Create an application that displays the grade details of students in a user-specified course. Allow the user to select the course name from a drop-down list. Then, display a grid that contains all the grade details of students in that specific course on a pop-up form (use the "Schools" database).

18. Create an application that will display the customer and corresponding booking details at a hotel. Allow insert, delete, and update operations (use the "Hotel" database).

CHAPTER

sixteen **Crystal Reports**

chapter **OVERVIEW**

447

16.1　*Introduction*

So far, we have used Windows forms to display information that can be viewed, edited, and saved. However, in many scenarios where we need to compile a large amount of information, it is more suitable to provide a report or summary of information than displaying tens or hundreds of records on the screen. For example, consider monthly utility bills, phone bills, and student transcripts. Reports are better suited than forms for presenting such information. Reports allow us to compare, summarize, group, and present data to users in a variety of formats including professional invoices, purchase orders, mailing orders, and monthly bills. In many business applications, it is desirable to present information in the form of charts rather than as plain text. Reports also allow us to plot charts on Windows forms. When connected to the database, query results can be summarized, grouped, and presented in the form of charts to the user.

Crystal Reports is one of the world's leading software packages for creating interactive reports. It is widely used and has become the de facto standard for reports. The Crystal Reports package is integrated and distributed along with the Visual Studio package and must be selected for installation while installing Visual Studio .NET. We utilize the Visual Studio IDE to design reports and integrate them in database applications to display charts and summarized information on Windows Forms or Web Forms (see Chapter 19). Crystal Reports .NET provides a rich collection of features such as grouping, sorting, summarizing, analyzing, applying selection criteria, selecting display styles, and graphically presenting data using charts. Figure 16.1 illustrates some examples of Crystal Reports.

Due to its correspondence with Visual Studio, Crystal Reports .NET offers several benefits to database developers. It leaves the ADO .NET architecture unperturbed, allowing us to interact with databases in the manner we accessed them through Windows forms. Crystal Reports can be built on existing or new data sources or on other ADO .NET objects, making the development process faster and easier.

16.1.1　Topics

This chapter discusses the following topics:

- How to create a simple data-bind Crystal Report.
- How to use Crystal Report's *Expert* wizard.
- How to specify the data source of a Crystal Report.
- How to build various charts in Crystal Reports.
- How to display a Crystal Report on a Windows form.
- How to create a Crystal Report based on a parameter query.
- The different sections of a Crystal Report.
- How to customize and enhance the appearance of an existing Crystal Report.

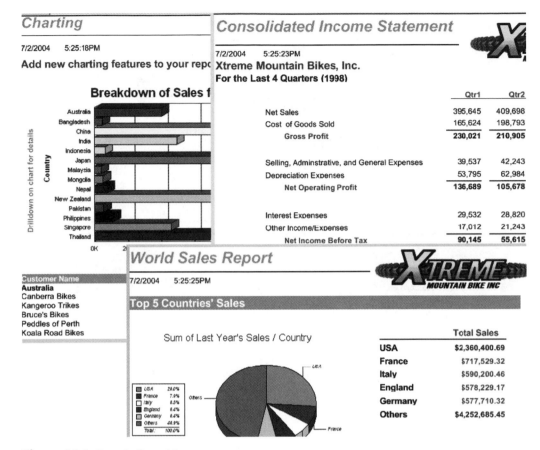

Figure 16.1 Sample Crystal Reports.

16.2 *Crystal Report Primer: A Simple Student Report*

This primer walks us through the steps that are necessary to create a *Student Report* using Crystal Report .NET in a Windows application. We make use of the *Standard Expert* Wizard to build the report. This section is divided into several subsections that correspond to the steps of the Crystal Report development process. We also summarize these steps in the succeeding hands-on tutorial.

The requirements for the student report (see Figure 16.2) are as follows:

- The report should display the contact information (name, email, and phone) of students in the Industrial Engineering (ISE) department, grouped by student classes.
- The report should also display a bar chart for the number of ISE students in each of the five student classes.

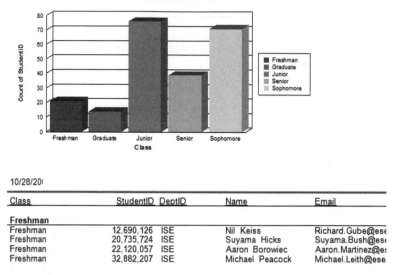

Figure 16.2 The student report.

16.2.1 Set Up the Application, Database Connection, and a Data Source

We first create a new application and establish connectivity with the University database. We also create a Data Source for our application.

1. Create a new Windows application named *CrystalReports*, using the *New Project* dialog box.
2. Choose the Data | Show Data Sources option from the main menu to open the Data Sources Window. Click *Add New Data Source* to start the *Data Source Configuration Wizard*.
3. In the *Data Source Configuration Wizard*, create a new connection to the University database; copy the database to the current project folder when prompted; choose the student, department, college, and faculty tables from the table's nodes on the last page. Click *Finish*.

16.2.2 Adding a Report to the Application

Crystal reports can be added to the existing application as a new item, similar to Windows forms, classes, and modules.

4. Choose Project | Add New Item from the main menu. This opens the *Add New Item* dialog box. Locate and select the *Crystal Report* option. Name the report as "Student Report.rpt" in the *Name* TextBox and click *Add* (see Figure 16.3).

A separate tab appears in Visual Studio IDE for the student report. The *Crystal Reports Gallery* dialog box is automatically displayed and serves as a starting point of the report design.

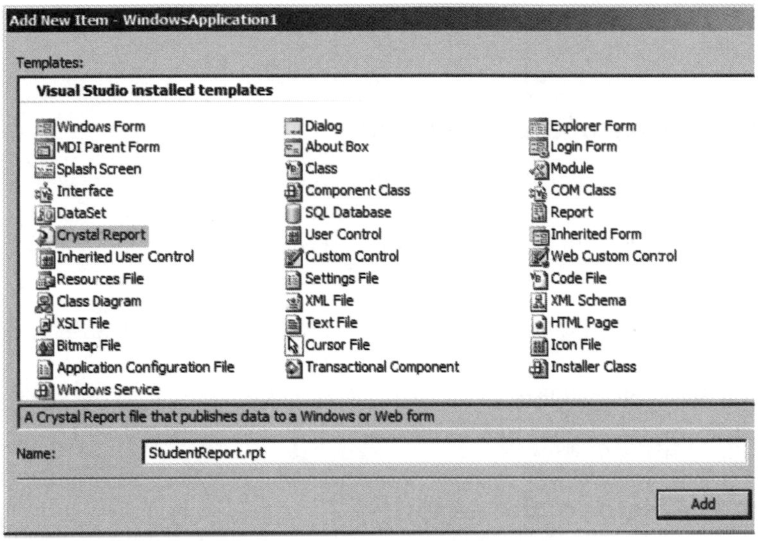

Figure 16.3 Adding a Crystal Report to the application.

16.2.3 Using the *Report Expert Wizard*

We choose the mode of the Crystal Report creation in the *Crystal Reports Gallery* dialog box. The following are the available options:

- **Using the Report Wizard:** When this option is selected, we can choose from a variety of *Experts* in the bottom half of the dialog box (see Figure 16.4). These experts create different types of reports and are, arguably, the most popular methods of creating new reports.
- **As a Blank Report:** Advanced users can build reports from a blank report. No *Expert* Wizards are available for this option.
- **From an Existing Report:** This option imports an existing report, which is used as the basis for a new report. Again, *Experts* Wizards are unavailable with this option.

Selecting the *Using the Report Wizard* option allows us to choose from three different *Experts*. Table 16.1 lists these *Experts* with a brief description. In this chapter, we focus on the *Standard Expert* wizard.

Table 16.1 Crystal Report *Experts*.

Expert	Description
Standard	It is the most generic and frequently used *Expert*. It is used to create columnar reports. It has features such as grouping, sorting, summary options, filtering, and charts. We can also choose from pre-defined styles for new reports.
Cross-Tab	This row-column grid report looks similar to a spreadsheet. It summarizes grouped data across rows and columns similar to cross-tab queries in the MS Access DBMS.
Mail Label	As the name suggests, this *Expert* prints multi-column mail labels and can combine the text object and database fields.

5. For the student report example, keep the default selections, *Using the Report Wizard* and *Standard Expert*. Click *OK*.

16.2.4   Specifying Source of the Report Data

On the next page (*Data* page), the Wizard enables us to choose the data we wish to report. There are different options available in the *Available Data Sources* pane of the Wizard page. We utilize the Project Data | ADO .NET Datasets option to specify the *UniversityDataSet* as the source of our report's data (the Data Source we added in Section 16.2.1).

6. Collapse the Project Data | ADO .NET DataSets | CrystalReports.UniversityDataSet nodes to see the list of data tables.

7. Add the student table from the *Available Data Sources* pane to the *Selected Tables* pane. Click *Next* (see Figure 16.5).

16.2.5   Selecting the Fields of the Report

The Wizard then moves to the *Fields* page, where we can choose the information to display on the report. We select fields from the *Available Fields* pane and add them to the *Fields to Display* pane. In our example, we are interested in the student's contact information (*Name*, *Email*, and *Phone*) and a method to count the number of ISE (*DeptID*) students (primary key—*StudentID*) for each student class (*Class*).

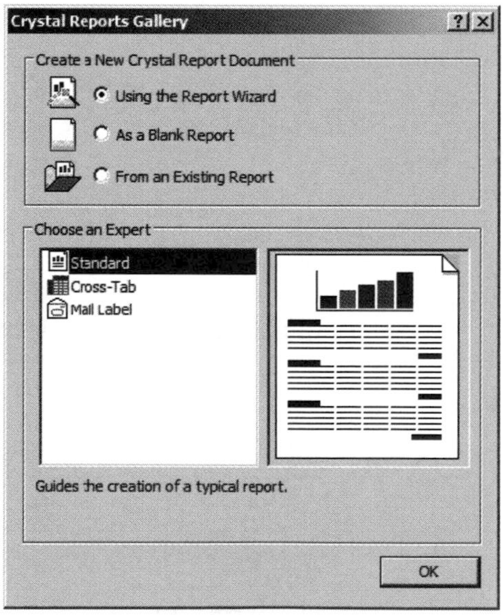

Figure 16.4 The *Crystal Reports Gallery* dialog box.

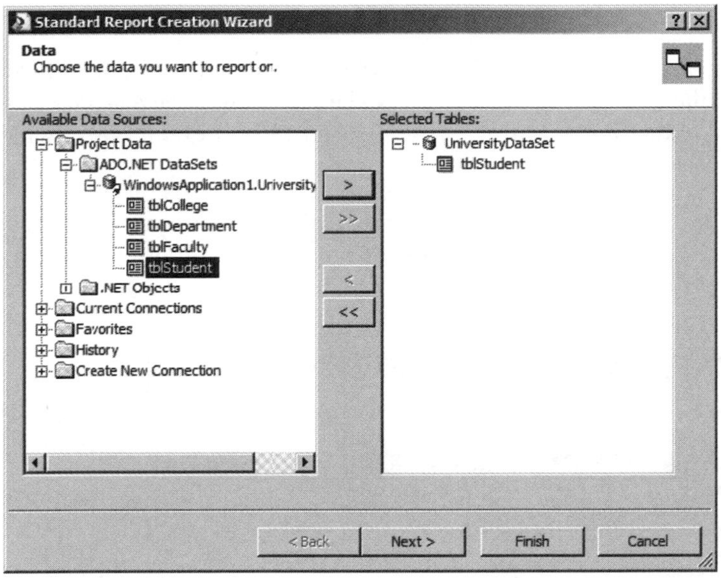

Figure 16.5 Using the *tblStudent* data table of the *UniversityDataSet* as the report's data source.

8. Collapse the *tblStudent* node to view its available fields. Add the *StudentID*, *DeptID*, *Name*, *Class*, *Email*, and *Phone* fields of the student table from the Available Fields pane to the *Fields to Display* pane. Click *Next* (see Figure 16.6).

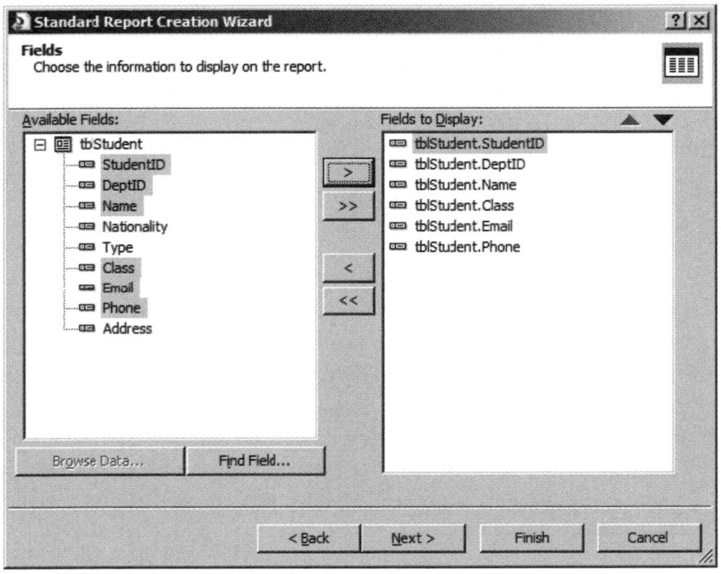

Figure 16.6 Selecting relevant fields for the report.

16.2.6 Performing Grouping Operations

The Wizard then displays the *Grouping* page, where we can specify the fields based on which we wish to group the information. These fields can be chosen from the *Available Fields* pane on the left and added to the *Group By* pane on the right side. In our example, we would like to group students based on student classes.

9. Add the *tblStudent.Class* field from the *Available Fields* pane to the *Group By* pane. Accept the default "*in ascending order*" sorting order at the bottom of the Wizard page and click *Next* (see Figure 16.7).

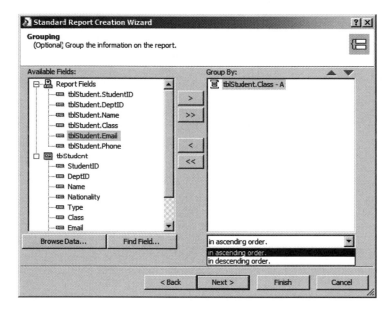

Figure 16.7 *Group By* field of the report.

16.2.7 Performing Summary Operations

We can add summary information to the report using the *Summaries* page of the Wizard. Specifically, we can choose fields and summary operations on the selected fields using this page. There are many summary operations available in the drop-down list at the bottom of the Wizard. The commonly used operations are Sum, Average, Count, Minimum, and Maximum.

Summary fields are closely related to the *Group By* fields we have added in the previous step. When we group student records based on student classes, it indicates that we are interested in the summary about each group. In our example, we are interested in counting the number of students in each group. The best way to count students is to count the primary key, namely, *StudentID*.

10. If required, add the *tblStudent.StudentID* field from the *Available Fields* pane to the *Summarized Fields* pane.
11. Select the *StudentID* summary field from the *Summarized Fields* pane and choose the *Count* operation from the drop-down list below that pane. Click *Next* (see Figure 16.8).

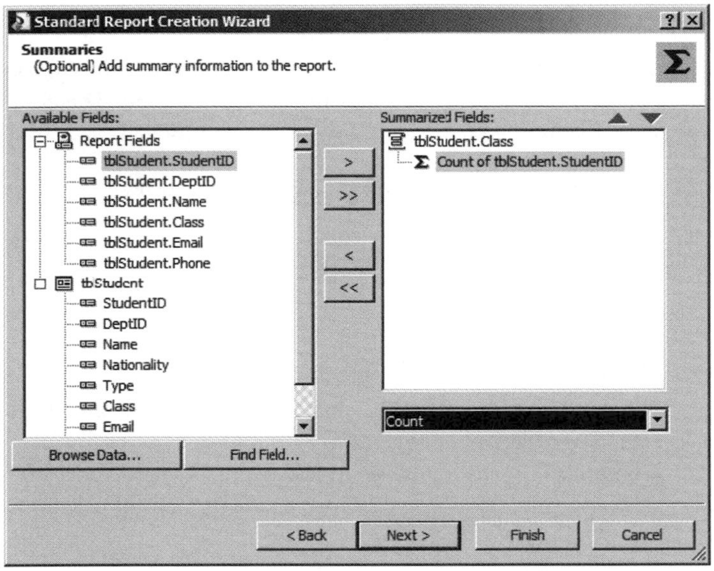

Figure 16.8 Counting the number of students.

16.2.8   Using the Group Sorting Feature

The *Group Sorting* page of the Wizard enables us to sort groups based on the summarized totals. In our example, we have groups based on student classes, and we are counting the number of students in each group. We can display the top 5 or bottom 5 classes based on the count value of the group. To display all the groups (classes), we select the *None* option (see Figure 16.9). For multiple *Group By* fields, we choose each group from the drop-down list one at a time, and then we apply the desired sorting feature for each selected group.

> **12.** On the *Group Sorting* page, accept the default *None* option for the *Class* group and click *Next* (see Figure 16.9).

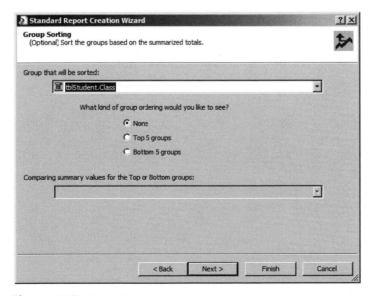

Figure 16.9 *Group Sorting* options.

16.2.9 **Using the Chart Option**

Chart is one of the most attractive features of the Crystal Reports. On the *Chart* page of the Expert Wizard, we can specify the chart type, chart title, and chart data. The chart types serve as templates for the chart design. We have the following three options for the chart design:

- **Bar Chart**: A bar chart uses vertical or horizontal bars to show the relationship between data.
- **Line Chart**: A line chart uses lines along a grid to present the data.
- **Pie Chart**: A pie chart is a circle divided into segments, with each piece of the pie representing the data.

To specify the chart data, we use two drop-down lists: "*On change of*" and "*Show summary.*" These two values are the two dimensions of the chart. In the case of the bar chart and line chart, the field selected in the "*On change of*" drop-down list supplies X-axis values, while the field selected in the "*Show summary*" drop-down list supplies values for the Y-axis. In the case of pie charts, the field values in the first drop-down list decide the number of pie slices, while the field values in the other decide the size of each slice.

13. Select the *Bar Chart* radio button. Select *tblStudent.Class* as the "*On change of*" field (X-axis) and *Count of tblStudent.StudentID* as the "*Show summary*" field (Y-axis). Name the chart title as shown in Figure 16.10. Click *Next*.

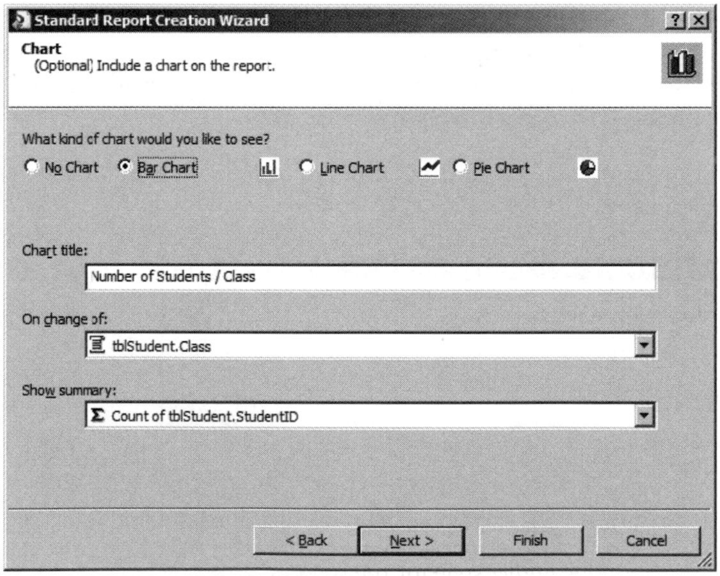

Figure 16.10 Selecting the chart type as a bar chart.

16.2.10 Filtering in the Report

As an option on the *Record Selection* page, we can apply filtering criteria to report fields. We move fields from the *Available Fields* pane to the *Filter Fields* pane, and then apply filtering criteria on each field. The filtering expression and its value are specified using the drop-down list at the bottom of the page. The following are the examples of filtering expression: "is equal to," "is not equal to," "is less than," "is greater than," "is between," "is like," and so forth. In our student report example, we want to display the records of students who are in the ISE department. We use the "is equal to" expression with "ISE" value to filter out desired records.

14. Move the *tblStudent.DeptID* field from the *Available Fields* pane to the *Filter Fields* pane.
15. Select the *DeptID* field in the *Filter Fields* pane, and choose the "*is equal to*" item from the drop-down list. Assign the value of the expression "*ISE*" in the second drop-down list (see Figure 16.11) and click *Next*.

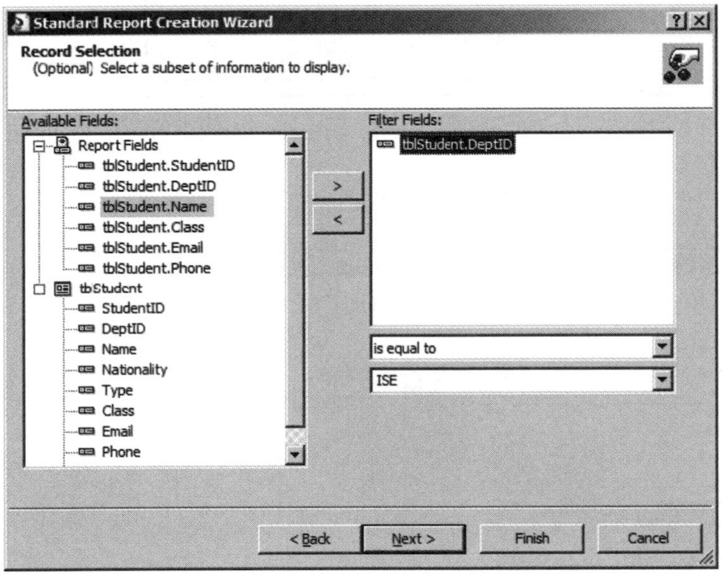

Figure 16.11 Applying filtering criteria to select the student records from the ISE department.

16.2.11 Selecting the Report Style

On the last page of the Wizard, *Report Style*, we select a formatting style for the report from a list of pre-defined styles. The *Expert* Wizard features ten different styling options that differ primarily in terms of color and font selection.

16. Select the *Red/Blue Border* style for the student report (see Figure 16.12). Click *Finish* to add the report to the application. Figure 16.13 shows the IDE with the report's design view.
17. Select the bar chart object from the report header and right-click the selection. Choose the Chart Options | Template option from the shortcut menu. This should open the *Chart Option* dialog box. Select the *Use Depth* CheckBox control and click *OK*.

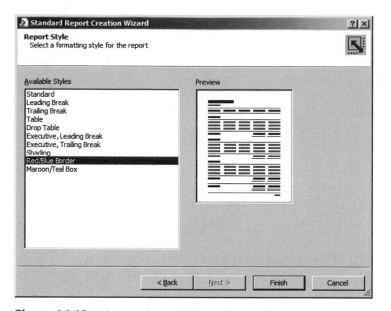

Figure 16.12 Selecting the *Red/Blue Border* style for the student report.

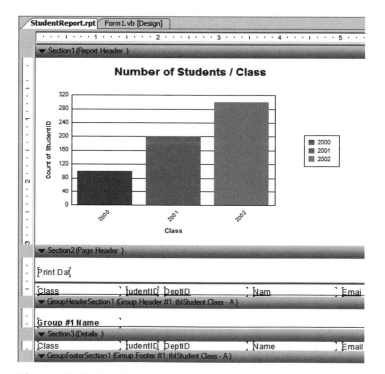

Figure 16.13 The Crystal Report's design environment.

16.2.12 Adding a CrystalReportViewer

So far, we have designed the student report with the required data. The student report file (*Student Report.rpt*) should appear as a separate entry under the Solution Explorer Window. Now, we shall demonstrate how to integrate this Crystal Report with a Windows form using a CrystalReport Viewer control.

> **18.** Open *Form1* in the Design Window. Drag and drop the CrystalReportViewer control under the *Crystal Reports* tab in the Toolbox on *Form1* (see Figure 16.14).

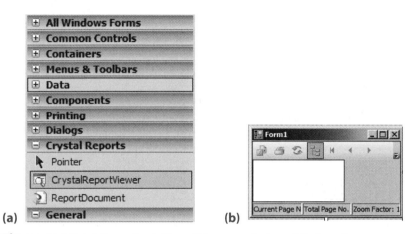

(a)   **(b)**

Figure 16.14 Adding a CrystalReportViewer control to a Windows form.

16.2.13 Binding the Report

We now associate the student report file, *StudentReport.rpt*, with the CrystalReportViewer control. We perform this task programmatically using the form's *Form_Load* event.

> **19.** Double-click on the *Form1* header (or anywhere on the form) to open the Code Window. Replace *Form1*'s *Form_Load* event with the code in Figure 16.15. Press Ctrl+F5 to run the application (see Figure 16.2 for running application).

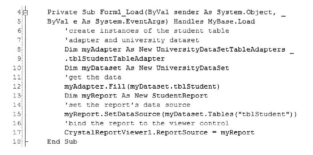

```
4    Private Sub Form1_Load(ByVal sender As System.Object, _
5    ByVal e As System.EventArgs) Handles MyBase.Load
6        'create instances of the student table
7        'adapter and university dataset
8        Dim myAdapter As New UniversityDataSetTableAdapters _
9        .tblStudentTableAdapter
10       Dim myDataset As New UniversityDataSet
11       'get the data
12       myAdapter.Fill(myDataset.tblStudent)
13       Dim myReport As New StudentReport
14       'set the report's data source
15       myReport.SetDataSource(myDataset.Tables("tblStudent"))
16       'bind the report to the viewer control
17       CrystalReportViewer1.ReportSource = myReport
18   End Sub
```

Figure 16.15 Crystal report binding code.

Figure 16.15 Explained:

We divide the explanation into two parts: getting the data and binding the report file.

Getting the Data

Recall that we have based the student report on the *tblStudent* data table. In order to display the bar chart, we must fill the data into the *tblStudent* data table. Like any other application we have developed before, we make use of the *TblStudentTableAdapter* to fill the *tblStudent* data table. We could add a *TblStudentTableAdapter* on the form, using one of the following options:

1. Drag the *tblStudent* data table from Data Sources Window on *Form1* to create the table adapter, data set, and related objects.
2. Create the table adapter and dataset programmatically at runtime.

We choose the second option for this primer and instantiate the *TblStudentTableAdapter* adapter and a dataset of type *UniversityDataSet* in lines 8–10. Line 12 actually fills the data in the *tblStudent* data table.

Binding the Report

To bind the report file with the CrystalReportViewer control, we should first create the report object (line 13). The object's data source is set to the filled data table (line 15), and finally the object is set as the report source of the viewer control (line 17).

16.3 *Crystal Report Sections*

If we look at the Crystal Report file in the Design Window, we notice several report sections. A Crystal Report consists of a number of sections (see Figure 16.16); we shall now briefly introduce some of the important sections of the report.

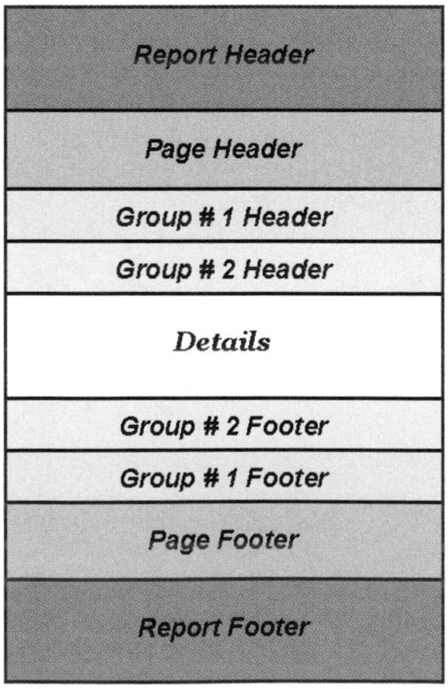

Figure 16.16 Crystal Report sections.

Every report has report header and report footer sections. The entities inside the report header and the report footer sections appear at the beginning of the report and at the end of the report, respectively. For example, the student report has a chart object in the report header and the total number of students in the report footer. The contents of the report header and report footer section appear once in the entire report.

Reports often have multiple pages. A report has page header and page footer sections that appear only once on each page of the report. The page header in our example includes the report title, date, and the column titles; these appear at the top of every report page. By default, the page number is included in the page footer and appears at the bottom of every page.

The core section of a report, the details section, appears once for each record in the report; this section displays columns of information. In our example, the contact information of students is displayed in the details section.

Finally, if the report includes multiple groups of records, then the group header and group footer sections appear automatically for each group. In our example, a student class group header and footer appear on the chart. In the student report, the group header includes the name of the groups: freshman, sophomore, senior, etc., while the group footer includes the summary for the groups, i.e., the number of students in each class.

Summary

Crystal Report Integration Summary:

1. Create the Crystal Report using the *Standard Expert* Wizard. Specify the report fields, group-by fields, summary fields, chart fields, and filter fields.
2. Add a CrystalReportViewer control on a Windows form.
3. Bind the report file with the CrystalReportViewer control in the VB code.

16.4 *Customizing Reports: Exploring the Design Environment*

We often modify the report created by the *Expert* Wizard to do the following:

1. Make it look more appealing (formatting)
2. Alter any design fields (editing)

In this section, we explore different options available for report formatting and editing in the Crystal Report designing environment.

16.4.1 Formatting Charts and Fields

Charts appear in the report header section. Formatting a chart includes modifying the chart type, editing its title, layout, data labels, axis labels, and grid lines settings.

1. Open the *StudentReport.rpt* file from the Solution Explorer to view the report's design.

2. Right-click on the chart object in the report header (Section 1) to display its formatting options. Choose the *Chart Options* item (see Figure 16.17).

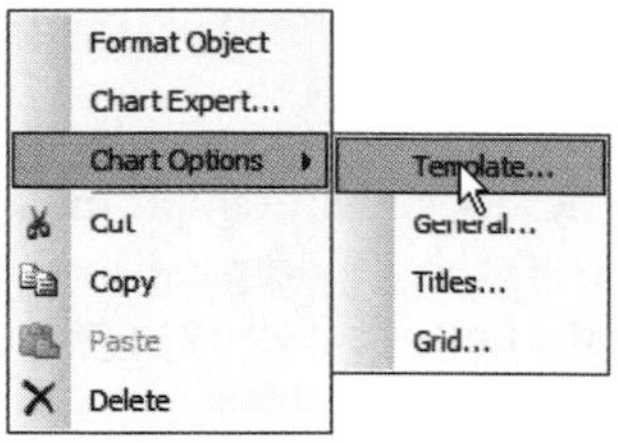

Figure 16.17 *Chart Options* item for chart formatting.

There are four different options available in the *Chart Options* menu to format a chart. These options are summarized in Table 16.2.

Table 16.2 *Chart Options* summary.

Chart options	Description
Template	We can choose different chart types using this option or enhance existing type settings such as selecting 3D riser and using chart depth, etc.
General	We can alter general options such as data labels and chart layout.
Titles	We can modify chart title and axis labels using this option.
Grid	This is one of the most effective formatting options. We can decide between major or minor grid lines and scale of the axes with this option.

The selected fields appear in the details section (Section3) of the report. The ability to format fields, page, and group headers helps us enhance the visual appeal of a report. We can change the length, width, and position of fields and separator lines. We can also alter their font and colors.

In general, for any object (chart or fields) in the report, we can format it by manipulating its properties in the Properties Window (see Figure 16.18). The Properties Window gives us fine control over formatting of each report element.

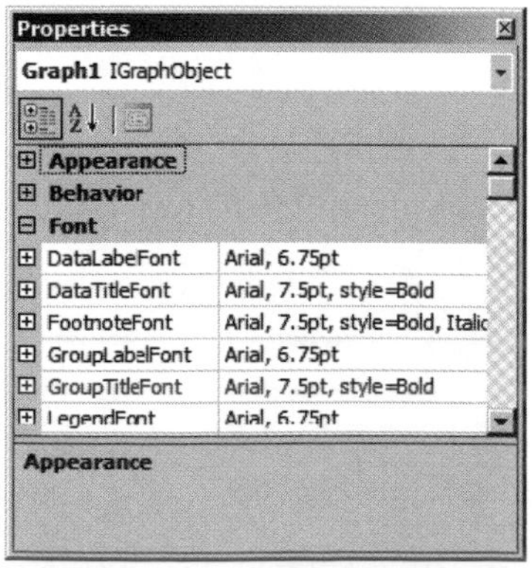

Figure 16.18 Properties of report charts and fields.

16.4.2 Editing Chart Design

Often, we need to alter some selections from the *Expert* Wizard. For example, we may add or remove fields from the report, change the *Group By* field, the sorting order, or alter filtering criteria. To edit any of the *Expert* Wizard options, we right-click *outside* the chart object in the report header section and choose the appropriate option from the shortcut menu (see Figure 16.19).

Figure 16.19 Editing chart design.

If we choose the *Select Expert* option, it should open the *Record Selection* page of the Wizard with existing filter criteria. Similarly, the *Group Expert* option should open the *Grouping* page of the Wizard, where we can add or remove *Group By* fields, and so forth.

16.5 *Properties of a CrystalReportViewer Control*

We can further enhance report appearance and behavior by manipulating properties of the CrystalReportViewer control (the report container). In this section, we briefly discuss important properties of the CrystalReportViewer control. The CrystalReportViewer control properties can be manipulated using the Properties Window, or alternatively, we can manipulate them programmatically at runtime. Table 16.3 summarizes some of the important properties.

Table 16.3 CrystalReportViewer control's properties.

Property	Description
BackColor	Gets/Sets the background color used to display text and graphics in the control.
DisplayGroupTree	Indicates whether the group tree on the left-hand side should be visible or hidden.
DisplayToolbar	Indicates whether the toolbar at the top should be visible or hidden.
ShowCloseButton	Indicates whether the viewer toolbar should contain buttons (Close, Export, and Print) to perform actions.
ShowExportButton	ShowPrintButton
Name	Gets/Sets the name used in the code to identify the control.
ReportSource	Determines which report to display inside the viewer control.

Hands-On Tutorial: Creating a Pie Chart to Display Faculty Salaries

In this hands-on tutorial, we will display the average faculty salaries for each department on a pie chart. The steps for this exercise are similar to the student report primer, except that we use the faculty table and an average aggregate function, and we plot a pie chart. The purpose of this section is to reiterate the Crystal Report integration process with another simple example. This section covers the following How-to topics:

- How-to: create a Crystal Report.
- How-to: add a Crystal Report on a Windows form.
- How-to: use the CrystalReportViewer control.
- How-to: plot a pie chart using Crystal Reports.

Creating the Report

1. Add *Form2* to the *CrystalReports* application.
2. Choose the Project | Add New Item option from the main menu to invoke the *Add New Item* dialog box. Choose the *Crystal Report* item, and name the report *FacultySalary.rpt*. Click *Add* to create a new Crystal Report.
3. Select the default *Using the Report Wizard* option with the *Standard Expert* selection in the *Crystal Reports Gallery* dialog box. Click *OK*.
4. On the *Data* page of the Wizard, select the *tblFaculty* data table under Project Data | ADO.NET Datasets in the *Available Data Sources* pane, and add it to the *Selected Tables* pane (see Figure 16.20). Click *Next*.

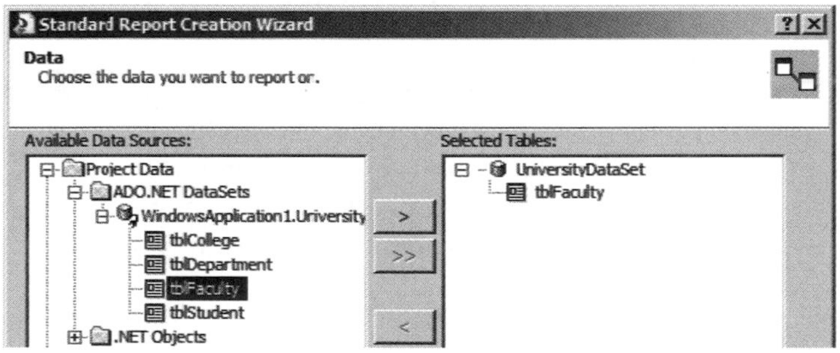

Figure 16.20 Choosing the *tblFaculty* data table for the faculty report.

5. On the *Fields* page, select and add the *FacultyID*, *DeptID*, and *Salary* fields to the *Fields to Display* pane. Click *Next*.
6. On the *Grouping* page, select and add the *DeptID* field to the *Group By* pane. Click *Next*.
7. On the *Summaries* page, remove the *Sum of tblFaculty.FacultyID* field from the *Summarized Fields* pane (use "<" button). For the *tblFaculty.Salary* field, choose the *Average* summary option from the drop-down list at the bottom of the page (see Figure 16.21). Click *Next*.

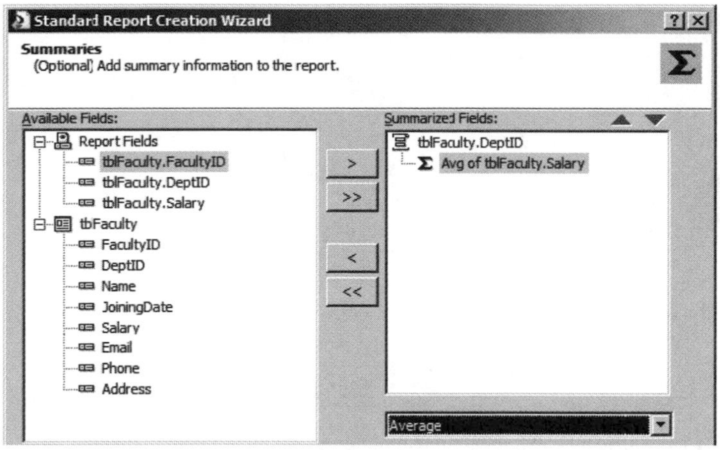

Figure 16.21 Assigning the *Average* function for the *Salary* field.

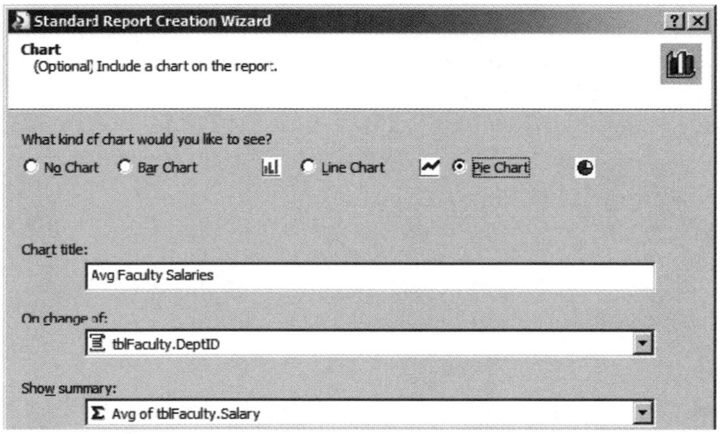

Figure 16.22 Setting up a pie chart to display average faculty salaries.

8. On the *Group Sorting* page, select the *None* ordering option and click *Next*.
9. On the *Chart* page, choose the *Pie Chart* option. Change the *Chart Title* box as shown in Figure 16.22. Accept default values for the *On Change of* and *Show summary* drop-down lists. Click *Finish*.

   Note that we do not need to select any filtering criteria or report styles; hence, we can bypass these pages of the Wizard.
10. In the *FacultyReport.rpt*'s design view, remove all the fields in the various report sections except for the chart object in the report header.
11. Select the chart object from the report header and right-click the selection. Choose Chart Options | General item from the shortcut menu. This should open the *Chart Options* dialog box.
12. Navigate to the *Data Labels* tab and configure it as shown in the Figure 16.23.

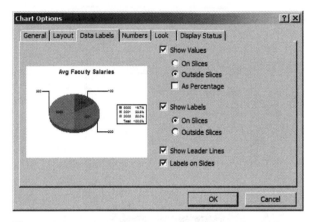

Figure 16.23 Configuring *Data Labels* on the pie chart.

Binding the Report

13. Add a CrystalReportViewer control from the ToolBox on *Form2*.

14. Using the Properties Window of the control, change its *Dock* property from *Fill* to *None*, and set its *DisplayGroupTree* property to *False* (see Figure 16.24). Adjust its length and width on the form.

15. Drag and drop the *tblFaculty* data table from the Data Sources Window on *Form2*. This creates a DataGridView control, a ToolStrip control, and related objects in the Component tray.

16. Remove the auto-created DataGridView control and the ToolStrip control from *Form2*. We will use the *TblFacultyTableAdapter*, *TblFacultyBindingSource*, and *UniversityDataSet* objects in the Component tray while binding the report (recall from Section 16.2.13 that this is a design-time alternative to create table adapter and dataset objects), for example, see Figure 16.25.

(a)	(b)

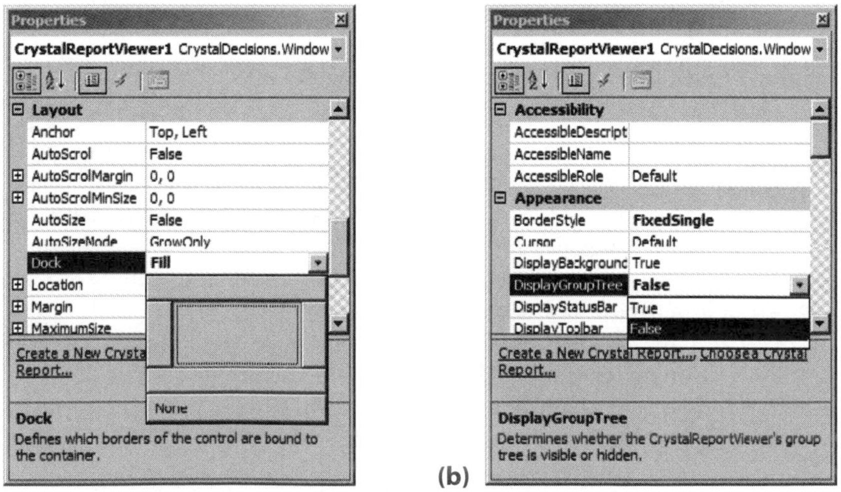

Figure 16.24 Un-docking the CrystalReportViewer control.

UniversityDataSet   TblFacultyBindingSource   TblFacultyTableAdapter

Figure 16.25 The *TableAdapter, BindingSource* and *Dataset* components for the chart's data.

```
 4    Private Sub Form2_Load(ByVal sender As System.Object, _
 5    ByVal e As System.EventArgs) Handles MyBase.Load
 6        'get the data from the dataset
 7        Me.TblFacultyTableAdapter.Fill(Me. _
 8        UniversityDataSet.tblFaculty)
 9        'create report instance
10        Dim myReport As New FacultyReport
11        'set its data source
12        myReport.SetDataSource _
13        (UniversityDataSet.Tables("tblFaculty"))
14        'bind the report to the viewer control
15        CrystalReportViewer1.ReportSource = myReport
16    End Sub
```

Figure 16.26 Binding code for the faculty report.

17. Replace the form's *Form_Load* event with the code shown in Figure 16.26. Note that we have used the table adapter and dataset objects from the Component tray to get the data (line 5) instead of creating them in the code.

18. Set the *Form2* as the start-up form and run the application (see Figure 16.27).

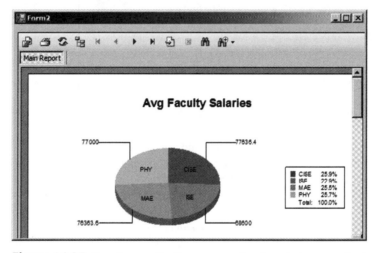

Figure 16.27 Running application: average faculty salaries on a pie chart.

16.7 Hands-On Tutorial: Creating a Crystal Report Based on Multiple Tables

In this section, we illustrate how to create a Crystal Report based on the data from the join of two or more tables. We plot a line chart of average student grades for each calendar year. In the University database, the grade information is stored in the transcript table for each student-section pair, while the year in which the sections are offered is stored in the section table. Thus, to get the average grades per calendar year, we must join the transcript and section tables. Our line chart will be based on this join. This hands-on tutorial covers the following How-to topics:

- ■ How-to: create a line chart.
- ■ How-to: create a Crystal Report based on the join of two or more tables.

Setting Up the Data Table

Unlike previous reports, we do not have a *DataTable* in the Data Sources Windows that can be directly used for the grades chart. We create a new *TableAdapter* (and thus a *DataTable*) using the Select query with the join of multiple tables. Recall from Section 15.5 the steps to add a new *TableAdapter* object using *Dataset Designer*.

1. Open the *Dataset Designer* (double-click the *UniversityDataSet.xsd* file in the Solution Explorer Window). Right-click anywhere in the designer, and choose the *Add TableAdapter* option from the shortcut menu. This should open the *TableAdapter Configuration* Wizard.

2. On the *Enter an SQL Statement* page of the Wizard, build the SQL query as shown in Figure 16.28, and finish the Wizard.

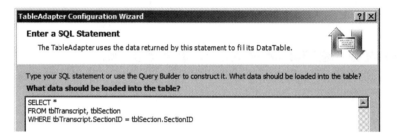

Figure 16.28 Average grade line chart's base query.

Note that we have only joined two tables, and no WHERE clause has been added to the query. The grouping operation of the *Year* field and average aggregation on the *Grade* field will be performed in the *Report Expert* Wizard. We keep *DataTables* in the Data Sources Windows as generic as possible so that they can be used for other application functionalities as well.

3. The Wizard adds a *DataTable* and *TableAdapter* in the Data Sources Window. Rename these objects as *tblGrades* and *tblGradesTableAdapter* as shown in Figure 16.29.

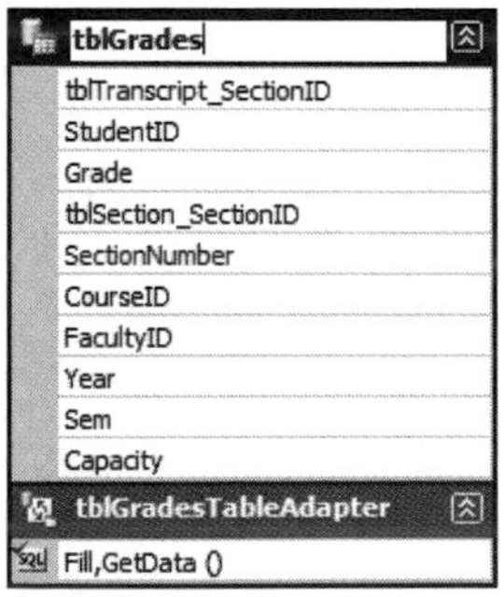

Figure 16.29 A *TableAdapter* and *DataTable* objects for the join query.

Creating the Report

4. Add *Form3* to the *CrystalReports* application.

5. Add an *AverageGrades.rpt* report to the application.

6. Accept the default selections in the *Crystal Reports Gallery* dialog box and click *OK*.
7. Select the *tblGrades* data table under the Project Data | ADO .NET Datasets item and add it to the *Selected Tables* pane (see Figure 16.30).

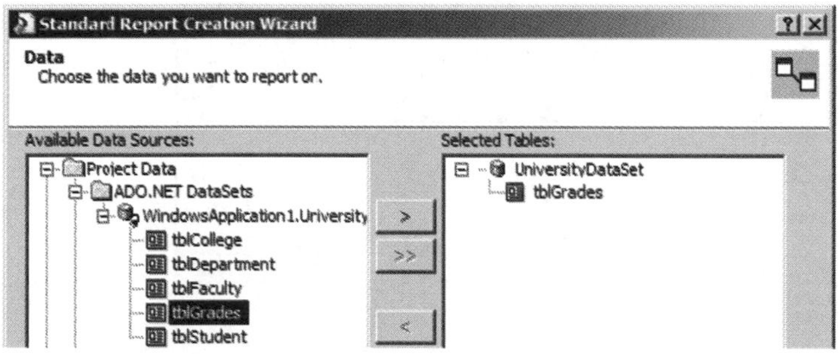

Figure 16.30 Choosing data for the grades report.

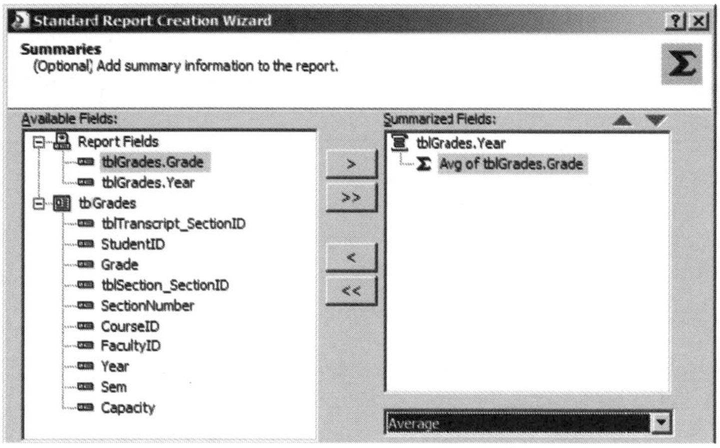

Figure 16.31 Choosing average function for the *Grade* field.

8. On the *Fields* page, select and add the *Year* and *Grade* fields to the *Fields to Display* pane. Click *Next*.
9. On the *Grouping* page, select and add the *Year* field to the *Group By* pane. Click *Next*.
10. On the *Summaries* page, remove any additional fields from the *Summarized Fields* pane. For the *tblSection.Grade* field, choose the *Average* summary option (see Figure 16.31). Click *Next*.
11. On the *Group Sorting* page, accept the default *None* ordering option and click *Next*.
12. On the *Chart* page, choose the *Line Chart* option. Change the *Chart Title* box as shown in Figure 16.32. Accept default values for the "*On change of*" and "*Show summary*" drop-down lists. Click *Finish*.

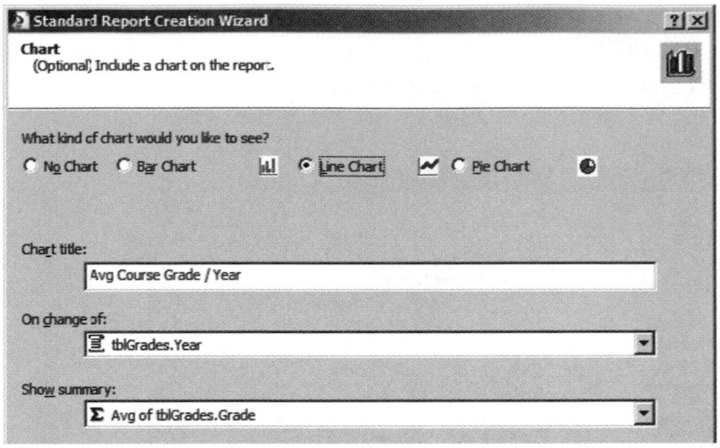

Figure 16.32 Setting up the line chart to display average grades per calendar year.

Note that we do not need to select any filtering criteria or report styles; hence, we can bypass these pages of the Wizard.

13. In the report's design view, remove all the fields in the various report sections except the chart object in the report header.

14. Select the chart object from the report header and right-click the selection. Choose Chart Options | Template from the shortcut menu. This should open the *Chart Option* dialog box. Check the *Use Depth* CheckBox control and click *OK*.

15. Now choose Chart Options | Titles from the same shortcut menu, and change the Y-axis title to *Average Grade*. Click *OK* to accept changes.

16. Next, choose the Chart Options | Grid option, and navigate to the *Scales* tab in the *Numeric Axis Grids & Scales* dialog box. Set up the scales as shown in Figure 16.33. This restricts our display to average grade values in the range 2–4.

17. Also on the same dialog box, navigate to the *Grids* tab and check the *Use Manual Grid* CheckBox control. Set the interval value to 0.5. This determines the spacing between the grid lines on the Y-axis.

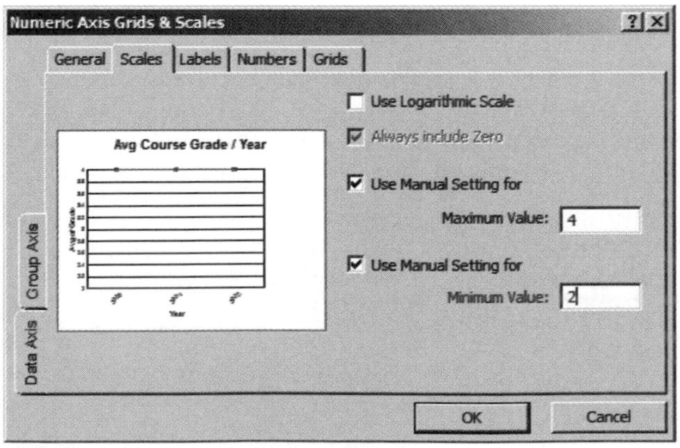

Figure 16.33 Adjusting Y-axis scales.

Binding the Report

18. Open *Form3* in the Design Window, and add the CrystalReportViewer control from the Toolbox. Change the viewer control's *Dock* property from *Fill* to *None*. Adjust its length and width. Also use the Property Window to set the *DisplayGroupTree* property of the control to *False*.

19. Drag and drop the newly created *tblGrades* data table from the Data Sources Window on *Form3*. This should create a DataGridView control, a ToolStrip control, and related objects in the Component tray.

20. Remove the auto-created DataGridView control and the ToolStrip control. We will use the *TblGradesTableAdapter* and *UniversityDataSet* objects in the Component tray while binding the report (see Figure 16.34).

UniversityDataSet   TblGradesBindingSource   TblGradesTableAdapter   TblGradesBindingNavigator

Figure 16.34 The *TableAdapter* and *Dataset* components for chart data.

```
3   Private Sub Form3_Load(ByVal sender As System.Object, _
4   ByVal e As System.EventArgs) Handles MyBase.Load
5       'Get the data
6       Me.TblGradesTableAdapter.Fill(Me.UniversityDataSet.tblGrades)
7       'Crystal report binding
8       Dim myReport As New AverageGrades
9       myReport.SetDataSource(UniversityDataSet.Tables("tblGrades"))
10      CrystalReportViewer1.ReportSource = myReport
11  End Sub
```

Figure 16.35 Binding code for average grades line chart.

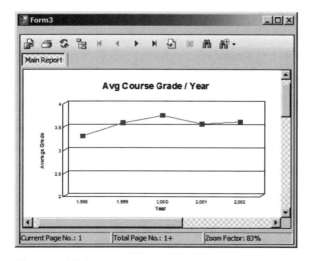

Figure 16.36 Running application: line chart of average grades per calendar year.

21. Replace the form's *Form_Load* event with the self-explanatory code in Figure 16.35.

22. Set *Form3* as the start-up form and run the application (see Figure 16.36).

Hands-On Tutorial: Creating Parameterized Crystal Reports

So far, we have discussed static reports—"static" in the sense that reports were designed to display information with certain fixed characteristics. For example, consider our simple student report in the primer section. The report displays contact information and the number of students per class for all Industrial Engineering (ISE) students. Appropriately this report displays information as new students are added or removed from the database, but the fact that the report displays information for only ISE students remains a constraint. What if a decision maker is interested in similar statistics for another department? Are we required to create a report per department?

We have dealt with a similar situation in Chapter 15 by using parameterized queries to display information based on parameter values. Can we base our reports on parameterized queries? In this section, we extend the simple student report developed in Section 16.2 to display contact information and a class bar chart for any user-selected department. The department selected by the user becomes a parameter for the report query, and the query result is displayed on the report *dynamically*. The following hands-on tutorial covers the following How-to topics:

- How-to: edit a copy of an existing Crystal Report and bind it to a different dataset.
- How-to: create reports using parameterized queries.

Edit a Copy of an Existing Report to Remove the Record Selection

1. In the Solution Explorer Window, select the *StudentReport.rpt* created in the primer section. First choose Edit | Copy from the main menu, and then choose Edit | Paste. Note that there exists a new file in the Solution Explorer, *Copy of StudentReport.rpt*. Use the Properties Window to rename it as *ParamStudentReport.rpt*

2. Double-click on *ParamStudentReport.rpt* to open it in the Design Window. Right-click anywhere on the report outside the chart object, and choose Report | Select Expert from the shortcut menu (see Figure 16.19). This should open the *Select Expert* dialog box.

3. Click *Delete* to remove the existing selection criterion, "*is equal to*" ISE. Click *OK* to accept the changes (see Figure 16.37).

The important thing to understand for this hands-on tutorial is that we will execute the parameter query outside the report and then feed the query results (list of students for user-specified department) to the report design for grouping and aggregation.

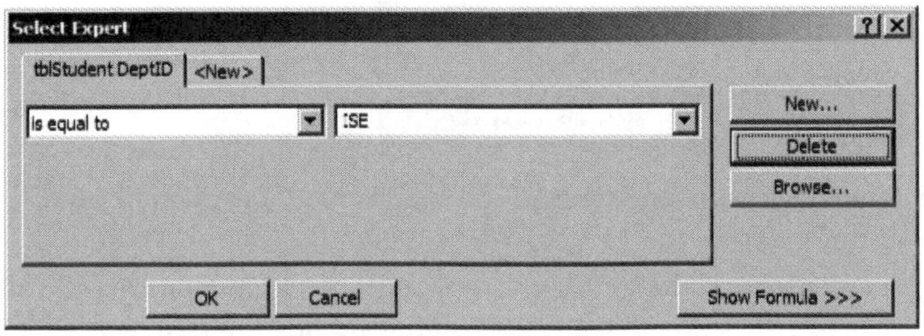

Figure 16.37 Removing selection criteria from an existing report.

Adding a Parameter Query to the Table Adapter

We have previously added parameter queries to the *TableAdapter* in a variety of ways. In this step, we add a *DeptID* parameter query to the *TblStudentTableAdapter*.

4. Open the *Dataset Designer*, locate and select the *TblStudentTableAdapter*, and right-click to choose the *Add Query* option. The *TableAdapter Query Configuration* Wizard appears.

5. On the page *Specify a SQL SELECT Statement*, enter the SQL query as shown in Figure 16.38 (or use the *Query Builder* option) and click *Next*.

6. On the next page, name the methods *FillByDeptID* and *GetDataByDeptID*, and click *Finish*. A new parameter query should get added to the *TableAdapter*.

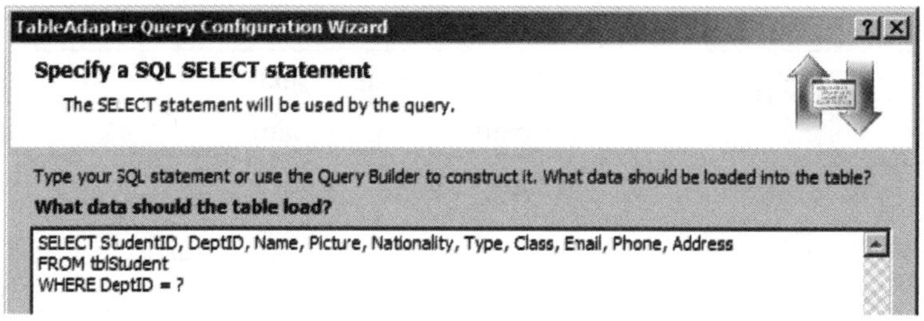

Figure 16.38 Parameterized query for the student report.

Adding a ToolStrip Control to Accept Parameter Values

Recall from Section 15.4 the steps to add a ToolStrip control for a Parameter query. We have added an existing query (designed in the *Dataset Designer*) to the *TableAdapter* object in the Component tray that automatically created a ToolStrip and associated binding code for us. However, for this report we have created the *TableAdapter* object programmatically at run-time. Thus, we must also configure the ToolStrip in VB code as we create the *TableAdapter* object. This step covers the following How-to topic:

■ How-to: manually add and bind a ToolStrip control

7. Add a new form *Form4* to the *CrystalReports* application. Drag and drop the CrystalReportViewer control under the *Crystal Reports* tab in the Toolbox.

8. Set the *Dock* property of the newly added *CrystalReportViewer1* control to *None*. Add a ToolStrip control from the *All Windows Forms* tab of the Toolbox on *Form4* (see Figure 16.39). This adds an empty ToolStrip control on the form and an icon in the Component tray.

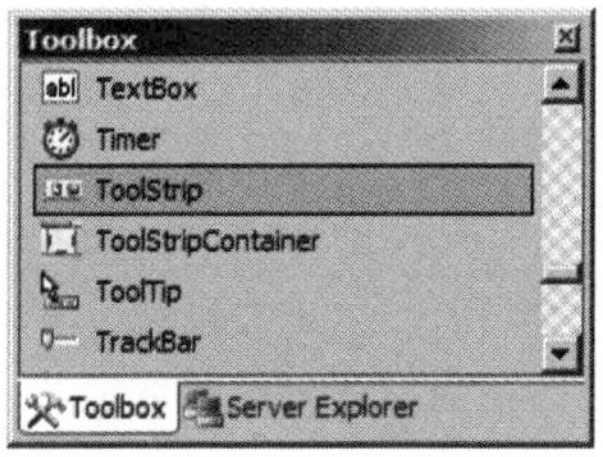

Figure 16.39 Adding a ToolStrip control to the form.

9. Position the ToolStrip on top of the page. Use the drop-down list on the ToolStrip control to add a Label control (see Figure 16.40).

10. Select the newly added Label control and alter its *Text* property using the Property Window (see Table 16.4).

11. Similarly, add a TextBox and Button controls to the ToolStrip. Manipulate their properties as shown in Table 16.4. We want a Textbox for the user to enter the *DeptID* and the *Click* event of a Button control to run the parameter query with *DeptID* parameter. The report is then displayed based on the Parameter query result.

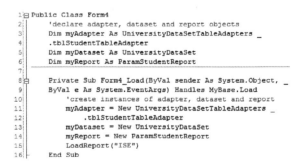

Figure 16.40 Adding controls to the ToolStrip control.

Table 16.4 Property values for controls in the ToolStrip.

Control	Property	Value
Label	Text	Enter Dept ID
TextBox	Name	tspDeptID
Button	Name	tspShowReport
	Text	Show Report
	Display Style	Text

Binding the Report

We had created a *TableAdapter*, *DataSet*, and a report object programmatically at runtime for the simple student report (see Figure 16.15) in the primer section. In this extended hands-on tutorial, we will be loading the report on the *Form_Load* event as well as on the *Click* event of the ToolStrip button. However, this time we define the *TableAdapter*, *DataSet*, and report objects globally (lines 3–6) in Figure 16.41 and instantiate them once on *Form_Load* event (lines 11–15). This avoids recreation of these objects on every click of ToolStrip's Button control.

12. Enter the code shown in Figure 16.41 for the *Form4*. Enter the code shown in Figure 16.42 for the *Click* event of the command button in the ToolStrip.

```
1  Public Class Form4
2      'declare adapter, dataset and report objects
3      Dim myAdapter As UniversityDataSetTableAdapters _
4      .tblStudentTableAdapter
5      Dim myDataset As UniversityDataSet
6      Dim myReport As ParamStudentReport
7
8      Private Sub Form4_Load(ByVal sender As System.Object, _
9      ByVal e As System.EventArgs) Handles MyBase.Load
10         'create instances of adapter, dataset and report
11         myAdapter = New UniversityDataSetTableAdapters _
12             .tblStudentTableAdapter
13         myDataset = New UniversityDataSet
14         myReport = New ParamStudentReport
15         LoadReport("ISE")
16     End Sub
```

Figure 16.41 *Form_Load* event code for a parametric student report.

```
18    Private Sub tspShowReport_Click(ByVal sender As _
19    System.Object, ByVal e As System.EventArgs) _
20    Handles tspShowReport.Click
21        LoadReport(tspDeptID.Text)
22    End Sub
23
24    Sub LoadReport(ByVal dept As String)
25        'get the data
26        myAdapter.FillByDeptID(myDataset.tblStudent, dept)
27        'set the report object's data source
28        myReport.SetDataSource(myDataset.Tables("tblStudent"))
29        'bind the report object to the viewer control
30        CrystalReportViewer1.ReportSource = myReport
31    End Sub
```

Figure 16.42 ToolStrip button's *Click* event code for a parametric student report.

Figure 16.41 and Figure 16.42 Explained:

We wrote the subroutine *LoadReport* to (i) get the data in the *DataSet* object, (ii) set the report object's data source to the filled *DataSet*, and (iii) bind the report object to the viewer control (lines 24–31). A *DeptID* parameter string is passed as one of the input parameters to the subroutine. Both the *Form_Load* and *Click* events call the *LoadReport* subroutine with the appropriate input parameter (lines 15 and 21). In lines 3–6, the *Form_Load* event instantiates the required objects as well.

13. Set *Form4* as the start-up form and run the application. Test the application by entering different *DeptID*s in the ToolStrip's TextBox control. Figure 16.43 shows the running application when a parameter "MAE" is entered for the *DeptID*.

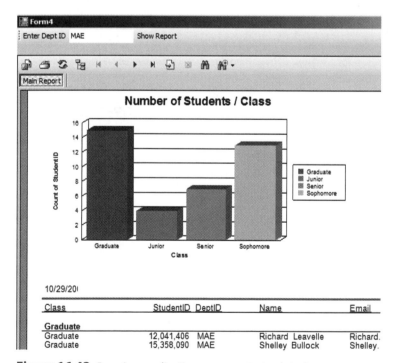

Figure 16.43 Running application: a parameterized student report.

16.9   *In-Class Assignment*

In this section we assign a simple problem that covers most of the features we have discussed in this chapter. We are interested in plotting a bar chart for the number of students in each department. We may not display any record fields in the report, the chart being the only requirement. Further, users should be able to view the bar chart for any college they select from a drop-down list of all colleges in the university.

16.10   *Summary*

- Reports are the best way to create a printed copy of information. They allow us to compare, summarize, and subtotal large data sets in the form of well-designed and professional invoices, purchase orders, mailing orders, monthly bills, etc.
- *Crystal Report* is one of the world's leading software packages for creating interactive reports. Crystal Reports are widely used and have set the standard for reports.
- Adding Crystal Reports on a Windows form involves the following steps:
  1. Add a Crystal Report to the application.
  2. Use the *Report Expert* to specify the report data source, report fields, group-by fields, aggregate function, selection fields, and filtering criteria.

  3. In the *Expert* Wizard, specify a chart type, chart titles, and chart data.
  4. Add a CrystalReportViewer control on the Windows form.
  5. Either add the data source used for report design in the Component tray or create it programmatically at run-time.
  6. Bind the report to the viewer control.
- We can also build a report based on the *TableAdapter* that has a join of multiple tables. Finally, we introduce a powerful technique to parameterize reports, and we display reports based on the results of parameterized queries.

16.11   *Exercises*

16.11.1 **Review Questions**

1. Why do reports play an important role in a wide range of areas and environments? Provide examples. (Try to come up with examples that are related to your profession, life, or area of study.)
2. What are some of the advantages of integrating Crystal Report with the .Net environment?
3. What do you mean by the data source of a report, and how do you specify it?
4. In the *Report Expert*, what is the relationship between the *Group By* fields and the *Summary* fields?
5. Which is the best *Expert* that fits the needs of the following scenarios:
   a. You are required to design a program that fills and prints a bill with a predefined design. The output data should be printed on a blank predesigned bill.

   b. You are part of a new advertising company. They have to ship a large number of advertising brochures to many customers. They are looking for a system to create labels for these brochures.
6. How can you apply filtering criteria inside the *Report Expert* Wizard?
7. We select "report styles" on the last page of the *Expert* Wizard. Which fields of the report are these styles applicable to?
8. Describe various sections of a Crystal Report.
9. Why are charts included in the report header section by default?
10. List the steps to building a report based on the join of multiple tables.
11. What are some of the built-in summarizing functions available in the Expert Wizard?

12. How can we make reports display charts based on a parameterized query?

16.11.2 Hands-on Exercises

NOTE: *The database files for these hands-on exercises are available at: www.dssbooks.com.*

1. A local hospital keeps track of patients and their assigned doctors. They have requested that you create a report that displays the following fields:

  a. The doctor's full name

  b. The patient's full name

  c. The department of the doctor

  d. The name of the medication prescribed for the patient

  e. The description of the patient's case

  They have also requested that you create a bar chart that displays the number of patients assigned to each doctor. Create a report satisfying the given requirements using the "Hospital" database.

2. A survey collected data about the amount of money made by a number of movie theaters for a specific list of movies. The survey's main goal was to compare the collections received at those theaters. The movie theaters have asked you to create a simple application that can connect to their survey result and view the following in a report:

  a. The name of the theatre

  b. The title and category of the movie

  c. The leading actor's full name

  In addition, they want you to show in a pie chart the percentage that each theater made per the overall collections for all the theaters. Also, they want to view the three theaters with the highest earnings (use the "Movies" database).

3. For the previous problem, we want to reveal the distribution of the collection for the movie "Come To Me." We want to include the dates of all the shows and the net collection per show. In addition, we want to display the overall collection per theater in a line chart and compare each theater's collection to all the other theaters.

4. A certain university offers a number of classes that students at various levels (undergraduate, graduate, and post-doctorate) can enroll. The university wants you to create a report that will display the number and percentage of students from each level attending each course. Include the following information for each course:

  a. Its name

  b. Each student's first and last name

  c. The instructor's first and last name

  d. The student's level

  When viewing the report, the university wants the students within each class to be grouped by their category (use the "Schools" database).

5. Globe Airlines is an interstate airline. It keeps records of all its previous reservations, and it has asked you to create a customer report that displays the number of reservations made by each customer. It is offering some specials for its best customers. Create a report that includes the following information:

  a. The customer's full name

  b. The route of the flight

  c. The cost of the flight

  d. The class of the customer's seat

  In addition, list the five most active customers by how many flights they have taken (use the "Airline" database).

6. Globe Airlines' manager (from the previous problem) liked your report. So, she has decided to hire you to develop another report. This time, the report should display the distribution of each flight's class reservations in a pie chart. Globe offers three travel classes: business, club, and economy. In the report, the user should be able to view all the reservations made for each class. In addition, the report should display the percentage of each class reserved with reference to the overall number of reservations.

7. This problem refers to the previous two problems. You have now been asked to combine the previous two reports into a single application. (*Hint:* You do not have to remake the reports; you can use the same two reports you already created.) The application should be a simple desktop application that consists of an empty page and two buttons. The buttons should be as follows:

  a. "Customers Report." When this button is clicked, the report from Exercise 5 should be shown.

  b. "Reservations Report." When this button is clicked, the report from Exercise 6 should be shown.

8. You are working on a project that implements a system to help people view information about a collection of books. Create a simple report based on the "Books" database with the following requirements:

   a. List all the publishers in the database, and summarize the total sale for each book published by a publisher.

   b. Also plot a pie chart displaying the total sales amount (book price × quantity sold) for each publisher.

9. Consider the "Books" database discussed in the previous hands-on exercise. In this exercise we report various authors listed in the database with the following requirements:

   a. Let the user select an author name from a drop-down list. For the selected author, display contact information and summarize the total sale for each book written by that author.

   b. Plot a pie chart displaying the total sales amount (book price × quantity sold) for each of the books written by a selected author.

   c. Also plot a bar chart displaying the total royalty (royalty × quantity sold) earned for each of the books written by a selected author.

10. Open the database Post Office.mdb to view the entire database. Review the existing tables and relationships in this database and create the following queries and reports:

    The shipping costs for a package depend on its weight and the mailing rate per ounce. There is also an additional one-time cost for certified mail packages. Queries can be used to calculate the shipping costs of a package based on its particular characteristics.

   a. Build a query that computes the shipping cost of all standard packages that weigh more than one ounce. Save this query as "QryStdCost."

   b. A manager is interested in knowing the total shipping paid by customers for each shipping mode. Plot a bar chart that displays the total shipping cost for each distinct shipping mode.

11. Using the "Post Office" database, create a report that reports the following information for all post offices in the database:

   a. Post office details and a list showing all the addresses for packages sent from those post offices.

   b. A bar chart showing the total package values for each post office in the database.

12. Consider the "Hotel" database. Continue improving the functionalities of this database by creating reports and appropriate charts based on the following queries:

   a. Calculate the total amount earned for each hotel room type. Include any pet fines while calculating the total amount earned for each booking.

   b. For each customer who had a room booked in the hotel between user-specified dates, show the split of amount spent on food, room charges, and pet fines.

PART FOUR

Web Application Development with ASP .NET

seventeen Web Introduction and Essential HTML

chapter OVERVIEW

17.1   *Introduction*

The Windows applications are practical for single-user personal computers and are effective, to a certain extent, for network solutions. However, the era of the Internet has taken network sharing to new heights, allowing millions of users to share information on the *World Wide Web* (WWW) or *Web* simultaneously. The Windows applications can be upgraded or *Web-enabled* to access them over the Internet. We discuss the development of Web-enabled applications in this part of the book. To begin our discussion, we introduce various Web terminologies and a Web interface language—HyperText Markup Language (HTML)—in this chapter.

17.1.1   Topics

This chapter discusses the following topics:

- Internet terminologies
- What is an HTTP request-reply cycle?
- What are the essential features of HTML?
- How do HTML forms and controls work?

17.2   *Internet, Web, and Related Terminologies*

In the past, computers operated in complete isolation. However, as more and more users relied on computers in their work, they increasingly felt the need to share information between machines. This need gave birth to floppy drives and other portable media storage devices. As computers increased in number and amount of information to share grew exponentially, the computer community devised Local Area Networking (LAN). In a LAN, computers belonging to a local area, such as the offices in a department, are connected together through network cables to facilitate information sharing. Given its benefits, LAN quickly grew in size to encompass organizations, cities (Wide Area Network—WAN), states, countries, and then, with the *Internet*, the entire world.

Internet   The *Internet* is a network of networks that links computers all over the world. The Internet itself does not contain any data. It is simply a means of transporting information from one computer to another via networks. The Internet provides a variety of services, including electronic mail, file sharing, and the World Wide Web.

World Wide Web   The *World Wide Web* (WWW) or simply, the *Web* is a network of computers that communicate with each other through a communication standard called HTTP (HyperText Transfer Protocol). The Web employs the Internet as its backbone for communication. In other words, the Internet acts as hardware for the Web. The Web allows us, among other things, to retrieve files, read text, view images, and listen to sound files from other connected computers.

Web Browser   A *Web browser* or simply a *browser* is a client software application that allows us to read Web pages on the Web.

Examples: Internet Explorer, Netscape, Mozilla Firefox, and Opera.

Some of the early browsers were limited to displaying only text and images. However, the latest browsers have multimedia capabilities and display video, audio, and animation.

Web Server   *Web server* is a piece of software that provides a service using information that we can share with other computers on the Internet.

Examples: Internet Information Server (IIS), Apache, and Tomcat.

In this part of the book, we use IIS to host the Web pages developed in the hands-on tutorial and use the Internet Explorer Web browser to view these pages. IIS software is integrated with the Visual Studio environment and is installed along with the Visual Studio package.

Web Pages   Web applications are stored on the Web server in the form of *Web pages*. A Web page is a file written in a HyperText Markup Language (HTML). A Web page has an *htm* or *html* extension. Web browser programs are designed to interpret HTML Web pages and display them to the user.

17.2.1   HTTP Cycle: Request and Response

The communication between a Web server and a Web client consists of a *request* and *response* cycle. A client requests a Web page from a server, and the server responds with the requested file. For example, the Web client (Sally's PC) wants to see an "index.htm" file stored on the Web server (Harry's PC). Sally should send the request to Harry, and Harry will respond to Sally with the requested file (see Figure 17.1).

The Web client requests a file from the Web server using a Web browser. Sally enters the Web address "http://www.harry.com/index.htm" in the Web browser (Internet Explorer) to send a request to Harry. The request sent over the Internet to Harry is termed an HTTP request, as it is sent using a well-known HTTP protocol (see HTTP request line in Figure 17.1). The Web address Sally entered is known as a *Uniform Resource Locator* (URL), which is used to uniquely locate Harry's computer and the file of interest on his computer.

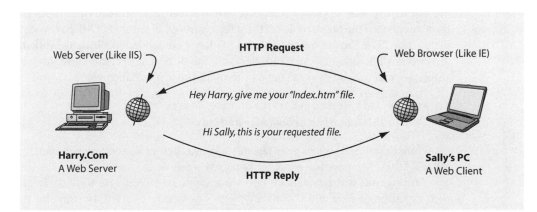

Figure 17.1 The HTTP request-response cycle.

Upon receiving an HTTP request, a Web server program serves the requested file to the client using the same HTTP standard, and therefore it is termed HTTP response. In our example, when the IIS software on Harry's computer sees Sally's request, it sends the "index.htm" file to Sally's PC (see HTTP Reply line the Figure 17.1).

When Sally's computer receives the requested file, the browser (Internet Explorer) on her computer knows how to read the HTML file, and therefore Sally can see what Harry has written in the file.

Summary

The request-response cycle:

- ■ The browser takes a URL and sends an HTTP request to the server.
- ■ The server responds by sending the requested Web document to the client.
- ■ The browser reads the incoming Web document and displays its contents to the user.

17.3 HyperText Markup Language (HTML)

HyperText Markup Language, or HTML, is designed to specify the logical organization of a Web document. Files with HTML codes are stored on the Web server and are interpreted by the Web browser to display Web data. The Web browser interprets an HTML code by means of HTML tag structure. HTML uses *tags* to mark selections of text (hence the name "Markup") and to specify its format. Consider, for example, the following line of HTML code:

```
<b> This is marked as bold face text. </b>
```
Output: **This is marked as bold face text.**

The `<b>` and `</b>` are the starting and ending tags. The text included between these tags is marked to display in bold face. Therefore, when a Web browser reads this line of code, it displays the text between the tags in bold on the screen. Almost all tags in HTML have a starting and ending portion. The former has the appropriate letter embedded in brackets, while the latter has a forward slash before the command. Tags can also be nested to create formatting effects. For example, we can use the `<i></i>` tag pair to mark the text as italic:

```
<b><i> This is marked as bold face italic text. </i></b>
```
*Output: **This is marked as bold face italic text.***

Note that tag `<i>` starts after tag `<b>` and ends before it. Tags are completely nested within others. An HTML page is a sequence of tagged statements.

Throughout this chapter, we develop a single-page Web site to illustrate various HTML tags, explaining where and how to use them. The example we will be using for this application is very simple but interesting. We will build a home page for the well-known scientist Albert Einstein. The goal is to provide general information about this scientist and display his picture and his famous $E = mc^2$ equation on a Web page.

Definitions

■ The *Internet* is a network of networks that links computers all over the world.
■ A *Web browser* is a client software application that allows us to read Web pages on the Web.
■ *Web server* is a piece of software that provides a service using information that we can share with other computers on the Internet.
■ An HTML page is a sequence of tagged statements.

17.3.1 Setting Up the Web Site Using Visual Studio

In this section, we illustrate how we can use the Visual Studio environment to develop HTML pages and write HTML codes.

Create a New Web Site Project

1. Choose the File | New Web Site option from the main menu (see Figure 17.2). This opens a *New Web Site* dialog box with a list of templates.
2. Select the *Empty Web Site* template, and accept the default Web site name.

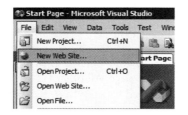

Figure 17.2 Creating a new Web site.

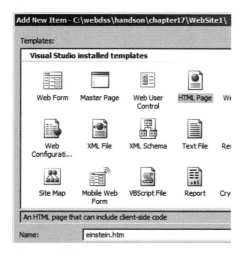

Figure 17.3 Adding a new HTML page to the Web site.

Adding an HTML Page   Once we have created a Web site project, we can add Web pages (with HTML extension) to it.

3. Choose the Web site | Add New option from the main menu to open the *Add New Item* dialog box.
4. Select the *HTML Page* template, and enter the file name "einstein.htm" (see Figure 17.3).

17.3.2 Structure of an HTML Page and HTML Tags

In the Solution Explorer, if we right-click on the newly added Web page and select *View Markup* option, we see the HTML code shown in Figure 17.4.

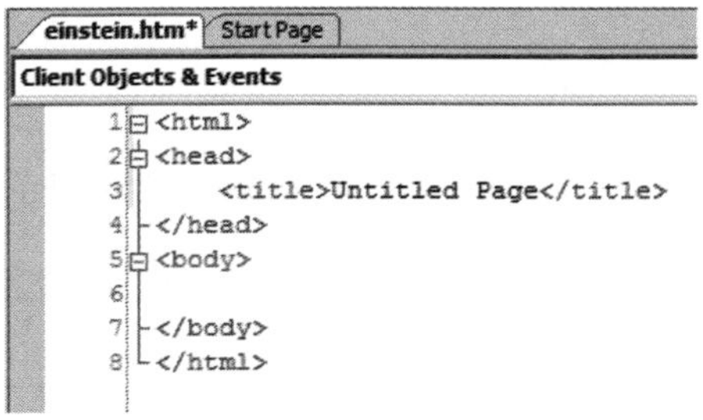

Figure 17.4 An HTML page.

As mentioned before, an HTML page comprises various HTML tags. The HTML tags `<html></html>` make the starting and ending of an HTML page. All other HTML tags go inside this pair (see line 1 and line 8 of Figure 17.4). The text entered between these two tags is called the HTML page.

An HTML page is divided into two broad sections: the *head* and the *body*. The head is marked by the `<head></head>` tag pair. The head section stores the metadata of a page, namely, the page title, author names, and relationships to other documents and scripts. Tags inside the head sections are never displayed to the user in the Web browser window. The body section is marked by the `<body></body>` tag pair. It contains tags that form the *body* of an HTML page. Figure 17.5 shows these sections of an HTML page.

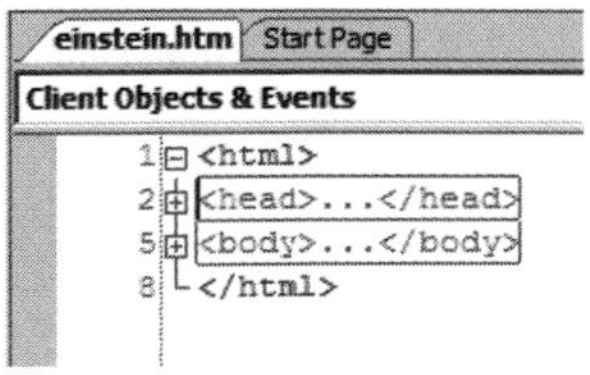

Figure 17.5 Structure of an HTML page.

Continuing with the Einstein's example, we now add a page title to our Web page.

5. Change the title tag to read, "Albert Einstein's Home Page," as shown in Figure 17.6, line 3. The contents of the `<title>` tag appear in the title bar of the browser window.
6. Press Ctrl + F5 from the keyboard to run the application. This should open the default browser window with an empty page. Verify the page title in the title bar of the window.

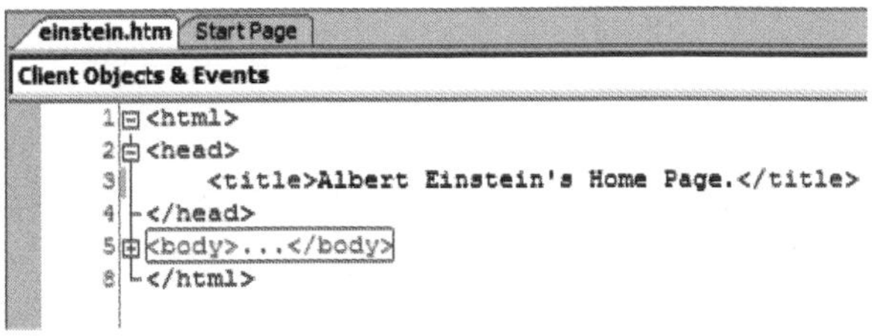

```
  einstein.htm  Start Page
Client Objects & Events
1  <html>
2    <head>
3        <title>Albert Einstein's Home Page.</title>
4    </head>
5    <body>...</body>
6  </html>
```

Figure 17.6 Editing the page title.

Summary

- An HTML page is marked by `<html></html>` tags. All other tags are placed inside this tag pair.

- An HTML page has a head and a body section marked by `<head></head>` and `<body></body>` tags, respectively.

- We can also use any text editor, such as WordPad or Notepad, to write an HTML code similar to the ones we will be writing in the Visual Studio. However, we use Visual Studio's integrated environment throughout our Web development process.

17.4 Essential Text Formatting

Text data is a primary means of communication for most Web sites. The visual presentation of text data has an impact on the appearance of a Web site. A designer must consider features such as font face, size, and color, as well as the appearance of the background and foreground. The objective of this section is to illustrate how to create headings, paragraphs, and lists for Web pages and also to explain the features associated with text formatting.

17.4.1 Displaying Text Data on a Web Page

The content of a Web page is present in its body section, enclosed between the `<body></body>` tags. Any text presented between these tags is displayed in the Web browser window.

7. Enter the text as shown in Figure 17.7 inside the `<body></body>` tags. We may use the text files provided in Chapter 17's folder from the book Web site to copy and paste the above the text.

8. Run the application to see the Web page shown in Figure 17.8.

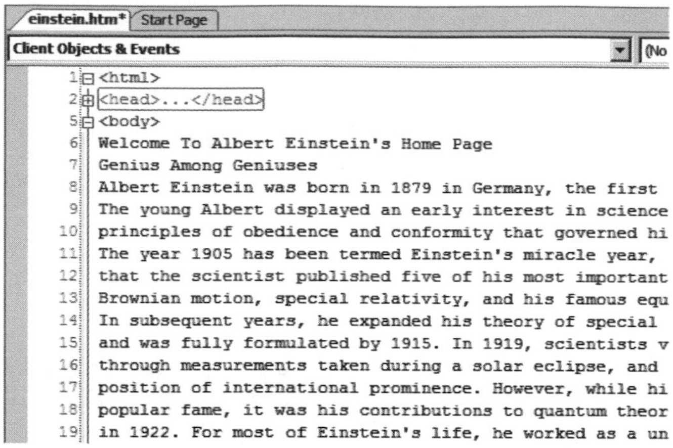

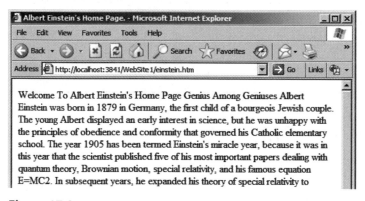

Figure 17.7 Entering introductory information about Einstein between body tags.

Figure 17.8 The Web page with unformatted text.

What we see in Figure 17.8 is the plain, unformatted text we have entered. Note that the text in lines 6 and 7 also appears as unformatted text on a single line. Unless we mark-up the text data with tags, the browser is not aware of where to end lines and paragraphs, and which text is a heading. HTML has a rich collection of formatting tags to make text data more presentable, which we describe next.

17.4.2   The Heading Tags

HTML headings are the equivalent of headings in paper-based documents. Headings provide the reader with an idea of the subject of a document. HTML <h1> through <h6> tags can be used for headings of six different sizes.

9. Add the <h1> tag at the beginning of line 6 (the first text line). Notice that Visual Studio's IntelliSense feature will automatically pop up a menu to help with adding HTML tags (see Figure 17.9). Then, add the ending </h1> tag at the end of the line.

10. Mark up the line 7 with <h3></h3> tag pair (see Figure 17.10).

11. Press Ctrl + F5 to view the Web page in the browser (see Figure 17.11).

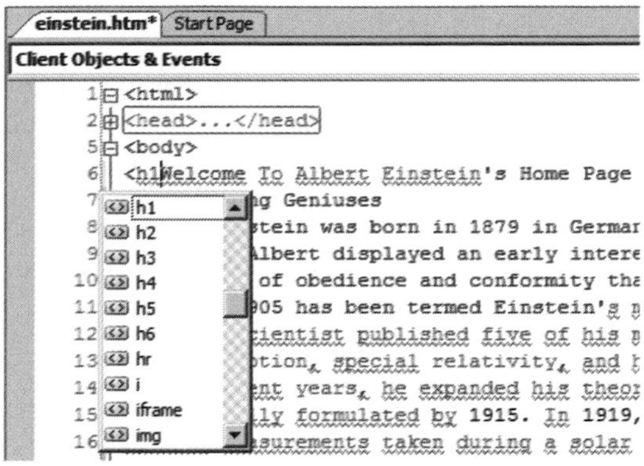

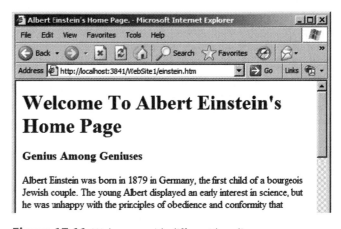

Figure 17.9 Adding heading tags.

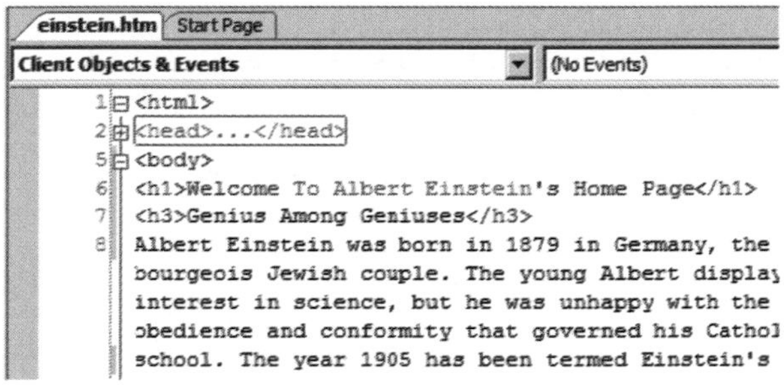

```
einstein.htm   Start Page
Client Objects & Events                    (No Events)
 1  <html>
 2  <head>...</head>
 5  <body>
 6  <h1>Welcome To Albert Einstein's Home Page</h1>
 7  <h3>Genius Among Geniuses</h3>
 8  Albert Einstein was born in 1879 in Germany, the
    bourgeois Jewish couple. The young Albert display
    interest in science, but he was unhappy with the
    obedience and conformity that governed his Cathol
    school. The year 1905 has been termed Einstein's
```

Figure 17.10 Heading tags embedded within the body tag.

Figure 17.11 Web page with different heading.

Note that the first two lines of our text now appear as article headings. Further, notice that the font size of these two heading tags are different, giving us the effect of a primary title and a secondary title. In general, the heading sizes decrease from heading tag <h1> to <h6>. As expected for a heading, the heading tags automatically add line breaks and appropriate line spacing between the header and the following text.

17.4.3   Paragraphs

A paper-based document uses paragraphs to organize its text. Similarly, HTML pages can add paragraphs to organize Web content. Paragraphs are defined with the <p></p> tag pair. We enclose the text that we want to appear as a paragraph between <p> and </p> tags. Paragraph tags always add an extra blank line before and after the paragraph.

> **12.** Add paragraph tags to Einstein's introductory description as shown in Figure 17.12 (lines 8-10).
>
> **13.** Press Ctrl + F5 to view the output (see Figure 17.13).

```
 6   <h1>Welcome To Albert Einstein's Home Page</h1>
 7   <h3>Genius Among Geniuses</h3>
 8   <p>Albert Einstein was born in 1879 in Germany, the first child of
     a bourgeois Jewish couple. The young Albert displayed an early
     interest in science, but he was unhappy with the principles of
     obedience and conformity that governed his Catholic elementary
     school.</p>
 9   <p>The year 1905 has been termed Einstein's miracle year, because
     it was in this year that the scientist published five of his most
     important papers dealing with quantum theory, Brownian motion,
     special relativity, and his famous equation E=MC2.</p>
10   <p>In subsequent years, he expanded his theory of special
     relativity to general relativity and was fully formulated by 1915.
```

Figure 17.12 Adding paragraph tags.

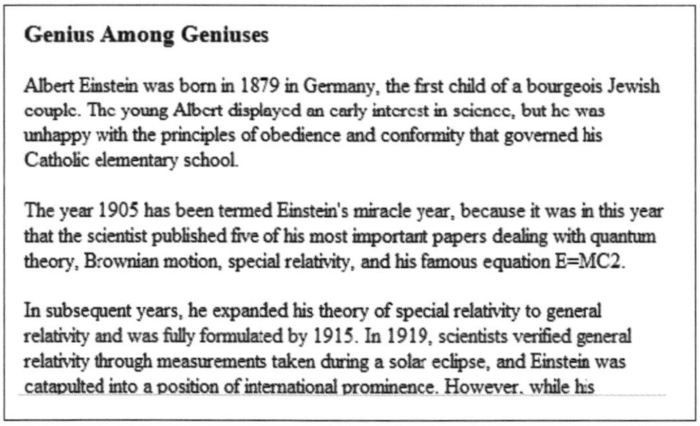

Genius Among Geniuses

Albert Einstein was born in 1879 in Germany, the first child of a bourgeois Jewish couple. The young Albert displayed an early interest in science, but he was unhappy with the principles of obedience and conformity that governed his Catholic elementary school.

The year 1905 has been termed Einstein's miracle year, because it was in this year that the scientist published five of his most important papers dealing with quantum theory, Brownian motion, special relativity, and his famous equation E=MC2.

In subsequent years, he expanded his theory of special relativity to general relativity and was fully formulated by 1915. In 1919, scientists verified general relativity through measurements taken during a solar eclipse, and Einstein was catapulted into a position of international prominence. However, while his

Figure 17.13 The Web page with paragraphs.

17.4.4   Tag Attributes

Almost all HTML tags can have attributes included in their opening tag. *Attributes* are the properties of an HTML tag. They control the appearance and behavior of the text marked up by the tags. Attributes help further enhance a tag's functionality. For example, the *Align* attribute of a paragraph tag allows us to align the text marked up by the paragraph tags.

Attributes can be assigned different values. For example, the *Align* attribute takes the values *left*, *right*, or *center* and accordingly aligns the paragraph text. The attribute and its value are always specified inside the opening tag. For example, if we would like to right-align the text inside a paragraph, we would write an HTML tag similar to the following line:

```
<p align=right>Paragraph text goes here</p>
```

If not specified, attributes take their default values. For example, if we do not include *Align* attribute in the paragraph tag, the paragraph text will be left-aligned by default. We present attributes of various HTML tags in the remainder of the chapter.

17.4.5 The Font Tag

The font tag pair `<font></font>` is probably one of the most frequently used tags for text formatting. The font tag allows us to select different font faces (for example, Arial or Georgia), font styles (for example, italic or bold), font colors, and font sizes (for example, 10pt or 14pt) using its attributes. The attributes of Font tag are familiar text formatting options in editors such as MS Word.

The tag pairs `<b></b>` can also be used for boldface, `<u></u>` for underline, and `<i></i>` for italics in association with the Font tag. Table 17.1 depicts some of the font tag attributes and their domain values.

Table 17.1 Font tag and its attributes.

Tag Example	Attribute	Values	Value Examples
`<font face=Arial></font>`	face	Name of font type	Arial, Courier New, Georgia, Verdana, etc.
`<font face=Arial color=Navy></font>`	color	Color name/code	Navy, Gray, Black, Red, etc.
`<font face=Arial color=Navy size=10></font>`	size	N as integer	10, 12, 14, etc.
`<b></b>`	Use for boldface style		
`<u></u>`	Use for underline style		
`<i></i>`	Use for italic style		

We further enhance titles of our example Web page using the Font tag.

14. Add font tags with *face* and *color* attributes as shown in Figure 17.14 (lines 6 and 9).

15. Run the application to see the Web page with different fonts as shown in Figure 17.15.

```
5   <body>
6   <h1><font face="Monotype Corsiva" color=maroon>
7   Welcome To Albert Einstein's Home Page</font></h1>
8   <br />
9   <h3><font face=arial color=navy>
10  Genius Among Geniuses</font></h3>
11  <p>Albert Einstein was born in 1879 in Germany, the first child of
    a bourgeois Jewish couple. The young Albert displayed an early
    interest in science, but he was unhappy with the principles of
    obedience and conformity that governed his Catholic elementary
    school.</p>
12  <p>The year 1905 has been termed Einstein's miracle year, because
```

Figure 17.14 Adding font tags.

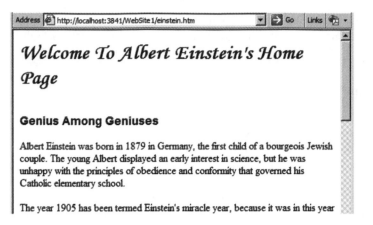

Figure 17.15 The Web page with different fonts.

17.4.6 List Tags

Bulleted or numbered lists are common in paper-based documents and are encouraged for point-wise descriptions. HTML also supports two types of listings: Ordered Listing (OL) and Unordered Listing (UL). Ordered lists enumerate items (or lines) using letters or numbers, while unordered lists render items using bullets. We use the tag pair `<ol></ol>` for an ordered listing of items and the tag pair `<ul></ul>` for an unordered listing. Each *list item* (LI) is included inside the `<ol>` or `<ul>` tag pairs using the `<li></li>` tag pair. Table 17.2 describes some of the common attributes of list tags.

Table 17.2 List tags and their attributes.

Tag Example	Attribute	Values	Description
`<ul type=circle></ul>`	type	disc, circle, square	Sets the shape of the bullet. Default is disc.
`<ol type=A></ol>`	type	1, A, a, I, i	Labels items with a number, an upper- or lowercase letter, and/or a Roman numeral.
`<ol start=5></ol>`	start	n (integer)	Starts the listing.
`<li type=disc></li>`	type	Same as `<ol>` or `<ul>`	Overrides the value of `<ol>` or `<ul>` tags.
`<li value=2></li>`	value	n (integer)	Starts the ordered listing.

We add more information about Einstein to our example Web page. We list some of his famous quotes.

16. Add a Navy colored heading, "Einstein's Quotes" (lines 14 and15).
17. Add Einstein's quotes as shown in Figure 17.16 (use the text files on book Web site to copy from). Mark the quotes using an unordered bulleted list.
18. Run the application for the output shown in Figure 17.17.

Note that the text inside each `<li>` tag appears as a bullet on the Web page. Also, the list tags automatically add a line break after each list item.

```
25  <h3><font face="arial" color="navy">
26  Einstein's Quotes</font></h3>
27  <ul>
28      <li>"Imagination is more important than knowledge."</li>
29      <li>"Gravitation is not responsible for
30      people falling in love."</li>
31      <li>"I want to know God's thoughts;
32      the rest are details."</li>
33      <li>"The only real valuable thing is intuition."</li>
34      <li>"Everything should be made as simple as possible,
35       but not simpler."</li>
36      <li>"Common sense is the collection of prejudices
37      acquired by age eighteen."</li>
38      <li>"Science is a wonderful thing if one does not
39      have to earn one's living at it."</li>
40  </ul>
```

Figure 17.16 Adding list tags to the Web page.

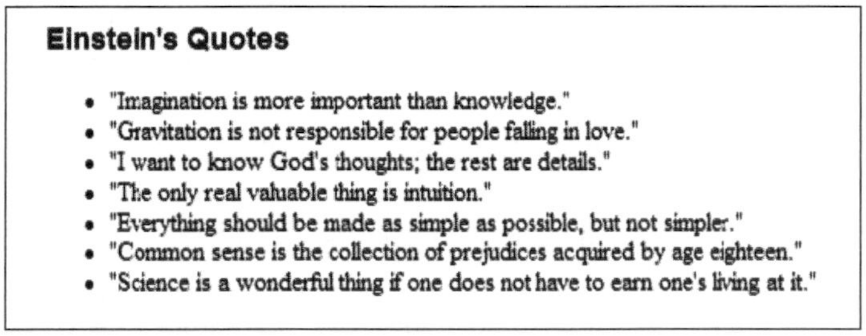

Einstein's Quotes

- "Imagination is more important than knowledge."
- "Gravitation is not responsible for people falling in love."
- "I want to know God's thoughts; the rest are details."
- "The only real valuable thing is intuition."
- "Everything should be made as simple as possible, but not simpler."
- "Common sense is the collection of prejudices acquired by age eighteen."
- "Science is a wonderful thing if one does not have to earn one's living at it."

Figure 17.17 The Web page with list of Einstein's quotes.

17.5   *HTML Hyperlinks*

Hyperlinks are special areas on a Web page that can be activated (usually with a mouse click) to redirect to a different section of the same or another Web page. They can link to any of the Web resources including Web pages, images, sound, or video files. Hyperlinks can appear as text or graphics links on a Web page. They can also be used to send email or submit a form, among other functions.

HTML `<a></a>` (anchor) tags are used to mark the hyperlinks. The text or image embedded within a `<a></a>` tag pair is referred as a link label. Link labels are the links a user sees on Web pages.

The href Attribute   The *href* attribute of an anchor tag is assigned the address to which the document is linked. The value of the *href* attribute is the destination of the hyperlink and is usually specified as a URL. Figure 17.18(a) shows an example of a hyperlink.

When a user clicks on a hyperlink's link label (e.g., NOVA Web site), the browser is redirected to the Web page referred value of an *href* attribute (see Figure 17.18(b)). Hyperlinks are extremely useful in Web development. Although it is impossible to include all information about Einstein on a single Web page, we can direct the user to additional information using hyperlinks. Hyperlinks connect the documents in context to enhance readability and conciseness of the text.

```
41   To read more about Einstein, visit
42   <a href="http://www.pbs.org/wqbh/nova/einstein"
43   target=_blank>NOVA website.</a>
```

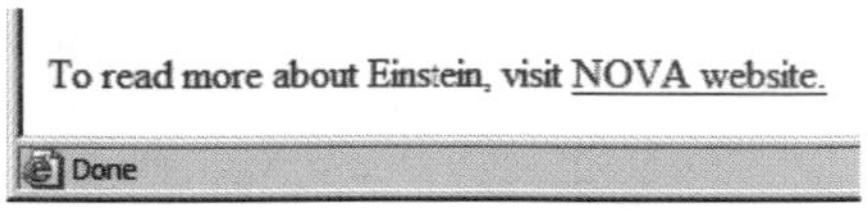

To read more about Einstein, visit <u>NOVA website.</u>

🖹 Done

(a)   **(b)**

Figure 17.18 (a) Adding a hyperlink in HTML code; (b) Functional hyperlink to NOVA Web site.

19. Add a hyperlink to Nova Web site as shown in Figure 17.18(a). This link gives wealth of information about Einstein.

17.6   *Page Backgrounds*

Adding colors and patterned images to the background of Web pages makes them presentable and attractive to the user. The HTML tag <body> has inherent attributes, *background* and *bgcolor* to enable the addition of background colors and images to the entire Web page. This is intuitive since background features apply to the entire document or *body* of an HTML page. We set the background color of a Web page, by assigning either the name or the hexadecimal code of the color to the *bgcolor* attribute. If we decide on a particular background image, we use the *background* attribute with the image path as its value.

Continuing with our example Web site, we add a background color to the Web page as follows:

20. Click on the body tag and add the bgcolor attribute with "AntiqueWhite" color value (see Figure 17.19).
21. Press Ctrl + F5 to see the background color effect (see Figure 17.20).

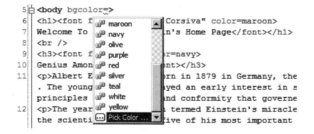

Figure 17.19 Setting the *bgcolor* attribute to apply a background color to the Web page.

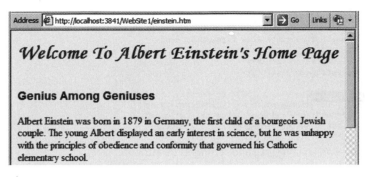

Figure 17.20 The Web page with a colorful background.

Arguably, the page looks more presentable as compared to the previous sections. Selecting the right color and background images for a Web page is an important decision of the design process.

17.7 Adding Graphics to Web Pages

The `<img>` tag is used to add images on Web pages. Images are one of the most important aspects of any document as a picture is worth a thousand words. The `<img>` tag and its attributes provide a powerful means to add images to HTML documents. The attributes of the `<img>` tag are summarized in Table 17.3.

Table 17.3 Attributes of the image tag.

Attribute	Value	Description
src	Image path	This specifies the location of an image as a path.
alt	String	This indicates the alternative text to be used for the link if the browser does not display the image.
height	N (integer)	The height of the image.
width	N (integer)	The width of the image.
align	Center, left, right, top, bottom	Alignment options.

We illustrate the image tag by adding Einstein's image on the example Web page.

22. Add the image tag just below the second heading (line 11 in Figure 17.21). Set the *src* attribute to an image file "Einstein.jpg." Note that if we add image files to the project folder, IntelliSense lists those images as we assign a value to the *src* attribute. The image files for this project can be found on the book Web site in the Chapter 17's folder.
23. Press Ctrl + F5 to view the default left aligned image in the browser window (see Figure 17.22).

```
 5 <body bgcolor=AntiqueWhite>
 6 <h1><font face="Monotype Corsiva" color=maroon>
 7 Welcome To Albert Einstein's Home Page</font></h1>
 8 <br />
 9 <h3><font face=arial color=navy>
10 Genius Among Geniuses</font></h3>
11 <img src=
12 <p>Alb  [einstein.jpg]  was born in 1879 in Germany, the
   . The  [...] Pick URL ...  displayed an early interest in sc
   principles of obedience and conformity that governed
13 <p>The year 1905 has been termed Einstein's miracle
```

Figure 17.21 Adding an image tag and setting its *src* attribute.

Genius Among Geniuses

Albert Einstein was born in 1879 in Germany, the first child of a bourgeois Jewish couple. The young Albert displayed an early interest in science, but he was unhappy with the principles of obedience and conformity that governed his Catholic elementary school.

Figure 17.22 The Web page with Einstein's picture.

17.8 *Structuring Web Pages Using HTML Tables*

Displaying data in a tabular format is a powerful way of presenting data to the user. Tables help in developing structured and easily readable Web pages. The HTML table tag arranges text data, images, and links into cells of table rows and columns.

The `<table>` tag marks the beginning of a table. A table can have one or more rows and columns. Each *table row* is marked by a pair of `<tr></tr>` tags. The *table data* (or column) inside each table row is marked by the `<td></td>` pair. The `<td>` tag is always nested inside a `<tr>` tag, and a `<tr>` is always nested inside the `<table>` tag. For example, consider the tag structure shown in Figure 17.23.

```
12 <table border=1>
13 <tr>
14 <td>This is Row1, Column1</td>
15 <td>This is Row1, Column2</td>
16 </tr>
17 <tr>
18 <td>This is Row2, Column1</td>
19 <td>This is Row2, Column2</td>
20 </tr>
21 </table>
```

Figure 17.23 An example of a table tag structure.

The first <tr> tag in line 13 (the first table row) includes two <td></td> tag pairs (two columns). They represent lines 13-16 in the previous code snippet. The second <tr> tag in line 17 (the second row) also has two <td></td> tag pairs as shown in lines 18-19. The output of these lines of code is shown in Figure 17.24.

This is Row1, Column1	This is Row1, Column2
This is Row2, Column1	This is Row2, Column2

Figure 17.24 Output of a simple table structure.

Note that we have added a *border* attribute to the <table> tag and set its value to 1. This draws a border of 1 pixel width around the table. Some of the important attributes of a table tag are listed in Table 17.4.

Table 17.4 Attributes of the table tag.

Attribute	Value	Description
border	N (Integer)	The width of the table border in pixels
height	N (integer)	The height of the image in pixels
width	N (integer)	The width of the image in pixels
valign	Center, left, right, top, bottom	Vertical Alignment options

```
 5  <body bgcolor=AntiqueWhite>
 6    <h1><font face="Monotype Corsiva" color=maroon>
 7    Welcome To Albert Einstein's Home Page</font></h1>
 8    <br />
 9    <h3><font face=arial color=navy>
10    Genius Among Geniuses</font></h3>
11    <table border=0>
12    <tr valign=top>
13    <td><img src=einstein.jpg /></td>
14    <td>
15    <p>Albert Einstein was born in 1879 in Germany, the first
      . The young Albert displayed an early interest in science
      principles of obedience and conformity that governed his
```

Figure 17.25 HTML table used for aligning Einstein's picture.

In our example, we would like to align Einstein's image in line with the text as shown in Figure 17.26. We achieve this by using a table structure and put the image in one column and the text data in another column.

    24. Modify the HTML code to resemble code in Figure 17.25.
    25. Press Ctrl+F5 to run the application. Figure 17.26 shows the output.

Figure 17.25 Explained:

Line 11 marks the beginning of a table with border zero. This ensures that we don't see the table border in the output. Line 12 creates the only row we want for this page. Line 13 adds the first column or data cell with an image tag. Line 14 marks the start of second column.

Welcome To Albert Einstein's Home Page

Genius Among Geniuses

Albert Einstein was born in 1879 in Germany, the first child of a bourgeois Jewish couple. The young Albert displayed an early interest in science, but he was unhappy with the principles of obedience and conformity that governed his Catholic elementary school.

The year 1905 has been termed Einstein's miracle year, because it was in this year that the scientist published five of his most important papers dealing with quantum theory, Brownian motion, special relativity, and his famous equation E=MC2.

Figure 17.26 The Web Page displaying image and text data in an HTML table.

17.9   *Using Visual Studio's Design View: WYSIWYG*

As mentioned before, we can develop or write HTML code in any text editor. Though we have written HTML code in Visual Studio's *Source* tab so far (see bottom of Figure 17.27), Visual Studio's *Design* tab provides a graphical user interface to easily and quickly develop Web pages.

In the *Design* tab, we can add text and format the same, similar to writing to a Word document. Thus, we can see the page in *Design* tab identical to what it will look like in the browser window. This property is popularly known as WYSIWYG (What You See Is What You Get).

We add Einstein's elegant equation $E = mc^2$ using *Design* tab of the Visual Studio window.

26. To access the *Design* tab, click the *Design* icon on the bottom left hand corner of the Visual Studio window.
27. Add the equation text as shown in Figure 17.27. Use various options including *Style* option in the *Format* menu of the main menu to design the page.
28. Switch to the *Source* tab and review the code generated by the Visual Studio (see Figure 17.28). Note that the `<h3>`, `<font>` and `<p>` tags are added along with the new text.

Elegant Equation

It's difficult to separate the enormous legacy of $E = mc2$ fro directly out of Einstein's work on special relativity, which is the theory of general relativity.

On the most basic level, the equation says that energy and of the same thing. Under the right conditions, energy can be that way—how can a beam of light and a walnut, say, be di

| ▫ Design | ▣ Source | | ◁ | `<body>` | `<p>` |

Ready

Figure 17.27 *Design* tab with "Elegant Equation" text.

```
33  <h3><font face=arial color=navy>Elegant Equation</font></h3>
34  <p>It's difficult to separate the enormous legacy of E = mc2 from E
    legacy as a whole. After all, the equation grew directly out of Ein
    on special relativity, which is a subset of what most consider his
    achievement, the theory of general relativity.</p>
35  <p>On the most basic level, the equation says that energy and mass
36  interchangeable; they are different forms of the same thing. Under
    conditions, energy can become mass, and vice versa. We humans don't
     way—how can a beam of light and a walnut, say, be different forms
    thing?—but Nature does.</p>
37  </body>
38  </html>
```

Figure 17.28 The auto-generated code for the "Elegant Equation" text.

17.10 — *Web Form and HTML Controls*

So far, we have illustrated HTML tags that display data to the user. HTML is not constrained by "display" tags, but also supports tags that allow the user to enter data on a Web page. In this section, we illustrate HTML control tags (or just HTML controls). TextBox, ComboBox, RadioButton, CommandButton, ListBox controls are some examples of HTML controls. These HTML controls appear and function similarly to Windows controls discussed in Chapter 13. An HTML control can be added to a Web page using one of the following methods:

- Using HTML tags in an HTML code
- Dragging and dropping an HTML control from the Toolbox on *Design* tab of the HTML page

We request users to enter data on a Web page by filling out various "forms," such as a data-entry form, or an inquiry form, etc. HTML supports a form tag indicated by the `<form></form>` tag pair. All HTML control tags are always nested inside a `<form></form>` tag pair. The `<form>` tag marks the beginning of the area where a user is required to enter the data. This structure is identical to Windows forms. Windows forms include Windows controls; similarly HTML forms include HTML controls.

Most of the HTML controls are marked by an `<input>` tag. The *type* attribute of an `<input>` tag determines the type of the control to be displayed on the Web page. Consider the examples of HTML controls in Table 17.5.

Table 17.5 HTML controls tags.

HTML Tag	HTML Control Displayed
`<input type="text" />`	TextBox
`<input type="radio" />`	RadioButton
`<input type="checkbox" />`	CheckBox
`<input type="button"/>`	CommandButton
`<textarea cols="20" rows="2"></textarea>`	ListBox
`<select><option selected="selected"> </option> </select>`	ComboBox with one entry

Creating an HTML Form

We add an HTML form to Einstein's page which illustrates the elegant equation $E = mc^2$. The idea behind this is to input values of *m* and *c* from the user and display the *E* value on the Web page. We use two TextBox controls to input values from the user and another TextBox control to output the calculated value. The Button control is used to submit the user request. We arrange these HTML controls in a table structure.

29. Switch to the *Design* tab.

30. Open the Toolbox from the menu by choosing View | Toolbox option.

31. Add a table (2 rows, 3 columns) under the "Elegant Equation" heading. Use Layout | Insert Table option from the main menu to invoke the *Insert Table* dialog box. Use this dialog box to insert the table.

32. Drag and drop three TextBox and a Button control from the Toolbox (see Figure 17.29) on individual rows of the table (see Figure 17.30).

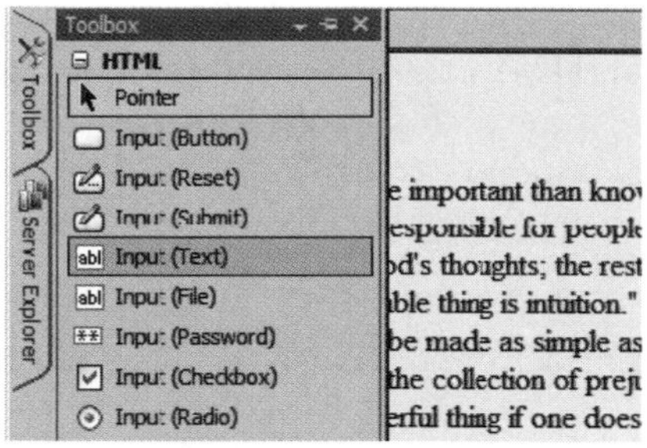

Figure 17.29 Toolbox showing HTML controls.

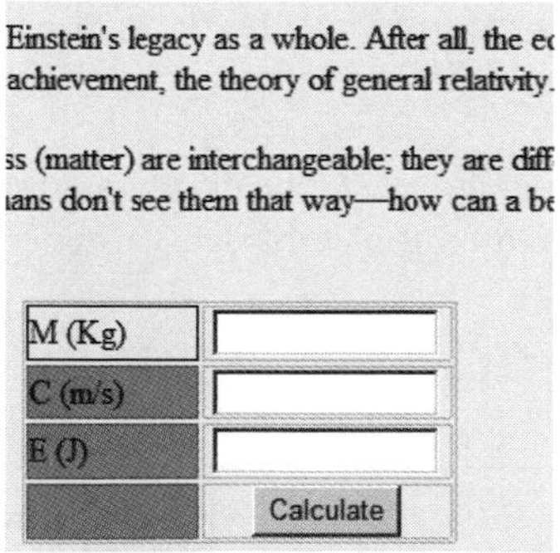

Figure 17.30 Setting-up the form for user input.

Similar to the controls in a Window application, we can manipulate the appearance and behavior of HTML controls using its properties in the Properties Window.

33. Individually select the TextBox controls and alter their properties as shown in Figure 17.31. Use Table 17.6 to set properties of various controls on the page.

34. Switch to the *Source* tab. Add the `<form></form>` tags as shown in line 50 and 76 of Figure 17.32.

35. Press Ctrl + F5 to run the application. Figure 17.33 shows the output.

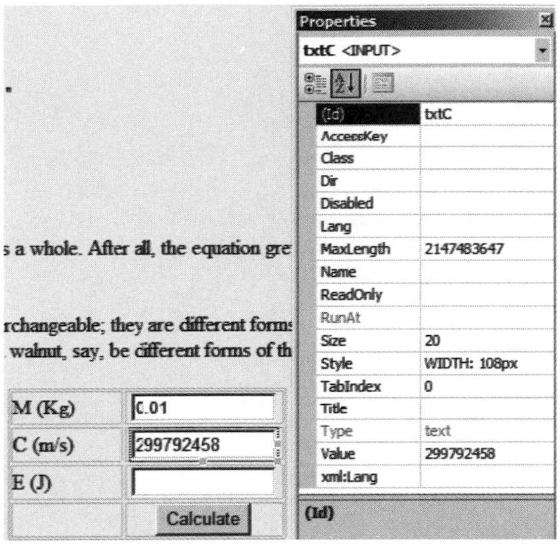

Figure 17.31 Properties of a TextBox control.

Table 17.6 HTML controls and their property values for example Web page.

Control	Property	Value
M TextBox	ID	txtC
	Value	0.01
C TextBox	ID	txtM
	Value	299792458
Button	Value	Calculate

```
50 <form name="eleganteq">
51 <table align="center">
52 <tr>...</tr>
57 <tr>
58    <td align="left" style="width: 82px;
59    height: 26px;">C (m/s)</td>
60    <td align="center" style="width: 117px;
61     height: 26px;">
62    <input id="txtC" style="width: 108px"
63    type="text" value="299792458" /></td>
64 </tr>
65 <tr>...</tr>
70 <tr>...</tr>
75 </table>
76 </form>
```

Figure 17.32 HTML code for the controls added on the example Web page.

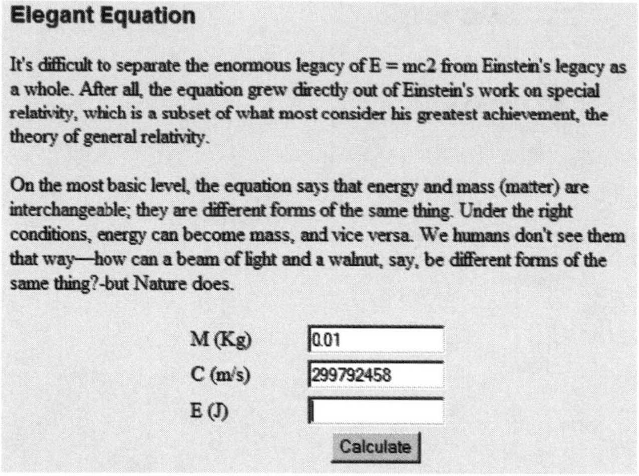

Figure 17.33 Einstein's page with an HTML form.

The four table rows carry four different HTML controls. Figure 17.32 shows the second row for the *C* value TextBox control. The HTML control tag is displayed in line 62-63.

Note that, we do not derive any result when we click on *Calculate*, since we have not written a code that will evaluate the equation to output the *E* value. We need more than HTML tags to perform mathematical operations. In the next chapter, we introduce server-side scripting which enables us to make our form functional.

Static Pages vs. Dynamic Pages   The Web pages are either designed as static or dynamic pages. Static HTML pages are the ones that display the same contents every time they are requested. Dynamic HTML pages are ones that may display different contents subject to change in request. For example, a dynamic Web page can be used to display database tables to the users. The HTML code of this page is "dynamically" generated based on the current state of the database table.

There are several scripting languages that support dynamic HTML page development. ASP.NET, JSP, and PHP are few popular examples for the same. We will discuss ASP.NET in depth in subsequent chapters.

17.11   *In-Class Assignment*

Develop your own home page. Make sure to use various HTML tags and the attributes introduced in this chapter. Apply image, table, and hyperlink HTML tags while building your Web page.

17.12 *Summary*

- **HTML page:** An HTML page is a sequence of tagged statements. An HTML page is marked by `<html></html>` tags. An HTML page has a head and a body section marked by `<head></head>` and `<body></body>` tags, respectively.

- The metadata of a page is placed inside the head section and is not visible to the user. All other tags are placed inside the body section.

- **Formatting tags:** Headings provide the reader with an idea about the subject of a document. HTML uses `<h1>` through `<h6>` tags for headings in six different sizes. We add paragraphs to Web contents in HTML pages using the `<p></p>` tag pair. The `<font></font>` tag pair and its attributes are used to control the font face, font color, and font size.

- **Listing tags:** HTML supports two types of listings: Ordered Listing (OL) and Unordered Listing (UL). Ordered lists enumerate items using letters or numbers, while unordered lists enumerate items using bullets. We use the `<ol></ol>` tag pair for an ordered listing and the `<ul></ul>` tag pair for an unordered listing of items.

- **Hyperlinks:** HTML uses hyperlinks to link to other documents on the Web. The `<a></a>` (anchor) tag pair is used to create a hyperlink. The *href* attribute of an anchor tag is assigned the address to which the document is linked. The value of the *href* attribute is the destination of the hyperlink.

- **Images:** The `<img>` tag and its attributes provide a powerful means to add images to HTML documents.

- **Tables:** The HTML table tag structures, text data, images, and links into cells of rows and columns. The `<table>` tag marks the beginning of a table. Each table row is marked by the `<tr></tr>` tag pair and each column is marked by the `<td></td>` tag pair.

- **HTML Controls:** HTML provides controls like TextBox, ComboBox, RadioButton, CommandButton, ListBox etc. Most of the HTML controls are marked by an `<input>` tag. The type attribute of an `<input>` tag determines the type of control to display (for example, `<input type="text"/>` is a TextBox control).

17.13 *Exercises*

17.13.1 Review Questions

1. What is the World Wide Web?
2. What is the relationship between the Internet and the World Wide Web?
3. What is a Web server? Give some examples.
4. Describe the HTTP request-response cycle.
5. What is the function of a URL?
6. What is HTML used for?
7. What are the pieces of information stored by the *head* section of an HTML page?
8. In a Web page, where should we place information that should not be visible to the user? In contrast, where should we place information we want to display on the Web page?
9. What are the types of listings supported by HTML?
10. What are hyperlinks? Which HTML tag is used to create a hyperlink?
11. How do we specify the destination address of a hyperlink in HTML?
12. Suppose, a user is using a text-only browser such as "Lynx." How will you convey the information you have currently displayed as a graphics image using the `<img>` tag in HTML?
13. What are the vertical alignment options available with the `<table>` tag in HTML?
14. How are dynamic Web pages different from static Web pages?
15. What are the languages used to generate static and dynamic Web pages?

17.13.2 Hands-On Exercises

1. Use HTML heading, font and list elements to create a Web page that looks like the following figure:

This is a level-2 heading.

The following is an ordered list:

1. **This is bold Arial font.**
2. *This is italic Verdana font.*
3. <u>This is underlined Georgia font.</u>

2. Create an HTML page with the title "My Hobbies and Interests." In the body of the page, add the following first-level headings in Times New Roman Italic, *Red* color font: "About Me," "My Interests and Hobbies." Under each heading, add a relevant paragraph in an appropriate color. Change the background color of this page to *Tan* color.

3. Create an HTML page with the title "My Contact Information." Create a table with a border of 2 pixels width. Add the following details in the table rows: Email, Phone, and Address. For each row, the label should be in Verdana Bold font and values should be in Arial Italic font.

4. Create an HTML page with the title "Useful Links." In the body of this page, create second-level headings in a bold font to group links into categories, such as News, Weather, and Email. Provide hyperlinks to the frequently visited Web sites like www.google.com, www.yahoo.com, www.aol.com etc., under each category. Assign meaningful names to the text of these hyperlinks.

5. Create an HTML page with the title "My Weekly Time Table." Create a table similar to the one shown below. The table is used for displaying the timetable of the current semester. Also add appropriate data.

	Mon	Tue	Wed	Thu	Fri
Period 1					
Period 2					
Period 3					

6. Create a Web page with links to the Web pages of all-time great scientists. Generate a list with the following scientists' names (for example):
   - Albert Einstein
   - Isaac Newton
   - Benjamin Franklin
   - Alfred Nobel
   - Richard Feynman

   Use an Internet search engine to find the most authoritative Web page with information about these scientists and provide a link to it. Keep the scientists' names as link labels.

7. It is a professional practice to provide one's resume as part of one's homepage. In this exercise, we shall create a resume in the HTML format. Use table rows to add information about each of the following bullets:
   - Contact Details
   - Educational Background
   - Work Experience
   - Skills
   - Projects
   - Extra-curricular Activities

8. In this exercise, we will create a photo Web page. Create an HTML page and add a table with two columns. In each row, add an image using the `<img>` tag in the first column and add some comments about the photo in the second column. Choose any personal images to create this album.

9. Often, we would like to receive feedback about our Web page from visitors. In this exercise, we shall create a "guestbook" for visitors to leave feedback. The form should have the heading "Sign my Guestbook" and the following fields:
   - Name
   - Email
   - Comments

   Create an HTML form page for the guestbook. Use text boxes for user input and provide a *Submit* button.

10. Create an HTML form to represent a simple survey. The form should have the heading "Student Survey." Provide an ordered list of fields and appropriate controls for user input:
    - Name: TextBox control
    - Age: TextBox control
    - Sex: RadioButton control (Values: Male, Female)
    - Class: CheckBox control (Values: Freshman, Sophomore, Junior, Senior, Graduate)
    - Citizenship: TextBox control

Introduction to ASP .NET

18.1   *Introduction*

In the previous chapter, we discussed HTML as a standard language for data presentation on Web pages. HTML forms and controls can take user inputs and process input data to some extent using client side scripts such as Java scripts or VB scripts (not discussed in this book). However, these features are not powerful enough for many application needs. For example, consider the functionalities offered by VB .NET Windows applications discussed in Chapters 14–16: obtaining data from databases, displaying and further manipulating query results, and displaying bar and line charts. Active Server Pages (ASP) .NET allows us to combine HTML and VB .NET to have these functionalities in Web application as well. Using ASP .NET, we can build front-end (interface) HTML files and associate back-end (code behind) VB .NET files to perform database retrievals, data manipulation, and data presentation. Thus, we can utilize the power of VB .NET programming in a Web environment by means of ASP .NET. However, there is a subtle difference between a Windows application and a Web application. In a Windows application, the application files, forms, and controls are typically stored and viewed on the same computer (or within a local network). In a Web application, however, application files are stored on a Web server and are viewed on client machines by several users at a time.

18.1.1   Topics

This chapter discusses the following topics:

- ASP .NET Web forms and controls.
- *AutoPostBack* property of Web controls.
- How to validate the user input using Validation controls.
- How to pass parameters through URL.
- How to create user controls in ASP .NET.

18.2   *ASP .NET Primer: Sum of* N *Numbers*

In this primer, we create our first Web page using ASP .NET. We have selected a simple application for this primer, sum of N numbers. We will ask the user for an integer number N and display the sum of all numbers from 0 to N. This primer covers the following How-to topics:

- How-to: create an ASP.NET Web Site project.
- How-to: add controls onto a Web form.

  1. Select File | New Web Site option from the main menu. In the *New Web Site* dialog box that opens, choose the *ASP.NET Web Site* option under *Visual Studio installed templates* (see Figure 18.1).
  2. In the *Location* drop-down list, enter the name and the path of the Web site as shown in Figure 18.1.
  3. Visual studio opens a default file named "Default.aspx" in the Design Window. Use the Properties Window to rename the file as "Sum.aspx" (see Figure 18.2).
  4. We can view the HTML source of the page (see Figure 18.3) by clicking on the *Source* button at the bottom of the page.

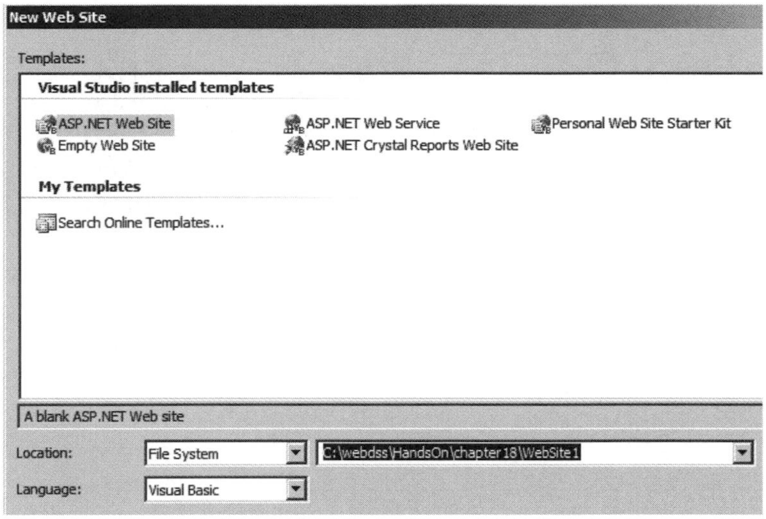

New Web Site

Templates:

Visual Studio installed templates

ASP.NET Web Site   ASP.NET Web Service   Personal Web Site Starter Kit
Empty Web Site   ASP.NET Crystal Reports Web Site

My Templates

Search Online Templates…

A blank ASP.NET Web site

| Location: | File System | ▼ | C:\webdss\HandsOn\chapter18\WebSite1 | ▼ |
| Language: | Visual Basic | ▼ | | |

Figure 18.1 Creating a new Web site.

Properties   ▼ ╬ ✕

Sum.aspx Web File Properties   ▼

☐ **Misc**

| File Name | Sum.aspx |
| Full Path | C:\webdss\HandsOn\chapter18\We |

Figure 18.2 Renaming the ASP Web page.

Sum.aspx

Client Objects & Events   ▼   (No Events)

```
 1  <%@ Page Language="VB" AutoEventWireup="false"
 2  CodeFile="Sum.aspx.vb" Inherits="Sun" %>
 3
 4  <!DOCTYPE html PUBLIC "-//W3C//DTD XHTML 1.0 Transitional//EN"
 5  "http://www.w3.org/TR/xhtml1/DTD/xhtml1-transitional.dtd">
 6
 7  <html xmlns="http://www.w3.org/1999/xhtml" >
 8  <head runat="server">
 9      <title>Untitled Page</title>
10  </head>
11  <body>
12      <form id="form1" runat="server">
13      <div>
14
15      </div>
16      </form>
17  </body>
18  </html>
```

Figure 18.3 Auto-generated HTML source for the *Sum.aspx* page.

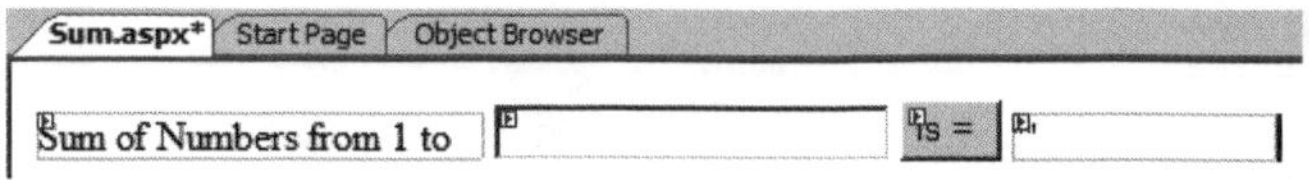

Figure 18.4 Adding Web controls to the *Sum.aspx* page in the Design Window.

Table 18.1 Controls to be added to the *Sum.aspx* page and their properties values.

Control	Attribute	Value
Label	ID	lblDisplay
	Text	"Sum of Numbers from 1 to "
TextBox	ID	txtEnd
Button	ID	btnCal
	Text	"is = "
Label	ID	lblSum
	Text	" "

5. Switch to design mode by clicking on the Design button at the bottom left-hand corner of the window.

6. Drag and drop two Label controls, a Button, and a TextBox control from the Toolbox onto the form (see Figure 18.4). Note that these are the Web controls listed under the *Standard* tab and not the HTML control listed under *HTML* tab of the Toolbox Window. The Web controls and their properties values are listed in Table 18.1.

7. Double-click on the Button control to open its *Click* event code in the Code Window, and enter the code as shown in Figure 18.5.

8. Run and test the application by pressing Ctrl + F5. Enter a number 50 in the TextBox control, and click on the command button to see the results (See Figure 18.6).

```
5    Protected Sub btnCal_Click(ByVal sender As Object, _
6    ByVal e As System.EventArgs) Handles btnCal.Click
7        Dim i, sum As Integer
8        sum = 0
9        For i = 1 To CInt(txtEnd.Text)
10           sum += i
11       Next
12       lblSum.Text = CStr(sum)
13   End Sub
14 End Class
```

Figure 18.5 Code for handling the *Click* event of the Button control.

Figure 18.6 The running application.

18.3 *Hands-On Tutorial: Currency Conversion Example*

In this hands-on tutorial, we consider another simple example. We will add a new Web page to the Web site created in the previous section. The Web page should convert the currency value entered by the user from US dollars to Euros. This hands-on tutorial covers the following How-to topics:

- How-to: add a new Web form to an existing Web site.
- How-to: set the start-up page for a Web site project.

1. In the *WebSite1* project created in the previous hands-on tutorial, open the *Add New Item* dialog box by choosing Website | Add New Item option from the main menu. Alternatively, use the Solution Explorer Window and right-click on the Web site name to choose Add | Add New Item option from the shortcut menu.
2. In the *Add New Item* dialog box, locate and select the *Web Form* item. In the *Name* box, name the new page as "Currency.aspx." Click the *Add* button to add the new page to the project (see Figure 18.7).
3. Drag and drop two Label controls, a Button, and a TextBox control from the *Standard* tab of the Toolbox onto the *Currency.aspx* form (see Figure 18.8). The controls and their properties values are listed in Table 18.2.

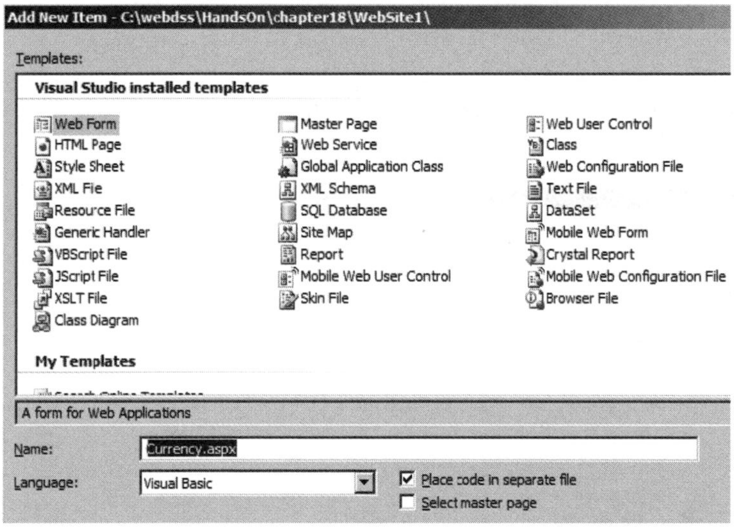

Figure 18.7 Adding a new Web form to an existing Web site.

| Currency.aspx* | Sum.aspx.vb | Surr.aspx | Start Page | Object Browser |

| | US Dollar to Euro | Convert | lblAnswer |

Figure 18.8 Design Window with Web controls for the currency page.

Table 18.2 Currency page—Web controls and their properties.

Control	Attribute	Value
TextBox	ID	txtInput
Label	ID	lblDisplay
	Text	"US to Dollar to Euro"
Button	ID	btnConvert
Label	ID	lblAnswer
	Text	" "

4. Double-click on the Button control to open its *Click* event code in the Code Window, and enter the code as shown in Figure 18.9.

```
5   Protected Sub btnConvert_Click(ByVal sender As Object, _
6   ByVal e As System.EventArgs) Handles btnConvert.Click
7       Dim temp As Double
8       temp = CDbl(txtInput.Text) * 0.782
9       lblAnswer.Text = CStr(Math.Round(temp, 2))
10  End Sub
```

Figure 18.9 Code for handling the *Click* event of the Button control.

Figure 18.10 Setting currency page as the *Start Page* of the application.

5. In the Solution Explorer, right-click on the "Currency.aspx" and select the *Set as Start Page* option (see Figure 18.10). This should make the currency page as the start-up page of the application.

6. Run and test the Application by pressing Ctrl + F5. Enter a number 11 in the TextBox control, and click on the command button to see the results (see Figure 18.11).

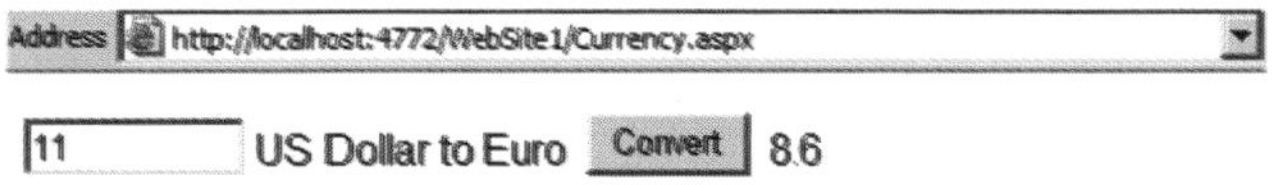

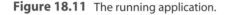

Address [🔵] http://localhost:4772/WebSite1/Currency.aspx

| 11 | US Dollar to Euro | Convert | 8.6 |

Figure 18.11 The running application.

18.4 *Extending the Currency Conversion Example—The* AutoPostBack *Property*

In this section, we will mainly learn about the *AutoPostBack* property of Web controls. We will modify the Web page created in the previous section by allowing the user to select various currency conversions. We will also learn about ListBox Web control and how to add HTML tables in IDE window as we work on this extension. This section covers the following How-to topics:

- ■ How-to: add HTML tables in IDE window.
- ■ How-to: use a ListBox Web control.
- ■ How-to: set the *AutoPostBack* property of Web controls.

18.4.1 Creating a Web Page Layout

Displaying data in a tabular format is a powerful way to present data to the user. It helps us in developing a clean, easily readable Web page. In Chapter 17, we have seen how to organize data in an HTML table. In this section, we use *Layout* menu of the IDE window to add an HTML table to the Web page.

1. In *WebSite1*, open the *Add New Item* dialog box by choosing Web Site | Add New Item from the main menu.

2. In the *Add New Item* dialog box, locate and select the *Web Form* item. In the *Name* box, name the new page as "CurrencyNew.aspx." Click the *Add* button to add the new page to the project.

3. Open the *Insert Table* dialog box by choosing Layout | Insert Table option from the main menu (see Figure 18.12).

4. The *Insert Table* dialog box allows us to specify table design parameters such as number of rows and columns, table width and alignment, and its cell properties. Set the table properties as shown in Figure 18.13 and click *OK*. Set the column heading text of the table as shown in Figure 18.14.

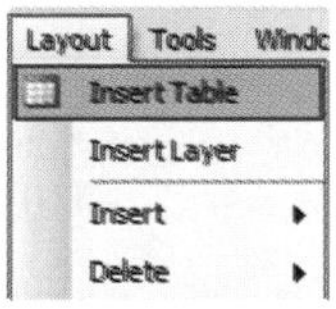

Figure 18.12 Inserting an HTML table using the *Layout* menu.

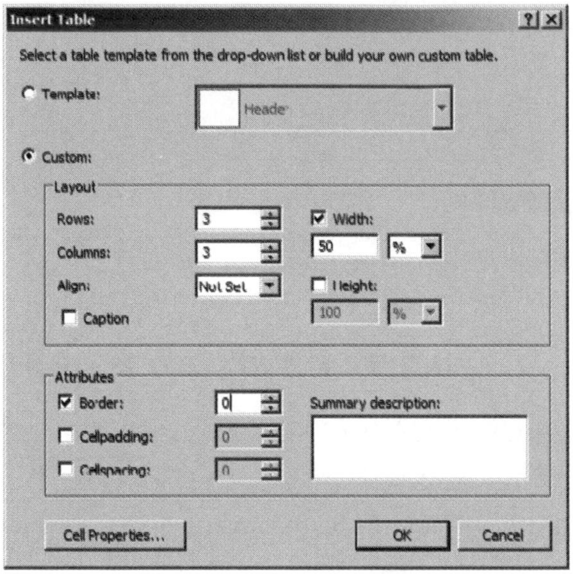

Figure 18.13 Creating a custom template for the table.

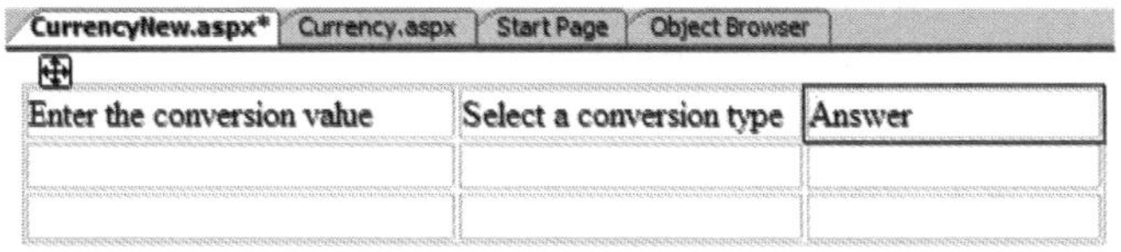

Figure 18.14 HTML table in the Design Window.

18.4.2 Using a ListBox Web Control

The ListBox control presents a list of choices to the user. Users can select one or more choices from the ListBox control displayed as a vertical column. Each display choice is associated with a value. We will add few currency conversion choices to the ListBox control.

5. Drag and drop a TextBox control from the *Standard* tab of the Toolbox onto the third row, first column cell of the table. Set its ID property to *txtInput*. Similarly, drag and drop a ListBox Web control in the third row, second column cell of the table (see Figure 18.15). Set its ID property to *lbxType*.

6. Click on the ListBox control and select the smart tag on the top right-hand corner of the control. In the ListBox's Tasks list that appears, select the *Edit Items* option (see Figure 18.15). This should open the *ListItem Collection Editor* dialog box.

7. We add items in the ListBox control using its *ListItem Collection Editor* dialog box. Click on the *Add* button four times to add four items to the ListBox control. For each item, we set its *Text* and *Value* properties. Set the *Text* properties of these four items as shown in Figure 18.16. For the *Value* property, enter appropriate conversion ratio values. Also, for the first list item we set its *Selected* property to *True* to let the user see a default selected value in the ListBox control. Click *OK* to close the dialog box.

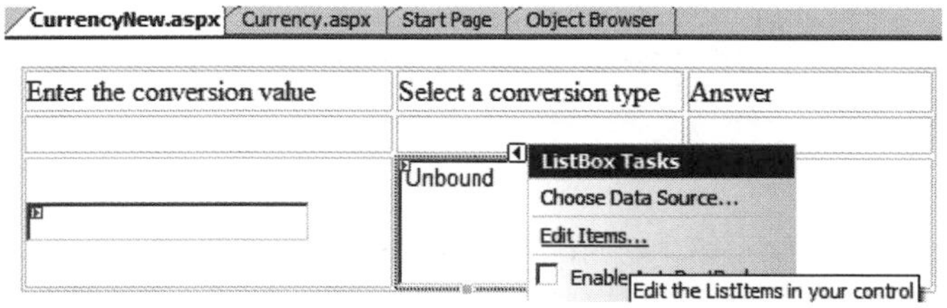

Figure 18.15 Opening the ListBox control's *ListItem Collection Editor* dialog box.

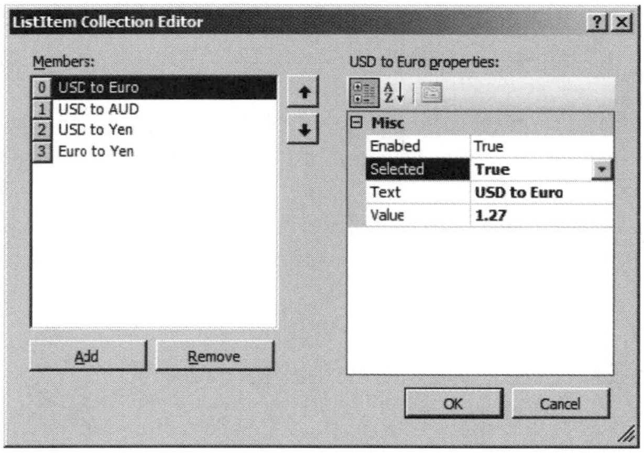

Figure 18.16 Adding items to a ListBox control and setting their properties.

8. Drag and drop a Label control from the *Standard* tab of the Toolbox onto the third row, third column cell of the table (see Figure 18.17). The Label control will display the converted currency value. Set its *ID* property to *lblAnswer* and *Text* property to an empty string.

9. In the previous section, we have seen how to do currency conversion on a click of the command button. In this section, we would like to perform the same operation *SelectedIndexChanged* event of the ListBox control. This event is called whenever a user changes a selection in the ListBox control. To access the event handler code, double-click on the ListBox control in the Design Window. Enter the code shown in Figure 18.18.

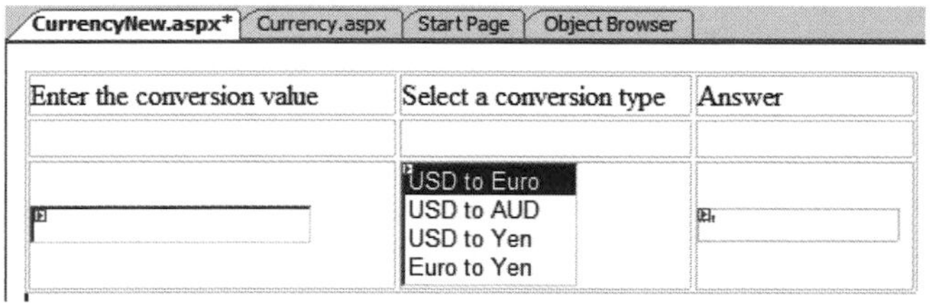

Figure 18.17 Layout for the *CurrencyNew.aspx* Web form.

```
 5      Protected Sub lbxType_SelectedIndexChanged(ByVal sender As Object, _
 6      ByVal e As System.EventArgs) Handles lbxType.SelectedIndexChanged
 7          Dim val As Double
 8          val = CDbl(txtInput.Text) / CDbl(lbxType.SelectedItem.Value)
 9          lblAnswer.Text = CStr(Math.Round(val, 2))
10      End Sub
```

Figure 18.18 Code for handling *SelectedIndexChanged* event of the ListBox control.

Figure 18.18 Explained:

In line 8, the user input from the TextBox control is divided by the value of the selected item of the ListBox control (*lbxtype.SelectedItem.Value*). In line 9, the converted currency value is rounded to two decimal positions and is displayed in the *lblAnswer* Label control.

10. Right-click on the *CurrencyNew.aspx* in the Solution Explorer Window and set it as the start page of the application. Run and test the application.

When we enter a value in the TextBox control and select an item from the ListBox control, we expect to see the results. Though we have entered the code correctly, the application does not run as expected.

18.4.3 Web Client to Web Server to Web Client, a Round Trip

Let us first understand how the Web application in the previous section worked. When the user clicked the command button to convert the currency value from USD to Euro, the value in the TextBox control was sent to the Web server. The event code associated with the command button actually got executed on the Web server. The converted value was sent back to the user for display. The process of sending data from a Web page to the Web server is known as "*post back.*" The Web pages are *post back* for server-side processing when event occurs on the client-side (for example, user clicks the command button).

However, there can be several events occurring on a Web page; a mouse movement, a mouse click on a page, and so forth. If post back occurs for each and every event on the Web page, it may deteriorate the Web page performance with multiple client-server round trips. We would like to send data to the Web server exactly when we would like to process it. This is why not all events automatically trigger a Web page post back. The *Click* event of a Button control is, however, designed for automatic post back every time it is clicked. That is the reason why our application worked in the previous section without performing any additional steps. The ListBox control is not designed for the auto post back and hence our extension is not working.

18.4.4 The *AutoPostBack* Property

AutoPostBack is a property of Web controls that indicates whether auto post back will be triggered for the control. For all the Web controls except the Button control, the *AutoPostBack* is set to *False*. The *AutoPostBack* is set to *True* for a Button control. We can access the *AutoPostBack* property for a Web control either using its Tasks list, or like any other property using the Properties Window.

For the currency conversion extension, we must set the *AutoPostBack* property of the List-Box control to True. This should trigger the post back of the Web page when ListBox's *Selected IndexChanged* event is invoked.

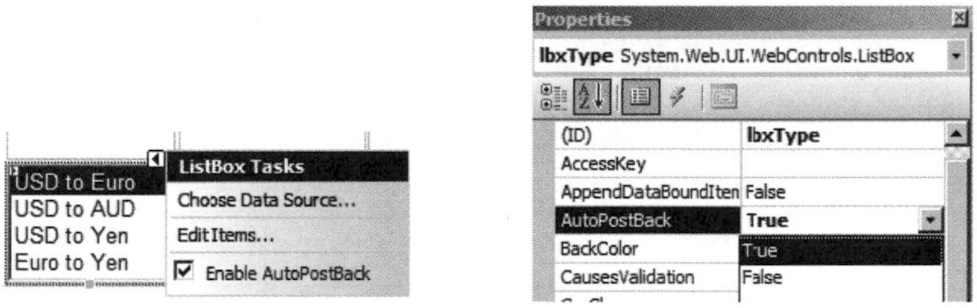

(a)   **(b)**

Figure 18.19 Enabling the *AutoPostBack* property using a Tasks list or the Properties Window.

    11. Click on the smart tag of the ListBox control to view its Task list. Select Enable *AutoPostBack* option from the Tasks list (see Figure 18.19).

    12. Run and test the application (see Figure 18.20).

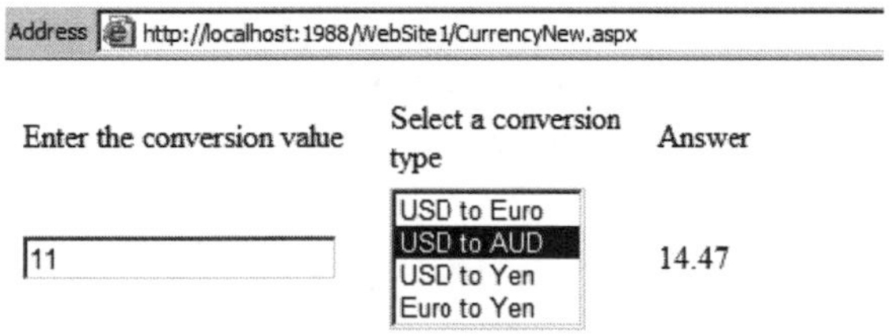

Figure 18.20 Testing the Web page by selecting between various conversion options.

18.5 *Using the* Page_Load *Event and* IsPostBack *Property*

In the previous section, we developed an extension to currency conversion application. Note that when we load the page for the first time, there is no default value assigned to the TextBox control. Sometimes it is a good design practice to assign default values to the controls. We can assign default values to Web controls in the *Page_Load* event code of a Web page. The *Page_Load* event of a Web page is triggered every time a page is refreshed in the Web browser. This section covers the following How-to topic:

    ■ How-to: use *IsPostBack* method with *Page_Load* event handler.

Let us add a code to the *Page_Load* event of the Web page created in the previous section.

    1. Open the *CurrencyNew.aspx* page and double-click anywhere on the page to open the Code Window with the *Page_Load* event handler.

2. Enter the as shown in Figure 18.21. Run and test the application (see Figure 18.22).

```
1  Partial Class CurrencyNew
2      Inherits System.Web.UI.Page
3
4      Protected Sub Page_Load(ByVal sender As Object, ByVal e As _
5      System.EventArgs) Handles Me.Load
6          txtInput.Text = CStr(10)
7          lblAnswer.Text = Convert()
8      End Sub
9
10     Protected Sub lbxType_SelectedIndexChanged(ByVal sender As Object, _
11     ByVal e As System.EventArgs) Handles lbxType.SelectedIndexChanged
12         lblAnswer.Text = Convert()
13     End Sub
14
15     Function Convert() As String
16         Dim val As Double
17         val = CDbl(txtInput.Text) / CDbl(lbxType.SelectedItem.Value)
18         Return CStr(Math.Round(val, 2))
19     End Function
20 End Class
```

Figure 18.21 The *Page_Load* event for the *CurrencyNew.aspx* Web form.

Figure 18.21 Explained

We have encapsulated the code for currency conversion in the *Convert* function (lines 15–19). The function is called in lines 7 and 12 to assign converted value to the *lblAnswer* Label control. The *Page_Load* event handle code is presented in lines 4–8. We assign a default value "10" to the TextBox control (line 6) every time the page is loaded.

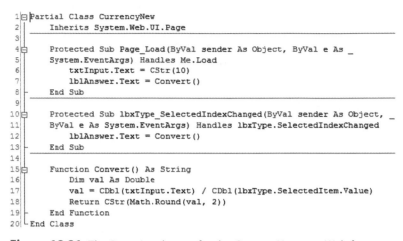

Figure 18.22 Conversion value in the textbox changes upon changing ListBox selection.

When we run the application, the default value shows up in the TextBox control. When we click any of the options in the ListBox control, we see the converted value on the Web page. However, when we change the default input value to some other number in the TextBox control, we observe unexpected behavior of the Web page. If we enter a value, say 20, in the TextBox control and click on one of the conversion options, we do see the correct conversion in the answer Label control, but the TextBox control shows a default value "10" rather than our input value "20."

Note that when we click one of the options in the ListBox control, the post back occurs. The Web page is sent to the Web server for currency conversion calculations. When the Web server responds with the converted value, the page is again *loaded* in the Web browser with the conversion answer. This is why we see the default value assigned to the TextBox control (line 6 of Figure 18.21) and the correct answer in the Label control.

How do we reconcile? How can we add a code to the *Page_Load* event handler that will get executed only when the page is loaded for the very first time? The *IsPostBack* method tells us if the page is loaded for the first time or if it is a post back. The *IsPostBack* method returns *True* if the page is getting loaded after a post back. It returns *False* if the page is getting loaded for the very first time.

We now modify the *Page_Load* event for the *CurrencyNew.aspx* page and assign the TextBox control its default value only when the page is loaded for the very first time.

3. Modify the *Page_Load* event handler code as shown in Figure 18.23. Run and test the application.

```
 4   Protected Sub Page_Load(ByVal sender As Object, ByVal e As _
 5   System.EventArgs) Handles Me.Load
 6       If Not IsPostBack Then
 7           txtInput.Text = CStr(10)
 8           lblAnswer.Text = Convert()
 9       End If
10   End Sub
```

Figure 18.23 Using the *IsPostBack* property in the *Page_Load* event handler code.

18.6 *Working with the Page Directive*

Page directive is a special ASP .NET tag that appears at the beginning of the HTML code of a Web page (see line 1–2 in Figure 18.24). The *Page* tag governs many aspects of appearance and behavior of a Web page using its properties. The *Page directive* supports eight different properties. In this section, we will discuss few important properties of a page directive.

```
CurrencyNew.aspx  CurrencyNew.aspx.vb  Currency.aspx  Start Page  Object Browser
Client Objects & Events              ▼  (No Events)
 1   <%@ Page Language="VB" AutoEventWireup="false"
 2   CodeFile="CurrencyNew.aspx.vb" Inherits="CurrencyNew" %>
```

Figure 18.24 Page directive for the *CurrencyNew.aspx* Web page.

- **Language:** This property indicates the language in which the inline code within the HTML code for the ASP.NET page will be written (the code between "<%" and "%>" tags). The value of this property can be C#, VB, or JS.
- **CodeFile:** This property indicates the name of the code behind file. The code behind file is the file with "VB" extension in which we write the VB .NET code that gets executed on the Web server.
- **AutoEventWireup:** When *AutoEventWireup* is *True*, ASP.NET does not require events to specify event handlers like *Page_Load*. Thus, we need not mention the `Handles` keyword in Visual Basic code next to the event subroutine declaration. The default value of this property is *False*.
- **Inherits:** This property indicates a qualified class module from which this ASP.NET page should be inherited. Generally, this is the name of the class in the *CodeFile*.
- **ErrorPage:** This property allows us to provide a URL to which the user will be redirected if an unhandled error occurs on the Web page. Visual Studio .NET also allows us to provide a similar URL in the "*Web.config*" file.

18.7 *Validation Controls*

Validation is a procedure that is used to check for the correctness of the data entered by users. As the name suggests, the validation controls are used to validate users' input. Validation controls can be attached any Web control to check the values assigned to the control.

There are various types of validation controls available under the *Validation* tab in the Toolbox Window. However, we will discuss the RequiredFieldValidator and RegularExpression-Validator controls in this section. The RequiredFieldValidator control forces the user to enter a value for a Web control, whereas the RegularExpressionValidator control checks the format of the value entered by the user.

In this section, we will create a Web page that will accept personal details from the user such as name, email, and phone. It is required for the user to enter her name and enter her email and phone in standard format. We validate this using Validation controls. This section covers the following How-to topic:

■ How-to: use RequiredFieldValidator and RegularExpressionValidator controls.

18.7.1 Adding Validation Controls to a Web Form

We use a RequiredFieldValidator control for the *Name* field and the RegularExpressionValida-tor control for *Email* and *Phone* fields.

1. Add a new a Web page to the *WebSite1* Web site using the *Add New Item* dialog box. Name the page as "Validation.aspx."
2. Add an HTML table as shown in Figure 18.25 to layout the page. Add Label controls and the TextBox controls to the page for user input. Also add a "*Validate*" Button control and *lblMsg* Label control to the page (see Figure 18.25).

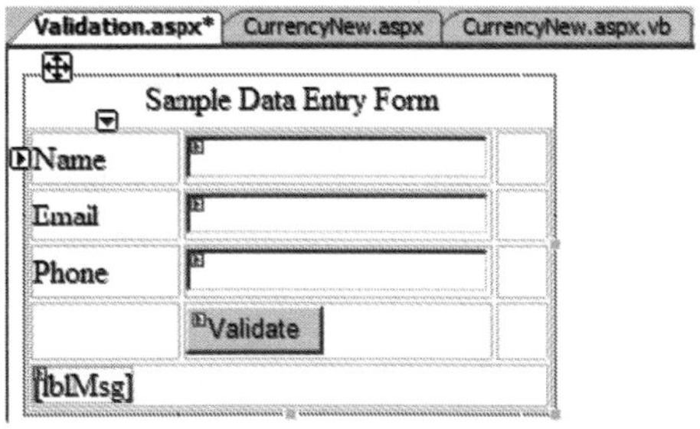

Figure 18.25 Layout for the *Validation.aspx* Web page.

3. Enter the code shown in Figure 18.26 for the *Click* event handler of the *Validate* Button control. The code displays the name, email, and phone number entered in TextBox controls on a click of the Button control.
4. Run and test the application. Enter the values as shown in Figure 18.27.
5. Now test the application by leaving the *Name* TextBox controls empty and by entering invalid values for the *Email* and *Phone* TextBox controls. We should not get any error message.

```
5┌     Protected Sub btnSend_Click(ByVal sender As Object, _
6│     ByVal e As System.EventArgs) Handles btnSend.Click
7│        lblMsg.Text = txtName.Text & "'s Phone:" & _
8│        txtPhone.Text & " & Email:" & txtEmail.Text
9└     End Sub
```

Figure 18.26 *Click* event handler code for the *Validate* Button control.

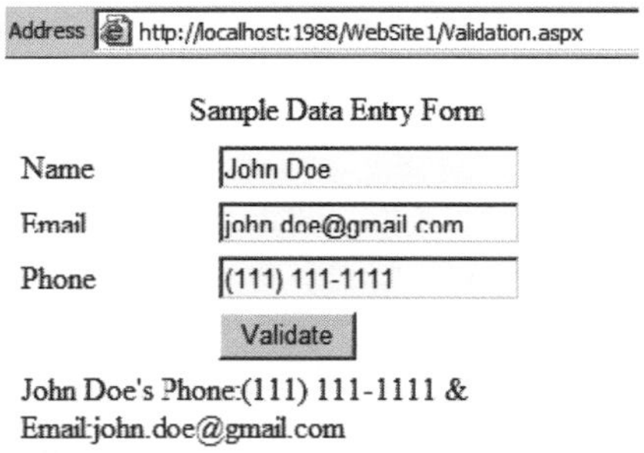

Address http://localhost:1988/WebSite1/Validation.aspx

Sample Data Entry Form

Name   John Doe

Email   john.doe@gmail.com

Phone   (111) 111-1111

Validate

John Doe's Phone:(111) 111-1111 &
Email:john.doe@gmail.com

Figure 18.27 Testing the running application.

18.7.2 The RequiredFieldValidator Control

To make sure that the user enters a value for the *Name* TextBox control, we add a RequiredField-Validator control and link it to the *txtName* TextBox control. The RequiredFieldValidator is a control that is attached to another control to check whether data has been entered into a connected control.

6. From the Toolbox, drag and drop the RequiredFieldValidator control (see Figure 18.28) onto the *Validation.aspx* page beside the *Name* TextBox control.
7. Once we have dropped the RequiredFieldValidator control onto the page, we access its properties of using the Properties Window. Change the *Display* property of the control to *Dynamic* and the *ErrorMessage* property to "*.*" Select *txtName* as the control to validate using *Control* property (see Figure 18.29).
8. Run and test the application for the *Name* TextBox control.

(a)

(b)

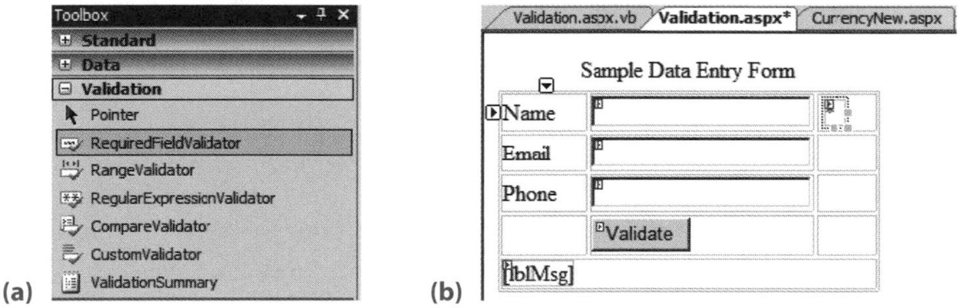

Figure 18.28 Adding a RequiredFieldValidator to the *Validation.aspx* Web page.

Figure 18.29 Attaching the RequiredFieldValidator control and setting its properties.

18.7.3 The RegularExpressionValidator Control

To make sure that the user enters a value in a valid format for the *Email* and *Phone* TextBox controls, we add RegularExpressionValidator controls and link them to the *txtEmail* and *txtPhone* TextBox controls. The RegularExpressionValidator is a control that is attached to another control to check the format of the data entered into a connected control. The format is checked against the specified *regular expression*.

9. From the Toolbox, drag and drop the RegularExpressionValidator control onto the form next to the *Email* and *Phone* TextBox controls (see Figure 18.31).

10. Access the properties of the RegularExpressionValidator control besides the *Email* TextBox control using Properties Window. Set the *Display* property to *Dynamic* and the *ErrorMessage* property to "*Invalid.*" Select *txtEmail* as the control to validate using *Control* property.

    The Display property, when set to Dynamic option, displays the error message as user enters values in the TextBox control. Also the error message is cleared as soon as user makes the necessary correction.

11. Locate the *ValidationExpression* property and click the available *Build* (...) button (see Figure 18.30). This should open the *Regular Expression Editor* dialog box.

12. Scroll through the list of options and select the *Internet e-mail address* option, and click *OK* (see Figure 18.30). The *Regular Expression Editor* dialog box allows us to quickly pick a regular expression for many standard fields.

13. From the Toolbox, drag and drop another RegularExpressionValidator control onto the form next to the *Phone* TextBox control (see Figure 18.31).

14. Access the properties of the RegularExpressionValidator control besides the *Phone* TextBox control using Properties Window. Set the *Display* property to *Dynamic* and the *ErrorMessage* property to "*Invalid.*" Select *txtPhone* as the control to validate using *Control* property.

15. Locate the *ValidationExpression* property and click the available *Build* (...) button (see Figure 18.30). Scroll through the list of available options in the *Regular Expression Editor* dialog box and select the *U.S. phone number* option, and click *OK*.

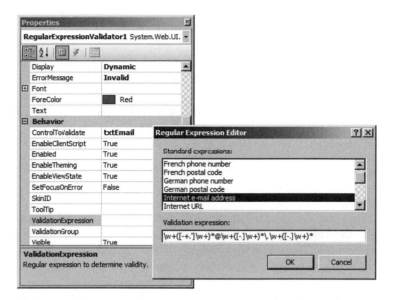

Figure 18.30 Setting properties and building a validation expression for the email address validation control.

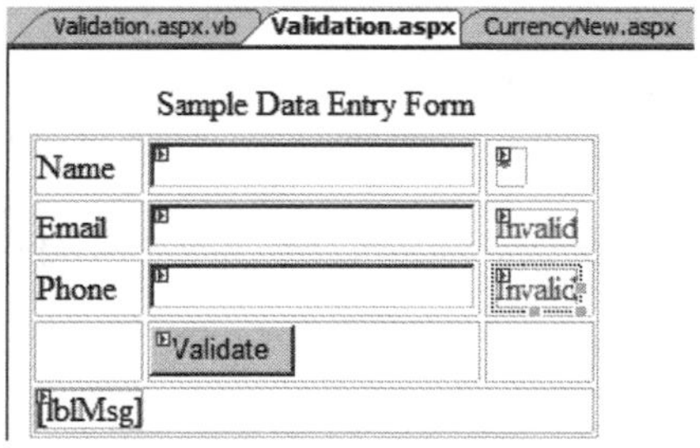

Figure 18.31 *Validation.aspx* page showing validation controls for name, email and phone fields.

16. Run and test the application. Do not enter any value for the name field, enter "john.doe@mailcom" in for the email field, and 111 1111 111 in the phone field. Even before clicking on the *Validate* button, we see that that the page displays a "*" mark beside the name field and *Invalid* message beside the email and phone fields (see Figure 18.32).

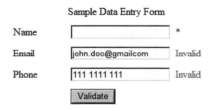

Figure 18.32 Testing the validation controls with empty name field and incorrect email and phone fields.

18.8 *Passing Parameters through URL*

Passing values from one Web page to another is a very common task in Web development. However, the importance of it has faded with ASP .NET's inherent support for post back forms and Session variables (see Chapter 20). But regardless, passing parameter values through URL remains as one of the simplest and most efficient ways of passing data from one Web page to another.

The query string is the string that is added at the end of a URL, separated by a question mark (?). For example, to open a Web page, *Page2.aspx* along with parameter values, we could use the following query string:

```
Page2.aspx?Name=bookreader&Phone=1729172917
```

The *Name* and *Phone* are the parameters with values *bookreader* and *1729172917*, respectively. We use an ampersand (&) operator to concatenate multiple parameters into a single query string. The parameter and their values are accessible on the *Page2.aspx*.

In this section, we extend the application developed on the *Validation.aspx* Web page in the previous section. We add a Button control to the page that when clicked, redirects a user to a new Web page and displays the data entered by the user on *Validation.aspx* Web page. We use query string to pass user entered values on the *Validation.aspx* page to the new Web page. This section covers the following How-to topic:

■ How-to: pass parameter values through URL.

1. Open the Validation.aspx page and add a Button control to it. Set the ID property of the Button control to "*btnRedirect*," and the Text property to "*Redirect Display*" (see Figure 18.33).
2. Double-click the *Redirect Display* command button and enter the code shown in Figure 18.34.

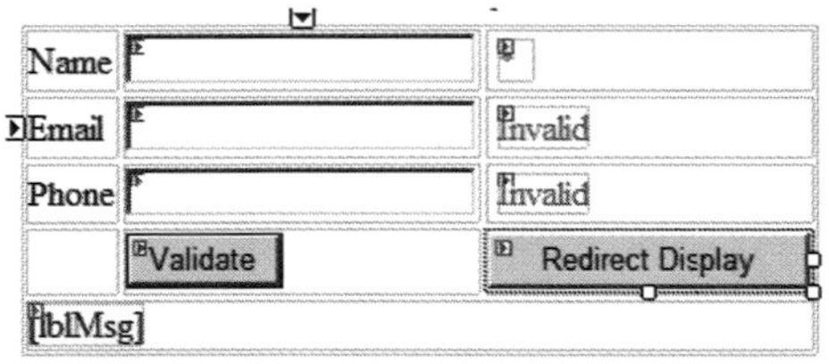

Figure 18.33 *Validation.aspx* page with the *Redirect Display* Button control.

```
11    Protected Sub btnRedirect_Click(ByVal sender As Object, _
12    ByVal e As System.EventArgs) Handles btnRedirect.Click
13        Dim query As String = "name=" & txtName.Text & "&"
14        query &= "ph=" & txtPhone.Text & "&"
15        query &= "email=" & txtEmail.Text
16        Response.Redirect("ValidationNew.aspx?" & query)
17    End Sub
```

Figure 18.34 Creating the query string and redirecting with parameter values.

Figure 18.34 Explained:

In lines 13–15, we create the query string using values of the TextBox controls. In line 16, we call the *Response.Redirect* function to redirect the user to a new page. The query string is appended with the URL.

3. Add a new Web page, "*ValidationNew.aspx*," to the Web site.
4. In the *Page_Load* event handler code of the new Web page, enter the code shown in Figure 18.35.
5. Run and test the application (see Figure 18.36).

```
4   Protected Sub Page_Load(ByVal sender As Object, ByVal e As _
5   System.EventArgs) Handles Me.Load
6       Dim name As String = Request.Item("name")
7       Dim phone As String = Request.Params("ph")
8       Dim email As String = Request.Params("email")
9       Response.Write(name & "'s phone#" & phone & _
10      " and email:" & email)
11  End Sub
```

Figure 18.35 Displaying the parameters from URL on a Web page.

Figure 18.35 Explained:

We access the parameter values in the query string using the *Request.Item* or *Request.Params* functions (lines 6–8). Each of these functions takes the name of the parameter that is present in the query string as its input and returns the value associated with the requested parameter. We use *Response.Write* function to write parameter values on a Web page. The *Request* and *Response* functions here can be thought of as *Request* and *Response* parts of the request-response cycle discussed in Chapter 17.

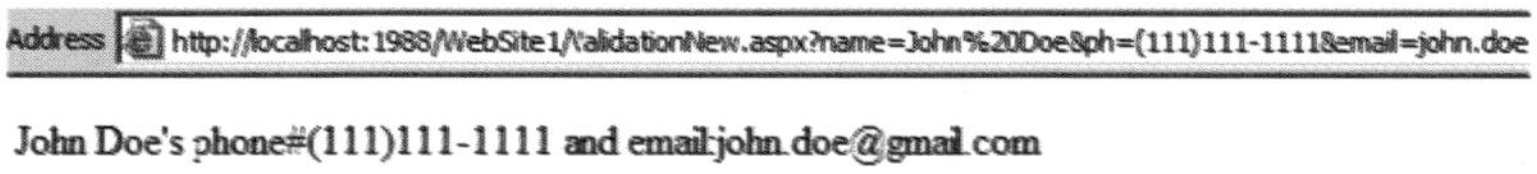

Address 🔲 http://localhost:1988/WebSite1/ValidationNew.aspx?name=John%20Doe&ph={111}111-1111&email=john.doe

John Doe's phone#(111)111-1111 and email:john.doe@gmail.com

Figure 18.36 Running application showing the output on the redirected page.

18.9   *User-Defined Controls*

Till now we have used the Web controls that already existed in the Toolbox. Although these controls provide a great deal of functionality, they may not satisfy all application requirements. User-defined Web controls enable us to easily define and design controls as required by applications. A user-defined Web control can be added to a Web page and work just like any other existing Web control.

In this section, we create a user-defined control that features a top banner. The banner consists of an image and a label showing the current date and time. We can then include the *Top-Banner* user-defined control to any Web page as a page header. This section covers the following How-to topics:

- How-to: create a user-defined control.
- How-to: add a user-defined control on a Web page.
- How-to: add a *Property* to a user-defined control.

18.9.1   Creating a User-Defined Control

1. Choose Web Site | Add New Item option from the main menu to open *Add New Item* dialog box. Select the *Web User Control* icon and specify its name as "TopBanner.ascx." Click *Add* to add the user-defined control to the Web site (see Figure 18.37).

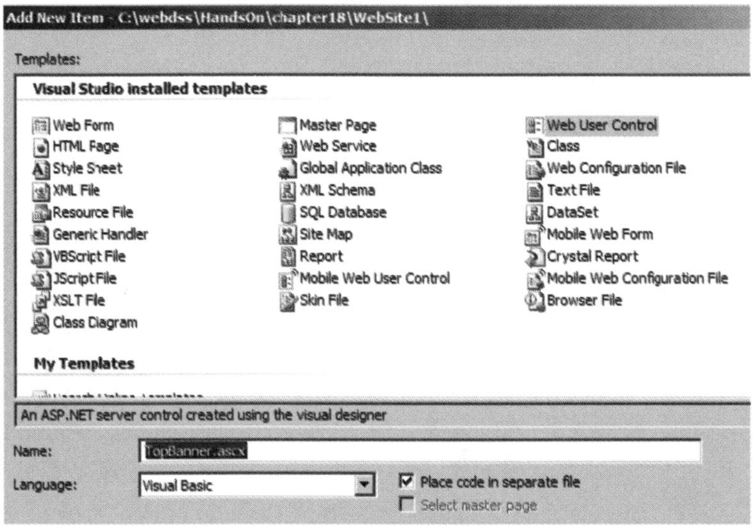

Figure 18.37 Adding a user-defined control to the Web site.

2. Add an Image control from the Toolbox onto TopBanner.ascx. In the Properties Window, set the *ImageURL* to the *banner1.jpg* file from the Chapter 18 folder available on the book Web site. Add a Label control and set its ID property to *lblWhen* (see Figure 18.38).

3. Double-click anywhere on the page to open its *Page_Load* event code. Enter the code as shown in Figure 18.39. In line 6 we assign current data and time to the *lblWhen* Label control.

4. Save the control by choosing the File | Save option from the main menu.

Figure 18.38 Layout for the *TopBanner* user-defined control.

```
5      Protected Sub Page_Load(ByVal sender As Object, ByVal e _
6      As System.EventArgs) Handles Me.Load
7          lblWhen.Text = "Login On: " & DateTime.Now
8      End Sub
```

Figure 18.39 Displaying current Date and Time.

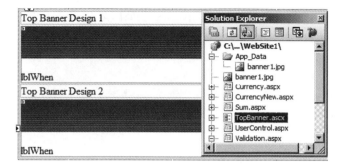

Figure 18.40 Layout for the *UserControl.aspx* Web page with two instances of the *TopBanner* control.

18.9.2 Adding User Control to a Web form

5. Add a new Web page named "UserControl.aspx" to the Web site.
6. Insert an HTML table as shown in Figure 18.40. Drag and drop the *TopBanner.ascx* from the Solution Explorer Window onto the Web page (see Figure 18.40). Enter the text "Top Banner Design 1" in row 1 and "Top Banner Design 2" in row 3 of the HTML table.
7. Set the *UserControl.aspx* page as the start page of the application using (use Solution Explorer Window). Run and test the application (see Figure 18.41).

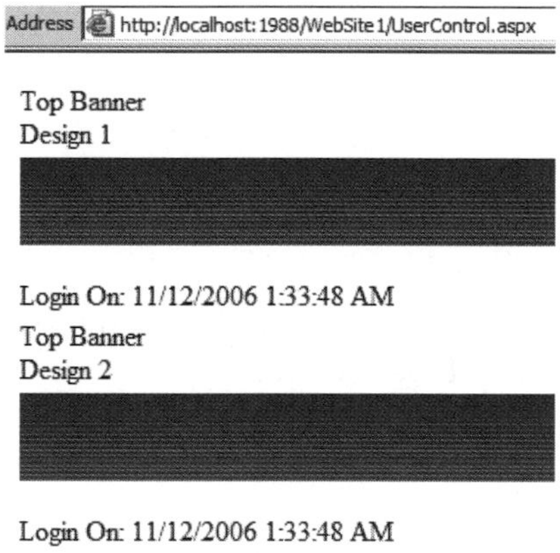

Address | http://localhost:1988/WebSite1/UserControl.aspx

Top Banner
Design 1

Login On: 11/12/2006 1:33:48 AM
Top Banner
Design 2

Login On: 11/12/2006 1:33:48 AM

Figure 18.41 Testing the Web form with two instances of the user control.

18.9.3 Adding a Property to a User-Defined Control

Just as existing Web controls have their own properties that govern their appearance and behavior; user-defined controls have their own properties as well. We extend the *TopBanner* user-defined control designed in the previous subsection. We add a *Color* property to the control, which, when set to a desired color, changes the color of the date and time label on the control.

1. Open the "TopBanner.ascx.vb" code file by double-clicking the file from the Solution Explorer Window.

2. As shown in Figure 18.42, add an *Imports System.Drawing* statement (line 1). Also, declare a global variable *thisColor* of type Color (line 6), and assign it a default value of *Black*.

```
1   Imports System.Drawing
2
3   Partial Class TopBanner
4        Inherits System.Web.UI.UserControl
5
6        Dim thisColor As Color = color.Black
```

Figure 18.42 Declaring a global variable of type Color.

3. Add the property declaration code shown in Figure 18.43. The code between the Get and End Get statements is used to return the value stored in the property. The code between Set and End Set is used to assign a value to the property (also see 12.6.5).

4. Modify the *Page_Load* event as shown in Figure 18.44. We set the *ForeColor* property of the Label control *lblWhen* to *thisColor* global variable.

```
14       Property color() As Color
15           Get
16               Return thisColor
17           End Get
18           Set(ByVal value As Color)
19               thisColor = value
20           End Set
21       End Property
```

Figure 18.43 Adding the Get and Set methods for the *Color* property.

```
8        Protected Sub Page_Load(ByVal sender As Object, ByVal e _
9        As System.EventArgs) Handles Me.Load
10           lblWhen.ForeColor = thisColor
11           lblWhen.Text = "Login On: " & DateTime.Now
12       End Sub
```

Figure 18.44 Setting the *ForeColor* property of the Label control.

```
5        Protected Sub Page_Load(ByVal sender As Object, _
6        ByVal e As System.EventArgs) Handles Me.Load
7            TopBanner1.color = Drawing.Color.Blue
8            TopBanner2.color = Drawing.Color.Red
9        End Sub
```

Figure 18.45 Using the *Color* property of the user-defined controls.

5. Open the "UserControl.aspx" form, and double-click anywhere on the form to open its *Page_Load* event handler code. Set the value of the *Color* property of the *TopBanner1* control to *Drawing.Color.Blue*. Similarly, set the *Color* property for the *TopBanner2* control to *Drawing.Color.Red* (see Figure 18.45). An alternative to set the value for the *Color* property is to make use of the Properties Window (see Figure 18.46).

6. Run and test the application. We should see the Web page with the date and time Label control in the user-defined control being displayed in two different colors (see Figure 18.47).

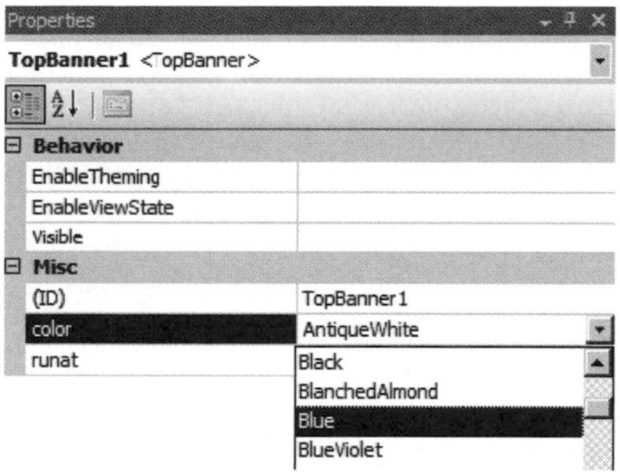

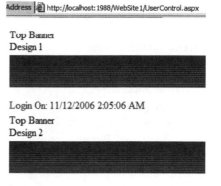

Figure 18.46 Using the *Color* property of a user-defined control using the Properties Window.

Figure 18.47 Running application with different colors for the Label control in the user-defined control.

18.10   *In-Class Assignment*

Recall the greeting card windows application we developed in Chapter 14. Now, we will develop a similar greeting card Web page. Use Web controls to take in user input for various parameters of the card such as background color, font type, size and color, and border style. Also, take in user input for the greeting text. Make sure that we set the *AutoPostBack* property wherever required. Also make sure to validate the user inputs. (*Hint:* Use RequiredFieldValidator controls.)

18.11   *Summary*

■ ASP .NET combines HTML front-end with VB .NET back-end to utilize the power of VB .NET programming in a Web environment.

■ The process of sending data from a Web page to the Web server is known as "*post back*." The Web pages are *post back* for server-side processing when events occur on the client-side (for example, user clicks the command button).

■ *AutoPostBack* is a property of Web controls that indicates whether *Auto post back* will be triggered for the control. The *AutoPostBack* property of a Button control is set to *True* by default.

■ The *IsPostBack* method tells us if the page is loaded for the first time or if it is a post back. The *IsPostBack* method returns *True* if the page is getting loaded after a post back. It returns *False* if the page is getting loaded for the very first time.

■ *Page directive* is a special ASP .NET tag that appears at the beginning of the HTML code of a Web page. The *Page* tag governs many aspects of appearance and behavior of a Web page using its properties.

■ Validation is a procedure that is used to check for the correctness of the data entered by users. The validation controls are used to validate users' input. To make sure that the user enters a value for a control, we add a RequiredFieldValidator control and link it to the validating control. To make sure that the user enters a value in valid format for a control, we add a RegularExpressionValidator control and link it to the validating control.

■ Passing values from one Web page to another is a very common task in Web development. Passing parameter values through URL remains as one of the simplest and most efficient ways of passing data from one Web page to another.

■ User-defined Web controls enable us to easily define and design controls as required by applications. A user-defined Web control can be added to a Web page and it will work just like any other existing Web control.

18.12.1 Review Questions

1. What is the difference between a Windows application and a Web application?

2. Which control is the *SelectedIndexChanged* event associated with? When is it triggered?

3. What is the significance of a Button control with regard to post back in Web pages?

4. What is the use of setting the *AutoPostBack* property of a control?

5. How can we populate controls with required default values?

6. Which event handler is invoked whenever a post back occurs?

7. What is the significance of the *IsPostBack* method?

8. What are the functions of *Page directives*? What are its properties?

9. Why is it important to validate user inputs, especially when we store the input values in a database?

10. What is the significance of setting the *Display* property of a validation control to *Dynamic*?

18.12.2 Hands-On Exercises

1. Create a simple Web page that asks a user to input a number *N*. When the user submits the input, write the code to check if the given number is Prime (refer to Chapter 12, Hands-On Exercise 2). Use a Label control to display the result ("Prime" or "Not Prime").

2. Create a Web application that asks a user to input a number *N* and compute its factorial (refer to Section 12.3). When the user submits the input, write code to compute the factorial of *N*, and display it on the page.

3. A certain restaurant offers three different meals (Combo1, Combo2, and Combo3). The client has three different choices for the meal size (Small, Medium, and Large). Create a Web form that displays all the options to the user. When the user submits the order by clicking on a *ViewOrder* command button, display the select meal type and its size to the user.

4. Create a Web form for a temperature conversion page. Provide a TextBox control for user input and a ListBox control with two options, "Convert Fahrenheit to Centigrade" and "Convert Centi-grade to Fahrenheit." Arrange all the controls inside an HTML table. Whenever the user enters a value in the TextBox control and selects a ListBox control option, display the output in a Label control.

5. Mimic Chapter 13, Hands-On Exercise 2 on a Web page. Provide CheckBox controls for the user to select the page background color. As the user checks the background color Check Box controls, we should modify the background color of the page (*Hint*: Use *AutoPostBack* property of a CheckBox control). If the user selects more than one color, the background color should be set as a combination of the selected colors.

6. Create a Web application for secure user registration. We will create a Web form that will allow the user to create a new username and a password for secure login. Since the password is sensitive data, we need to make sure that the user does not mistype it. So, we will ask the user to re-enter it for confirmation. After entering the data, the user must click the *Submit* button to register. Validate user input for the following conditions:

   a. That the user entered all the required information.

   b. That the username is at least eight characters in length.

   c. That the text in the Password field is identical to that in the Verify Password field.

   Indicate any missing or incorrect information on the page. If the data is valid, display a simple message, "Thank you for signing up." Provide a "Reset" button that clears all the controls on click.

7. Create a Web page for student login with the following fields: Name, StudentID, Email, Phone, and Degree Program (BS, MS, and PhD). Validate the input values for all the fields. Use TextBox controls for user input for the first four fields and a ListBox control for the fifth field. Populate a Label control with the student's category based on the following rules:

   a. If degree is BS, label should read "Undergraduate."

   b. If degree is MS or PhD, label should read "Graduate."

8. A university's Computer Science department is collecting information about its students' areas of

interest. Create a Web application that can be used as an interface for this task. Design a Web form that has controls for taking in user input for the following fields for each student: Name, Student number (must be eight digits), Date of birth, Gender, and Areas of interest.

Choose a Web control that is appropriate for the type of information it is collecting. Validate user input as the user is entering the data. Invalid data may result from one of the following:

a. The student did not enter name or student number.

b. The student number does not contain eight characters.

c. The student did not choose any area of interest.

If there are no errors in data input, display a message to the student indicating that the data was valid.

9. Create a Web application for Fibonacci series generation. We should take in the user's input number *N* on the first page, validate the input (refer to Section 12.3.1), and pass it to another page as a parameter through URL. On the new page, we should write the code to: extract the number *N* from the query string, generate the Fibonacci series, and display it in a ListBox control.

10. Recall the Guest Book application we developed in Chapter 17 (Hands-On Exercise 9). In this exercise, we develop a Web application to display a "Thank You" page following the Guest Book entry. From the guestbook form, pass the name of the user to a new form through a URL query string. Display the message "Thank you <user name> for your comments. We appreciate your feedback."

11. User-defined controls can be used on every Web page that we design. In this exercise, we design a page footer that we can use at the bottom of all Web pages. Create a Web user-defined control called *PageFooter*. Include a Horizontal Rule from the Toolbox and two Label controls. Use one of the labels to display the text "Last login:," and write the code to display the current time in the second label on the *Form_Load* event.

12. In this exercise, we design a navigation pane user-defined control that we can use in almost all our pages. Use an HTML table to represent the navigation pane. Include Label controls with text denoting the often-used pages (Home, Contact, About Us, and People).

nineteen Database Connectivity in Web Applications

chapter OVERVIEW

19.1 *Introduction*

In the previous chapter, we introduced the ASP .NET Web programming language and illustrated how ASP .NET combines HTML and VB .NET to build dynamic Web pages. We also introduced Web controls, which constitute the building blocks of ASP .NET Web pages. Web controls are more appealing when used to display and manipulate data that resides in databases. A Web-based, data-driven application is a program that allows users to manipulate data in a DBMS through a Web interface. The databases are typically stored on a Web server and are accessed from a Web client using a Web browser program. Online shopping sites such as Amazon.Com and Buy.com, driving-direction providers, such as Mapquest.com and Yahoo Maps, and movie information portals, such as Imdb.com, are excellent examples of Web-based, data-driven applications.

In this chapter, we will learn how to use the Visual Studio environment to develop Web-based, data-driven applications using ASP .NET and an MS Access database. We introduced database programming in Chapter 14 and discussed several advanced database connectivity topics in Chapter 15. These chapters serve as useful background material for the topics discussed in this chapter. We therefore highly recommend readers to revisit Chapters 14–16 before proceeding with the material in this chapter.

19.1.1 Topics

This chapter discusses the following topics:

- How to display data and images from a database on a Web page.
- How to display the result of a query with a join of multiple tables on a Web page.
- How to add look-up and filter functionalities to a Web page.
- How to programmatically access database tables.
- How to add Crystal Reports in ASP .NET Web application.

19.2 *Connecting to the Access Database Using the Server Explorer Window*

The Server Explorer Window is used to create and manipulate database connections. It provides an easy yet powerful way to view and modify the contents of a database. To create a connection to an Access database, we perform the following steps. This section covers the following How-to topic:

- How-to: add a database connection using the Server Explorer Window in a Web application.

    1. Create a new ASP .NET Web site named *WebDBConnectivity*.
    2. Open the Server Explorer Window by choosing the View | Server Explorer option from the main menu.

3. In the Server Explorer Window, right-click on the *Data Connections* icon, and select the *Add Connection* option (see Figure 19.1). This should open the *Add Connection* dialog box.

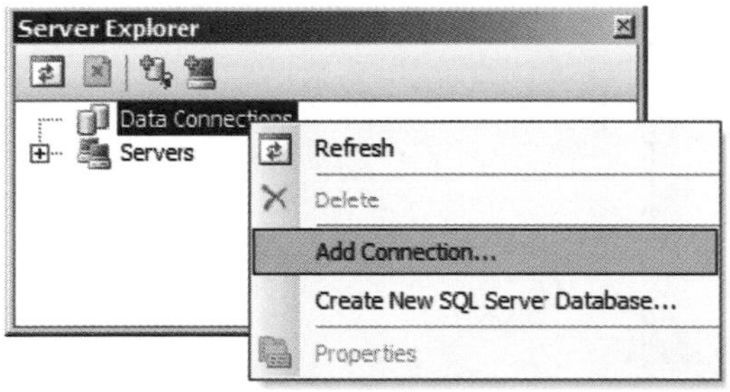

Figure 19.1 Invoking the *Add Connection* dialog box using the Server Explorer Window.

4. In the *Add Connection* dialog box, select the database that we would like to create a connection to (see Figure 19.2). Click the *Browse* button, and locate and select the "University.mdb" database file for Chapter 19 (see book Web site to download related files).
5. Click on the *Test Connection* button to verify the database connection. Click the *OK* button to add the connection.

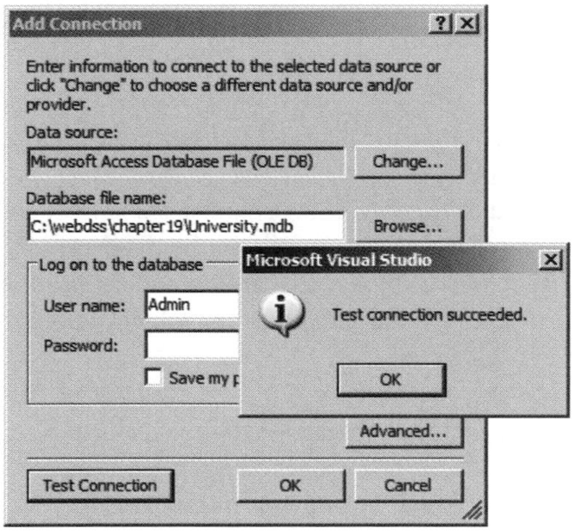

Figure 19.2 Connecting to the University database.

The new connection appears as an entry under the *Data Connections* icon in the Server Explorer Window (see Figure 19.3).

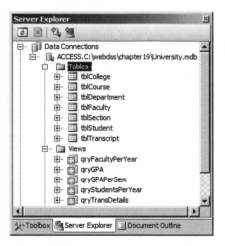

Figure 19.3 Server Explorer Window showing tables and queries of the University database.

19.2.1 Exploring Database Tables and Views

We can use the Server Explorer Window to view the table and query listing of a connected Access database. We can also view and modify contents of database tables using the Server Explorer Window. Visual Studio IDE thus provides a single environment to develop Web applications, and to access connected databases. This section covers the following How-to topic:

■ How-to: view and modify the data in an Access database using the Server Explorer Window.

1. In the Server Explorer Window for the *WebDBConnectivity* project, open (or collapse) the newly added connection node.
2. To access the database tables and queries, collapse the *Tables* and *Views* nodes. This should present a list of available tables and queries in the database (see Figure 19.3).
3. To view a database table, right-click on the listed table and select the *Show Table Data* option from the shortcut menu. This should open the table in a separate tab in the Design Window of Visual Studio IDE.

The database tables are presented as a grid-like structure, very much like in Access's Datasheet View (see Chapter 6). We can view and edit columns' values using this grid interface. Figure 19.4 shows the *tblCollege* table opened from the Server Explorer Window.

Figure 19.4 Viewing table data in the Visual Studio environment.

19.3 *Hands-On Tutorial: Displaying Data on a Web Page*

In this hands-on tutorial, we will display the student table on a Web page and enhance its appearance using the *AutoFormat* feature of a GridView control. This hands-on tutorial covers the following How-to topic:

- How-to: display contents of a database table on a Web page.

1. Add a Web page named "*Page1.aspx*" to the *WebDBConnectivity* project.
2. Drag and drop the *tblStudent* table from the Server Explorer Window onto *Page1.aspx* in the Design Window. This should automatically create an AccessDataSource control and a GridView control. The drag-and-drop also configures the GridView control and sets its *DataSourceID* property to the AccessDataSource control (see Figure 19.5).
3. Run the application (Ctrl+F5) to view the student table on a Web page (see Figure 19.6).

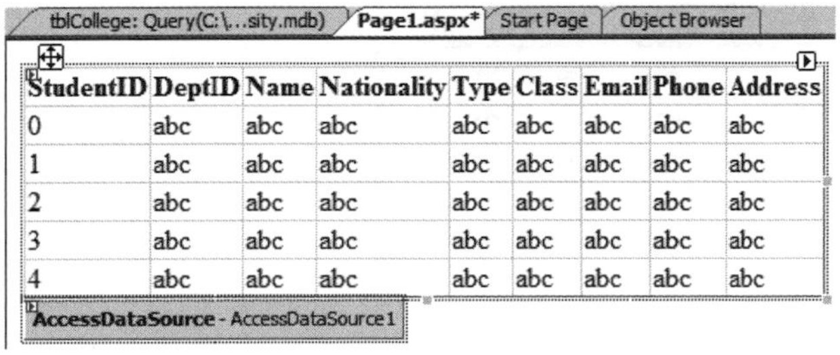
tblCollege: Query(C:\...sity.mdb)
Page1.aspx*
Start Page
Object Browser
StudentID DeptID Name Nationality Type Class Email Phone Address
0 abc abc abc abc abc abc abc abc
1 abc abc abc abc abc abc abc abc
2 abc abc abc abc abc abc abc abc
3 abc abc abc abc abc abc abc abc
4 abc abc abc abc abc abc abc abc
AccessDataSource - AccessDataSource1

Figure 19.5 Adding an AccessDataSource control and data-bind GridView control to a Web page.

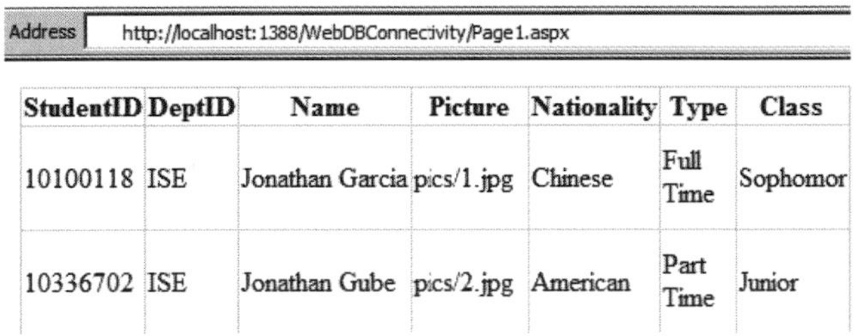
Address
http://localhost:1388/WebDBConnecivity/Page1.aspx
StudentID DeptID Name Picture Nationality Type Class
10100118 ISE Jonathan Garcia pics/1.jpg Chinese Full Time Sophomor
10336702 ISE Jonathan Gube pics/2.jpg American Part Time Junior

Figure 19.6 The student table displayed on a Web page.

We can modify the appearance of the GridView control by manipulating its properties. This step covers the following How-to topic:

- How-to: modify the appearance of a GridView control using its *AutoFormat* feature.

4. Select the GridView control and click on its smart tag, which is located on the top-right corner of the control (see Figure 19.7). Select the *AutoFormat* option.
5. This should pop up an *AutoFormat* dialog box. Select from the available pre-defined formatting schemes, and click the *OK* button (see Figure 19.8).

We now review the HTML code generated by Visual Studio when we dragged and dropped the student table on the Web page. We review HTML code in the *Source* tab of the Design

Window. Figure 19.9 shows an ASP tag for the data-bind GridView control (lines 13–19). Note that the *DataSourceID* property of the GridView control is set to the *AccessDataSource1* control, which was created due to the drag-and-drop of the student table (line 15). Also, note that the *DataKeyNames* property is set to the primary key of the student table, *StudentID* (line 14).

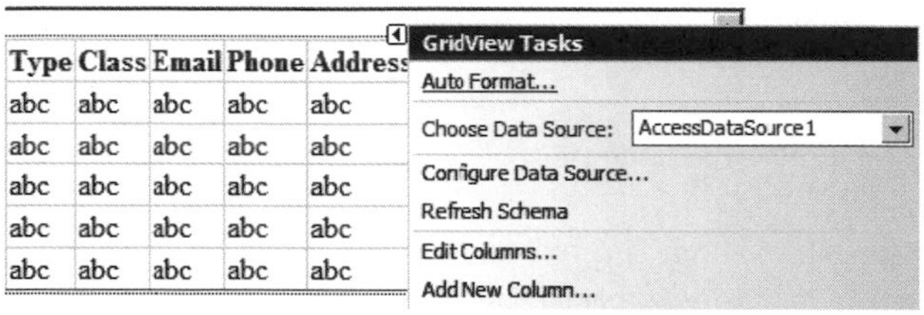

Figure 19.7 Formatting a GridView control using its *AutoFormat* feature.

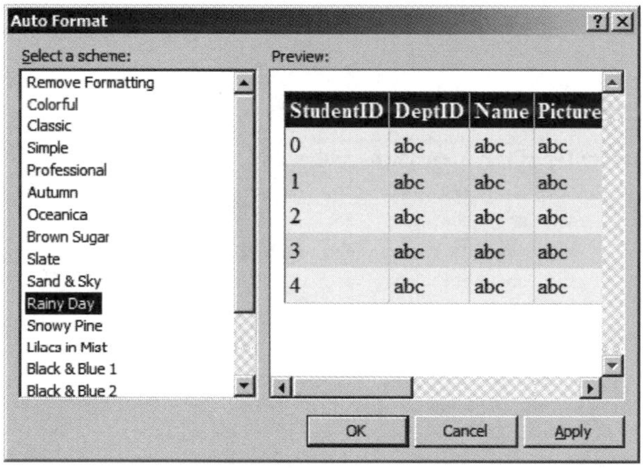

Figure 19.8 Selecting a pre-defined formatting scheme for a GridView control.

```
13    <asp:GridView ID="GridView1" runat="server"
14    AutoGenerateColumns="False" DataKeyNames="StudentID"
15    DataSourceID="AccessDataSource1"
16    EmptyDataText="There are no data records to display."
17    BackColor="White" BorderColor="#999999"
18    BorderStyle="None" BorderWidth="1px" CellPadding="3"
19    GridLines="Vertical">
```

Figure 19.9 ASP tag for data-bind GridView control.

19.4　*Reconfiguring SQL Query in an AccessDataSource*

Often we would like to change the query associated with an existing AccessDataSource. For example, we accepted the default SELECT * query for the AccessDataSource created in the previous section. Recall from Chapter 15 that there are two ways we can reconfigure an SQL query in an AccessDataSource control: (i) use the *Configure Data Source* Wizard at design-time, and (ii) programmatically access it at runtime. In this section, we illustrate the first approach. The discussion of the second approach is deferred to Section 19.12.

We continue with the example from the previous section and illustrate how we can reconfigure an SQL query in an existing AccessDataSource. Specifically, we modify the application to display only the "full-time" and "graduate" students from the database on a Web page. This section covers the following How-to topic:

■ How-to: edit an SQL query associated with an existing AccessDataSource.

1. Open the Web page, *Page1.aspx*, created in the previous section. Select the auto-generated *AccessDataSource1* control below the GridView control.
2. Click on the smart tag of *AccessDataSource1* to view its Tasks list. Select the *Configure Data Source* option from the Tasks list (see Figure 19.10). This should open a *Configure Data Source* Wizard.

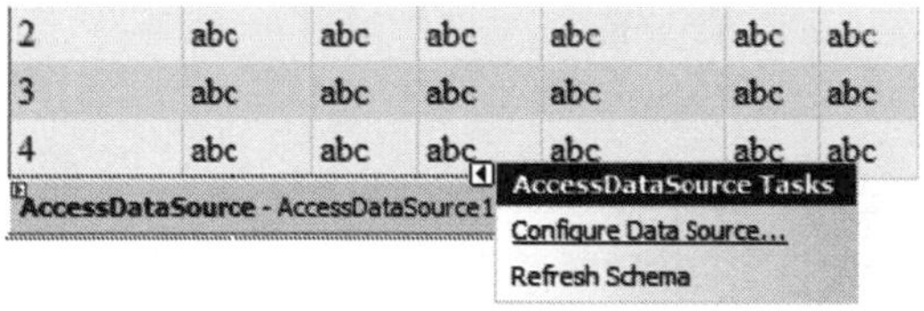

Figure 19.10 Configuring an AccessDataSource using its Tasks list.

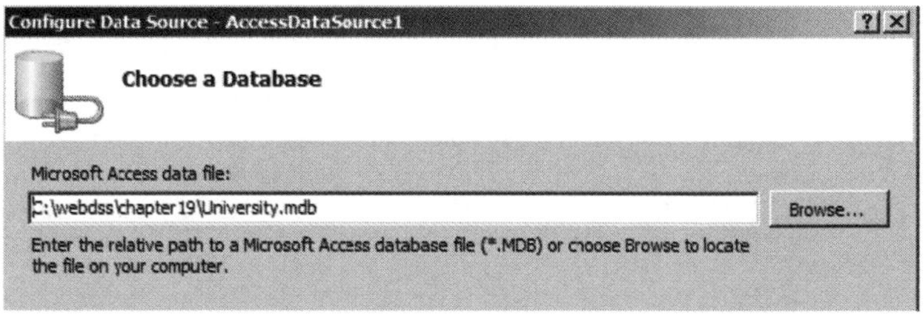

Figure 19.11 *Choose a Database* page of the Wizard: selecting the University database file.

3. On the first page of the *Configure Data Source* Wizard, we select the Access database file to connect. Since we have created the database connection before, the Wizard page displays the path of a connected database (see Figure 19.11). We accept this default path. Click the *Next* button.
4. On the *Configure the Select Statement* page, we select the *tblStudent* table from the *Name* drop-down box. We select the table columns from the *Columns* area as shown in Figure 19.12.
5. On the same Wizard page, click the *WHERE* button to add a WHERE clause to the query statement. This should pop up the *Add* WHERE *Clause* dialog box (see Figure 19.13).
6. In the *Add* WHERE *Clause* dialog box, select the *Class* column from the *Column* drop-down box. Enter the criteria "= Graduate" using the *Operator* and *Value* input areas (see Figure 19.13). Click the *Add* button to add the selection criterion to the query. Similarly add the criterion "Class = Full Time" (see Figure 19.14). Click *OK* to return to the Wizard page.

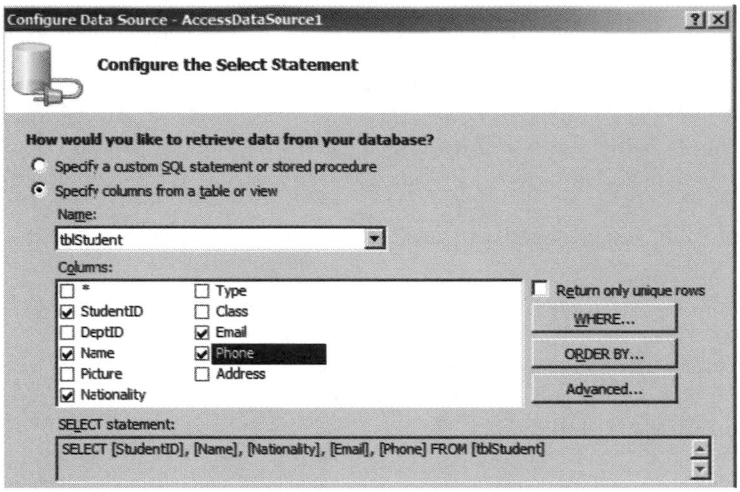

Figure 19.12 Reconfiguring a select query statement.

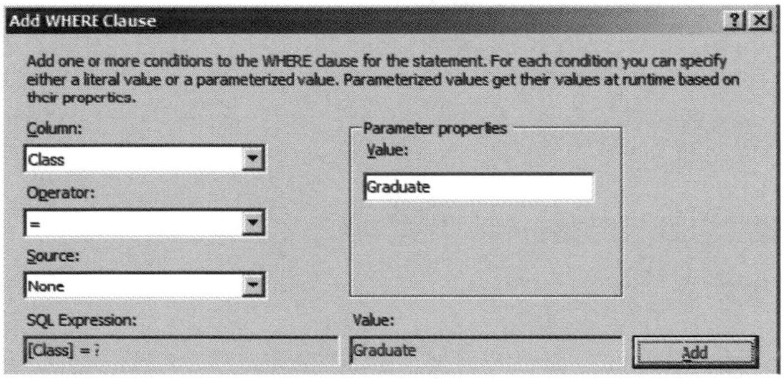

Figure 19.13 Adding a WHERE clause to the query.

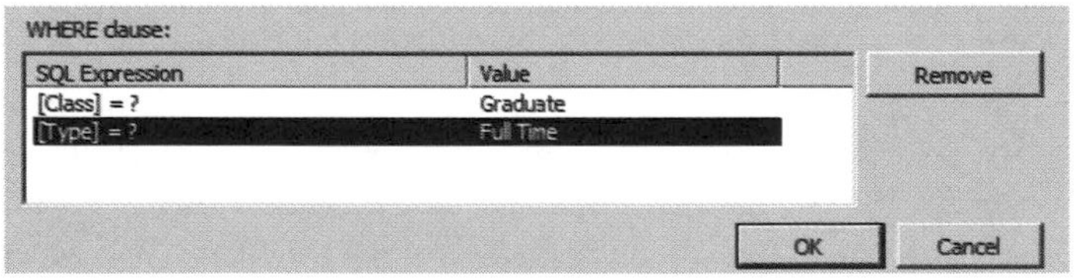

Figure 19.14 Selection criterion for the WHERE clause.

7. Next, on the *Configure the Select Statement* page, click the *ORDER BY* button to add an *ORDER BY* clause to the query. This should open the *Add ORDER BY Clause* dialog box. Select the *Name* column from the *Sort by* drop-down list, and specify *ascending* sorting order (see Figure 19.15). Click *OK* to return to the Wizard page.

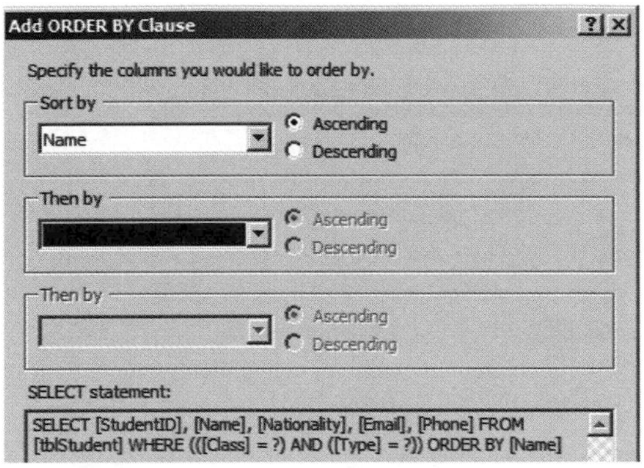

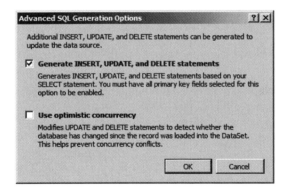

Figure 19.15 Adding an ORDER BY clause to the query.

8. Now click on the *Advanced* button on the *Configure the Select Statement* page. This should pop up the *Advanced SQL Generation Options* dialog box. We use this dialog box to generate INSERT, UPDATE, and DELETE SQL statements of an AccessDataSource control (see Figure 19.16). Select the generate CheckBox control, and click the *OK* button to return to the Wizard page.

Figure 19.16 Generating INSERT, UPDATE, and DELETE SQL queries for a data source.

9. Click the *Next* button on the *Configure the Select Statement* page to open the *Test Query* Wizard page. Use the *Test Query* button to test the query.
10. Click the *Finish* button to close the Wizard. Since we have changed the columns of the GridView control, Visual Studio asks us for a confirmation. Click the *Yes* button to refresh the columns and the key of the GridView control.
11. Test the application to verify the change. Note that the output records are now sorted in ascending order of the *Name* column (see Figure 19.17).

Address	http://localhost:1388/WebDBConnectivity/Page1.aspx

StudentID	Name	Nationality	Email	Phone
22025882	Aaron Duong	Indian	Davis.Burke@eserver.com	(352) 935-5823
48323414	Alex Carlos	American	Alex.Mapson@eserver.com	(352) 406-5118
81675687	Andre Carlos	German	Andre.Lueck@eserver.com	(352) 320-6380
64294504	Anthony Robinson	Indian	Bradley.Farruggio@eserver.com	(352) 596-7101
71525998	Bonifacio Alexander	American	Bonifacio.Goodman@eserver.com	(352) 734-5017
70991150	Bonifacio Boivin	Chinese	Bonifacio.Augustyn@eserver.com	(352) 195-6580

Figure 19.17 Student page with reconfigured SQL query.

We now review the HTML code for the *AccessDataSource1* control after reconfiguration. Switch to the *Source* tab and locate the AccessDataSource ASP tag (see Figure 19.18).

```
34 <asp:AccessDataSource ID="AccessDataSource1" runat="server"
35 DataFile="C:\webdss\chapter19\University.mdb"
36 DeleteCommand="DELETE FROM [tblStudent] WHERE [StudentID] = ?"
37 InsertCommand="INSERT INTO [tblStudent] ([StudentID], [Name],
38 [Nationality], [Email], [Phone]) VALUES (?, ?, ?, ?, ?)"
39 SelectCommand="SELECT [StudentID], [Name], [Nationality],
40 [Email], [Phone] FROM [tblStudent] WHERE (([Class] = ?)
41 AND ([Type] = ?)) ORDER BY [Name]"
42 UpdateCommand="UPDATE [tblStudent] SET [Name] = ?,
43 [Nationality] = ?, [Email] = ?, [Phone] = ? WHERE [StudentID] = ?">
```

Figure 19.18 The AccessDataSource ASP tag showing changes due to query reconfiguration.

The ASP tag for the AccessDataSource has been modified to reflect the new SQL query that we have just reconfigured using the *Configure Data Source Wizard*. Furthermore, the HTML code also reflects the Insert, Update, and Delete queries generated for the AccessDataSource.

19.5 *Paging, Sorting, and Data Manipulation in a GridView Control*

If a data source has a few tens or hundreds of records to display, it may clutter a Web page. The GridView control provides a well-structured and well-formatted solution to the problem. The control allows us to display a large number of records on multiple pages. These pages are part of the GridView control and are displayed on the same Web page that the GridView control belongs to. Thus, users can view a fixed number of records at a time and should navigate through multiple GridView control pages to view all the records. This feature of the GridView control is known as *paging*. Paging thus leads to a very compact and easy-to-navigate interface. Also, when the data-bind GridView control's data source supports a sorting operation, the GridView controls can be easily extended to provide this functionality on the Web interface. In this section, we will see how to enable *paging* and *sorting* features for a GridView control. We will also see how to *select*, *edit* and *delete* a row in a GridView control. This section covers the following How-to topics:

■ How-to: enable paging and sorting for a GridView control.
■ How-to: manipulate (select, edit, and delete) the data displayed in a GridView control.

We will continue with the Web page (*Page1.aspx*) we have reconfigured in the previous sections.

1. Click on the smart tag of the GridView control to view its Tasks list.
2. Check the *Enable Paging, Enable Sorting, Enable Editing, Enable Deleting,* and *Enable Selection* options from the Tasks list as shown in Figure 19.19.

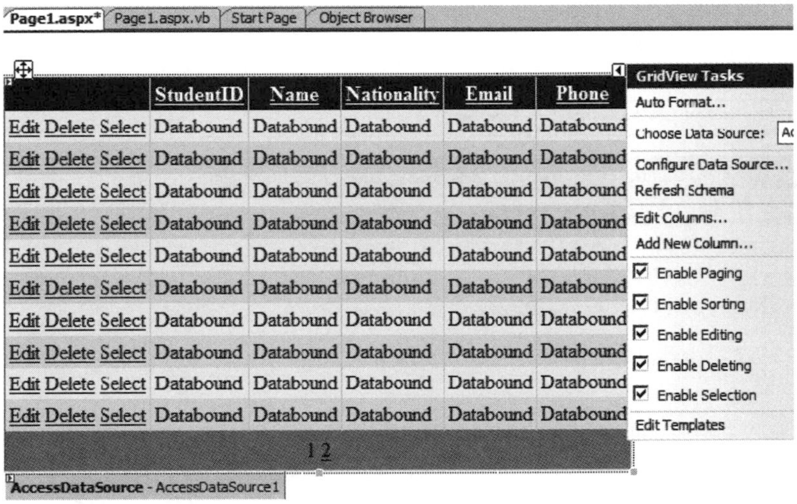

Figure 19.19 Using GridView control's Tasks list to enable Paging, Sorting, Editing, Deleting, and Selection operations.

Note that we can see the *Enable Editing* and *Enable Deletion* links because we have added the Insert, Update, and Delete queries to the data source. If we are not able to add these queries to the data source (because the select query is based on multiple tables or we have not included the primary key in the select query), we must add Insert, Update, and Delete queries to the data source programmatically at runtime. We discuss this option in Section 19.12.

3. Run and test the application.

The links in the column headings allow us to sort the records. For example, click on the *Nationality* column to sort records by students' nationality. Click the *Nationality* column heading one more time to reverse the sorting order.

The first column of the grid lets us select, edit, and delete records. When we click on the *Select* link, the selected record gets highlighted. The *SelectedIndex* property of the GridView control is set to the selected record (see Figure 19.20). When we click on the *Edit* link, the GridView control automatically displays the TextBox controls for each column in the row to edit. It also shows the *Update* and *Cancel* links to respectively accept or reject changes made in the TextBox controls (see Figure 19.21). Note, that the *StudentID* column remains as a read-only column when we click the *Edit* link. This is because the *StudentID* column is set as the data key column of the GridView control (see Figure 19.9) and therefore cannot be updated.

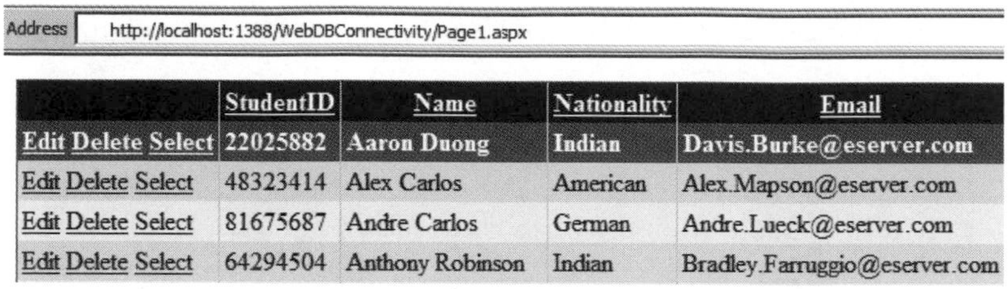

Address http://localhost:1388/WebDBConnectivity/Page1.aspx

	StudentID	Name	Nationality	Email
Edit Delete Select	22025882	Aaron Duong	Indian	Davis.Burke@eserver.com
Edit Delete Select	48323414	Alex Carlos	American	Alex.Mapson@eserver.com
Edit Delete Select	81675687	Andre Carlos	German	Andre.Lueck@eserver.com
Edit Delete Select	64294504	Anthony Robinson	Indian	Bradley.Farruggio@eserver.com

Figure 19.20 Selecting a student record on a Web page.

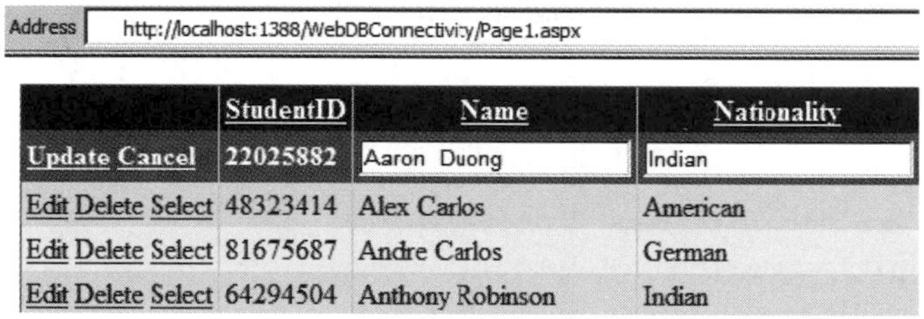

Address http://localhost:1388/WebDBConnectivity/Page1.aspx

	StudentID	Name	Nationality
Update Cancel	22025882	Aaron Duong	Indian
Edit Delete Select	48323414	Alex Carlos	American
Edit Delete Select	81675687	Andre Carlos	German
Edit Delete Select	64294504	Anthony Robinson	Indian

Figure 19.21 Updating a student record on a Web page.

Since we have enabled paging for the GridView, we will see ten rows per page. If we want to see records on other pages, we navigate to a page using page links in the footer section of the control (see Figure 19.22).

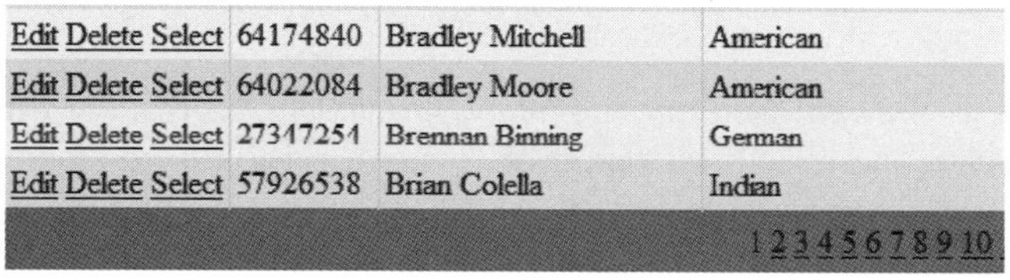

Edit Delete Select	64174840	Bradley Mitchell	American
Edit Delete Select	64022084	Bradley Moore	American
Edit Delete Select	27347254	Brennan Binning	German
Edit Delete Select	57926538	Brian Colella	Indian
			1 2 3 4 5 6 7 8 9 10

Figure 19.22 The Paging functionality of GridView control on a Web page.

19.6 *Hands-On Tutorial: Displaying Data on a Web Page from a Query with a Join of Multiple Tables*

In this section, we show how to add an AccessDataSource to a Web page without dragging a table from the Server Explorer Window. We also show how to add a multi-table query to the AccessDataSource to display the query result on a Web page. Specifically, we display the faculty and faculty-department information on a Web page. The application requires a join of the department and faculty tables. This section covers the following How-to topics:

- How-to: add and configure an SQL query with a join of multiple tables to an AccessDataSource.
- How-to: add a data-bind GridView control to a Web page.
- How-to: bind a GridView control to an existing AccessDataSource.

1. Add a new Web page (*Page2.aspx*) to the *WebDBConnectivity* project.
2. Open the Toolbox window by choosing the View | Toolbox option from the main menu.
3. Drag and drop the AccessDataSource control under the *Data* category in the Toolbox onto *Page2.aspx* (see Figure 19.23).
4. Click on the smart tag of the AccessDataSource control to view its Tasks list. Select the *Configure Data Source* option to open the *Configure Data Source* Wizard.
5. Browse and select the *University.mdb* database file, and click on the *Next* button (see Figure 19.24).

Figure 19.23 Adding an AccessDataSource from the Toolbox onto a Web page.

Figure 19.24 Selecting the existing database for an AccessDataSource.

6. On the *Configure the Select Statement* page, choose the *Specify a custom SQL statement or stored procedure* option, and click the *Next* button.

We can either enter an SQL statement or use Access's query Design View-like query builder to design the query. We will design a query to display the details of faculty members who joined the university after 1995 and have a salary of more than $50,000.

7. Click the *Query Builder* button on the *Define Custom Statements or Stored Procedures* page. The *Add Table* dialog box should pop up. Select the *tblFaculty* and *tblDepartment* tables from this dialog box, and click the *Add* button to add these tables to the *Query Builder* dialog box (see Figure 19.25). Refer to Chapters 14 and 15 for details of the *Query Builder* dialog box.

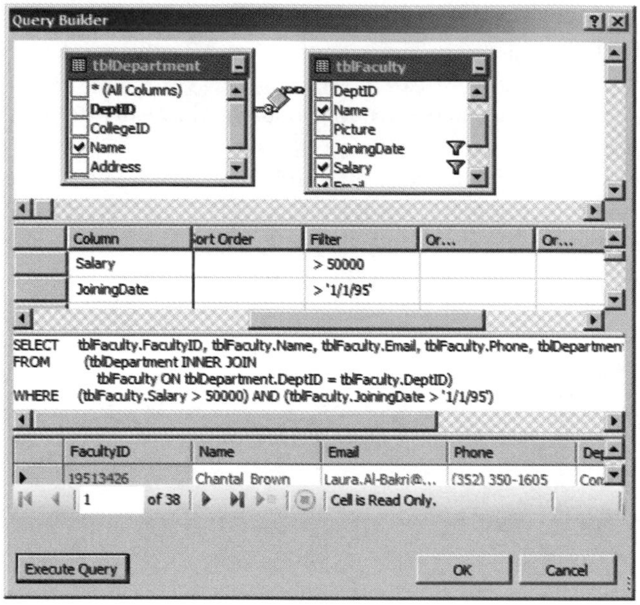

Figure 19.25 Designing a multi-table faculty query in the *Query Builder* dialog box.

8. In the *Query Builder* dialog box, select the columns as shown in Figure 19.25. In the *Filter* column of the grid, enter the comparison values for the *Salary* and *JoiningDate* fields. Click the *Execute Query* button at the bottom of the dialog box to test the query. Click the *OK* button to return to the Wizard page.

9. Click the *Finish* button to close the *Configure Data Source* Wizard.

We now add a GridView control to the Web page. We bind the GridView control to the AccessDataSource created in Steps 1–9. This should display the query result on the Web page.

10. Open the Toolbox and drag and drop the GridView control onto *Page2.aspx*. The GridView control is listed under the *Data* tab of the Toolbox.

11. Click on the smart tag of the GridView control to view the Tasks list. Use the *Choose Data Source* drop-down list to select the *AccessDataSource1* data source created in Steps 1–9 (see Figure 19.26).

12. Select the *AutoFormat* option, and choose the *RainyDay* template for the GridView control.

13. Select the *Enable Paging, Enable Sorting*, and *Enable Selection* options for the GridView control as shown in Figure 19.26.

14. We must set the new page as the starting page of the application. Right-click on the *Page2.aspx* in the Solution Explorer Window, and select the *Set As Start Page* option from the shortcut menu.

15. Run and test the application (see Figure 19.27).

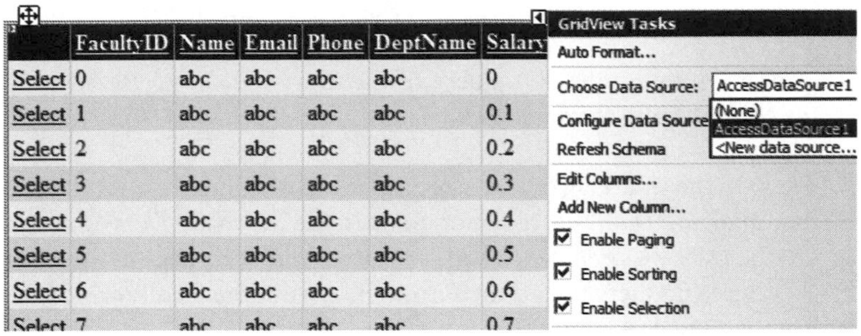

Figure 19.26 Binding a GridView control to an AccessDataSource.

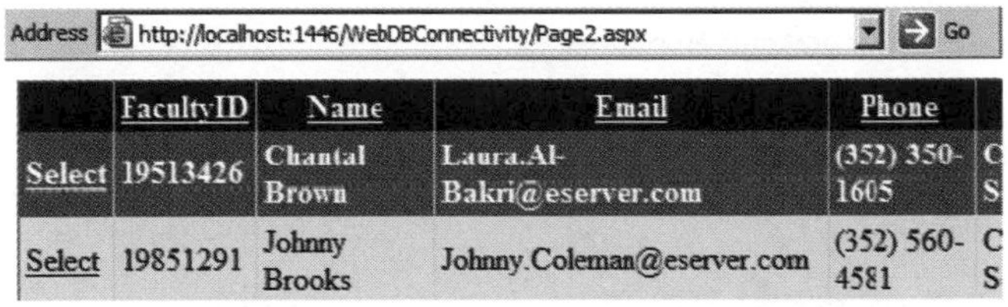

Figure 19.27 List of faculty members on a Web page.

We now review the associated HTML code shown in Figure 19.28. In this section, we have configured an AccessDataSource and added a multi-table select query to it. When we look at the HTML code for the page, we see that an ASP tag is added for the AccessDataSource control. The *DataFile* property is assigned the relative path of the database, and the query that we have designed using the *Query Builder* dialog box is assigned to the *SelectCommand* property of the AccessDataSource tag.

```
31 <asp:AccessDataSource ID="AccessDataSource1" runat="server"
32   DataFile="~/University.mdb" SelectCommand="SELECT tblFaculty.
     FacultyID,tblFaculty.Name,  tblFaculty.Email, tblFaculty.Phone,
     tblDepartment.Name AS DeptName, tblFaculty.Salary FROM
     (tblDepartment INNER JOIN tblFaculty ON tblDepartment.DeptID =
     tblFaculty.DeptID) WHERE (tblFaculty.Salary > 50000) AND
     (tblFaculty.JoiningDate > '1/1/95')">
33 </asp:AccessDataSource>
```

Figure 19.28 AccessDataSource ASP tag for the faculty application.

19.7   *Hands-On Tutorial: Displaying Data-Bind Images in a GridView Control*

In this hands-on tutorial, we continue with the faculty application from the previous section. We show how we can edit the columns of the data source and GridView controls to add data-bind images on the Web page. Specifically, we add a faculty image column to the GridView control. Thus, we should see a faculty thumbnail in front of each faculty member on the Web page. This hands-on tutorial covers the following How-to topic:

■ How-to: display data-bind images in a GridView control.

We first reconfigure the SQL query of the *AccessDataSource1* control to add a faculty image column from the database.

1. Click on the smart tag of the *AccessDataSource1* control to view its Tasks list. Choose the *Configure Data Source* option to open the *Configure Data Source* Wizard.
2. On the *Define Custom Statements or Stored Procedures* page of the Wizard, modify the existing SQL query to add the *Picture* field from the faculty table (see Figure 19.29).
3. Run and test the application.

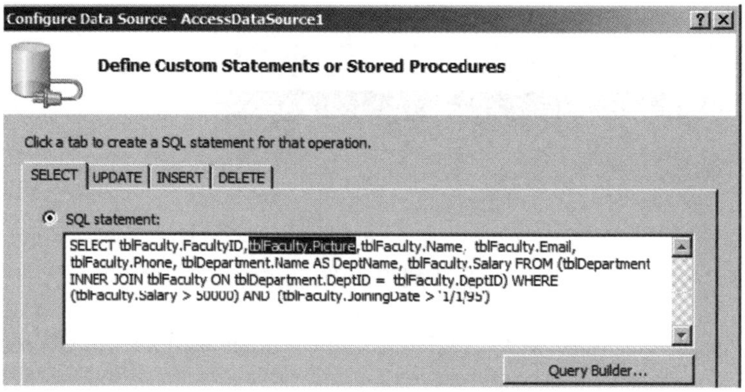

Figure 19.29 Adding the Picture field from the faculty table to the SQL query.

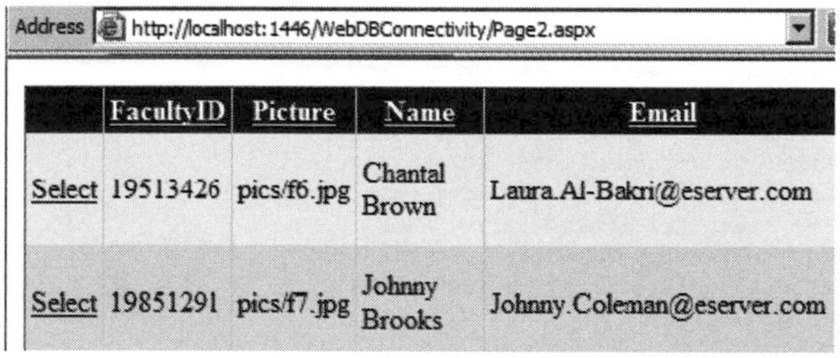

Figure 19.30 Faculty information with the new *Picture* column.

We should see the *Picture* column showing the path of the image file rather than the image itself (see Figure 19.30). This is because the table column actually has image paths stored, and actual images are stored externally to the database. We must modify the *Picture* column to show the faculty images from the path currently specified by the *Picture* column. We achieve this by adding a data-bind *ImageField* to the GridView control.

4. Open the GridView control's Tasks list, and select the *Edit Columns* option (see Figure 19.31). This should pop up the *Fields* dialog box.
5. We first delete the existing *Picture* column from the GridView control, which is set to display the text data. Select the *Picture* column from the list under the *Selected fields* area, and click the *Delete* button to remove the column (see Figure 19.32). Note that

removing the *Picture* field from the GridView control does not remove it from the AccessDataSource.

6. Now, from the list under the *Available fields* area, select the *ImageField* entry and click on the *Add* button (see Figure 19.33). The field should get added to the list under the *Selected fields* area.

7. Select the newly added *ImageField*, and view its properties in the *ImageField Properties* pane. Set the *HeaderText* property to the text "Picture" and the *DataImageUrlField* property to the data source column, *Picture* (select the available data source column from the drop-down list shown in Figure 19.34.) Click the *OK* button to return to the Design Window.

8. Run and test the application (see Figure 19.35).

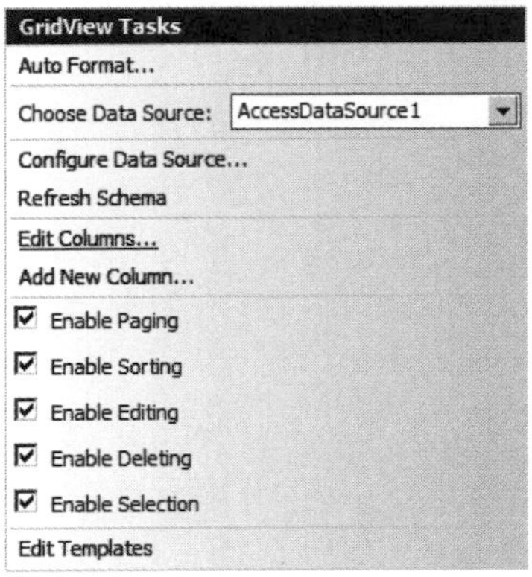

Figure 19.31 Accessing the *Edit Columns* option of a GridView control.

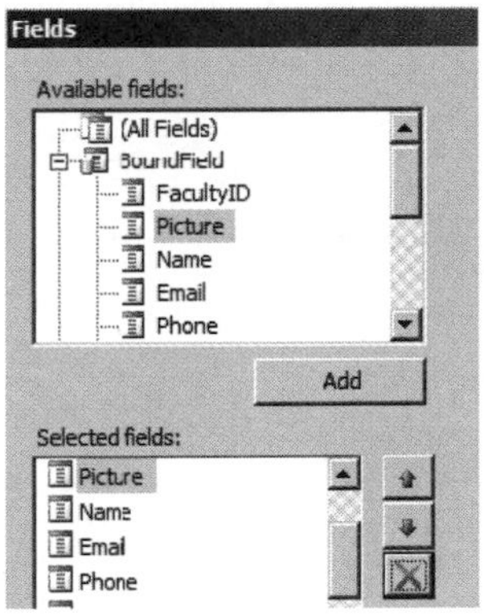

Figure 19.32 Removing the *Picture* field from the GridView.

Figure 19.33 Adding an *ImageField* to the GridView control.

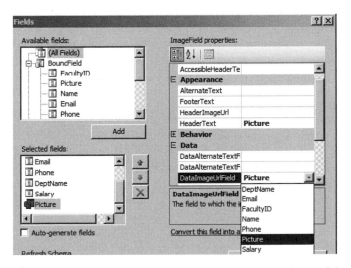

Figure 19.34 Binding the *ImageField* to the *Picture* column of the AccessDataSource.

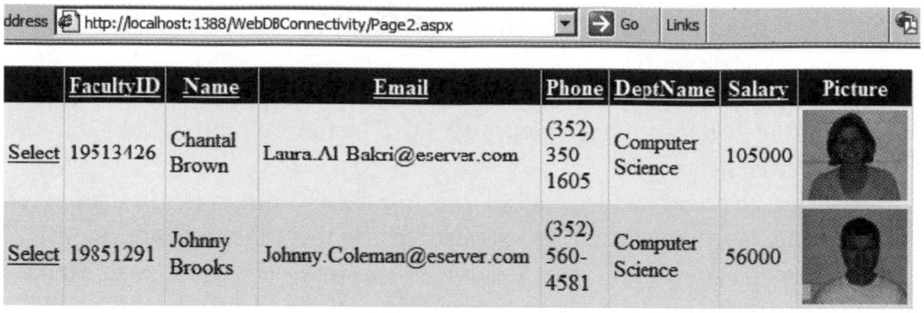

	FacultyID	Name	Email	Phone	DeptName	Salary	Picture
Select	19513426	Chantal Brown	Laura.Al Bakri@eserver.com	(352) 350 1605	Computer Science	105000	
Select	19851291	Johnny Brooks	Johnny.Coleman@eserver.com	(352) 560-4581	Computer Science	56000	

Figure 19.35 Running application with an *ImageField.*

We now review the HTML code behind the page in the *Source* tab (see Figure 19.36). The HTML code for the GridView control is now modified to include the *ImageField* (line 24). The *DataImageUrlField* property is assigned to the *Picture* column, and the *HeaderText* property is set to the "Picture" string.

```
23                <asp:BoundField DataField="Salary" HeaderText=
   "Salary" SortExpression="Salary" />
24                <asp:ImageField DataImageUrlField="Picture"
   HeaderText="Picture">
25                </asp:ImageField>
```

Figure 19.36 The *ImageField* ASP tag.

19.8 *Hands-On Tutorial: Adding Lookup and Filter Functionalities to a Web Page*

In this section, we create a simple Web application to illustrate lookup and filter functionalities in ASP .NET. We use a ComboBox control and a parameterized query to provide these functionalities. We design a Web page that allows a user to select a university department from the drop-down list of departments. As the user selects a department, we show a list of students from the selected department in a GridView control. This hands-on tutorial covers the following How-to topics:

- How-to: use parameterized queries in a Web application.
- How-to: provide the lookup and filter functionalities on a Web page.
- How-to: bind a DropDownList control to an AccessDataSource.

1. Add another page (*Page3.aspx*) to the *WebDBConnectivity* project.
2. Add an AccessDataSource from the Toolbox Window onto the Web page.
3. Click the smart tag of the AccessDataSource, and choose the *Configure Data Source* option to open the *Configure Data Source* Wizard.
4. Select the *University.mdb* database file, and click the *Next* button.
5. On the *Configure the Select Statement* page, select *tblDepartment* from the *Name* drop-down list, and select the *DeptID* and *Name* columns as shown in Figure 19.37.

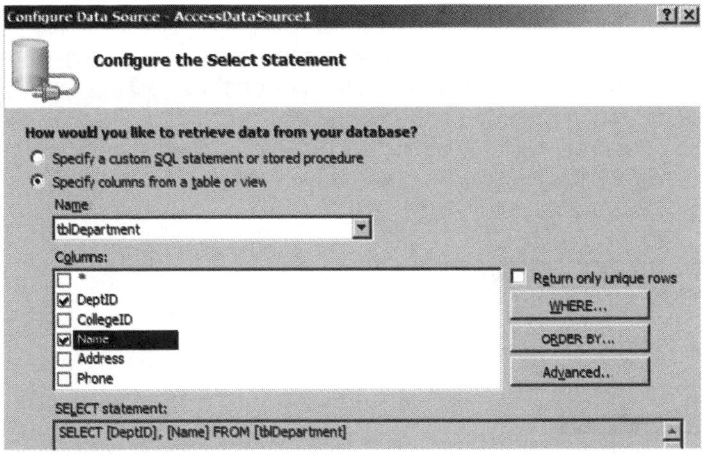

Figure 19.37 Configuring an AccessDataSource to query the *tblDepartment* table.

6. Drag and drop the DropDownList control from the Toolbox onto the *Page 3.aspx* page.
7. Click the smart tag of the DropDownList control to open its Tasks list (see Figure 19.38). Select the *Choose Data Source* option. This should open the *Data Source Configuration* Wizard with the *Choose Data Source* page on top.
8. Select the *AccessDataSource1* control from the *Select a data source* drop-down list. Select the *Name* field for the field to display and *DeptID* field for the value field (see Figure 19.39). Click on the *OK* button to return to the Design Window.
9. From the DropDownList control's Tasks list, check the *Enable AutoPostBack* option to set the *AutoPostBack* property of the control.

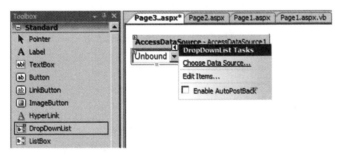

Figure 19.38 Adding a DropDownList control to a Web page and selecting its data source.

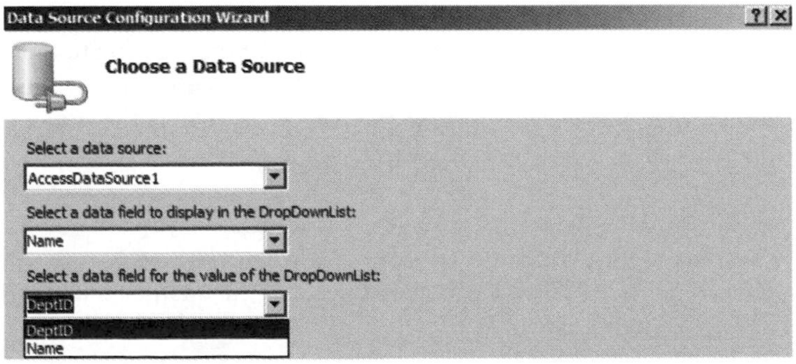

Figure 19.39 Specifying data source and the display and value fields of a DropDownList control.

10. Drag and drop a Label control from the Toolbox on the Web page just above the DropDownList control, and set its Text property to "Select a Department:."

11. In the Solution Explorer Window, right-click on the *Page3.aspx*, and select the *Set as Start Page* option from the short-cut menu.

12. Run and test the application developed so far. The DropDownList control should display the list of departments from the University database (see Figure 19.40).

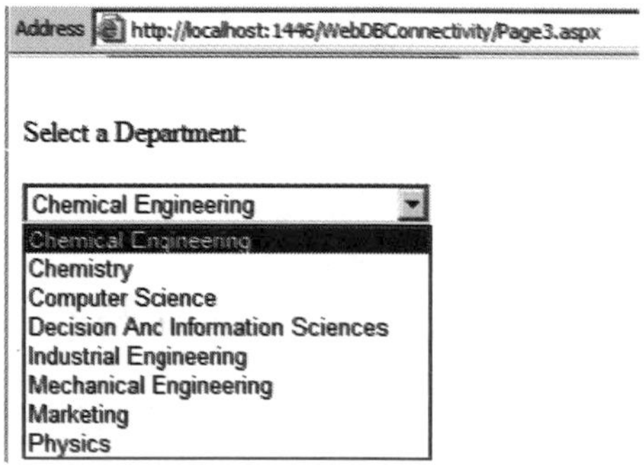

Address http://localhost:1446/WebDBConnectivity/Page3.aspx

Select a Department:

Chemical Engineering ▼
Chemical Engineering
Chemistry
Computer Science
Decision Anc Information Sciences
Industrial Engineering
Mechanical Engineering
Marketing
Physics

Figure 19.40 Testing the department DropDownList.

We now review the HTML code that was automatically added for the Page3.aspx (see Figure 19.41).

```
12         <asp:AccessDataSource ID="AccessDataSource1" runat=
    "server" DataFile="~/University.mdb"
13             SelectCommand="SELECT [DeptID], [Name] FROM
    [tblDepartment]"></asp:AccessDataSource>
14         <br />
15         <asp:Label ID="Label1" runat="server" Text="Select a
    Department:"></asp:Label><br />
16          </div>
17         <asp:DropDownList ID="DropDownList1" runat="server"
    DataSourceID="AccessDataSource1"
18             DataTextField="Name" DataValueField="DeptID"
    AutoPostBack="True">
```

Figure 19.41 The DropDownList and AccessDataSource tags for the department listing.

The AccessDataSource ASP tag appears in line 12 with its *SelectCommand* property set to the query we designed in the *Configure Data Source* Wizard. The DropDownList ASP tag appears in line 17. The *AutoPostBack* property of the tag is set to *True*, the *DataSourceID* property of the tag is set to *AccessDataSource1*, the *DataTextField* property of the tag is set to the *Name* column, and the *DataValueField* property of the tag is set to the *DeptID* column.

We now add another AccessDataSource to the Web page to fetch the student details for the selected department in the DropDownList control.

13. Drag and drop the AccessDataSource control onto the page. Use AccessDataSource control's Tasks list to open the *Configure Data Source* Wizard.

14. On the *Configure the Select Statement* page, select the *tblStudent* table and its columns as shown in Figure 19.42.

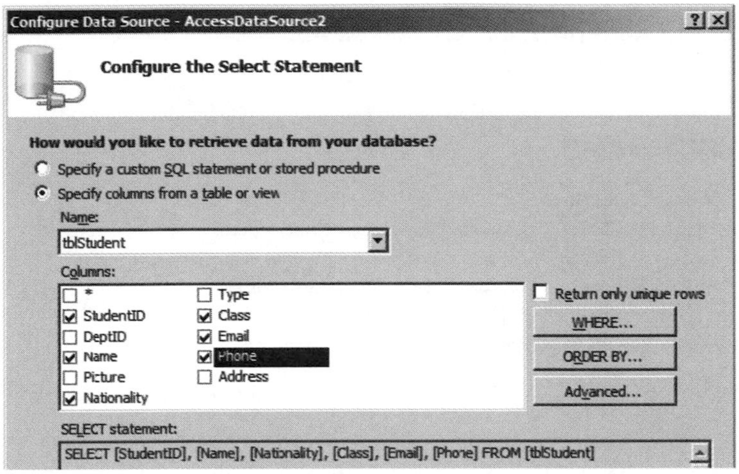

Figure 19.42 Selecting fields for the student query.

> **15.** Click the *WHERE* button to add the WHERE clause to the query design. Set the *Add WHERE Clause* dialog box as shown in Figure 19.43. Click the *Add* button to add the selection criteria.

Since we would like to filter records based on the *DeptID* field of the student table, we add a WHERE clause on the *DeptID* field. Also, we know that the value of the *DeptID* parameter must be the same value the user has selected in the department drop-down list. Therefore, we set the parameter value source to the *DropDownList1* control (see Figure 19.43).

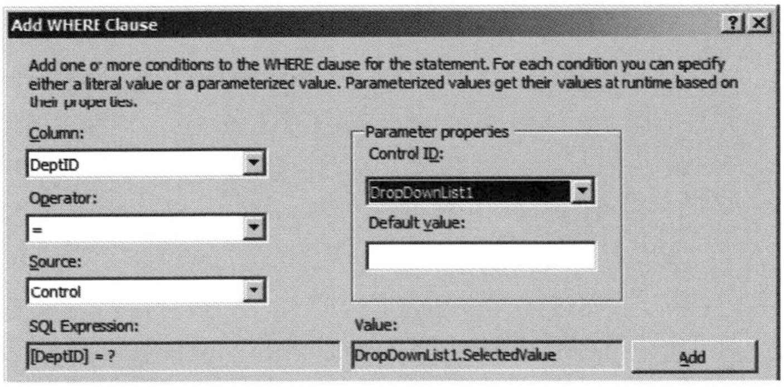

Figure 19.43 Adding a WHERE clause; specifying a parameter and its value source.

> **16.** Test the query and click *Finish* to close the *Configure Data Source* Wizard.
> **17.** Now, drag and drop a GridView control onto the Web page (*Page3.aspx*). Use the GridView control's Tasks list to set its data source to the *AccessDataSource2* control created in Step 13. Also, choose the *Enable Paging* option from the GridView control's Tasks list.
> **18.** Run and test the application (see Figure 19.44).

Select a Department:

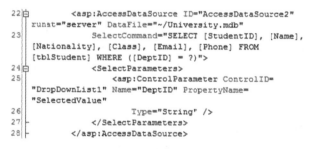

StudentID	Name	Nationality	Class	Email
12041406	Richard Leavelle	Chinese	Graduate	Richard.Juanez@eserver.com
13890452	Mac Ochoa	German	Sophomor	Mohan.Evans@eserver.com
15358090	Shelley Bullock	French	Graduate	Shelley.Michael@eserver.com
16864467	Cheryl Moss	Chinese	Sophomor	Cheryl.Deacon@eserver.com
18497630	Laura Luitze	Chinese	Junior	Laura.Bracher@eserver.com

Figure 19.44 Application output: department lookup and filtered student records.

We now review the HTML code behind the page in the *Source* tab (see Figure 19.45). The ASP tag for the *AccessDataSource2* is similar to the ones we have seen in the previous sections except for the nested *SelectPrameters* tag (lines 24–27). Since the query is a parameterized query, the *SelectPrameters* tag is used to specify the parameter source, the *DropDownList1* control.

```
22      <asp:AccessDataSource ID="AccessDataSource2"
   runat="server" DataFile="~/University.mdb"
23          SelectCommand="SELECT [StudentID], [Name],
   [Nationality], [Class], [Email], [Phone] FROM
   [tblStudent] WHERE ([DeptID] = ?)">
24      <SelectParameters>
25          <asp:ControlParameter ControlID=
   "DropDownList1" Name="DeptID" PropertyName=
   "SelectedValue"
26              Type="String" />
27      </SelectParameters>
28      </asp:AccessDataSource>
```

Figure 19.45 AccessDataSource ASP tag for the student query.

19.9　*Hands-On Tutorial: Displaying Related Data in a DetailsView Control*

In this hands-on tutorial, we extend the application developed in the previous section. We have listed the students' information in a GridView control based on the department selection in the DropDownList control. GridView controls are useful when we have to "list" the brief information (i.e., fewer numbers of columns) in a compact representation. If we would like to display detailed information, a DetailsView control is an ideal choice. For example, we can use a DetailsView control to display detailed student information including the student's picture and courses taken per semester. The DetailsView control is also useful to display related information on a Web page. For example, we can let users select a student record from the GridView control and display the detailed information for the selected student in a DetailsView control.

In this hands-on tutorial, we add a DetailsView control to the *Page3.aspx* page, and as the user selects the student from the GridView control, we display the student's detailed information in a DetailsView control. We also illustrate how to show a student's picture in a DetailsView control. This hands-on tutorial covers the following How-to topics:

- How-to: use the DetailsView control to show detailed information about a record.
- How-to: use the DetailsView control to display related data on a Web page.
- How-to: add an ImageField to a DetailsView control.

1. Open the *Page3.aspx* file of the *WebDBConnectivity* project.
2. Click on the smart tag of the GridView control to open its Tasks list. Check the *Enable Selection* option from the list. This should add a *Select* link to the GridView control. When the user clicks this *Select* link, we display detailed information about the selected student.
3. Add another AccessDataSource control, *AccessDataSource3*, to the Web page. We will fetch the student's details using this data source.
4. As before, use AccessDataSource control's Tasks list to invoke the *Configure Data Source* Wizard.
5. Choose the University database on the first page of the Wizard. On the second page, *Configure the Select Statement*, select the *tblStudent* table and its columns as shown in Figure 19.46.

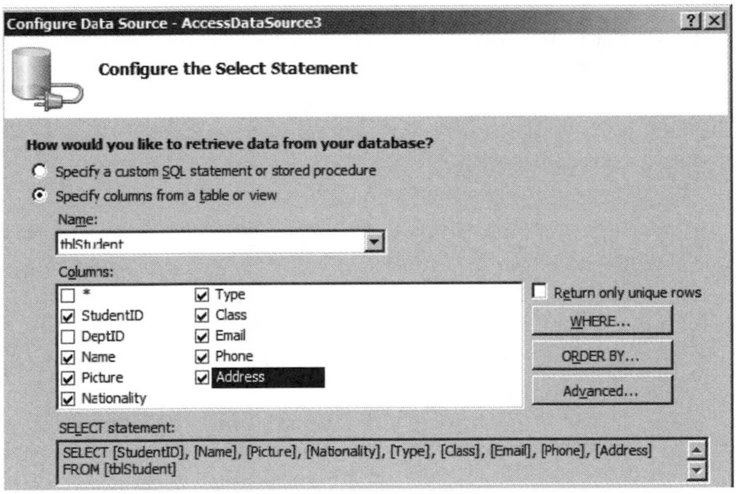

Figure 19.46 Configuring a select query for the DetailsView control's data source.

Since we are going to fetch a student's records based on the student row selected in the GridView control, we create a parameter query for the DetailsView control's data source. We assign the *StudentID* field as a parameter in the WHERE clause and link its value source to the GridView control.

6. Click on the *WHERE* button to add the WHERE clause to the select query. Use Figure 19.47 to set the *Add WHERE Clause* dialog box. Click the *Add* button to add the clause. Click the *OK* button to return to the *Configure Data Source* Wizard.
7. On the same page of the Wizard, click the *Advanced* button, and select the *Generate INSERT, UPDATE, and DELETE statements* option to automatically generate these commands for the student table. We select this option to add Update, Insert, and Delete record functionalities to the DetailsView control.

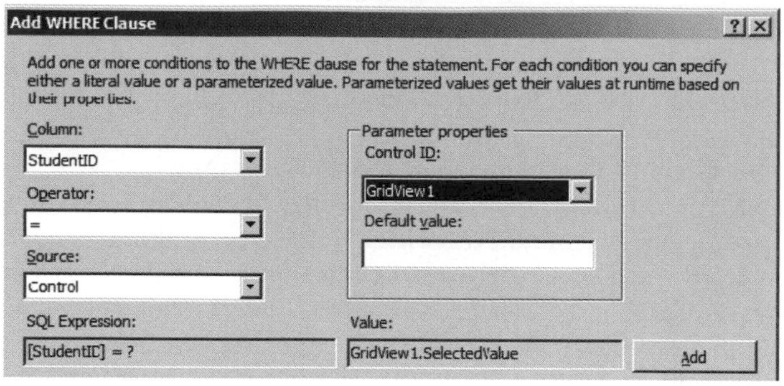

Figure 19.47 Specifying the WHERE clause and linking its value source to the GridView control.

8. Drag and drop the DetailsView control from the Toolbox onto the Web page. The DetailsView control is listed under the *Data* tab of the Toolbox Window (see Figure 19.48).

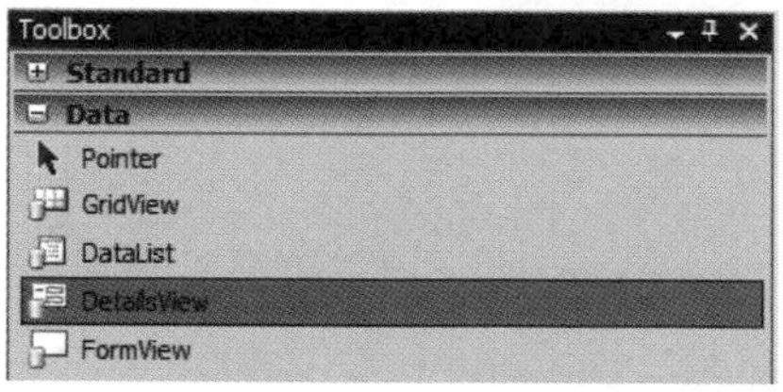

Figure 19.48 Adding a DetailsView control onto the Web page.

9. Click on the smart tag of the DetailsView control to view its Tasks list. In the *Choose Data Source* drop-down list, select the *AccessDataSource3* control to assign the Details View control's data source.

10. Just like in a GridView control, check the *Enable Inserting*, *Enable Editing*, and *Enable Deleting* options (see Figure 19.49) to enable inserts, updates, and deletions from the DetailsView control. Also, use the *AutoFormat* option to set the formatting of the De-tailsView control (like we did for the GridView control).

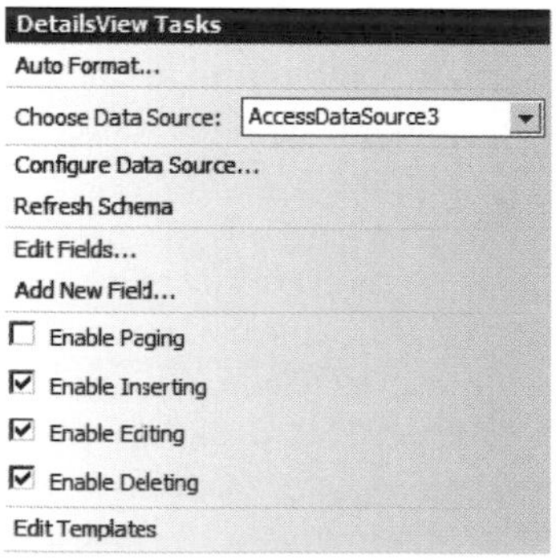

Figure 19.49 Binding the DetailsView control to *AccessDataSource3* and enabling its Insert, Up-date, and Delete functions.

11. Run and test the application (see Figure 19.50).

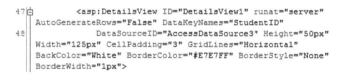

Figure 19.50 Running application with the DetailsView control for a student record.

Since we have enabled selection for the GridView control, beside every row we observe a *Select* link. When we click on this link for any row, the particular details for the selected student are shown in the DetailsView control. Since we have enabled editing, inserting, and deletions for the DetailsView control, we see *Edit*, *New*, and *Delete* links at the bottom of the DetailsView control (see Figure 19.50).

We now review the associated HTML code shown in Figure 19.51. The DetailsView ASP tag is shown in line 47. Note that the *DataSourceID* property is set to the *AccessDataSource3*, and the *DataKeyNames* property is set to the *StudentID* field. It is not hard to see that a DetailsView control is not much different from a GridView control; the former displays one record at a time and the latter displays multiple records at once.

```
47       <asp:DetailsView ID="DetailsView1" runat="server"
    AutoGenerateRows="False" DataKeyNames="StudentID"
48          DataSourceID="AccessDataSource3" Height="50px"
    Width="125px" CellPadding="3" GridLines="Horizontal"
    BackColor="White" BorderColor="#E7E7FF" BorderStyle="None"
    BorderWidth="1px">
```

Figure 19.51 The DetailsView ASP tag.

We also notice that the student's picture is not displayed in the DetailsView control. We saw how to resolve this before when we added an *ImageField* to the GridView control. We can resolve the problem here in a similar fashion. We edit the fields of the DetailsView control and add a custom picture field to it.

12. Click the *Edit Fields* option from the Tasks list of the DetailsView control (see Figure 19.49). This should open the *Fields* dialog box. The Fields dialog box for DetailsView works very much like the Fields dialog box for the GridView control we discussed in Section 19.7.

13. First remove the existing *Picture* field from the list under the *Selected fields* area. Then add an *ImageField* from the *Available fields'* list to *Selected fields'* list.

14. Select the newly added *ImageField*, and view its properties in the *ImageField's properties* pane. Set the *HeaderText* property to the string "*Picture*," and set the *DataImageUrl-Field* property to the data source field, *Picture* (select the column from the drop-down list as shown in Figure 19.52). Click the *OK* button to return to the Design Window.

15. Run and test the application (see Figure 19.53).

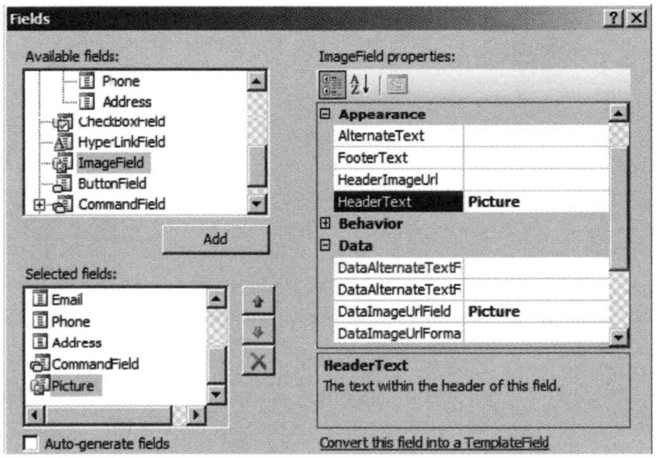

Figure 19.52 Adding a template *ImageField* and binding it to the student *Picture* field.

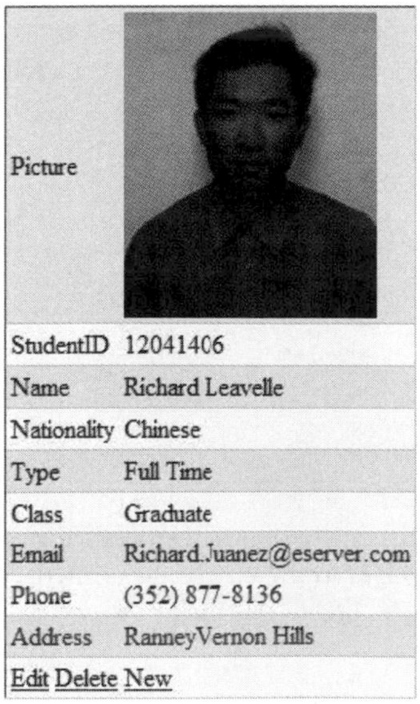

Figure 19.53 DetailsView displaying a student's picture.

We now review the associated HTML code shown in Figure 19.54. The HTML code for the DetailsView is now modified to include the *ImageField* tag inside the *Fields* tag. The *DataImageUrl-Field* property is set to the *Picture* field, and the *HeaderText* property is set to the "*Picture*" string.

```
47    <asp:DetailsView ID="DetailsView1" runat="server"
      AutoGenerateRows="False" DataKeyNames="StudentID"
48          DataSourceID="AccessDataSource3" Height="50px" Width=
      "125px" CellPadding="3" GridLines="Horizontal" BackColor="White"
      BorderColor="#E7E7FF" BorderStyle="None" BorderWidth="1px">
49        <Fields>
50            <asp:ImageField DataImageUrlField="Picture"
      HeaderText="Picture">
51            </asp:ImageField>
52            <asp:BoundField DataField="StudentID" HeaderText=
      "StudentID" ReadOnly="True" SortExpression="StudentID" />
```

Figure 19.54 *Fields* tag of the DetailsView control showing *ImageField* ASP tag.

When we click on the *Edit* link at the bottom of the DetailsView control, we see that the fields in the DetailsView are automatically changed into TextBox controls (see Figure 19.55). This allows us to modify the contents of the fields. Also note that the *Edit* link is changed to *Update* and *Cancel* links to accept or reject the updates, respectively.

If we click on the *New* link at the bottom of the DetailsView control, all the fields in the DetailsView control are automatically changed into empty TextBox controls. Once we enter the field values in the TextBox controls, we click the *Insert* link to insert data into the database tables.

Figure 19.55 Ability of a DetailsView control to update records.

19.10 *Hands-On Tutorial: Working with the Repeater Control*

In this section, we illustrate the Repeater control. This control displays database records in a custom template in a repeated fashion. The Repeater control does not have a built-in rendering of its own, which means that we must provide the layout for the Repeater control by creating a template. When the page is displayed, the Repeater control loops through the records in the data source and renders each record as dictated by the defined template.

In this section, instead of using the GridView control, we will display the faculty information using the Repeater control. This hands-on tutorial covers the following How-to topics:

- How-to: add a Repeater control to a Web page.
- How-to: bind a Repeater control to a data source.
- How-to: display images in a Repeater control.

1. Add another page (*Page4.aspx*) to the *WebDBConnectivity* project.
2. Drag and drop a Repeater control from the Toolbox control onto the page. The Repeater control is listed under the Data tab in the Toolbox (see Figure 19.56).

Figure 19.56 Adding a Repeater control to the Web page.

3. Drag and drop an AccessDataSource control to the Web page, and configure it using the *Data Source Configuration* Wizard. Use Figure 19.57 to configure the Select query statement of the data source.

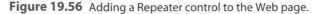

Figure 19.57 Configuring faculty information for the Repeater control's data source.

4. Click on the smart tag of the Repeater control to open its Tasks list (see Figure 19.58). Select the *AccessDataSource1* data source from the *Choose Data Source* drop-down list.

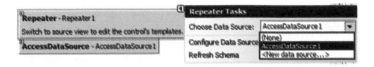

Figure 19.58 Binding the Repeater control to the AccessDataSource.

Now for the first time, we will write HTML code to define the template of the Repeater control. As mentioned before, we should define a template that will be used to display each record of the data source.

5. Switch to the *Source* tab of the *Page4.aspx* file, and write the code shown in Figure 19.59 for the ItemTemplate tag under the ASP Repeater tag.

```
12      <asp:Repeater ID="Repeater1" runat="server" DataSourceID=
   "AccessDataSource1">
13    <ItemTemplate>
14      <font face="arial" color="navy" size="2">
15      <table border="1" cellpadding="4" >
16      <tr><td>Name:</td><td><%#Eval("Name")%></td></tr>
17      <tr><td>Email:</td><td><%#Eval("Email")%></td></tr>
18      <tr><td>Phone:</td><td><%#Eval("Phone")%></td></tr>
19      <tr><td>Department:</td><td><%#Eval("DeptID")%></td></tr>
20      <tr><td>Joining Date:</td><td><%#Eval("JoiningDate")%></td></tr>
21      </table>
22      </font>
23      <br />
24    </ItemTemplate>
25    </asp:Repeater>
```

Figure 19.59 Defining a template of a Repeater control.

In the HTML code, we define an ItemTemplate tag within the Repeater tag. Inside the ItemTemplate tag, we define the layout for each record to display. In line 15, we add an HTML Table tag. In lines 16 to 20, we add one table row for each column of the data source. Each row is divided into two columns: one for field label and one for field value. The field value is specified using an *Eval* function. The function takes the column name as its input parameter and gives the field value as output. Note that the *Eval* function is an ASP function nested in "<%" and "%>" symbols.

6. In the Solution Explorer Window, set the *Page4.aspx* as a start page of the application. Run and test the application (see Figure 19.60).

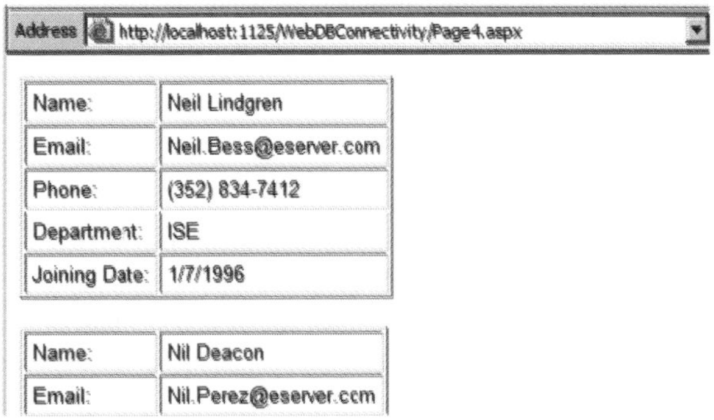

Address http://localhost:1125/WebDBConnectivity/Page4.aspx

Name:	Neil Lindgren
Email:	Neil.Bess@eserver.com
Phone:	(352) 834-7412
Department:	ISE
Joining Date:	1/7/1996

| Name: | Nil Deacon |
| Email: | Nil.Perez@eserver.com |

Figure 19.60 Faculty list displayed in the Repeater control.

In the previous examples, we showed the image alongside the faculty details. We will see how we can add the *ImageField* to a Repeater control.

7. Modify the page's HTML source by adding the code in lines 16 and 17 as shown in Figure 19.61. This is similar to what we have seen so far. We display the picture using the Image ASP tag. The *ImageUrl* property is set to the output of the *Eval* function called with *Picture* column as its input parameter. This *Eval* function returns the relative path of the picture and, hence, is assigned to the *ImageUrl* property.

8. Run and test the application. The picture for each faculty member is now displayed alongside the faculty details (see Figure 19.62).

```
15    <table border="1" cellpadding="4" >
16    <tr><td rowspan="6">
17    <asp:Image ID="Image1" ImageUrl=<%#Eval("Picture")%> runat =
"server" /> </td></tr>
```

Figure 19.61 Adding an ASP Image tag to the Repeater control's item template. 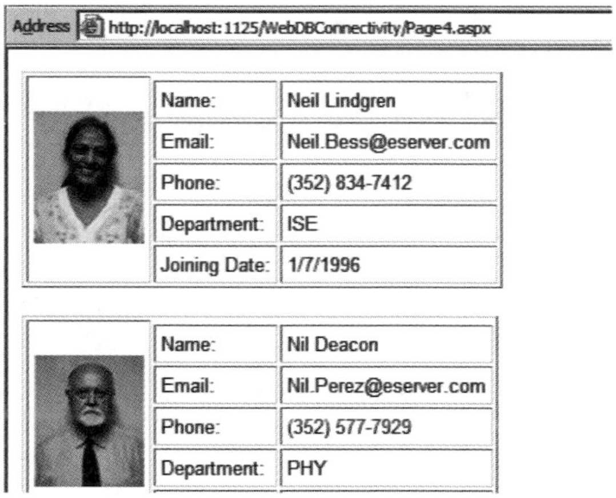

Figure 19.62 Faculty Repeater control with faculty picture.

19.11   *Web-based Crystal Reports*

So far we have seen how to process and display information on Web pages. We now illustrate how we can leverage the power of Crystal Reports and display charts on Web pages (refer to Chapter 16 for an introduction to Crystal Reports).

In this section, we will design a simple crystal report with the following requirements:

■ The report should display the students' contact information (Name, Email, and Phone) for all students from the Industrial and Systems Engineering (ISE) department. Group the records by student class.

■ The report should display a bar chart for the number of ISE students in each of the five student classes.

1. Add a new page (*Page5.aspx*) to the Web site we have developed so far.

2. Add a new crystal report to the project by selecting a *Crystal Report* item in the *Add New Item* dialog box. Name the report, "*StudentReport.rpt*."

3. A *Report Expert* Wizard should start and open the first Wizard page, *Crystal Reports Gallery* (refer to Section 16.2.3 for an explanation of the various options on this page). Select the default *Using the Report Wizard* option and the *Standard* option in the *Choose an Expert* list (See Figure 19.63). Click *OK*.

4. On the Data page, choose the *Access/Excel DAO* item under the *Create New Connection* option in the *Available Data Sources* pane. This should open the *Connection* dialog box. Browse and select the "*University.mdb*" file (see Figure 19.64), and click *Finish* to return to the Wizard page.

5. All the tables and views of the University database are now available to us on the *Data* page. Collapse the *Tables* node and select the *tblStudent* table. Click on the ">" button to move it to the *Selected Tables* pane (see Figure 19.65). Click the *Next* button.

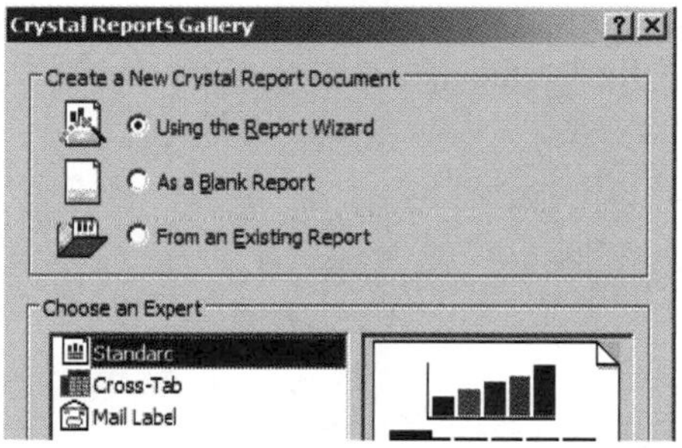

Figure 19.63 Selecting the *Report Expert*.

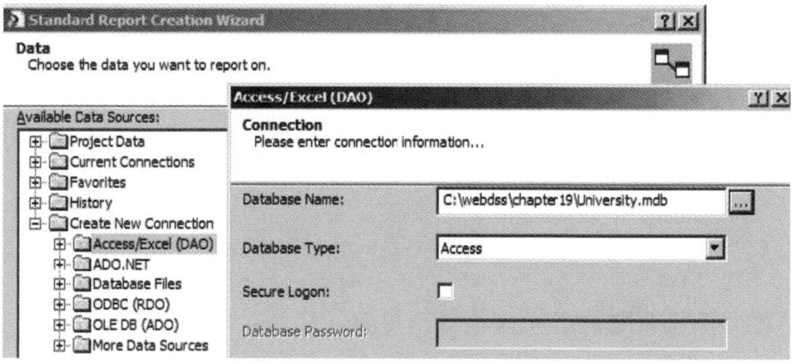

Figure 19.64 Selecting a data connection for the report.

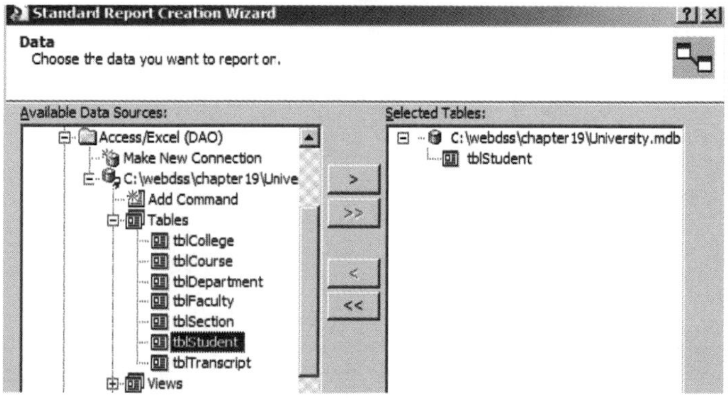

Figure 19.65 Selecting the data source table for the report.

6. On the *Fields* page, collapse the *tblStudent* node to view available fields for the report. Add the *StudentID*, *DeptID*, *Name*, *Class*, *Email*, and *Phone* fields of the student table from the *Available Fields* pane to the *Fields to Display* pane (see Figure 19.66). Click the *Next* button.

7. On the *Grouping* page, specify the fields in which we would like to group student information. In our example, we would like to group students based on student class. Add the *tblStudent.Class* field from the *Available Fields* pane to the *Group By* pane. Accept the default "*in ascending order*" sorting, and click the *Next* button (see Figure 19.67).

8. On the *Summaries* page, we add summary information to our report by choosing fields and relevant summary operations on the selected fields. In our example, we are interested in counting the number of students from each class. For this, we add the *tblStudent.StudentID* field from the *Available Fields* pane to the *Summarized Fields* pane.

9. Select the *StudentID* summary field in the right pane, and choose the *Count* operation from the drop-down list below that pane (see Figure 19.68). Click the *Next* button.

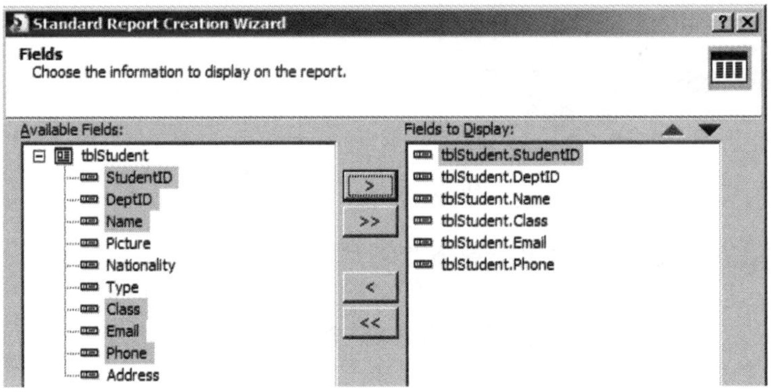

Figure 19.66 Selecting the required fields for the report.

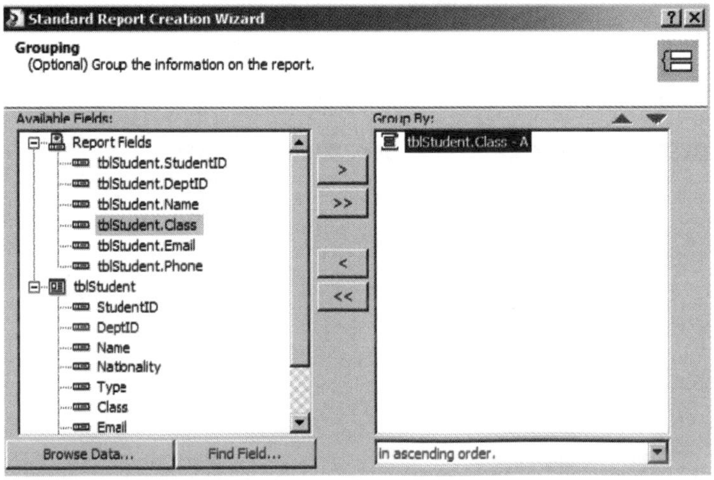

Figure 19.67 Selecting the *Group By* field for the report.

10. On the *Group Sorting* page of the Wizard, we sort groups based on student class (see Figure 19.69). Accept the default selection and click the *Next* button.

11. On the *Chart* page of the *Expert* Wizard, we specify the chart type, chart title, and chart data. Choose the *Bar Chart* type. Select *tblStudent.Class* as the "*On Change of*" field (X-axis) and *Count of StudentID* as the "*Show summary*" field (Y-axis) (see Figure 19.70). Appropriately name the chart title, and click the *Next* button.

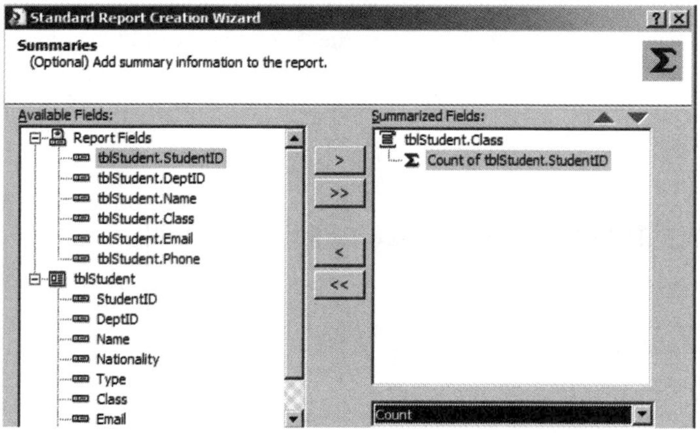

Figure 19.68 Selecting the Summary field for the report.

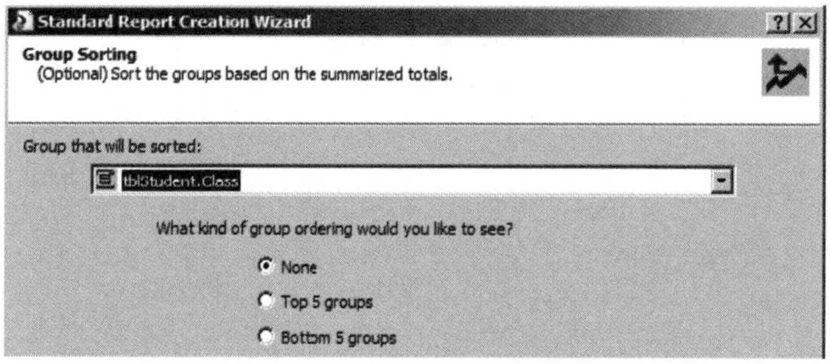

Figure 19.69 Selecting the group ordering for the report.

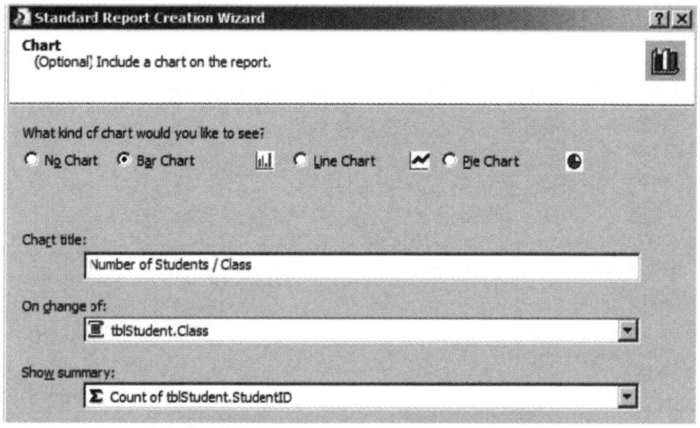

Figure 19.70 Selecting the chart type, title, and data.

12. On the *Record Selection* page, we can optionally apply filtering criteria to report fields. In our example, we want to display records of students who are in the ISE department alone, and, hence, we move the *tblStudent.DeptID* field from the *Available Fields* pane to the *Filter Fields* pane.

13. We select the *DeptID* field in the *Filter Fields* section and choose the "*is equal to*" item from the drop-down list. We assign the value of the expression to ISE in the drop-down list as shown in Figure 19.71. Click the *Next* button.

14. On *Report Style*, the last page of the Wizard, we select the *Shading* format style for the report. Click the *Finish* button to close the Wizard and to add the report to the project.

Now that we have designed our crystal report, we integrate this report with a Web page using a CrystalReportViewer control.

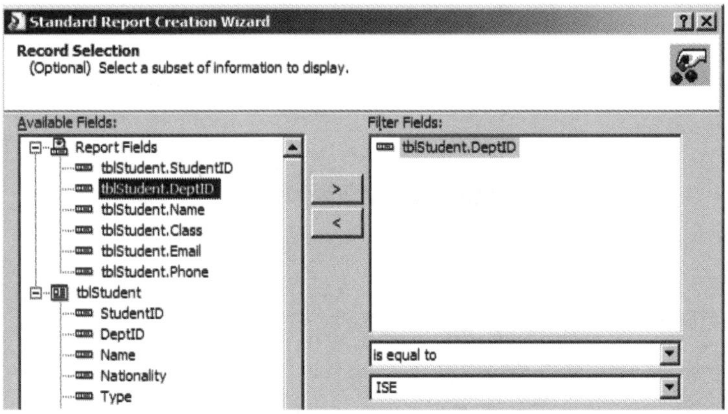

Figure 19.71 Applying filtering criteria to select student records from the ISE department.

15. Open the *Page5.aspx* page. Drag and drop a CrystalReportViewer control from the Toolbox on the Web page (see Figure 19.72).

16. Now, we must bind *StudentReport.rpt* to the CrystalReportViewer control. Click on the smart tag of the CrystalReportViewer control to view its associated Tasks list. In the *Choose Report Source* combo box, select the *New Report Source* option (see Figure 19.73). This should open the *Create a CrystalReportSource Control* dialog box.

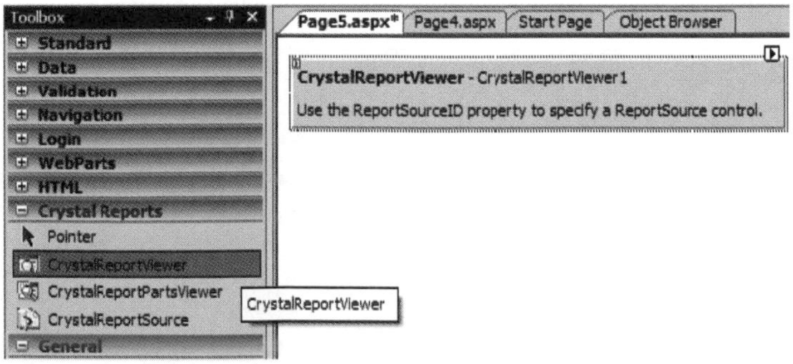

Figure 19.72 Adding a CrystalReportViewer control to a Web page.

Figure 19.73 Choosing the CrystalReportViewer control's report source.

17. In the *Create a CrystalReportSource Control* dialog box, accept the default control name. In the *Specify a Crystal Report* drop-down list, select *StudentReport.rpt* (see Figure 19.74). Click *OK* to bind the student report with the viewer control.

18. In the Solution Explorer, set *Page5.aspx* as a start page. Run and test the application (see Figure 19.75).

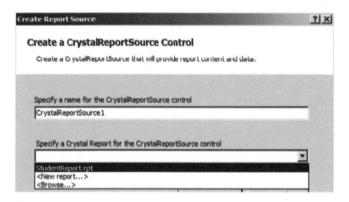

Figure 19.74 Creating a CrystalReportSource.

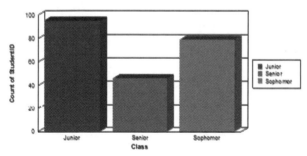

Figure 19.75 Web page displaying the student crystal report.

We discuss more complicated Web-based crystal reports and programmatically binding crystal reports and CrystalReportViewer control in the case studies part of this book. Please refer to Chapters 21 and 22 for more examples.

19.12   *Programmatically Accessing the Database*

In this section, we show how we can perform database access programmatically at runtime. Accessing database in the VB program gives us flexibility and more control over the development process. The application we will develop for illustration should display in a drop-down list of the courses offered by the department selected. This section covers the following How-to topic:

■ How-to: access a database programmatically at run-time.

1. Add another page (*Page6.aspx*) to the application.
2. Drag and drop the GridView control onto the Web page, and set its *ID* to "*grvCourses.*" Format the grid using the *AutoFormat* option.
3. Drag and drop the DropDownList control onto the page, and set its *ID* to "*cmbDept.*" Also, add a Label control, "Select Department," next to the drop-down list. Click on the smart tag of the DropDownList control to view its Tasks list, and check the *Enable AutoPostBack* option.

Until now we have seen that the data gets populated from the AccessDataSource control. We have not written any code to actually fetch the data from the database and bind it to the controls. In this section, we will write Visual Basic code (in *Page6.aspx.vb* file) that will fetch the data from the database into an *OledbDataReader* object. To fetch the data, we need to know the location of the database, which is specified using the *OledbConnection* object. We also need to specify what data to fetch from the database. This is done using the *OledbCommand* object, which executes the SQL query against the database and post the results into an *OledbDataReader* object.

4. To use the discussed *Oledb* objects, we must include the reference to the *OleDb* library. This is done using the *Imports* command (lines 1–2 of Figure 19.76). The location of the database is stored in the *connString* variable (line 7).

```
1  Imports System.Data.OleDb
2  Imports System.Data
3
4  Partial Class Page6
5      Inherits System.Web.UI.Page
6
7      Din connString As String = "Provider=Microsoft.Jet.OLEDB.
       4.0;Data Source=C:\webdss\HandsOn\chapter19\WebDBConnectivity
       \University.mdb"
8      Din univDB As OleDbConnection
```

Figure 19.76 Importing the *OleDb* library.

5. Enter the code shown in Figure 19.77 for the *Page_Load* event of the Web page. This code will be executed when a page is loaded for the first time (line 11) and populates the list of departments into the DropDownList control.

```
10    Protected Sub Page_Load(ByVal sender As Object, ByVal e
      As System.EventArgs) Handles Me.Load
11        If Not IsPostBack Then
12            Dim cmdDept As OleDbCommand
13            Dim drdDept As OleDbDataReader
14            univDB = New OleDbConnection(connString)
15            cmdDept = New OleDbCommand("SELECT * FROM
      tblDepartment", univDb)
16
17            Try
18                univDb.Open()
19                drdDept = cmdDept.ExecuteReader
20                cmbDept.DataSource = drdDept
21                cmbDept.DataTextField = "Name"
22                cmbDept.DataValueField = "DeptID"
23                cmbDept.DataBind()
24                drdDept.Close()
25            Catch ex As Exception
26            Finally
27                univDb.Close()
28            End Try
29        End If
30    End Sub
```

Figure 19.77 *Page_Load* event populating the DropDownList with the list of departments.

Figure 19.77 Explained:

We declare an *OledbCommand* object (line12) that hosts the SQL query that fetches the details of the *tblDepartment* table (line 15). In line 14, we create a new connection connecting to the *University.mdb* Access database file. We use the *ExecuteReader* command on the *OledbCommand* object to read the details from the database into the *OledbDataReader* object (line 19). We then bind the *OledbDataReader* object to the DropDownList control. We first specify the *DataTextField* and *DataValueFields* properties of the DropDownList control (lines 20–22). To bind a *DataReader* to a *DropDownList*, we call the *Databind* function of the DropDownList control (line 23). Finally, we close the *DataReader* and *Connection* objects.

```
32    Protected Sub cmbDept_SelectedIndexChanged(ByVal sender
      As Object, ByVal e As System.EventArgs) Handles cmbDept.
      SelectedIndexChanged
33        UpdateSource()
34    End Sub
35
36    Sub UpdateSource()
37        Dim cmdCourse As OleDbCommand
38        Dim odaCourse As OleDbDataAdapter
39        Dim dsCourse As DataSet
40        univDB = New OleDbConnection(connString)
41        cmdCourse = New OleDbCommand("SELECT * FROM tblCourse
      WHERE DeptID=@DID", univDb)
42        cmdCourse.Parameters.AddWithValue("@DID", cmbDept.
      SelectedValue)
43        odaCourse = New OleDbDataAdapter(cmdCourse)
44        dsCourse = New DataSet
45        odaCourse.Fill(dsCourse)
46        grvCourses.DataSource = dsCourse
47        grvCourses.DataBind()
48    End Sub
```

Figure 19.78 Update course details for a selected department in the grid view.

6. Whenever we change our selection in the DropDownList control, we should update the course details in the GridView. Enter the code shown in Figure 19.78 in the Drop-DownList control's *SelectedIndexChanged* event handler to facilitate this.

Figure 19.78 Explained:

We write a subroutine, *UpdateSource*, to perform these updates. We need to declare an *Oledb-Command* object (line 37) that hosts the SQL query that fetches the details from the *tblCourse* table (line 41). The SQL query we are using is a parameterized query, and, hence, before executing the query, we must supply values for its parameter (line 42). A variable beginning with "@" is used to represent a parameter in a query. The *SelectedValue* property of the DropDownList control gives us the *DeptID* of the selected department (line 42). Now instead of using the *DataReader* object, we use the *Dataset* and *DataAdapter* objects to fetch the data from the database (lines 38, 39, 43, 44). We have used the *Dataset* and *DataAdapter* extensively in the VB.NET section of this book. We then execute the *Fill* method of the *DataAdapter* object that executes the SQL query and return the result in the *Dataset* object (line 45). To bind the *Dataset* object to the GridView control, we set the control's *DataSource* property to the dataset name (line 47) and call the GridView control's *DataBind* method.

7. In the Solution Explorer, set the *Page6.aspx* as the start page. Run and test the application (see Figure 19.79).

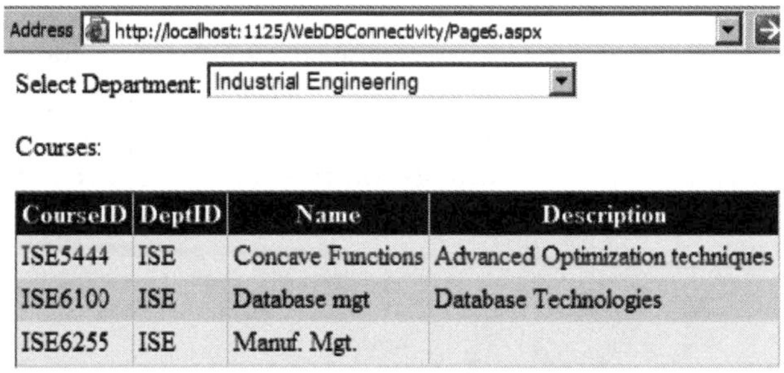

Figure 19.79 Running the application displaying courses from the selected department.

19.13 *In-Class Assignment*

In this assignment, we design a Web application that retrieves and displays student name, picture, type, class, and grade in a GridView control based on the section number selected from a drop-down list. (*Hint*: use the lookup and filter functionalities to retrieve data from the transcript, section, and student tables.) Include a DetailsView control that displays the details of the section selected from the drop-down list. Enable edit operations for the DetailsView control. Present well-formatted views of the GridView and DetailsView control. (*Hint*: use the *AutoFormat* option.)

19.14 *Summary*

- A Web-based, data-driven application is a program that allows users to manipulate data in a DBMS through a Web interface.

- The Server Explorer is used to create and manipulate database connections. Using the Server Explorer, we can view and edit the data in database tables.

- Instead of displaying all the records in the data source on a single Web page, the GridView control automatically puts them on multiple pages. This feature is called *Paging*. When the GridView control is data-bind to a data source that supports sorting, the sorting functionality can be easily

extended by the GridView control to allow record sorting on Web pages.

- We use parameterized queries to provide filtering capability to a Web page.

- The DetailsView control is used to display related information on a Web page. DetailsView control is an ideal choice for displaying one record at a time on a Web page.

- The Repeater control does not have a built-in rendering of its own. Hence, we must provide the layout for the Repeater control by creating templates.

19.15 *Exercises*

19.15.1 Review Questions

1. In a Web-based, data-driven application, where is the database stored, and how is it accessed by a Web client?

2. How can we view table data from a Server Explorer?

3. What are the two methods to change the query associated with an existing AccessDataSource?

4. Which tool is used to enhance the appearance of data-driven controls such as GridView in ASP .NET?

5. How can we enable paging and sorting for a GridView control?

6. How can we ensure that updates made using edit links on a Web page get passed on to the database on the server?

7. How can we sort a column in a grid in a running Web application?

8. What gets stored in the DataFile and Select Command attributes of an AccessDataSource ASP tag?

9. What is the use of the Select parameters tag in the ASP source file of a Web page?

10. How can you configure the data source of an AccessDataSource control?

11. What is the function of the Repeater control?

12. Which function must be called in order to bind data to a DropDownList control?

13. What is the role of the *Fill* function of a *DataAdapter* object?

14. How can you bind a Web-based crystal report to a CrystalReportViewer?

19.15.2 Hands-On Exercises

NOTE: *The database files for these hands-on exercises are available at: www.dssbooks.com.*

1. Create a Web page for a furniture company that displays its products on a well-formatted grid (use the "Furniture" database).

2. Create a Web page for a hotel that displays the details of its customers who are from California (use the "Hotel" database).

3. Design a Web page for a hospital to display in a grid control the details of its doctors who are general physicians (use the "Hospital" database).

4. Create a Web page for Megabucks bank to display the account details of all currently active accounts that have a balance greater than $1,000 (use the "Megabucks" database; an active account is one for which the *Close* date field is null).

5. A restaurant wants you to design a Web page that displays the various menu items and provides the users the capability to edit, insert, or delete menu items. Also, since they expect to include a large number of items, they want you to include paging and sorting by price functionalities (use the "Menu" database).

6. Using the "Movies" database, create a Web page that allows a user to select a state from a drop-down list. With this information, populate a second drop-down list that allows the user to select a city from those available in the selected state. Display a list of movie theaters in that city, and allow the user to select one. Finally, display the appropriate movie data for that theater in a grid control.

7. A post office wants you to create a simple Web page that provides a listing of all its offices along with the respective manager and handler information (use the "Post Office" database).

8. Create a simple Web page for a bottling company that displays the details of the bottles used for water and lemonade drinks in a well-formatted table (use the "Bottling" database).

9. Create a Web page for a restaurant that displays the ingredients of every menu item. Allow the user to select a particular menu item from a drop-down list, and then display all the ingredients of that item along with the price and recipe number in a GridView control (use the "Menu" database).

10. Using the "Megabucks" database, create a Web application that displays the details of all customers whose accounts have a current balance greater than $1,000 and who currently have a loan from the bank. Perform a join of the Accounts, Loans, and Customer tables to extract the required information, and display the retrieved customer details in a grid control.

11. An airline company has asked you to create a simple Web application with the features listed below (use the "Airline" database):

   a. The user must be able to choose a certain flight from a drop-down list of all available flights.

   b. The system should be able to display all the customer reservations and preferences for the selected flight in a grid control.

12. A bottling company is performing a study to analyze and improve its processes. As a part of this study, you are to design a Web application that will display the details of the lines whose maximum fraction of non-conforming bottles is less than 0.1 for any sample. Display the line details in a well-formatted grid control (use the "Bottling" database).

13. A school employs you to develop a Web application that will display the student details in a grid control. You must provide selection functionality for each student row. On the click of the Student ID field, populate the courses taken by that particular student in another grid control on the same Web page. On the click of the Course ID field, provide the details about that particular course in a DetailsView control (use the "Schools" database).

14. Globe Airlines is an interstate airline. It keeps records of all its previous reservations, and it has asked you to create a Web-based customer report that displays the number of reservations made by each customer. It is offering some specials for its best customers. Create a Web-based crystal report that includes the following information:

   a. The customer's full name

   b. The route of the flight

   c. The cost of the flight

   d. The class of the customer's seat

   In addition, list the five most active customers by how many flights they've taken (use the "Airline" database).

15. Create a Web page that displays the meal orders in a restaurant in a page-by-page fashion. Display the order number, menu item name, price, and date and time of order, and sort the list in ascending order of price. (*Hint*: Join *tblOrders* and *tblMenuItems* of the "Menu" database.)

16. Design a Web page for a post office that provides a clerk the ability to select a particular customer from a drop-down list and view all the package information for that customer. Also, compute and display the cost of shipping each package according to the shipment type, package weight, and shipping rate. Sort the packages in ascending order by package weight (use the "Post Office" database). (*Hint*: Join *tblPackages* and *tblRates*.)

17. Create a Web page that displays the list of students who have earned about 60% in a user-specified course. Allow the user to select a specific course from a drop-down list of courses. Also, whenever the user clicks on a specific student ID, display the details of that student in a DetailsView control (use the "Schools" database).

18. Create a Web page for a bottling company that displays the details of lines where the equipment age is at most two years. Whenever the user clicks on a particular line, display the details of the associated bottle in a details view control (use the "Bottling" database).

19. A hospital would like you to identify and display on a Web page the patients who have spent between $100 and $250 on medicines starting on January 1, 2002. Arrange the results in alphabetical order by the patients' last names. On the click of the patient name, provide the details of the patient in a DetailsView (use the "Hospital" database).

20. A hospital wants you to design a Web page that will display its billing information with each bill in a separate table for ease of printing and issuance of bills to patients. Use the Repeater control and design a table template through HTML code to create the Web application (use the "Hospital" database).

21. A furniture company would like you to create a Web page with its product information displayed in a repeated fashion. Use the Repeater control and design a suitable template for displaying records. Separate each product record using a suitable line separator (use the "Furniture" database).

22. Create a Web application that displays flight information in a repeating fashion for flights whose travel time is greater than two hours. Use the Repeater control and design the page (use the "Airline" database).

23. Create a Web page that displays the customer details for a hotel in a repeating fashion. Use a Repeater control to design the Web page (use the "Hotel" database).

24. A university wants you to develop a Web-based report that displays the average faculty salaries for each department on a pie chart. The steps for this exercise are very similar to the student report we have created in this chapter, except we use the faculty table, use an average aggregate function, and plot a pie chart (use the "University" database, and refer to Section 16.6 for a similar report).

25. Create a Web-based crystal report for a school that displays the average percentage earned by students in each course as a line chart (use *tblStudentCourse* of the "Schools" database).

26. Create a Web-based crystal report for a hotel that displays in a bar chart the total amount paid by each customer for various bookings (use *tblBilling* of the "Hotel" database).

one Online Book Store

CS1.1 *Introduction*

Online Book Store is an ASP .NET case study featuring the "*Universal Books and Tech. Center*" Web site. The center relies on this Web site to sell its books and handle book order transactions. The Web site lists all the books from the database and also allows its users to search books using a variety of pre-defined options such as book titles, book authors, etc. A user can get detailed book information and buy books by adding them to an online shopping cart. Once all desired items are collected, the user can checkout and make online payments for her orders.

The case study is a simple, scaled-down version of today's online shopping sites like Amazon.com and Buy.com. Here, we illustrate how various ASP .NET components can be combined to design a complete business-oriented Web site. Almost all the features used in this case study are discussed in Chapters 17–19. We also illustrate the concept of *Session Variables* and *Master Page* in this case study. We elaborate further on session variables in Section CS1.4.6 and on the master page in Section CS1.3.

The case study code and the complete application can be found on the book Web site. We strongly recommend readers to download and install the case study and browse through the application pages before going through the details described in this chapter. We will not discuss the nuances of the Web page setup and interface design in the chapter, but they are visible in the downloaded application. Since we do not present the case study as a hands-on tutorial, we recommend that the reader develop the case study as we explain various Web pages. We also suggest that the reader open the underlying database file and understand the database design before proceeding with the case study. Figure CS1.1 shows the Relationships Window of the bookstore database used in this case study.

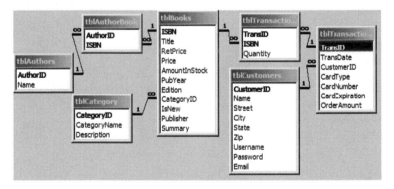

Figure CS1.1 The Relationships Window for the *Universal Books'* database.

CS1.2 *Application Functionalities and Assumptions*

Although the application is a simple version of a real-life online bookstore, it provides myriad functionalities to its users. These functionalities are listed below:

Book Search (Search and Sort): The application can list all available books and allow the user to *search books* by *Book Title*, *Book Author*, *ISBN*, and *Book Category*. For each of these search criteria, the user can specify the "search keyword," and all the books that include the keyword are listed back to the user. The user can also *sort the list* based on *ISBN*, *Title*, or *Price* fields.

Book Details (Drill Down): Once the books (all or searched) are listed on the page, the user can *view detailed information* for desired books by clicking on the "View Details" button available next to each listed book. Details include publisher, publication year, edition information, amount in stock, and book summary information.

Add-To-Cart (Multiple Selections): Once the user browses the book information, she can *select one or more books* from the list and add them to an online shopping cart.

Order Editing (Inventory Management): A user can edit shopping carts to choose the desired quantity of selected books, either to purchase or remove them from the cart. When the user is satisfied with the selection, she can check out to purchase the books. On checkout, we update the stock quantities of selected books and database tables accordingly. If a particular item is out-of-stock or lacks the requested quantity, we display the appropriate message to the user.

Shopping Cart (Session Variables): Web applications are typically accessed by multiple users at the same time. It is important for online shopping applications to provide a personalized view of the shopping carts to the users as they browse and add items to purchase. *Session variables* and *Internet cookies* are two popular methods used to support this functionality. In this case study, we introduce session variables to keep track of information across Web pages individually for each user. A session variable can be thought of as a variable in programming languages that gets initialized by an event on a Web page and holds the desired piece of information as long as the Web browser is open.

Login (Authentication): As a user checks out an online shopping cart, we authenticate her on the login page. To login, the user is required to enter a username and password. We then confirm the input information against the stored username and password in the database. A user must be registered with the Web site before login. We do not illustrate user registration in this case study, as this task is left as a part of the case study extensions.

Checkout (Validation Controls): Once logged-in, the user enters her personal information, shipping address, and payment information to place the order. The checkout involves several user inputs, which are validated using validation controls (see Chapter 18).

Order Confirmation (Populating Database Tables): Once the user confirms her list of books and checks out, we insert the ordered items, ordered quantities, shipping addresses, and payment information in multiple database tables for order processing.

Master Page (Unified View): A master page is an essential feature for large Web site designs. A master page is a template of all Web pages in an application. Designs for page header, page footer, and navigation menu created on the master page are reflected on every Web page, uniformly and in a consistent manner.

CS1.2.1 The Application Flow

The flow of the *Online Book Store* application is depicted in Figure CS1.2.

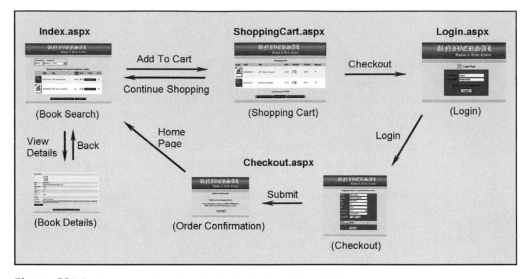

Figure CS1.2 The application flow for the *Online Book Store Web site*.

The names of the Web pages are depicted on top of the Web page, while their functionalities are shown at the bottom of the respective thumbnails. The names on flow arrows indicate the buttons on Web pages that lead to the required page. The *Book Search* and *Book Details* functions are embedded on the same page, "Index.aspx." As the user clicks the *View Detail* button, she can view the book details on the same page just below the book listing. Similarly, the *Checkout* and *Order Confirmation* functions are also put together on a single page, "Checkout.aspx." We let the user browse the book database to choose desired books to purchase, and when she is ready to check out, we ask for her login information. On successful login, we redirect her to the checkout page.

We shall now enumerate details of each Web page of this application. We discuss the main design issues and the code behind these pages. We will first discuss the master page of this application (not shown in the application flow).

CS1.3   *The Master Page*

A master page is the template to all Web pages of an application. A master page typically contains a design and a code that is common to all Web pages, including page header, page footer, logos, and page navigation menu. A master page is essential for large Web site design. It not only offers a uniform view of Web pages, but also provides a single editing point. That is, changes made on the master page are automatically reflected to all Web pages that are designed based on the master page template.

We can add a master page to an application at any time, but it is recommended to create a master page before designing other pages. To add a master page to the new application, we do the following:

■ How-to: add a master page to a Web application.

1. Select the Web site | Add New Item option from the main menu. This opens the familiar *Add New Item* dialog box.
2. Choose the *master page* option and name it appropriately (see Figure CS1.3).

Figure CS1.3 Adding a master page to a Web application.

3. Design the page similarly to other Web pages by adding desired controls and codes behind controls.

We show the master page for this application in Figure CS1.4. The page features a page header and a page borders design in HTML tables. We also add a ContentPlaceHolder control to the page that acts like a placeholder and features the main contents of a Web page. The images required for this page are available in the *Images* folder of the application. For the sake of brevity, we do not provide every detail of the page setup and leave it to the reader to examine the actual application files for details.

Figure CS1.4 The master page for *An Online Book Store* application.

CS1.4 *The Index Page*

The index page is the starting page of the application. The snapshot of the index page is shown in CS1.5. The page, when loaded for the first time, displays the list of all "New Arrival" books. It then provides the user with the following options:

- Search books
- List search results
- Show book details
- Select and add books to the shopping cart

We discuss these functions in separate subsections to follow.

Figure CS1.5 The index page (searched books by author keyword).

CS1.4.1 Applying the Master Page

Every time we add a new Web page to the application, we can create the page design based on the master page. The page header and other design setup for the index page in Figure CS1.5 are part of the master page in Figure CS1.4. To create a new Web page using a master page, do the following How-to topic:

- How-to: apply a master page to a new or an existing Web page.

    1. Invoke the *Add New Item* dialog box to add a new Web page, and choose the *Select master page* option to apply the master page (see Figure CS1.6).
    2. When we click the *Add* button to create a new page, the *Select a Master Page* dialog box appears. We select the previously designed master page and click *OK* (see Figure CS1.7).

Figure CS1.6 Appling the master page to the index page.

Figure CS1.7 Choosing the master page to apply.

We can apply a master page to an existing Web page by manipulating its *Page* directive (see Chapter 18). We use the *MasterPageFile* attribute in the *Page* directive (the first line in the HTML source code) and assign it a path of the master page file as in Figure CS1.8. The "~" symbol is used to denote the root folder of the Web application.

Figure CS1.8 Appling the master page to an existing Web page with the *Page* directive.

CS1.4.2 Book Search

The user can search books based on the keywords entered in the *Keyword* TextBox control and the option selected in the *Search By* DropDownList control. We set various options in the *Search By* DropDownList control as shown in Figure CS1.9.

Figure CS1.9 The *Search By* DropDownList control options.

The *Search* button executes one of the six queries listed in Table CS1.1 based on the values in the *Search By* DropDownList control and *Keyword* TextBox control (see Figure CS1.10). The *SearchBooks* subroutine (line 96) is a member function we developed for this case study (see Section CS1.4.3 for the subroutine details). This subroutine takes two input parameters that correspond to values of the *Search By* DropDownList control and *Keyword* TextBox control. Inside the subroutine, it executes the appropriate query, based on input parameter values, and the query result is displayed to the user in a GridView control (discussed in the next subsection).

```
93      'This event is invoked when user clicks Search button
94      Protected Sub btnSearch_Click(ByVal sender As Object, ByVal e As _
95      System.EventArgs) Handles btnSearch.Click
96          SearchBooks(cboSearchBy.SelectedValue, txtKeyword.Text)
97      End Sub
```

Figure CS1.10 *Search* button's *Click* event.

Further, as the user performs different searches with options in the DropDownList control, we assign a default keyword value in the TextBox control and also list the search result in a Grid-View. This functionality provides better application flow and also illustrates its utilities efficiently. The code for the *SelectedIndexChanged* event of the DropDownList control is given in Figure CS1.11. The event code features a Select-Case structure (lines 74–90). Based on the "case" of the *Search By* DropDownList control, a value is assigned to the *Keyword* TextBox control. A call to the *SearchBooks* member function is then made with appropriate input values.

Also, note that when we load the index page for the first time, we display the "New Arrival" books. The code for the *Page_Load* event is shown in Figure CS1.12.

```
70      'This event is invoked when user changes selection in the search box
71      Protected Sub cboSearchBy_SelectedIndexChanged(ByVal sender As _
72      Object, ByVal e As System.EventArgs) Handles cboSearchBy. _
73      SelectedIndexChanged
74          Select Case cboSearchBy.SelectedValue
75              Case "All"
76                  txtKeyword.Text = "New Arrivals"
77                  SearchBooks(cboSearchBy.SelectedValue, txtKeyword.Text)
78              Case "Title"
79                  txtKeyword.Text = "ASP"
80                  SearchBooks(cboSearchBy.SelectedValue, txtKeyword.Text)
81              Case "Category"
82                  txtKeyword.Text = "Technical Books"
83                  SearchBooks(cboSearchBy.SelectedValue, txtKeyword.Text)
84              Case "Author"
85                  txtKeyword.Text = "Anthony , Landry"
86                  SearchBooks(cboSearchBy.SelectedValue, txtKeyword.Text)
87              Case "ISBN"
88                  txtKeyword.Text = "0201760401"
89                  SearchBooks(cboSearchBy.SelectedValue, txtKeyword.Text)
90          End Select
91      End Sub
```

Figure CS1.11 *Search By* DropDownList control's *SelectedIndexChanged* event.

```
61      Protected Sub Page_Load(ByVal sender As Object, _
62      ByVal e As System.EventArgs) Handles Me.Load
63          'If page being loaded first time i.e. without
64          'a postback then show user the new arrivals
65          If Not IsPostBack Then
66              SearchBooks("All", "New Arrivals")
67          End If
68      End Sub
```

Figure CS1.12 *Page_Load* event of the Index.aspx page.

CS1.4.3 Search Results in the GridView

As the *Search* button's *Click* event executes the *SearchBooks* member function, the search results—a book list—are displayed to the user in a GridView control, *grdBookSearchResults*. Each grid row features a book entry with book thumbnail image, ISBN, book title, and its price. The Design View of *grdBookSearchResults* is shown in Figure CS1.13. We use the GridView control's properties to set up the *grdBookSearchResults*. Specifically, we use a set of *Style* properties to set the grid interface; *Columns* property is used to set the *Details* (Button Field) and *Check* (CheckBox Field) columns. The *Column* property for the *Details* column is shown in Figure CS1.14.

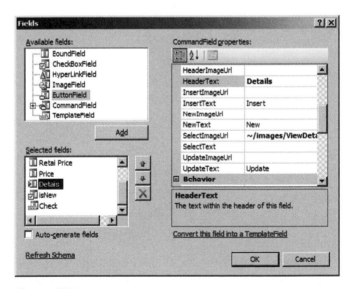

Figure CS1.13 Design View of *grdBookSearchResults* on the index page.

Figure CS1.14 Adding *Details* column with *View Detail* button to the *grdBookSearchResults*.

All other columns of the *grdBookSearchResults* are *databound* and acquire values from the search query result. The data source of the *grdBookSearchResults* is an AccessDataSource, *dbBookStore* (see bottom of Figure CS1.13). When we add this data source to the index page using the

Configure Data Source dialog box, we set its SELECT statement to execute the pre-defined Access query (see Figure CS1.15). Since we display the newly arrived books on page load, we set the default statement to "*exec qryGetNewArrivals.*" The "*exec*" is a command to run the existing queries of the connected database.

Figure CS1.15 Configuring *dbBookStore* data source.

As discussed before, when a user searches for books using the *Search* button, we execute the *SearchBooks* member function, with the search criteria and the search keyword as input parameters. We use these parameters in the *SearchBooks* member function to reassign a SELECT statement to the *dbBookStore* data source. Figure CS1.16 depicts the code for the *SearchBooks* member function.

```
14      Private Sub SearchBooks(ByVal strSearchByField As String, _
15      ByVal strSearchValue As String)
16          lblTitle.ForeColor = Drawing.Color.Black
17          lblTitle.Text = "Search Results by: '" & strSearchByField & "'"
18          If strSearchValue <> "" Then
19              lblTitle.Text = lblTitle.Text & " for keyword: '" _
20              & strSearchValue & "'"
21          End If
22          'Change the SelectCommand of DataSource based on "SearchBy" value
23          'in the Combo Box and "Keyword" in the Text Box
24          If cboSearchBy.SelectedValue = "All" And txtKeyword.Text = _
25          "New Arrivals" Then
26              dbBookStore.SelectCommand = "exec qryGetNewArrivals"
27          Else
28              dbBookStore.SelectCommand = "exec qryGetBooksBy" & _
29              strSearchByField & " '" & strSearchValue & "'"
30          End If
31      End Sub
```

Figure CS1.16 *SearchBooks* member function.

Figure CS1.16 Explained:

Lines 24–30 reassign the SELECT statement (or *SelectCommand*) to the *dbBookStore* data source. There are two distinct cases here. The first (lines 24–26) is when the search criteria is "All" and the search keyword is "New Arrival." In this case, we execute the "qryGetNewArrival" as before. The second case (lines 27–30) executes other search options and is selected from one of the queries listed in Table CS1.1 based on the search criteria. Note that all queries in the second case are Access Parameter queries, and the search keyword is passed as a parameter to the query in line 29.

Table CS1.1 Access queries for the index page.

Query Name	Query Function	SQL Statements
qryGetBooksByAll	Fetching all books books	SELECT ISBN, Title, retPrice, Price, CategoryName,'./images/thumbnails/'+ [ISBN]+'.gif' AS Thumbnail FROM tblCategory, tblBooks WHERE Category.CategoryID=Books.CategoryID;
qryGetBooksByAuthor	Fetch books by Author	Same as "qryGetBooksByAll" with additional WHERE clause: `Authors.Name Like "%" + [?] + "%"`
qryGetBooksByCategory	Fetch books by Category	Same as "qryGetBooksByAll" with additional WHERE clause: `Category.CategoryName Like "%"+[?]+"%"`
qryGetBooksByISBN	Fetch books by ISBN	Same as "qryGetBooksByAll" with additional WHERE clause: `Book.ISBN = [?]`
qryGetBooksByTitle	Fetch books by Title	Same as "qryGetBooksByAll" with additional WHERE clause: `Book.Title Like "%" + [?] + "%"`
qryGetNewArrivals	Fetch newly arrived books	Same as "qryGetBooksByAll" with additional WHERE clause: `Book.isNew = Yes`
qryBookDetails	Fetch book details	SELECT Books.ISBN, Title, retPrice, Price, AmountInStock, PubYear, Edition, Publisher, Summary, Authors.Name, './images/thumbnails/'+[Books.ISBN]+'.gif' AS ThumbNail FROM tblBooks, tblAuthors, tblAuthorBook WHERE Authors.authorID = AuthorBook.AuthorID AND Books.ISBN = AuthorBook.ISBN AND Books.ISBN=[?];

CS1.4.4   Book Details in the DetailView

The DetailView control, *detBookDetails*, gives the detailed information for the books selected in the *grdBookSearchResults* (see Figure CS1.17(a)). The Design View of the *detBookDetails* is shown in Figure CS1.17(b). As with the *grdBookSearchResults*, we use the *Style* and *Items* properties to set the interface of the *detBookDetails*.

The data source of the *detBookDetails* is an AccessDataSource, *BookDetails* (see Figure CS1.17(b)), and hosts the "qryBookDetails" listed in the Table CS1.1 (see Figure CS1.18). The only parameter of this query—an ISBN—is supplied from the *grdBookSearchResults*' row, for which the *View Details* button is clicked, i.e., the selected index of the *grdBookSearchResults* is changed (see Figure CS1.19).

(a)

(b)

Figure CS1.17 *GrdBookSearchResults* (a) in the running application; (b) in the Design View.

Figure CS1.18 Configuring the data source for *detBookDetails*.

```
 99      'This event is invoked when user clicks View Details button
100      Protected Sub grdBookSearchResults_SelectedIndexChanged _
101      (ByVal sender As Object, ByVal e As System.EventArgs) _
102      Handles grdBookSearchResults.SelectedIndexChanged
103          pnlDetailView.Visible = True
104          BookDetails.SelectCommand = "exec qryBookDetails '" _
105          & grdBookSearchResults.SelectedRow.Cells(COL_ISBN).Text & "'"
106          btnBackToGridView.Focus()
107      End Sub
```

Figure CS1.19 *SelectedIndexChanged* event of the *grdBookSearchResults*.

Figure CS1.19 Explained:

The *detBookDetails* is placed inside the *pnlDetailView* panel control. The panel is visible in line 103 on the *Click* event of the *View Detail* button in the *grdBookSearchResults*. The query "qry-BookDetails" and the ISBN parameter (a value from the *ISBN* column of the selected row of *grd-BookSearchResults*) are assigned as the *SelectCommand* of the *BookDetails* data source (line 105). COL_ISBN is the member variable that indicates the index of the ISBN column in the *dbBook-Store* data source (see line 7 of the "Index.aspx.vb" file).

When the user clicks the *Back* button at the bottom of the *detBookDetails*, we make the *det-BookDetails* invisible and focus on the *grdBookSearchResults* (see Figure CS1.20).

```
109   'This event is invoked when user clicks Back button
110   Protected Sub btnBackToGridView_Click(ByVal sender As Object, ByVal _
111   e As System.Web.UI.ImageClickEventArgs) Handles btnBackToGridView.Click
112       pnlDetailView.Visible = False
113       grdBookSearchResults.SelectedIndex = -1
114   End Sub
```

Figure CS1.20 *Click* event of the *Back* button.

CS1.4.5   Selecting and Adding Books to the Shopping Cart

The three buttons at the bottom of the index page, *Add To Cart*, *Select All*, and *Clear All*, permit the user to select and add books to the online shopping cart. The *Select All* and *Clear All* buttons select or de-select all the books in the *grdBookSearchResults*, respectively. The code behind the *Click* event of the *Select All* button is shown in Figure CS1.21. We iterate over rows of the *grdBook-SearchResults* in a For-Each-Next loop (lines 149–152) and select the check boxes in the last column of the *grdBookSearchResults* for each row. The code for the *Add To Cart* button is shown in Figure CS1.22.

```
143       'This event is invoked when user clicks Select All button
144       Protected Sub btnSelectAll_Click(ByVal sender As Object, _
145       ByVal e As System.Web.UI.ImageClickEventArgs) _
146       Handles btnSelectAll.Click
147           Dim row As GridViewRow
148           'Go over all the checkboxes and select them
149           For Each row In grdBookSearchResults.Rows
150               CType(row.Cells(COL_SELECTED).FindControl _
151               ("chkSelected"), CheckBox).Checked = True
152           Next
153       End Sub
```

Figure CS1.21 *Click* event of the *Select All* button.

```
116       'This event is invoked when user clicks Add To Cart button
117       Protected Sub imgAddToCart_Click(ByVal sender As Object, _
118       ByVal e As System.Web.UI.ImageClickEventArgs) _
119       Handles btnAddToCart.Click
120           Dim row As GridViewRow
121           Dim bSelected As Boolean
122           Dim strISBN As String
123           For Each row In grdBookSearchResults.Rows
124               'Check if any book is selected
125               bSelected = CType(row.Cells(COL_SELECTED). _
126               FindControl("chkSelected"), CheckBox).Checked
127               If bSelected Then
128                   strISBN = row.Cells(COL_ISBN).Text
129                   'Add this ISBN book to the cart
130                   AddToCart(strISBN)
131               End If
132           Next
133           'If cart is empty, do not redirect to the next page
134           If Not Cart_Empty() Then
135               Response.Redirect("ShoppingCart.aspx", True)
136           Else
137               lblTitle.Text = "No items selected to add !"
138               lblTitle.ForeColor = Drawing.Color.Red
139           End If
140
141       End Sub
```

Figure CS1.22 *Click* event of the *Add To Cart* button.

Figure CS1.22 Explained:

As with the *Select All* button code, we iterate over all rows of the *grdBookSearchResults* (lines 123–132). For each row where the check box is checked (lines 127–131), we add the ISBN of the corresponding book to the cart (line 130). *AddToCart* is the member function that takes the book ISBN to add as an input parameter. After going over all the books in the *grdBookSearchResults*, if the cart is not empty (line 134), we redirect the user to the "ShoppingCart.aspx" page (line 135). If the user tries to add books to the cart without any selection in the *grdBookSearchResults*, we display an error message in line 137. The *Cart_Empty* is also a member function. The function, when called, determines if the cart is currently empty or not. We now discuss the *AddToCart* and *Cart_Empty* functions in detail.

CS1.4.6   Simulating Shopping Cart Using Session Variables

The *AddToCart* member function takes the ISBN of the book the user intends to add to the cart. The selected book is added to the cart by storing its ISBN in a session variable. *Session variables* are Web variables that allow us to store and retrieve data, similar to a variable in the programming language. These variables are initialized using a keyword *Session*. Session variables store any value assigned to them in a text format. The value of a session variable is valid as long as the user's browser or *session* is open. Another advantage of session variables is that they are automatically initialized for each new session. If multiple users access the same application in different browser windows, multiple session variables will be initialized. This feature is useful to support the personalized view of an online shopping cart.

For this application, we store a string of comma-separated ISBNs in the session variable. As the user adds a book to the cart, we append the book's ISBN to the string of existing ISBNs. The *AddToCart* function code is shown in Figure CS1.23. Lines 37–41 check if the session variable "*UserCart*" is empty. If it is non-empty, we retrieve already added ISBNs (line 38) and append the input ISBN to it. We assign the new, appended string back to the session variable (line 42).

```
33    'Stores the ISBN book values in the Session Variable.
34    'The Shopping cart is hence maintained in the Session state
35    Private Sub AddToCart(ByVal strISBN As String)
36        Dim strCart As String
37        If Not Session("UserCart") Is Nothing Then
38            strCart = Session("UserCart").ToString
39        Else
40            strCart = ""
41        End If
42        Session("UserCart") = strCart & strISBN & ","
43    End Sub

45    Private Function Cart_Empty() As Boolean
46        If Not Session("UserCart") Is Nothing Then
47            If Session("UserCart").ToString = "" Then
48                Return True
49            Else
50                Return False
51            End If
52        Else
53            Return True
54        End If
55    End Function
```

Figure CS1.23 *AddToCart* and *Empty_Cart* member functions.

The *Empty_Cart* function is a Boolean function that returns *True* if the cart is currently empty. If the session variable is not defined before (check in line 46) or it is defined and is empty (check in line 47), we return *True*; otherwise, we return *False* (see Figure CS1.23).

CS1.5 *The Shopping Cart Page*

The shopping cart page displays the user's book selection so far—the items the user has added to the cart using the index page. The snapshot of ShoppingCart.aspx is shown in Figure CS1.24.

The ISBNs for the books to be displayed on the shopping cart page are first retrieved from the *UserCart* session variable. Using these ISBNs, we avail book information from the database and display it to the user in a GridView control, *grdShoppingCart*. The *grdShoppingCart* is set up just like the *grdBookSearchResults* grid view on the index page. The DropDownList control column, *Quantity*, however, is added as an *ItemTemplate* field in the *Columns* property dialog box of the *grdShoppingCart*. We then open the HTML source code and locate the *grdShoppingCart* tag to add the template code. We add a ComboBox control to the template as shown in Figure CS1.25.

Figure CS1.24 The ShoppingCart.aspx page.

```
<asp:TemplateField HeaderText="Quantity" FooterText="Total Amount">
    <ItemTemplate>
        <asp:DropDownList ID="cboQuantity" runat="server" AutoPostBack="True"
        OnSelectedIndexChanged="cboQuantity_SelectedIndexChanged">
            <asp:ListItem Selected="True">1</asp:ListItem>
            <asp:ListItem>2</asp:ListItem>
            <asp:ListItem>3</asp:ListItem>
            <asp:ListItem>4</asp:ListItem>
            <asp:ListItem>5</asp:ListItem>
        </asp:DropDownList>
    </ItemTemplate>
    <HeaderStyle HorizontalAlign="Left" />
    <ItemStyle HorizontalAlign="Left" />
</asp:TemplateField>
```

Figure CS1.25 *Quantity* column's *ItemTemplate*.

Table CS1.2 Access queries for the shopping cart page.

Query Name	Query Function	SQL Statements
qryGetBooksAddedToCart	Fetching all books added to the cart	SELECT ISBN, Title, retPrice, Price, './images/thumbnails/'+[ISBN]+'.gif' AS ThumbNail FROM tblBooks WHERE [?ISBN] Like ('%'+[ISBN]+',%');
qryActionReduceStock	Reduce the stock for the books added to the cart	UPDATE tblBooks SET AmountInStock = (AmountInStock-[?Quantity]) WHERE ISBN=[?ISBN];
qryGetLastTransID	Get the last transaction ID	SELECT Max(TransID) FROM tblTransactions;
qryAction_NewTransaction Detail	Insert shopping cart book details	INSERT INTO tblTransactionDetails (transID, ISBN, Quantity) SELECT [transID], [ISBN], [Quantity];

The data source of the *grdShoppingCart* is the *dbBookstore* AccessDataSource that hosts the Parameter SQL query "qryGetBooksAddedToCart" listed in Table CS1.2. When the shopping cart page is loaded, we assign the UserCart session variable as an input to dbBookstore's parameter query (see Figure CS1.26).

```
99   'This event is invoked every time the page is loaded
100  Protected Sub Page_Load(ByVal sender As Object, _
101  ByVal e As System.EventArgs) Handles Me.Load
102      If Not IsPostBack Then
103          If Not Session("UserCart") Is Nothing Then
104              dbBookStore.SelectCommand = _
105              "exec qryGetBooksAddedToCart '" & _
106              Session("UserCart").ToString & "'"
107          End If
108      End If
109  End Sub
```

Figure CS1.26 *Page_Load* event code for the shopping cart page.

Also, every time we refresh *dbBookstore's SelectCommand*, we calculate the total value of the shopping cart and display it to the user at the bottom of the book listing (see Figure CS1.27). We access each row of the *grdShoppingCart* (line 177). For each row accessed, we get its *Amount* column's cell value (line 178). We sum all amounts to calculate the total amount.

```
171  'Invoked when grid's databinding is refreshed
172  Protected Sub grdShoppingCart_DataBound(ByVal sender As Object, _
173  ByVal e As System.EventArgs) Handles grdShoppingCart.DataBound
174      Dim row As GridViewRow
175      Dim totalAmount As Decimal
176      'Sum the "Amount" of each row to get the "Total amount"
177      For Each row In grdShoppingCart.Rows
178          totalAmount += CDbl(row.Cells(COL_AMOUNT).Text)
179      Next
180      lblTotalAmount.Text = totalAmount.ToString
181  End Sub
```

Figure CS1.27 *DataBound* event of the AccessDataSource.

The shopping cart page allows the user to change the quantity of selected books using the *Quantity* DropDownList control column. If the DropDownList control value is changed for any book row, we update its *Amount* column as well as the *Total Amount* field on the page (see Figure CS1.28).

```
111    'Invoked when any of the GridView's combo box value is changed.
112    Protected Sub cboQuantity_SelectedIndexChanged(ByVal sender _
113    As Object, ByVal e As System.EventArgs)
114        Dim ShoppingCartRow As GridViewRow
115        Dim strISEN As String
116        Dim newQuantity As Integer
117        Dim price, total, oldAmount As Double
118
119        ShoppingCartRow = CType(CType(sender, DropDownList).Parent. _
120        Parent, GridViewRow)
121
122        'Get current state of the row and total amount
123        strISBN = ShoppingCartRow.Cells(COL_ISBN).Text
124        oldAmount = CDbl(ShoppingCartRow.Cells(COL_AMOUNT).Text)
125        price = CDbl(ShoppingCartRow.Cells(COL_PRICE).Text)
126        newQuantity = CInt(CType(ShoppingCartRow.Cells(COL_QUANTITY). _
127        FindControl("cboQuantity"), DropDownList).SelectedValue)
128        total = CDbl(lblTotalAmount.Text)
129
130        'Update the TotalAmount for newQuantity
131        total -= oldAmount
132        ShoppingCartRow.Cells(COL_AMOUNT).Text = price * newQuantity
133        lblTotalAmount.Text = total + (price * newQuantity)
134    End Sub
```

Figure CS1.28 *SelectedIndexChanged* event of a *Quantity* DropDownList control.

Figure CS1.28 Explained:

The *SelectedIndexChanged* event is invoked when a new quantity value is selected for *any* of the DropDownList controls in the *Quantity* column. The event is invoked with the "sender" object as an input parameter to the event subroutine (line 112). This object is a changed DropDownList control on *grdShoppingCart*. We obtain the grid row of a changed DropDownList control in line 119–120. The parent of the DropDownList control object is the cell object of the grid, and the parent of the cell object is the row object of the grid. We then obtain various values from the *grdShoppingCart*'s row in lines 123–128 and use them to calculate the new amount (line 132) and, thus, the new total amount (line 133).

The shopping cart page also allows the user to remove items from the shopping cart. The user checks the items to remove in the last check box column, *Remove*, of the *grdShoppingCart*. The checked items are removed on the click of the *Remove Items* button (see Figure CS1.29). To remove the checked books from the cart (line 144–145), we remove their ISBNs from the *UserCart* session variable (line 148) and hide the corresponding row in the *grdShoppingCart* (line 151). We update the total amount on the page by subtracting the amount associated with the deleted items (line 149–150).

The *RemoveFromCart* is the member function that takes the ISBN to remove as an input parameter. The code for the member function is depicted in Figure CS1.30. We use the *Replace* method of the *String* class to replace the *strISBN* with an empty string in line 26.

```
136        'Invoked when user clicks the remove button
137    Protected Sub imgRemove_Click(ByVal sender As Object, ByVal e _
138    As System.Web.UI.ImageClickEventArgs) Handles imgRemove.Click
139        Dim row As GridViewRow
140        Dim bSelected As Boolean
141        Dim strISBN As String
142        'Remove the selected books
143        For Each row In grdShoppingCart.Rows
144            bSelected = CType(row.Cells(COL_SELECTED).FindControl _
145            ("chkSelected"), CheckBox).Checked
146            If bSelected Then
147                strISBN = row.Cells(COL_ISBN).Text
148                RemoveFromCart(strISBN)
149                lblTotalAmount.Text = CStr(CDbl(lblTotalAmount.Text) _
150                - CDbl(row.Cells(COL_AMOUNT).Text))
151                row.Visible = False
152            End If
153        Next
154    End Sub
```

Figure CS1.29 *Click* event of the *Remove Item* button.

```
21        'Remove the strISBN from UserCart session variable
22    Private Sub RemoveFromCart(ByVal strISBN As String)
23        Dim strCart As String
24        If Not Session("UserCart") Is Nothing Then
25            strCart = Session("UserCart").ToString
26            strCart = strCart.Replace(strISBN + ",", "")
27            Session("UserCart") = strCart
28        End If
29    End Sub
```

Figure CS1.30 *RemoveFromCart* member function.

The shopping cart page enables the user to shop more and add new books to the shopping cart. With the *Continue Shopping* button, we redirect the user to the "Index.aspx" page. Finally, if the user decides to check out books currently in the cart, we provide checkout functionality on the click of the *Proceed To Checkout* button (see Figure CS1.31). Specifically, we perform the following four operations: (1) for each book in the shopping cart, we deduct the quantity purchased from the units in stock (a call to *ReduceInventory* member function in line 165); (2) save the transaction details such as ISBNs and quantities of purchased books (a call to *SaveTransactionDetails* member function in line 166); (3) save the total order amount in the session variable so that it is accessible on the checkout page (line 167); and (4) redirect the user to the login page for authentication (line 168). The *ReduceInventory* and *SaveTransactionDetails* member functions are depicted in Figure CS1.32 and Figure CS1.33, respectively.

```
162        'Invoked when user clicks the checkout button
163    Protected Sub imgCheckout_Click(ByVal sender As Object, ByVal e _
164    As System.Web.UI.ImageClickEventArgs) Handles imgCheckout.Click
165        ReduceInventory()
166        SaveTransactionDetails()
167        Session("TotalAmount") = lblTotalAmount.Text
168        Response.Redirect("Login.aspx")
169    End Sub
```

Figure CS1.31 *Click* event of the *Proceed To Checkout* button.

```
31   'Reduce inventory from tblBooks
32   Private Sub ReduceInventory()
33       Dim row As GridViewRow
34       Dim dsReduceInventory As New AccessDataSource
35       Dim quantity As Integer
36       dsReduceInventory.DataFile = DATA_FILE
37       For Each row In grdShoppingCart.Rows
38           quantity = CInt(CType(row.Cells(COL_QUANTITY).FindControl _
39           ("cboQuantity"), DropDownList).SelectedValue)
40           dsReduceInventory.UpdateCommand = _
41           "exec qryActionReduceStock '" & CStr(quantity) & "','" _
42           & row.Cells(COL_ISBN).Text & "'"
43           dsReduceInventory.Update()
44       Next
45   End Sub
```

Figure CS1.32 *ReduceInventory* member function.

Figure CS1.32 Explained:

For each row of the *grdShoppingCart* (line 37), i.e., for each book in the cart, we reduce the *AmountInStock* value in the *tblBook* by the number of books selected by the user for purchase (line 38–19). The database table update is performed by executing the Access Update query "qry-ActionReduceStock" (see Table CS1.2) for each book in the cart. The update parameters, ISBN and the quantity to reduce, are supplied in lines 41–42. The Access query is executed using an AccessDataSource object created in line 34. We set its *DataFile* (line 36) and *UpdateCommand* (line 40) properties before performing updates in line 43. We refer the reader to the "Member Variable" code region in the "ShoppingCart.aspx.vb" file for the DATA_FILE, COL_ISBN, and COL_QUANTITY variables.

```
60   'STEP 1
61   queryStr = _
62   "INSERT INTO tblTransactions (TransDate, CustomerID) VALUES (" _
63   & Now.Date & ", 49)"
64   cmdQuery.CommandType = CommandType.Text
65   cmdQuery.CommandText = queryStr
66   cmdQuery.ExecuteNonQuery()
67
68   'STEP 2
69   Dim transID As Integer
70   cmdQuery.CommandType = CommandType.StoredProcedure
71   cmdQuery.CommandText = "qryGetLastTransID"
72   transID = CType(cmdQuery.ExecuteScalar, Integer)
73
74   'STEP 3
75   Dim row As GridViewRow
76   Dim dsTransactionDetails As New AccessDataSource
77   dsTransactionDetails.DataFile = DATA_FILE
78   For Each row In grdShoppingCart.Rows
79       'Only visible rows are valid rows
80       If (row.Visible) Then
81           'Execute INSERT query for each valid row
82           dsTransactionDetails.UpdateCommand = _
83           "exec qryAction_NewTransactionDetail '" & transID.ToString _
84           & "','" & row.Cells(COL_ISBN).Text & "','" & CType(row. _
85           Cells(COL_QUANTITY).FindControl("cboQuantity"), _
86           DropDownList).SelectedValue & "'"
87           dsTransactionDetails.Update()
88       End If
89   Next
```

Figure CS1.33 *SaveTransactionDetails* member function.

Figure CS1.33 Explained:

Inserting the transaction and transaction detail information in *tblTransaction* and *tblTransaction-Details* tables, respectively, is a three-step process. In Step 1, we insert a transaction into *tblTransaction* with the current date and a dummy *CustomerID* (lines 60–66). We update the dummy *CustomerID* in this table once the user authenticates herself on the login page. We use the *cmdQuery*, an *oleDbCommand* object, to execute this insert query. In Step 2, we obtain the auto-generated transaction ID for the newly inserted transaction in the *tblTransaction*. This time we use the *cmdQuery* object with the existing stored procedure (an Access query) "qryGetLastTransID" (see Table CS1.2) in lines 70–71. The *ExecuteScalar* option is used because the query output is known to be a single identification number (line 72). In Step 3, we insert transaction details such as transaction ID, books purchased, and their quantities (lines 83–86) in the *tblTransactionDetails*. We use the Access Parameter query "qryAction_NewTransactionDetail" (see Table CS1.2) to insert values in the target table. This time we use an AccessDataSource, *dsTransactionDetails*, to perform the insert operation (lines 75–89).

Note that we have used the *oleDbCommand* object in Steps 1 and 2 of Figure CS1.33. In order to use this object, we must import it (see Figure CS1.34(a)). Also, when we created an Access-DataSource object in the code, we configured it using the connection and database file strings from the "web.config" file of the application (see Figure CS1.34(b)).

```
1   Imports System.Data
2   Imports System.Data.OleDb
3
4   Partial Class ShoppingCart
5       Inherits System.Web.UI.Page
```

Figure CS1.34 (a) Importing *OleDb* objects.

```
<appSettings>
<add key="ConnString" value="Provider=Microsoft.Jet.OLEDB.4.0;Data
Source=C:\webdss\casestudies\OnlineBookShopping\database\universalbooks.mdb"/>
<add key="DataBaseFile" value=".\database\universalbooks.mdb"/>
</appSettings>
```

Figure CS1.34 (b) Database connection setting in "web.config" file.

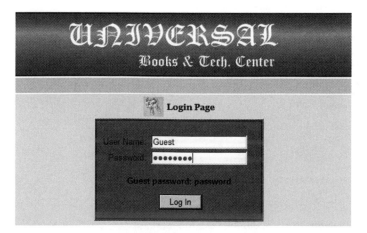

Figure CS1.35 The login page.

CS1.6 *The Login Page*

The login page authenticates the user when she tries to check out the items in her shopping cart. The page snapshot is shown in Figure CS1.35. The page first requests the user to enter the username and password and then confirms the user input against the existing username and password pair in the database table. If confirmed, the user is redirected to the "Checkout.aspx" page for checkout. If the authentication fails, an error message is shown to the user (see Figure CS1.36).

```
7     Dim connString As String = _
8     ConfigurationSettings.AppSettings("ConnString")
9
10    'This event is invoked when user clicks Login button
11    Protected Sub LoginButton_Click(ByVal sender As Object, ByVal e _
12    As System.EventArgs) Handles LoginButton.Click
13        'Verify if user's credentials password/username pair
14        Dim custID As Integer
15        Dim qryStr As String = ""
16        Dim connDb As OleDbConnection
17        connDb = New OleDbConnection(connString)
18        connDb.Open()
19        Dim cmdQuery As OleDbCommand
20        cmdQuery = New OleDbCommand(qryStr, connDb)
21        cmdQuery.CommandType = CommandType.StoredProcedure
22        qryStr = "qryUsernamePassword '" & UserName.Text & "','" _
23        & Password.Text & "'"
24        cmdQuery.CommandText = qryStr
25        custID = CType(cmdQuery.ExecuteScalar, Integer)
26        connDb.Close()
27        If custID <> 0 Then
28            Session("CustomerID") = custID
29            Response.Redirect("Checkout.aspx")
30        Else
31            lblErrorMessage.Visible = True
32        End If
33    End Sub
```

Figure CS1.36 *Click* event of the *Login* button.

Figure CS1.36 Explained:

We executed the Access Parameter query "qryUsernamePassword" (see Table CS1.3) that takes username and password as its parameters and returns a *CustomerID* that satisfies the query criteria (lines 22–23). If a match is not found, the query returns "0." The query is executed using the *OleDbCommand* object, and its scalar output is checked in line 27. A valid *CustomerID* is stored in the session variable (line 28), and the user is redirected to the checkout page (line 29).

CS1.7 *The Checkout Page*

The checkout page requests that the user enter personal and payment information that is required to process the order. The information includes customer name, shipping address, and credit card information. The snapshot the checkout page is shown in Figure CS1.37.

Figure CS1.37 The checkout page.

The user input is validated using validation controls. We use *RequiredFieldValidator* for each control on the page and *RegularExpressionValidator* for the *Zip* TextBox control. When the user clicks the *Submit* button, the order and payment information is updated in the *tblTransaction*. Upon successful database update, we display a confirmation message to the user (see Figure CS1.38). We now present the *Click* event of the *Submit* button (see Figure CS1.39) and the related *SubmitOrder* function (see Figure CS1.40).

Figure CS1.38 Order confirmation message.

```
39  Protected Sub btnTrans_Click(ByVal sender As Object, _
40  ByVal e As System.EventArgs) Handles btnTrans.Click
41      pnlCheckOut.Visible = False
42      pnlOrderConfirmation.Visible = True
43      If SubmitOrder() Then
44          lblConfirmationMessage.Text = _
45          "<br>Thanks for shopping with us<br>"
46          lblConfirmationMessage.Text += _
47          "<br>Your Confirmation number is  UFRIG PYTR" & 10000 * Rnd()
48          lblConfirmationMessage.Text += _
49          "<br>Write it down or print it out for your record.<br>"
50      Else
51          lblConfirmationMessage.Text = _
52          "Some error occured, please try over again"
53      End If
54
55  End Sub
```

Figure CS1.39 *Click* event of the *Submit* button.

Figure CS1.39 Explained:

There are two different Panel controls in the checkout page. The *pnlCheckout* panel contains the user input controls, and the *pnlOrderConfirmation* panel displays the confirmation message to the user. On the click of the *Submit* button, we make the *pnlOrderConfirmation* panel visible (line 42) and call the Boolean member function *SubmitOrder* (explained next) in line 43 to submit the order. If the order submission is successful, we print the confirmation message to the *lblConfirmation-Message* TextBox control (lines 44–49).

```
12  Private Function SubmitOrder() As Boolean
13      If Session("CustomerID") Is Nothing _
14      Or Session("transID") Is Nothing Then
15          Return False
16      End If
17      Dim dsUpdateTransactionDetails As New AccessDataSource
18      dsUpdateTransactionDetails.DataFile = DATA_FILE
19      dsUpdateTransactionDetails.UpdateCommand = _
20      "exec qryAction_UpdateTransaction '" & Now.ToShortDateString & _
21      "','" & CInt(Session("CustomerID")) & "','" & _
22      cboCardType.SelectedValue & "','" & txtCardNo.Text & "','" & _
23      Me.cboMonth.SelectedValue & "/" & Me.cboYear.SelectedValue & _
24      "','" & Session("TotalAmount").ToString & "','" & _
25      Session("transID").ToString & "'"
26      dsUpdateTransactionDetails.Update()
27      Return True
28  End Function
```

Figure CS1.40 The *SubmitOrder* member function.

Figure CS1.40 Explained:

The *SubmitOrder* member function actually inserts the checkout information in the *tblTransaction*. The function makes use of the Access Parameter query "qryAction_UpdateTransaction" (see Table CS1.3) to update the table (lines 19–25). The parameters of this query are user input values and three session variables for total order amount, customer ID, and transaction ID fields. Lines 12–16 invalidate the transaction if the session variables, *CustomerID* and *transID*, are invalid. This validation is useful when the user accidentally accesses the checkout page without visiting prior pages. No order will be submitted in this scenario.

Table CS1.3 Access queries for the login and checkout pages.

Query Name	Query Function	SQL Statements
QrypasswordQuery Customer	Verify user authenticity	SELECT CustomerID FROM tblCustomers WHERE Username=[?username] AND Password=[?password];
qryAction_Update Transaction	Update Transaction details	UPDATE tblTransactions SET CustomerID = [?customerID], CardType = [?cardType], CardNumber = [?cardNumber], CardExpiration = [?cardExpiration], OrderAmount = [?OrderAmount] WHERE TransID=[?transID];

CS1.8 *Summary*

- "Online Book Store" is an ASP .NET case study featuring Universal Books and Tech. Center's Web site.
- Although the application is a simple version of a real-life online bookstore, it provides myriad functionalities to its users including the following: book search, detail view of book information, adding selected books to the online shopping cart, editing orders, authenticating user information, and checkout and payment functionalities.
- We introduce and illustrate the concept of Session Variables and Master Page in this case study. A session variable can be thought of as a variable in programming languages that gets initialized by an event on a Web page and holds the desired piece of information until the Web browser is open.
- A master page is the template to all Web pages of an application. A master page typically contains page header, page footer, logos, and page navigation menu. A master page not only offers a uniform view of Web pages, but also provides a single editing interface.

CS1.9 *Extensions*

1. The index page permits users to add books to the shopping cart. In the current design, the user can view the shopping cart only when she adds books to the cart. In this extension, we provide an additional button, "View Cart," on the index page, which will allow the user to view her existing items in the cart.

2. As discussed in Section CS1.2, we currently do not have the support to register a new customer on the shopping Web site. Add this functionality to the login page. Add a button "Register a New User," which should open a new page and ask the user for necessary registration information. Add validation controls to username and password fields and store the input information in appropriate database tables.

3. We further extend the functionality built in Extension 2. Upon successful registration, we redi-rect the user to the checkout page and direct her toward completion of her order.

4. The current application is mainly designed for customers. In this extension, we add a product entry page to the application. Assume that only administration personnel have access to this page. On the product entry page, we permit administration personnel to enter a new book in the database. Use appropriate controls and validations to add a new book entry (make this page accessible through the index page).

5. As an additional support for the administrative personnel, we also add a Web page through which we allow them to search books and update the book inventory (make this page accessible through the index page).

two Portfolio Management and Optimization

CS2.1 *Introduction*

This case study allows users to create and/or edit their portfolio as well as optimize their investments. To create a portfolio, users can choose from a list of stocks in an Access database and add them to or remove them from their portfolio. The stocks are listed by name and category. These stocks can also be compared using their historical annual returns and changes in market price. Once users have created their portfolio, they may also edit it at any time. Users may then optimize their investment by specifying a desired return on their portfolio and the amount available for investing. The application solves an optimization problem that minimizes users' risk on their selected portfolio. The suggested investment strategy is then displayed to the users. The model base for this DSS uses a heuristic algorithm coded in VB .NET to perform an optimization that minimizes the users' risk on the portfolio investments. (To find out more about calculating risk by variance in market price, please refer to the book *Investment Science* by Luenberger.) This application also allows users to interact with the database of stock information and the knowledge base of comparative statistics.

   The case study code and the complete application can be found on the book Web site. We strongly recommend that readers download and install the case study and browse through the application pages before going through the details described in this chapter. We also recommend that readers open the Portfolio database file and study its Relationships window (see Figure CS2.1). The database features three main tables to store information about investors, their portfolios, and available stocks. The other two tables of the database store historical stock data and details of each portfolio created by an investor.

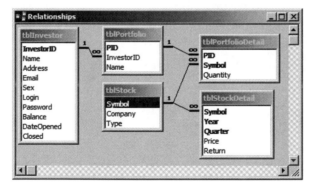

Figure CS2.1 The Relationships window for the *Portfolio* database.

CS2.2 *Application Functionalities and Assumptions*

The Portfolio application supports numerous functionalities to manage and optimize investment portfolios. The application also introduces two new concepts: the Menu control and how to write optimization codes in VB .NET. We also extensively use Session Variables, introduced in the Book Store case study chapter (Case Study 1). The portfolio management and optimization-related functionalities are listed as follows:

Login: Investors (users) must log in using their user name and password to enter the personalized Web site. Only the stock comparison page is accessible without user login. For all other pages of the application, users must log in to view personalized Web pages. As with the previous case study, we left the task of user registration as a part of the case study extensions.

Personal Information: The application allows investors (users) to view and edit their personal information. The personal information includes fields such as name, address, email, account balance, user name, and password. The account balance field dictates the amount investors can invest in buying different stocks for their portfolios, whereas the user name and password are used to authenticate investors.

Portal Page: The Portal page is a one-stop review page for investors. After successful login, investors are directed to their individual personal portal page, where they can view their existing portfolios and portfolio details such as stock symbols, companies, and stock quantity owned. Investors have options to edit, delete, and optimize any of the selected portfolios through the Portal page. Finally, their page displays a pie chart for logged-in investors, summarizing their investment in different portfolios.

Portfolio Operations: This application supports these portfolio-related operations: create new portfolio, add stocks to existing or newly created portfolio, delete selected stocks from existing portfolios, and update quantities of stocks in existing portfolios. The portfolio operation page provides all these functionalities.

Compare Stocks: This is one of the most important functionalities of the application. Investors must be able to compare various available stocks in the database before deciding whether to add them to existing portfolios. We compute and display the average price and average return for each selected stock. Users can select multiple stocks (one at a time) to compare their statistics. We also display a line chart for each selected stock showing the stock's historical price and return values for the last five years.

Portfolio Optimization: With multiple stocks added to a portfolio, users can optimize the investment in each of the selected stocks (i.e., determine the optimal number of stocks to purchase). Portfolio optimization takes the total amount to invest and the maximum risk investors are willing to accept as inputs and it returns the investment amount in each stock such that the total returns are maximized.

Master Page: The master page for this application features the top banner of the application and the navigation menu on the left. The master page introduces the Menu control used to build the navigation menu.

CS2.2.1 The Application Flow

The flow of the *Portfolio Management and Optimization* application is depicted in Figure CS2.2.

The navigational menu gives access to all Web pages of the application. The Problem Information or Login page gives a problem description and lets investors log in to the system. All Web pages except the Compare Stock page require user login. On successful login, users are redirected to the Portal page. The Portal page gives users the options of editing and optimizing portfolios. The Edit and Add portfolio operations are supported on a single Web page, *PortOps.aspx*. We will discuss the design of these pages in the remainder of this case study.

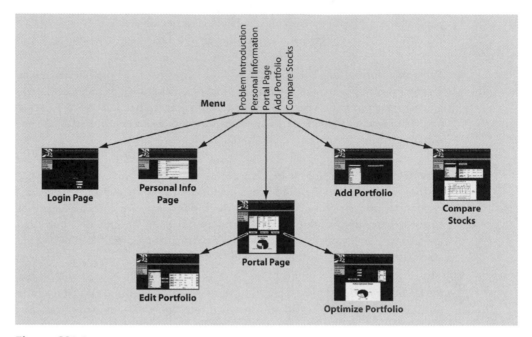

Figure CS2.2 The application flow.

CS2.3   *The Master Page*

A master page is the template for all Web pages of an application. The master page for the Portfolio application is shown in Figure CS2.3. We introduced master pages in the previous case study chapter. Refer to Section CS1.3 for details on how to add a master page to the Web application and to Section CS1.4.1 for how to add master page content to a Web page designer. The master page of the Portfolio case study features a top banner and a navigational menu. We have used the HTML table structure and image controls to design the top banner. The navigational menu introduces a new Web control, Menu control. We discuss the Menu control in this section.

Figure CS2.3 The master page for the Portfolio application.

Figure CS2.4 Adding a Menu control to the Web page.

The Menu control is available under the *Navigation* tab in the Toolbox (see Figure CS2.4). We add a Menu control to the Web page just like any other Web control and use the Property Window to add menu items to the Menu control. We would like to add links shown in Figure CS2.3 to the Menu control. Each link should open the respective page on a click.

■ How-to: add and set an item link to the Menu control.
  1. Add a Menu control from the *Navigation* tab of the Toolbox on the Web page (see Figure CS2.4).
  2. Select the Menu control and open the Property Window. Click on the *Items* property collection to open the *Menu Item Editor* dialog box (see Figure CS2.5).
  3. Use the *Items* toolbar to add nodes and sub-nodes (menus and sub-menus) to the Menu control.
  4. Use the *Properties* area to assign *NavigateUrl* and *Text* to each menu. Click *OK* to return to the Web page. We can use the *Build* button available in the *NavigateUrl* property line to browse existing files in the application folder.

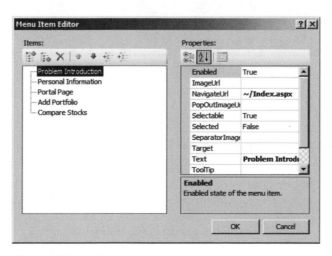

Figure CS2.5 *Menu Item Editor* dialog box to add and manipulate menu items.

CS2.4   *The Index Page*

The Index page is the starting page of the application. A snapshot of the Index page is shown in Figure CS2.6. The Index page gives a problem description and lets investors (or users) log in to the system. Users must be registered in the database before they can log in (see the Extension section at the end of the case study chapter). The login code is very similar to the code we discussed in the Book Store case study. Refer to Section CS1.6 for details of the login logic and code explanation.

If we open the code behind the Index page, we will find that after successful login, we store the unique identification number of each investor, *InvestorID*, in a Session variable. The identification number is used on subsequent Web pages to retrieve personalized information for logged-in investors. Refer to Section CS1.4.6 for an introduction to Session variables.

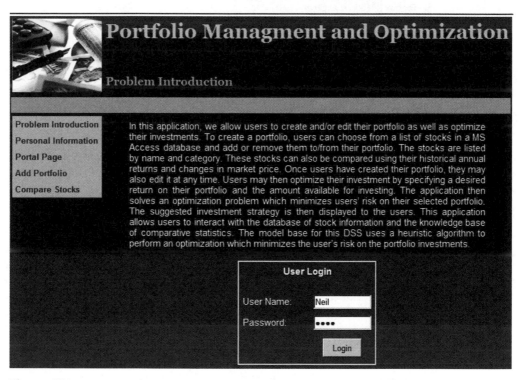

Figure CS2.6   The Index page (problem introduction and user login).

CS2.5   *The Personal Information Page*

The Personal Information page displays personal information such as name, address, email, account balance, user name, and password for logged-in investors. A snapshot of the page is shown in Figure CS2.8. The page makes use of the *InvestorID*, stored in the Session variable, to display personal information to users. Users can also edit and update displayed information.

Figure CS2.7 The Personal Information page.

The AccessDataSource control used for this page is set up using the following SQL query.

```
SELECT    Name, Sex, Address, Email, Balance, Login, Password, InvestorID
FROM      tblInvestor
WHERE     InvestorID =?
```

The only parameter of the query, *InvestorID*, gets its value from the *InvestorID* Session variable. We also create an update and insert query for the AccessDataSource control in the *Configure Data Sources* Wizard. If the Session variable is not defined or is empty, we redirect users to the Login page. This code is assigned to the *Page_Load* event of the Web page as shown in Figure CS2.8. Also, note that in the Figure CS2.8, we use another Session variable, *PageTitle*, in line 8. The master page uses this Session variable to assign the page title. For every Web page of the application, we set this Session variable to display the appropriate page title in the master page's top banner.

```
 5  Protected Sub Page_Load(ByVal sender As Object, _
 6  ByVal e As System.EventArgs) Handles Me.Load
 7      If Not Session("InvestorID") Is Nothing Then
 8          Session("PageTitle") = "Personal Information"
 9      Else
10          Response.Redirect("Index.aspx")
11      End If
12  End Sub
```

Figure CS2.8 *Page_Load* event of the Personal Information page.

We then add a DetailsView control to the page to display the contents. In the Tasks list of the DetailsView control, we assign the data source of the DetailsView control and enable the editing option.

CS2.6 *The Stock Comparison Page*

This application allows investors to compare stock performances using the Stock Comparison pages before they add them to one or more of their portfolios (see Figure CS2.9).

Figure CS2.9 The Stock Comparison page.

The Stock Comparison page provides the following functionalities:

1. It displays all the available stocks and stock categories on the page for investors to select from (the ComboBox and ListBox controls).
2. It displays the required information, average price, and average return values for all selected stocks for comparison (the DataGridView control).
3. It shows the historical price and return values for the currently selected stock on a line chart (the Crystal Report and CrystalReportViewer control).
4. Users can clear the selected stocks and the line chart and start over.

We now discuss the design setup and code behind the Stock Comparison page.

We set the ComboBox control *cmbType* at design time with various values for the stock categories. As users choose a category value (or the *All* option) from the ComboBox control, we display the stock from the selected category in the ListBox control. The AccessDataSource

Table CS2.1 Various queries for the Stock Comparison page.

Control/Query Name	Function	Command
AccessDataSource: *dsStock*	Fetch all the stock names for the category in the *cmbType* ComboBox control	SELECT Type, Symbol, Company FROM tblStock WHERE Type LIKE '%' + ? + '%'; [*parameter value*: *cmbType*.SelectedValue]
AccessDataSource: *dsStockComparisonData*	Fetch stock details for all the stocks in the Session variable *Stocks*	exec qryGetStockComparisonData '" & Session("Stocks").ToString & "'";
MS Access: *qryGetStockComparisonData*	Fetch stock details for all the stocks in the Session variable *Stocks*	SELECT tblStock .Symbol, Company,Type, Round(Avg(Price),2) AS [Avg Price], Round(Avg(Return)*100,2) AS [Avg Return] FROM tblStock, tblStockDetail WHERE tblStock.Symbol = tblStockDetail.Symbol GROUP BY tblStock.Symbol, Company, Type HAVING ([?Symbol]) Like ('%'+[tblStock.Symbol]+',%');
MS Access: *qryStockPerformance*	Fetch all stock prices and return values for the selected stock	SELECT Symbol, Year, Quarter, Price, 100*Return AS Returns FROM tblStockDetail;

dsStock is used to source the ListBox control. Table CS2.1 shows the Select command for the *dsStock* AccessDataSource and its details. Next, as users select stocks from the ListBox control, we add those stocks and their performance details to the DataGridView control. The AccessDataSource *dsStockComparisonData* is used to source the DataGridView control. Table CS2.1 shows the Select command for the *dsStockComparisonData* AccessDataSource and its details.

Figure CS2.10 shows the *SelectIndexChanged* event of the ListBox control. Every time users select a stock in the ListBox control, we append the selected stock to the Session variable "Stocks" (lines 17–22). We then refresh the Select command of the *dsStockComparisonData* AccessDataSource with the Session variable value (lines 23–25). Appending stocks to the Session variable and using the appending string in the query execution is similar to appending a book's ISBN to the Session variable and using it to populate the shopping cart, as shown in the Book Store case study (Case Study 1—refer to Section CS1.5 for details).

```
14  Protected Sub lstStock_SelectedIndexChanged _
15    (ByVal sender As Object, ByVal e As System.EventArgs) _
16    Handles lstStock.SelectedIndexChanged
17      If Not Session("Stocks") Is Nothing Then
18        Session("Stocks") = Session("Stocks").ToString _
19          & lstStock.SelectedValue & ","
20      Else
21        Session("Stocks") = lstStock.SelectedValue & ","
22      End If
23      dsStockComparisonData.SelectCommand = _
24        "exec qryGetStockComparisonData '" & _
25        Session("Stocks").ToString & "'"
26      BindReport(lstStock.SelectedValue)
27  End Sub
```

Figure CS2.10 *SelectIndexChanged* event of the ListBox control.

Note that in line 26 of Figure CS2.10, we refresh the line chart for the selected stock in the ListBox control. This is done by calling a *BindReport* subroutine, as shown in Figure CS2.11.

```
45   Sub BindReport(ByVal symbol As String)
46       Dim myConnection As New OleDbConnection
47       Dim myCommand As New OleDbCommand
48       Dim myDA As New OleDbDataAdapter
49       Dim myDS As New DataSet
50
51       myConnection.ConnectionString = _
52       ConfigurationManager.AppSettings("connString")
53       myCommand.Connection = myConnection
54       myCommand.CommandText = "Select * from qryStockPerformance " _
55       & "where Symbol = '" & symbol & "'"
56       myCommand.CommandType = CommandType.Text
57       myDA.SelectCommand = myCommand
58       myCommand.Connection.Open()
59       myDA.Fill(myDS, "qryStockPerformance")
60       Dim oRpt As New CrystalDecisions.CrystalReports.Engine.ReportDocument
61       oRpt.FileName = "C:\webdss\casestudies\Portfolio\rptStockPerformance.rpt"
62       oRpt.SetDataSource(myDS)
63       rptViewer1.ReportSource = oRpt
64       myCommand.Connection.Close()
65   End Sub
```

Figure CS2.11 *BindReport* subroutine.

Figure CS2.11 Explained:

We use an OleDbAdapter object (line 48) and a DataSet object (line 49) to provide the data for the Crystal Report. In lines 51–53, we set the connection object, and in line 54, we set the command text of the adapter object. We execute the query *qryStockPerformace* (see Table CS2.1) with the stock value for which we wish to display the line chart as its parameter. We execute the query and fill the DataSet object in line 59. The report object, *oRpt*, is set in line 60–62. The Crystal Report, *rptStockPerformace*, is added to the project at design time (refer to Chapter 19 for details). For the report object, we specify the file name and the data source (the DataSet object). Finally, we bind the report object to the CrystalReportViewer control in line 63.

Figure CS2.12 A snapshot of the *Portal* page.

CS2.7 *The Portal Page*

The Portal page is the heart of the Portfolio application. The page lists the portfolios and their details for the logged-in investors. It also shows investors a pie chart of their investment in various portfolios and lets investors edit, delete, or optimize existing portfolios. A snapshot of the Portal page is shown in Figure CS2.12. In this section, we discuss the design setup and code behind the portal page.

The Portal page design involves a ListBox control (*lstPort*) to display the list of all portfolios for logged-in investors, a DataGridView control (*grdPortDetails*) to display the details of the portfolio selected in the *lstPort*, a CrystalReportViewer control (*rptViewer1*) to display the pie chart of logged-in users' investments, and three Button controls to let investors edit, delete, and optimize the portfolio selected in the *lstPort*. We use two AccessDataSource controls (*dsPortfolio* and *dsPortfolioDetails*) to provide the data for the *lstPort* and *grdPortDetails* controls. The data for the pie chart is provided by the OleDbAdapter and DataSet objects created at run-time. We give the details of the queries used to design these data sources in Table CS2.2.

We now discuss the event handler code behind the Portal page. We discuss four events: the *Page_Load* event and the *Click* events of three command buttons used to edit, delete, and optimize selected portfolios. The *Page_Load* event is shown in Figure CS2.13. If the Session variable InvestorID is defined before (line 11), we assign an appropriate title to the page (line 12). If the page is getting loaded for the first time (i.e., it is not a postback), we select the first portfolio in the *lstPort* (line 18). Finally, we load the Crystal Report to display the investment pie chart. The *loadReport* subroutine is very similar to the *BindReport* subroutine discussed in Section CS2.6, Figure CS2.11, and the report file for this report (*rptPieChart.rpt*) is set at design time using the Access query *qryForOneInvID* (see Table CS2.2).

The *Click* event of the three command buttons is shown in Figure CS2.14. The edit and optimization buttons redirect investors to the portfolio operation and optimization pages, respectively (lines 26 and 32). We store the portfolio (*PID* value) to edit or optimize in the Session variable *SelectedPID* before redirection (lines 25 and 31). The click of the delete command button removes the selected portfolio from the database. We define an AccessDataSource in the code (line 38), assign a delete query to its *DeleteCommand* property (lines 41–43), and execute the query in line 44. We refresh the Portal page by self-redirection in line 46.

Table CS2.2 Various queries for the Portal page.

Control/Query Name	Function	Command
AccessDataSource: *dsPortfolio*	Fetch the list of portfolios for logged-in investors	SELECT PID, Name FROM tblPortfolio WHERE InvestorID =? [*parameter value*: Session("*InvestorID*")]
AccessDataSource: *dsPortfolioDetails*	Fetch details for the portfolio selected in the *lstPort*	SELECT Symbol, Company, Type, Quantity FROM qryGetPortfolioDetails WHERE PID =? [*parameter value*: *lstPort*.SelectedValue]
MS Access: *qryGetPortfolioDetails*	Fetch details for the portfolio selected in the *lstPort*	SELECT Symbol, Company, Type, Quantity, PID FROM tblStock, tblPortfolioDetail WHERE tblStock.Symbol = tblPortfolioDetail.Symbol;
Crystal Report: *qryForOneInvID*	Fetch investment details for logged-in investors	Refer Access database file for the query design in the Design View.

```
 9  Protected Sub Page_Load(ByVal sender As Object, _
10  ByVal e As System.EventArgs) Handles Me.Load
11      If Not Session("InvestorID") Is Nothing Then
12          Session("PageTitle") = "Investor's Portal"
13      Else
14          Response.Redirect("Index.aspx")
15      End If
16      'Select the first portfolio
17      If Not IsPostBack Then
18          lstPort.SelectedIndex = 0
19      End If
20      loadReport() 'Load the crystal report
21  End Sub
```

Figure CS2.13 *Page_Load* event of the Portal page.

```
23  Protected Sub cmdEdit_Click(ByVal sender As Object, _
24  ByVal e As System.EventArgs) Handles cmdEdit.Click
25      Session("SelectedPID") = CInt(lstPort.SelectedValue)
26      Response.Redirect("PortOps.aspx?op=Edit")
27  End Sub
28
29  Protected Sub cmdOpt_Click(ByVal sender As Object, _
30  ByVal e As System.EventArgs) Handles cmdOpt.Click
31      Session("SelectedPID") = CInt(lstPort.SelectedValue)
32      Response.Redirect("Optimization.aspx")
33  End Sub
34
35  Protected Sub cmdDelete_Click(ByVal sender As Object, _
36  ByVal e As System.EventArgs) Handles cmdDelete.Click
37      Session("SelectedPID") = CInt(lstPort.SelectedValue)
38      Dim dsDeletePortfolio As New AccessDataSource
39      Dim deleted As Integer
40      dsDeletePortfolio.DataFile = "./database/Portfolio.mdb"
41      dsDeletePortfolio.DeleteCommand = _
42      "DELETE FROM tblPortfolio WHERE InvestorID=" _
43      & Session("InvestorID") & " AND PID=" & Session("SelectedPID")
44      deleted = dsDeletePortfolio.Delete()
45      lblMsg.Text = deleted & " row(s) deleted."
46      Response.Redirect("Portal.aspx")
47  End Sub
```

Figure CS2.14 *Click* event of the command buttons.

CS2.8   *Portfolio Operations*

The *PortOps.aspx* page supports two portfolio operations—add a new portfolio and edit existing portfolio. The page allows users to create a new portfolio if the page is requested with the URL parameter "Add" and to edit an existing portfolio if the page is requested with the URL parameter "Edit." When users click the "Add Portfolio" link in the navigational menu, we redirect the users to PortOps.aspx?op=Add. Whereas, when users click the "Edit Portfolio" button on the Portal page, we redirect the users to PortOps.aspx?op=Edit. The URL parameter *op* is used to set up the *PortOps.aspx* page, as shown in Figure CS2.15.

```
14    Protected Sub Page_Load(ByVal sender As Object, _
15    ByVal e As System.EventArgs) Handles Me.Load
16        If Not Session("InvestorID") Is Nothing Then
17            Session("PageTitle") = Request.Params("op") & " Portfolio"
18            If Request.Params("op") = "Edit" Then
19                txtPortName.Visible = False
20                cmdCreate.Visible = False
21            ElseIf Request.Params("op") = "Add" Then
22                cmdAdd.Visible = False
23                cmdDelete.Visible = False
24                dgrPortDetails.Visible = False
25            End If
26            lblMsg.Text = ""
27        Else
28            Response.Redirect("Index.aspx")
29        End If
30    End Sub
```

Figure CS2.15 *Page_Load* event of the command buttons.

Figure CS2.15 Explained:

In line 16, we make sure that the Session variable *InvestorID* has a value (i.e., the user is logged in). We then use the `Request.Params` to access the value of the URL parameter *op*. If the value of the *op* parameter is "Edit" (line 18), we hide the *Portfolio Name* TextBox control and the *Create Portfolio* command button on the form (lines 18–19). If the parameter value is "Add," we hide the portfolio editing controls (lines 22–24).

Snapshots of the *PortOps.aspx* page are shown in Figure CS2.16 (an add operation) and Figure CS2.17 (an edit operation). We will first discuss the add operation. For the add operation, users are required to enter the name of the new portfolio in the *txtPortName* TextBox control. The *Click* of the *Create* command button adds a new portfolio to the database, as shown in Figure CS2.18.

Figure CS2.16 Creating a new portfolio.

Figure CS2.17 Editing an existing portfolio.

```
32    Protected Sub cmdCreate_Click(ByVal sender As Object, _
33    ByVal e As System.EventArgs) Handles cmdCreate.Click
34        Dim dsCreateNewPortfolio As New AccessDataSource
35        'Get the new PID
36        Session("SelectedPID") = GetMaxPID() + 1
37        dsCreateNewPortfolio.DataFile = "./database/Portfolio.mdb"
38        dsCreateNewPortfolio.InsertCommand = _
39        "INSERT INTO tblPortfolio (PID,InvestorID,Name) VALUES (" _
40        & Session("SelectedPID") & "," & Session("InvestorID") & _
41        ",'" & txtPortName.Text & "')"
42        dsCreateNewPortfolio.Insert()
43        Response.Redirect("PortOps.aspx?op=Edit")
44    End Sub
```

Figure CS2.18 *Click* event of the *Create* command button.

Figure CS2.18 Explained:

We use the AccessDataSource object (line 34) to add a new portfolio to the *tblPortfolio* table of the database. The Insert query is set up in lines 38–41. The new portfolio name, the logged-in investor's ID, and the next ID number for the portfolio (line 36) are used to populate the new database entry. The query is executed in line 42. Once we create an entry for the new portfolio, we simply redirect users to the edit page to edit the newly created, empty portfolio. Note that we called a function *GetMaxPID* in line 36. This function is shown in Figure CS2.19. The function executes the Access query *qryGetLastPID* and returns the last PID in the database. We can then create a new portfolio with the next highest PID value (line 36).

The code in Figure CS2.19 is an excellent example of executing "Stored Procedures" in a VB .NET application. All Access special queries appear as Stored Procedures in the Explorer Window and can be incorporated in a VB .NET application in a similar manner.

```
103    Public Function GetMaxPID() As Integer
104        Dim connDb As New OleDbConnection(connString)
105        Dim cmdQuery As New OleDbCommand("", connDb)
106        Dim pid As Integer
107        connDb.Open()
108        cmdQuery.CommandType = CommandType.StoredProcedure
109        cmdQuery.CommandText = "qryGetLastPID"
110        pid = CInt(cmdQuery.ExecuteScalar)
111        connDb.Close()
112        Return pid
113    End Function
```

Figure CS2.19 *GetMaxPID* subroutine.

We now turn our attention to the more involved edit operation. The edit operation supports three sub-operations:

- Adding stocks to the portfolio
- Deleting stocks from the portfolio
- Updating quantities of stocks in the portfolio

The available stocks from the database are listed in the ListBox control. The ListBox control is set up exactly as the stock ListBox control is on the Stock Comparison page (see Section CS2.6). The stocks in the profile selected for editing are displayed in the DataGridView control. The DataGridView control is set up exactly as the portfolio details DataGridView control is on the Portal page (see Section CS2.7). We support the addition and deletion operations on the click of the command button (see Figure CS2.20 and Figure CS2.21 and their explanations). The update quantity operation is supported using the DataGridView control's Update functionality. The code to update the database is shown in Figure CS2.22.

```
61    Private Sub cmdAdd_Click(ByVal sender As System.Object, _
62    ByVal e As System.EventArgs) Handles cmdAdd.Click
63        Dim dsInsertPortfolioDetail As New AccessDataSource
64        If lstStock.SelectedIndex = -1 Then
65            lblMsg.Text = "Please select the stock to add!!"
66            Exit Sub
67        End If
68        dsInsertPortfolioDetail.DataFile = "./database/Portfolio.mdb"
69        dsInsertPortfolioDetail.InsertCommand = _
70        "INSERT INTO tblPortfolioDetail (PID,Symbol,Quantity) VALUES (" _
71        & Session("SelectedPID") & ",'" & lstStock.SelectedValue & "',10)"
72        Try
73            dsInsertPortfolioDetail.Insert()
74            dgrPortDetails.DataBind()
75        Catch
76            lblMsg.Text = "The stock already exists in the portfolio."
77        End Try
78    End Sub
```

Figure CS2.20 *Click* event of the *Add* button.

Figure CS2.20 Explained:

We add a stock to the portfolio by inserting a selected stock from the *lstStock* ListBox control to the *tblPortfolioDetail* table of the database. We perform database insertion using an Access-DataSource object (line 63) and set up its *InsertCommand* property (line 69–71). Note that we use the Session variable "SelectedPID" to associate the selected *PID* and the default quantity of 10 with the selected portfolio.

```
80   Private Sub cmdDelete_Click(ByVal sender As System.Object, _
81   ByVal e As System.EventArgs) Handles cmdDelete.Click
82       Dim deleted As Integer
83       Dim symbol As String
84       Dim dsDeletePortfolioDetail As New AccessDataSource
85       If dgrPortDetails.SelectedIndex = -1 Then
86           lblMsg.Text = "Please select the stock to delete!!"
87           Exit Sub
88       End If
89       symbol = dgrPortDetails.SelectedRow.Cells(1).Text
90       dsDeletePortfolioDetail.DataFile = "./database/Portfolio.mdb"
91       dsDeletePortfolioDetail.DeleteCommand = _
92       "DELETE FROM tblPortfolioDetail WHERE Symbol='" & symbol _
93       & "' AND PID=" & Session("SelectedPID")
94       deleted = dsDeletePortfolioDetail.Delete()
95       dgrPortDetails.DataBind()
96       lblMsg.Text = deleted & " row(s) deleted."
97   End Sub
```

Figure CS2.21 *Click* event of the *Delete* button.

Figure CS2.21 Explained:

The delete operation is very much like the add operation. We delete the stock selected in the DataGridView control from the portfolio under consideration. We do so by deleting the stock from the *tblPortfolioDetail* table of the database. We use an AccessDataSource object (line 84) and set up its *DeleteCommand* property (lines 91–93). We execute the delete query in line 94. Note that we retrieve the symbol of the stock to delete from the first cell of the selected row of the DataGridView control (line 89). The DataGridView control is refreshed when we call its DataBind method in line 95.

```
46   Protected Sub dgrPortDetails_RowUpdating(ByVal sender As Object, _
47   ByVal e As System.Web.UI.WebControls.GridViewUpdateEventArgs) _
48   Handles dgrPortDetails.RowUpdating
49       Dim quantity As Integer
50       Dim symbol As String
51
52       quantity = CInt(CType(dgrPortDetails.Rows _
53       (dgrPortDetails.EditIndex).Cells(4).Controls(0), TextBox).Text)
54       symbol = dgrPortDetails.Rows(dgrPortDetails.EditIndex).Cells(1).Text
55       dsPortfolioDetails.UpdateCommand = _
56       "UPDATE tblPortfolioDetail SET Quantity=" & quantity & _
57       " WHERE Symbol='" & symbol & "' AND PID=" & Session("SelectedPID")
58       dsPortfolioDetails.Update()
59   End Sub
```

Figure CS2.22 *RowUpdating* event of the DataGridView control.

Figure CS2.22 Explained:

To update the quantity of the existing stock (i.e., the one present on the DataGridView control), we use the existing AccessDataSource *dsPortfolioDetails*. The *dsPortfolioDetails* is the design-time setup and is used to provide the data for the DataGridView control. We set its *Update-Command* in the code using the Session variable *SelectedPID*, the selected stock symbol (lines 54–55), and the quantity users have updated in the DataGridView control (lines 52–53).

The Optimization Page

Investors can optimize their portfolio by selecting a portfolio on the Portal page and clicking the Optimize Portfolio button. The Portfolio page (see Figure CS2.23) implements the portfolio optimization logic.

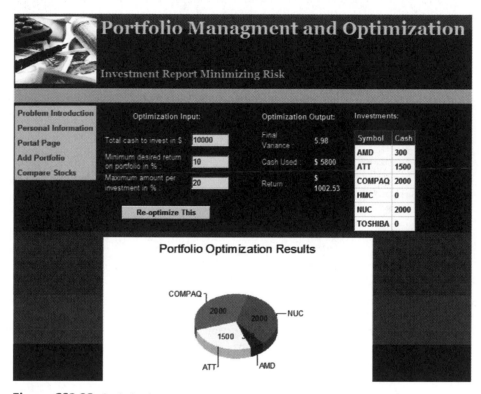

Figure CS2.23 *Optimization* page.

CS2.9.1 Model Definition and Assumptions

The underlying model for optimizing the portfolio investment plan minimizes risk as the objective function and subject to certain constraints. These constraints include the following: the cash invested must be less than or equal to the cash available for investing; the return on the portfolio must be greater than or equal to the minimum return desired for the entire portfolio; and the amount invested per stock must be less than or equal to a maximum amount to be invested in each stock.

We will now outline this model mathematically. Let x_i be the amount we invest per stock i in the portfolio. The index i varies from 1 to n, where n is equal to the number of stocks in the portfolio. Let r_i represent the expected return on stock i. The expected returns are determined based on each stock's historical data of annual returns from the database. Let v_i represent the variance of stock i. This variance is calculated based on the historical data of quarterly market prices.

We can now define the risk of the portfolio, z, as the sum of the product of the square of the investment and the variance over all stocks in the portfolio:

$$z = \sum_{i=1}^{n} z_i^2 \; * \; v_i$$

We would like to mention that the above formulation is accurate with the assumption that the stock values are independent of each other. In real life, however, this might not always be true. For example, stock values tend to increase or decrease depending on how other stocks from the same category are doing. This *correlation* can be mathematically modeled by adding a *co-variance* term in the above equation. However, to keep the model simple, we ignore the covariance term and assume that stock values are independent of each other.

We define the return on the portfolio as the sum of the product of the investment amount and the expected return over all stocks:

$$\sum_{i=1}^{n} x_i * r_i$$

Let us represent the optimization inputs from the users as follows: C = total cash available for investing; D = desired return on the portfolio; and M = maximum amount to invest per stock. We can now finalize the mathematical model representation:

```
Minimize      z = ∑ⁿᵢ₌₁ xᵢ² * vᵢ                              (1)
```

$$\text{Minimize} \quad z = \sum_{i=1}^{n} x_i^2 * v_i \tag{1}$$

Subject to:

$$\sum_{i=1}^{n} x_i \text{ " } C \qquad\qquad \text{for } i = 1 \text{ to } n \tag{2}$$

$$\sum_{i=1}^{n} (x_i * r_i) \text{ "} \qquad\qquad \text{for } i = 1 \text{ to } n \tag{3}$$

$$x_i \text{ " } M \qquad\qquad\qquad \text{for } i = 1 \text{ to } n \tag{4}$$

CS2.9.2 Optimization Input

- For each stock in the selected portfolio, we require the stock's annual return and market price change to calculate the expected return and price variance.
- Total cash for investing
- Minimum return desired
- Maximum amount to invest per stock

CS2.9.3 Optimization Output

The output reported to the users after the optimization is complete consists of the following:

- Minimum return
- Cash used
- The final variance (i.e., risk)
- Amount to invest per stock in a DataGridView control and on the pie chart

CS2.9.4 A Heuristic Algorithm for the Optimization Problem

We solve the optimization problem sketched in Section CS2.9.1 using a heuristic algorithm. Typically, a heuristic is an approximate algorithm which uses a rule-of-thumb to find a solution to an optimization problem. For each stock, we define its *worth* w = Average (Return) / Var (Price). Intuitively, stocks with larger worth give maximum return at minimum risk for a given investment. The heuristic used to solve the optimization problem can be explained through the following steps.

Step 1: Get the worth of each stock in the portfolio (see Figure CS2.24)

Find the worth of each stock in the portfolio that is under consideration for optimization. The Access query *qryOptimization* is used to calculate the worth of stocks (see database file). The query takes a portfolio ID as its input parameter (see line 43) and outputs the following four columns: (i) stock symbol, (ii) average stock return, (iii) Variance of stock price, and (iv) worth. The query result is stored in the *dsGetStockWorth* DataSet object (see line 46) for further processing.

```
36      'Step 1: Determine the worth of each stock in the selected PID
37      Dim connGetStockWorth As New OleDbConnection
38      Dim cmdGetStockWorth As New OleDbCommand
39      Dim daGetStockWorth As New OleDbDataAdapter
40      Dim dsGetStockWorth As New DataSet
41      connGetStockWorth.ConnectionString = ConfigurationManager.AppSettings("connString")
42      cmdGetStockWorth.Connection = connGetStockWorth
43      cmdGetStockWorth.CommandText = "exec qryOptimization '" & Session("SelectedPID") & "'"
44      daGetStockWorth.SelectCommand = cmdGetStockWorth
45      connGetStockWorth.Open()
46      daGetStockWorth.Fill(dsGetStockWorth)
47      connGetStockWorth.Close()
```

Figure CS2.24 Optimization step 1: Get the worth of each stock in the portfolio.

Step 2: Set up initial values and data structures (see Figure CS2.25)

We take the optimization input (see Section CS2.9.2) and store it in program variables (lines 68–70). The variable for number of stocks, *numStocks*, is set to the number of rows in the *ds-GetStockWorth* (line 53). We define two data structure arrays (lines 56 and 66), *worth* and *weights*. The first array holds the worth of each stock (lines 58–64), whereas the second array is used to hold stock weights. We weigh each stock on a scale of 0–1, representing the fraction of total available cash allocated or invested in the stock. To start, the weight of each stock is set to zero. We set the variable *bestStock* to the index of the stock with highest worth (lines 60–63). This is the stock with which we will start our investment in step 3.

```
49      'Step 2: Setup initial values and data structures
50      Dim i, bestStock As Integer
51      Dim cashUsed, currentReturn, finalReturn, finalVariance As Double
52
53      Dim numStocks As Integer = dsGetStockWorth.Tables(0).Rows.Count
54      'Stores worth of each stock; worth = avg price / std Dev of return
55      'We set the stock with the highest worth as the bestStock
56      Dim worth(numStocks - 1) As Double
57      Dim maxWorth As Double = 0
58      For i = 0 To numStocks - 1
59          worth(i) = CDbl(dsGetStockWorth.Tables(0).Rows(i).Item(3))
60          If (worth(i) > maxWorth) Then
61              bestStock = i
62              maxWorth = worth(i)
63          End If
64      Next
65      'Stores the stock weights; initial value = 0; investment = cash * weight
66      Dim weights(numStocks - 1) As Double
67
68      Dim CASH As Double = CDbl(txtCash.Text)
69      Dim MINRET As Double = CDbl(txtMinRet.Text) / 100
70      Dim MAXWT As Double = CDbl(txtMaxInv.Text) / 100
71      lblVar.Text = "Infinity"
72      lblReturn.Text = 0 & "  $"
73      lblCashUsed.Text = 0 & "  $"
74      lblError.Text = ""
```

Figure CS2.25 Optimization step 2: Set up initial values and data structures.

```
76      'Step 3: Execute the heuristic algorithm
77      'Loop until the currentReturn is the required return
78      Do While (currentReturn < MINRET)
79
80          Dim delta As Double = 0.01
81          Dim AR As Double = CDbl(dsGetStockWorth.Tables(0).Rows(bestStock).Item(1))
82          Dim VAR As Double = CDbl(dsGetStockWorth.Tables(0).Rows(bestStock).Item(2))
83
84          'When the room for an investment is less than the delta increment
85          If (MAXWT - weights(bestStock)) < delta Then
86              delta = MAXWT - weights(bestStock)
87          End If
88
89          weights(bestStock) += delta
90          currentReturn += delta * AR
91          worth(bestStock) = AR / (VAR + ((weights(bestStock) ^ 2) * VAR))
92
93          'Find the bestStock after this delta investment
94          maxWorth = 0
95          For i = 0 To numStocks - 1
96              If ((worth(i) > maxWorth) And (weights(i) < MAXWT)) Then
97                  bestStock = i
98                  maxWorth = worth(i)
99              End If
100         Next
101         If (maxWorth = 0) Then
102             lblError.Text = "Infeasible solution. Input is too constrained."
103             Exit Sub
104         End If
105
106     Loop
```

Figure CS2.26 Optimization step 3: Running the heuristic algorithm.

Step 3: Running the heuristic algorithm (see Figure CS2.26)

We start out investing a very small amount (1% of the total cash) in the stock indicated by the *bestStock* (lines 80 and 89). Every time we invest in a particular stock, we do the following: (i) increase the weight of the stock in line 89; (ii) increase the current return value by average return multiplied by the weight increment in line 90 (the average return for the *bestStock* is retrieved from the *dsGetStockWorth* in line 81); and (iii) re-calculate the worth of the stock as shown in line 91. The variance of the *bestStock* is retrieved from the *dsGetStockWorth* in line 82.

The process of investment in the best stock is continued until the current return is raised to the desired minimum return value (line 78 and (3) in Section CS2.9.1). The new *bestStock* with the highest worth is determined in lines 94–100 of the loop. The constraints (2) and (4) in Section CS2.9.1 are satisfied by lines 85–87 and line 96. These lines of the code make sure not to exceed the investment limit for a single stock and also adjust the increment value *delta* for the last iteration when the amount of cash left for the stock is less than the default increment of 1%.

Step 4: Retrieving optimization solution (see Figure CS2.27)

The optimization outputs (see Section CS2.9.3)—total final return value (line 109), cash used (*weight × available cash*), and the final variance (lines 111–112)—are shown to users in lines 115–117.

```
108    'Step 4: Set the final output of the optimization problem
109    finalReturn = currentReturn
110    For i = 0 To numStocks - 1
111        cashUsed += weights(i) * CASH
112        finalVariance += (weights(i) ^ 2) * _
113        CDbl(dsGetStockWorth.Tables(0).Rows(i).Item(2))
114    Next
115    lblVar.Text = Math.Round(finalVariance, 2).ToString
116    lblReturn.Text = "$ " & Math.Round((finalReturn * CASH), 2)
117    lblCashUsed.Text = "$ " & cashUsed
```

Figure CS2.27 Optimization step 4: Retrieving optimization solution.

Step 5: Showing optimization solution on the form (See Figure CS2.28)

We display the investment in individual stocks of the portfolio to users in a DataGridView control and on a pie chart (Crystal Report). For simplicity, we insert the optimization solution (stock symbol and optimal investment) to the existing database table (lines 123–128). We set the AccessDataSource *dsOptTable* and bind it with the DataGridView control at design-time. We refresh this binding in line 131 to show the current result on the form. Note that since the database table used to insert the optimization result is a temporary table, we delete its content before inserting any new results (lines 121–122). We plot the pie chart using the same temporary table *tblOptimization* in lines 138–149. Refer to Sections CS2.6 and CS2.7 for details on Crystal Report code.

```
119    'Step 5: Show the suggested investment to the user
120    'Insert the results into the tblOptimization table
121    dsOptTable.DeleteCommand = "DELETE * from tblOptimization"
122    dsOptTable.Delete()
123    For i = 0 To numStocks - 1
124        dsOptTable.InsertCommand = _
125            "INSERT INTO tblOptimization (Symbol,Cash) VALUES ('" _
126            & dsGetStockWorth.Tables(0).Rows(i).Item(0) & "'," _
127            & Math.Round((weights(i) * CASH), 2) & ")"
128        dsOptTable.Insert()
129    Next
130    'Show results on the DataGridView control
131    dataGridResults.DataBind()
132    'Show the pie-chart crystal report
133    Dim myConnection As New OleDbConnection
134    Dim myCommand As New OleDbCommand
135    Dim myDA As New OleDbDataAdapter
136    Dim myDS As New DataSet
137
138    myConnection.ConnectionString = ConfigurationManager.AppSettings("connString")
139    myCommand.Connection = myConnection
140    myCommand.CommandText = "Select * from tblOptimization"
141    myCommand.CommandType = CommandType.Text
142    myDA.SelectCommand = myCommand
143    myCommand.Connection.Open()
144    myDA.Fill(myDS, "tblOptimization")
145    Dim oRpt As New CrystalDecisions.CrystalReports.Engine.ReportDocument
146    oRpt.FileName = "C:\webdss\casestudies\Portfolio\rptOptimization.rpt"
147    oRpt.SetDataSource(myDS)
148    rptViewer1.ReportSource = oRpt
149    myCommand.Connection.Close()
```

Figure CS2.28 Optimization step 5: Showing optimization solution on the form.

CS2.10 *Summary*

- This case study allows users to create and/or edit their portfolio as well as optimize their investments.

- The portfolio database features three main tables to store information about investors, their portfolios, and available stocks. The other two tables of the database store historical stock data and details of each portfolio created by an investor.

- The application allows investors (users) to view and edit their personal information.

- The Portal page of the application is a one-stop review page for investors.

- The application supports these portfolio-related operations: create new portfolio, add stocks to existing or newly created portfolio, delete selected stocks from existing portfolios, and update quantities of stocks in existing portfolios.

- In the application, the stocks in the database are listed by name and category. These stocks can also be compared using their historical annual returns and changes in market price.

- Users may optimize their investments by specifying a desired return on their portfolio and the amount available for investing. The application solves an optimization problem that minimizes users' risk on their selected portfolio.

CS2.11 *Extensions*

1. The index page permits users to log in and view the Portal page. Add a user registration page to the application that registers new users' user name and password in the database.

2. The Stock Comparison page can currently be reached without logging into the system. We are about to extend functionality provided by this page and make it personalized for the logged-in investor. Like the Portal page or Personal Information page, make the Stock Comparison page accessible only to the logged-in investors.

3. The Stock Comparison page let users compare existing stocks before they can add them to the portfolio. In the application, however, users have to use the Edit Portfolio option on the Portal page to add stocks to the existing portfolio. Modify the application for the following functionality. As users finish comparing different stocks on the Stock Comparison page, they should be able to add the stocks in the DataGridView control on that page to the existing portfolio (*Hint*: Use the pop-up window and Session variables to ask users for the target portfolio ID). Display the *PortOps.aspx* page with the added stocks so that users can further edit the stock quantities in the portfolio or delete unwanted stocks.

4. In the current version of the application, users can create portfolios and add stocks to the newly created or existing portfolios using the *PortOps.aspx* page. However, there is no check done as to whether the total amount invested across all portfolios is exceeding a user's account balance. Add this check as users add stocks to the new or existing portfolios.

5. We further extend the functionality developed in the previous extension. When users exceed their investment while adding a particular stock, we compute the minimum number of stocks they can buy with the current account balance and suggest the feasible quantity to the users. If the feasible quantity is less than one, we redirect users to the Personal Information page with a message suggesting to increase the account balance.

6. Solve the optimization discussed in this case study by maximizing returns instead of minimizing risk.

three Television Advertisement Allocation

CS3.1 *Introduction*

Television is the most popular medium of entertainment. Considering its impact on us, it is natural to make optimal use of this medium for advertisement and entertainment programs. Generally, a cable service provider can track information for each household: which channel and the period for which viewers are tuned in on any particular channel. This information, along with data about customers, television programs, episodes, and show times, can be used to develop a decision support system. We allocate advertisements and episodes based on some predetermined criteria as one of the functionalities of the DSS. For example, given a set of advertisements, their target age group, race, and income group, an advertisement budget, and cost of advertising per program, we optimally allocate these advertisements to different TV programs to maximize the viewership per dollar spent. The model base for the advertisement allocation problem makes use of the greedy algorithm for the knapsack problem (Winston and Venkataramanan [2002]) programmed in VB .NET.

The case study code and the complete application can be found on the book Web site. We strongly recommend readers download and install the case study and browse through the application pages before going through the details described in this chapter. We also recommend that users open the TVProject database file and study its Relationships window (see Figure CS3.1). The database features five main tables to store information about customers, channels, programs and their episodes, and advertisement information. The other two tables of the database link customer-episode and advertisement-episode tables.

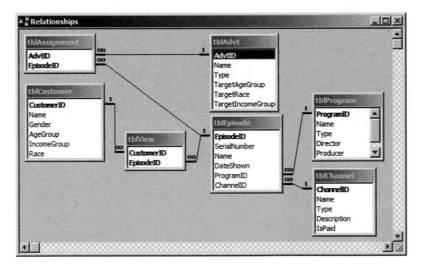

Figure CS3.1 The Relationships Window for the *TVProject* database.

CS3.2 *Application Functionalities*

The functionalities of the application are listed as follows:

Channel Information: For each channel in the database we display its viewership. The viewership is displayed for different categories of age range, gender, race, and income group. For example, if the user selects the age range as the selection criteria, then we display the viewership of all channels for categories such as Adult, Kids, Old, and Youth. The database is queried for these pre-defined categories to retrieve data, which is then displayed in the GridView control for the user. The user can select a channel from the GridView control to view the categorized viewership on a bar chart and detailed channel information in the DetailsView control. This functionality is provided by the Channel Information page of the application.

Program Information: The Program Information page of the application is exactly like the Channel Information page, except that it shows the categorized viewership information for all the programs in the database. The user can select a program from the grid view to view the categorized viewership on a bar chart and detailed program information in the DetailsView control.

Customer Preference: The Customer Preference page of the application shows the customer's penchant for different program types. Each piece of the pie chart on the page depicts a unique program type, and the size of the piece indicates the number of customers preferring the program type. We further provide categorized customer preferences. For example, the form shows the customer's preferences for all program types only for the age groups kids or adult, the income groups high or low, and so forth. See the Extension section of this chapter for the categorized customer preferences.

Trend Lines: A trend line is a line chart that shows the program viewership of a selected program over time. Any spikes or dips in the trend line are of interest for advertisement decisions. Trend lines can also be categorized based on age, race, income, and gender to capture very specific information. Multiple trend lines can be shown for a channel to view patterns and more. Trend lines are discussed in the Extension section of the chapter.

Advertisement Allocation: Each advertisement may have a target age group, race, gender, and income group. Additionally, each advertisement must have an advertisement budget and target viewership. Further, there is a cost of advertisement associated with each program. The Advertisement Allocation page solves the optimization problem to allocate the selected advertisement to programs to maximize viewership with the constraints of available budget and target categorized viewership. The model base for the advertisement allocation problem makes use of the greedy algorithm for the knapsack problem programmed in VB .NET.

The flow of the *Television Advertisement Allocation* application is depicted in Figure CS3.2.

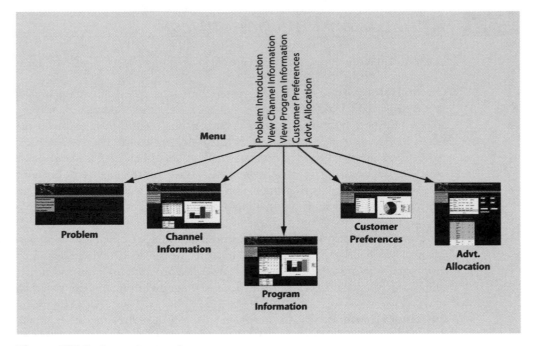

Figure CS3.2 The application flow.

The Channel Information and Program Information Pages

In this section, we discuss the design and code behind the Channel Information page and the Program Information page. The Channel Information page shows the viewership information for all the channels in the database based on one of the selection criteria (see Figure CS3.3). The page also displays the detailed channel information and a bar chart of viewership for a selected channel. The Program Information page displays viewership information for all the programs in the database.

The Channel Information Page Setup

We use a Master page to create all the pages of this case study. Master pages and related topics are discussed in depth in Case Study 1 (see Section CS1.3). The Master page provides the page header, page title, and the side navigation menu for each application page that is based on the Master page.

The Channel page features a RadioButtonList (for selection criteria), a GridView (for channel viewership information), a DetailsView (for selected channel details), and a CrystalReportViewer control (for bar chart of a selected channel). The RadioButtonList control groups the multiple RadioButton controls and lets the user choose exactly one option from the list (see Figure CS3.4). We use this control to choose from age, gender, income, and race options.

Based on the selection in the RadioButtonList control, we populate the GridView with the viewership information. For each selection criteria, we execute the Crosstab query in the MS Access database (refer to the application database file). The Crosstab queries are designed to group

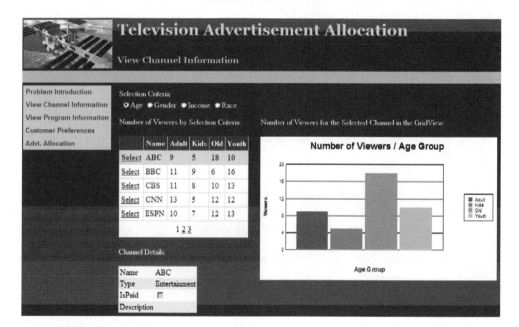

Figure CS3.3 The Channel Information Page.

Figure CS3.4 The RadioButtonList control in the Toolbox.

the viewership information based on the pre-defined categories. For example, the age selection criterion has categories such as Adult, Kids, Old, and Youth; the gender criterion is divided into male and female categories, and so forth (refer to Chapter 8 for more about Crosstab queries).

Since the source of the GridView is determined at runtime based on the selection criteria selected by the user, we set up the GridView columns and data source in the code at runtime (see the next subsection). However, the formatting of the grid and its *DataKeyNames* property are set at design-time. Recall that the *DataKeyNames* property indicates which GridView column provides the value of the selected row. We set this property to the *Name* column (see Figure CS3.5). Whenever the user selects the channel in the GridView control, we get the channel name as the *SelectedValue* of the GridView control.

```
29   <asp:GridView ID="gvData" runat="server" BackColor="White"
30   BorderColor="#CC9966" BorderStyle="None" BorderWidth="1px"
31   DataKeyNames="Name" CellPadding="4">
```

Figure CS3.5 The ASP tag for the channel list GridView control; setting up the *DataKeyNames*.

We set up the DetailsView control at design-time. The DetailsView control displays the detailed channel information for the channel selected in the GridView control. The query used to set the AccessDataSource of the DetailsView control is shown in Figure CS3.6. The Name parameter gets its value from the *SelectedValue* of the GridView control.

Figure CS3.6 The query for the DetailsView control.

The Event Handler Code

We now move to the code behind the Channel Information page. We mainly discuss the *Page_Load* event of the page, the *SelectedIndexChanged* event of the GridView control (see Figure CS3.7). On page load, we first set the page title using a Session variable (line 9). The data for the selected criteria is populated in the GridView control using the *LoadData* subroutine (line 12). The *LoadData* subroutine is shown in Figure CS3.8. The Crystal Report is displayed using the *Plot* subroutine (lines 14 and 19). We discuss the *Plot* subroutine in the next subsection.

```
 6    Protected Sub Page_Load(ByVal sender As Object, _
 7    ByVal e As System.EventArgs) Handles Me.Load
 8        If Not IsPostBack Then
 9            Session("PageTitle") = "View Channel Information"
10            rblistSelectCriteria.SelectedIndex = 0
11        End If
12        LoadData()
13        gvData.SelectedIndex = 0
14        Plot()
15    End Sub
16
17    Protected Sub gvData_SelectedIndexChanged(ByVal sender As Object, _
18    ByVal e As System.EventArgs) Handles gvData.SelectedIndexChanged
19        Plot()
20    End Sub
```

Figure CS3.7 The event handler for the Channel Information page.

```
26    Sub LoadData()
27        dsData.DataFile = "~\database\TVProject.mdb"
28        Dim choice As Integer = rblistSelectCriteria.SelectedIndex
29        Select Case choice
30            Case 0
31                dsData.SelectCommand = "exec qryChannelAge"
32            Case 1
33                dsData.SelectCommand = "exec qryChannelGender"
34            Case 2
35                dsData.SelectCommand = "exec qryChannelIncome"
```

(continues)

Figure CS3.8 The *LoadData* subroutine to populate the GridView control.

```
36        Case 3
37            dsData.SelectCommand = "exec qryChannelRace"
38        End Select
39        dsData.DataBind()
40        gvData.DataSource = dsData
41        gvData.AutoGenerateColumns = True
42        gvData.AutoGenerateSelectButton = True
43        gvData.AllowPaging = True
44        gvData.PageSize = 5
45        gvData.DataBind()
46    End Sub
```

Figure CS3.8 (*continued*)

Figure CS3.8 Explained:

The *Load* subroutine sets the *dsData* AccessDataSource on the page and then sets the *gvData* GridView control. The *DataFile* property of the *dsData* is set to the *TVProject* database in line 27. Next, we set the *SelectCommand* property of the *dsData* based on the selection criteria selected by the user (line 28). In the Select-Case statement (lines 29–38), we assign the appropriate Crosstab query to the *SelectCommand* property. The selected Crosstab query is data-bound to the *dsData* using its *DataBind* method in line 39. Next, we set the *gvData* GridView control. The *DataSource* of the *gvData* is set to *dsData* in line 40. Since each Crosstab query returns a different number of columns (corresponds to the categories of the selection criteria), we set the *AutoGenerateColumns* property of the *gvData* to *True* in line 41. We would also like the user to select the channel in *gvData* to view its details and bar chart of viewership. We therefore provide the *Select* link for each row by setting the *AutoGenerateSelectButton* property to *True* (line 42). We then allow paging and set the page size for the *gvData* in lines 43–44. Finally, we data-bind *gvData* to *dsData* using their *DataBind* methods in line 45.

The Crystal Report

We now discuss the Crystal Report of the Channel Information page. We would like to show the viewership information for the channel selected in the GridView control on a bar chart (see Figure CS3.3). As with any Crystal Report design, two things are involved in this report design: (i) setting up the report file and (ii) populating the report's data source and showing the report file in the CrystalReportViewer control. The first step requires the schema of the data source so that we can use columns of the data source in the report design, whereas the second step requires actual data to be filled in the data source to display the report.

Step 1A: Adding DataSets for the Crystal Report

We know that the schema of the reports is the schema of the Crosstab query used for the Grid-View control, and the actual data is the single row of the Crosstab query output that is selected by the user in the GridView control. So, instead of creating new parameterized Crosstab queries, we use the schema of the Crosstab queries to create the report. We create new DataSets at design-time based on four Crosstab queries used to source the GridView control. These four DataSets serve as the schema for the four report designs, one for each selection criteria.

Figure CS3.9 Adding a Dataset to the project.

To add the DataSet to the Web application at design-time, do the following How-to topics:

- How-to: add a DataSet to the Web application.
- How-to: use DataSet design in the Web application.
  1. Choose the Project | Add New Item option from the main menu. This should open the *Add New Item* dialog box.
  2. Select the *DataSet* item from the *Templates* pane, name the new *DataSet*, and click *Add* (see Figure CS3.9). This should open the *DataSet Designer* window and *TableAdapter Configuration Wizard*.
  3. Specify the source SQL query on the Enter a an SQL Statement page of the Wizard (see Figure CS3.10). Use the appropriate Crosstab query for the DataSet.
  4. Accept all other default settings and click Finish. This should create the required DataSet in the DataSet Designer window (see Figure CS3.11).
  5. Create four DataSets for four selection criteria (see Figure CS3.12).

Figure CS3.10 The query for the *DsChannelInfoAge* Dataset.

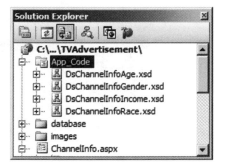

Figure CS3.11 The *DsChannelInfoAge* Dataset in the *DataSet Designer*.

Figure CS3.12 DataSets for the Crystal Report design.

Step 1B: Setting up the Crystal Report

Now that we have the data source schema ready, we create four report files. All four reports are very similar to each other. We show the few steps for one of the reports.

- On the *Data* page of the *Crystal Report* Wizard, select the Project Data | ADO .NET DataSets option, and then add the desired DataSet from the *Available Data Sources* pane to the *Selected Tables* pane (see Figure CS3.13).
- On the *Chart* page of the Crystal Report Wizard, navigate to the *Data* tab and set the page as shown in Figure CS3.14.

Step 2: Populate the Report's Data Source and Display the Report

We perform this step in the code at runtime (see Figure CS3.15). Based on the selection criteria selected by the user (line 55), we first populate the DataSet in the Select-Case statement (lines 56–73). We use the *PopulateDataSet* subroutine with the appropriate DataSet as its input parameter (see Figure CS3.16). We then assign the corresponding report file to the report object (lines 59, 63, 67, and 71) and set the data source of the report object to the populated DataSets (lines 60, 64, 68, and 72). Finally, the report object is assigned as the report source of the CrystalReportViewer control on the page (line 74).

Figure CS3.13 *Data* page of the *Crystal Report* Wizard; selecting the DataSets.

Figure CS3.14 *Chart* page of the *Crystal Report* Wizard; setting up the bar chart.

```
48  Sub Plot()
49      Dim oRpt As New CrystalDecisions.CrystalReports.Engine.ReportDocument
50      Dim DsChannelInfoAge1 As New DsChannelInfoAge
51      Dim DsChannelInfoGender1 As New DsChannelInfoGender
52      Dim DsChannelInfoIncome1 As New DsChannelInfoIncome
53      Dim DsChannelInfoRace1 As New DsChannelInfoRace
54
55      Dim choice As Integer = rblistSelectCriteria.SelectedIndex
56      Select Case choice
57          Case 0
58              PopulateDataSet(DsChannelInfoAge1)
59              oRpt.FileName = "C:\webdss\casestudies\TVAdvertisement\ChannelInfoAge.rpt"
60              oRpt.SetDataSource(DsChannelInfoAge1)
61          Case 1
62              PopulateDataSet(DsChannelInfoGender1)
63              oRpt.FileName = "C:\webdss\casestudies\TVAdvertisement\ChannelInfoGender.rpt"
64              oRpt.SetDataSource(DsChannelInfoGender1)
65          Case 2
66              PopulateDataSet(DsChannelInfoIncome1)
67              oRpt.FileName = "C:\webdss\casestudies\TVAdvertisement\ChannelInfoIncome.rpt"
68              oRpt.SetDataSource(DsChannelInfoIncome1)
69          Case 3
70              PopulateDataSet(DsChannelInfoRace1)
71              oRpt.FileName = "C:\webdss\casestudies\TVAdvertisement\ChannelInfoRace.rpt"
72              oRpt.SetDataSource(DsChannelInfoRace1)
73      End Select
74      rptViewer1.ReportSource = oRpt
75  End Sub
```

Figure CS3.15 The *Plot* subroutine for the Crystal Report display.

```
77  Sub PopulateDataSet(ByRef dataset As Data.DataSet)
78      Dim dRow As Data.DataRow = dataset.Tables(0).NewRow
79      Dim i As Integer
80      For i = 0 To dataset.Tables(0).Columns.Count - 2
81          dRow.Item(i) = gvData.SelectedRow.Cells(i + 2).Text
82      Next
83      dataset.Tables(0).Rows.Add(dRow)
84  End Sub
```

Figure CS3.16 The *PopulateDataSet* subroutine.

Figure CS3.16 Explained:

To populate the DataSets, we could execute the appropriate Crosstab query again for the selected channel name. However, we can simply copy the selected row from the GridView control into the DataSet. We only need to plot the data shown for various categories in the selected row of the GridView control. We first create a temporary *DataRow* in line 78. We then determine how many columns we must copy from the GridView control. Since the number of columns varies based on the categories in the selection criteria, we get the current column count of the DataSet (line 80). For each column, we copy the value from the *SelectedRow* cell to the columns of the temporary DataRow (line 81). Finally, we add the new row to the DataSet in line 83.

The Program Information Page Setup

The Program Information page is exactly the same as the Channel Information page except that it displays the viewership information for all the programs in the database. We set up the Program Information page just like the Channel information page (see Figure CS3.17). The controls used on this page and their behavior are the similar to the one on the Channel Information page. In fact, we use the same set of DataSets and Crystal Report files to set up the Program Information page. Only the Crosstab queries used to source the data are different. The Crosstab queries bring similar categorized information, but for each program rather than for different channels. Thus, the outputs of these Crosstab queries and the one used for the Channel Information page is similar in the sense that the queries' schema is the same, but the actual data is different. This is why we could use the same DataSet objects and report files to set up the program page.

The DetailsView now shows the detailed program information for the program selected in the GridView control and is set accordingly. The code behind the Program Information page is also no different from the code behind the Channel Information Page except that it executes the Crosstab queries designed to retrieve program viewership (see project database file).

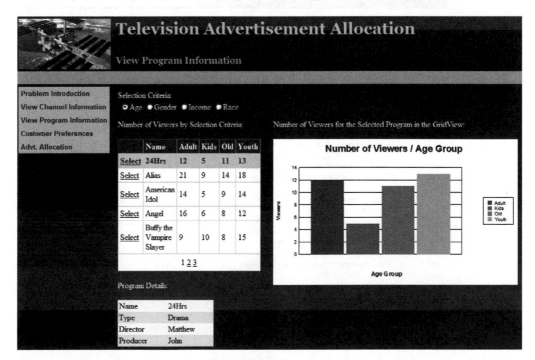

Figure CS3.17 The Program Information page.

CS3.4   *The Customer Preferences Form*

Different customers usually prefer different programs. The database stores the program types such as drama, comedy, action, adventure, and so forth. The Customer Preference page displays the viewership for different types of programs. The data is displayed in the GridView control and in a pie chart on the Crystal Report (see Figure CS3.18). The GridView control is set at design-time, and the *qryCustPref* MS Access query is used to set the AccessDataSource for the GridView control. The code for the Crystal Report is shown in Figure CS3.19 and is similar to the report code seen in previous case studies.

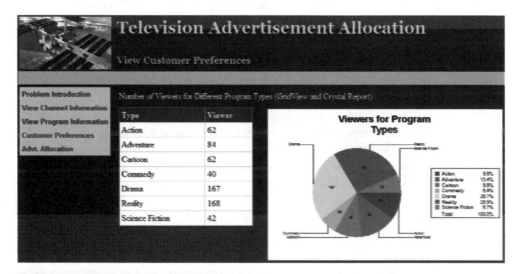

Figure CS3.18 The Customer Preferences page.

```
15        Sub Plot()
16            Dim myConnection As New OleDbConnection
17            Dim myCommand As New OleDbCommand
18            Dim myDA As New OleDbDataAdapter
19            Dim myDS As New DataSet
20
21            myConnection.ConnectionString = _
22            ConfigurationManager.AppSettings("connString")
23            myCommand.Connection = myConnection
24            myCommand.CommandText = "qryCustPref"
25            myCommand.CommandType = CommandType.StoredProcedure
26            myDA.SelectCommand = myCommand
27
28            myCommand.Connection.Open()
29            myDA.Fill(myDS)
30            Dim oRpt As New CrystalDecisions.CrystalReports.Engine.ReportDocument
31            oRpt.FileName = "C:\webdss\casestudies\TVAdvertisement\CustPref.rpt"
32            oRpt.SetDataSource(myDS)
33            rptViewer1.ReportSource = oRpt
34            myCommand.Connection.Close()
35        End Sub
```

Figure CS3.19 The code behind the Customer Preferences page.

Figure CS3.19 Explained:

We populate the *myDS* DataSet with the result of the *qryCustPref* query (line 29). The report object's *FileName* property is set to the report file in line 31, and the data source is set to the *myDS* in line 32. Finally, the report object is set as the report source of the CrystalReportViewer control (line 33).

CS3.5 *The Advertisement Allocation Page*

The Advertisement Allocation page displays the list of all the advertisements in the database, sorted by the advertisement type. Each advertisement has a target age group, race, gender, and income group. Likewise, each program in the database has its fixed advertisement cost and viewership information. The advertisement allocation algorithm determines the programs to which a selected advertisement can be assigned to maximize the viewership subject to the constraints of available budget and target audience type of the advertisement (see Figure CS3.20).

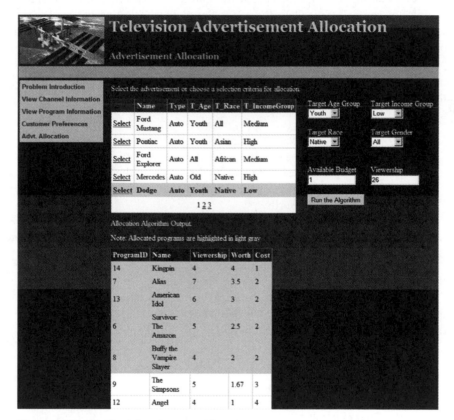

Figure CS3.20 The Advertisement Allocation Page.

On the Advertisement Allocation page, we first display the list of all the advertisements in a GridView control *gvAdvt*, sorted by the advertisement type. The select query used in the AccessDataSource *dsAdvt* is shown in Table CS3.1. The *dsAdvt* is set as the data source for *gvAdvt*. We use the GridView control's *Fields* dialog box (Tasks list | Edit Columns option) to add the *Select* link to each row and to hide the *AdvtID* field in the GridView control (see Figure CS3.20). When the user selects the advertisement in the *gvAdvt* for optimized allocation, we populate the advertisement's target selection criteria such as target age, income group, and race in the ComboBox controls on the page (see Figure CS3.21).

```
66    Protected Sub gvAdvt_SelectedIndexChanged(ByVal sender As Object, _
67    ByVal e As System.EventArgs) Handles gvAdvt.SelectedIndexChanged
68        'GridCols: (0) Select (1) [AdvtID], (2) [Name], (3)[Type],
69        ' (4)[TargetAgeGroup],(5)[TargetRace], (6)[TargetIncomeGroup]
70        cmbAge.SelectedValue = gvAdvt.SelectedRow.Cells(4).Text
71        cmbRace.SelectedValue = gvAdvt.SelectedRow.Cells(5).Text
72        cmbIncome.SelectedValue = gvAdvt.SelectedRow.Cells(6).Text
73    End Sub
74  End Class
```

Figure CS3.21 The GridView control's selection change event.

Note that the user can also change the values of the selection criteria directly through the ComboBox controls. This allows the user to fine-tune the selection criteria. We then ask the user to enter the available budget for the selected advertisement and run the optimization algorithm on the click of the command button. The Advertisement Allocation page solves the optimization problem to allocate the selected advertisement to the programs to maximize the viewership with the constraint of available budget. The model base for the advertisement allocation problem makes use of the greedy algorithm for the knapsack problem programmed in VB .NET. The algorithm steps are stated as follows:

1. For each program, we determine its worth as viewership per unit cost. The higher the worth, the higher the viewership per dollar invested in that program.
2. All the programs are listed in descending order of their worth (greedy approach).
3. We start allocating the programs to the selected advertisement beginning with the program with highest worth.
4. Every time we select the program, we increase the viewership of the advertisement by the viewership of the selected program, and we decrease the available budget by the cost of advertisement with that program.
5. The algorithm terminates when the available budget is not enough for further allocation.

We use an MS Access query to perform the first two steps of the algorithm. The MS Access query *qryProgWorth* computes the worth of all programs in the database and sorts the output in descending order of worth (see Table CS3.1).

Table CS3.1 Queries for the Advertisement Allocation page.

Control Name	Query Function	SQL Statements
AccessDataSource —*dsAdvt*	Fetch all advertisements	SELECT Name, Type, TargetAgeGroup AS T_Age, TargetRace AS T_Race, TargetIncomeGroup AS T_IncomeGroup FROM tblAdvt ORDERBY Type;
MS Access —*qryProgWorth*	Fetch worth of all programs (Also see the project database file for query Design View)	SELECT ProgramID, Name, Count(CustomerID) AS Viewership, Round (Count([CustomerID]/[Cost]),2) AS Worth, Cost FROM tblProgram, tblEpisode, tblCustomer, tblView WHERE tblCustomer.CustomerID = tblView.CustomerID AND tblEpisode.EpisodeID = tblView.EpisodeID AND tblProgram.ProgramID = tblEpisode.ProgramID AND Gender Like [?Gender] AND AgeGroup Like [?AgeGroup] AND IncomeGroup Like [?IncomeGroup]) AND Race Like [?Race] GROUP BY ProgramID, Name, Cost ORDER BY Round (Count([CustomerID]/[Cost]),2) DESC;

On the click of the *Run Algorithm* command button, we call the *LoadData* subroutine to perform steps 1 and 2 of the algorithm (see Figure CS3.22, line 22). The *LoadData* subroutine executes the MS Access query *qryProgWorth* and stores the query result in the DataSet object for further processing (see Figure CS3.23).

```
19   Protected Sub btnRunAlgorithm_Click(ByVal sender As Object, _
20   ByVal e As System.EventArgs) Handles btnRunAlgorithm.Click
21       'Step 1: Get the worth of each program
22       LoadData()
23       'Step 2: Run the greedy algorithm
24       txtViewerShip.Text = RunAlgorithm(txtBudget.Text)
25   End Sub
```

Figure CS3.22 *Click* event of the *Run Algorithm* command button.

```
27   Sub LoadData()
28       Dim qry As String
29       qry = "exec qryProgWorth '" & cmbGender.SelectedValue & "','" _
30       & cmbAge.SelectedValue & "','" & cmbIncome.SelectedValue & "','" _
31       & cmbRace.SelectedValue & "'"
32
33       connWorth.ConnectionString = ConfigurationManager.AppSettings("ConnString")
34       cmdWorth.Connection = connWorth
35       cmdWorth.CommandText = qry
36       daWorth.SelectCommand = cmdWorth
37       connWorth.Open()
38       daWorth.Fill(dsWorth)
39       connWorth.Close()
40
41       gvProg.DataSource = dsWorth
42       gvProg.AutoGenerateColumns = True
43       gvProg.DataBind()
44   End Sub
```

Figure CS3.23 The *LoadData* subroutine.

Figure CS3.23 Explained:

We first create the query statement along with the parameter values (i.e., values of the ComboBox controls) in lines 28–31. The Connection, Command, Data Adapter, and DataSet objects are declared globally outside any procedure. We set the Connection and Command objects in lines 33–36. The query is executed in line 38, and the result is saved in the DataSet object. Lines 41–43 show the DataSet contents on a GridView control *gvProg*.

Next, we execute steps 3–5 of the algorithm by calling the *RunAlgorithm* subroutine (see Figure CS3.24). The subroutine goes over all the rows in the DataSet (i.e., program ordered by their worth, and for each program, the available budget is reduced by the cost of the program (line 52) and the viewership value is incremented by the program viewership value in line 53 (step 4 of the algorithm). We also highlight the row of the GridView control in line 54 to show the selection to the user. The allocation is continued either until we exhaust the entire available budget (line 51) or when we have accessed all the rows of the DataSet (line 50).

```
46  Function RunAlgorithm(ByRef budget As Integer) As Integer
47      'Query Col: (0) ProgramID, (1) Name, (2) Viewership, (3) Worth, (4) Cost
48      Dim i As Integer
49      Dim viewership As Integer
50      While (i < dsWorth.Tables(0).Rows.Count)
51          If (budget - CInt(dsWorth.Tables(0).Rows(i).Item(4))) >= 0 Then
52              budget -= CInt(dsWorth.Tables(0).Rows(i).Item(4))
53              viewership += CInt(dsWorth.Tables(0).Rows(i).Item(2))
54              gvProg.Rows(i).BackColor = System.Drawing.Color.LightGray
55          End If
56          i += 1
57      End While
58      If i = 0 Then
59          lblMsg.Text = "No programs meet the criteria!"
60      Else
61          lblMsg.Text = "Note: Allocated programs are highlighted in light gray"
62      End If
63      Return viewership
64  End Function
```

Figure CS3.24 The *RunAlgorithm* subroutine.

The user can change the value of the selection criteria and available budget to re-run the optimization problem multiple times.

CS3.6 *Summary*

- Television is most popular medium of entertainment. Considering its impact on us, it is natural to make optimal use of this medium for advertisement and entertainment programs.
- The case study database features five main tables to store information about customers, channels, programs and their episodes, and advertisement information. The other two tables of the database link customer-episode and advertisement-episode tables.
- The Channel Information page of the case study displays the viewership for each channel in the database. The viewership is displayed for different categories such as age range, gender, race, and income group. The Program Information page displays similar information, but for each program in the database.

- The Customer Preference page of the application shows the customer's penchant for different program types. Each piece of the pie chart on the page depicts a unique program type, and the size of the piece indicates the number of customers preferring the program type.
- Each advertisement may have a target age group, race, gender, and income group. Additionally, each advertisement must have an advertisement budget and target viewership. Further, there is a cost of advertisement associated with each program. The Advertisement Allocation page solves the optimization problem to allocate the selected advertisement to the programs to maximize the viewership with the constraints of available budget and target categorized viewership.

CS3.7 *Extensions*

1. Add new data entry pages to the application in which the user can add/edit channel, program, customer, and episode information in the database. Add appropriate links to the navigational menu on the Master page.

2. The Customer Preference page of the application shows the customer's liking for program types. We would like to extend this page to display categorized customer preference. The user should be able to choose from one of the following

selection criteria: age group and income group. For a given selection criteria, we would like to display the program types preferred by each category of the selection criteria. For example, if the user selects the age group as the selection criteria, then we show program types preferred by each category: kids, youth, adult, and old. Display this information on a GridView control.

3. We discussed trend lines in Section CS3.2. A trend line is a line chart that shows program viewership over time. Add a new page to the application. Show the list of all programs on the page for selection. Also add two Calendar controls on the page. The user selects the start and end date from the Calendar controls. As the user selects the program and dates, we display the program viewership between the start and end dates on a line chart (*Hint*: Use the existing MS Access query *qryTrendLine*). Add the Trend Lines link to the navigational menu on the Master page.

4. Trend lines can also be categorized based on age, race, income, and gender to capture very specific information. We extend the Trend Line page created in the previous exercise to display the categorized trend lines for race ad gender selection. For example, if the user selects Female gender, we display all female viewership information for the selected program and dates.

5. Multiple trend lines can be used to view interesting viewership patterns of the programs shown on a channel. Add a new page to the application that shows the trend lines similar to the one discussed in Extension 3, but for the channel selected by the user. For the selected channel, we show a line for each program broadcasted on that channel.

6. Add a new page to the application in which the user can assign the advertisements to the programs as suggested by the Advertisement Allocation page. We should populate the *tblAssigment* table using this page. Provide appropriate controls for the user to select the existing advertisement and the program for assignment. Link this page as the pop-up page from the Advertisement Allocation page.

four **Voyage Prophesy**

case study

OVERVIEW

CS4.1 *Introduction*

Voyage Prophesy is the case study developed to illustrate how Windows applications can be enhanced with the aid of external software. Microsoft MapPoint is a software program that allows users to view, edit and integrate maps. This mapping software is designed to visualize and analyze included data geographically. Maps and geographic information are gaining importance in today's mobile world. In this case study, we discuss how Windows applications can embed functionalities of MapPoint software. We develop the Voyage Prophesy application to assist users in finding a nearby airport, hotel, bus or gas station, restaurant, or city attraction and also provide driving directions to the selected location. The MapPoint software has its own database of maps, streets, and related information. We exploit MapPoint objects and access the MapPoint database in the Windows application to develop the Voyage Prophesy application.

The case study code and the complete application can be found on the book Web site. We strongly recommend that readers download and install the case study and browse through the application pages before going through the details described in this chapter. Users are also required to have Microsoft MapPoint software installed in order to successfully develop and execute this application. A copy of the latest version of MapPoint software can be obtained from the Microsoft Web site. The students in the Microsoft academic alliance universities can obtain their free copy of MapPoint from the MSDNAA Web site.

CS4.2 *Application Functionalities*

The functionalities of the application are listed as follows:

Search Locations: The search form allows the user to choose between various options available for finding a nearby airport, hotel, bus or gas station, restaurant, or city attraction. For example, minor airport-major airport, bus station-gas station-train station, Asian-Italian-Indian-Mexican restaurants, and so forth. The form also takes from the user the address, the radius (r) in miles, and the maximum number of output results (n) to display. The input address is used as the center of the search circle, and up to n results within r miles of the radius are returned to the user on the Show Map form.

Map Representation: The Show Map page shows the result of the search on the map and in the text format. The map provides ample functionalities to users. They can zoom in, zoom out, and pan the map for a better view.

Driving Directions: Once the user has selected the desired location, the application asks the user for the starting address and provides the driving directions of the shortest path from the starting location to the desired location. The directions are shown on an intractable map as well as in the text format along with distance and estimated travel time. Users can also print the directions for their reference.

User controls and MapPoint control: This case study illustrates how user controls can be created and used on all Windows forms. The case study also shows how the MapPoint controls can be added to the Toolbox and used in the Windows application.

The flow of the *Voyage Prophesy* application is depicted in Figure CS4.1.

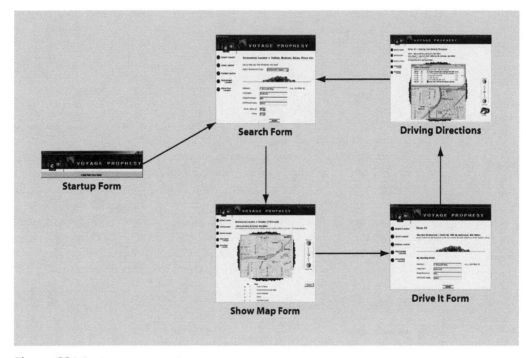

Figure CS4.1 The application flow.

The Startup Form, User Controls, and MapPoint Reference

In this section, we cover a few preliminary setups for this application. They include the startup form, two user controls, and the addition of the MapPoint control.

The Startup Form and the Main Procedure
Unlike we have done in any previous case study, we start this application with a flashing startup form. Recall from Section 13.13 how we can use the *Main* procedure to flash a startup form and then redirect the user to the main form of the application. We use the Startup form (not shown here) along with the *Main* procedure (see Figure CS4.2). This buys some time to load the referenced MapPoint objects into the application. Note that this *Main* procedure is declared inside the *GlobalVar* module, and the *SearchForm* and *SearchFor* are two module-level global variables. These variables correspond to the main search form of the application that the *Main* procedure opens after the Startup form.

```
 3      Public Sub Main()
 4          Dim fForm As New Startup
 5          fForm.Show()
 6          fForm.Refresh()
 7          System.Threading.Thread.Sleep(1500)
 8          fForm.Close()
 9
10          SearchFor = "Restaurant"
11          Application.Run(mainSearchForm)
12      End Sub
```

Figure CS4.2 The starting Main procedure.

User Controls

All application pages have a form header and a navigational menu on the left-hand side of the form. The menu provides navigation to various search options (see Figure CS4.3). As in Web applications, we can create user controls in the Windows application and add them to the Toolbox and then on every form of the application. We add two such user controls to this application: (i) the form header (*Header.vb*) and (ii) the side menu (*Menu.vb*).

To add a user control to the application, choose the Project | Add User Control option from the main menu. Name the user control file and click *OK* to open the design view of the control. The design of the *Header* user control is fairly straightforward and involves setting up images available in the application folder. The *Menu* control is more involved and is discussed next.

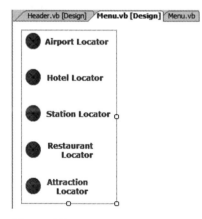

Figure CS4.3 The *Menu* user control.

We set up the menu control as shown in Figure CS4.3. Each of these links is a LinkLabel control with its *Image* property set to the image seen in the screenshot. The code for the *LinkClicked* event of these links gives users different search options (see Figure CS4.4). On the click of these links, we call the *Open* subroutine, which sets the global variable *SearchFor* with the appropriate string value (line 40), calls the *InitForm* method of the Search form in line 41 (discussed later), and closes the form on which this Menu control is present, i.e., the *Parent* form (lines 42–44).

Note that the Search form is the main form of the application, whereas the menu control will be included on all forms to give the user an option to restart the search from any of the application forms. Therefore, when the user clicks any of the menu items from a form other than the Menu form, we close the parent form of the *Menu* user control and expose the already open Search form.

```
 5    Private Sub lnkAirport_LinkClicked(ByVal sender As System.Object, _
 6    ByVal e As System.Windows.Forms.LinkLabelLinkClickedEventArgs) _
 7    Handles lnkAirport.LinkClicked
 8        open("Airport")
 9    End Sub


39    Sub open(ByVal op As String)
40        SearchFor = op
41        mainSearchForm.InitForm()
42        If Not Parent.GetType Is Voyage.SearchForm.GetType Then
43            CType(Parent, Form).Close()
44        End If
45    End Sub
```

Figure CS4.4 The code behind the *Menu* user control.

Adding a MapPoint Reference

Next, we add a MapPoint reference to the Windows application. MapPoint is the external software to the Voyage Prophesy application, and we must include its reference to the project to access its objects, controls, and their functionalities. We must install the full version of MapPoint to find and add its references.

To add a reference, open the *Property* page of the application from the *Project* list of the main menu. Navigate to the *References* tab and click the *Add* button (see Figure CS4.5). This should open the *Add Reference* dialog box. Navigate to the *Browse* tab and locate the two DLL files provided with the application folder (see Figure CS4.6). Add these files as a reference to the project. These files provide access to all MapPoint objects we need for this application. Click *OK* to return to the property page.

Figure CS4.5 The *Reference* tab of the project property page.

Adding Controls to the ToolBox

We would like to add the *Header* and *Menu* user controls to the Toolbox so that we can drag and drop them on Windows forms just like any other Windows control. To add user controls to the Toolbox, all we need to do is build the application once. Press Ctrl+F5 to run the application, and the user controls should automatically get added to the ToolBox under a separate tab, as shown in Figure CS4.8.

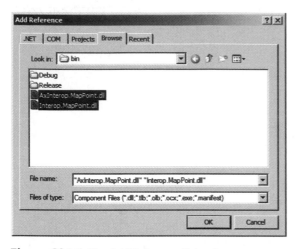

Figure CS4.6 The *Add Reference* dialog box.

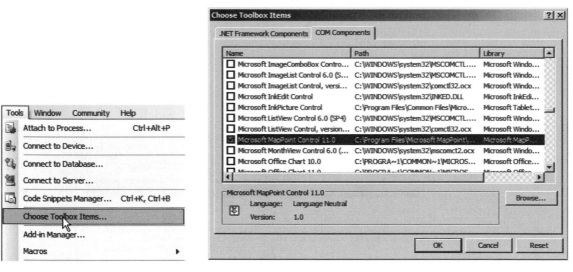

(a)   (b)

Figure CS4.7 Adding the MapPoint control to the ToolBox.

Figure CS4.8 The ToolBox with the user controls and MapPoint control.

We will also use controls provided by the MapPoint software in our application, specifically, to display the maps on the Windows forms. We can add controls from other software packages to the ToolBox as follows:

How-to: add controls from external software packages to the ToolBox.

1. Choose the Tools | Choose Toolbox Items option from the main menu (see Figure CS4.7(a)). This should open the *Choose Toolbox Items* dialog box.
2. In the *Choose Toolbox Items* dialog box, navigate to the *COM Components* tab and locate the *Microsoft MapPoint Control 11.0* (or your version) option.
3. Select the option and click *OK* to add the control to the ToolBox.

We are now ready to discuss the design and code behind the four core forms of the application shown in the application flow diagram, Figure CS4.1.

CS4.4 *The Search Form*

The Search form collects the following information from the user (see Figure CS4.9):

- Type of the locator (*cmbType* ComboBox control)
- Address as the center of the search circle (TextBox controls)
- Radius of the search circle (*cmbRad* ComboBox control)
- Maximum number of search results to display (*cmbShow* ComboBox control)

Figure CS4.9 The Search form

The most important procedure of the Search form is its *InitForm* subroutine that sets up the form (see Figure CS4.10). Based on the locator (airport, hotel, station, etc.) selected by the user, i.e., value of the *SearchFor* global variable, the *InitForm* subroutine populates the *cmbType* ComboBox control with various options (lines 29–73). We write these lines of code as part of a separate subroutine rather than as part of the *Form_Load* subroutine because we call the *InitForm* subroutine every time the user clicks the navigation links in the Menu user control on any of the application pages (see Figure CS4.4).

Another important event subroutine is the click of the *Submit* button. When users submit the search request, we save the information on the Search form in global variables so that the values can be accessed on other Windows forms (see Figure CS4.11). These global variables are declared in the *GlobalVar* module of the project (not shown here).

```
26  Public Sub InitForm()
27      cmbType.Items.Clear()
28      lblType.Text = "Select " & SearchFor & " Type"
29      Select Case SearchFor
30          Case "Airport"
31              lblTitle.Text = "Airport Locator > Major or Minor"
32              With cmbType.Items
33                  .Add("Airports - Minor")
34                  .Add("Airports - Major")
35              End With
36          Case "Hotel"
37              lblTitle.Text = "Hotel Locator > Hotels and Motels"
38              With cmbType.Items
39                  .Add("Hotels and Motels")
40              End With
41          Case "Restaurant"
42              lblTitle.Text = "Restaurent Locator > Italian, Mexican,
43              With cmbType.Items
44                  .Add("Restaurants - Asian")
45                  .Add("Restaurants - Italian")
46                  .Add("Restaurants - Chinese")
47                  .Add("Restaurants - French")
48                  .Add("Restaurants - Indian")
49                  .Add("Restaurants - Mexican")
50              End With
```

Figure CS4.10 The *InitForm* subroutine.

```
10  Private Sub cmdSubmit_Click(ByVal sender As System.Object, _
11  ByVal e As System.EventArgs) Handles cmdSubmit.Click
12      Maptitle = SearchFor & " Locator > Results"
13      Address = txtAddress.Text & ", " & txtCity.Text & ", " _
14      & txtState.Text & "," & txtZip.Text
15      Type = cmbType.SelectedItem
16      Rad = CDbl(cmbRadius.SelectedItem)
17      Showval = CInt(cmbShow.SelectedItem)
18      Dim MapForm As New ShowMap
19      MapForm.Show()
20  End Sub
```

Figure CS4.11 The *Click* event of the *Submit* button.

The Show Map Form

The Show Map form is one of the core forms that display the search results to the user on a map as well as in the text format. The page setup is shown in Figure CS4.12. The four directional image buttons around the MapPoint control are used for the map panning functionality, while the zoom in/out bar along the side of the MapPoint control is used for the zooming functionality of the map. We add the MapPoint control to display the map of the search results, and we set it up in the program at runtime. Also, the search result in the text format is displayed at the bottom of the MapPoint control. We add a set of RadioButton controls and Label controls in the code at runtime to display the text search result.

Figure CS4.12 The Show Map form.

There are three main event codes we explain in this section. They are as follows:

- *Page_Load* event of the Show Map form—Perform the search and display it on the map and in the text format (see Figure CS4.13).
- *Click* event of the *DriveIt* command button—Save the destination selected by the user and open the next form of the application (see Figure CS4.14).
- Pan and Zoom operation-related events—Allow user to pan or zoom in/out on the map to view the search results (see Figure CS4.15).

```
10    Dim i, numShow As Integer
11    Dim oLoc As MapPoint.Location
12    MapControl.NewMap(MapPoint.GeoMapRegion.geoMapNorthAmerica)
13
14    ' Search for nearby location by type
15    MapControl.ActiveMap.PlaceCategories.Visible = MapPoint.GeoTriState.geoFalse
16    MapControl.ActiveMap.PlaceCategories(Type).Visible = True
17    oLoc = MapControl.ActiveMap.FindResults(Address)(1)
18    oLoc.GoTo()
19    oFound = oLoc.FindNearby(Rad)
20
21    lblTitle.Text = Maptitle & " (" & oFound.Count & " found)"
22    lblAddress.Text = Address
23    numShow = Showval
24    If oFound.Count < Showval Then numShow = oFound.Count
25
26    'Display the output
27    For i = 1 To numShow
28        Dim l1, l2 As New Label
29        Dim r1 As New RadioButton
30        r1.Text = ""
31        r1.Location = New System.Drawing.Point(255, (710 + ((i - 1) * 30)))
32        r1.Size = New System.Drawing.Size(15, 25)
33        If i = 1 Then r1.Checked = True
34        Me.Controls.Add(r1)
35        l1.Text = CStr(i)
36        l1.Location = New System.Drawing.Point(300, (710 + ((i - 1) * 30)))
37        l1.Size = New System.Drawing.Size(25, 25)
38        Me.Controls.Add(l1)
39        l2.Text = oFound.Item(i).Name
40        l2.Location = New System.Drawing.Point(360, (710 + ((i - 1) * 30)))
41        l2.Size = New System.Drawing.Size(200, 25)
42        Me.Controls.Add(l2)
43        oFound.Item(i).Highlight = True
44        oFound.Item(i).GoTo()
45    Next
```

Figure CS4.13 *Page_Load* event of the Show Map form.

Figure CS4.13 Explained:

We define a MapPoint *Location* object in line 11. The *Location* object in MapPoint holds all the information about a particular location including its address. Similarly, we define Dim oFound As MapPoint.FindResults as a MapPoint *Results* object in line 3 (not shown in the figure) that can hold all the locations of the search results. In line 12, we create a new map instance and associate it with the MapPoint control on the form. Lines 15–19 perform the actual location search. Lines 15–16 make only the location of interest (the type selected by the user on the Search form) visible. In line 17, we first locate and save the "Address" specified as the center of the search circle. The *FindNearBy* method of the *Location* object is used in line 19 to find all locations of interest within the specified search radius. Lines 27–45 dynamically add each search result up to the maximum desired number of search results on the form. For each result, we add a RadioButton control (line 34), a Label control for the serial number (line 38), and a Label control with the location name (line 42). A call to the *GoTo* method of the location in the *oFound* collection actually adds the search location on the map (line 44).

```
54  Private Sub cmdDrive_Click(ByVal sender As System.Object, _
55      ByVal e As System.EventArgs) Handles cmdDrive.Click
56
57      Dim obj As New Control
58      Dim idx As Integer = 1
59
60      For Each obj In Me.Controls
61          If obj.GetType.ToString = "System.Windows.Forms.RadioButton" Then
62              If CType(obj, RadioButton).Checked Then
63                  dLoc = oFound.Item(idx)
64                  Exit For
65              End If
66              idx += 1
67          End If
68      Next
69
70      Dim DriveForm As New DriveIt
71      DriveForm.Show()
72
73  End Sub
```

Figure CS4.14 *Click* event of the *DriveIt* command button.

Figure CS4.14 Explained:

On the click of the *DriveIt* command button, we iterate over all the RadioButton controls on the form sequentially and see which one the user has selected (line 60–68). For the selected or checked RadioButton control, we save the corresponding location object from the *oFound* collection in the global variable *dLoc* (destination Location object). We open the next application form in lines 70–71. Note that we do not close the Show Map form. Closing the form essentially destroys the search results and therefore the saved destination location is not accessible for the rest of the application forms. We ask the reader to extend this application to remove this dependency in the Extension section at the end of the chapter.

```
93   Private Sub picZoomIn_Click(ByVal sender As System.Object, _
94       ByVal e As System.EventArgs) Handles picZoomIn.Click
95       MapControl.ActiveMap.ZoomIn()
96       If tbarZoom.Value = 10 Then
97           MessageBox.Show("Can not ZoomIn more!!")
98           Exit Sub
99       End If
100      ZoomLevel += 1
101      tbarZoom.Value += 1
102  End Sub
103
104  Private Sub picZoomOut_Click(ByVal sender As System.Object, _
105      ByVal e As System.EventArgs) Handles picZoomOut.Click
106      MapControl.ActiveMap.ZoomOut()
107      If tbarZoom.Value = 0 Then
108          MessageBox.Show("Can not ZoomOut more!!")
109          Exit Sub
110      End If
111      ZoomLevel -= 1
112      tbarZoom.Value -= 1
113  End Sub
114
115  Private Sub panNorth_Click(ByVal sender As System.Object, _
116      ByVal e As System.EventArgs) Handles panNorth.Click
117      MapControl.ActiveMap.Pan(MapPoint.GeoPanCmd.geoNorth)
118  End Sub
```

Figure CS4.15 Zoom and pan operations code.

Figure CS4.15 Explained:

Although the MapPoint control itself provides the pan and zoom in/out functionalities, we further illustrate the use of MapPoint objects and their methods to perform a map-related operation. We provide four image controls for four directional pans and a zoom sliding bar for the zoom in/out operations. We discuss zoom in and north pan event codes here. Other related event codes are identical and are easy to follow after this explanation. Every time the zoom in click event occurs (lines 93–102), we call the *ZoomIn* method of the active map to zoom in by a pre-defined percentage (line 95). We also set the global variable *ZoomLevel* and value of the TrackBar control accordingly. For the pan operation, we call the *Pan* method of the active map with the desired direction to pan the map by a pre-defined distance (line 117).

CS4.6   *The DriveIt Form*

The DriveIt form is one of the simplest forms in the application and simply collects the starting address from the user. The form setup is shown in Figure CS4.16. When the form is opened, we use the global destination *Location* (dLoc) object (populated on the Show Map form) to show the destination address on the DriveIt form (see line 5 of Figure CS4.17). Once the user enters the starting address and clicks the *Submit* button, we store the starting address in the *Address* global variable (see lines 10–11 of Figure CS4.17). The starting address and the *dLoc* location object are used on the Direction form to give driving directions to the user.

Figure CS4.16 The DriveIt form.

```
 3 ┌  Private Sub DriveIt_Load(ByVal sender As System.Object, _
 4 │  ByVal e As System.EventArgs) Handles MyBase.Load
 5 │      lblAddress.Text = dLoc.Name & " : " & dLoc.StreetAddress.Value
 6 └  End Sub
 7
 8 ┌  Private Sub cmdSubmit_Click(ByVal sender As System.Object, _
 9 │  ByVal e As System.EventArgs) Handles cmdSubmit.Click
10 │      Address = txtAddress.Text & ", " & txtCity.Text & ", " _
11 │          & txtState.Text & "," & txtZip.Text
12 │      Dim DirectForm As New Directions
13 │      DirectForm.Show()
14 │      Me.Close()
15 └  End Sub
```

Figure CS4.17 The code behind the DriveIt form.

CS4.7 *The Direction Form*

The last form of the application flow displays the driving directions, total distance, and estimated travel time to the user. The starting address provided by the user on the DriveIt form and the destination selected from the search result on the Show Map form are used for the driving directions. The form shows the driving directions on the map as well as in the text (see Figure CS4.18). We also provide the zoom in/out and pan operations for the map and the ability to print the directions (see the Extension section of the chapter).

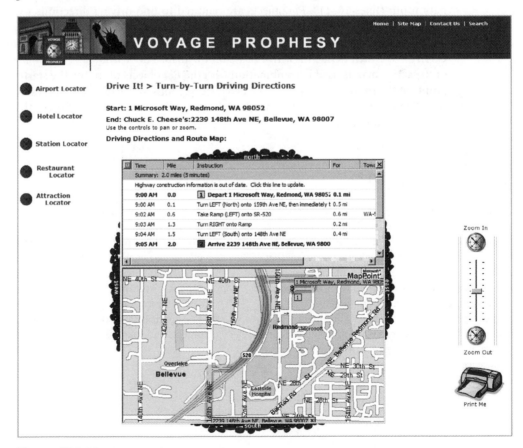

Figure CS4.18 The Direction form.

```
 3   Private Sub Directions_Load(ByVal sender As System.Object, _
 4   ByVal e As System.EventArgs) Handles MyBase.Load
 5
 6       MapControl.NewMap(MapPoint.GeoMapRegion.geoMapNorthAmerica)
 7       Dim actMap As MapPoint.Map = MapControl.ActiveMap
 8
 9       sLoc = actMap.FindResults(Address)(1)
10       sPin = actMap.AddPushpin(actMap.FindResults(Address)(1))
11       dPin = actMap.AddPushpin(actMap.FindResults(dLoc.StreetAddress.Value)(1))
12       sPin.BalloonState = MapPoint.GeoBalloonState.geoDisplayName
13       dPin.BalloonState = MapPoint.GeoBalloonState.geoDisplayName
14       actMap.ActiveRoute.Waypoints.Add(sPin)
15       actMap.ActiveRoute.Waypoints.Add(dPin)
16       actMap.ActiveRoute.Calculate()
17
18       lblStart.Text = "Start: " & sLoc.StreetAddress.Value
19       lblEnd.Text = "End: " & dLoc.Name & ":" & dLoc.StreetAddress.Value
20
21   End Sub
```

Figure CS4.19 The code behind the Direction page.

Figure CS4.19 Explained:

On the form load, we first create a new map instance for the map control on the form (line 6). We then locate the starting address and store the location in the global variable *sLoc* (starting *Location* object) in line 9. We then add two *Pin* objects to the map, the starting pin and the destination pin (lines 10–11). *Pin* objects are required to find driving directions from point A to point B. We use the *AddPushpin* method of the active map with the *Location* object (where to add the pin) as its input parameter. Lines 12–13 add the pin address on the map (see Figure CS4.18). We then define the active route on the map. The *ActiveRoute.Waypoints.Add* method of the active map is used in combination with the *Pin* objects to specify the starting and ending points of the route (lines 14–15). The driving directions, travel distance, and estimated time are calculated and displayed on the map by calling the *Calculate* method of the active route on the active map (line 16).

CS4.8   *Summary*

- Voyage Prophesy is the case study developed to illustrate how Windows applications can be enhanced with the aid of external software.
- Microsoft MapPoint is a software program that allows users to view, edit, and integrate maps. This mapping software is designed to visualize and analyze included data geographically.
- The application assists users in finding a nearby airport, hotel, bus or gas station, restaurant, or city attraction and also provides driving directions to the selected location. The MapPoint software has

its own database of maps, streets, and related information.

- The application allows users to search nearby places, shows them on the map representation, lets the user specify the starting address, and provides driving directions from the starting address to the selected location.
- The application also illustrates how to use map objects and map operations such as zoom in/out and pan.

Extensions

1. The Driving form has a setup for the map zoom in/out and pan operations. However, there is no code behind these controls on the form. Complete these functionalities similar to the Show Map form of the application.

2. The Driving form also has an image control to print the driving directions, but it is not functional in the current design. Add the code to the print image to provide this functionality (*Hint*: use the *ActiveMap.PrintOut* method).

3. The Search form allows the user to enter the address as the center of the search circle. MapPoint also has a provision to accept "places" (e.g., Space Needle, Century Tower) as the location address. Extend the Search form to accept either an address or a place (use the RadioButton control) from the user and set it as the center of the search circle.

4. As in the previous extension, extend the DriveIt form to accept a "place" as the starting address of the route.

5. Both the Search and DriveIt forms accept addresses or places (after the previous extensions) from the user. However, the current design assumes that the user has entered a valid location. This might not always be true. Add a code to error checking on these forms. Verify that (i) the user has entered the required fields of the address/places and (ii) the location is valid and present on the map (*Hint*: use *FindAddressResults* and *FindResults* methods).

6. We mentioned in the chapter that we should not close the Show Map form to preserve the search result and have it accessible to all the forms of the application. This constraint is because of map instances created locally in the form. A better design is to create all map-related objects in the global module and populate them in the application forms. Use this methodology to redesign the application. (*Hint*: create only one active map instance and associate it with the MapControl on the forms. Save all the related objects in the global module.)

7. The current application can provide directions from the starting and ending locations. Extend the application to let users design a three-point trip. That is, users should able to specify/search two destination locations and input the starting address/place to plan a trip. The application should provide the directions from the starting address to the first destination, from the first destination to the second destination, and back to the starting location.

five ADO.NET and MS Excel

CS5.1   *Introduction*

So far, we have used ADO .NET objects such as table adapters and datasets within a Windows or Web application. In this case study, we use ADO .NET objects to link data in MS Access database's outside Windows or Web application to the Excel spreadsheet application. MS Excel spreadsheets have become one of the most popular software packages in the business world. A spreadsheet application can store and organize data, perform various calculations, and use additional packages, called add-ins, for more advanced problem-solving and analysis. With the aid of Visual Basic programming in Excel (Visual Basic for Applications, or VBA), its functions can be readily utilized to support the decision-making process.

The main objective of this case study is to illustrate the connectivity between MS Excel and VB .NET applications. We will illustrate how to take advantage of the powerful features of MS Excel such as Excel Solver (to solve optimization problems), Excel functions, and Excel charts (to present data in charts) to process data that resides in MS Access databases (see Figure CS5.1).

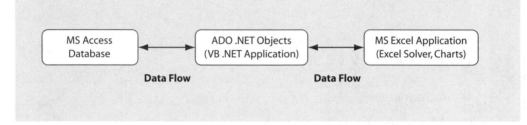

Figure CS5.1 MS Access databases and MS Excel linked though ADO .NET objects.

In Sections CS5.2 through CS5.6, we first present a forecasting case study. The forecasting case study illustrates the use of Excel functions, Excel charts, and transferring data from Access to ADO.NET objects to the Excel spreadsheet. In the remaining sections of the chapter, we introduce the Dynamic Production Problem (DPP) case study. The DPP case study illustrates the use of Excel Solver. In this case study chapter, we will specifically learn the following:

- How Excel reference is added to a Windows application.
- How Excel objects are used with ADO .NET objects to send data back and forth.
- How to use Excel charts, Excel functions, and Excel Solver from a Windows application.

CS5.2   *Forecasting Methods: Background and Theory*

Forecasting consists of estimating a variable's value at a future point in time. We usually perform a forecasting exercise to aid in decision making and when planning for the future. One classical application for forecasting is in inventory control and production planning. For instance, forecasting allows us to predict the demand for a product, which enables us to control the raw materials and finished goods inventory and to plan the production schedule. The prominent fields for practical forecasting are investments and economic policies. Moving Averages, Single/Double Exponential Smoothing, Holt's Method for Trends, and Winter's Method for Seasonality are a few examples of the methods for forecasting. All of these methods observe historical data and contain a mathematical model to estimate future data values.

For any forecasting method, the timescale involved, that is, how far into the future we are trying to forecast, is an important factor. A forecasting period can be as short as the next period and as long as several periods in the future. Let us consider the Single Exponential Smoothing model in order to forecast the demand for an industry product. We will discuss the general formula for forecasting for any future period.

The basic idea behind Single Exponential Smoothing is rather straightforward. We expect the most recent observations to be a better indicator of the future than past ones. To incorporate this fact into a mathematical model, the Exponential Smoothing technique gives more *weight* to the recent observations than to older observations. Therefore, for any period t, its forecasted demand (F_t) is represented by the following equation:

$$F_t = \alpha \cdot D_{t-1} + \alpha \cdot (1 - \alpha) \cdot D_{t-2} + \alpha \cdot (1 - \alpha)^2 \cdot D_{t-3} + \ldots \qquad \ldots \text{(i)}$$

where,

D_i: is the demand for period i and,
α : is the smoothing constant that takes a value between 0 and 1.

The smoothing constant acts as a weighting factor for demand values, and its value exponentially decays for older demands (hence the name "Exponential Smoothing"). The sensitivity of the smoothing can be adjusted by carefully selecting the value of the α constant. The smoothing equation (i) above can be re-written in its recurrent form as follows:

$$F_t = \alpha \cdot D_{t-1} + (1 - \alpha) \cdot F_{t-1} \qquad \text{where,} \quad F_1 = D_1 \qquad \ldots \text{(ii)}$$

Equation (ii) suggests that to forecast for a period t, we need the actual demand and the *forecasted demand* from the previous period, *t-1*. Because of its effectiveness and its simplicity, Single Exponential Smoothing is often applied to large-scale statistical forecasting problems.

Since there can be an element of error in any forecast, we need a mechanism to judge the reliability of a method's estimated forecast. At the basic level, the forecasting error is determined as follows:

$$\text{Error } (E_i) = \text{Forecast } (F_i) - \text{Actual Value } (D_i) \qquad \ldots \text{(iii)}$$

It is a common practice to take the square value of an error calculated in equation (iii) and then average the square value over all the forecasting periods to determine a mean square error or MSE (see equation (iv)). An MSE value is used to judge the accuracy of a forecasting method.

$$\text{MSE} = [\ (E_t)^2 + (E_{t+1})^2 + \ldots + (E_{t+n})^2\ ] \ / \ n+1 \qquad \ldots \text{(iv)}$$

Input for the Single Exponential Smoothing method:

- Historical demand for a product over period 1 to n (i.e., D_1 to D_n)
- The initial period, T_i (usually 2)
- The final period, T_f (greater than n)
- The smoothing constant, α (between 0 and 1)

Output of the Single Exponential Smoothing method:

- The forecasted demand values for periods n+1 to T_f
- An MSE value

CS5.3   *Forecasting Methods: Application Functionalities and Assumptions*

The Forecasting Methods application provides the following functionalities to its users:

1. The application retrieves the historical data for the demand per period from an Access database and displays it in a data grid for the users to add/remove/update demand values.
2. The application uses the MS Excel application for forecasting. The historical demand values from the Windows application (data grid) are first stored in an Excel spreadsheet. Then, Excel functions are used to evaluate equation (ii) and equation (iv), described in the previous section. Finally, the output of the Single Exponential Smoothing is shown to the users using Excel charts.
3. The users can re-run the application several times with different input parameters—the initial period, the final period, and the smoothing constant—to observe the forecasting sensitivity for its input parameters.

Application Flow

Figure CS5.2 shows a simple and self-explanatory application flow for the forecasting application.

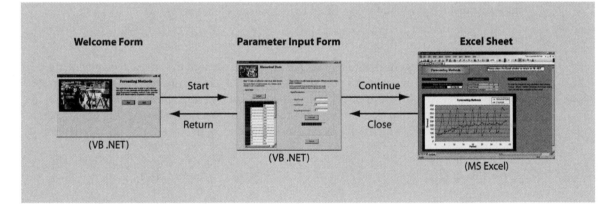

Figure CS5.2 Forecasting application flow.

CS5.4   *Setting up the Parameter Input Form and the Excel Sheet*

The main design-time setups for this application are the Parameter Input form and the Excel sheet. The Parameter Input form is depicted in Figure CS5.3. The form has the following three main setups:

- A DataGridView control to display the historical demand data from the Access database table.
- Three TextBox controls to obtain input parameters: the initial period, the final period, and the smoothing constant.

Figure CS5.3 A snapshot of the Parameter Input form.

- A ProgressBar control (available under the *All Windows Forms* tab in the Toolbox) indicating the progress of the running application. (See Figure CS5.3.)

Next, we need to set up the Excel sheet "ForecastingMethods.xls" (provided with the application folder). The Excel file has two main sheets, the Method sheet and the HistData sheet. We perform all forecasting calculations using Excel functions in the HistData sheet, and the result of the forecasting is plotted in the Method sheet for the user. The main setup involved in these sheets is naming the Excel cells. In Excel, we can name the cells so that the names can be used in the Visual Basic programs to refer to the cells. We use the Insert | Names | Defines option from the main menu of the Excel sheets to view existing names and to define new names. When we click the cell on the Excel sheet, we see the cell's name in the *Name Box* on the top-left of the Excel toolbar (See Figure CS5.4). We expect readers to be somewhat familiar with Excel and Excel charts to perform or to review Excel file setups. We set up these sheets as follows:

- Method Sheet: Named cells for the initial period, the final period, the smoothing constant, and the output MSE value. An Excel line chart set with the chart title, the legend, the axis titles, and other cosmetic settings (See Figure CS5.4). We will provide the data source for the chart at runtime.
- HistData Sheet: The sheet has four named columns for the period, the demand, the forecast, and the MSE values. (See Figure CS5.5.)

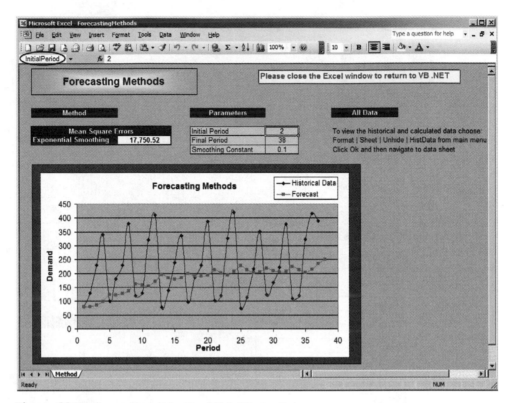

Figure CS5.4 A snapshot of the Excel file's "Method" sheet.

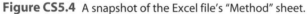

Figure CS5.5 A snapshot of the Excel file's "HistData" (hidden) sheet.

CS5.5 *The Code Behind the Parameter Input Form*

In this section, we explain the VB .NET code behind the Parameter Input form that actually executes the forecasting logic and the dataflow from the Access database to the VB .NET form and then to the Excel sheet. The code behind the Parameter Input form mainly consists of three event handlers:

- *Form_Load* event of the form: retrieving Access data on VB .NET form
- *Click* event of the "Update" button: updating modified data on VB .NET form back to the database
- *Click* event of the "Continue" button: executing forecasting logic

As described earlier in Chapters 14–15, we create a Data Source for the application and drag and drop the *tblHistData* table on the form to create the grid control and related objects. The auto-generated code for the *Form_Load* event retrieves historical data from the Access database table on a DataGridView control (see Figure CS5.6). As we drag and drop the data table on the form, it creates the ToolStrip control with the "Save" button to update the data in the grid control. We use the same code of the *Click* event of the "Update" button (see Figure CS5.7).

```
16   Private Sub frmHistData_Load(ByVal sender As System.Object, _
17   ByVal e As System.EventArgs) Handles MyBase.Load
18      Me.TblHistDataTableAdapter.Fill(Me.ForcastingDataSet.tblHistData)
19   End Sub
```

Figure CS5.6 *Form_Load* event of the Parameter Input form.

```
21   Private Sub cmdUpdate_Click(ByVal sender As System.Object, _
22   ByVal e As System.EventArgs) Handles cmdUpdate.Click
23      Me.Validate()
24      Me.TblHistDataBindingSource.EndEdit()
25      Me.TblHistDataTableAdapter.Update(Me.ForcastingDataSet.tblHistData)
26   End Sub
```

Figure CS5.7 *Click* event of the 'Update" button.

The *Click* event of the "Continue" button is the core of the application. On the click of this button, we transfer the data from ADO .NET objects on the form to pre-defined locations on the Excel sheet. We use Excel functions to calculate forecasted demands and their MSE values. We then use this data in the Excel sheet to plot the Excel chart. We perform all these tasks in the VB .NET code. Finally, we open the Excel sheet and display the chart to the user. We have divided these tasks into the following six code segments:

1. Check the input parameters' validity.
2. Open and set the Excel application file object.
3. Copy data from the ADO .NET dataset to the Excel spreadsheet.
4. Run the Single Exponential Smoothing algorithm.
5. Update the Excel charts and the final result.
6. Open the Excel file for the user.

Step 1: Input Validation

We first validate the user input by calling a *ValidateInput* function in line 35 (see Figure CS5.8). The *ValidateInput* function (see Figure CS5.9) checks the validity of three input parameters as follows:

- Smoothing constant between 0 and 1 (lines 123–129), stored in the *Alpha* variable.
- Initial period between 2 and total period +1 (lines 131–138), stored in the *IntialPeriod* variable.
- Final period greater than initial period (lines 140–146), stored in the *FinalPeriod* variable.

These input parameters are stored in the global variables (see Figure CS5.10). The function also stores the total number of periods, i.e., the number of rows in the DataGridView control in the global variable *TotalHistPeriods* (line 121).

```
28     Private Sub cmdCont_Click(ByVal sender As System.Object, _
29     ByVal e As System.EventArgs) Handles cmdCont.Click
30
31         Dim i As Integer
32         Dim fPath As String = "C:\webdss\casestudies\Forcasting\ForecastingMethods.xls"
33
34         '***Step 1: Validate input parameters
35         If Not ValidateInput() Then
36             Exit Sub
37         End If
```

Figure CS5.8 Call to the *ValidateInput* function.

```
116    Public Function ValidateInput() As Boolean
117
118        barProgress.Value = 0
119
120        'Get the total number of periods for which historical data is available
121        TotalHistPeriods = ForcastingDataSet.Tables("tblHistData").Rows.Count
122
123        'Set the smoothing constant
124        If txtConst.Text >= 1 Or txtConst.Text <= 0 Then
125            MessageBox.Show("The Smoothing Constant must be between 0 and 1.")
126            Return False
127        Else
128            Alpha = txtConst.Text
129        End If
130
131        'Set the initial period
132        If txtInitial.Text < 2 Or txtInitial.Text > TotalHistPeriods + 1 Then
133            MessageBox.Show("For Exponential Smoothing, the Initial Period must be greater " & _
134                "than 1 and less than the total number of periods + 1.")
135            Return False
136        Else
137            InitialPeriod = txtInitial.Text
138        End If
139
140        'Set the final  period
141        If txtFinal.Text <= txtInitial.Text Then
142            MessageBox.Show("Final period should be greater than intial")
143            Return False
144        Else
145            FinalPeriod = txtFinal.Text
146        End If
147
148        barProgress.Value = 5
149        Return True
```

Figure CS5.9 The *ValidateInput* function.

```
1  Public Class frmHistData
2
3      Dim TotalHistPeriods As Integer
4      Dim Alpha As Double
5      Dim InitialPeriod As Integer
6      Dim FinalPeriod As Integer
7      Dim MSE As Double
```

Figure CS5.10 Global variables for the Parameter Input form.

Step 2: Open and Set the Excel Application

Just as we open an Excel file by first starting the Excel application and then browsing and opening the desired file, we must start (or create) an Excel application object and then open the "ForecastingMethods.xls" file. We create the Excel application and two Excel worksheet objects in lines 40–42 (see Figure CS5.12). These objects are assigned with the "ForecastingMethods.xls" file and its HistData and Method sheets (lines 43–45).

We create Excel objects such as Excel applications, worksheets, cells, etc. using the reference `Microsoft.Office.Interop.Excel.` We must add this reference to the library of Excel objects before we can use it in VB .NET code. To add a reference of external libraries, we do the following:

1. In the Solution Explorer Window, right–click the project title and choose the *Add Reference* option from the short-cut menu (see Figure CS5.11(a)). This should open the *Add Reference* dialog box.

2. In the *Add Reference* dialog box, navigate to the *COM* tab, find and select the *Microsoft Excel 11.0 Object Library* (or available version of Excel) listing, and click *OK* to add the reference to the project (see Figure CS5.11(b)).

3. Verify the addition by opening the project property dialog (choose the Project | Forecasting properties option from the main menu). Navigate to the *Reference* tab to view the added reference (see Figure CS5.11(c)).

(a)

(b)

(c)

Figure CS5.11 Adding an Excel library reference.

```
39    '***Step 2: Open and set the excel file
40    Dim ForcastFile As New Microsoft.Office.Interop.Excel.Application
41    Dim DSheet As New Microsoft.Office.Interop.Excel.Worksheet
42    Dim MSheet As New Microsoft.Office.Interop.Excel.Worksheet
43    ForcastFile.Workbooks.Open(fPath)
44    DSheet = ForcastFile.ActiveWorkbook.Worksheets("HistData")
45    MSheet = ForcastFile.ActiveWorkbook.Worksheets("Method")
46    barProgress.Value = 10
```

Figure CS5.12 Creating Excel application and worksheet objects.

Step 3: Copy Data from the ADO .NET Dataset to the Excel Sheet

In this step, we copy the historical data, periods, and demand values from the DataGridView control (i.e., *ForecastingDataset*) to the *HistData* worksheet of the Excel sheet (see Figure CS5.13). We will later use Excel functions to run the Single Exponential Smoothing algorithm on this copied data.

```
48    '***Step 3: Copy data from ADO .NET dataset to Excel sheet
49    'Clear the existing data, if any
50    DSheet.Activate()
51    DSheet.Range(DSheet.Range("Period").Offset(1, 0), _
52    DSheet.Range("SqError"). _
53    End(Microsoft.Office.Interop.Excel.XlDirection.xlDown)).ClearContents()
54
55    'Consume ADO .NET dataset in Excel Sheet
56    For i = 0 To TotalHistPeriods - 1
57        DSheet.Range("Period").Offset(i + 1, 0).Value = _
58        ForcastingDataSet.Tables("tblHistData").Rows(i).Item(0)
59        DSheet.Range("Demand").Offset(i + 1, 0).Value = _
60        ForcastingDataSet.Tables("tblHistData").Rows(i).Item(1)
61    Next
```

Figure CS5.13 Step 3, copy data from ADO .NET dataset to the Excel sheet.

Figure CS5.13 Explained:

We activate the *HistData* worksheet (*DSheet* object) in line 50. Just as we choose the worksheet in Excel before we can work with it, we must activate the worksheet to use it in the program. We then clear any previous values in the worksheet. We use the named cells (heading of the four columns) to select the columns and call the *ClearContents* method of the Excel cell range to delete existing values (lines 51–53). We then copy the data from the ADO .NET dataset to the *HistData* worksheet in the For-Next loop (lines 56–61). Note that we have used the *Range* and *Offset* methods of Excel objects extensively to choose Excel cells in a particular order. Refer to an Excel reference book to learn more about these methods.

Step 4: Run the Single Exponential Smoothing Algorithm

We now run the Single Exponential Smoothing algorithm with the data copied in the *HistData* worksheet. Note that the reason we copied the data is that we would like to use the Excel function to run the algorithm. We also refer to the equations discussed in Section CS5.2 to explain the algorithm's execution (see Figure CS5.14).

Figure CS5.14 Explained:

We first set the initial values of the forecasted demand and the actual demand. The MSE value is zero for the first period, as we set both the forecasted demand and the actual demand to the demand of the first period (lines 66–68). We then go over all the periods to evaluate the forecasted demand as dictated by equation (ii) from Section CS5.2 (lines 71–76). We use the *FormulaR1C1* property to specify the Excel formulas. The $R[i]$ and $C[j]$ Excel notations are used to

```
64    '***Step 4: Run the Single Exponential Smoothing algorithm
65    '1. Setting F1 = D1 as per eqn (2). E1 = 0 as per eqn (3)
66    DSheet.Range("Forcast").Offset(InitialPeriod - 1, 0).Value = _
67    DSheet.Range("Demand").Offset(InitialPeriod - 1, 0).Value
68    DSheet.Range("SqError").Offset(InitialPeriod - 1, 0).Value = 0
69
70    '2. Now caluclate forcast and error for periods between initial and final
71    For i = InitialPeriod To FinalPeriod
72        DSheet.Range("Forcast").Offset(i, 0).FormulaR1C1 = _
73        "=" & Alpha & "*R[-1]C[-1] + " & (1 - Alpha) & "*R[-1]C"  'Eqn (2)
74        DSheet.Range("SqError").Offset(i, 0).FormulaR1C1 = "=(RC[-2]-RC[-1])^2" 'Eqn (4)
75        DSheet.Range("Period").Offset(i, 0).Value = i
76    Next
77
78    '3.Calculate the final Avg MSE and put them in Excel sheet
79    MSE = ForcastFile.WorksheetFunction.Average _
80        (DSheet.Range(DSheet.Range("SqError").Offset(InitialPeriod - 1, 0), _
81           DSheet.Range("SqError").Offset(FinalPeriod, 0)))
```

Figure CS5.14 Running Single Exponential Smoothing algorithm.

specify the Excel cells with desired *row* and *column* offsets with respect to the named cells. The formula $F_t = \alpha.D_{t-1} + (1 - \alpha).F_{t-1}$ transforms to "=Alpha * R[-1]C[-1] + (1-Alpha) * R[-1]C". The "R[-1]C[-1]" part means, "obtain the value of the cell one row up and one column left," i.e., the demand for the previous period, D_{t-1}. The "R[-1]C" part means, "obtain the value of the cell one row up and in the same column," i.e., the forecast for the previous period, F_{t-1}. The square error for each forecasted demand is evaluated in line 74 using equation (iv). Finally, in lines 79–81 we calculate the MSE, the average of the square error column. Note that here we have used the Excel function *Average* directly in the code (unlike using the *FormulaR1C1* property to specify the math formula) to calculate the MSE value.

Step 5: Refresh the Chart and Output Results

After executing the forecasting algorithm, we display the results in the *Method* worksheet. The forecasted values are plotted on an Excel line chart along with the historical data. The input parameters and output MSE values are displayed above the chart (see Figure CS5.4). The code is presented in Figure CS5.15.

```
84    '***Setp 5: Update the Excel Chart and put the final values
85    'Activate the Method sheet and hide the HistData sheet from user
86    MSheet.Activate()
87    DSheet.Visible = False
88
89    MSheet.ChartObjects(1).Activate()
90    With ForcastFile.ActiveChart
91        .SetSourceData(Source:=DSheet.Range(DSheet.Range("Period").Offset(1, 0), _
92                       DSheet.Range("Forcast").Offset(FinalPeriod, 0)))
93        .SeriesCollection(1).Name = "Historical Data"
94        .SeriesCollection(2).Name = "Forecast"
95        .Axes(Microsoft.Office.Interop.Excel.XlAxisType.xlCategory).MinimumScale = 0
96        .Axes(Microsoft.Office.Interop.Excel.XlAxisType.xlCategory).MaximumScale = FinalPeriod + 2
97    End With
98    barProgress.Value = 80
99    MSheet.Range("InitialPeriod").Value = InitialPeriod
100   MSheet.Range("FinalPeriod").Value = FinalPeriod
101   MSheet.Range("Alpha").Value = Alpha
102   MSheet.Range("MSE").Value = MSE
```

Figure CS5.15 Showing the algorithm's result on the *Method* sheet.

Figure CS5.15 Explained:

We first activate the *Method* sheet and the chart object on the *Method* sheet (lines 86 and 89). We hide the *HistData* sheet in line 87. We then set the Excel chart's data source (lines 90–91). The data for the line chart is pulled from the *HistData* sheet. The data source is specified as a range from the first cell in the period column to the last cell in the forecast column. We label the chart's X-axis and Y-axis and set its scales in lines 93–96. We then copy the input parameter values and output the MSE value on the Method sheet (lines 99–102).

Step 6: Open the Excel File

So far, we have performed all the tasks through VB .NET code using Excel objects. However, for the end user, the final results (the chart and the MSE value) must be displayed in an Excel sheet. We save the Excel file (line 106) and make it visible for the user (line 108). See the code lines in Figure CS5.16. We rely on the user to close the Excel file and thus the application object created in the code to return to the Windows application.

```
105        '***Step 6: Open the Excel file for the user
106        ForcastFile.ActiveWorkbook.Save()
107        barProgress.Value = 100
108        ForcastFile.Visible = True
```

Figure CS5.16 Making the Excel file and its worksheet visible to the user.

CS5.6 *Dynamic Production Problem (DPP) Application*

A production system produces products of multiple items. Each item has a given weight, space requirement, profit value, quota to satisfy, and limit on production. Each item production must meet its required quota but must not exceed its production limit. Also, the total weight and space requirements of produced items are limited by the shipping facilities. The goal of the application is to find the optimal production plan for different items that maximizes the system's profit. However, we want this production problem to be dynamic. In other words, we want the user to decide how many items to consider (limited to five for this application) and to provide the input for each item: its weight, space, profit, quota, and limit.

We illustrate the use of Excel Solver to solve this optimization problem. We accept the input parameters from the user on a Windows form in a Windows application and invoke Excel Solver to solve the optimization problem. Just as in the Forecasting Methods problem, we set up an Excel sheet and use Excel objects and Excel Solver to solve the optimization problem. Unlike the Forecasting Methods problem, we never expose the Excel sheet to the user, but the result of the optimization problem, an optimal production plan, is displayed to the user in the Window application. The application flow for the DPP problem is depicted in Figure CS5.17. The DPP application performs the following functions, it:

1. Transfers data from an ADO .NET dataset to an Excel sheet and from an Excel sheet back to the VB .NET controls.
2. Illustrates the use of an external optimization package (Excel Solver plug-in) in the Windows application to solve optimization problems.
3. Dynamically adds and removes controls from the Windows form to create the desired GUI for user input.

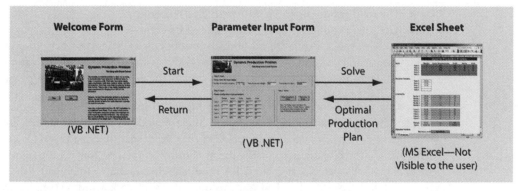

Figure CS5.17 Application flow for DPP application.

CS5.7 *DPP: Setting up the Parameter Input Form and the Excel Sheet*

For this application, we set up the Parameter Input form and the Excel sheet in the manner we did for the Forecasting Methods application. We ask the user for the following input parameters (see Figure CS5.18):

- Number of decision variables (number of different items to produce) using a NumericalUpDown control (available in the All Windows Controls tab in the Toolbox). We set the maximum value of this control to five.

Figure CS5.18 DPP: a snapshot of the Parameter Input form.

- The total production weight using a TextBox control.
- The total production space using a TextBox control.
- Weight, Space, Profit, Quota, and Limit values for each item. Each input is taken from the user in a TextBox control. The TextBox controls are added dynamically to the form based on the number of different items selected by the user in a NumericalUpDown control

Setting up an Excel sheet is more complicated. It involves two main setups, (i) the Excel sheet and its named ranges for the objective function and the constraint values, and (ii) writing VBA code to run the Excel Solver. Figure CS5.19 shows a snapshot of a pre-set Excel sheet, "Production.xls," which is included inside the application directory. Review the named cells of the *Production* worksheet. To view the VBA module *SolveMe* that actually runs the Excel Solver, press Atl + F11 from the Excel window to open the VBA code window (see Figure CS5.20). A discussion of the Solver VBA code is beyond the scope of this book, and we suggest the reader to refer to an Excel book to read more about Excel VBA and Excel Solver.

Figure CS5.19 DPP: a snapshot of an Excel optimization sheet.

Figure CS5.20 DPP: Excel VBA code to solve the optimization problem.

CS5.8 *DPP: The Code Behind the Parameter Input Form*

In this section, we take a detailed look at the VB .NET code that drives the application. We will discuss the following three event handlers:

(a) ***Form_Load event:*** We set the Windows form with five TextBox controls for each item for the number of decision variables selected by the user in the NumericalUpDown control.

(b) ***ValueChanged event of the NumericalUpDown control:*** If the user changes the value of the number of decision variables, we update the item parameter input TextBox controls accordingly.

(c) ***Click event of the Solver button:*** The core code of the application is embedded inside this event handler. The subroutine copies data to the Excel application, adds an Excel Solver plug-in to the Excel application, calls the SolveMe Excel VBA subroutine to solve the optimization problem, copies the solution back to the Windows application, and finally closes the Excel application.

Before we explain the code for these event handlers, we discuss various global variables used for the Parameter Input form (see Figure CS5.21).

```
 3  #Region "Global Variables"
 4
 5      Dim NumDv As Integer = 1 'By default 1 item
 6
 7      'Data structures for the production items
 8      Dim item(4) As Label            'Item# labels
 9      Dim inputVals(4, 4) As TextBox  'Input textboxes
10      Dim answer(4) As Label          'Labels for the production plan
11
12      'Default input values: weight, space, profit, quota, and limit
13      Dim itemVals() As Integer = {1, 200, 400, 10, 20}
14
15  #End Region
```

Figure CS5.21 Global variables for the DPP's Parameter Input form.

Figure CS5.21 Explained:

The integer variable *NumDv* (line 5) is used to store the value of the number of decision variables selected by the user in the NumericalUpDown control. In lines 8–10, we define three arrays to store control objects related to the item's input parameter. For each item, we need a Label control to display the item number, five TextBox controls to let the user enter the item's weight, space, profit, quota, and limit values, respectively, and a Label control to display the final answer (production plan) for the item (see Figure CS5.18). Since we constrained the number of items to be between one and five, we need a maximum of five Label controls for the item numbers, twenty-five TextBox controls, and another five Label controls for the answers. The array *itemValues* (a 2-D array) holds the default values for the item's input parameters (line 13).

(a) Creating and Adding Required Control Objects to the Windows Form

We now take a look at the *Form_Load* event code of the Parameter Input form. We primarily set all the input parameter controls in this code (see Figure CS5.22).

```
19  Private Sub frmParams_Load(ByVal sender As System.Object, _
20  ByVal e As System.EventArgs) Handles MyBase.Load
21
22      Dim i, j As Integer
23
24      For i = 0 To 4   'For each item
25          'Create a label in item array
26          item(i) = New Label
27          item(i).Font = New System.Drawing.Font("Arial", 9.75)
28          item(i).Text = "Item " & i + 1
29          item(i).Size = New System.Drawing.Size(50, 25)
30          item(i).Location = New System.Drawing.Point(25, 330 + i * 30)
31
32          'Create a label for the production plan in answer array
33          answer(i) = New Label
34          answer(i).Font = New System.Drawing.Font("Arial", 9.75)
35          answer(i).Size = New System.Drawing.Size(50, 25)
36          answer(i).Location = New System.Drawing.Point(425, 330 + i * 30)
37          answer(i).ForeColor = System.Drawing.Color.Navy
38
39          'Create 5 textboxes in inputVals array
40          For j = 0 To 4
41              inputVals(i, j) = New TextBox
42              inputVals(i, j).Text = itemVals(j)
43              inputVals(i, j).Size = New System.Drawing.Size(50, 25)
44              inputVals(i, j).Location = New System.Drawing.Point(85 + j * 65, 330 + i * 30)
45              inputVals(i, j).BackColor = System.Drawing.Color.LightGray
46          Next
47      Next
48
49      'Add the first item to the form
50      AddItem(0)
51
52  End Sub
```

Figure CS5.22 *Form_Load* event of the DPP's Parameter Input form.

Figure CS5.22 Explained:

On *Form_Load*, we create all the input parameter controls needed for this application. Note that we only create these controls. We do not add all these controls on the Parameter Input forms. The controls are added to the Windows form using an auxiliary subroutine *AddItem* (line 50). We discuss this subroutine next in the chapter. Since we have a maximum of five decision variables, the outer For-Next loop (lines 24–47) initializes controls for a single item at a time in its loop execution. Lines 26–40 create a Label control, add it to the *Item* array, and set its *Font*, *Text*,

Size, and *Location* properties. Lines 33–37 create a Label control in the *Answer* array in a similar manner. The inner For-Next loop (lines 40–46) creates five TextBox controls for an item and sets their properties. Note that the *inputVals* array is used to assign a default value to the TextBox controls (line 42). Finally, in line 50 we call the *AddItem* subroutine to add the controls for the first item (the default value for the *NumDV* variable) on the Windows form.

The auxiliary subroutine AddItem is shown in Figure CS5.23. We add a Label control (line 178) and five TextBox controls (lines 179–181) to the *Controls* collection of the form. We send the GroupBox control back to make newly added controls on the form (line 182). Note that adding controls to the *Controls* collection of the form programmatically is equivalent to dragging and dropping controls from the Toolbox onto Windows forms.

```
173    'Adds an item row to the form
174    Public Sub AddItem(ByVal idx As Integer)
175
176        Dim i As Integer
177
178        Me.Controls.Add(item(idx))              'Add an item label
179        For i = 0 To 4
180            Me.Controls.Add(inputVals(idx, i))  'Add item textboxes
181        Next
182        grpBox2.SendToBack()                    'Make them visible
183
184    End Sub
```

Figure CS5.23 *AddItem* subroutine to add controls to the Windows form.

(b) The *ValueChanged* event of the NumericalUpDown Control

As the user changes the value of the number of decision variables, we add and remove input controls from the Windows form. Note that we do not delete or create controls in the arrays that hold all required controls, but only change the GUI (see Figure CS5.24).

```
138    Private Sub updDvars_ValueChanged(ByVal sender As System.Object, _
139    ByVal e As System.EventArgs) Handles updDvars.ValueChanged
140
141        Dim i As Integer
142
143        ClearLastSolution() 'We can clear the last solution
144        If NumDv > updDvars.Value Then
145            For i = updDvars.Value To NumDv - 1
146                RemoveItem(i)
147            Next
148        ElseIf NumDv < updDvars.Value Then
149            For i = NumDv To updDvars.Value - 1
150                AddItem(i)
151            Next
152        End If
153        NumDv = updDvars.Value
154
155    End Sub
```

Figure CS5.24 *ValueChanged* event subroutine of the NumericalUpDown control.

Figure CS5.24 Explained:

Note that the default value of the *NumDv* variable is one. If the user selects the value in the *upDvars* NumericalUpDown control that is less than the current value of the *NumDv* variable, we remove items (line 146) from the user-selected number to *NumDv -1* from the form (lines 144–147). If the selected value is greater than the current value of the *NumDv* variable, we add items (line 150) from the *NumDv* to the user-selected number to the form (lines 148–152).

Finally, we save the selected value of the NumericalUpDown control in the *NumDv* variable (line 153).

Note that we call a subroutine *ClearLastSolution* in line 143. This subroutine clears any previous solution controls from the form (see Figure CS5.25). This is required because as the user selects a different value in the NumericalUpDown control, the user is interested in running or re-running the optimization problem, and, therefore, we must clear any previous solution to re-run the problem afresh. The *ClearLastSolution* code removes the solution Labels controls, the production plan, and the maximum profit from the Windows form.

We call the *RemoveItem* subroutine in line 146 to remove an item's input controls from the Windows form. The remove item subroutine (see Figure CS5.26) removes the item number Label control (line 166) and five TextBox controls (lines 167–169) for an item from the Windows form.

```
186        'Removes solution labels from the form
187        Public Sub ClearLastSolution()
188
189            Dim i As Integer
190
191            lblSol1.Visible = False
192            lblSol2.Visible = False
193            lblSol3.Visible = False
194            For i = 0 To NumDv - 1
195                Me.Controls.Remove(answer(i))
196            Next
197
198        End Sub
```

Figure CS5.25 The *ClearLastSolution* subroutine.

```
161        'Removes an item row from the form
162        Public Sub RemoveItem(ByVal idx As Integer)
163
164            Dim i As Integer
165
166            Me.Controls.Remove(item(idx))              'Removes an item label
167            For i = 0 To 4
168                Me.Controls.Remove(inputVals(idx, i))   'Removes item textboxes
169            Next
170
171        End Sub
```

Figure CS5.26 The *RemoveItem* subroutine.

(c) *Click* Event of the *Solver* Button

As described earlier, on the click of the *Solver* button we perform the following five main tasks:

1. Create and set the Excel application with the "Production.xls" file.
2. Clear any previous values in the Excel sheet and copy the new item's input values to the Excel sheet. Name the various ranges in the sheet that are used by the Solver code.
3. Add the *Solver* plug-in to the Excel application and run the optimization code by calling the *SolveMe* Excel VBA subroutine.
4. Get the optimization solution back to the Windows form from the Excel sheet.
5. Close and exit the Excel application

(1) Create and Set the Excel Application: Figure CS5.27 depicts the code to create and set the Excel application. We open the "Production.xls" file and assign it to the Excel application object (line 67). The only sheet of the file (hence, active sheet) is assigned to the Excel sheet object in line 68. Note that we must add an Excel library reference to the project to access the `Microsoft.Office.Interop.Excel` library (refer to Section CS5.5 Step 2).

```
64    '****** Step 1: Open and setup the Excel file ******
65    Dim excelApp As New Microsoft.Office.Interop.Excel.Application
66    Dim wsheet As New Microsoft.Office.Interop.Excel.Worksheet
67    excelApp.Workbooks.Open("C:\webdss\casestudies\ExcelSolver\Production.xls")
68    wsheet = excelApp.ActiveWorkbook.ActiveSheet
69
70    If excelApp Is Nothing Then 'Error checking
71        MessageBox.Show("Couldn't start Excel")
72        Exit Sub
73    End If
```

Figure CS5.27   Step 1: Creating and setting the Excel application.

(2) Set the Excel Sheet: Figure CS5.28 depicts the code to set up the Excel sheet. We first clear any existing values on the worksheet (lines 77–78). We then copy the data from the item's input parameter controls to the pre-defined locations in the Excel worksheet (lines 81–89). We then name the various ranges in the Excel sheet (lines 93–99). The named ranges are used by the Excel VBA code SolveMe to solve the optimization problem (see Figure CS5.20).

(3) Excel Solver: Figure CS5.29 depicts the code that first adds the Excel Solver plug-in to the Excel application (line 103). We run the *Solver* plug-in in line 104. We then call the *SolveMe* subroutine of Excel VBA to solve the optimization problem (line 105).

```
75    '****** Step 2: Put input values in the Excel sheet ******
76    'Clear any old values in the Excel sheet
77    wsheet.Range("C4:G8").ClearContents()
78    wsheet.Range("C11:C15").ClearContents()
79
80    'Put input values from the form in the Excel sheet
81    wsheet.Range("E30").Value = txtProdWt.Text
82    wsheet.Range("E31").Value = txtProdSp.Text
83    For i = 0 To NumDv - 1
84        wsheet.Range("C4").Offset(i, 0).Value = inputVals(i, 0).Text
85        wsheet.Range("D4").Offset(i, 0).Value = inputVals(i, 1).Text
86        wsheet.Range("E4").Offset(i, 0).Value = inputVals(i, 2).Text
87        wsheet.Range("F4").Offset(i, 0).Value = inputVals(i, 3).Text
88        wsheet.Range("G4").Offset(i, 0).Value = inputVals(i, 4).Text
89    Next i
90
91    'Name various ranges in the Excel sheet. This is required for Excel Solver code
92    'to work. Solver code refer Excell cell by their names
93    wsheet.Range("C11", wsheet.Range("C11").Offset(NumDv - 1)).Name = "ProdDecVar"
94    wsheet.Range("C11", wsheet.Range("C11").Offset(NumDv - 1)).Value = 0
95    wsheet.Range("C4", wsheet.Range("C4").Offset(NumDv - 1)).Name = "Weight"
96    wsheet.Range("D4", wsheet.Range("D4").Offset(NumDv - 1)).Name = "Space"
97    wsheet.Range("E4", wsheet.Range("E4").Offset(NumDv - 1)).Name = "Profit"
98    wsheet.Range("F4", wsheet.Range("F4").Offset(NumDv - 1)).Name = "Quota"
99    wsheet.Range("G4", wsheet.Range("G4").Offset(NumDv - 1)).Name = "Limit"
```

Figure CS5.28   Step 2: Setting up the Excel sheet.

```
101    '****** Step 3: Run the Solver ******
102    'Add the Solver.xla reference and execute it
103    excelApp.AddIns.Add("C:\Program Files\Microsoft Office\OFFICE11\Library\SOLVER\SOLVER
104    excelApp.Run("Solver.xla!Auto_Open")
105    'Run the Solver code stored in a macro inside the Excel file
106    'Open the Excel file and press Alt+F11 to view this code
107    excelApp.Run("Module1.SolveMe")
```

Figure CS5.29   Step 3: Using Excel Solver to solve the optimization problem.

```
109    '****** Step 4: Get the solution from the Excel file ******
110    'See if solution in A4 cell of excel sheet is feasible
111    If wsheet.Range("A4").Value <> 5 Then
112        lblSol1.Visible = True
113        lblSol2.Visible = True
114        lblSol3.Visible = True
115        'The Max Profit is saved in D34 cell of excel sheet
116        lblSol3.Text = wsheet.Range("D34").Value
117
118        'The production plan is saved in C11-C15 cells of excel sheet
119        For i = 0 To NumDv - 1
120            answer(i).Text = wsheet.Range("C" & 11 + i).Value
121            Me.Controls.Add(answer(i))
122        Next
123        grpBox2.SendToBack()      'Make it visible
124        MessageBox.Show("Sucess!! You may re-run with different values", _
125        "Answer Msg", MessageBoxButtons.OK, MessageBoxIcon.Information)
126    Else
127        ClearLastSolution()       'Clear any old solution
128        MessageBox.Show("No feasible solution found, please re-try", _
129        "ExcelSolver", MessageBoxButtons.OK, MessageBoxIcon.Error)
130    End If
```

Figure CS5.30 Step 4: Getting the optimization solution back to the Windows application.

(4) Retrieving Optimal Solution: We first check whether we have a feasible optimal solution. The Excel Solver returns a code "5" if the solution is infeasible for the given input parameters. If the solution is infeasible, we display an error message and clear any previous solution from the Windows form (lines 127–129). If the solution is feasible, we make all solution Label controls visible (lines 112–114) and copy the answers from pre-determined Excel cells to the Label controls (lines 116–122).

CS5.9   *Summary*

- In this case study chapter, we illustrated how the data from ADO .NET objects such as datasets can be transferred to an Excel spreadsheet.
- We also showed how to use Excel features such as Excel functions (to perform calculations), Excel charts (to show results in graph format), and Excel Solver (to solve the optimization problems) within the Windows application to assist in the decision-making process.
- We also explained how to add an Excel library reference to a Windows application. We must add the library reference in order to access the Excel objects in VB .NET code.

CS5.10   *Application Extensions*

1. Extend the DPP case study to add an option for the user to open the Excel file and view the optimization worksheet setting. Perform this operation on the click of a Button control on a Windows form.

2. Extend the Forecasting case study to display the *HistData* worksheet of the Excel file to the user when the final Excel chart is displayed to the user.

References

We have composed a list of references for each part of the text. These references provide some, but not all, of the materials used to compose the book text, example files, exercise files, and case studies. The reader may refer to these sources to learn more details about database design, database development, and database application development. We also list several general references that discuss decision support systems, GUI design, and programming principles.

Part I—Principles of Good Database Design

Connolly, T., and Begg, C. *Database Systems: A Practical Approach to Design, Implementation, and Management.* Addison Wesley, 2004.

Elmasri, R., and Navathe, S. *Fundamentals of Database Systems.* Pearson Education, 2006.

Garcia-Molina, H., Ullman, J., and Widom, J. *Database Systems: The Complete Book.* Pearson Education, 2004.

Part II—Database Development with MS Access

Andersen, V. *MS Access 2003: The Complete Reference.* McGraw Hill, 2003.

Cassel, P., Eddy, C., and Price, J. *Teach Yourself Microsoft Access 2002 in 21 Days.* SAMS, 2001

Groff, J., and Weinberg, P. *SQL: The Complete Reference.* McGraw Hill, 2002.

Prague, C., Irwin, M., and Reardon, J. *Access 2003 Bible.* Wiley Publishing, 2003.

Part III—Windows Application Development with VB .NET

Blair, R., Crossland, J., Reynolds, M., and Willis, T. *Beginning VB.NET (Programmer to Programmer).* Wrox, 2002.

Deitel, H., Deitel, P., Yaeger, C., and Nieto, T. *Visual Basic .NET For Experienced Programmers.* Prentice Hall Pearson Education, 2002.

Dobson, R. *Programming Microsoft Visual Basic .NET For Microsoft Access Databases.* Microsoft Press, 2002.

Holzner, S. *Visual Basic .NET Black Book.* Coriolis, 2002.

McAmis, D. *Crystal Reports: A Beginner's Guide*. McGraw Hill, 2001.

McAmis, D. *Professional Crystal Reports for Visual Studio .NET*. Wrox, 2004.

Oliver, D., and Morrison, M. *Teach Yourself HTML and XHTML in 24 Hours*. SAMS, 2003.

Part IV—Application Development with ASP .NET

Kauffman, J., and Thangarathinam, T. *ASP.NET 2.0 Databases Beta Preview*. Wrox, 2005.

Keogh, J. *ASP.NET 2.0 Demystified*. McGraw Hill, 2005.

Lee, W. *ASP.NET 2.0 A Developer's Notebook*. O'Reilly, 2005.

MacDonald, M. *The Complete Reference ASP .NET*. McGraw Hill, 2002.

Smith, S. *ASP.NET By Example*. Que, 2001.

Part V—Case Studies

Ahuja, R., Magnanti, T., and Orlin, J. *Network Flows: Theory, Algorithms and Applications*. Prentice Hall, 1993.

Luenberger, D. *Investment Science*. Oxford University Press, 1998.

Winston, W., and Albright, S.C. *Practical Management Science*. Brooks/Cole, 2001.

Winston, W., and Venkataramanan, M. *Introduction to Mathematical Programming*. Brooks/Cole, 2003.

Winston, W., *Decision Making Under Uncertainty with Risk Optimizer*. Palisade Corp., 1999.

Winston, W., *Introduction to Operations Research: Applications and Algorithms*. Duxbury Press, 1994.

Winston, W., *Introduction to Probability Models*. Brooks/Cole, 2004.

General References

Ahuja, R., and (Şeref) Hanna, M. Decision Support Systems Development: An Essential Part of OR Education. *Operations Research Letters* 31, 2004.

Caron, R. Microsoft Corporation: Coding Techniques and Programming Practices. http://msdn.microsoft.com/library/default.asp?url=/library/en-us/dnvsgen/html/cfr.asp, Feb 2000.

Geoffrion, A., and Krishnan, R. Prospects for operations research in the e-business era. *Interfaces* 31, 2001.

Johnson, J. *GUI Bloopers*. Morgan Kaufmann, 2000.

Mandel, T. *Elements of User Interface Design*. John Wiley & Sons, 1997.

Power, D., and Sharda, R. Model-Driven DSS: Concepts and Research Directions, *Decision Support Systems*, special issue on Integrated Decision Support, (In Publication).

Power, D. *Decision Support Systems: Concepts and Resources for Managers*. Quorum Books, 2002.

Power, D. *DSS Resources*, 2006. URL = http://www.dssresources.com

Turban, E., and Aronson, J. *Decision Support Systems and Intelligent Systems*, Prentice-Hall, 2001.

About the Authors

Abhijit A. Pol

Abhijit Pol is a researcher in the Department of Computer and Information Science and Engineering at the University of Florida, Gainesville. His research focus is in the area of databases, with special interests in approximate query processing and physical database design. Abhijit has taught the course *Developing Web-Enabled Decision Support Systems* (DSS) several times in the Department of Industrial and Systems Engineering at the University of Florida. He has presented several tutorials at workshops and conferences on the need and importance of teaching DSS material, and he has also taught at two instructor-training workshops on DSS development. Abhijit has presented research papers at several prestigious database conferences and performed research at the Microsoft Research Lab.

Ravindra K. Ahuja

Ravindra Ahuja is a professor at the University of Florida, Gainesville, in the Department of Industrial and Systems Engineering. He specializes in mathematical modeling, state-of-the-art network optimization techniques, and solving large-scale scheduling problems arising in logistics and transportation. He founded the company Innovative Scheduling, Inc. (www.InnovativeScheduling.com) to bring cutting-edge operations research and optimization techniques to the field of transportation and scheduling. He has developed innovative models and algorithms for several scheduling problems that were previously considered intractable; these models are now being packaged into interactive web-enabled decision support systems. He is winner of the 1993 *Lanchester Prize* for the best contribution of the year in Operations Research, the 2003 *Pierskalla Award* for the best paper on Operations Research in Health Applications, and the 2006 *Daniel H. Wagner Award* for Excellence in Operations Research Practice. He is a coauthor of the widely used text and reference book, "*Network Flows: Theory, Algorithms, and Applications.*" He is also a coauthor of the companion book, "*Developing Spreadsheet-Based Decision Support Systems,*" which describes how to build decision support systems using Excel and VBA for Excel.

Index